Modern Studies in Property Law

Volume 6

Edited by

Susan Bright

• HART •
PUBLISHING

OXFORD AND PORTLAND, OREGON

2011

Hart Publishing
16C Worcester Place
Oxford
OX1 2JW
United Kingdom
Telephone: +44 (0)1865-517530
Fax: +44 (0)1865-510710
E-mail: mail@hartpub.co.uk
Website: http://www.hartpub.co.uk

Published in North America (US and Canada) by
Hart Publishing
c/o International Specialized Book Services
920 NE 58th Avenue, Suite 300
Portland, OR 97213-3786
USA
Tel: +1 (503) 287-3093 or toll-free: +1 (800) 944-6190
Fax: +1 (503) 280-8832
E-mail: orders@isbs.com
Website: www.isbs.com

British Library Cataloguing in Publication Data
Data Available

ISBN: 978-1-84946-185-6

Typeset by Criteria International

Printed and bound in Great Britain by
CPI Antony Rowe, Chippenham and Eastbourne

Modern Studies in Property Law

The Modern Studies in Property Law Conference has become well-known as a unique opportunity for property lawyers to meet and confer both formally and informally. The eighth biennial conference was held at the University of Oxford in March 2010, and this book is the sixth in the series Modern Studies in Property Law. The volume is a refereed and revised selection of the papers given at the Oxford conference, covering a broad range of topics of contemporary importance, both nationally and internationally. The book includes chapters written by the key speakers at the conference: Lady Justice Arden, Professor Kevin Gray and Law Commissioner, Professor Elizabeth Cooke.

Previous volumes in this series:

Modern Studies in Property Law: Volume 1
Edited by Elizabeth Cooke

Modern Studies in Property Law: Volume 2
Edited by Elizabeth Cooke

Modern Studies in Property Law: Volume 3
Edited by Elizabeth Cooke

Modern Studies in Property Law: Volume 4
Edited by Elizabeth Cooke

Modern Studies in Property Law: Volume 5
Edited by Martin Dixon

Preface

This book is the sixth volume in the Modern Studies in Property Law series. As many readers will know, the origins of this series lie in the conference that was hosted at the University of Reading in 1996. The preface to the book that resulted from that conference, *The Reform of Property Law*, gave no hint that what was there described as the Inaugural Conference of the Centre of Property Law would become a key feature in the world of property law scholarship. We now know that the biennial conference, newly branded as the Modern Studies in Property Law Conference, has become *the* leading conference for property law scholars attracting participants from around the world. There is also a small band of practitioners who come to the conference, and their contributions to discussions have been most valuable: there is much to be learned by increasing dialogue between the practising profession, the judiciary and academics. Having initially been based at the University of Reading the conference became peripatetic in 2008 when it was hosted at Cambridge University. It has now very definitely come of age and is beginning to roam around England under the auspices of an editorial board, currently chaired by Professor Elizabeth Cooke. The 2010 conference had three key speakers, all of whom were in some way or other involved with that Inaugural Conference as well, and I am delighted that the book contains a contribution from each: Professor Elizabeth Cooke (as Law Commissioner of England and Wales), Lady Justice Arden, and Professor Kevin Gray.

This current volume reflects a selection of the papers given at the conference at the University of Oxford in March 2010. The range of topics covered by the various conference delegates made the task of first selecting papers for inclusion, and secondly grouping them into Parts for this book, a challenging one. The selected papers contain elements which are eclectic in nature and so the book could quite legitimately be grouped as a collective whole spanning the various dimensions of property law, without subdivision. However, such an approach would betray the important links between various chapters, and deprive the reader of the opportunity to gain a broader perspective of the topic in question. Therefore, while the book is split into parts to illustrate the strong links which tie together certain papers, the reader should not feel confined to approaching the book in accordance with the structure suggested by the Parts.

Part I examines the 'propertiness' of property: the extent of proprietary protection and when it can be acquired, used, abused, and in some cases, lost. Kevin Gray examines when real property can lose its 'real'ness in the context of state takings both in America and in the UK, where real property rights are taken away in exchange for monetary compensation. Paul Davies discusses how one may use their property rights, specifically rights to light, and when, if ever, that use may amount to abuse. Lady Justice Arden's chapter looks at water and its proprietary status; a subject of fascinating intellectual depth and one which may assume enormous importance in years to come. The joint chapter by David Capper, Heather Conway and Lisa Glennon looks at the important but rather neglected area of law to do with charging orders, and suggests that the power to convert unsecured contractual debts into security with proprietary attributes needs to have stronger procedural protection built into it. Finally, examining the recent clashes between the European Court of Human Rights and the House of Lords and Supreme Court of the UK in the context of Article 8 and possession orders, Sarah Nield explores whether the procedural safeguards accompanying Convention rights give rise to a new form of proprietary protection.

In Part II the authors look at various types of property rights, with an emphasis on doctrinal development through the years. Jill Morgan discusses the role the tenancy at will has played in the past, and the role it will continue to play in the future. Lisa Whitehouse looks at the English law of mortgage, noting its impressive stability in spite of its operating in ever-changing social circumstances. Finally, John Mee tracks the development of the doctrine of proprietary estoppel from the mid-nineteenth century into the present day, examining the principles which are subsumed within the doctrine and questioning the recent decision by the House of Lords in *Yeoman's Row Management Ltd v Cobbe*.[1]

No doubt prompted by the topicality of the issue as a result of the Law Commission's ongoing work, several chapters touch on the law of easements, covenants, and profits à prendre. Most of these chapters are contained in Part III, with a particular focus on law reform. Elizabeth Cooke and Lu Xu provide us with a sandwich looking at these 'appurtenant interests', a descriptive label that, as discussed in these chapters, is itself controversial. At the conference, we had the benefit of a paper in two halves delivered by Elizabeth Cooke, the first dealing with various issues raised by the Law Commission's proposed reform to easements, covenants and profits à prendre, and the second responding to points raised by Lu Xu. It is Lu Xu's chapter that forms the meat of this sandwich of law reform. Rowena Meager looks at the law of prescription and the inconsistencies in the courts' approach to the user as of right test, with a particular focus on the village green case law that has mushroomed in recent years. Chapters in other Parts of the book also explore aspects of these rights; in particular Ben McFarlane's chapter in Part V and Paul Davies' chapter in Part I.

With the new regime of land registration in England and Wales now firmly bedded down, in Part IV Aruna Nair, Matthew Harding and Robin Hickey examine the scheme from different perspectives. Aruna Nair examines the principles the courts of England and Wales should use when interpreting the land registration rules, arguing that they cannot be properly understood except

1 [2008] UKHL 55, [2008] 1 WLR 1752.

by reference to their interaction with principles of property law, including those pertaining to unregistered land, taken as a coherent whole. Taking a multi-jurisdictional view, Matthew Harding and Robin Hickey build on the important work of Pamela O'Connor on the bijural ambiguity which can occur within land registration systems, and identify a number of normative principles which the authors assert underlie many seminal decisions involving land registration.

Lastly, Part V delves into the more theoretical-based studies in property law. Ben McFarlane takes a fresh look at the *numerus clausus* doctrine and the implications of the principle for reform of restrictive and positive covenants over land. Amy Goymour examines the outer edges of property law from the perspective of the tort of conversion, arguing that unjust enrichment provides a superior form of legal protection for contractual rights. The role of intellectual property in property law is examined by Andreas Rahmatian, whose chapter places intellectual property rights at the conceptual core of property law, alongside real and personal property rights.

This book is being published by Hart Publishing. Richard Hart has been a wonderful supporter of this conference over the years and we are most grateful to him for his continuing commitment to publication of this book. This year he also gave an interesting session during the conference, together with Martin Dixon, on 'Getting Published'. I now understand just how much work goes into book production at his end, as well as at 'ours', and how grateful we should all be to publishers who are willing to 'take a punt' on books that may not be destined to be bestsellers. I am also very grateful to other publishers who sponsored the conference: LexisNexis and Oxford University Press. Various people have given generously of their time to enable this project to come to fruition: a Committee of Faculty members at my own University who helped in the selection of papers for the conference; the 'team' of distinguished anonymous referees who have taken great time and care and have provided many valuable pointers to authors; and Farrah Ahmed who helped me throughout the pre-conference planning as well as during the conference itself. I am most grateful to them.

I want especially to thank Nick Macklam. Nick has been a complete star: he helped during the conference but the bulk of his work has been helping with the editing of these chapters – biting off rather more than he anticipated I think! But I could not have asked for a better person to work on the editing.

I am delighted to be handing over organisation of the next conference in 2012 to Nick Hopkins at Southampton University. In the meantime, enjoy this collection.

Sue Bright
New College, Oxford
October 2010

Contents

Table of Cases

Table of Legislation

United States

Other

European Union

International

I

The 'Propertiness' of Property

1

Recreational Property

Kevin Gray*

It is a good idea, from time to time, to take stock of the current status of property as a jural category. When we refer to 'property', what exactly do we mean? Does the terminology of 'property' have much substantive content and, if so, what? Property lawyers – of all people – tend to leave such questions unaddressed, happy instead to explore the procedural mechanics of property as a subject of gift, exchange and security. Many of us have devoted our professional lives to property – but does it exist? The present chapter tackles this question from the perspective of compulsory acquisition. As in so many other matters, we tend to know the true meaning of something only when it is taken away.

Across the world a legal movement is occurring with surprising symmetry. We have entered a new age of taking – often dignified as taking by the state 'for higher and better use' – a phenomenon that prompts fresh curiosity about the inner reality of property as a human or social institution. The taking process is usually (but not always) concerned with land. Last year, for example, the government of New South Wales proposed legislation enabling the compulsory purchase of private homes in Sydney in order to facilitate large-scale coordinated housing construction.[1] Not so long ago a building in central London was compulsorily acquired because it was not making a 'proper contribution' to local housing stock – the premises were, in fact, being used for purposes of prostitution.[2] The land was then sold on to private developers. Last year, again, New York courts approved the

* For invaluable help in the preparation of this chapter, thanks are owed to David and Moira Milne, Claire and David Sladden, and Peter Zawada. Several related papers can be found at http://www.trin.cam.ac.uk/kevingray.

[1] 'Keneally slams "scaremongering" as she refuses to rule out compulsory purchase of private land' *Sydney Morning Herald* (Sydney 12 March 2010) <http://www.smh.com.au/nsw/keneally-slams-scaremongering-as-she-refuses-to-rule-out-compulsory-purchase-of-private-land-20100312-q2wz.html> accessed 8 October 2010.

[2] *Ainsdale Investments Ltd v First Secretary of State* [2004] EWHC 1010 (QB); [2004] HLR 956.

razing of an area of Brooklyn in order to make way for a number of building constructions including, principally, a new basketball arena for the New Jersey Nets.[3]

Such takings are, of course, accompanied by some sort of money compensation for those affected. Precisely for this reason, these takings reinforce the suggestion that real property may no longer be 'real'; that property rules have dwindled into mere liability rules;[4] and that a new, and not always equitable, doctrine of conversion routinely turns acres into sovereigns.[5] If this is true, proprietary rights in land may connote nothing more than defeasible entitlements that are readily transmutable into money. In so far as private individuals and private corporations can harness the state's monopoly of violence toward this end, there is a real danger that the rich and powerful in society may be enabled, at any time of their choosing, to impose mandatory buy-outs upon the poor and vulnerable.[6]

There was a time when the expropriation of physical resources occurred most conspicuously on a grand scale. Conquistadors and colonists dispossessed entire peoples and took over vast tracts of land – at a price to be paid, if at all, only by much later successors of the invaders. Such takings lie at the root of many of the world's current ills. Nowadays the process of taking is usually a more modest, localised and subtle affair. Takings tend to be narrowly targeted toward the achievement of specific projects or purposes that promise social welfare or environmental benefits for the whole community. Roads must be built or widened; hospitals and schools must be constructed. Most people agree that pressing public need may justify the mandatory erosion of private ownership. But the objectives toward which takings are directed are themselves capable of adaptation to changing times. In a progressively secular and hedonistic society, where sheer survival is generally no longer a matter of struggle, social imperatives have now begun to focus more closely on non-material goods of a recreational or experiential nature. In the words of Jeremy Rifkin, the commodification of work brought about by the industrial era has given way to the 'commodification of play'.[7] People increasingly want to be entertained. Contemporary mores are marked, on an almost global scale, by twin pre-occupations with material accumulation and leisure opportunity. These concerns are tied up in a complex of supportive links aimed at the maximisation of personal satisfaction. But they are also sometimes caught in relationships of mutual antagonism. The imperative of

[3] *Matter of New York State Urban Development Corp (Atlantic Yards Land Use Improvement and Civic Project – Phase 1* (No 32741/09) 26 Misc 3d 1228A (1 March 2010).

[4] See G Calabresi and A D Melamed, 'Property Rules, Liability Rules, and Inalienability: One View of the Cathedral' (1971–72) 85 *Harv L Rev* 1089.

[5] See *Chandler v Pocock* (1880) 15 Ch D 491 (CA) 496.

[6] See *Griffiths v Minister for Lands, Planning and Environment* (2008) 235 CLR 232 [127]–[133], [153].

[7] J Rifkin, *The Age of Access: How the Shift from Ownership to Access is Transforming Capitalism* (Penguin Books, London 2000) 7.

one citizen's recreational or leisure experience may demand encroachments upon the conventionally recognised property rights of others. This collision of values has become an increasingly common dilemma of modern public ethics.

Accordingly the present chapter directs a spotlight on a highly symbolic issue of takings law, namely the degree to which derogations from property rights can be justified by enhanced access to various sorts of recreational entertainment or leisure engagement. What legal value should be accorded to concerns that earlier, less affluent generations may well have considered as ranking low in terms of social priority? How do we calculate the legal traction of often harmless, but nevertheless ephemeral or even self-indulgent, recreational or sporting interests? May your property be taken away just so that other people – perhaps lots of other people – can have fun? What price recreational property?

With all of this in prospect, let me take you on a detour, first to an island of fantasy and then to the land of cold reality.

A property theorist's fantasy

The dream of all property theorists is to discover a pristine island, rich in resources, on which a sizeable group of intelligent, fair-minded and deeply rational human beings has been abandoned. During the period following their arrival on the deserted island the castaways have drawn up, *de novo*, a scheme for their own governance and, in particular, for the allocation and exploitation of the island's terrain and its natural assets. Force of circumstance has caused this isolated community to formulate from first principles a body of rules to control its social, political and economic relations. These people have managed to establish some kind of legal or constitutional structure for their mutual dealings. The result is Rawls in practice rather than Rawls in theory.

Now if such a fascinating collection of individuals were ever found, close observation of its arrangements would surely provide answers to some of the big questions about property – not least the quandary as to whether the term has much significant meaning. Important light would be thrown upon the true nature of proprietary perception and upon the irreducible content of proprietary experience. Extrapolating from this remarkable experiment we could begin to frame better informed hypotheses about the role and utility of proprietary concepts within human groupings which are intent on collective survival. But, alas, there is no juristic laboratory of the kind just described. The desert island and its inhabitants have never existed – except in our imagination.

Or is this necessarily so? In 1787 a judge in North Carolina observed that, following the War of Independence, the settlers in the American colonies had been 'thrown into a similar situation with a set of people ship wrecked and cast on a maroon'd island – without laws, without magistrates, without government, or any legal authority' and that 'being thus circumstanced, the people of this country, with a general union of sentiment, ... formed that system or those fundamental principles comprised in the constitution'.[8] These Argonauts of the Western Atlantic promptly set about fashioning for themselves a workable scheme of property law. They based this scheme on a unique store of proprietary first principles, some derived from their religious beliefs, some from distant recollections of Magna Carta, and some from those English law books that had made it across the ocean. The foundational tenets of the scheme were incorporated in state and federal constitutions and are richly evidenced in the extraordinary body of jurisprudence recorded in the law reports covering the first century of American independence. From these sources we can now glean much of what was then deemed *a priori* about the concept of property. We can catch a glimpse of a lost world of legal experimentation, discovery and self-realisation. We can learn something about the ground rules of proprietary awareness – indeed, of elementary proprietary morality.

The early American experience

It is clear that the dominating impulse behind the North American novation of property ideology was the colonists' insistent desire to escape forever the despotic power from which they had just freed themselves.[9] References to despotic control became a recurring feature of their early case law,[10] the spectre of despotism being pictured variously by analogy to an 'Asiatic prince'[11] or a 'Russian autocrat'[12] or indeed the English Parliament itself.[13] Never again, in the sensitive matters of property and taxation, should citizens be exposed to an 'absolute disposition and unlimited control' of their affairs.[14] Hence that large American theme which reaches through to the present day, the 'essential principle' that '[i]ndividual freedom finds tangible

[8] *Den d Bayard v Singleton* (1787) 1 NC 5, 1 Mart (NC) 48. See also *Vanhorne's Lessee v Dorrance* (1795) 2 US (2 Dall) 304, 308. It should be said immediately, of course, that the American colonists did *not* land on uninhabited territory. They too were invaders and takers – a fact that they promptly and conveniently overlooked.

[9] There remains, of course, some debate as to whether the American struggle for independence was ultimately a 'just war'. See the controversy provoked by the recent contribution of Georgetown University's Professor John Keown (I J Keown, 'America's War for Independence: Just or Unjust?' (2009) 6 *Journal of Catholic Social Thought* 277).

[10] See *Bloodgood v Mohawk & Hudson Railroad Co* (1837) 18 Wend 9, 31 Am Dec 313, 329–31, 334, 352–53; *Taylor v Porter and Ford* (1843) 4 Hill 140, 145, 40 Am Dec 274, 278; *People, ex rel Fountain v Board of Supervisors of Westchester County* (1848) 4 Barb 64.

[11] *Vanhorne's Lessee v Dorrance* (1795) 2 US (2 Dall) 304, 308. See likewise *Bloodgood v Mohawk & Hudson Railroad Co* (1837) 18 Wend 9, 31 Am Dec 313, 343 (referring to 'Asiatic despotism').

[12] *Sharpless v Mayor etc of Philadelphia* (1853) 21 Penn 147, 59 Am Dec 759, 764.

[13] *Vanhorne's Lessee v Dorrance* (1795) 2 US (2 Dall) 304, 310; *Bloodgood v Mohawk & Hudson Railroad Co* (1837) 18 Wend 9, 31 Am Dec 313, 329–30.

[14] *Loan Association v Topeka* (1874) 87 US (20 Wall) 655, 662. See similarly *Calder v Bull* (1798) 3 US (3 Dall) 386, 387–88; *Wilkinson v Leland* (1829) 27 US (2 Pet) 627, 657.

expression in property rights'.[15] The Declaration of Rights in the Pennsylvania Constitution of 1776 set the tone, affirming that all men are born equally free and independent and have, among other entitlements, the right of 'acquiring, possessing and protecting property'.[16] The tenure of property was conceived as a natural, original and pre-legal right[17] or, alternately, as an entitlement derived from, and sanctioned by, 'the sovereign power of the political body' by way of some grant, franchise or 'contract'.[18] It is never perhaps entirely clear whether, as a jural category, property predates contract or vice versa.[19] But, whichever is the case, the jealous protection of the early American citizen's property was said to be grounded on 'a fundamental principle of right and justice'.[20] In a 'free republican country' the enjoyment of private property 'should always be held sacred and inviolable'[21] and indeed, in the words of Pennsylvania's Supreme Court, 'as sacred as life'.[22] Secure possession and undisturbed enjoyment of property by individuals were considered 'the great cement of the social compact'[23] and, in the words of John Locke,[24] the 'great end of Mens entering into Society'.[25] Such sentiments were rapidly enshrined as enduring articles of faith in state constitutions[26] and pre-eminently (as early as 1791) in the Fifth Amendment to the Federal Constitution. As is well known, the latter provision stipulates that '[n]o person shall be ... deprived of ... property, without due process of law; nor shall private property be taken for public use, without just compensation'.

Few constitutional formulae have generated so much difficulty as the Fifth Amendment and its many state analogues. However, almost without exception from the earliest days of American jurisprudence, it has been agreed that the Fifth Amendment's 'takings clause' performs three distinct functions that define the role of property. *First*, the clause implicitly endorses a *Grundnorm* according to which private property is deserving of far-reaching protection by

[15] *United States v James Daniel Good Real Property* (1993) 510 US 43, 61, 81.

[16] Pennsylvania Constitution of 1776 art 1.

[17] See *Vanhorne's Lessee v Dorrance* (1795) 2 US (2 Dall) 304, 310–11; *Varick v Smith* (1835) 5 Paige Ch 137, 28 Am Dec 417, 421; *Bloodgood v Mohawk & Hudson Railroad Co* (1837) 18 Wend 9, 31 Am Dec 313, 354; *Bank of Toledo v Toledo* (1853) 1 Ohio St 622, 632.

[18] *West River Bridge Co v Dix* (1848) 47 US (6 How) 507, 532–33, 536, 539.

[19] See K J Gray, 'Property in a Queue' in G S Alexander and E M Peñalver (eds), *Property and Community* (OUP Inc, New York 2010) 165, 189–91.

[20] *Regents of University of Maryland v Williams* (1838) 9 Gill & John 365, 31 Am Dec 72, 96.

[21] *Bloodgood v Mohawk & Hudson Railroad Co* (1837) 18 Wend 9, 31 Am Dec 313, 331.

[22] *Sharpless v Mayor etc of Philadelphia* (1853) 21 Penn 147, 166, 59 Am Dec 759, 771. See likewise *Den d Bayard v Singleton* (1787) 1 Mart (NC) 48.

[23] *Bloodgood v Mohawk & Hudson Railroad Co* (1837) 18 Wend 9, 31 Am Dec 313, 353.

[24] J Locke, *Two Treatises of Government* (2nd critical edn by P Laslett CUP, Cambridge 1967): *The Second Treatise* Chapter XI, s 134 (373). See also *Entick v Carrington* (1765) 19 Howell St Tr 1029, 1066, 95 ER 807.

[25] For endorsement of the Lockean analysis in American law, see *Vanhorne's Lessee v Dorrance* (1795) 2 US (2 Dall) 304, 310; *Calder v Bull* (1798) 3 US (3 Dall) 386, 388; *Taylor v Porter and Ford* (1843) 4 Hill 140, 145, 40 Am Dec 274, 277.

[26] See, for example, the Virginia Declaration of Rights 1776 arts I, VI; Pennsylvania Declaration of Rights 1776 arts I, VIII.

government. Once vested in a citizen-owner, property is 'encircle[d]' by the Constitution and rendered 'an holy thing'.[27] On any other hypothesis, as the United States Supreme Court observed in 1848,[28] 'the law of property would be simply the law of force', all owners being mere 'tenants at will' holding at the arbitrary pleasure of the strongest within their community.[29] *Second*, the clause acknowledges that in extraordinary circumstances privately held property may require to be yielded up under the ultimate threat of state coercion.[30] The potentiality of expropriation for the sake of the common good is itself a component of the 'social compact':[31] *salus populi suprema est lex*.[32] *Third*, and precisely in view of the 'despotic' nature of this emanation of state power,[33] several equitable constraints or preconditions are imposed on the taking of private property. Any taking must be carried out by 'due process of law'; the taking must be 'for public use'; and, finally, 'just compensation' must be paid.

American jurisprudence thus recognised, in effect, that the state was invested with a 'supereminent dominion'[34] which, under strictly controlled conditions, could mandate the compulsory transfer of privately owned assets in order to meet a public necessity. Notwithstanding subsisting claims of private property, 'eminent domain, the highest and most exact idea of property, remains in the government', by which was clearly meant 'the aggregate body of the people in their sovereign capacity'.[35] But the prerequisites for the exercise of this 'sovereign or transcendental propriety'[36] were both fierce and fiercely enforced in the early days of American independence.

The requirement of just compensation

For example, state taking without the provision of full monetary compensation came to be condemned, in fairly unrestrained language, as an act of 'legalized

[27] *Vanhorne's Lessee v Dorrance* (1795) 2 US (2 Dall) 304, 311.

[28] *West River Bridge Co v Dix* (1848) 47 US (6 How) 507, 532.

[29] See *Vanhorne's Lessee v Dorrance* (1795) 2 US (2 Dall) 304, 316 ('[w]retched situation, precarious tenure'); *Bloodgood v Mohawk & Hudson Railroad Co* (1837) 18 Wend 9, 31 Am Dec 313, 343.

[30] '[P]rivate rights must yield to public exigencies' (*Calder v Bull* (1798) 3 US (3 Dall) 386, 400).

[31] *Livingston v Mayor etc of New York* (1831) 8 Wend 85, 22 Am Dec 622, 633; *Bloodgood v Mohawk & Hudson Railroad Co* (1837) 18 Wend 9, 31 Am Dec 313, 353.

[32] *West River Bridge Co v Dix* (1848) 47 US (6 How) 507, 545.

[33] The early American cases recognised frankly the 'despotic' and 'arbitrary' nature of the power to expropriate. See *Vanhorne's Lessee v Dorrance* (1795) 2 US (2 Dall) 304, 311, 315; *Bloodgood v Mohawk & Hudson Railroad Co* (1837) 18 Wend 9, 31 Am Dec 313, 327.

[34] *Bloodgood v Mohawk & Hudson Railroad Co* (1837) 18 Wend 9, 31 Am Dec 313, 353–54.

[35] *Beekman v Saratoga & Schenectady Railroad Co* (1831) 3 Paige Ch 45, 22 Am Dec 679, 683. See also *West River Bridge Co v Dix* (1848) 47 US (6 How) 507, 535.

[36] *Bloodgood v Mohawk & Hudson Railroad Co* (1837) 18 Wend 9, 31 Am Dec 313, 354. See similarly *Cooper v Williams* (1831) 4 Ohio 253, 286, 22 Am Dec 745, 749 ('transcendent sovereignty'); *Scudder v Trenton Delaware Falls Co* (1832) 1 Saxton Ch 694, 23 Am Dec 756, 764.

plunder'[37] or 'rapine',[38] a form of 'moral piracy'[39] that alike violated 'universal law',[40] 'natural equity'[41] and a 'deep and universal sense of ... justice'.[42] The 'great and sacred principle of private right' demanded that compensation be 'an indispensable attendant' on the exercise of eminent domain.[43] Only on payment of an indemnity to the affected owner could the burden of necessary public works be made to fall, not on a single individual, but 'equally upon every member of the State'.[44] Uncompensated taking would be a 'monster in legislation', not only 'inconsistent with the principles of reason, justice and moral rectitude', but also 'incompatible with the comfort, peace, and happiness of mankind ... [and] contrary to the principles of social alliance in every free government'.[45]

The requirement of public use

There was, furthermore, overwhelming agreement that, even if coupled with an offer of full compensation, the non-consensual taking of a citizen's property could never be justified on the basis of purely private requirement or necessity.[46] No man could be compelled to surrender his property merely in order to serve another man's narrowly conceived self-interest. Whereas publicly motivated taking might be tolerable in view of its diffused social benefits, any expropriation aimed at conferring private gain or benefit upon some individual or corporation was anathema.[47] Expropriation was valid only if directed toward a 'public use'.

[37] *In the Matter of the Mayor etc of New York* (1885) 99 NY 569, 577.

[38] *East Hartford v Hartford Bridge Co* (1850) 51 US (10 How) 511, 531–32 (argument of counsel).

[39] *Heyward v Mayor etc of New York* (1852) 7 NY 314, 324.

[40] J Kent, *Commentaries on American Law* (12th edn by O W Holmes Little, Brown & Co, Boston 1873) vol II, 389; *People, ex rel Fountain v Board of Supervisors of Westchester County* (1848) 4 Barb 64.

[41] *Gardner v Village of Newburgh* (1816) 2 Johns Ch 162, 7 Am Dec 526, 529; *Bloodgood v Mohawk & Hudson Railroad Co* (1837) 18 Wend 9, 31 Am Dec 313, 369; *Hale v Lawrence* (1848) 21 N J Law 714, 729.

[42] *Gardner v Village of Newburgh* (1816) 2 Johns Ch 162, 7 Am Dec 526, 529; *Bloodgood v Mohawk & Hudson Railroad Co* (1837) 18 Wend 9, 31 Am Dec 313, 338. See also *Cooper v Williams* (1831) 4 Ohio 253, 286, 22 Am Dec 745, 749; *Hale v Lawrence* (1848) 21 N J Law 714, 738.

[43] *Gardner v Village of Newburgh* (1816) 2 Johns Ch 162, 7 Am Dec 526, 530. See also *People v Platt* (1819) 17 Johns 195, 8 Am Dec 382, 389; *Rogers and Magee v Bradshaw* (1823) 20 Johns 735; *Beekman v Saratoga & Schenectady Railroad Co* (1831) 3 Paige Ch 45, 22 Am Dec 679, 683.

[44] *Taylor v Porter and Ford* (1843) 4 Hill 140, 143, 40 Am Dec 274, 276.

[45] *Vanhorne's Lessee v Dorrance* (1795) 2 US (2 Dall) 304, 310, 312 ('contrary to the eternal principles of justice, as well as the sacred principles of the social contract').

[46] *Beekman v Saratoga & Schenectady Railroad Co* (1831) 3 Paige Ch 45, 22 Am Dec 679, 683–84; *Varick v Smith* (1835) 5 Paige Ch 137, 28 Am Dec 417, 421; *People v Morris* (1835) 13 Wend 325, 328; *Bloodgood v Mohawk & Hudson Railroad Co* (1837) 18 Wend 9, 31 Am Dec 313, 316, 355, 358; *Taylor v Porter and Ford* (1843) 4 Hill 140, 147–48, 149, 40 Am Dec 274, 280; *Bradford v Cole* (1859) 8 Fla 263, 265.

[47] See K J Gray, 'There's No Place Like Home!' (2007) 11 *Journal of South Pacific Law* 73, 74–75.

A prohibition on private-to-private taking

It followed that no sovereign power was entitled, under colour of statutory authority, to take the property of one citizen for the sole purpose of transferring it to another private party or applying it to the latter's exclusive use.[48] Any purported legislation to this effect was 'contrary to the great first principles of the social compact'.[49] Indeed American courts refused to dignify such enactments as 'law' at all,[50] preferring instead to describe them as a 'sentence',[51] a 'rescript',[52] or a 'mere decree between private parties'.[53] Privately motivated eminent domain smacked of attainder and a legislature could no more confiscate for private use than it 'could order an innocent man to be put to death without trial'.[54] Private-to-private taking by legislative command was 'against common right, as well as against Magna Charta' and 'therefore, *ipso facto*, void'.[55] Any other conclusion, said the Supreme Court of Ohio in 1840, would 'break down all the distinctions between *meum* and *tuum*, and annihilate them forever, at the pleasure of the state'.[56]

Thus emerged the consistent theme of early American case law that privately sponsored expropriation of a citizen was none other than 'robbery',[57] 'plunder',[58] or 'spoliation'.[59] Such expropriation threatened to 'subvert the foundation principle upon which the government was organized, and resolve the political community into its original chaotic elements'.[60] If ever endorsed by the courts, unconsented private-to-private transfers would cause ownership to dwindle into a 'frail and precarious' tenure, dependent on the 'whim or caprice of a legislature',[61] thereby 'mocking the citizen who would thus be despoiled

[48] The authorities are legion, starting with *Vanhorne's Lessee v Dorrance* (1795) 2 US (2 Dall) 304, 311–12 and *Calder v Bull* (1798) 3 US (3 Dall) 386, 388.

[49] *Calder v Bull* (1798) 3 US (3 Dall) 386, 388.

[50] *Calder v Bull* (1798) 3 US (3 Dall) 386, 388.

[51] *Regents of University of Maryland v Williams* (1838) 9 Gill & John 365, 31 Am Dec 72, 99 (quoting William Blackstone, *Commentaries on the Laws of England* (1765–1769) (*Bl Comm*) vol 1, 44).

[52] *Sharpless v Mayor etc of Philadelphia* (1853) 21 Penn 147, 167, 59 Am Dec 759, 772.

[53] *Sharpless v Mayor etc of Philadelphia* (1853) 21 Penn 147, 173, 59 Am Dec 759, 779. See similarly *Loan Association v Topeka* (1874) 87 US (20 Wall) 655, 664.

[54] *Sharpless v Mayor etc of Philadelphia* (1853) 21 Penn 147, 167, 59 Am Dec 759, 772.

[55] *Bowman v Middleton* (1792) 1 SCL (1 Bay) 252. See similarly *Matter of Albany Street* (1834) 11 Wend 149, 151, 25 Am Dec 618, 620 (a 'violation of natural right'); *Varick v Smith* (1835) 5 Paige Ch 137, 28 Am Dec 417, 421; *Matter of John and Cherry Streets, New York* (1838) 19 Wend 659, 676–77.

[56] *Buckingham v Smith* (1840) 10 Ohio 288, 297. See also *Sutton's Heirs v City of Louisville* (1837) 5 Dana 28, 32.

[57] *Loan Association v Topeka* (1874) 87 US (20 Wall) 655, 664.

[58] *Sharpless v Mayor etc of Philadelphia* (1853) 21 Penn 147, 169, 59 Am Dec 759, 774.

[59] *Riley v Charleston Union Station Co* (1905) 51 SE 485, 496.

[60] *Bloodgood v Mohawk & Hudson Railroad Co* (1837) 18 Wend 9, 31 Am Dec 313, 353.

[61] *Bloodgood v Mohawk & Hudson Railroad Co* (1837) 18 Wend 9, 31 Am Dec 313, 343. See similarly *Concord Railroad v Greely* (1845) 17 NH 47, 56 (referring to 'the arbitrary discretion of the legislature in a matter of mere private right').

of his land to enrich another'.[62] State mandate would displace contractual negotiation. As the Supreme Court of New York pointed out in 1843, '[t]he power of making bargains for individuals has not been delegated to any branch of the government ... [W]hen one man wants the property of another ... the Legislature cannot aid him in making the acquisition'.[63]

The balance between public and private

From the viewpoint of European or Australasian observers, the foregoing focus on the recently independent North American colonies may seem, at first, unnecessary or even misplaced. Nevertheless the law of the nascent American jurisdictions is quite remarkable, not because it is unparalleled elsewhere, but because it elaborated, at an extremely early stage and in a particularly pure form, the bedrock principles and perceptions that were to inform the global law of expropriation for a long time to come. During the intervening centuries little new has actually been said about the subject of taking or about the peculiar political and ideological difficulties which it throws up. The judicial insights disclosed in the incipient American case law are both detailed and acute; the range and tenor of juristic debate strangely modern.

To be sure, takings doctrine underwent further mutation in the late nineteenth and twentieth centuries. But, from the very outset, the American courts were sensitively apprised of that single most difficult issue of takings jurisprudence, namely the identification of the 'public use' that legitimises the mandatory expropriation of private individuals or businesses.[64] A variety of interpretative approaches ensued. Over the years the doctrinal understanding of the 'public use' requirement wavered ambivalently between initial connotations of public accessibility or openness to the public and more expansive concepts of public usefulness, public benefit, public welfare and public purpose – even a blunt test of generalised 'public prosperity'.[65] When construed in terms of promotion of the public interest, the constitutional precondition of 'public use' became a powerful lever for the provision of much needed networks of transport, power, communications, water supplies and sanitation. More controversial was the subsequent employment of eminent domain for purposes of urban regeneration[66] and economic development.[67] Even in the early American case law, however, there was never any universally accepted rule that the state's eminent

[62] *Harding v Goodlett* (1832) 11 Tenn (3 Yerger) 41, 24 Am Dec 546, 550.

[63] *Taylor v Porter and Ford* (1843) 4 Hill 140, 143, 147, 40 Am Dec 274, 276, 280. See likewise *Heyward v Mayor etc of New York* (1852) 7 NY 314, 324.

[64] *Bloodgood v Mohawk & Hudson Railroad Co* (1837) 18 Wend 9, 31 Am Dec 313, 352 ('one of the most difficult, and perhaps altogether the most important question that has ever been presented to this court').

[65] See *Harvey v Thomas* (1840) 10 Watts 63, 67, 36 Am Dec 141, 144.

[66] *Berman v Parker* (1954) 348 US 26.

[67] *Kelo v City of New London, Connecticut* (2005) 545 US 469.

domain power should not be made available on behalf of private commercial interests[68] or that substantial private sector profits might not result from the exercise of such power.[69] Nevertheless, amid the various intellectual migrations apparent in the case law, one overarching principle remained constant. Private property must not be forcibly transferred to new private ownership except for reasons which were demonstrably public, rather than private, in their overall nature and impact.[70] Any other approach amounted to some form of state-sanctioned theft.[71]

In retrospect it was perhaps inevitable that the assembling of much of America's burgeoning industrial and communications infrastructure was entrusted to private corporations endowed with delegated facilities of eminent domain. This recourse to eminent domain by private actors meant, of course, that the divide between public and private could never be clean or decisive. The American cases of the early nineteenth century recognised that the interests of private enterprise and the promotion of public purpose might sometimes coincide and that public advantage was often secured at the hand of private sector agents by 'quickening and rewarding their diligence by a grant of the profits'.[72] It was not necessarily fatal that compulsorily acquired land ended up in the ownership of private entrepreneurs, provided always that compensation was paid and the public interest served.

Ultimately, however, the question was inescapable. At what point did a purported exercise of eminent domain cross the borderline between beneficial state intervention and impermissible preferment of another's private commercial advantage? Where was the threshold of unprincipled encroachment upon claims of private ownership? Such enquiries required not only a sophisticated analysis of the ratio of public and private benefit flowing from any expropriation, but also a hard-hitting evaluation of the relative social worth of expropriatory objectives. The result was a fascinating, and remarkably accurate, index of a society's collective values.

Thus, for example, the American courts usually had little difficulty in recognising the paramountly public benefits associated with new railroads built by private corporations with the help of borrowed powers of eminent domain.[73]

[68] See *Bloodgood v Mohawk & Hudson Railroad Co* (1837) 18 Wend 9, 31 Am Dec 313, 346.

[69] See *Bloodgood v Mohawk & Hudson Railroad Co* (1837) 18 Wend 9, 31 Am Dec 313, 317, 322, 324, 345, 361.

[70] It has been pointed out that this prohibition prevented the state 'from invoking its eminent domain power as a means of transferring property from one private owner to another who has found more favor with state officials, or who promises to use the land in a way more to the state's liking' (*Matter of Goldstein v New York State Urban Development Corp* (2009) 921 NE 2d 164, 186).

[71] Thus, for example, eminent domain could not properly be invoked in order to take another's land for the purpose of a private road (*Taylor v Porter and Ford* (1843) 4 Hill 140, 147–48, 40 Am Dec 274, 280) or the provision of a private burial ground (*In the Matter of Deansville Cemetery Association* (1876) 66 NY 569, 573–74).

[72] *Cotrill v Myrick* (1835) 3 Fair 222. See likewise *Matter of Niagara Falls & Whirlpool Railway Co* (1888) 15 NE 429, 432.

[73] See *Matter of Niagara Falls & Whirlpool Railway Co* (1888) 15 NE 429, 433.

The private commercial profit derived from the new railroad company's operations was more than counter-balanced by the 'beneficial influence of railroads in their effects upon the vast and increasing business relations of the nation, and the promoting, sustaining, and perpetuating the happiness, prosperity, and liberty of the people'.[74] Moreover, the 'common carrier' regulations governing railroad companies guaranteed every citizen's equal right to fair, reasonable and non-discriminatory service.[75] By contrast, eminent domain could not appropriately be harnessed for the purpose of causing one man's land to be handed over to another for the construction of a privately operated saw mill or paper mill. Such commercial undertakings had 'no public character', being 'wholly for the private use' of the proponents of the transfer and unaccompanied by any 'common carrier' responsibility toward the public at large. In these circumstances the exercise of eminent domain would be simply a 'violation of the rights of one man for the private benefit of another'.[76] As the United States Supreme Court emphasised in 1874, the use of government power to bestow a citizen's property 'upon favored individuals to aid private enterprises and build up private fortunes, is none the less a robbery because it is done under the forms of law'.[77]

Still less were American courts attracted to the employment of eminent domain 'for purposes of public ornament or pleasure'[78] as distinct from purposes connected with public health. Thus, for example, the mere desire to expand the recreational rights of groups of individuals to hunt or fish in privately owned areas did not point toward any sufficiently strong 'public use' that could validate the taking of private property.[79] In such cases, said one court in 1904, the advantage sought was 'private, rather than public' and eminent domain could not properly be exercised 'to furnish a means of amusement or sport to the few persons who have the inclination and the leisure for such pastime'. The public utility to be subserved by such indulgence was 'imperceptible'.[80] In much the same vein the New York Court of Appeals had earlier denied, in *Matter of Niagara Falls & Whirlpool Railway Co*,[81] that any 'public use' would be promoted by a proposed compulsory purchase of land aimed at affording fee-paying sightseers an enhanced opportunity to view the wonders of the Niagara River from a railway

[74] *Bloodgood v Mohawk & Hudson Railroad Co* (1837) 18 Wend 9, 31 Am Dec 313, 346. See now *Kelo v City of New London, Connecticut* (2005) 545 US 469, 477.

[75] See K J Gray, 'Regulatory Property and the Jurisprudence of Quasi-Public Trust' (2010) 32 *Syd L Rev* 221, 232–36.

[76] *Harding v Goodlett* (1832) 11 Tenn (3 Yerger) 41, 24 Am Dec 546, 549 (contrasting the business operations of a grist miller, who conventionally ranked as a 'public servant'). See similarly *Matter of Eureka Basin Warehouse & Mfg Co of Long Island* (1884) 96 NY 42, 48.

[77] *Loan Association v Topeka* (1874) 87 US (20 Wall) 655, 664.

[78] See *Gardner v Village of Newburgh* (1816) 2 Johns Ch 162, 7 Am Dec 526, 529; *Bloodgood v Mohawk & Hudson Railroad Co* (1837) 18 Wend 9, 31 Am Dec 313, 354–55.

[79] *Albright v Sussex County Lake & Park Commission* (1904) 57 A 398, 400–01. See similarly *Peavy-Wilson Lumber Co, Inc v County of Brevard* (1947) 31 So 2d 483, 486–87.

[80] *Albright v Sussex County Lake & Park Commission* (1904) 57 A 398, 400.

[81] (1888) 15 NE 429, 432–33.

car. Said Andrews J, the fact that the projected railroad would enable visitors 'more easily or more fully to gratify their curiosity' did not justify 'the exercise of the high prerogative of sovereignty invoked in aid of this enterprise'.[82]

The drift of modern American law

The development of modern American takings law is a story of gradual accommodation to the idea that community objectives can often be secured only by allowing substantially free rein to private profit. The provision of public goods is frequently driven by the power of the mighty dollar. The evolving understanding of the 'public use' requirement now endorses any taking that can be said to be 'rationally related to a conceivable public purpose'.[83]

It was on this basis that in 2005, in *Kelo v City of New London, Connecticut*,[84] the United States Supreme Court upheld by a bare majority the expropriation of a group of homeowners in Connecticut in order to further a local plan for economic regeneration. This plan was to be effectuated by private enterprise and was intended to serve the housing needs and social convenience of the Pfizer Corporation, a large pharmaceuticals company that hoped to expand its operations in the area.[85] The holdouts in the *Kelo* case had declared themselves unwilling to sell at any price and saw no reason why they should be compelled to give up their homes simply to make way for the profitable construction of new and fancier homes and facilities for more affluent citizens. The outcome in *Kelo* plainly shocked the American public conscience. The legal firestorm provoked by the decision revolved around the fear that if eminent domain powers could be activated in this way for private commercial advantage, property as a jural category would have a severely diminished content. In effect, property would become a mere ticket entitling the holder, at the election of the state (or of its private sector delegate), to some form of monetary pay-off. Even worse, local government could employ eminent domain as a deliberate fiscal strategy. Provided some public interest were served (however indirectly), there would be no obstacle to compulsory purchase from one private party in order that his or her assets should be sold on profitably to another private party accompanied by the added value of a development consent granted by local government itself.[86]

[82] The Court contrasted the legitimate use of eminent domain in the provision of public parks, observing that such amenities 'contribute to the health … of the people' ((1888) 15 NE 429, 433). The mere 'enjoyment or convenience of those who may visit the [Niagara] Falls' was not enough.

[83] *Hawaii Housing Authority v Midkiff* (1984) 467 US 229, 241.

[84] (2005) 545 US 469.

[85] Notwithstanding the eviction of local residents, the envisaged development in New London never reached fruition. In November 2009 the Pfizer Corporation announced that it was pulling out of the city and cancelling 1,400 jobs: see P McGeehan, 'Pfizer to Leave City That Won Land-Use Case' *New York Times* (New York 12 November 2009) <http://www.nytimes.com/2009/11/13/nyregion/13pfizer.html> accessed 21 September 2010.

[86] Exactly such a strategy has recently been disallowed by the High Court of Australia (see *R & R Fazzolari Pty Ltd v Parramatta City Council* (2009) 237 CLR 603).

Since 2005 more than 40 American states have legislated to cut back the scope of *Kelo*, thus rendering eminent domain largely unavailable for the purpose of privately sponsored commercial development. However, the takings jurisprudence of the Supreme Court and of a handful of states remains unchanged. Here, of course, 'just compensation' must still be tendered in respect of all takings, but in other respects it appears that privately owned assets represent nothing more than a quantum of social and economic resource to be reallocated at will by the state. The only constraint is the slender requirement that the reallocation should bear some rational relation to a 'conceivable public purpose' and that any private benefits conferred should be incidental or secondary to the public advantage achieved.[87] This curtailed perception of the durability of ownership certainly underscores an increasingly prevalent understanding that property rights are limited by social ends and are valid only in so far as their exercise conduces to general community welfare. There is nevertheless a danger that we may lose sight of the longstop role of the phenomenon of property. The minimal and irreducible component of proprietary entitlement is simply the protection that it affords against acts of sheer predation by strangers. It is for this reason that purely or predominantly private benefit cannot properly found the assertion of eminent domain. Powers of compulsory purchase should never be made available to those who walk the earth seeking whom they may devour.

Take, for example, the case of Vera Coking, a 70 year-old widow who had lived for over three decades in Atlantic City, New Jersey in a house immediately adjacent to what later became a Trump Plaza hotel-casino. Availing itself of eminent domain powers vested in a state agency (New Jersey's Casino Reinvestment Development Authority), the Trump Organization, under the controlling influence of the billionaire entrepreneur Donald J Trump, attempted during the 1990s to obtain title to Coking's house. Trump hoped to tarmac over the site and to use it, at least initially, as a limousine parking area adjacent to the hotel-casino.[88] In *Casino Reinvestment Development Authority v Banin*[89] the courts rejected the condemnation action against Coking, who had long proved resistant to offers of purchase. Noting that the action, if successful, would have given Trump a 'blank check' for future extension of the hotel-casino, New Jersey's Superior Court ruled that the primary interest served by the proposed expropriation was 'a private rather than a public one' and that any potential public benefit was 'overwhelmed' by the private advantage that Trump would have derived by way of 'assemblage and future control over development and use of parcels of prime real estate in Atlantic City'.[90] Even in the murky

[87] See *Kelo v City of New London, Connecticut* (2005) 545 US 469, 490–91, where Kennedy J, albeit one of the majority judges, referred to the need for judicial vigilance in cases of alleged 'impermissible favoritism to private parties', repeating the formula that 'transfers intended to confer benefits on particular, favored private entities, and with only incidental or pretextual public benefits, are forbidden by the Public Use Clause.'

[88] Two other adjoining properties, an Italian restaurant and a pawnshop, were also included in the proposed condemnation.

[89] (1998) 727 A 2d 102.

[90] (1998) 727 A 2d 102, 111.

area of eminent domain there is a discernible distinction between economic regeneration and aggressive profit-taking by private developers of real estate. Or, as a Pennsylvania court said way back in 1795, it is 'difficult to form a case, in which the necessity of the state can be of such a nature, as to authorize or excuse the seizing of landed property belonging to one citizen and giving it to another citizen'.[91]

Nevertheless the danger remains. In the *Banin* case itself the Court did not definitively exclude the possibility of a successful condemnation action in the future. The message is stark: if you happen to own something that a very rich person really wants, you had better watch out! Chances are that, if you refuse to sell it to him, he will try to take it anyway.

American 'takers' come to Britain

There is a further reason why the early part of this chapter has focused upon the American experience of eminent domain. Quite simply, American 'takers' have now come to Britain: Donald Trump himself has arrived!

At the time of writing, a battle is being fought out on a pristine stretch of Scottish coastline a few miles north of Aberdeen. In 2006 Donald Trump purchased part of the Menie Estate, an area of some 1,400 acres, which one of his corporate arms, Trump International Golf Links Scotland (TIGLS), now proposes to develop as a £1 billion golf resort. This resort is envisaged as comprising two 18-hole championship links (predicted by Trump to become 'the world's greatest golf course'), a clubhouse, a golf academy, an equestrian centre, a spa, a nine-storey five-star Victorian-style hotel and a residential village of 950 holiday homes and 500 luxury homes, together with shops and restaurants. The location is certainly spectacular, but the golf course, dramatically positioned beside the sea, will invade a Site of Special Scientific Interest and threaten a fragile dune system. The entire project is opposed by a number of conservation and heritage groups.[92] The resort proposal was eventually called in by the Scottish Ministers. Following a public inquiry, the Ministers overrode all objections and, citing likely benefits for the local economy, granted outline planning consent in December 2008.[93] Not surprisingly, Trump's plans have aroused much controversy and popular protest. Among the opponents of the scheme are the actress Tilda Swinton and the film director, Bill Forsyth, whose 1983 film 'Local Hero' revolved around themes similar to those being played out at Menie.

[91] *Vanhorne's Lessee v Dorrance* (1795) 2 US (2 Dall) 304, 311.

[92] A Black, 'Saga of Tycoon's golfing vision' *BBC News* (London 3 November 2008) <http://news.bbc.co.uk/1/hi/scotland/7706703.stm> accessed 21 September 2010.

[93] — 'Trump's £1bn golf resort approved' *BBC News* (London 3 November 2008) <http://news.bbc.co.uk/1/hi/scotland/north_east/7700074.stm> accessed 21 September 2010. Some have speculated that the Menie development may offer the largest boost to the Scottish economy since the North Sea oil boom.

The only substantial impediments to the realisation of the scheme now consist in the presence of several dwelling-houses and some farm land, not yet purchased by TIGLS but located in the centre of the development site.[94] A small number of private owners have refused to sell to TIGLS, even though offered free access for life to the resort's golfing facilities together with an opportunity to purchase new homes within the development.[95] Among the holdouts are Dr David Milne and Moira Milne, who live in a renovated coastguard station that enjoys a 40-mile view north and south along the coast. An 85 year-old lady, Mrs Molly Forbes, occupies a pre-fab home (named 'Paradise') situated on land owned by her son, Michael Forbes, who is likewise opposed to sale. At an early stage TIGLS suggested that Aberdeenshire Council should use its powers of compulsory purchase in order to remove the holdouts, a possibility that the Council has expressly refused to rule out. The atmosphere quickly turned nasty, Donald Trump describing Michael Forbes as 'a village idiot' and 'a loser'[96] living in a 'pig sty'.[97] Molly Forbes announced poignantly that 'I never expected in my life to face eviction from my home, let alone for a golf course'.[98]

Although full planning permission has yet to be obtained for the hotel and housing development, consent to preparatory work on the sand dunes was given in November 2009.[99] Within a week work had commenced to plant the marram grass that supposedly stabilises the dunes over which the golf course is, in part, to be laid. Molly Forbes promptly challenged this grant of planning permission and sought from the Court of Session an interim interdict against further works. In January 2010 she failed on the grounds, inter alia, that she could not show a prima facie case of 'sufficient interest' and that, expensive works already being underway, the balance of convenience did not warrant any interim order.[100] One month later Donald Trump unveiled his 'masterplan' for the proposed development, the aerial view sketches indicating that all the holdout properties had mysteriously disappeared. Since then matters

[94] One parcel, a parking lot half an acre in size, was owned by Aberdeenshire Council. In January 2010 the local area planning committee granted TIGLS 'special purchaser' status in respect of this half-acre parcel, thereby shutting out a number of competitive bids that were being prepared by objectors to the overall scheme. See 'Trump given clearance over land' *BBC News* (London 19 January 2010) <http://news.bbc.co.uk/1/hi/scotland/north_east/8467401.stm> accessed 21 September 2010.

[95] G Harris, 'We're not selling, Donald Trump' *The Sunday Times* (London 18 October 2009) <http://www.timesonline.co.uk/tol/news/uk/scotland/article6879278.ece> accessed 21 September 2010.

[96] 'Trump blasts golf resort village idiot' (STV 24 November 2009) <http://news.stv.tv/scotland/north/139473-trump-blasts-golf-resort-village-idiot> accessed 8 October 2010.

[97] F Urquhart, '"Trump's men grabbed my land" – Forbes' *The Scotsman* (Edinburgh 5 August 2010) <http://thescotsman.scotsman.com/news/39Trump39s-men-grabbed-my-land39.6460647.jp > accessed 21 September 2010.

[98] 'Trump golf course plan faces legal challenge' *BBC News* (London 23 November 2009) <http://news.bbc.co.uk/1/hi/scotland/north_east/8374330.stm> accessed 21 September 2010.

[99] Ref FIAPP/2009/2479.

[100] *Petition of Mary Buchan Forbes v Aberdeenshire Council and Trump International Golf Links* [2010] CSOH 01 [26], [47].

have deteriorated. The possibility of compulsory purchase still hangs over the dissentient owners.[101] Allegations of vandalism and theft by anti-Trump protesters have been countered by claims of trespass committed by Trump contractors. Michael Forbes has begun to sell joint ownership of one of his acres to members of the public in an attempt to render any process of acquisition slow and administratively unwieldy.[102] At the date of submission of this chapter, the central issue of potential expropriation remains unresolved.

The Vice-President of TIGLS has declared that '[t]he whole impetus behind the [golf resort] development is Trump's love of the game'.[103] Donald Trump is certainly a determined collector of golf courses, his commercial organisations having developed eight or nine premier courses in the United States alone. In 2006 his plans to construct a massive golf resort in upstate New York were finally defeated by local residents' objections, based in part on the pollution threat to the water supply posed by runoff fertiliser and pesticides.[104] It seems that Trump turned his attention instead to another jurisdiction where the law of eminent domain may not impinge as strictly on private developers as it now does in many American states.

The social and legal value of recreational interests

Developments such as the golf resort project at Menie raise a curiously prevalent modern question about the social and legal evaluation of sporting and other recreational interests. To what extent can one citizen's legitimate desire to have fun, entertainment or recreational fulfilment validate a state-endorsed and non-consensual taking of rights that other citizens regard as their property? Can privately held land be compulsorily converted into sporting or entertainment

[101] In early March 2010 the Trump team disclaimed any immediate intention to seek compulsory purchase orders, but the holdout owners have expressed little confidence that this stance is final or conclusive. See R Crighton, 'We are tired of fighting over golf plan, says Trump team' *The Press and Journal* (Aberdeen 5 March 2010) <http://www.pressandjournal.co.uk/Article.aspx/1632901> accessed 21 September 2010.

[102] Green MP Caroline Lucas and Body Shop co-founder Gordon Roddick, together with multiple other purchasers, are reported to have become joint owners of the plot in question. See Press Association, 'Caroline Lucas joins campaign to "trip up" Donald Trump' *The Guardian* (London 8 August 2010) <http://www.guardian.co.uk/politics/2010/aug/08/caroline-lucas-donald-trump-golf> accessed 21 September 2010.

[103] B Ferguson, 'Challenges "made Trump more determined"' *The Scotsman* (Edinburgh 3 March 2010) <http://news.scotsman.com/aberdeen/Challenges-made-Trump-more-determined 39.6121947.jp> accessed 21 September 2010.

[104] S Hodara, 'Trump's Golf Course Plan Seen as Threat to Water' *New York Times* (New York 18 March 2001) <http://www.nytimes.com/2001/03/18/nyregion/environment-trump-s-golf-course-plan-seen-as-threat-to-water.html> accessed 22 September 2010. Trump eventually donated the land for use as park land bearing his own name, the tax benefits of this donation being reputed to have been substantial: E Brenner, 'The Ultimate in Luxury Parks' *New York Times* (New York 23 April 2006) <http://query.nytimes.com/gst/fullpage.html?res=9C07E7D8143FF930A15757C0A9609C8B63> accessed 22 September 2010.

space? How does one balance public benefit against personal loss? Is it relevant that certain recreation-related ventures may entail huge private profits for those in charge of their implementation? Do socially motivated doctrines of 'higher and better use' justify compulsory purchase from owners who profess themselves unwilling to sell at any price? What about the Benthamite (or felicific) calculus that elevates the greatest happiness of the greatest number? What price bread and circuses? What price jobs? What price property?

In the case of the golf resort at Menie, these queries pose themselves in a particularly stark form. Should uncooperative citizens be evicted from their homes in order that a number of rich people can play golf at a luxury resort in a beautiful coastal location? Graded instances of the same kind of question crop up almost everywhere today. Let me highlight several examples that may help to pinpoint the threshold beyond which sport- or entertainment-related takings may be thought to be unacceptable.

The Atlantic Yards development in New York

For some years the massive Atlantic Yards project in downtown Brooklyn has engaged the attention of courts in New York. Here the American property tycoon Bruce Ratner spearheaded a proposal that the state's eminent domain power be used on behalf of his corporate alter ego, the Forest City Ratner Companies, to clear 22 acres for a publicly subsidised $4.9 billion mixed-use development. The development was advertised as inclusive of condominiums, offices, retail outlets and (most significantly) a splendid 18,000-seat arena to house the New Jersey Nets.[105] The Nets are a professional basketball franchise currently based across the Hudson River and owned, coincidentally, by Bruce Ratner. The new arena is intended to be publicly owned, but leased to the Nets on extremely generous terms. More generally, the Atlantic Yards proposal has necessitated the compulsory purchase of over 100 parcels of land, variously in residential and commercial use (including popular bars and restaurants and a homeless shelter). In 2008 the Second Circuit Court of Appeals declined to hold that the raison d'être of the regeneration scheme was simply the enrichment of 'the private individual who proposed it and stands to profit most from its completion'.[106] Instead the Court ruled that the revitalisation plan promoted 'several classic public uses' which conferred constitutional sufficiency upon the project, although no attempt was made to single out the degree in which the provision of the basketball venue in itself represented an element of public benefit conducing to this result.[107] In 2009 New York's state courts similarly

[105] Some predict that the new arena will rival Manhattan's Madison Square Garden (see A Mensch, '"Upon Further Review": Why a Sports Stadium Can Justify an Eminent Domain Taking' (2008) 40 *Conn L Rev* 1623, 1642).

[106] *Goldstein v Pataki* (2008) 516 F 3d 50, 52–53, cert den (2008) 128 S Ct 2964, 171 L Ed 2d 906.

[107] (2008) 516 F 3d 50, 63.

rejected the contention that the Ratner proposal, taken as a whole, served no 'public use, purpose, or benefit' or that such benefit was 'merely incidental' to the private benefit to be realised by the developer.[108] Further appeal elicited only a general affirmation that the removal of urban blight is indisputably a 'proper, and, indeed, constitutionally sanctioned predicate for the exercise of the power of eminent domain'.[109] In March 2010 the Supreme Court of New York turned down yet another appeal against the proposed condemnations.[110] Although at this point a number of key opponents of the scheme finally gave up their uneven struggle, others were still seeking, as of August 2010, to reopen the environmental findings of 'blight' that supposedly supported the acquisitions in question.[111] The litigation rumbles on.

The London Olympics and Legacy project

The Atlantic Yards case is perhaps difficult. Any calculation of the human cost versus the social benefit of attracting the New Jersey Nets to Brooklyn is complicated by the fact that the basketball arena project was coupled[112] with a more general scheme aimed at palpable 'revivification of the urban landscape'.[113] The same, too, can be said of litigation in England over the compulsory purchase of

[108] *Matter of Goldstein v New York State Urban Development Corp* (2009) 879 NYS 2d 524, 535–36.

[109] *Matter of Goldstein v New York State Urban Development Corp* (2009) 921 NE 2d 164, 170–71. See also *Matter of Develop Don't Destroy (Brooklyn) v Urban Development Corp* (2009) 874 NYS 2d 414, 420.

[110] *Matter of New York State Urban Development Corp (Atlantic Yards Land Use Improvement and Civic Project – Phase 1* (No 32741/09) 26 Misc 3d 1228A (1 March 2010).

[111] N Oder, 'Surreal morning in court: finally, belatedly a wholesale assault on the Atlantic Yards project, but before a detached judge' (Watchdog blog) <http://atlanticyardsreport.blogspot.com/2010/08/surreal-morning-in-court-finally.html> accessed 22 September 2010. Even those judges who ruled in favour of the Atlantic Yards condemnations felt that the 'blight' bar had probably been 'set too low' and that it was now overly easy for environmental impact studies paid for by developers to 'constitute a predicate for the invasion of property rights and the razing of homes and businesses' (*Matter of Goldstein v New York State Urban Development Corp* (2009) 921 NE 2d 164, 172). Under New York law, however, such environmental findings are exposed to a less than robust judicial scrutiny. Other judges in the Atlantic Yards litigation deprecated more forthrightly the 'deplorable lack of transparency' in the official survey of the environmental impact of the development project, noting that there had been absent 'the candor that the public was entitled to expect' (*Develop Don't Destroy (Brooklyn), Inc v Empire State Development Corp* (No 114631/09) 26 Misc 3d 1236A (10 March 2010)). See also Catterson J's reference to 'a less than admirable sleight of hand' on the part of the quasi-governmental body charged with overseeing the environmental assessment (*Matter of Develop Don't Destroy (Brooklyn) v Urban Development Corp* (2009) 874 NYS 2d 414, 429).

[112] Even this remains a matter of some doubt. The Atlantic Yards project was planned as two phases of construction, the first phase comprising principally the new basketball arena. Opponents of the scheme have pointed out that the second phase need not be implemented for several decades and that the developer could ultimately decide to abandon this phase completely (see *Develop Don't Destroy (Brooklyn), Inc v Empire State Development Corp* (No 114631/09) 26 Misc 3d 1236A (10 March 2010)).

[113] *Matter of Goldstein v New York State Urban Development Corp* (2009) 921 NE 2d 164, 173.

large areas of land in the Lower Lea Valley. This land has been acquired by the London Development Agency in preparation for the 2012 Olympic Games and the so-called 'Legacy' development that is envisaged as extending the Games' regenerative effects throughout a blighted district of East London.

In *Sole v Secretary of State for Trade and Industry*,[114] the High Court rejected a human rights challenge to the expropriation of residential land owned and run by the Peabody Trust. The land was required for the construction of the Olympic Athletes' Village and other sports facilities. The Secretary of State's Inspector concluded that the undoubted private loss comprised in the dislocation of local residents was more than amply outweighed by the anticipated benefits on an 'unimaginable scale' flowing from the Olympic and Legacy projects.[115] The Secretary of State's decision letter confirming the compulsory purchase order emphasised that 'the staging of the Games and fulfilling the Legacy are in the interest of the economic well-being of the country'.[116] This 'much needed regeneration' of parts of the East End represented 'one of the most important and significant development projects planned for the United Kingdom for some considerable time'.[117] In this context the special interests of sports participants and sports spectators were enveloped within, and overshadowed by, a rejuvenation scheme of huge national prestige and importance.

Sport and recreational entertainment as forms of social capital

A purer test of the social ethics of eminent domain presents itself where the relocation of sports arenas is less closely allied with infrastructural projects aimed at economic development or urban regeneration. Typical is the case of the professional football club which simply wants to exchange its ageing ground for a new state-of-the-art stadium in a comparable urban setting. Frequently this objective cannot be achieved without the compulsory purchase of homes and business premises within the targeted relocation site. The mix of competing interests now more obviously pits the disbenefit of individual loss against the social dividends of football, against the environmental impact of the project, and against the anticipated profits of both the developer and the shareholder-owners of the football club itself.[118]

[114] [2007] EWHC 1527 (Admin), (2007) 151 SJLB 746.

[115] *Report to the Secretary of State for Trade and Industry by David Rose (Inspector) on the Application by The London Development Agency for confirmation of The London Development Agency (Lower Lea Valley, Olympic and Legacy) Compulsory Purchase Order 2005* (16 October 2006) [6.5.3.].

[116] [2007] EWHC 1527 (Admin), (2007) 151 SJLB 746 [42]. Compare, however, J Cheyne, 'Olympian Masterplanning in London' (2009) 10 *Planning Theory & Practice* 404.

[117] [2007] EWHC 1527 (Admin), (2007) 151 SJLB 746 [15]. See similarly *Smith v Secretary of State for Trade and Industry* [2007] EWHC 1013 (Admin), [2008] 1 WLR 394 [45]–[50].

[118] It should not be forgotten that in recent years majority share ownership and effective control of many of England's leading football clubs have been increasingly vested in a motley array of extremely wealthy foreign investors and entrepreneurs.

Sport is increasingly recognised as a significant cultural form in the modern world. The broader advantages brought about by spectator engagement with sport are not inconsiderable. There exists a small, but interesting, body of literature concerning the intangible non-economic benefits that successful professional sports teams confer upon their fan-base and the surrounding community. Shared partisanship in support of one team's efforts undoubtedly has a certain collegial or integrative dimension. Sport is a 'socially-consumed commodity'[119] – a non-trivial form of social capital – providing a constant and convenient reference point for everyday interaction and interpersonal exchange. In some cases – as with the major European soccer clubs – sporting affiliations have become a truly globalised brand, generating a medium of communication that is understood as readily in Bangkok as in Birmingham or Barcelona. Much is at stake, ranging from a sense of local identity or civic pride to community bonding and important measures of vicariously derived self-esteem or reflected glory.[120] Personal perceptions of well-being and self-worth often fluctuate with the fortunes of the object of one's sporting affection. In a phrase often attributed to the revered Bill Shankly, manager of Liverpool Football Club during the 1960s and 1970s, 'football isn't a matter of life and death: it's much, much more important than that!'

In many instances, therefore, the social significance of fan support and spectator participation may seem to afford a powerful argument in favour of compulsory purchase.[121] American courts have long recognised that 'a sports arena, even one privately operated for profit, may serve a public purpose'.[122] It should never be forgotten that three decades ago precisely such factors precipitated a bizarre twist in the history of eminent domain law. In 1982 the Oakland Raiders, a professional football team in the NFL, announced its intention to move to Los Angeles. The City of Oakland, fearing a negative impact on the local community, successfully asserted eminent domain in order to buy up the intangible rights – the choses in action – constituted by the players' contracts with the Raiders, thereby keeping the Raiders for the time being safely in Oakland.[123] The Supreme Court of California upheld the expropriation of the Raiders' franchise rights on the ground that 'providing access to recreation to its citizens in the form of spectator sports is an appropriate function of city

[119] A R Sanderson, 'In Defense of New Sports Stadiums, Ballparks and Arenas' (1999–2000) 10 *Marq Sports L J* 173, 189.

[120] It has frequently been noted, however, that intangible public goods of this kind are not traded in a market where their value can be quantified (D Coates and B R Humphreys, 'The Stadium Gambit and Local Economic Development' (2000) 23(2) *Regulation* 15, 16–18). See also D Coates and B R Humphreys, 'Professional Sports Facilities, Franchises and Urban Economic Development' (2003) 3 *Public Finance and Management* 335, 344–46.

[121] See A Mensch, '"Upon Further Review": Why a Sports Stadium Can Justify an Eminent Domain Taking' (2008) 40 *Conn L Rev* 1623.

[122] *Matter of Develop Don't Destroy (Brooklyn) v Urban Development Corp* (2009) 874 NYS 2d 414, 424. See likewise *Murphy v Erie County* (1971) 268 NE 2d 771, 774; *Matter of Kaur v New York State Urban Development Corp* (2010) 15 NY 3d 235, 258.

[123] *City of Oakland v Oakland Raiders* (1982) 183 Cal Rptr 673.

government'.[124] In this respect the Court's conclusion mirrored a much earlier judicial statement that municipal corporations are 'not limited to providing for the material necessities of their citizens', but have a duty to 'please and amuse their inhabitants'.[125] A modern equivalent, in other words, of the ancient Roman *panes et circenses* – the bread and circuses which only the more cynical perceived to be deliberate distractions from the pressing problems of everyday life and from the constant failures of government.

The social ethics of personal dislocation

Where recreational participation is facilitated by acts of eminent domain, the benign personal and emotional by-products must, of course, be measured against the human and other costs of expropriation. Displacement, it has been said, is the 'defining feature' of mega-events such as the Olympic Games.[126] Indeed, it has been estimated that successive Olympiads have displaced more than 2 million people during the past 20 years, a large proportion by the 2008 Beijing Games alone. This darker side of sporting mega-events, with their potential for human rights violations, 'stands in stark contrast to the admirable universal ideals that are often cited at their opening ceremonies'.[127] Nor, by any means, are the dislocation consequences of promoting and celebrating sport limited to regularly recurring global sporting festivals.[128] What Frank Michelman famously termed the 'demoralization cost' of takings is felt no less keenly by those who are forced to surrender their homes in order that a new football stadium be built in their own locality.[129] As the Supreme Court of Ohio observed in *City of Norwood v Horney*,[130] '[f]or the individual property owner, the appropriation is not simply the seizure of a house. It is the taking of a home – the place where ancestors toiled, where families were raised, where memories were made'.

Thus, for example, when Everton Football Club proposed in 2007 to relocate from Goodison Park to a brand new stadium in Kirkby, a grandmother, Dot Reid, led a resistance movement directed against the scheme's major proponent,

[124] (1982) 183 Cal Rptr 673, 680.

[125] *Meyer v City of Cleveland* (1930) 171 NE 606, 606–07. See similarly *Martin v Philadelphia* (1966) 215 A 2d 894, 896.

[126] L Porter, 'Planning Displacement: The Real Legacy of Major Sporting Events' (2009) 10 *Planning Theory & Practice* 395. See also D Eby, 'Closing Ceremonies: How Law, Policy and the Winter Olympics are Displacing an Inconveniently Located Low-Income Community in Vancouver' (2009) 10 *Planning Theory & Practice* 408.

[127] *Fair Play for Housing Rights: Mega-Events, Olympic Games and Housing Rights* (Centre on Housing Rights and Evictions, Geneva 2007) 9–11. 'Nobody should be forcibly evicted for the sake of a sporting event' (ibid 10).

[128] See M Jaconelli, '"Just a Person in a Wee Flat": Being Displaced by the Commonwealth Games in Glasgow's East End' (2009) 10 *Planning Theory & Practice* 399.

[129] F I Michelman, 'Property, Utility, and Fairness: Comments on the Ethical Foundations of "Just Compensation" Law' (1966–67) 80 *Harv L Rev* 1165, 1214.

[130] (2006) 853 NE 2d 1115, 1122.

Sir Terence Leahy. Leahy, a lifelong Everton fan, also happened to be the chief executive of the Tesco supermarket chain. Dot Reid's home in Kirkby was one of 72 houses which stood to be demolished in order to make way for a 55,000-seat stadium and home for Everton FC as part of a more general £400 million redevelopment scheme which would, by chance, have incorporated a Tesco superstore. Said Mrs Reid:

> What we have built here is a proper community, a lovely place to live … I don't think this area is right for a football stadium and won't accept watching this street we worked hard to build turned into a Tesco car park.[131]

So angered was Mrs Reid that she submitted a planning application requesting permission to demolish Sir Terence Leahy's luxury home 100 miles away in Hertfordshire, with the stated objective of converting the property (together with its swimming pool and gymnasium) into a community garden for pensioners complete with water features. Welwyn Hatfield Council solemnly announced that it would consider this application as it would consider any other.[132] Sadly, however, the confrontation came to naught when in November 2009 Everton's proposed move to Kirkby was rejected, at least for the time being, by John Denham, the Secretary of State for Communities and Local Government.

The Emirates Stadium in North London

The first stadium-led compulsory purchase in Britain seems to have been that involving Arsenal Football Club.[133] In 2002 Islington London Borough Council granted planning permission for a scheme which would enable Arsenal FC to move from its dilapidated 38,500-seat facility at Highbury to a magnificent £350 million 60,000-seat stadium to be built half a mile away. The permission was subject to a 'section 106 agreement',[134] under which a range of 'planning gains' were supposedly secured for the local community. The Council subsequently made a compulsory purchase order under which the new stadium site, together with substantial surrounding land, was to be turned over to Arsenal FC. The surplus land was then intended to be sold on by Arsenal FC for housing and commercial development, the profits generated by these transactions helping to fund the construction of the new stadium and the various non-commercial facilities needed as substitutes for facilities displaced by the new arena. The

[131] G O'Keeffe, 'We will fight to save our homes and stop Blues' Kirkby stadium' *Liverpool Echo* (Liverpool 3 April 2007) <http://www.library./+fight+to+save+our+homes+and+stop+Blues'+Kirkby+stadium%3B...-a0161496553> accessed 9 October 2010.

[132] M Hughes, 'Home of Tesco boss "should be bulldozed"' *The Independent* (London 12 April 2008) <http://www.independent.co.uk/news/uk/this-britain/home-of-tesco-boss-should-be-bulldozed-808152.html> accessed 30 April 2010.

[133] See *The London Borough of Islington (Ashburton Grove and Lough Road, Islington) Compulsory Purchase Order 2002: Conclusions of Rupert Grantham, Inspector* (2003) [685].

[134] See Town and Country Planning Act 1990 s 106.

CPO covered 134 plots of land currently being used for business or residential purposes.

After objections to the scheme from local owners and following a six-week public inquiry, the Secretary of State's Inspector, Rupert Grantham, recommended that the CPO should not be confirmed. In his view, the deployment of compulsory purchase powers was not sustainable either by the 'desire to bolster the club's chances of future success'[135] or on the ground of any 'civic pride' flowing from Arsenal FC's presence in Islington. Only five per cent of season ticket holders for Highbury Stadium actually lived within the Borough of Islington.[136] Moreover, in the Inspector's opinion, the level of regenerative benefit likely to accrue from the overall scheme was 'disappointingly low'.[137] This conclusion mirrors more general research findings that the presence of a major sports team or stadium in a particular area is no guarantee of local economic benefit or growth.[138] Objective studies 'consistently show building sports stadiums to be a poor investment for cities'.[139] Islington Council's approach, said the Inspector, had been marked by an understandable element of 'opportunism' and there was 'a danger that the benefits to the community [would] be overly constrained by private interests'.[140] Local employment prospects, particularly for poorer members of the community, might well be damaged by an influx of new households into the area.[141] Even the much vaunted provision of affordable local housing promised by the scheme involved high density blocks of flats wrapped around a new waste and recycling centre positioned in the least desirable part of the CPO site. Any short term benefits were 'far outweighed by the long term social consequences of consolidating the area's reputation as an area of low income households'.[142] The Inspector concluded that economic regeneration arguments had been 'retrofitted' to what was, in effect, a privately motivated redevelopment scheme.[143] The new stadium would 'cater mostly for

[135] *Inspector's Conclusions* (n 133) [684].

[136] *Inspector's Conclusions* (n 133) [715], [736].

[137] *Inspector's Conclusions* (n 133) [737].

[138] *Inspector's Conclusions* (n 133) [707]. See A R Sanderson, 'In Defense of New Sports Stadiums, Ballparks and Arenas' (1999–2000) 10 *Marq Sports LJ* 173, 187; D Coates and B R Humphreys, 'The Stadium Gambit and Local Economic Development' (2000) 23(2) *Regulation* 15, 18–20; V Bovo, 'Keeping the Public in the Public Use Requirement' (2006) 16 *Seton Hall J Sports & Ent L* 289, 311; C F Hartzog, 'The "Public Use" of Private Sports Stadiums: *Kelo* Hits a Homerun for Private Developers' (2006–07) 9 *Vand J Ent & Tech L* 145, 159.

[139] P Weinberg, 'Eminent Domain For Private Sports Stadiums: Fair Ball Or Foul?' (2005) 35 *Envtl L* 311, 321. '[T]he real benefit goes to the private corporations that profit from constructing, developing, and selling the land that was basically handed over to them' (E A Stanton, 'Home Team Advantage? The Taking of Private Property for Sports Stadiums' (2005–06) 9 *NY City L Rev* 93, 106). See also D Coates and B R Humphreys, 'Professional Sports Facilities, Franchises and Urban Economic Development' (2003) 3 *Public Finance and Management* 335, 350.

[140] *Inspector's Conclusions* (n 133) [690]. In particular, it seemed highly likely that Arsenal FC could sell the surplus purchased land on to private developers for significantly more than the Council paid in compensation' (*Inspector's Conclusions* (n 133) [774]).

[141] *Inspector's Conclusions* (n 133) [735].

[142] *Inspector's Conclusions* (n 133) [722].

[143] *Inspector's Conclusions* (n 133) [693].

people living outside the area, whereas the adverse side effects of the increased capacity and frequency of events would be felt locally'.[144] All of these contra-indications disinclined the inspector to find any 'compelling case in the public interest' that the CPO should be confirmed.[145]

The Inspector's recommendation was in due course rejected by the then Secretary of State, John Prescott, who found that the 'need to secure a comprehensive regeneration scheme' for the area was overwhelming.[146] This decision was, in its turn, challenged in the High Court on the ground that compulsory purchase powers could not properly be used to enable a privately owned football club to construct a replacement stadium. However, in *Alliance Spring Co Ltd v First Secretary of State*[147] Collins J held that the Secretary of State had been entitled to conclude that local regeneration was the 'main purpose' of the challenged CPO, 'albeit that the trigger for the scheme was the desire of [Arsenal FC] for a new stadium with a substantially increased capacity'. Collins J expressed a natural sympathy for the individuals whose lives were to be 'disrupted by a scheme which benefits [the Club]', but added that it was entirely irrelevant that the scheme was led by and largely dependent on a private developer.[148] Although the Inspector had declined to examine the objectors' European Convention rights (precisely because he recommended against confirmation of the CPO),[149] Collins J, in a worryingly brief reference, felt sure that these rights had been fully and properly considered by the Secretary of State.[150]

The upshot was, of course, the construction of the strikingly handsome Emirates Stadium in North London. It has since emerged, nevertheless, that many of the ancillary benefits pledged by Arsenal Football Club in its original planning application have not been realised.[151] A sum of £7.6 million set aside for the upgrading of nearby underground stations was withdrawn after Transport for London discontinued its plans for such renovation works; and instead of building a new local sports centre, the Club merely announced that it would contribute £1 million to unspecified local sports facilities. Perhaps most disconcertingly, the Club has now admitted that the transition to the new stadium was motivated only by the need to raise increased income by absorbing more of the fans waiting on lists for season tickets. As two leading American commentators have observed, professional sports may actually be 'a drain on local economies rather than an engine of economic growth'. In the view of

[144] *Inspector's Conclusions* (n 133) [736].

[145] *Inspector's Conclusions* (n 133) [780].

[146] *Alliance Spring Co Ltd v First Secretary of State* [2005] EWHC 18 (Admin), [2005] 3 PLR 76 [17].

[147] [2005] EWHC 18 (Admin), [2005] 3 PLR 76 [19]–[20].

[148] [2005] EWHC 18 (Admin), [2005] 3 PLR 76 [19]–[23].

[149] *Inspector's Conclusions* (n 133) [784].

[150] [2005] EWHC 18 (Admin), [2005] 3 PLR 76 [21].

[151] D Conn, 'Shadow of Arsenal's grand design hangs over the little people' *The Guardian* (London 3 May 2006) <http://www.guardian.co.uk/football/2006/may/03/sport.comment1> accessed 22 September 2010.

these analysts, 'one thing is clear ... [that is] that owners are reaping substantial benefits in the value of their teams because they are so skilled at the stadium gambit'.[152]

Some American contrasts

Although the record is far from uniform, the vast corpus of American eminent domain law throws up several stern instances of judicial unwillingness to sanction compulsory purchase for mere purposes of sport or public entertainment.[153] Thus, for example, in *Peavy-Wilson Lumber Co, Inc v County of Brevard*[154] the Supreme Court of Florida refused to allow the compulsory acquisition of a parcel of 'wild and rural' land in order that it be made 'available to a group who may have the leisure and inclination to hunt and fish'. The Court thought it irrelevant that the proposed park land would attract sportsmen and tourists from all over the world and would be open to the public. The 'forms of amusement' envisaged had a private rather than public quality. Eminent domain, said the Court, was aimed at the provision of goods that are 'basically essential', such as public buildings to carry on governmental functions, public roads, schools, drainage projects, and the like. The constitutional protection of property had been 'promulgated as a compact, by all in the first instance, to shield minorities from majorities'.[155] More recently, a court in Massachusetts objected to an exercise of eminent domain which would have enabled the grant of a leasehold estate to a private entity in order that the latter could build a stadium for its professional baseball team. Given that not a dime in rent was to be payable on the lease, the 'potential private windfall' for profit-making assignees of the lease rendered the public purpose of the acquisition somewhat less than clear, even though the concomitant 'revitalization of the central business district would increase public pride and spirit'.[156]

One of the more notable rejections of recreation-related eminent domain occurred in *Southwestern Illinois Development Authority v National City Environmental, LLC.*[157] Here the Supreme Court of Illinois threw out a proposed acquisition of a block of privately owned land that had been intended to increase the parking facilities adjacent to a privately operated automobile racetrack. The Court conceded that it might be true that spectators at the track 'would benefit greatly' and that economic development was a legitimate

[152] D Coates and B R Humphreys, 'The Stadium Gambit and Local Economic Development' (2000) 23(2) *Regulation* 15, 18, 20.

[153] It has even been suggested that the condemnation of land for recreational purposes involves a different, and higher, standard of judicial review than in ordinary eminent domain proceedings (*Hillsborough County v Lutz Realty & Investment Co* (1989) 553 So 2d 1320, 1324).

[154] (1947) 31 So 2d 483, 486.

[155] (1947) 31 So 2d 483, 487.

[156] *City of Springfield v Dreison Investments Inc* (2000) 11 Mass L Rep 379.

[157] (2002) 768 NE 2d 1.

rationale for eminent domain. However, it emerged that, equipped with the additional parking, the track was likely to attract new race opportunities worth many millions of dollars in spectator revenue and also, crucially, that it was cheaper for the racetrack owner to request that 'quick-take' eminent domain be exercised on its behalf than to construct enhanced parking on its existing parcel of land. In the light of these factors the Supreme Court regarded the private-to-private transfer for commercial profit as disclosing no recognisable public purpose.[158] In the words of the Court:

> If property ownership is to remain what our forefathers intended it to be, if it is to remain a part of the liberty we cherish, the economic by-products of a private capitalist's ability to develop land cannot justify a surrender of ownership to eminent domain.[159]

Hallmarks of impermissible taking

This chapter has attempted, against the backdrop of various forms of recreational or entertainment-led user, to identify the boundary of permissible takings of property and, correlatively, the threshold of unconsented and *impermissible* takings. The question has haunted global jurisprudence for centuries: 'Where, then, shall the line be drawn …?'[160] Let us first establish certain realistic points of departure; and in this context the early wisdom of the American courts again proves helpful. Remember that, throughout this chapter, we have been using the old case law of the United States as a laboratory of elementary proprietary ideas.

Few would deny that eminent domain or compulsory purchase is an indispensable feature of the contemporary legal landscape: it is simply a fact of life. Without it,

> … the means of social and commercial intercourse might be petrified, and remain for ages, like the fossil remains in sandstone, unaltered, and the government … be paralyzed in every important public improvement.[161]

Eminent domain thus has a vital social function; it is required for the administration of the 'affairs of a state … in the most beneficial manner'.[162] There is no doubt that the process must be accompanied by the proffering of monetary compensation. The power of compulsory acquisition may be delegated to or made available on behalf of private parties, but it is always

[158] (2002) 768 NE 2d 1, 8–11 ('the true beneficiaries of this taking are private businesses and not the public').

[159] (2002) 768 NE 2d 1, 10.

[160] *Scudder v Trenton Delaware Falls Co* (1832) 1 Saxton Ch 694, 23 Am Dec 756, 769.

[161] *West River Bridge Co v Dix* (1848) 47 US (6 How) 507, 547. See likewise *Concord Railroad v Greely* (1845) 17 NH 47, 58.

[162] *Harding v Goodlett* (1832) 11 Tenn (3 Yerger) 41, 24 Am Dec 546, 548.

'of a high and extraordinary character, and ought to be exercised with great caution and deliberation'.[163] Constant vigilance is required to 'secure the citizen from the capricious abuse of the sovereign right of eminent domain'.[164] In the old days American courts even went so far as to attach a fiduciary status to the recipients of eminent domain authority. '[S]overeign franchises' and the powers of acquisition which they carried 'must be held in trust for the general good'.[165] The exercise of eminent domain was, in truth, the 'execution of the trust'.[166] In a more modern setting, compulsory acquisition is recognised to be a power of last resort for the good of the public. It is 'not simply a vehicle for cash-strapped municipalities to finance community improvements'.[167] Still less can a taking be allowed to confer a private benefit on a particular private party.[168]

It is equally clear that public objectives have frequently been met through the harnessing of private commercial enterprise or public-private partnerships. Particularly during the past thirty years the drive toward privatisation has rendered the definition of public purpose, public benefit and public use even more obscure and controversial. Nor need there be any misunderstanding of the motivation behind corporate involvement in the provision of the infrastructure of modern life. Even in 1832 the Chancellor of New Jersey was able to declare that altruistic private corporations 'are not to be found. Private interest or emolument is the *primum mobile* in all. The public interest is secondary and consequential'.[169] The New York courts of that same era were no less realistic. Incorporated companies 'are often irresponsible'[170] and 'have no consciences, nor souls to commiserate the condition of others … [and are] proverbial for their keenness and sagacity in amassing wealth, and not too unfrequently at the expense of others'.[171] Hence the substantial reluctance of these courts to acknowledge that 'the highest responsibilities of the government may be devolved on a moral nonentity, which from its nature is incapable of exercising political responsibilities'.[172]

It has long seemed to me that the unacceptable face of eminent domain is best identified in the language of *predation* or *plunder*. Until this point is

[163] *Boston Water Power Co v Boston & Worcester Rail Road Corpn* (1839) 40 Mass (23 Pick) 360, 395–96. See *Bl Comm Vol 1* (n 51) 135.

[164] *Sutton's Heirs v City of Louisville* (1837) 5 Dana 28, 32. See *Southwestern Illinois Development Authority v National City Environmental, LLC* (1999) 710 NE 2d 896, 904 ('Eminent domain is an intrusive power, and the potential for its abuse is boundless').

[165] *Messenger v Pennsylvania Railroad Co* (1873) 36 N J Law (7 Vroom) 407, 413, 13 Am Rep 457, 462. See also *Messenger v Pennsylvania Railroad Co* (1874) 37 N J Law (8 Vroom) 531, 533, 18 Am Rep 754, 756; K J Gray, 'Regulatory Property and the Jurisprudence of Quasi-Public Trust' (2010) 32 *Syd L Rev* 221, 233.

[166] *Rogers and Magee v Bradshaw* (1823) 20 Johns 735.

[167] *Beach-Courchesne v City of Diamond Bar* (2000) 95 Cal Rptr 2d 265, 279; *City of Norwood v Horney* (2006) 853 NE 2d 1115, 1141.

[168] *Hawaii Housing Authority v Midkiff* (1984) 467 US 229, 245.

[169] *Scudder v Trenton Delaware Falls Co* (1832) 1 Saxton Ch 694, 23 Am Dec 756, 769.

[170] *Bloodgood v Mohawk & Hudson Railroad Co* (1837) 18 Wend 9, 31 Am Dec 313, 328.

[171] Ibid, 341.

[172] Ibid, 366.

reached, I myself have no real quarrel with the assertion of expropriatory power. But when taking for the common good crosses a borderline and becomes a predatory act, there the process of state-sanctioned expropriation begins to sour. To be sure, this does not happen often. But when expropriation in the public interest slides into an acquisition heavily dedicated to an overweening private interest, the taking starts to resemble theft.[173] Or, to use the terminology of the early American cases, the outcome is analogous to 'robbery'[174] or 'plunder'.[175] Another description – again to be found in the American case law – is the label of 'spoliation'.[176] This was a term later adopted (although I think unconsciously) by the Northern Irish courts as a *Leitmotiv* in their construction of the interesting prohibition on uncompensated taking of property that was enshrined in the Government of Ireland Act 1920.[177] Nor, in the more general context, are we far from connotations of piracy or the pillaging of the goods of those who lose on the field of battle.

The difficulty is, of course, to articulate the criteria that might sensibly discriminate between legitimate and illegitimate takings. There follows here an attempt, albeit very tentative, to outline a number of overlapping indicators which may more closely identify the intuitively perceived category of *predatory* taking. None of these indicators is in itself conclusive, but in some combination or other they may evidence the hallmarks of impermissible acquisition. They comprise giveaway signals that a proposed compulsory purchase of privately held property is, in some way, suspect.

The 'balance of power' test

Predatory taking is almost invariably associated with a gross imbalance of economic power. The suspect category extends indicatively to instances where the relatively poor and vulnerable are targeted by the taker and are picked off in turn.[178] Superior resources enable the taker to deploy overwhelming

[173] As is well known, the Convention for the Protection of Human Rights and Fundamental Freedoms (European Convention on Human Rights, as amended) (ECHR) prescribes that '[n]o one shall be deprived of his possessions except in the public interest' (Protocol No 1 art 1). Furthermore, any interference with a person's right to respect for his private and family life and home must be shown to be 'necessary in a democratic society in the interests of national security, public safety or the economic well-being of the country, for the prevention of disorder or crime, for the protection of health or morals, or for the protection of the rights and freedoms of others' (ECHR art 8).

[174] *Loan Association v Topeka* (1874) 87 US (20 Wall) 655, 664.

[175] *Sharpless v Mayor etc of Philadelphia* (1853) 21 Penn 147, 169, 59 Am Dec 759, 774.

[176] *Riley v Charleston Union Station Co* (1905) 51 SE 485, 496.

[177] *Northern Ireland Road Transport Board v Benson* [1940] NI 133, 158. See K J Gray, 'Can environmental regulation constitute a taking of property at common law?' (2007) 24 *EPLJ* 161, 172–73.

[178] For an insightful analysis, see A J van der Walt, *Property in the Margins* (Hart Publishing, Oxford and Portland 2009), 205–07: 'Ownership (and strong property rights) are not necessarily strong in themselves. It is strong owners that are strong'.

legal assistance and services in promotion of the forced acquisition, while the 'takees' – to use a term coined in the Northern Ireland case law[179] – are isolated and uncoordinated in their resistance. There is here a strong aspect of opportunism, exploitation and instrumentalism. The expropriated person (together with the land he or she owned) is treated merely as a means to a desired fiscal or commercial end. As the Supreme Court of Alberta once pointed out in an analogous context, the owner is 'victimize[d]' in order to maximise the private advantage of the stronger party.[180] A good (but, in its way, very bad) example can be found in a recent use of compulsory acquisition in Australia's Northern Territory that enabled a private citizen to acquire land for purposes of farming, tourist and other commercial enterprises liberated from the hard-won native title rights which had previously encumbered that land.[181]

The 'net effect' test

A potent index of predatory taking focuses on what might be termed the 'net effect' of the transaction in question. Where does the compulsory acquisition leave the parties? Predatory takings tend to correlate with significant transfers of valued resource from one set of owners to another. Such takings are marked by a substantial disparity of final outcome and represent the polar opposite of a Pareto-optimal trade. The takee's subjective valuation of an asset (which may not have much to do with its monetary value) is conclusively subordinated to the taker's declared interest and private advantage. The takee stands to lose pretty much everything that he or she originally valued in the resource, while the predator is ideally placed to carry on toward a privately conceived objective and to exclude the rest of the world from its benefits.

The taker's goal may be (and commonly is) the accumulation of financial gain, an objective not of course shared by any takee whose stance is one of unwillingness to sell at any price. In such cases, as Justice Breyer observed during the oral hearing in the *Kelo* case,[182] somebody is being expropriated 'just so some other people can get a lot more money'. Here the taking has a clear rent-seeking dimension – the promotion of private profit. The process is described by some as the 'fiscalization' of land use,[183] ie the turning of land to its highest value as a generator of cash. The key element is the diversion of advantage to

[179] See *Belfast Corporation v O D Cars Ltd* [1960] AC 490 (HL) 508 (argument of counsel).

[180] *Re Murphy Oil Co Ltd and Dau* (1969) 7 DLR (3d) 512, 520. See also *Cottonwood Christian Center v Cypress Redevelopment Agency* (2002) 218 F Supp 2d 1203 (an unsuccessful attempt by Costco to take over a church site for use as a supermarket).

[181] *Griffiths v Minister for Lands, Planning and Environment* (2008) 235 CLR 232. See K J Gray, 'There's No Place Like Home!' (2007) 11 *Journal of South Pacific Law* 73.

[182] *Kelo v City of New London, Connecticut*: Transcript of Oral Argument (22 February 2005) 50.

[183] See M Brnovich, *Condemning Condemnation: Alternatives to Eminent Domain* (Goldwater Institute Policy Report No 195, 14 June 2004).

the total (or virtually total) exclusion of the takee.[184] Predation, in this context, has the unattractive character of asset-stripping.

And the greater the financial windfall for the taker, the more closely does the taking resemble an act of plunder – a perception stressed in *City of Springfield v Dreison Investments, Inc*[185] (the baseball stadium case referred to earlier in this chapter). Likewise in *Southwestern Illinois Development Authority v National City Environmental, LLC*[186] the Supreme Court of Illinois pointedly observed that the deployment of sovereign power for the private purpose of 'maximising corporate profits' was truly a 'misuse of the power entrusted by the government'. Things are, if anything, even worse if the taker is so fantastically rich that the imperative of private profit is rivalled or overshadowed by a desire to indulge some idiosyncratic non-commercial ambition. At this point the harnessing of the state's powers of compulsory acquisition becomes simply a means by which a wealthy élite can be facilitated in the gratification of economically irrational interests and capricious personal concerns.

The 'initiative' test

A pointer toward the predatory character of a taking is frequently to be found in the identity of the party who has initiated the suggestion of compulsory acquisition. It may be hugely significant that the initial pressure for compulsory purchase emanates from a private commercial party who stands to gain from the expropriation (as in the case of the golf resort proposed by Trump International Golf Links Scotland). In perhaps the most notorious example, *Poletown Neighborhood Council v City of Detroit*,[187] the General Motors Corporation was able to secure the expropriation of the elderly Polish-American population of a Detroit suburb in order to clear a site for a new assembly plant for its operations. '[W]hat General Motors wanted, General Motors got'[188] as the price of offering to maintain its presence in a city deeply affected by chronic unemployment. Indeed, General Motors orchestrated the entire process of expropriation. It selected the site for condemnation, fixed the cost, established deadlines for clearance of the area and even demanded twelve years of tax concessions. The Poletown residents were bought out for a total of $200 million, of which General Motors paid only $8 million.[189] History reveals

[184] *Housing Authority of City of Atlanta v Johnson* (1953) 74 SE 2d 891, 893; *Edens v City of Columbia* (1956) 91 SE 2d 280, 281–82 (referring to parties 'who could have no interest in acquiring ... property other than as a means to make money').

[185] (2000) 11 Mass L Rep 379.

[186] (2002) 768 NE 2d 1, 11.

[187] (1981) 304 NW 2d 455.

[188] (1981) 304 NW 2d 455, 470.

[189] (1981) 304 NW 2d 455, 469. 'Behind the frenzy of official activity', said the dissenting Justice Ryan, was 'the unmistakable, guiding and sustaining, indeed controlling, hand of the General Motors Corporation' ((1981) 304 NW 2d 455, 468).

that the proposed plant was never built and General Motors later sold the site on at a substantial profit.[190]

A variant of the compromised role of the city agency in the *Poletown* case can be found in those instances where the acquiring authority acts as a 'default broker' for the purpose of enabling private commercial entities to obtain assets otherwise than through the normal functioning of the market. For example, in *Southwestern Illinois Development Authority v National City Environmental, LLC*[191] it was evident that the development authority entrusted with powers of eminent domain had advertised that, for a fee, it would assist private developers to secure the compulsory acquisition of land which those developers were unable to purchase through voluntary bargain. Echoing a view taken elsewhere,[192] the Supreme Court of Illinois regarded this *modus operandi* with extreme disfavour.[193]

The 'location' test

The locality of expropriation may also be deeply significant. The potentially predatory aspect of any taking is generally regarded as intensified where a proposed expropriation relates to a dwelling place. In this context, as in many others,[194] the home is thought of as having a special or privileged status. The 'sanctity of a man's home' has always commanded high respect.[195] It was Justice Oliver Wendell Holmes who long ago declared the distinction between the home and 'open fields' to be 'as old as the common law'.[196] As the Supreme Court of Ohio emphasised in *City of Norwood v Horney*,[197] compulsory acquisition of a home involves 'more than a battle over a plot of cold sod in a farmland pasture or the plat of municipal land on which a building sits'. It concerns the destruction of an organic institution and a way of life. In relation to this theme much more might be said. But it is clear that where a home is at stake,

[190] The jurisprudence behind the *Poletown* decision was finally overturned by the Supreme Court of Michigan in *Wayne County v Hathcock* (2004) 684 NW 2d 765.

[191] (2002) 768 NE 2d 1, 10

[192] See *Bartrum v Manurewa Borough* [1962] NZLR 21, 26–27; *Prentice v Brisbane City Council* [1966] Qd R 394, 410.

[193] See Town and Country Planning Act 1990 s 226(1), (1A), as amended by Planning and Compulsory Purchase Act 2004 s 99, empowering local authorities in England and Wales to acquire land if they think that development, redevelopment or improvement of that land is likely to promote or improve the economic, social or environmental well-being of their area. See also *Standard Commercial Property Securities Ltd v Glasgow City Council* [2006] UKHL 50, 2007 SC (HL) 33; E Waring, 'The legality of back-to-back agreements and compulsory purchase' [2007] *Conv* 265.

[194] K J Gray and S F Gray, 'Civil Rights, Civil Wrongs and Quasi-Public Space' (1999) 4 *EHRLR* 46, 91–92.

[195] *Boyd v United States* (1886) 116 US 616, 630, citing *Entick v Carrington* (1765) 19 Howell's State Trials 1029, 95 ER 807. See also *Payton v New York* (1980) 445 US 573, 601.

[196] *Hester v United States* (1924) 265 US 57, 59.

[197] (2006) 853 NE 2d 1115, 1122.

a heightened responsibility bears upon a taker to demonstrate the social worth or public utility of the purpose which underlies the acquisition. Some observers will, of course, react with raw incredulity to the suggestion, for instance, that a person's home may be taken away in order that others may enjoy a game of golf.

The 'social merit' test

There is a more general sense in which the net social dividend produced by a compulsory purchase may highlight the predatory aspect of the proposed expropriation. There can be significant calibrations of expropriatory objective: policy-based evaluations of outcome are inescapable. The minimal social worth of an intended mandatory acquisition tends to indicate that the project is aimed principally, if not exclusively, at a divesting of privately held assets for purely personal or corporate profit. Can absolutely *any* activity that might conceivably be termed 'recreational' or 'leisure-related' justify the employment of privately directed powers of compulsory purchase? As one American judge has recently queried, 'would anyone seriously suggest, for example, that … private casinos or adult video stores … qualify as "public" uses' for the purpose of attracting the exercise of eminent domain?[198] Similar questions of social merit would doubtless surround a compulsory purchase of premises for use as a lap-dancing club or as a cigarette factory. Enterprises of these kinds may facilitate certain leisure preferences, but the accommodation of such preferences can scarcely be described as life-enhancing or as promoting the public interest in any sensible way.

The 'environmental' test

A further telltale sign of predatory activity lies in the nature and extent of the environmental impact involved in any exercise of eminent domain. Does a proposed acquisition generally improve or impoverish the local ecology? Predatory taking tends to be marked by a self-interested disregard for the environmental quality of the terrain in question. Predation correlates with 'waste' (to use the latter term in its more accurate, historic, sense). Predatory takers tend to be relatively unperturbed if they lay waste to the earth; they do not particularly care if they trash the environment. By contrast, increasingly prevalent theories of stewardship nowadays emphasise that the landowner is at most a tenant for life, encumbered by corresponding duties toward later generations.[199] The more extreme the taker's unconcern for the environmental damage likely to ensue from compulsory acquisition, the more probable it is

[198] *Matter of Kaur v New York State Urban Development Corp* (2010) 15 NY 3d 235, 263.
[199] See K J Gray, 'Equitable Property' (1994) 47(2) *CLP* 157, 188–206.

that the taker's motivations have a conspicuously non-altruistic character that qualifies for stigmatic description in terms of pillage or plunder.

Conclusion

So where does all of this leave us? How stable or substantial is our contemporary notion of property?

Property – if it exists – is intrinsically and inescapably about the ranking of moral and social (rather than economic) priorities. If property were purely about the endorsement of rationally calculated commercial interests, we would still support the institution of slavery and its implicit affirmation of the economic value of coerced human labour-power.

What we *can* say is that proprietary entitlement revolves around some specifically enforceable expectation of autonomous control over valued resources or opportunities. The categories of thing that are ring-fenced in this way are defined by collective perceptions of moral or social worth. These perceptions are never absolute in quality, requiring instead a constant arbitration between the various goals that we wish to achieve. The individual's expectation of specific performance – that is, of effectual decisional control over a resource or opportunity – is generally, but not always, realised. The expectation is just that – a relatively fortified hope or *spes* which is so commonly fulfilled by default that we rarely recognise its inbuilt limitations. But in some instances a readjustment of the initial rankings of moral and social concern may indeed be necessary. In these cases we allow expectations to be diminished for the sake of a greater community good and we accept that the citizen's claim to specific enforcement of his or her entitlement can and should be converted into a form of monetary satisfaction. This is the traditional field of compulsory acquisition or eminent domain.

So far, so good. Property remains relatively stable, although liable to mutation in unusual (and frequently unforeseeable) circumstances that call for a rearrangement of priorities. But make no mistake – property in land is not everything it is cracked up to be. It can be here today and gone tomorrow, leaving you with just a bag of coins in your hand. For those who think they own land, the clear message is that money is the sole asset to which their claim of 'property' can ultimately refer. Realty is always monetisable at the command of the state: money is fast becoming the measure of all value. Nowadays it often seems that the idea of property – in the shape of an indefeasible entitlement of control – is actualised only in the context of ideas themselves. Intellectual property is the new Wild West. Here property, once seized, really *means* something. But many of the moral and social priorities that currently regulate the exploitation of intellectual property (in areas ranging from copyrights to drug patents) will one day appear to us as abhorrent as the concept of property in slaves. Compulsory acquisition of the products of the human intellect will soon come.

But back to real property. Here a new danger is beginning to appear. Money talks. Property in land does not – and can always be commuted compulsorily into a money form. Today we are increasingly confronted by the emergence of an incredibly wealthy élite – in both individual and corporate guise – whose resources and ambitions cause all other social and economic stratifications to fade into insignificance. The modern super-rich can easily harness powers of compulsory purchase with the connivance of weak, subservient, short-sighted or corruptible agencies of government. Those embraced within the euphemistic contemporary designation of 'high net worth' can then do exactly as they please under some pretence of conferring public benefit or creating a 'trickle-down effect', but remaining all the while beyond the reach of any genuine political control or scrutiny. This is a new species of predator of whom we should all be extremely wary.

The founding fathers of the United States Constitution would turn in their graves if they knew of the modern betrayal of their instinctive revulsion against one human's plunder of another for purposes of private gain or gratification. The danger was clearly recognised in *Southwestern Illinois Development Authority v National City Environmental, LLC*[200] (the automobile racetrack case to which reference was made earlier). Here Kuehn J voiced the fear that 'the inalienable right to own and enjoy property to the exclusion of others will pass to a privileged few who constitute society's élite'. He added: 'The rich may not inherit the earth, but they most assuredly will inherit the means to acquire any part of it they desire'.[201] This, it might be said, is a prospect worth avoiding.

Coda

A short coda, if I may, to a central theme of this chapter, namely the relative weighting of recreational interests against the claims of proprietary ownership. To what extent, it has been asked, may sport, leisure or entertainment concerns be allowed to encroach upon, diminish or abrogate private rights of property?

It is well known that in recent years Britain has seen a dramatic statutory expansion of pedestrian access for purposes of open-air recreation.[202] The so-called 'right to roam' introduced in England and Wales by the Countryside and Rights of Way Act 2000 was rapidly followed in Scotland by the confirmation of even more extensive access rights pursuant to the Land Reform (Scotland) Act 2003. In November 2009 the successful parliamentary passage of the Marine and Coastal Access Bill brought within prospect the creation of a new long-

[200] (1999) 710 NE 2d 896, 906.

[201] Kuehn J likened oppressive powers of compulsory purchase to 'the tyranny our forefathers fled. Our heritage stems in part from the aversion to the King's use of property to convey favor upon a privileged nobility.'

[202] I have attempted to analyse and rationalise this development in K J Gray, 'Pedestrian Democracy and the Geography of Hope' (2010) 1 *Journal of Human Rights and the Environment* 45.

distance walking route 'allowing two people to walk comfortably abreast' along a virtually continuous four metre-wide access corridor around the 4,000 km entirety of the English coast.[203] Although these statutory initiatives have been criticised in some quarters as unwarranted invasions of the proprietary rights of landowners, it seems tolerably plain that none involves, in any sense, the element of privately motivated *predation* or *plunder* which for many observers marks out the threshold of unacceptable interferences with ownership.

If therefore, in days to come, you find yourself a few miles north of Aberdeen in the vicinity of a golf course operated by Trump International Golf Links Scotland, you should be aware of the following. Under the Land Reform (Scotland) Act 2003 you have an entitlement of access to the golf course for recreational and educational purposes,[204] provided that you do not interfere with the activities of lawful golfers.[205] Here the one recreational activity foreclosed to you as a citizen is, of course, the game of golf itself.[206] But otherwise, while you traverse a beautiful area and gaze at its complementary seascape, your claim of right is in no way lessened by the fact that, out of sheer civility, you occasionally stand back and let the golfers play through down the fairways.[207] As is increasingly affirmed by contemporary property theorists, the stuff of modern property involves a consonance of entitlement, obligation and mutual respect – in other words, a phenomenon characterised by accommodation and reciprocity rather than by predatory acts of self-interested taking.

With luck you might even be able to stroll over to their respective homes and say hello to Michael and Molly Forbes, David and Moira Milne and their immediate neighbours.

[203] Marine and Coastal Access Act 2009 ss 296–97; National Parks and Access to the Countryside Act 1949 ss 51, 55A. See Natural England, *Coastal Access: Natural England's outline scheme* (April 2008) [2.1.1.], [4.3.8.].

[204] Land Reform (Scotland) Act 2003 s 1.

[205] Land Reform (Scotland) Act 2003 ss 2, 6(1)(e), 7(7).

[206] Land Reform (Scotland) Act 2003 s 9(g).

[207] See *R (Lewis) v Redcar and Cleveland BC (No 2)* [2010] UKSC 11, [2010] 2 WLR 653 [36], [48].

2

Lighting the Way Ahead: The Use and Abuse of Property Rights

Paul S Davies*

This chapter considers the extent to which individuals may use, and perhaps abuse, their property rights. The focus of this analysis will be disputes concerning rights to light. Easements to light are property rights. The 'owner' of such a right may well wish to protect that right against a neighbour who intends to carry out building works such that the right to light would be infringed. There are two potential remedies available to the party who benefits from the right to light: an injunction and monetary compensation.

The court should first determine whether injunctive relief is appropriate, and only if it is not does the question of damages arise. Quantifying the damages to be awarded in lieu of an injunction raises a host of difficult issues, and much has been written on the nature of this remedy.[1] However, less attention has been paid to the logically prior question of when damages should be awarded instead of an injunction. This chapter seeks to redress that imbalance.

Rights to light provide an interesting focus of study.[2] Such rights often hinder planned developments: it is not uncommon for owners to demand very large sums from developers in return for releasing their property rights. Developers feel as if they are being held to ransom, whereas owners insist that they can make use of their rights in any way they see fit. Can owners expect an injunction to protect their rights, and therefore demand a 'ransom price' in order to sell their rights? Do such demands constitute an 'abuse' of a property right? The

* Fellow, Gonville and Caius College, Cambridge. I am grateful to those who attended the Conference for their helpful advice, and to Stuart Bridge, Matthew Conaglen, David Fox, Colin Oakley, Emma Waring and the anonymous reviewer for commenting on various drafts of the chapter. The usual disclaimers apply.

[1] Eg C Rotherham, 'Wrotham Park damages and accounts of profits: compensation or restitution?' [2008] *LMCLQ* 25.

[2] And may soon be investigated by the Law Commission: Law Commission, 'Annual Report 2008–09' (Law Com No 316 HC 811, 2009) [6.11].

approach of the courts appears to have oscillated regarding the respect to be afforded to rights to light.[3] This is problematic: if the parties do not know the likelihood of an injunction being granted, it means that they cannot be sure of the strength of their respective bargaining positions. This in turn hinders the chances of a settlement being successfully concluded, even if the owner is willing to release his right for a fee.

This chapter will initially consider whether it is ever possible to abuse a property right. It will then be necessary to consider whether easements should be protected through injunctive relief. Courts generally rely on the decision of the Court of Appeal in *Shelfer v City of London Electric Lighting Company*,[4] but it will be suggested that this test may afford insufficient protection to those who 'own' property rights. Recent cases concerning rights of light will then be analysed. It will be argued that the problem of valuing a property right should generally be left to the parties themselves; the owner of a property right should be able to use the powerful bargaining chip of an injunction. Only very rarely indeed will this right be 'abused', and the courts refuse injunctive relief. This should ensure that the parties know the strength of their respective bargaining positions, which should, in turn, aid settlement negotiations. If the developer fails to offer the owner of a property right enough money for the owner to release his right, then the developer should not be allowed to infringe the owner's right.[5]

Property rights: freedom to use and abuse?

An absolutist approach towards property law suggests that an individual can exploit his property right to any extent he sees fit.[6] If correct, then the 'owner' of an easement of light should, in principle, be able simply to refuse to release his right, or demand any (extortionate) sum he wishes from a developer. This would seem to follow from the decision in *Bradford Corporation v Pickles*.[7]

Edward Pickles owned land from which water flowed into a reservoir on land owned by the Bradford Corporation. In 1890, Pickles sank a shaft deep into his land, which polluted the water supply and diverted it away from the Corporation's property. The Corporation had no proprietary right to the water, but argued that Pickles could not divert the water because he was motivated

[3] See recently *Regan v Paul Properties Ltd* [2006] EWCA Civ 1391, [2007] Ch 135; *Midtown Ltd v City of London Real Property Co Ltd* [2005] EWHC 33 (Ch), [2005] 1 EGLR 65; *Tamares (Vincent Square) Ltd v Fairpoint Properties (Vincent Square) Ltd* [2007] EWHC 212 (Ch), [2007] 1 WLR 2167.

[4] [1895] 1 Ch 287 (CA).

[5] The major exceptions concern compulsory purchase and the public interest: text to n 65–75.

[6] W Morrison (ed), *Blackstone's Commentaries on the Law of England* (vol 1, Routledge-Cavendish, London 2001).

[7] [1895] AC 587 (HL). See M Taggart, *Private Property and Abuse of Rights in Victorian England: The Story of Edward Pickles and the Bradford Water Supply* (OUP, Oxford 2002); A W B Simpson, *Victorian Law and the Industrial Spirit* (Selden Society, London 1995).

solely by malice. The trial judge found as a matter of fact that Pickles was not acting in good faith, and solely in order to extract money from the Corporation.[8]

Was Pickles 'abusing' his property rights? The Corporation was outraged at being held to 'ransom' and convinced that Pickles' acts were tantamount to blackmail. However, Pickles succeeded in the House of Lords. The judges were convinced that he could use his land however he saw fit. Lord Macnaghten emphasised that '[i]t is the act, not the motive for the act, that must be regarded. If the act, apart from motive, gives rise merely to damage without legal injury, the motive, however reprehensible it may be, will not supply that element'.[9]

This decision supports the notion that it is permissible for the owner of a property right to seek to exploit his right in any way he deems appropriate, and not to sell for anything less than a 'ransom price'. Moreover, the House of Lords was not entirely convinced that Pickles' acts were motivated by malice. Lord Macnaghten asked: 'where is the malice? Mr. Pickles has no spite against the people of Bradford. He bears no ill-will to the Corporation. They are welcome to the water, and to his land too, if they will pay the price for it'.[10] Pickles may not have acted in a very neighbourly way, but he was not *solely* motivated by a desire to harm the Corporation;[11] indeed, if Pickles could have gained a higher price for his land without diverting the water supply he may well have done so.

Nevertheless, there remains a feeling that Pickles was lucky to triumph.[12] But why is there such sympathy for the Corporation? After all, it refused to countenance compulsory purchase.[13] Lord Herschell LC, after hearing argument in the Court of Appeal, informed counsel for the Corporation that if it were to apply to Parliament for compulsory power to take the water, the Court of Appeal would adjourn its decision. The Corporation refused to avail themselves of this opportunity; it did not wish to make even the small payment which would be associated with compulsory purchase. Given such stubbornness and reluctance to invoke the legislative regime, it may be thought that the Corporation did not deserve to succeed.[14]

Pickles remains a seminal case. The selfish conduct of Pickles does not seem entirely in tune with communal living, but the law clearly refused to limit the *reasons* for which he could use his property. This may be because establishing the reasons why people act is very hard; it is difficult to totally exclude the possibility that Pickles truly believed there were valuable stones under his land which he intended to mine.[15] In any event, it is suggested that the Court of Appeal's

[8] [1894] 3 Ch 53 (Ch) 67–68.

[9] [1895] AC 587 (HL) 601.

[10] Ibid. Note too that malice is not a stable concept: see eg Lord Herschell in *Allen v Flood* [1898] AC 1 (HL). See too J B Ames, 'How Far an Act May Be a Tort Because of the Wrongful Motive of the Actor' (1905) 18 *Harv L Rev* 411.

[11] J Finnis, 'Intention in Tort Law' in D G Owen (ed), *Philosophical Foundations of Tort Law* (OUP, Oxford 1997).

[12] *Simpson* (n 7). *Taggart* (n 7), *Ames* (n 10).

[13] Taggart even asks, 'Who was the Baddy in *Pickles*?' (n 7) 71.

[14] See text to n 65.

[15] As Pickles argued, albeit with little supporting evidence.

preference for the matter to be resolved by Parliament rather than the courts is understandable. The court is not best placed to decide upon the necessity of expropriating a private individual's property rights.[16] The Corporation should have made use of the compulsory purchase regime. By not doing so, the public interest aspect of the dispute became of much less importance, and the case became a simple one where one private party wanted to dictate what should be done with another private party's property. But the Corporation was not willing to pay the price demanded by Pickles. The court could not force Pickles to release his right for nothing. Nor could it make Pickles accept a reasonable price – not, at least, without the support of the compulsory purchase legislation.[17]

Abuse restrained?

Pickles has often been taken to be authority for the principle that English law does not recognise a general principle of abuse of rights. The idea that the reasons *why* a person acts are irrelevant if the act itself is lawful has been cited by judges on numerous occasions.[18] But other cases have made it clear that motive *may* be a relevant consideration. In *Christie v Davey*, for instance, the court held that the level of noise made by the defendant would not have constituted a nuisance if made innocently, but since the noise was made with a direct intent to harm, the law could not tolerate it.[19]

This might suggest a less 'absolutist' conception of property, and that more importance be given to motive than the wide dicta in *Pickles* might suggest. However, the claimant in *Christie* had a right to quiet and peaceful enjoyment of his property. By contrast, the Bradford Corporation enjoyed no right to the water. The cases may be reconciled on the basis that *Pickles* concerned a 'non-right'.

The distinction between 'right' and 'non-right' cases has been criticised: if the essence of the cases concerns the defendant's motive, the focus should be on the acts of the person 'abusively' exerting his rights, regardless of the status of the claimant. A general principle of abuse of rights may be considered to be morally appealing,[20] but a major problem lies in the fact that it is difficult to

[16] See text to n 65–75.

[17] Courts will not sanction the expropriation of rights from one individual to another: see text to n 64.

[18] Eg *Allen v Flood* (n 10); *Chapman v Honig* [1963] 2 QB 502 (CA); *Margaronis Navigation Agency Ltd v Henry W Peabody & Co of London Ltd* [1965] 2 QB 430 (CA).

[19] [1893] 1 Ch 316 (Ch). See also *Keeble v Hickeringill* (1707) 11 East 574, 88 ER 945; *Hollywood Silver Fox Farm Ltd v Emmett* [1936] 2 KB 468 (KB); A W B Simpson, *Leading Cases in the Common Law* (OUP, Oxford 1995).

[20] *Ames* (n 10), *Finnis* (n 11), even recognised by H C Gutteridge, 'Abuse of Rights' (1933) 5 *CLJ* 22. T Honore, 'The Morality of Tort Law' in D G Owen (ed), *Philosophical Foundations of Tort Law* (n 11). Cf the 'prima facie tort' doctrine in America: *Tuttle v Buck* (1909) 107 Minn 145; K J Vandevelde, 'The Modern Prima Facie Tort Doctrine' (1991) 79 *Ky LJ* 519.

ascertain exactly what is meant by 'abuse'. In its most limited form, it may mean only 'disinterested malevolence',[21] and this may not cover *Pickles*.[22] Alternatively, 'abuse' may mean that the right has been exercised for an improper purpose.[23] Although superficially appealing, this test is difficult to apply; identifying the proper purposes for which a right can be exercised is often a thankless task. Similarly, equating 'abuse' with 'malice' does not make matters clearer.[24] A wider test of 'abuse' has been encapsulated in the Netherlands, which considers the exercise of a right to be abusive if 'its holder could not reasonably have decided to exercise it, given the disproportion between the interest to exercise the right and the harm caused thereby'.[25] However, such a wide doctrine of 'abuse' which extends to 'unreasonableness' may well lead to uncertainty.

The inability to provide a satisfactory definition of 'abuse' may be the reason why a general principle of 'abuse of right' is not recognised in English law.[26] Nevertheless, it might be considered unsatisfactory that the law should tolerate conduct motivated solely by the desire to harm. Yet any doctrine of 'abuse of right' should be of very limited scope; a party's freedom to act should not be unduly curtailed.[27]

Instances of abuse are often dealt with through the intervention of Equity. This is particularly so where the claimant seeks equitable relief, which is discretionary. Important equitable maxims include 'a claimant must not sit on his rights', and must have 'clean hands'. The role of Equity is of crucial importance when deciding whether or not to protect a right to light through an injunction.

Discretion in equity: to injunct or not to injunct?

Protecting easements: property rules or liability rules?

The above discussion of *Pickles* suggests that the owner of a property right may exploit his right in any way he sees fit. This may logically lead to the conclusion that the claimant owner of an easement to light may prevent a defendant developer from infringing the former's right. Indeed, such instances may be analysed as 'non-right' cases: the defendant does not have a right to build such that the property rights of others will be infringed. Since the claimant has a

[21] Eg *Tuttle v Buck* (n 20).

[22] Since Pickles was simply trying to increase the value of his property.

[23] Eg L M Katz, 'A Jurisdictional Principle of Abuse of Right' (SSRN, February 8 2010) http://ssrn.com/abstract=1417955 (accessed 25 August 2010).

[24] Text to n 10.

[25] Article 3:13(2) of the Nieuw Burgerlijk Wetboek (New Civil Code).

[26] Also, perhaps, because the focus of English law appears to be on remedies rather than rights: *Kingdom of Spain v Christie, Manson & Woods Ltd* [1986] 1 WLR 1120 (Ch).

[27] T Weir, *Economic Torts* (Clarendon Law Lectures, OUP, Oxford 1997).

right to protect and exploit, and the defendant does not,[28] the existing rights of the former should prevail over the mere hope of the latter that he will be able to build without restraint. Just as Pickles could exploit his land and the Bradford Corporation could not object as it had no right which required protection, so can the owner of a right to light protect his property: the developer enjoys no right which allows him to object.

However, there has been some reluctance to protect rights to light to the same extent as Pickles' property rights.[29] It is possible that rights to light would be more appropriately protected by a 'liability rule' rather than a 'property rule'. A property rule would favour injunctive relief, whereas a liability rule would allow the developer to infringe the easement and then simply pay damages.[30]

There has been much discussion about the relative efficiency of 'liability rules' and 'property rules' from a law and economics perspective.[31] In a world of no transaction costs, it would not matter which rule was chosen:[32] the parties would bargain with one another to reach an efficient outcome in any event.[33] In the real world, however, there are costs. In the right to light context, transaction costs may often be low. In many instances, it should be relatively easy for the developer to find out which neighbouring estates may be affected by the proposed development: easements of light cannot exist in gross, but must benefit a dominant tenement. Thus the developer will only need to negotiate with his neighbour, and two neighbours should be able to negotiate quite readily. Given low transaction costs, a property rule may be considered to be the more efficient. However, many neighbouring properties could be affected by the development, and there may be many claimants who each seek to protect their individual right to light; one neighbour might intend to 'hold-out' and not reach any bargain with the developer at all. In such cases, transaction costs may be high, and this might lead to a liability rule being preferred.

Nevertheless, it is far from obvious that a property rule would be less efficient even in these instances. Although the transaction costs may be high, 'assessment costs' will also be high:[34] courts have found the assessment of damages to be very troublesome.[35] Damages are awarded on a 'loss of bargain' basis, but

[28] At least when a prohibitory injunction is sought; the defendant has perhaps acquired a right if a mandatory injunction is required: text to n 78.

[29] Text to n 83–111.

[30] G Calabresi and A D Melamed, 'Property Rules, Liability Rules and Inalienability: One View of the Cathedral' (1972) 85 *Harv L Rev* 1089.

[31] As well as *Clabresi and Melamed* (n 30), see eg A M Polinsky, 'Resolving Nuisance Disputes: The Simple Economics of Injunctive and Damage Remedies' (1980) 32 *Stan L Rev* 1075; L Kaplow and S Shavell, 'Property Rules versus Liability Rules: An Economic Analysis' (1996) 109 *Harv L Rev* 713; J E Krier and S J Schwab, 'Property Rules and Liability Rules: the Cathedral in Another Light' (1995) 70 *NYU L Rev* 440; R Epstein, 'A Clear View of *The Cathedral:* The Dominance of Property Rules' (1996) 106 *Yale LJ* 2091.

[32] Assuming the owner of a right would be willing to bargain for its release.

[33] R H Coase, 'The Problem of Social Cost' (1960) 3 *JLE* 1.

[34] *Polinsky* (n 31).

[35] Indeed, some judges have resorted to saying that the final award must simply 'feel right': *Tamares* (n 3) [21]–[22] (Gabriel Moss QC), citing *Amec Developments Ltd v Jury's Hotel Management (UK) Ltd* [2001] 1 EGLR 81 [35] (Anthony Mann QC).

the 'bargain' the courts assess is entirely hypothetical, between two fictional 'reasonable' parties, keen to negotiate a settlement. This is clearly a difficult exercise for the courts, which involves significant assessment costs. Moreover, there is the very real danger that the monetary sum awarded fails adequately to compensate the claimant owner. This is particularly acute since the sentimental value[36] which the owner attaches to the property is difficult to quantify, and may indeed be what leads the claimant owner to demand more money than the maximum the developer is prepared to pay.[37]

The importance of a person's subjective valuation of his property emphasises the significance of distributional goals when choosing between property rules and liability rules. In particular, the security and stability of property should be defended.[38] For example, R might be an Olympic swimmer, desperate to put a swimming pool in her garden so that she can practise regularly in the hope of winning a gold medal at London 2012. However, her garden not being quite big enough, R would need to build on the garden of her next-door-neighbour, S, in order to have a swimming pool of the necessary size. S does not care about whether or not he has a garden; S's garden is an overgrown mess. However, if S refuses to allow R to build on his land, the court should not even contemplate forcing S to sell his land to R. S has the right to choose whether or not to sell his property at any given price. This is an important incident of property ownership: the ability to choose whether or not to sell. The fact that, objectively, damages are thought to be 'adequate' misses the point: the objective assessment of the court should not trump the subjective valuation and priorities of the owner.

However, while it is clear that a person may 'own' land, it is perhaps less intuitive to state that a person 'owns' or 'possesses' an easement.[39] Yet easements do need to be appurtenant to dominant land; the proprietary basis of rights to light is fundamental, so it should not be difficult to talk of a party 'owning' a right to light. Moreover, since there is no available market to which the owner of the right could turn in order to replace the easement to light if lost, it seems preferable to afford strong protection to such rights through a property rule. Endorsing a liability rule would be tantamount to condoning the expropriation of that right.[40]

[36] Or 'idiosyncratic value': *Kaplow and Shavell* (n 31). See also text to n 56.

[37] It may be true that giving the owner the right to light has a 'framing effect', such that he values the right at a level higher than he would be prepared to pay if he did not possess the right in the first place. This emphasises that the initial allocation of rights is important if an efficient allocation of resources is desired. However, it is suggested that this issue really concerns whether and how the right to light is acquired; if the law wishes to prevent a person from acquiring the easement to light, then reform of the law of prescription is required: see n 114. In any event, efficiency is not the sole goal of the law.

[38] *Epstein* (n 31).

[39] *Kaplow and Shavell* (n 31) 771–73 give the example of a hotel room which benefits from a view, and suggest that it is unclear whether a liability rule or property rule should be preferred because it is difficult to decide whether possessory rights are at issue.

[40] *Cowper v Laidler* [1903] 2 Ch 337 (Ch) 341; cf *Jaggard v Sawyer* [1995] 1 WLR 269 (CA) 287. This may be problematic in view of human rights considerations: n 60–69.

Favouring a property rule may encourage the parties to reduce transaction costs if forced to bargain amongst themselves.[41] It may also provide a degree of certainty which could facilitate negotiated settlements. This is very much lacking under the fictional hypothetical bargain measure: it is almost impossible to predict the amount of damages the court will award.[42] It might be suggested that it is insulting to the parties to suggest that they did not, in fact, act reasonably, and that the court should construct a hypothetical bargain for them. After all, *Pickles* laid down a general principle that an owner is able to exploit his property in a capricious manner.

The infringement of easements to light should be sanctioned through injunctive relief as a matter of course.[43] Only rarely should damages be preferred. Such instances may be examples of an owner 'abusing' his right, or of overriding considerations of public policy.

A 'good working rule': *Shelfer v City of London Electric Lighting Company*[44]

English law does not ruthlessly protect easements with property rules. Courts are able to award damages in lieu of injunctions as a result of Lord Cairns' Act, although the Act itself offers little guidance regarding when this jurisdiction should be exercised.[45] Guidelines have therefore been developed through caselaw. The most significant decision in this area is *Shelfer*. The case concerned a nuisance caused by the defendants carrying out noisy and disruptive work. The claimants sought an injunction to prevent further work continuing the nuisance. Kekewich J, at first instance, thought that an injunction was inappropriate and awarded damages in lieu. The Court of Appeal disagreed.

The approach of the appellate court was very conservative indeed. Lindley LJ thought that the jurisdiction to award damages 'ought not to be exercised … except under very exceptional circumstances'.[46] This restrictive approach was clearly shared by both Lord Halsbury and AL Smith LJ. The latter stressed that

[41] *Krier and Schwab* (n 31), R Craswell, 'Property Rules and Liability Rules in Unconscionability and Related Doctrines' (1993) 60 *U Chic L Rev* 1. And parties' bargains do tend to be efficient: see eg E Hoffmann and M L Spitzer, 'The Coase Theorem: Some Experimental Tests' (1982) 25 *JLE* 73.

[42] For example, in *Tamares* (n 3) 30% of the gains were awarded, but in *Forsyth-Grant v Allen* [2008] EWCA Civ 505, [2008] 2 EGLR 16 only 15% of the gains were awarded. Similarly, it is difficult to explain the final sum awarded in *Carr-Saunders v Dick McNeil Associates Ltd* [1986] 1 WLR 922 (Ch).

[43] Cf J Gaunt and P Morgan (eds), *Gale on Easements* (18th rev edn Sweet & Maxwell, London, 2008) [14–58]. In *Hunter v Canary Wharf Ltd* [1997] AC 655 (HL) 692, Lord Goff described an injunction as being the 'primary remedy' for nuisance. Mandatory injunctions may be more complicated: n 77–82.

[44] [1895] 1 Ch 287 (CA).

[45] Chancery Amendment Act 1958 s 2; see now Supreme Court Act 1981 s 50.

[46] *Shelfer* (n 44) 316.

a claimant is prima facie entitled to an injunction, emphasising that 'a person by committing a wrongful act ... is not thereby entitled to ask the Court to sanction his doing so by purchasing his neighbour's rights'.[47]

Shelfer is significant since it limits the very wide discretion afforded to judges on the face of Lord Cairns' Act. This is welcome: the sanctity of property rights is to be taken seriously. However, the passage from *Shelfer* which continues to be cited most often is the 'good working rule' of AL Smith LJ:

> (1) If the injury to the plaintiff's legal rights is small,
> (2) And is one which is capable of being estimated in money,
> (3) And is one which can be adequately compensated by a small money payment,
> (4) And the case is one in which it would be oppressive to the defendant to grant an injunction: -
>
> then damages in substitution for an injunction may be given.[48]

Despite being consistently used by courts, there has been little serious consideration whether this 'working rule' is appropriate and affords sufficient respect for the claimant's property right.[49]

Take the first limb: 'small' is relative to the facts of a given case, but its meaning is unclear, and some of the awards made under Lord Cairns' Act have been anything but small.[50] The goal appears to be that insignificant, trivial harm should lead to damages rather than an injunction; there may be a *de minimis* exception to the presumptive award of an injunction. Thus, in the rights to light context, it may be more difficult for a commercial claimant than a residential claimant to obtain an injunction, since the commercial claimant may use artificial lighting at all times, and not suffer at all if an easement to light is infringed.[51] Such a *de minimis* exception should be restrictively defined, but may, perhaps, be justified on the basis that a claimant who has not suffered any real injury may be considered to act unconscionably by seeking an injunction.[52]

The second limb is sensible, but if the injury is not capable of being estimated in money, then a court would not be able to award damages anyway: quantification would logically be impossible. The third limb is more problematic. If the injury can be adequately compensated by the award of damages, why has the claimant

[47] Ibid 322 (AL Smith LJ). See similarly Lindley LJ: the 'Court has always protested against the notion that it ought to allow a wrong to continue simply because the wrongdoer is able and willing to pay for the injury he may inflict' (ibid 315–16).

[48] Ibid 322–3.

[49] Although see J A Jolowicz, 'Damages in Equity – A Study of Lord Cairns' Act' (1975) 34 *CLJ* 224.

[50] Eg £150,000 was awarded in *Lane v O'Brien Homes* [2004] EWHC 303 (QB). In *Jaggard* (n 40) a strong Court of Appeal appeared to pay little heed to this first criteria. In *Regan* (n 3) the Court of Appeal thought £5,000 not to be small, contradicting the trial judge: see text to n 103.

[51] Cf *Midtown* (n 3), *Tamares* (n 3). Although it should be remembered that the interference needs to be more than minimal to constitute an actionable nuisance anyway: *Colls v Home & Colonial Stores Ltd* [1904] AC 179 (HL).

[52] However, even here care must be taken, since the right to light, once lost, is lost to successors in title also.

not accepted (or perhaps not even sought) damages?[53] The claimant probably does not agree that his injury *can* be adequately compensated by a small money payment, or at least considers that it is worth more than the highest amount offered by the defendant (and, perhaps, the objective value of the right). In such a case, it appears that the claimant values the right more than the defendant; absent overriding considerations of public interest, it is submitted that the court should not order the claimant to release the right to the defendant.[54]

The fourth limb is often the most crucial.[55] Courts appear very reluctant to grant an injunction if to do so would be oppressive to the defendant. This seems to be based on the idea that Equity will not intervene if to do so would lead to injustice. However, it is suggested that the focus of the fourth limb is too defendant-oriented; is it not oppressive to the claimant to expropriate a property right against his will? Supporters of the working rule in *Shelfer* may consider this not to be the case, since if the injury is small and can, objectively, be adequately assessed and compensated through damages, awarding damages should not be oppressive to the claimant. But the problem is that it deprives the claimant of a *choice* whether or not to sell. Rights to light are of real value to many.[56] Few people want to live in a dark home, and estate agents are keen to promote an abundance of natural light as a 'desirable feature'. It would be a mistake simply to conclude that because a defendant will be handicapped by being prevented from developing on his land that an injunction would be oppressive. It would not. The land never enjoyed the possibility of development;[57] development was always likely to be hindered by the rights to light enjoyed by neighbouring properties.[58] To allow the development to proceed would give the developer a right to develop in a way he never previously enjoyed. The court should be highly reluctant to allow this if there are not overriding considerations of public policy.

Human rights and public interest: the missing elements?

Shelfer was decided well over one hundred years ago, and it should be remembered that it is no more than a 'working rule'.[59] In the current legal climate, regard must

[53] Conversely, it should be noted that the fact that a defendant is willing to accept damages should not necessarily lead to an injunction (*Watson v Croft Promo-Sport Ltd* [2009] EWCA Civ 15, [2009] 3 All ER 249 [48]; cf Lindley LJ in *Shelfer* (n 44)). A willingness to accept damages of a certain amount should not be taken to mean that the claimant will accept what the courts might consider to be an objectively 'reasonable' amount.

54 A logical consequence of a 'property rule'.

[55] Richard Arnold QC in *Site Developments (Ferndown) Ltd v Barratt Homes Ltd* [2007] EWHC 415 (Ch) [64] called it the 'key question'.

[56] Although perhaps of less value to some commercial claimants: n 51.

[57] At least, not in a way which would infringe property rights.

[58] Indeed, prudent developers would always check and assess risks: n 80.

[59] Cf *Jaggard* (n 40) 287. *Daniells v Mendonca* (1999) 78 P & CR 401 (CA) described the equitable jurisdiction as 'unfettered'.

be had to considerations of human rights and public interest. When deciding whether or not to grant an injunction, these issues should feature prominently.

There are two potentially relevant provisions regarding human rights which might influence a court: Article 8 of the European Convention on Human Rights (ECHR) and Article 1 of the First Protocol to the ECHR (A1P1). The former provision protects the right to respect of a person's home. A significant deprivation of light probably does engage Article 8;[60] after all, a home which benefits from plenty of natural right is very different in nature from a home which does not. Although this right is not absolute, its infringement should only be allowed if proportionate and 'necessary'.[61] The strong presumption is that the right be respected rather than violated. Regarding the protection of rights to light, this means that even if the award of an injunction would be oppressive to a particular, individual defendant, it may not be *necessary* for the wider public interest to refuse an injunction.[62] Mention is made of the need to protect 'the rights and freedoms of others', but the defendant developer does not have the right to build such that rights to light will be infringed: his land is limited and does not enjoy such a right.

A1P1 is also relevant:

> Every natural or legal person is entitled to the peaceful enjoyment of his possessions. No one shall be deprived of his possessions except in the public interest and subject to the conditions provided for by law …
>
> The preceding provisions shall not, however, in any way impair the right of a State to enforce such laws as it deems necessary to control the use of property in accordance with the general interest … .

Disputes concerning rights to light engage this provision, and it is strongly arguable that awarding damages in lieu of an injunction represents a deprivation of possession, rather than a 'control' of the use of property (the property being the dominant land itself).[63] After all, the claimant no longer enjoys the right he previously had. A1P1 makes it plain that this can only be allowed if it would be in accordance with the public interest; the only pertinent question to ask is whether awarding an injunction and respecting a party's property right would be sufficiently damaging to the public interest.

It is difficult for the courts to decide that there is a 'public interest' in the defendant's expropriating the claimant's right, just because the defendant

[60] Cf *Lough v First Secretary of State* [2004] EWCA Civ 905, [2004] 1 WLR 2557; *Lopez Ostra v Spain* (App no 16798/90) (1995) 20 EHRR 277; *Guerra & Others v Italy* (App no 14967/89) (1998) 26 EHRR 357.

[61] Convention for the Protection of Human Rights and Fundamental Freedoms (European Convention on Human Rights, as amended) art 8(2).

[62] A 'liability rule' is not necessarily in the public interest: n 30–43.

[63] Compare S Bickford-Smith and A Francis, *Rights of Light: The Modern Law* (2nd edn Jordans Ltd, Bristol 2007) [15.29]. In *Midtown* (n 3) Peter Smith J heard full argument on A1P1 but did not need to decide the point: [49]. In *Ferndown* (n 55), concerning an injunction to protect a restrictive covenant, Richard Arnold QC expressed the view that A1P1 would not have been contravened, but did not have to decide on the facts. The reasoning of the judge appears to rely upon the finding that there was no expropriation.

intends to develop his property. As the European Court of Human Rights observed in *United Kingdom v James*, 'a deprivation of property effected for no reason other than to confer a private benefit on a private party cannot be "in the public interest"'.[64] Nor should the 'public interest' be assumed to prevail simply because the defendant is a public authority, or carrying out works for the public good.[65] Instead, public authorities should be encouraged to make use of the compulsory purchase regime. If a public body is unwilling to lend its support to a development and exploit the compulsory purchase procedure, then the court may be reluctant to usurp the legislative regime and deem there to be a sufficient public interest to allow the violation of the property right. Encouraging the use of compulsory purchase does put a burden on private developers to seek the help of public bodies, but if developers are unable to negotiate with right-holders for the release of their rights, then this path seems more appropriate than forcing courts into the difficult position of deeming the expropriation of a private right at the request of another private individual to be in the public interest. Recommendations to improve the compulsory purchase procedure have been made by the Law Commission, and these should be exploited.[66]

That compulsory purchase may be the preferable route was perhaps hinted at by Lindley LJ in *Shelfer* when he commented that:

> Expropriation, even for a money consideration, is only justifiable when Parliament has sanctioned it. Courts of Justice are not like Parliament, which considers whether proposed works will be so beneficial to the public as to justify exceptional legislation, and the deprivation of people of their rights with or without compensation.[67]

The support of public bodies in deciding that development is necessary in the public interest helps to placate fears that the courts are ordering expropriation of a person's property too readily. Even in cases of compulsory purchase, it will still need to be shown that the claimant's human rights are respected,[68] although proportionality is normally guaranteed through the award of a fair price in return for the expropriation of a right.[69]

Developers should not struggle to gain the support of local authorities if their developments are truly necessary in the public interest.[70] Developers could enter

[64] (App no 8795/79) (1986) 8 EHRR 123 [40].

[65] In *Shelfer* (n 44) itself, the Court of Appeal granted an injunction even though it would hinder works on the electricity supply.

[66] Law Commission, 'Towards a Compulsory Purchase Code: (2) Procedure: Final Report' (Law Com No 291 Cm 6406, 2004).

[67] *Shelfer* (n 44) 316.

[68] *Alliance Spring Co Ltd v First Secretary of State* [2005] EWHC 18 (Admin), [2005] 3 PLR 76.

[69] Assuming that the legislative regime is not exploited inappropriately, expropriation should be in the public interest; the decisions of public authorities are subject to judicial review.

[70] Governmental guidance emphases the importance of the compulsory purchase regime, and encourages local authorities to use their powers pro-actively: 'Ministers believe that compulsory purchase powers are an important tool for local authorities and other public bodies to use … Bodies possessing compulsory purchase powers – whether at local, regional or national level – are therefore encouraged to consider using them pro-actively wherever appropriate to ensure real gains

into 'back-to-back' agreements with local authorities. Under such agreements, a public body can agree to exercise its powers of compulsory purchase in order to ensure that the land can be developed, and later give the land back to the developer, in return for the developer undertaking to indemnify the public authority for the costs incurred in the process. In *Standard Commercial Property Securities Ltd v Glasgow CC*,[71] the House of Lords recently held that it is entirely permissible and appropriate for this practice to occur.

Indeed, greater use may be made of section 237 of the Town and Country Planning Act 1990.[72] This is desirable now that the scope of this provision has expanded. In *Thames Water Utilities Ltd v Oxford City Council* it was held that section 237, as it then stood, only provided for the temporary override of a private right for the duration of the development works, but not permanently.[73] Implementing Law Commission proposals, section 237(1A) has since been added, which allows a development to continue to be used in such a way that a private right is breached, even when the development works have finished.[74] In this way, a public authority which wishes to see land developed in the public interest, such that the property rights of private persons will be overridden, can lend its considerable support to the case by exploiting this provision.[75]

Type of injunctions

The award of a negative or prohibitory injunction should generally be straightforward. Such an injunction prevents the defendant from infringing a property right. Before commencing the development the defendant does not

are brought to residents and the business community without delay' (Department of Communities and Local Government, 'Compulsory Purchase and the Crichel Down Rules' (Office of the Deputy Prime Minister Circular 06/2004, 31 October 2004) <http://www.communities.gov.uk/documents/planningandbuilding/pdf/142928.pdf> accessed 25 August 2010. The circular replicated the wording contained in previous guidance: Department of Communities and Local Government, 'Compulsory Purchase Orders' (Office of the Deputy Prime Minister Circular 02/03, 26 February 2003) <http://www.communities.gov.uk/documents/planningandbuilding/pdf/156360.pdf> accessed 25 August 2010.

[71] [2006] UKHL 50; 2007 SC (HL) 33; E Waring, 'The legality of back-to-back agreements and compulsory purchase' [2007] *Conv* 265.

[72] Cf *Gaunt and Morgan* (n 43) vii.

[73] [1999] 1 EGLR 167. The case concerned a restrictive covenant.

[74] Implementing Law Commission, 'Towards a Compulsory Purchase Code: (2) Procedure: Final Report' (Law Com No 291 Cm 6406, 2004), the Planning Act 2008, sch 9 para 4(2) ensures that the Town and Country Planning Act s 237(1A) now reads:

> Subject to subsection (3), the use of any land in England which has been acquired or appropriated by a local authority for planning purposes (whether the use is by the local authority or by a person deriving title under them) is authorised by virtue of this section if it is in accordance with planning permission even if the use involves—
> (a) interference with an interest or right to which this section applies, or
> (b) a breach of a restriction as to the user of land arising by virtue of a contract.

[75] For discussion of the principles of compensation see generally: Law Commission, 'Towards a Compulsory Purchase Code: (1) Compensation' (Law Com No 286 Cm 6071, 2003).

enjoy a right to build such that a neighbour's property right will be infringed. The right to build is limited *ab initio*. The developer is therefore in a similar position to the Bradford Corporation in *Pickles* – it lacks a right to protect. It should not be able to force the claimant to release the right, absent wider considerations of public interest.

The onus is on the owner of a right to light to ensure that his property rights are fully respected. This can be achieved by bringing the matter to the courts promptly; an interim injunction should generally be sought before a final injunction. Different views have been expressed about whether a claimant should be granted a final injunction if he fails to seek an interim injunction at the outset.[76] A claimant may often be legitimately wary about seeking an interim injunction, since in order to succeed he must give an 'undertaking in damages' to compensate the defendant for any loss the defendant suffers if an interim injunction is granted and it later transpires that it ought not to have been.

A robust presumption that a final injunction be granted may encourage claimants to seek interim relief. Moreover, if the interim injunction is later overturned, it may well be inappropriate to make the claimant pay damages to the defendant. If the claimant has acted perfectly properly at all times, and simply sought to protect property which is rightfully his, it appears unduly harsh for that claimant then to have to pay damages to the defendant if the court finally decides that damages are more appropriate than an injunction. This is particularly so if it is the defendant who has acted badly.

Prohibitory injunctions are obviously less intrusive than mandatory injunctions, which force defendants to remove the infringing elements of developments. Mandatory injunctions are consequently more difficult to obtain. In *Wrotham Park Estate Co Ltd v Parkside Homes Ltd*, the judge thought that ordering the demolition of a building built in breach of a restrictive covenant would represent 'an unpardonable waste'.[77] Moreover, once the defendant has completed the envisaged development, it would seem that the defendant himself has acquired rights which he may seek to protect. Admittedly, such rights were obtained unlawfully, but have come into existence and deserve some recognition.[78]

Nevertheless, mandatory injunctions should still be available; in some circumstances the claimant may have been unable to ascertain the nature of the proposed development and contemplated infringement of the right.[79] In the context of restrictive covenants, one judge has observed that 'where there is

[76] By not seeking an interim injunction the claimant runs the risk that a final injunction be refused, eg *Gafford v Graham* (1999) 77 P & CR 73 (CA), although clearly a final injunction can still be granted, especially if the claimant raised an objection with the defendant: eg *Mortimer v Bailey* [2004] EWCA Civ 1514, [2005] 2 P & CR 9; G Watt, 'Building at risk of injunction' [2005] *Conv* 460.

[77] [1974] 1 WLR 798 (Ch) 811.

[78] In *Jaggard* (n 40) 283, Sir Thomas Bingham MR observed that 'the court cannot ignore the reality with which it is then confronted' at the time of trial.

[79] Cf *Daniells v Mendonca* (1999) 78 P & CR 401 (CA).

doubt as to whether a restrictive covenant applies ... the prudent party will get the matter sorted out before starting building'.[80] Quite right. And if a developer acts unconscionably in deliberately avoiding the issue, that developer deserves little sympathy if asked to remove the offending aspect of the work.

However, often the defendant will be unaware of private property rights which might restrict the building.[81] In such a scenario, it is not clear who deserves the more sympathy: the defendant who failed to ascertain what rights restricted the use of his land, or the claimant who has only just found out about the infringement. It may be that the fact that the claimant failed to protect his rights in good time means that he should not now be able to seek a mandatory injunction.[82] To seek an injunction so late in the day may even represent an abuse of right.

Rights to light: cases of confusion

Judicial discussion: how to protect rights of light?

Many judges have found it difficult to contemplate with equanimity the possibility of allowing a person to exploit a right to light to make 'ransom demands' from a neighbour.[83] For example, in *Colls v Home & Colonial Stores Limited*[84] the House of Lords overturned a decision to grant an injunction to prevent the defendant from developing his property such that the claimant's rights to light would be infringed. The House of Lords appeared to suggest that the courts have a fairly wide discretion to award damages in lieu of an injunction. Lord Macnaghten was 'disposed to think that the Court ought to incline to damages rather than to an injunction. ... the Court ought to be very careful not to allow an action for the protection of ancient lights to be used as a means of extorting money'.[85]

But why should the owner of a property right be prevented from exercising it in order to make a sizeable profit? After all, that appears to follow from the decision in *Pickles*, where the ability of an owner to make use of his property

[80] *Mortimer* (n 76) [41]. In *Jaggard* (n 40) 283, Sir Thomas Bingham MR pointed out that just as the claimant could obtain an interim injunction, so could the developer have obtained a declaration of right.

[81] For example, easements acquired by prescription do not appear on the Land Register. A developer's notice, similar to the procedures in the Party Wall etc Act 1996, may be beneficial: see eg A Francis, 'The Law of Light' (2008) 7317 *NLJ* 542.

[82] Provided there has been no sharp conduct on the part of the defendant.

[83] In *Isenberg v East India House Estate Co Ltd* (1863) De GJ & S 263, 273, Lord Westbury LC expressed concern that the defendant be 'bound hand and foot' to the claimant. This was cited with approval by Millett LJ in *Jaggard* (n 40) 287. The problem may be that rights to light tend to arise through prescription, which is itself controversial: see generally Law Commission, 'Easements, Covenants and Profits à Prendre' (Law Com Cp No 186, 2008) [4.151]–[4.256].

[84] [1904] AC 179 (HL).

[85] Ibid 193.

rights as he saw fit was emphasised. Lord Lindley, agreeing that an injunction should not be granted, observed that rights to light cases tended to be difficult and adopted a balancing approach, taking into account 'consideration for both sides'.[86] However, the balancing exercise should not start at a 'neutral' point: the scales should be heavily tipped in favour of an injunction. A property rule should be preferred to a liability rule.

Colls was thought to go further than the Court of Appeal in *Shelfer,* and suggest that courts should not presumptively award an injunction for breach of a right to light.[87] This was indeed the approach adopted in *Fishenden v Higgs and Hill Ltd*, [88] where the relevant considerations in cases concerning rights to light were thoroughly examined. The trial judge had held that, since the four criteria of AL Smith LJ were not satisfied, an injunction should be granted. This was emphatically overturned by the Court of Appeal. The appellate court strongly favoured damages over an injunction; Lord Hanworth MR cited with approval the opinion of Lord Macnaghten in *Colls* that the court ought to incline towards damages rather than an injunction.[89] All the judges agreed that the discretion the judges had was wider than the 'working rule' of *Shelfer*, but did not attempt to define the scope of that discretion.[90] Maugham LJ was openly critical of *Shelfer*, insisting that 'the working rule laid down by AL Smith LJ is not a universal or even a sound rule in all cases of injury to light'.[91]

Thus it generally appeared to be that the *Shelfer* principles were less helpful in rights to light cases.[92] The courts appeared to enjoy a wider discretion. In *Tamares (Vincent Square) Ltd v Fairpoint Properties (Vincent Square) Ltd*,[93] a rights to light dispute between two neighbouring property companies, Gabriel Moss QC refused to grant an injunction, commenting that *Shelfer* should not fetter the discretion of the courts.[94] Similarly, in *Midtown Limited v City of London Real Property Company Ltd* Peter Smith J was happy to depart from 'the strict requirements of the four requirements set out in *Shelfer*'.[95] That case also concerned a dispute between two companies, and the judge thought it would be oppressive to the defendant to grant an injunction.

[86] Ibid 213.

[87] See *Kine v Jolly* [1905] 1 Ch 480 (CA); *Price v Hilditch* [1930] 1 Ch 500 (Ch).

[88] (1935) 153 LT 128 (CA).

[89] Ibid 139.

[90] Although Romer LJ found that the *Shelfer* test was perhaps satisfied on the facts. Even if not, the claimant had acted badly in not bringing his concerns to the defendant's attention, and that may therefore bar his claim: see text to n 84.

[91] *Fishenden* (n 88) 144.

[92] Earlier editions of *Gale on Easements* thought that this was the result of *Colls*: see now *Gale on Easements* (*Gaunt and Morgan* n 43) [14–92].

[93] [2007] EWHC 212 (Ch), [2007] 1 WLR 2167.

[94] Citing Romer LJ in *Fishenden* (n 88) 141. Although perhaps *Shelfer* was nevertheless satisfied on the facts.

[95] [2005] EWHC 33 (Ch), [2005] 1 EGLR 65 [73].

Recently, however, the Court of Appeal has adopted a stricter approach to the question of when damages should be awarded in lieu of an injunction.[96] *Regan v Paul Properties Ltd* concerned a developer who wished to increase the height of his properties. This interfered with the claimant's right to light. In fact, the claimant's living room became very much darker as a result of the building. The claimant had consistently objected to the development, and refused all offers of settlement. He was solely motivated by the desire to have his rights to light specifically enforced.[97]

Stephen Smith QC, at first instance, considered cases such as *Colls*, *Fishenden* and *Midtown* and came to the conclusion that:

> ... in the case of an infringement of a right to light it cannot be said that refusing an injunction and leaving the claimant with an award of damages in lieu is an exceptional course. Indeed it seems to me ... that the onus is plainly on a claimant to persuade the court that he should not be left to a remedy in damages.[98]

The judge thought that the claimant had failed to discharge the burden on him to show that damages would not be an adequate remedy. However, he did then go on to apply the guidelines of *Shelfer*. He found that the injury was small,[99] capable of being estimated in money, and that damages would be an adequate remedy, whereas an injunction would be oppressive to the defendant.

By contrast, the Court of Appeal adopted a much stricter approach.[100] Mummery LJ, giving the only reasoned speech, emphasised that *Shelfer* should govern the question of whether or not to award damages in lieu of an injunction in cases concerning the infringement of a right to light. He rejected the contention that *Colls* had departed from the guidelines of *Shelfer*. Mummery LJ pointed out that in *Slack v Leeds Industrial Co-operative Society Ltd*,[101] the Court of Appeal had previously held that nothing said in *Colls* affected the *Shelfer* guidelines. Mummery LJ was adamant that the trial judge was wrong to suggest that the onus lay on the claimant to show that an injunction was appropriate, rather than on the defendant to show that damages represented a more appropriate substitute.[102] He emphasised that damages should only be awarded in lieu of an injunction in exceptional cases.

Contrary to the court below, the Court of Appeal held that the interference in question was not a 'small injury', and not adequately compensated by 'a small

[96] Although there have always been some cases which did seek to apply *Shelfer* strictly: eg *Slack v Leeds Industrial Co-operative Society Ltd* [1924] 2 Ch 475 (CA); *Pugh v Howells* (1984) 48 P & CR 298 (CA).

[97] [2006] EWHC 1941 (Ch) [23].

[98] Ibid [85].

[99] The value of the maisonette was reduced by £5,500.

[100] *Regan v Paul Properties Ltd* [2006] EWCA Civ 1391, [2007] Ch 135.

[101] [1924] 2 Ch 475 (CA).

[102] *Regan* (n 100) [58]. One commentator has expressed the opinion that the Court of Appeal chose 'to reverse the courts' longstanding developer-friendly approach to remedies in rights to light cases': P Chynoweth, 'Rights to light: radical consequences of an orthodox decision' [2007] *Conv* 175, 183.

money payment'. Mummery LJ explicitly stated that the fall in value of the claimant's property of £5,000 to £5,500 'is not a small figure',[103] and considered an injunction not to be oppressive to the defendants since they took a 'calculated risk'[104] in proceeding with the development when they knew that the claimant may have enjoyed a right to light. His Lordship concluded that '[t]he defendants who took and acted on the wrong advice must take the consequences and not throw them on to Mr Regan in order to deny him his prima facie right to protect his property by injunction'.[105]

This decision is welcome. It emphasises the importance which should be placed on protecting a person's property rights, and the general suitability of protecting property rights with a property rule. It also shows that if a substantial payment would be required, an injunction should be preferred. The trial judge and Court of Appeal clearly differed in their interpretation of a 'small' sum. It is submitted that the Court of Appeal was correct to view £5,000 as not a small sum in the context; the injury suffered was more than *de minimis*.

The decision of the Court of Appeal goes some way towards establishing a strong presumption that an injunction be awarded. Interestingly, Mummery LJ explicitly notes that the claimant's conduct may encourage a court to award damages in lieu; proper, open and timely steps to protect one's property should be taken. Mummery LJ also noted that there may be 'other' circumstances which justify the refusal of an injunction, but this should not be interpreted broadly. Such circumstances should be limited to the 'exceptional', and may perhaps be linked with the public interest. Only if there is a necessary public interest may the expropriation of a right to light be sanctioned.

But will the tenor of *Regan*, which favours the award of an injunction, be followed? It was cited in *Site Developments (Ferndown) Ltd v Barratt Homes Ltd*,[106] a case concerning rights of way and restrictive covenants, to remind the judge that an injunction should only be granted in exceptional cases. However, Richard Arnold QC nevertheless relied on *Jaggard v Sawyer*[107] and earlier authority to express the view that the key question was still whether the award of an injunction would be oppressive to the defendant, and that he would be inclined to award damages in lieu.[108] More promisingly, in *Watson v Croft Promo-Sport*[109] the Court of Appeal allowed an appeal from a decision that damages should be awarded in lieu where the noise made by the defendant constituted an actionable nuisance. The Chancellor emphasised that an injunction should be awarded unless there were exceptional circumstances. He also thought that,

[103] *Regan* (n 100) [71].
[104] Ibid [74].
[105] Ibid [74].
[106] [2007] EWHC 415 (Ch).
[107] [1995] 1 WLR 269 (CA) 287.
[108] Although the case only concerned an application for summary judgment, and there was clearly a 'reasonable prospect of success': [2007] EWHC 415 (Ch) [73]–[83].
[109] [2009] EWCA Civ 15, [2009] 3 All ER 249.

while the public interest alone could not negate the requirement of exceptional circumstances, it may be taken into account in 'a marginal case where the damage to the claimant is minimal'.[110] This restrictive approach is to be commended.

However, within the specific context of rights to light there remains a degree of scepticism concerning the proper level of respect which should be afforded to rights to light. *Tamares* was decided after *Regan* and only awarded damages, and the status of *Midtown* remains unresolved. It may be possible to reconcile those cases with *Regan* on the basis that the claimants were businesses who relied on artificial light anyway, as opposed to a residential owner who derived a real benefit from a living room with an abundance of natural light. Thus it may be argued that it was unconscionable for the companies to seek specific enforcement of their right to light. However, even in this context it is arguable that it would be preferable to force the parties to bargain with each other for the release of property rights, rather than for the courts to construct a hypothetical bargain.[111]

Conclusion

Owners of property rights should be able to exploit their rights as they see fit.[112] Thus they can demand a high price for the sale of their assets. This is not an abuse of right; it is an incident of property ownership. The language of 'abuse' is problematic, but, if it is to be used, should only really be invoked if claimants fail to protect their rights in good time, or act unconscionably in some way. In such instances, damages might be awarded in lieu of an injunction.

The discretion to award damages in lieu should be very limited. Equitable relief is discretionary, but principles must guide that discretion. In principle, property rights should be protected through property rules; injunctive relief should be readily available.[113] *Regan* will, hopefully, be seen as a turning point: injunctions should strongly be preferred, and the jurisdiction to award damages in lieu exercised only rarely.

While it is likely that *Shelfer* will continue to be cited for some time to come, human rights considerations and the compulsory purchase regime – particularly the enlarged powers under the revised section 237 of the Town and Country Planning Act 1990 – need to be brought to the fore when considering whether an injunction should be granted. Full use should be made of the compulsory purchase regime; it is doubtful whether the courts are best placed to determine the nebulous question of 'public interest'. For example, representations from

[110] Ibid [51].

[111] After all, assessing damages in lieu is no easy task, and a right, once lost, is lost to successors in title also.

[112] Unless there are overriding concerns of public interest: text to n 59–75.

[113] The arguments in this chapter may be equally relevant to other easements and restrictive covenants as they are to rights to light.

environmental groups can be taken into account under the compulsory purchase procedure, but are rarely presented to the court.[114]

Easements of light are property rights, and deserve to be protected through injunctive relief. It may be that the reason why rights to light cases have caused consternation among some observers lies in the method by which rights to light tend to be acquired: prescription. If so, then attention should be paid to the law of prescription as it affects the law of light.[115] But that is beyond the scope of this chapter. Once acquired, rights to light exist as property rights. They merit the protection of property rules.

[114] It may therefore be that even if easements are to fall within an expanded jurisdiction of s 84 of the Law of Property Act 1925, the Lands Tribunal is an inappropriate forum to determine the public interest of a development (Law Commission, 'Easements, Covenants and Profits à Prendre' (Law Com Cp No 186, 2008) part 14). Indeed, the Lands Tribunal appears to have been unwilling to exploit the 'public interest' ground for modifying a restrictive covenant under s 84(1)(aa) of the Law of Property Act 1925: see eg Law Commission, 'Easements, Covenants and Profits à Prendre' (Law Com Cp No 186, 2008) [14.57].

[115] The Law Commission has already raised the idea that the types of easement which can be acquired by prescription should perhaps be restricted: Law Commission, 'Easements, Covenants and Profits à Prendre' (Law Com Cp No 186, 2008) [4.186].

3

Water Matters: A Study of Water-Related Problems in Property Law

The Rt Hon Lady Justice Arden DBE*

As an island nation surrounded by water, whose favourite pastime is to complain about the weather, whose favourite recreations are frequently washed out, and whose homes are regularly flooded, it is quite surprising how we have failed to produce property lawyers who are intellectually curious about the rights and liabilities attaching to water. It took a gifted Australian academic, Dr Joshua Getzler, to write a fascinating account of the history of water law, and a New Zealand academic, the late Professor Taggart, to write an amusing book[1] on *Bradford Corporation v Pickles*.[2] We owe them an immense debt of gratitude, and I shall draw upon each of their learning. I also draw on the skill of Oliver Pegden, a judicial assistant in the Court of Appeal. When he first heard about my interest in writing about rights related to water, I sensed his disbelief. But, characteristically, he applied himself with great diligence and skill and provided a great deal of research. I hope to demonstrate that water rights is a subject which is full of interest and scope for study. Water rights raise some fundamental issues, and also provide a source of learning for the development of other property rights about resources; resources which will have to be carefully conserved in the years to come.

It goes without saying that water is an essential element of existence: we cannot do without it. It is also untameable. T S Eliot wrote:

> I do not know much about gods; but I think that the river
> Is a strong brown god – sullen, untamed and intractable,
> Patient to some degree, at first recognised as a frontier;
> Useful, untrustworthy, as a conveyor of commerce;

* Member of the Court of Appeal of England and Wales.

[1] M Taggart, *Private Property and Abuse of Rights in Victorian England: The Story of Edward Pickles and the Bradford Water Supply* (OUP, Oxford 2002).

[2] [1895] AC 587 (HL).

Then only a problem confronting the builder of bridges.
The problem once solved, the brown god is almost forgotten
By the dwellers in cities – ever, however, implacable,
Keeping his seasons and rages, destroyer, reminder
Of what men choose to forget … .[3]

Yet we do try to tame it: people, for instance, try to increase the height of banks of rivers to protect their land. But, if a person is successful at doing this, he may cause harm to those downstream. How are the benefits and burdens of water ownership shared out by the law? This is a question the reader should keep asking throughout this chapter.

This is a remarkable area of law. Let us start with some of the fundamental issues about water:

a. Is water a thing?
b. Can you own water if it is flowing?
c. What does it mean to own water? Is it enough to have a right to use the water or a right to exclude others from using the water?
d. Is water ever public property?

There is a treasure house of decided cases on water law. The cases often concern problems arising from the industrialisation of Britain. Disputes have arisen in relation to coal mining, the running of mills, the growth of towns and their need for reservoirs, the development of the United Kingdom's canal system and the need for water for industrial purposes. For instance, a mill owner may wish to divert a stream so as to use the water for his own mill, and then send the water back into the stream. Can he do this? And what about the landowner who receives decreased supplies of water and himself wants to use it? To take another example, can a water company abstract water not for the benefit of the land it owns, but for the benefit of the inhabitants of a city many miles away?

The old factual paradigms may not often occur today, thanks to technological developments and the intervention of Parliament. But we have an increasing need to consume water, and that increasing need for water is leading to pressure on global supplies. A single cup of coffee takes 140 litres of water to produce. A glass of beer takes about 45 litres to produce. A hamburger takes about 2,400 litres to produce and a 12oz steak takes a phenomenal 6,000 litres of water to produce.[4]

There are regularly hosepipe bans and water restrictions in the summer. Water has to be allocated between domestic, agricultural and industrial use. Who should have priority? The shortages which Kent suffers are likely to increase because of the general increase in water usage and because of the programme of building thousands of new houses in the region. And, if it is not enough to

[3] T S Eliot, 'The Dry Salvages' in his *Four Quartets* (Mariner Books, UK 1968).

[4] See K Cooke, 'Why Beer Needs Watering Down' *The Times* (London 4 March 2010) 41 at http://www.timesonline.co.uk/tol/news/science/eureka/article7041183.ece, accessed 14 September 2010.

think of the problems that may arise domestically, think of the problems around the world, particularly in Africa, India and the Middle East, where pressure on water resources may well lead to war and civil dissension.[5]

Nearer to home, if we are going to have water problems, it may fall to the courts to give the lead on how the law should be brought up to date so that we can all share equitably in this essential resource. In my view, the development of case law in this area – in any area – is like promoting sustainable development itself. The courts have to know how to use case law to get the best out of it for today's purposes, and yet leave a body of principled law for future generations to be governed by, and where appropriate develop themselves. So I am promoting the idea of sustainable development of case law in the higher courts, though the development of that idea must await another day.

I would just like to explain how I became interested in this area of law. The fascinating thing about water law is that it arises in the courts in many different contexts and on a regular basis. Let me give you some examples from my own period on the Bench:

Seahenge[6]

This may well be the only case where any Chancery judge has been addressed by Druids in full regalia! The case, which arose in 1999, concerned Seahenge, an early Bronze Age timber circle located on the beach at Holme-next-the-Sea, Norfolk. The site was an area of special scientific interest and home to thousands of migratory birds. When Seahenge was laid bare by the movement of sand-dunes, a large number of human visitors flocked to the area, including the Druids. Seahenge was within the private ownership of the Le Strange estate, because unusually the beach was owned by it and not the Crown. English Heritage decided that the best way for Seahenge to be preserved was for it to be excavated, and the Le Strange estate gave it a licence to do this. This caused enormous concern to the Druids. The Druids' case was that Seahenge was a cultural gem. They wanted to worship there. They said it was one of the few Druidic places of worship not destroyed by the Romans. One of the respondents said: 'Our ancestors brought the site there to honour all creation, and ownership, therefore, of the site does not come into the matter.' If this dispute had arisen after 2 October 2000 there might have been an issue to be tried as to how to resolve the conflict between the right to manifest one's religion under article 9[7] and the right to property guaranteed by article 1 of the First Protocol to the ECHR. However, despite the

[5] See, for example, A Roy, 'The Greater Common Good' (Website article, April 1999, available at http://www.narmada.org/gcg/gcg.html, accessed 14 September 2010).

[6] See M Champion, *Seahenge: a Contemporary Chronicle* (Barnwell's Print Ltd, Norfolk 2000).

[7] Convention for the Protection of Human Rights and Fundamental Freedoms (European Convention on Human Rights, as amended) (ECHR) art 9.

submissions of the Archdruid of Britain, private interests prevailed.[8] Seahenge is now located on dry land at Flag Fen, near Peterborough. The case was truly fascinating and there was no forewarning that it would come my way that day, but that is often the case with interlocutory work.

Arscott and others v The Coal Authority and others[9]

This case concerned the interaction of water rights with the law of nuisance. The homes of the 32 claimants had been flooded when the River Taff overflowed its banks in 1998. Before the flood the National Coal Board had deposited colliery spoil on the banks of the Taff up-river from the claimants' homes. As a result the banks were raised and flooding happened around the claimants' homes whereas it would previously have happened further upstream. The claimants sought damages in nuisance, and the National Coal Board sought to defend itself on the basis of the historic 'common enemy principle' by which a person could defend his land from future flooding notwithstanding that it may cause another's land to flood. The Court of Appeal held that acting to defend one's land from future flooding was a reasonable use of land, and thus could not give rise to liability for nuisance. The common enemy principle was upheld. The flood damage for the defendants downstream was not foreseeable. This principle may have very wide implications as river banks have been raised up and down the country to reduce the risk of flooding, but this is liable to increase the risk of flooding to those downstream.

Moore v British Waterways Board[10]

This was a recent appeal on a preliminary issue. The case has yet to go to trial, but it is concerned with a section of the River Brent which was canalised during the late eighteenth century pursuant to the Grand Junction Canal Act 1793 and which is now called the Grand Union Canal. The claimant lives in a houseboat moored by the side of the canal, but has been given notice to quit by the British Waterways Board which owns the Grand Union Canal. The claimant says that he has a right to remain by virtue of the common law public rights of navigation over the River Brent, which, he says, survived the canalisation. One of the issues raised by the case is whether a public right of navigation, or alternatively a private riparian right, includes a right to moor. As I said, there has yet to be a trial of this case.

[8] *The Historic Buildings & Monuments Commission for England v Nolan and others* (Ch) (Arden J) 6 July 1999.

[9] [2004] EWCA Civ 892, [2005] Env LR 6.

[10] [2010] EWCA Civ 42, [2010] CP Rep 21.

Water law, therefore, is a living and expanding area of law. I intend to divide my subject into five sections. First, I intend to examine some of the legal theories which have underpinned the development of the common law in relation to the use and ownership of water. Secondly, I intend to examine the features of the modern riparian doctrine. Thirdly, I intend to examine some of the case law in relation to flooding. Fourthly, I intend to examine how the modern statutory regime covering water use interacts with common law water rights. Fifthly, I intend to offer some answers to those fundamental questions which (as previously indicated) water poses.

Different theories

The common law of water rights has a long history and the various theories which have underpinned its development are diverse and complex. It is not possible for me to give a fully-textured picture of the theoretical background. Instead my approach is a simplified one: I want to examine two competing doctrines in water law. One is the 'appropriation theory', and the other is 'natural rights theory', also known as riparianism. It is accepted that it is natural rights theory which is the doctrine behind modern water law, but, in order properly to understand it, it is important to understand how it differs from its predecessor, appropriation theory. Surprisingly, the common law drew on both American law and civil law in the course of its evolution. This section of this chapter culminates in a discussion of the great case of *Bradford Corporation v Pickles*.

Appropriation theory

As the name of the doctrine suggests, appropriation theory grants ownership of water to the person who appropriates it. To take a trivial example, if you put water in your bucket it belongs to you. Under this theory water is classified as a form of property. An individual may acquire the ownership of water by using it. Although water in this theory is considered to be property, it is also considered to be 'transient'. Because water is transient it cannot be permanently appropriated. It is only owned whilst it is appropriated. So, to use the words of the old lyric, if there is a hole in my bucket, dear Liza, and the water seeps out, I lose my ownership of it.

Appropriation theory in its modern form may be traced to William Blackstone's *Commentaries on the Law of England*.[11] Dr Getzler reduces Blackstone's expression of the doctrine to five key points. The first three of those points are the most important for current purposes, they are:

[11] See J Getzler, *A History of Water Rights at Common Law* (Oxford Studies in Modern Legal History, OUP, Oxford 2004) 154.

(1) Water is a type of corporeal right, a transient element available to the public but subject to a qualified individual property or title during use.
(2) The first appropriator of water wins title under a natural principle of defending occupation.
(3) Title subsists only during time of use, as water cannot be possessed or appropriated in the manner of land.[12]

Blackstone drew upon a host of influences, including scripture and Roman law, in the process of defining his appropriation theory of water law, but underpinning the theory are just two key ideas: firstly, the idea that occupation (in other words, appropriation) is the foundation of title; and, secondly, the idea that water cannot be occupied in the same way as land because of its fluid nature – in Blackstone's own words:

> For water is a moveable wandering thing and must of necessity continue common by the law of nature so that I can only have a temporary, transient, usufructary, property therein … .[13]

In appropriation theory, unused water remains common property, or one of the *res communes*. There are thus two key Roman law influences on the doctrine: the first is the notion that occupation gives rise to title; the second is the notion that unused water in the natural environment is *publici juris*. Of these two the first has primacy: the essence of appropriation theory therefore is that title in water persists in an individual only for so long as that individual puts the water to use. Although unused water is recognised as public property, in this theory water is not really treated as a communal resource. Instead under appropriation theory the first appropriator may take it all without regard to the fact that he may leave other people short of water in the process. Put another way, there is no concept here of reasonable use.

It is important to note that the upstream user is not necessarily the first appropriator. Where an upstream user increases the amount of water he appropriates, he may deprive an already existing downstream appropriator, and it is that downstream appropriator who, in these circumstances, is the first appropriator.

By the early nineteenth century appropriation theory had become one of the dominant doctrines, if not the dominant doctrine, in English water law. In the case of *Bealey v Shaw*,[14] two mill owners disputed the use of water in the River Irwell. The downstream plaintiff complained that the upstream defendant was diverting more water to his mill than he had done previously, thereby depriving the plaintiff of the flow that he was used to for the purposes of using his own mill. The four judges found in favour of the plaintiff, and two did so on the basis of a pure adherence to the appropriation doctrine. Where an upstream

[12] Ibid.
[13] *Getzler* (n 11) 173–74.
[14] (1805) 6 East 208; 102 ER 1266.

user had hitherto left water unappropriated, that water was left available to be appropriated by successive downstream users. If the upstream user then increased the amount of water that he appropriated, he thereby interfered with the established first appropriation of those below him. That gave rise to an actionable wrong.

Bealey v Shaw can be contrasted with *Williams v Morland*.[15] In that case, the plaintiff complained that he had lost the benefit and advantage of a stream on his land since the defendant had built a dam upstream. The issue for the court was whether the plaintiff could simply complain of an interrupted flow without showing some use had been interfered with. The court rejected the plaintiff's arguments that he had some inherent right to the natural flow of the water on his land, and held that to bring a claim he had to show some injury to the existing appropriation of the water flow. On the facts, the court held that it was essential that a plaintiff should demonstrate that he had been putting the relevant water to some use. It was not sufficient simply to say that flow had been disrupted. The decision in *Williams v Morland* thus demonstrates the courts' acceptance of the appropriation theory.

Appropriation theory also illustrates the concept of *damnum sine injuria*, meaning that there is no actionable injury despite damage. That is because it was necessary to show actual interference with use. Even if the flow of water had been interrupted, no action was available if there was no use which had been interfered with. I shall have more to say about *damnum sine injuria* later on.

Natural rights theory

Natural rights theory had been a feature of the English common law of water rights in the seventeenth and eighteenth centuries. It was abandoned in favour of appropriation theory in the early nineteenth century as I have described, but in the mid-nineteenth century it re-established itself and it has persisted since then as one of the foundations of the common law of water rights.

Natural rights theory in essence provides that the right to water is a natural incident to the ownership of the contiguous land. The key difference between natural rights theory and appropriation theory is that in natural rights theory the rights in the relevant water do not depend upon the landowner putting the water to use.

Like appropriation theory, natural rights owes much to Roman law concepts and I wish to emphasise two of those. In the first place, natural rights theory draws upon the Roman law notion of the right to water as a praedial (or property) right.[16] In other words, emphasis was placed upon the right to water being a right

[15] (1824) 2 B & C 910; 107 ER 620.

[16] As to Roman praedial doctrine, see *Getzler* (n 11) 72.

arising from and attached to the contiguous land. The right was said to extend from the land abutting the river to the midway point of the river, or the *medium filum*. That had not been a key feature of appropriation doctrine, and although the difference might seem to be academic, by the end of the nineteenth century technological advances had meant that the use (or appropriation) of water was possible without owning adjoining land. Accordingly it became important to define whether the right to water was attached to neighbouring land or not.[17]

The second key Roman influence was water as one of the *res communes*. Whereas this had been a secondary influence under appropriation theory, it was dominant in natural rights theory. This meant that water was residually owned by the public.

The growth of the emphasis upon water as a communal property went hand in hand with a growth in emphasis upon the requirement to use water reasonably, that is, with the good of the community in mind. As part of natural rights theory a 'reasonable use' doctrine developed. From an early stage in English law the requirement to limit oneself to 'reasonable use' was explained in terms of the maxim *sic utere tuo ut alienum non laedas* (so use your own property as not to cause injury or nuisance to property of another).

Natural rights theory, unlike appropriation theory, did not accord the first appropriator the right to deprive all others, but rather required that a balance of reasonable use should be struck for the benefit of all. Natural rights theory thus represented not only a distinct set of *legal* principles governing the use of water, but also a distinct set of political and ideological principles. In appropriation theory the absolute right to own property had primacy: it was only water's fluid form that prevented it from being owned outright. On the other hand natural rights theory provided that water could not be owned because it *should* not be owned by individuals, regardless of whether its physical form made it possible.[18]

Natural rights theory was dominant in American law in the early nineteenth century, and by the middle of that century it had become prevalent in England and Wales. The key case in this regard was *Embrey v Owen*,[19] in which the downstream plaintiff sought damages from an upstream defendant for the wrongful diversion of the flow of water, in circumstances where there was no appreciable damage to the plaintiff's use of the river. Parke B, giving the judgment of the court, held that it was not necessary for there to have been damage for there to be an action for interference with the flow of the river. However, Parke B held that not all interferences with flow would be actionable, since allowance had to be made for the upstream defendant's right to make reasonable use of the river as *publici juris*. Accordingly, only unreasonable use by the upstream user could give rise to an action, albeit that that unreasonable use did not have to cause actual damage. Ultimately the court found in favour

[17] *Getzler* (n 11) 44.
[18] *Getzler* (n 11) 43–45.
[19] (1851) 6 Exch 353; 155 ER 579.

of the defendant on the basis that there had been no sensible diminution of the flow, and that, crucially, his use had been reasonable.

Natural rights theory allowed for instances of *injuria sine damno* or actionable injury without damage. That is because it was only necessary for a plaintiff to show that there had been an interference with the flow, not that he had suffered actual damage or the interference with any particular use.

In *Miner v Gilmour*,[20] the plaintiff complained that the defendant had diverted flow away from his (the plaintiff's) tannery to the defendant's mill. The defendant's defence was that the plaintiff had known about the mill before he bought his property and thus could not complain about it. The Privy Council confirmed that the general rule was that there was no need for actual damage for an action to lie. However, the Privy Council also held that allowance had to be made for everyone's reasonable use of the water. Reasonable use could not give rise to an action even if it caused actual damage. On the facts the defendant's use of the water for his mill was reasonable, given that it was longstanding, and accordingly damage to the plaintiff was not actionable.

In *Miner* the court explained that although there was no requirement for a plaintiff to show damage, he nevertheless had to show that his right had been materially interfered with. Thus the two requirements for an action were (1) an unreasonable use of the water by the defendant; and (2) a material interference with the plaintiff's right to reasonable use himself.

Chasemore v Richards[21] finally confirmed natural rights theory as the basis of the English common law of water rights. *Chasemore* really concerned the status of underground water (discussed below), but in the process of reaching its decision the House of Lords confirmed that the right to flowing water was a natural right attached to the land over which water flows, and subject to the limit of reasonable use.

Rights to fish and rights in fish: appropriation theory and natural rights theory side-by-side

A short recreational diversion may help to illustrate appropriation theory and natural rights theory. In the fourth edition of his work, *The Compleat Angler*, published in 1668, Izaak Walton included a fascinating passage in relation to seventeenth century water law in so far as it was relevant to anglers. It represents an interesting juxtaposition of appropriation theory in relation to fish with natural rights theory in relation to water.

In appropriation theory, wild animals including fish were treated in much the same way as water. In expounding his understanding of appropriation theory, Blackstone explained that water was to be compared with:

[20] (1858) 12 Moo PC 131; 14 ER 861.
[21] (1859) 7 HLC 349; 11 ER 140.

> ... those animals which are said to be *ferae naturae*, or of wild and untameable disposition: which any man may seise upon and keep for his own use or pleasure ... but if once they escape from his custody, or he voluntarily abandons the use of them, they return to the common stock and any man else has an equal right to seise and enjoy them afterwards.[22]

In *The Compleat Angler*, Walton described the property in fish in appropriation theory terms. He explained that in a river:

> ... the fish are said to be *ferae naturae*, and the taking of them with an angle is not trespass for that no man is said to have a property in them until he hath caught them, and then it is trespass to take them from him.[23]

What is interesting about the passage is that Izaak Walton proceeds on the basis that fishing rights in a river (as opposed to a pond or several fishery)[24] attach to the land *contiguous* to the water. But, because of the application of appropriation theory to the fish in the river, he concludes that, as long as you have the right to be on that land, you are not abusing your right to be there by taking fish from the river. In his own words:

> If a man have a licence to enter into a Close or Ground for such a space of time; there though he practise angling all that time, he is not a trespasser because his fishing is no abuse of his licence.[25]

So, Izaak Walton is at one and the same time reflecting both the appropriation theory (in relation to the fish) and also the idea that the ownership of land potentially confers rights in respect of the contiguous water. The latter is an expression of the natural rights theory. As explained, this was the current legal theory in the seventeenth century when Izaak Walton was writing.

Modern riparian doctrine

Key features

The modern riparian doctrine can thus be summarised as follows:

- riparian rights arise for an owner of water flowing in a defined natural watercourse;

[22] *Getzler* (n 11) 173.

[23] I Walton and C Cotton, *The Compleat Angler* (OUP, Oxford 2008) 230–33.

[24] A several right of fishery is an exclusive right of fishing in a given place. The passage cited in *Walton* (n 22), states that the owner of a several fishery also has to own the land over which the several fishery was claimed to exist. Today, however, a several fishery can exist without ownership of the soil: see *Halsbury's Laws of England* vol 1(2), [805].

[25] *Walton and Cotton* (n 23).

- the riparian owner has a right to the flow of water on to and away from his property regardless of whether he is putting it to use;
- the prima facie rule is that his rights in the water extend to the *medium filum*;
- the riparian owner has the right to make reasonable use of the water flow although that may cause damage to another riparian user; and
- although a riparian owner need not suffer damage before he can enforce his riparian rights, he must show some interference with his right – this is the *de minimis* principle.[26]

The significance of natural flow: standing surface water, subterranean water and artificial watercourses

Standing Surface Water

What about standing surface water? The position in relation to standing water was established in *Broadbent v Ramsbotham*.[27] In that case the plaintiff complained that the defendant was draining standing water from the surface of his (the defendant's) land in such a way as to deprive him (the plaintiff) of the flow of water to his mill. The court held that there was no right to the flow of water beyond the right to the flow of water in the brook itself. Accordingly the defendant was free to treat his standing surface water as he pleased. Flow in a defined channel was essential for an actionable wrong.

In this regard it is important to note that, in relation to ponds and lakes (which do give rise to riparian rights) less emphasis is inevitably placed on the flow, and more on the existence of a defined channel (for example, the bed of the lake or pond).[28]

Subterranean water in a defined stream

Non-percolating subterranean water, that is, water which forms part of a defined subterranean stream also attracts riparian rights. This is established by *Dickinson v Grand Junction Canal Co*,[29] in which the court held that an action lay for the diversion of a defined underground watercourse just as it lay for a defined over-ground watercourse. This was also the approach in *Grand Junction Canal Co v Shugar*.[30]

[26] See generally: J Bates, 'Rights in Waters and Pipes' in his *Water and Drainage Law* (vol 2, Sweet & Maxwell, London 1990).

[27] (1856) 11 Exch 602; 156 ER 971.

[28] *Bates* (n 26) [1.126]–[1.134].

[29] (1852) 7 Exch 282; 155 ER 953; See also *Getzler* (n 11) 296.

[30] (1870–71) LR 6 Ch App 483 (CA).

Artificial Watercourses

Since the modern riparian doctrine attaches primary significance to *natural* flow in a defined channel, riparian rights do not arise in relation to artificial water courses. That is because, although water may flow in artificial watercourses, it is not natural flow. On this issue, *Bates on Water and Drainage Law* cites the Privy Council decision *Rameshur Pershad Narain Singh v Koonj Behari Pattuck*,[31] in which Sir Montague Smith held that:

> There is no doubt that the right to the water of a river flowing in a natural channel through a man's land and the right to water flowing to it through an artificial watercourse ... do not rest on the same principle.[32]

Subterranean percolating water

Similarly water percolating underground does not give rise to riparian rights.[33] In this regard the courts have often justified their decisions on the basis of practical considerations. The leading nineteenth century authority on this issue was *Acton v Blundell*.[34] In that case the plaintiff owned mills and in them used water drawn from a well. The neighbouring defendant sank a mine into his own land, and thereby cut off the percolating supply of water to the plaintiff's well. The court held that the plaintiff had no right to the percolating water in the well. The predominant justification was that underground water is out of sight and there is therefore no means of monitoring changes to the flow. *Chasemore*[35] confirmed that percolating water was not subject to riparian rights, and, again, the justification was practical. The issue was deemed to be evidential: percolating water was out of sight and therefore changes to flow and the causes of any such changes could not be proved. As I have explained, however, subterranean water in a defined stream *is* subject to riparian rights, and accordingly the underlying basis for the decision in *Chasemore* seems to have been doctrinal rather than practical.

The best known case on the subject of subterranean percolating water is *Bradford Corporation v Pickles*.[36] The facts can be shortly summarised. Bradford was a growing industrial town. It needed water for its inhabitants. Bradford Corporation formed a new statutory company to look for water for the inhabitants of Bradford. They found the perfect place, a gushing spring known as Many Wells. Perfect – or so they thought. They had not reckoned on the fact that Mr Pickles was the owner of a neighbouring farm called East Many Wells farm. The water which emerged at Many Wells collected under

[31] (1878–79) 4 App Cas 121 (PC).
[32] Ibid 126.
[33] *Bates* (n 26) [1.146]–[1.150].
[34] (1843) 12 M & W 324; 152 ER 1223.
[35] See above (n 21).
[36] [1895] AC 587 (HL).

Mr Pickles' farm. Mr Pickles wanted to mine the minerals under his land and to achieve this purpose proposed to drain the water under his land and then pipe it back into the river many miles away. Needless to say, this plan caused great consternation in Bradford. Bradford Corporation relied on a private Act of Parliament to prevent Mr Pickles from carrying out his plan, but that only prevented an unlawful diversion of water. Bradford Corporation therefore had to show that Mr Pickles was interfering with its common law water right to percolating water.

The problems which Bradford Corporation faced are immediately apparent. Mr Pickles was operating on his own land and was intercepting percolating water. Since the water was not part of a defined stream, and it was not *publici juris*, he was entitled to do with it as he pleased. The House of Lords relied upon *Chasemore v Richards* for the proposition that Mr Pickles was entitled to the percolating water under his land.

In those circumstances Bradford Corporation sought to establish that Mr Pickles was abusing his rights by acting maliciously and to succeed against him on that basis. The Corporation failed on this argument too. The House of Lords held that, given that Mr Pickles' actions were lawful, his motives were irrelevant. This was neatly expressed by Lord Macnaghten as follows:

> If the act, apart from motive, gives rise merely to damage without legal injury, the motive, however reprehensible it may be, will not supply that element.[37]

The key point to note from the case is that the reasonable use theory had no application outside the existing parameters of riparian doctrine. If there was no cause of action, then the fact that the defendant had been acting unreasonably was irrelevant. The reasonable use doctrine could not apply. Lord Macnaghten's well-known dictum is one of the high water marks of the rigidity of the common law.

It appears that Scots law offers a much more flexible approach. It contains a useful, if little used, doctrine of *aemulatio vicini*. My research[38] suggests that the role of this doctrine is to provide a remedy in cases where the harm caused is *damnum absque injuria*. Thus, this doctrine can be invoked to qualify the near absolute rights of another to intercept underground percolating water. It is true that doubts were expressed by Lord Watson in *Bradford Corporation v Pickles*, but *Stair* considers that Lord Watson did not accurately state the effect of Scots law. The doctrine depends upon an act, which is otherwise lawful, being rendered unlawful if done with a malicious intent of injuring a neighbour. Just think what possibilities this doctrine might offer for insisting on greater neighbourliness throughout property law: suppose that you have a wonderful view over a lake and then the owner of a property between you and

[37] Ibid 601.

[38] 'Nuisance' in R Black, J Thomson and K Miller (eds), *Stair Memorial Encyclopaedia* (Butterworths Law, Scotland 1991) [34] '*Aemulatio vicini in modern Scots law*'.

the lake decides to plant a woodland of fast-growing Sitka spruce which quickly removes your view. You would have no cause of action in English law. It adopts an absolute rule about motive. It is possible that there would be a different result in Scots law.

Nuisance actions, riparian rights and flooding

Actions taken against the infringement of riparian rights most commonly fall within the parameters of the law of nuisance, which protects the enjoyment of real property. But what if you are not seeking to protect the enjoyment of your own right to water? What if you are simply seeking to protect yourself from another's use or misuse of water? A claimant who complains of flooding from a defendant's land, for example, is not seeking to enforce any right that he has to enjoyment of water; on the contrary, he is seeking to be protected from another's water use. This is no longer strictly a question of water rights, but it is still within the broader parameters of water-related nuisance.

The basic rule in relation to the discharge of water is that a lower occupier has no cause of action against the higher occupier for the natural drainage or percolation of water on to his (the lower occupier's) land. Conversely, the higher occupier has no action against the lower occupier if the latter prevents such drainage from the higher land onto his own. This position was confirmed by the Court of Appeal in *Palmer v Bowman*.[39] In this case, the claimant landowners brought an action against the owners of neighbouring land. They claimed that they were entitled to an easement, acquired by lost modern grant for the percolation of water from their land on to their neighbour's land, and that that drainage right had been interfered with by the defendants. At first instance the judge held that, although there had been such an easement, it had since been extinguished. On appeal the defendants sought to uphold that decision, but in the alternative they cross-appealed the judge's finding that there had ever been an easement. The Court of Appeal held that, in order for a claim of lost modern grant to be successful, the subject-matter of the grant had first to be a right capable of existing as an easement. The court held that natural drainage of percolating and undefined surface water from one piece of land to another, lower, piece of land was not capable of existing as an easement. There is no right, then, to benefit from natural drainage, nor is there a right to be protected from it.

What if the flow from one piece of land to another is not natural, but artificial or at least artificially increased? The essential distinction to be made here is between flooding that occurs as a result of a defendant's natural use of land, and flooding that occurs as a result of the defendant's non-natural use. The former will not normally be actionable in nuisance, whereas the latter will be.

[39] [2000] 1 WLR 842 (CA); and see J Bates, 'Flooding and Private Rights' (2007) 18 *WL* 159.

In relation to waters that have been artificially contained, for example in a reservoir, and which then escape or are released, the well-known rule in *Rylands v Fletcher*[40] may attach strict liability to the occupier of the higher land. The facts of the case were, briefly, that the defendant landowner had built a reservoir over certain disused mineshafts which connected with the plaintiff's mine. Water from the reservoir burst through the disused shafts and flooded the plaintiff's mine. The court found that the owner of the flooded mine was entitled to damages. Lord Cranworth expressed the ratio succinctly as follows:

> If a person brings, or accumulates, on his land anything which, if it should escape, may cause damage to his neighbour, he does so at his peril.[41]

The essence of the rule in *Rylands* was thus, originally, that the relevant substance needed to have been artificially contained by the defendant. If it then escaped, the defendant would be strictly liable. That conception of the rule, however, not only made the rule in *Rylands v Fletcher* very wide, but it also gives rise to difficulties with regard to determining what is artificially contained and what is not.

These difficulties were partly dealt with when the rule in *Rylands v Fletcher* was considered by the Privy Council in *Rickards v Lothian*.[42] That case concerned the overflow of water from a sink and the court determined that the key question in relation to the rule in *Rylands v Fletcher* was not whether the escaping substance had been artificially contained, but whether the land had been put to some non-natural use which brought increased danger to others. This is a markedly more restricted approach to the *Rylands v Fletcher* rule in its original form.

These issues were revisited by the House of Lords in 1994 in *Cambridge Water Co Ltd v Eastern Countries Leather plc*[43] and more recently in 2003 in *Transco plc v Stockport MBC*.[44] Those cases confirm that the fundamental question is not whether the water is artificially contained, but whether the land is being put to some non-natural use which heightens the risk to others. *Transco* was a claim in respect of damage caused by a large amount of water which escaped from a pipe used to supply a block of flats. The claimant, Transco, sought damages from the defendant authority for loss caused by water flowing from a leak in the pipe. The court held that the piping of water by the authority was not a non-natural use, and therefore that strict liability could not be attached to the authority.

The instances, then, where a defendant may be made strictly liable for flooding his neighbour's land have been restricted by the recent jurisprudence on *Rylands*. In many cases, the use of the land which gave rise to the flooding will not be deemed 'non-natural' and in those circumstances a claimant will

[40] (1868) LR 3 HL 330 (HL).
[41] Ibid 340.
[42] [1913] AC 263 (HL) 280.
[43] [1994] 2 AC 264 (HL).
[44] [2003] UKHL 61, [2004] 2 AC 1.

have to try to bring his claim within nuisance without the help of the rule in *Rylands v Fletcher*.

It is important to note that the rule in *Rylands* may only apply to flooding where there has been a discharge from one piece of land to another. The court in *Transco* made it clear that, although the key question in *Rylands* was whether the use of the land was natural or non-natural, *Rylands* liability was *only* capable of arising where there had been escape of a substance from one tenement to another.[45]

Rylands thus does not cover circumstances where the defendant's non-natural use of his land causes water to flow on to the claimant's land from another source. In those circumstances, there will be no strict liability and the normal rules of foreseeability will apply.

Arscott[46] was a case in which nuisance was claimed in just those circumstances. The upstream coal authority had raised the banks of the river on its land in such a manner as to cause flooding downstream. By doing so it had in effect displaced the flood from its own land to the claimants' land. But, importantly, there had been no escape of water from the defendant's land to the claimant's land and so *Rylands* could not apply.

As the court made clear in *Arscott*, the 'common enemy defence' does not apply in circumstances where the flood water has already arrived on to the defendant's land. In other words, a defendant is not able deliberately to transfer flood waters on to his neighbour and in so doing use the common-enemy principle as a defence. In *Whalley v Lancs and Yorks Ry Co*[47] which the court cited in *Arscott*, the defendant cut channels into his land so as to drain flood water on to his neighbour's land and in those circumstances he was held to be liable. Cases such as this may be seen as instances of 'non-natural' use which, although they concern discharge from one piece of land to another, do not engage *Rylands* because the accumulation is not artificial. Alternatively they may be seen as an example of one of the instances where a defendant may be liable in nuisance notwithstanding that his use of his land was 'natural' – I will briefly discuss such cases now.

Can a defendant be liable in nuisance if his use of his land is 'natural'? In *Smith v Kenrick*,[48] waste water from the defendant's mine was discharged into the plaintiff's mine, and the plaintiff sought damages. The Privy Council held that a mine owner had no obligation to prevent the flow of water from his mine into a neighbour's mine. Modern commentators explain the decision in *Kenrick* on the basis that the mine was not being put to any unnatural use and on the basis that the waste water was never artificially accumulated or contained.[49]

[45] See ibid [9].

[46] *Arscott and others v The Coal Authority and others* [2004] EWCA Civ 892, [2005] Env LR 6.

[47] (1884) 13 QBD 131 (CA).

[48] (1849) 7 CB 515 (KB).

[49] See, for example, A Dugdale and M Jones (eds), *Clerk & Lindsell on Torts* (19th edn Sweet & Maxwell, London 2009) 21–34.

The court in *Kenrick* made clear that the defendant mine owner had the right to work his own mine as he saw fit and thereby cause prejudice to his neighbour 'so long as that does not arise from the negligent or malicious conduct of the party'. On the basis of *Kenrick*, then, no natural use of land will give rise to liability in nuisance unless it is negligent or malicious. That position may be seen as supportive of absolute property rights.

In modern cases, however, the courts have taken a slightly different approach. In *Arscott* the court held that in nuisance there were two important distinctions to make: (i) the distinction between natural and non-natural use; and (ii) the distinction between reasonable and unreasonable use. The court held that natural use might give rise to liability in nuisance if it was unreasonable, but reasonableness would never be a defence to liability for nuisance for the non-natural use of land.

Conclusion on flooding and nuisance

In summary, the case law that I have described in relation to flooding, like the cases described earlier concerning 'pure' riparian rights, evidences a development of the doctrine of reasonable use. That doctrine appeared in the distinction between 'natural' and 'non-natural' use, but reasonableness is now recognised as a separate concept. Even natural use of land may give rise to liability if it is unreasonable.

The impact of statute – codification of the reasonable use doctrine?

Statutory provisions affecting the common law on the use of water and riparian rights

The common law position described above now operates within an extensive statutory scheme which includes the Water Industry Act 1991, the Water Resources Act 1991, the Statutory Water Companies Act 1991, the Land Drainage Act 1991, the Land Drainage Act 1994, the Environment Act 1995, the Water Industry Act 1999, the Enterprise Act 2002 and the Water Act 2003. I will highlight some of the provisions of the Water Resources Act 1991, which is the most pertinent piece of legislation to the matters discussed above.

The Water Resources Act 1991 places significant constraints upon the way water may be used. In broad terms, it provides that no person may 'abstract' or 'impound' water from any inland waters without a licence.[50] The provisions of

[50] Water Resources Act 1991 ss 24 and 25.

the 1991 Act ultimately derive from the Water Resources Act 1963 under which, for the first time, the abstraction and impounding of water resources became regulated on a regional basis.

In the context of the terms of the Water Resources Act 1991 to 'abstract' means to remove water from the waterway either temporarily or permanently[51] and to 'impound' means to control water by means of a dam, weir or other similar works.[52]

The types of waterway covered by these rules are extensive. They include: any river, stream or other watercourse whether natural or artificial and whether tidal or not; any lake or pond, whether natural or artificial, or any reservoir or dock; and any underground strata. The restriction on abstraction is subject to a *de minimis* exception under section 27 of the Act. That section essentially provides that no licence is required to abstract water if the volume abstracted in any 24 hour period is less than 20 cubic metres.[53]

An individual may obtain a licence from the Environment Agency, but under section 35 of the Act his application will not be considered unless (1) he has, or at the time when the proposed licence is to take effect will have, a right of access to land contiguous to the inland waters at that place, or those places; and (2) he will continue to have such a right for the period of at least one year beginning with the date on which the proposed licence is to take effect, or until it is to expire if sooner.[54]

It is to be noted that the Water Resources Act 1991 section 70 provides that sections 24 and 25 of the Act (that is, those sections that I have described which proscribe abstraction and impounding) are not to be interpreted as conferring a right of action in any civil proceedings (other than proceedings for the recovery of a fine) in respect of any contravention of those restrictions. It is thus envisaged that the statutory scheme should operate alongside the common law and be distinct from it. But the statutory scheme may affect the nature and number of common law actions.

In many ways the statutory scheme preserves the DNA of riparian doctrine. As I have just described, licences may only be granted to those individuals who already have common law riparian rights by virtue of rights in the contiguous land. And, broadly speaking, the regime differentiates between standing or 'discrete' waters and flowing water forming part of a wider network of watercourses.

In other ways, however, the legislation represents a significant departure from riparian doctrine. For example, the regime extends restrictions on the use of water to include artificial watercourses and water percolating in underground strata. Under the common law, a landowner is free to treat those waters as he pleases.

[51] Water Resources Act 1991 s 221.
[52] Water Resources Act 1991 s 25.
[53] Water Resources Act 1991 s 27.
[54] Water Resources Act 1991 s 35.

Statutory provisions affecting the common law on flooding and nuisance

The Water Resources Act 1991 also contains provisions in relation to flooding and drainage. There are other relevant provisions in the Land Drainage Act 1991. The primary function of those provisions is to create a national infrastructure for dealing with flooding and drainage, in the form of local flood defence committees and drainage boards overseen by the Environment Agency.

The statutory regime also creates public obligations for riparian owners and others to ensure the proper flow of water in watercourses so as to avoid flooding. For example, the Land Drainage Act 1991 section 23 prohibits any person without the written permission of the relevant drainage board from erecting any dam, weir or other similar obstruction to any ordinary watercourse, or from altering any such obstruction. In this context ordinary watercourses exclude 'main rivers', but similar provisions in relation to main rivers are contained in the Water Resources Act 1991.

Conclusions on the statutory regime

On a broad level, the statutory regime can essentially be viewed as a codification of the doctrine of reasonable use. Matters which would previously have fallen solely within the scope of the common law are now within the scope of the public law statutory provisions. The judgment as to what is reasonable and what is not has to a certain extent been taken out of the hands of the courts, and placed into the hands of an executive agency.

The statutory regime also represents an expansion of the reasonable use doctrine because under it a greater number of instances of water use are subjected to the scrutiny of the state. It is noteworthy that Mr Pickles would probably have fallen foul of the provisions of the Water Resources Act 1991 if it had been in force at the end of the nineteenth century.

Some answers to questions originally posed

At the beginning of this article I suggested that water, by its nature, raises the following property law questions:

a. Is water a thing?
b. Can you own water if it is flowing?
c. What does it mean to own water?
d. Is water ever public property?

I now propose to offer some short answers to those questions.

Is water a thing?

Yes, water is a thing and it can properly be subject to property law. Nevertheless it is a unique thing from the perspective of property law because of the conjunction of its two important features: first, the fact that it is essential to life, and secondly, the fact that it is a liquid means that in its natural state it may be flowing.

Can you own water if it is flowing?

Yes and no. The natural rights theory, which underpins riparianism, provides that no one person owns the actual substance of water which is flowing. Nevertheless, riparian rights to water may in some ways result in water being capable of being described as property and therefore of being owned.

What does it mean to own water?

In *National Provincial Bank v Ainsworth*, Lord Wilberforce held that:

> Before a right or an interest can be admitted into the category of property, or of a right affecting property, it must be definable, identifiable by third parties, capable in its nature of assumption by third parties, and have some degree of permanence or stability.[55]

These requirements, particularly that of stability, pose difficulties for the ownership of water. Generally speaking, water is not capable of ownership until it is reduced into possession with some element of permanence. You can sell water in tanks. You can sell land with a lake on it. But the right is lost if the water is in a receptacle from which it drains away.

Is it ever public property?

If water is free-flowing, it is not *bonum vacans*. It has been held that in certain circumstances water is *publici juris*: public property. The courts have not worked out exactly what this means. However, there is an interesting discussion in a recent decision of the High Court of Australia.[56] This case also shows the difficulty of property ownership in water. The case concerned aquifers and the plaintiffs had licences to abstract water, which were replaced by the state by further licences. The plaintiffs complained that since the licences were for a

[55] [1965] AC 1175 (HL) 1248.

[56] *ICM Agriculture Property Ltd & others v The Commonwealth of Australia and others* [2009] HCA 51.

reduced amount of water the state had acquired property from them for no consideration, contrary to the constitution. However, the majority of the High Court of Australia held that in these circumstances there was no right of ownership in the water until it had been reduced into possession. They applied *Embrey v Owen* and held that water was *publici juris*, not *bonum vacans*. Accordingly, the state could validly be given a statutory right to regulate water without acquiring any property interests of the plaintiffs. The plaintiffs never had a right to water which was taken away from them. This case is particularly interesting because the water was percolating water.

Conclusions

In this study of water rights, we have seen that the common law courts often use theory to develop the law. They have also, unusually, used law from other sources: Roman law, civil law and American law. We see the conflict between the rights of owners and the rights of non-owners being played out. We saw how subterranean percolating water is treated differently. As to the absolute statement in *Bradford Corporation v Pickles* about motive not affecting or invalidating the exercise of rights, the English courts may have to look at that again. For example, in European Union law, in claims for damages for breach of member states' obligations, courts have to assess the seriousness of the breach and the good faith of the organ of the state.

We have seen that the law developed different theories of adjusting rights in water.[57] The doctrine of reasonable use is one that creates a great deal of interest. It constitutes an early use of the notion of proportionality. We tend to think that proportionality stems from the European Convention on Human Rights, but the idea may be much older than this. It is interesting to note that reasonable use was part of the weft and weave of water law. It holds out the possibility of an idea that could be used in the future: the development of public rights over private property and a way of securing sustainable use of vital resources.

There are many areas of water law that I have not even touched on – such as rights to the seashore, fishing, weirs, wharves and so on. A more modern problem perhaps is the problem of what happens when driving on a beach. Do you have do observe the rule of the road or the rule of the sea? Some of you will remember the A P Herbert story of a road accident on the Chiswick Mall, which

[57] Professor Lon Fuller notes, in 'Irrigation and Tyranny' (1965) 17 *Stan L Rev* 1021, 1039, that internationally there was a much greater diversity of legal rules affecting irrigation water. 'In actual practice, over the world and through history, the most diverse rules had been applied to the allocation of irrigation waters. These rules expressed every conceivable standard of distributive justice: first come, first served [appropriation theory and Islamic law]; to each according to his contribution [Near East]; to each according to his needs [Persia]; to each according to the needs of society [Persia and Egypt]; to each according to the luck of the throw [British colonial laws in India]' (words in square brackets added from footnote references given by Professor Fuller).

was temporarily flooded. Mr Haddock, A P Herbert's favourite character, had been driving on the wrong side of the 'road' and collided with another vehicle making the assumption that it was still the rule of the road which applied. But Mr Haddock pleaded that, as the Mall was flooded, the right rule was not the rule of the road but the rule of the sea which meant that he was obliged to drive on the starboard side. The action was dismissed.

I conclude with that improbable story, and express the hope I have said enough to encourage others to study this complex and fascinating area of law.

4

From Obligations to Proprietary Interests: A Critique of the Charging Orders System in England and Wales

David Capper, Heather Conway and Lisa Glennon*

Introduction

The recent global financial crisis has resulted in unprecedented levels of household debt throughout the UK, with the total personal debt recorded as £1,460 billion at the end of December 2009.[1] While mortgage loans account for a large proportion of this figure, the level of unsecured debt has also grown considerably with figures for the same period showing a £229,029 million deficit inclusive of credit card debts of £54,146 million.[2] The financial crisis has not only resulted in large-scale over-indebtedness of consumers at all income levels; it has also generated higher levels of financial exclusion as vulnerable consumers are squeezed out of the mainstream lending market and forced to rely on sub-prime lenders.[3] Such developments raise important questions about the

* School of Law, Queen's University Belfast.

[1] Credit Action, 'Debt Statistics – February 2010' (2010).

[2] Consumer Credit Counselling Service, 'Debt Dashboard Q3 2009' (CCCS Research) <http://www.cccs.co.uk/Portals/0/Documents/media/reports/dashboards/debt-dashboard-Q3-2009.pdf> accessed 4 October 2010. Research carried out by the housing charity Shelter also indicates that more than one million households in Britain have used credit cards to pay their mortgage or rent in the last twelve months – Shelter, '1m paying for homes by card' (report from YouGov poll carried out for Shelter's 'Roof' magazine, 11 January 2010) <http://england.shelter.org.uk/news/january_2010/1m_paying_for_homes_by_creditcard> accessed 4 October 2010. Shelter point out that, as credit card companies are not subject to the same rules as mortgage lenders when recovering their debt, defaulting on one's payments could result in repossession as the lender may obtain a charging order over the property. It is this order which is the subject-matter of this chapter.

[3] The Financial Inclusion Centre, 'From Feast to Famine: The Rationing of Consumer Credit in the Financial Crisis' (2009). The latest Bank of England Financial Stability Report indicates that levels of defaulting credit card debt reached £1.25 billion in the first quarter of 2010 alone, and that banks wrote off more than 10 per cent of their credit card loan balance in the same period,

mechanisms of debt recovery and the need for court procedure to take account of the fact that debtors may have more than one unsecured creditor: what might be described as a 'multiple debt' phenomenon. Given the growth and instability of the unsecured loans market, it has been predicted that 'lenders are likely to come under pressure to take aggressive action to protect their interests by using charging orders to convert unsecured debt into secured debt.'[4] While increased recourse to this particular remedy is hardly surprising in light of prevailing socio-economic conditions, the circumstances in which such orders can be granted and their impact on both debtors and other 'interested parties'[5] raise serious concerns which form the subject-matter of this chapter.

As is well-known, a charging order is a remedy available to an unsecured creditor in the enforcement of a judgment debt.[6] Once granted, it gives the creditor a charge over land owned by the debtor or in which he/she has a beneficial interest[7] as a means of enforcing the judgment, and transfers the enforcement of the creditor's rights from the law of obligations to the law of property.[8] In short, it 'converts what was at most a contractual debt into an enforceable security with proprietary attributes.'[9] The last decade has witnessed a 700 per cent increase in the number of charging orders applied for in England and Wales; a trend which is likely to continue in the current economic climate. Moreover, the same statistics also suggest an increase in the percentage total of orders being made by courts over the same time period, with a 61 per cent 'success rate' on successful applications by creditors in 2000 growing steadily to 82 per cent of applications made in England and Wales in 2008.[10] The underlying reasons for such a startling increase and their social significance for unsuspecting debtors cannot be adequately explained in the present chapter, and are part of an ongoing and much broader research project involving the three authors.

a record increase- Bank of England Financial Stability Report, Issue No 27 (June 2010) < http://www.bankofengland.co.uk/publications/fsr/2010/fsrfull1006.pdf> accessed 4 October 2010.

[4] The Financial Inclusion Centre, 'From Feast to Famine: The Rationing of Consumer Credit in the Financial Crisis' (2009).

[5] In other words, non-debtor occupants of the property in question and other creditors (both secured and unsecured).

[6] See the Charging Orders Act 1979, supplemented by CPR Part 73 and myriad case law.

[7] Charging Orders Act 1979 s 2. Under s 2 a charging order may also be granted over government stock, shares in companies, and funds in court held by the debtor, though the focus of this chapter will be on land and, in particular, the home as the subject-matter of most applications.

[8] Charging Orders Act 1979 s 3(4) states that a charging order has 'the like effect and shall be enforceable in the same courts and in the same manner as an equitable charge created by the debtor by writing under his hand'.

[9] K J Gray and S F Gray, *Elements of Land Law* (5th edn OUP, Oxford 2009) 709.

[10] Ministry of Justice, 'Judicial and Court Statistics 2007, Chapter 4' http://www.justice.gov.uk/publications/docs/judicial-court-stats-2007-full.pdf accessed 4 October 2010; 'Judicial and Court Statistics 2008, Chapter 4' <http://www.justice.gov.uk/publications/docs/judicial-court-statistics-2008-04-chapt4.pdf> accessed 4 October 2010. The 2008 percentage figure is the last year in which statistics are available for each of the four quarters. At the time of writing, figures for 2009 were only available until the end of the third quarter, and while they show a slight decrease in the number of court applications for charging orders in England and Wales, the percentage of successful applications is nevertheless 86% of orders sought for the last quarter.

One might assume that such a draconian and far-reaching remedy, which converts an unsecured creditor into a secured creditor with relative ease, has a well-articulated legislative rationale. However, this does not appear to be the case. Neither the earlier versions of the charging orders system nor its modern equivalent was preceded by any policy based or theoretical consideration of the appropriateness of granting this kind of relief.[11] The Report of the Law Commission which led to the current Charging Orders Act 1979 (the '1979 Act') was mainly concerned with specific technical problems in the existing charging orders procedure, rather than its fundamental principles.[12] While the Law Commission did express concern that a creditor could obtain priority in the debtor's insolvency too easily,[13] the only proposals it made for addressing this problem were that the court should have a full discretion whether to grant a charging order and should take account of the personal circumstances of the debtor and the position of other creditors. This remains the case today under the 1979 Act.[14] This chapter proceeds on the assumption that a reasonably clear rationale for charging orders exists, but has concerns that the current procedure for obtaining a charging order does not facilitate a full and proper consideration of all relevant circumstances. The recent financial crisis has made the availability of charging orders a more urgent policy question, particularly when the order is sought over the debtor's home. Since the home is likely to be the debtor's only (or most) significant asset, this will be the focus of the chapter.

The substantive law

Making the charging order

The first stage in seeking a charging order is the creditor's application for an interim order which is made without notice to the debtor.[15] This application will be dealt with by a judge without a hearing[16] and while, in theory, the judge has a full discretion whether or not to grant an order, in practice one is almost invariably made.[17] The judgment creditor is not obliged to make a case for a charging order, nor does he have to address any statutory criteria and persuade the judge that

[11] An earlier version appeared in the Law of Property Act 1925 (replacing the Judgments Act 1838 s 13 and the Land Charges Act 1900 s 2), and a later one in the Administration of Justice Act 1956 s 35. The 1956 Act followed a report by the Evershed Committee: 'Report of the Committee on Supreme Court Practice and Procedure' (1953) Cmd 8878, but its recommendations were mainly concerned with other matters and the charging orders system remained unaltered.

[12] Law Commission, 'Charging Orders' (Law Com No 74 Cm 6412, 1976).

[13] Ibid [40].

[14] See text to nn 20–26.

[15] CPR r 73.3(1) and 73.4. To make such an application, the applicant has to hold a High Court or county court money judgment against the debtor – Charging Orders Act 1979 s 1(1).

[16] CPR r 73.4(1).

[17] Although an interim charging order should not be made if the judgment is payable by instalments and the debtor has not failed to pay any instalments – County Courts Act 1984 s 86 (see n 87 and text below).

these have been satisfied. All that is required is a compilation of practical details such as the debtor's name and address; the size of the debt; the land to be charged and the debtor's interest in it.[18] Where the land is jointly owned, any co-owners must receive notice of the creditor's application. However, the debtor's other creditors find themselves in a more tenuous position since the applicant's only obligation is to inform the court of the identity of any other creditors known to it.[19] This means that the interim order may be made without a full picture of the debtor's circumstances – in particular, the size of the debt owed to the applicant creditor in relation to the amount owed to other creditors. No attempt is made to carry out a preliminary assessment which balances the competing interests of those affected by the order and, even if this were carried out, it would be an incomplete exercise as the full list of the debtor's other creditors may not be known.

When determining whether a final charging order should be made, section 1(5) of the Charging Orders Act 1979 instructs the court to consider 'all the circumstances of the case' and, in particular:

> ... any evidence before it as to —
> (a) the personal circumstances of the debtor, and
> (b) whether any other creditor of the debtor would be likely to be unduly prejudiced by the making of the order.[20]

Thus, any substantive challenge to the making of the order must wait until the final hearing when the court will, in theory, balance the interests of all interested parties. However, the Court of Appeal made clear in *Roberts Petroleum Ltd v Bernard Kenny Ltd*[21] that the debtor must 'show cause' why a final order should not be made, a principle which has been extended to domestic property.[22] This places the onus squarely on the debtor to bring countervailing considerations before the court despite the fact that no such statutory requirement exists under the 1979 Act. By contrast the applicant is not required, either at the interim application stage or the final hearing, to show why the order should be made. Therefore, a presumption seems to exist under which the interim order is affirmed unless the debtor, or other interested parties who are aware

[18] CPR, 'Practice Direction – Charging Orders, Stop Orders and Stop Notices' [1.2].

[19] Ibid [1.2(5)]. The court may direct that a copy of the interim order is served on the debtor's other creditors – CPR r 73.5(1)(b). See also C Harpum, S Bridge and M Dixon, *Megarry and Wade, The Law of Real Property* (7th edn Sweet & Maxwell, London 2008) 536. Of course, this will only be of use where the other creditors are known to the court.

[20] Section 3(1) of the 1979 Act further states that a charging order may be made absolutely or subject to certain conditions, including the timing of enforcement.

[21] [1982] 1 WLR 301 (CA). The House of Lords reversed the decision of the Court of Appeal but on grounds that detracted in no way from this point – *Roberts Petroleum Ltd v Bernard Kenny Ltd* [1983] 2 AC 192 (HL). Although the Court of Appeal did outline several principles which should be applied in deciding whether a final charging order should be made (see n 47 and text below), these do not add significantly to the aforementioned statutory criteria under s 1(5) of the 1979 Act.

[22] *First National Securities Ltd v Hegarty* [1985] QB 850 (CA). In practical terms, if the debtor wishes to prevent the making of a final charging order he/she must file in court and serve on the creditor written evidence stating the grounds of objection at least 7 days before the final charging order hearing – CPR 73.8(1).

of the proceedings, can bring forward reasons to counter this. Yet the interim application stage is little more than a paper-based (and potentially incomplete) 'roll call' of the parties to be affected by the order which does not justify the apparent 'presumption' in favour of making the order.[23] As the Court of Appeal stressed in *First National Securities v Hegarty*:[24]

> The making of a charging order is a discretionary remedy, but a judgment creditor, although not entitled to such an order as of right, is justified in expecting that such an order will be made in his favour unless the judgment debtor can persuade the court that in all the circumstances of the case the order should not be made.

One complicating factor appears to be where a non-debtor spouse has petitioned for divorce and ancillary relief proceedings are pending or already underway.[25] While this may displace the otherwise strong presumption in favour of making a charging order against the home or justify postponement of sale of the charged property,[26] this seems to be confined to that particular factual scenario and raises issues which are beyond the scope of this chapter.

Seeking sale

When seeking to enforce the charging order, the judgment creditor must apply to the court for an order for sale. Such an application is made under rule 73.10 of the Civil Procedure Rules 1998 where the debtor is the sole owner of the property in question or under the Trusts of Land and Appointment of Trustees Act 1996 (the '1996 Act') section 14 where the property is jointly owned.[27] Again, sale is at the court's discretion[28] and may be subject to such conditions as the court thinks appropriate. Section 15(1) of the 1996 Act requires the court to take account of specific factors when determining an application for sale under section 14, namely:

> (a) the intentions of the person or persons (if any) who created the trust,
> (b) the purposes for which the property subject to the trust is held,
> (c) the welfare of any minor who occupies or might reasonably be expected to occupy any land subject to the trust as his home, and

[23] Judicial statistics reveal that the majority of interim charging orders become final orders. In 2003, for example, 72% of interim orders were converted into a final order: see HC Written Answer by the then Parliamentary Under-Secretary of State for Justice, Bridget Prentice, 'Debt: Court Orders' Hansard HC vol 493 col 887WA (10 June 2009) <http://services.parliament.uk/hansard/Commons/ByDate/20090610/writtenanswers/part011.html> accessed 4 October 2010.

[24] *Hegarty* (n 22) 866.

[25] The leading authority on this point is *Harman v Glencross* [1986] Fam 81 (CA).

[26] *Austin-Fell v Austin-Fell* [1990] Fam 172 (Fam).

[27] In the latter scenario, it seems that the creditor can still apply under CPR 73.10 where both co-owners are debtors, though the more usual procedure is to invoke the Trusts of Land and Appointment of Trustees Act 1996 s 14 as well – *Close Invoice Finance Ltd v Pile* [2008] EWHC 1580 (Ch), [2009] 1 FLR 873.

[28] *Forrester Ketley & Co v Brent & Palette* [2009] EWHC 3441 (Ch) [52].

(d) the interests of any secured creditor or any beneficiary.

While CPR 73.10 does not instruct the court to do likewise, the decision in *Close Invoice Finance Ltd* v *Pile*[29] confirms that the same considerations should be taken into account in the exercise of the court's discretion. The notes accompanying CPR 73.10 acknowledge that 'sale is a draconian step to satisfy a simple debt' but is nevertheless likely to be ordered in cases of a debtor's 'contumelious neglect or refusal to pay or ....where in reality without a sale the judgment debt would not be paid.'[30] To a large extent, reported case law confirms this approach, and the fact that the prevailing consideration is that the creditor gets paid.[31] For example, in *C Putnam & Sons v Taylor*[32] a judgment creditor obtained an order for sale of a matrimonial home valued at £500,000 to discharge a debt of £60,000 incurred solely by the husband. In deciding to order sale, the court was sympathetic to the wife's position as an 'innocent' party and the husband's ongoing battle with cancer. Despite this however, the court felt that sale was the only realistic option, given that the creditor had already waited several years for repayment with the debt increasing all the time. In reaching this conclusion Judge Purle QC did 'not consider it ... right to put off the evil day indefinitely and effectively keep the claimant out of its money with no prospect of any recovery in the near future.'[33] Moreover, the same cases have confirmed that the power to enforce a charging order is compatible with the Convention for the Protection of Human Rights and Fundamental Freedoms (European Convention on Human Rights, as amended),[34] at least where the court takes the aforementioned factors into account when reaching its decision on whether or not to order sale of a home.[35]

[29] *Pile* (n 27).

[30] Reproduced in *Forrester Ketley* (n 28).

[31] According to the decision of Laddie J in *Barclays Bank plc v Hendricks* [1996] 1 FCR 710 (Ch), applications for sale by holders of charging orders are to be approached in similar fashion to applications for possession and sale by a trustee in bankruptcy. The apparent bias in favour of ordering sale at the request of a creditor is also apparent in bankruptcy situations – see the often cited comments of Nourse LJ in *Re Citro (A Bankrupt)* [1991] 1 FLR 71 (CA) 82 referring to the 'melancholy consequences of debt and improvidence with which every civilised society has been familiar.'

[32] [2009] EWHC 317 (Ch).

[33] Ibid [36]. See also *Forrester Ketley* (n 28) (debtor unwilling to face the reality of the sums owed and refusing to comply with the orders of the court), as well as *National Westminster Bank plc v Rushmer* [2010] EWHC 554 (Ch), [2010] 2 FLR 362 (wife's position as an 'innocent' party and child's learning difficulties insufficient to deny creditor's request for sale).

[34] See in particular the decision in *Pile* (n 27).

[35] *Forrester Ketley* (n 28) and *Rushmer* (n 33).

Defects in the charging orders system

> The Government believes that responsible creditors who are owed money and have gained judgment in a court should have the right to enforce that judgment. Equally, debtors should be protected from the oppressive pursuit of their debts.[36]

The premise of the current charging orders system is not in dispute, and has much to commend it. Where the debtor has defaulted and the creditor has obtained judgment one would expect the creditor to be afforded an appropriate enforcement mechanism. One might also assume that, when considering an application for a charging order, the exercise of the court's discretion is a balanced one which takes account of the interests of both the debtor and the creditor. At a cursory glance, section 1(5) of the Charging Orders Act 1979 seems to fulfil this requirement, given the specific factors which the court is directed to consider and the fact that there is no statutory presumption in favour of the creditor's application being granted. However, it is argued that there is a fundamental disconnect between the ethos of the system and how it is actually applied in practice, since the judicial starting point appears to be that an order will be made in the creditor's favour, and little more than passing reference is made to the statutory factors. As previously stated, this creates a judicially sanctioned expectation on the part of the creditor that a charging order will be granted.[37]

Under the 1979 Act section 1(5)(a), the court must take account of the personal circumstances of the debtor where such evidence has been brought before it. This generates two problems. First, the legislation does not specify what type of personal circumstances should inform the court's decision – for example, is this limited to the debtor's own financial situation in relation to the sums owed, or is it sufficiently broad to encompass the interests of, for example, non-debtor occupants of the home and their economic dependence on the debtor? Case law suggests that such broad considerations can inform the court's decision, although this appears to be confined to situations where a non-debtor spouse has instigated ancillary relief proceedings prior to the creditor's charging order application, and as such there is a competing claim to the debtor's interest in the home.[38] Beyond this, however, it does not appear that the debtor's obligations to family and other dependants will have a significant (if any) impact on the court's decision. Secondly, the court is only obliged to consider such evidence as is placed before it by the debtor. While the debtor has a vested interest in doing so, the fact that no guidance is provided as to how

[36] Ministry of Justice, 'Orders for Sale Consultation – Consultation on whether a minimum threshold should be imposed on Order for Sale applications in relation to Consumer Credit Act debts only' (CP2/10, February 2010) 7.

[37] See the comments of the Court of Appeal in *Hegarty* (n 22) (reproduced at text to n 24 above).

[38] *Harman* (n 25) although the Court of Appeal did stress that the position would be different if such proceedings had not yet been instigated.

the court should evaluate and balance these factors against the interests of the creditor makes this a problematic and potentially inconsistent exercise.[39]

A different problem emerges when looking at the 1979 Act section 1(5)(b), which directs the court to consider the interests of other creditors. This effectively turns on whether or not any other creditor would be prejudiced by the making of the charging order – something which is particularly important in the context of the current multiple debt phenomenon. As the decision of the House of Lords in *Roberts Petroleum Ltd v Bernard Kenny Ltd*[40] makes tolerably clear, charging orders are not designed to subvert the *pari passu* principle in insolvency. So when the debtor company entered liquidation after the making of an interim charging order, a final charging order should not then be made. However, putting this principle into practice is problematic because the court is unlikely to be aware of the debtor's full list of creditors, largely because this particular creditor-applicant has no easy means of identifying such persons and little incentive to put their interests before the court. The limitations of the charging orders system in this respect were exposed by the 2009 decision of the Court of Appeal in *Nationwide Building Society v Wright*.[41] For present purposes, a brief outline of the facts will suffice. Having obtained judgment for a £10,000 credit card debt in April 2006, an interim charging order was made against the debtor on 5 May 2006. This was followed by a final charging order on 26 June 2006. In the interim period however, a bankruptcy petition had been presented against the same debtor in the same court[42] (the date of petition was 17 May), with the debtor being adjudicated bankrupt on 12 July 2006. Fearful of the potential impact of the charging order on the debtor's general creditors, the trustee in bankruptcy applied to have the charging order set aside under the Charging Orders Act 1979 section 3(5) – an application which was eventually rejected by the Court of Appeal[43] on the basis that execution of the credit card company's debt had been *completed* before the bankruptcy adjudication.[44] Although technically correct, there is clearly some tension between this decision and the anti-priority gaining policy of *Roberts Petroleum*. The problem was caused by defects in the procedure for obtaining charging orders which did not

[39] One cannot assume that the interests of non-debtor occupants will be given sufficient consideration when an application for sale is made by the creditor. As noted previously, while the interests of such persons are taken into account at this stage, the creditor's interests will usually prevail – see nn 27–35 and text above. It has been suggested elsewhere that insufficient consideration is given to the interests of other occupants in possession and sale applications generally – see L Fox, *Conceptualising Home – Theories, Laws and Policies* (Hart Publishing, Oxford 2007).

[40] [1983] 2 AC 192 (HL).

[41] [2009] EWCA Civ 811, [2010] Ch 318. For comment see D Capper, 'Charging Orders and Bankruptcy' (2010) 29 *CJQ* 150.

[42] Northampton County Court, one of the bulk processing courts for charging orders.

[43] Both the deputy district judge and circuit judge on appeal had ruled in favour of the trustee in bankruptcy and discharged the order.

[44] Since the creditor was only adjudicated bankrupt on 12 July 2006, whereas the final charging order had been made some two weeks earlier, and s 346(1) of the Insolvency Act 1986 expressly provides that a creditor can retain, against the trustee in bankruptcy, any execution against the debtor's property which was completed before commencement of bankruptcy.

allow for evidence of the debtor's imminent bankruptcy to be brought before the court that granted the final charging order.

In short, it is unclear how the court should approach section 1(5)(a) of the 1979 Act – the provision seems to require some sort of evaluative exercise yet how the court is to approach this task is far from certain. Turning to section 1(5)(b) of the same Act, case law makes it clear that a creditor's expectation of obtaining a charging order is not absolute and may be qualified where a creditor finds itself in competition with other creditors.[45] While acceptable in principle, the fact that the court may not know the identity of other creditors leads to problems identified immediately above. Section 1(5) of the 1979 Act also states more generally that the court should take account of 'all the circumstances of the case', yet it is hard to imagine what other considerations might inform the court's decision-making process beyond factors (a) and (b). In the Court of Appeal decision in *Roberts Petroleum Ltd v Bernard Kenny Ltd*,[46] Lord Brandon set out several principles to be applied in deciding whether a final order should be made,[47] including the duty to take account of 'all the circumstances of any particular case' and the need to 'do equity, so far as possible, to all the various parties involved ... [namely] the judgment creditor, the judgment debtor, all other unsecured creditors.'[48] However, this merely replicates both the wording and intent of section 1(5) of the 1979 Act without clarifying either its interpretation or application. More importantly perhaps, the first two factors articulated by the Court of Appeal illustrate a core problem at the heart of the judicial decision-making process. According to Lord Brandon, the question of whether a final charging order should be made 'is one for the discretion of the court', yet the 'burden of showing cause why a charging order ... should not be made absolute'[49] falls squarely on the debtor. The juxtaposition of these factors illustrates the inherently contradictory nature of the judicial process – the jurisdiction cannot be truly discretionary when there is a judicially pre-determined onus in favour of the applicant creditor, despite the fact that no such presumption exists under the legislation. Moreover, this seems to run contrary to one intended purpose of the 1979 Act, based upon the Law Commission's criticisms of the system of enforcement which preceded this legislation. Commenting in 1976, the Law Commission stated:

> At present there is a tendency for the court to accede almost automatically to a judgment creditor's request for a charging order. We think this should not be so – not only because it makes priority gaining too easy, but also because it may result in charging orders being made in cases where they are really unfair to the debtor.[50]

[45] *Harman* (n 25).

[46] [1982] 1 WLR 301 (CA).

[47] As previously noted (see n 21 above), the House of Lords reached a different conclusion on the facts of the case but did not disagree with these specific factors which were set out by the Court of Appeal.

[48] [1982] 1 WLR 301 (CA) 307.

[49] Ibid.

[50] Law Commission, 'Charging Orders' (Law Com No 74 Cm 6412, 1976) [43].

Such criticisms are equally relevant to the current system under the 1979 Act.

These comments should not be taken to suggest that debtors should be able to evade their debts, not least because there are important social policy objectives in ensuring that creditors have an effective means of enforcing sums owed to them. As Judge Purle QC observed in *Close Invoice Finance Ltd v Pile*:[51]

> It ... [is] in the public interest to enforce charging orders generally, because of the economic importance of ensuring that there is an efficient machinery for the enforcement of debt obligations, even though, unlike in the case of a legal mortgagee, this was not a debt obligation which was voluntarily provided as a secured obligation.[52]

Strasbourg jurisprudence has also emphasised the public interest element in ensuring the repayment of contractual debts.[53] Moreover the European Court of Human Rights has specifically noted that a state would be in breach of its obligations under Article 6(1) of the European Convention on Human Rights if it failed to provide a functional system for the enforcement of court judgments.[54]

Social policy arguments aside, the current charging orders system has obvious benefits for both debtors and creditors. While the focus of this chapter has been on the home, charging orders may be made in respect of other types of property, such as commercial or investment properties, although these do not raise the same issues in terms of potential hardship. Likewise, one cannot assume that 'all judgment creditors are faceless corporations';[55] they might be private individuals or small businesses seeking payment for goods or services provided. The debtor's property may be his/her only significant asset, and therefore the only realistic recourse for enforcing the judgment. As such a charging order serves a valuable protectionist function, guarding against further dissipation of assets while simultaneously guaranteeing (insofar as is possible) that the creditor will be repaid if the property is sold in the future.[56] Moreover, some debtors may be content for a charging order to be made on the basis that it is simply giving the creditor some measure of security while maintaining the status quo, since the debtor can remain in the property (an important consideration where that property is a family home) and the creditor cannot insist on sale without a further application to the court. More generally, the economic importance of unsecured loans and their widespread availability was also highlighted by a recent

[51] *Pile* (n 27).

[52] Ibid [12].

[53] See the decision of the European Commission in *Wood v UK* (App no 32540/96) (1997) 24 EHRR CD69.

[54] *Hornsby v Greece* (App no 18357/91) (1997) 24 EHRR 250.

[55] *Harman* (n 25).

[56] Of course, this may not always work in the creditor's favour. The recent fall in house prices and corresponding increase in negative equity scenarios means that full repayment is not always guaranteed upon sale of the debtor's property. However, a recovery in house prices will once again strengthen the creditor's position in these situations – see I Ramsay, '"Wannabe WAGS" and "Credit Binges": The Construction of Over-Indebtedness in the UK' in J Niemi, I Ramsay and WC Whitford (eds), *Consumer Credit, Debt & Bankruptcy* (Hart Publishing, Oxford 2009) ch 4.

Ministry of Justice report on consumer debt.[57] Emphasising the importance of the charging orders system, the report cautioned against restricting such orders or their scope on the basis that this might discourage unsecured lending or lead to higher interest rates on such loans to off-set 'bad debts'.[58] The report also raised the possibility of unsecured lenders taking more drastic action against debtors – in particular, an increase in 'consumer bankruptcies' with even more disastrous consequences for the debtor.[59]

In light of these observations, this chapter is not recommending substantial changes to the current charging orders system; the defects which have been identified here can be remedied by a number of amendments to the procedure for seeking charging orders. One might think that these various defects are largely illusory given that a more holistic account of all the circumstances of the case and the interests of all relevant parties are adequately taken into account on an application for sale. However, this stage of the process is not without its problems. Aside from the fact that any priority gaining has already happened by this stage, the strong presumption in favour of sale tends not to be displaced by the interests of other parties.[60] More importantly perhaps, the court will not dispute the legitimacy of the applicant's security over the property at this stage: the transition from unsecured to secured status has long since occurred, and any distinctions between this and other types of secured lending are largely irrelevant. In addition, delaying consideration of the full circumstances until this stage of the process is arguably too late. Anecdotal evidence suggests that the charging order, by itself, has 'bite' with some debtors feeling compelled to sell the charged property to satisfy the debt even in the absence of an order for sale. This means that the charging order is being used, at times, as a tactic to force debtors to take disproportionate steps to repay what are relatively small debts.[61]

The proposed procedural amendments to the charging orders system are considered in the next section, and can be justified on a number of grounds. In addition to the problems mentioned earlier, the 1979 Act does not specify any minimum threshold of debt which must be owed to the creditor before a

[57] Ministry of Justice, 'Orders for Sale Consultation – Consultation on whether a minimum threshold should be imposed on Order for Sale applications in relation to Consumer Credit Act debts only' (CP2/10, February 2010).

[58] Ibid 18.

[59] Ibid 19.

[60] See nn 27–35 and text above. During the passage of the Charging Orders Bill through Parliament in 1979, concerns were expressed about the consequences of subjecting co-owned domestic property to a charging order. The Government did not address these concerns, relying on the misplaced assumption that the interests of non-debtor co-owners would be adequately considered on an application for sale under what was then the Law of Property Act 1925 s 30. However, it appears that this was not the case and that despite the more stringent legislative guidance under the Trusts of Land and Appointment of Trustees Act 1996 ss 14–15, the interests of creditors still tend to prevail – see L Fox, 'Co-owners, not co-owers: Legislative and judicial policy in relation to Charging Orders and Co-ownership' (1998) 29 *Cambrian Law Review* 9.

[61] Inside Money, 'Would You Credit It' BBC Radio 4 (22 July 2002).

charging order can be sought, which means that the use of this enforcement mechanism may be disproportionate to the amount owed.[62] While the decision in *Re Goldspan Ltd*[63] suggests that the court should refuse to make a charging order over a substantial asset in respect of a relatively small debt, anecdotal evidence suggests that this sometimes happens nonetheless as unsecured creditors are seeking charging orders before pursuing other means of securing repayment.[64] A recent report from the Citizens Advice Bureau has highlighted repeated instances of aggressive tactics by creditors, such as using charging orders (or the threat of one) to intimidate debtors into paying more than they can reasonably afford and ignoring good debt collection practices safe in the knowledge that a charging order will most likely be granted with minimal judicial fuss. It has been noted that:

> Some creditors are using the court process as a tactic to intimidate vulnerable debtors into paying unaffordable amounts. This is not only unfair to the individuals concerned who have offered payment towards their debts but it also unfair to other creditors.[65]

As argued previously, even where enforcement is justified, it appears that charging orders are often granted as a matter of course and sought in preference to other enforcement methods. To some extent this is probably due to the dysfunctional condition of the enforcement system in England and Wales.[66] However, it probably also owes much to the abolition of the requirement to obtain leave to inspect the land register as introduced by the Land Registration Act 1988.[67] It is noteworthy that in this last decade there has been a marked

[62] Section 94 of the Tribunals Courts and Enforcement Act 2007 proposed to insert a new provision into the Charging Orders Act 1979, giving the Lord Chancellor the power to specify financial thresholds below which a court could not make a charging order and/or an order for sale. However, this provision has not been implemented. In addition, the recent Ministry of Justice Consultation Paper only addressed the issue of whether there should be a minimum threshold for orders for sale but favoured leaving sale applications to the discretion of the court: Ministry of Justice, 'Orders for Sale Consultation – Consultation on whether a minimum threshold should be imposed on Order for Sale applications in relation to Consumer Credit Act debts only' (CP2/10, February 2010) 7.

[63] [2003] BPIR 93 (Ch) applying *Robinson v Bailey* [1942] Ch 268 (Ch).

[64] However, this may change under the new Coalition government in Britain – see n 92 and text below.

[65] Citizens Advice Bureau Chief Executive David Harkens commenting on the findings of the report by the Citizens Advice Bureau. See Citizens Advice Bureau, 'Out of Order – CAB evidence on the use of charging orders and orders for sale in debt collection' (2009) <http://www.citizensadvice.org.uk/index/pressoffice/press_index/press_20090625> accessed 4 October 2010.

[66] See J Baldwin and R Cunnington, 'The Crisis in Enforcement of Civil Judgments in England and Wales' [2004] *PL* 305; J Baldwin, 'The Enforcement in Undefended Claims in the Civil Courts in England and Wales' (2004) 23 *CJQ* 354. Enforcement of judgments has been the subject of a lengthy review which culminated in the Tribunals Courts and Enforcement Act 2007 but the enforcement provisions of this legislation are not going to be brought into force. On the latter see J Baldwin and R Cunnington, 'The Abandonment of Civil Enforcement Reform' (2010) 29 *CJQ* 159 as well as n 89 below.

[67] Members of the public can inspect the Land Register and obtain copies of information recorded against a particular title, subject to payment of the requisite fee – Land Registration Act 1988 s 1(1).

reduction in the number of applications under Part 71 of CPR 1998 for orders to obtain information from judgment debtors.[68] In light of this it is reasonable to think that some creditors are going straight to the Land Registry to ascertain whether the debtor has a house, and proceeding quickly back to court to seek a charging order on the basis that the debtor almost certainly has sufficient assets over which to obtain security. It may also be the case that, on occasion, debt collection agencies are purchasing the debt from the original lender and then seeking to enforce the debt immediately by applying for a charging order.[69]

Finally, it is argued that the seemingly routine availability of charging orders can lead to irresponsible lending practices. This contradicts the clear policy moves to secure both responsible lending and responsible borrowing practices, particularly in the current economic climate where lending transactions are subject to much greater public scrutiny. An important aspect of this is responsible arrears management where creditors engage with debtors about their ability to repay and to negotiate a realistic payment plan.[70] Indeed, the Council of Europe recently observed that, given that arrears will normally arise due to financial difficulties, court action and debt recovery should be seen as a last resort.[71] By contrast, however, it seems that 'savvy' creditors are seeking charging orders as a first resort instead of a last resort to enforce unsecured consumer debts, or using the threat of such orders to extract larger instalment payments from debtors.[72]

Reform

Where a creditor has obtained judgment for a particular debt it is axiomatic that the debtor has already defaulted. This default, whether it was in failing to pay for goods sold or services rendered, or was in one or more instalments on an unsecured loan, alters the basic assumptions that lie at the heart of the parties'

[68] From 61,247 in 2000 to 27,148 in 2007 – see The Stationary Office, 'Judicial and Court Statistics 2007' (Cm 7467) (TSO, London 2008) 79 and Table 4.22.

[69] It has been predicted that the rise in default rates on unsecured loans may result in mainstream lenders 'cutting their losses' by selling debts to debt collection agencies – The Financial Inclusion Centre, 'From Feast to Famine: The Rationing of Consumer Credit in the Financial Crisis' (2009). These specialist firms may be more inclined to pursue aggressive tactics to secure repayment.

[70] European Commission, 'Towards a Common Operational European Definition of Over-Indebtedness' (2008).

[71] Council of Europe, 'Recommendation of the Committee of Ministers to Member States on Legal Solutions to Debt Problems' (2007).

[72] N Hickman, 'Charging Orders and Their Impact on Creditors and Debtors' *Law Society Gazette* (London 7 January 2010) <http://www.lawgazette.co.uk/in-practice/benchmarks/Charging-orders-and-their-impact-creditors-and-debtors> accessed 4 October 2010. Judicial thinking suggests that, insolvency situations aside, there is nothing inherently wrong with the 'first past the post rule' in the enforcement system – *F G Hemisphere Associates LLC v Republic of Congo* [2005] EWHC 3103 (Comm) [14], applying *Pritchard v Westminster Bank* [1969] 1 WLR 547 (CA). However, it is suggested that this principle loses strength in today's multiple debt society with increasingly tactical applications for charging orders.

legal relationship. The creditor should not be expected to assume the risk of further default or the debtor's insolvency, and for this reason the elevation in status from unsecured to secured creditor is not difficult to justify.

However, this chapter argues that this is not an absolute principle and that the creditor's otherwise legitimate expectation is subject to three qualifications. First, a creditor has no right to expect payment in priority to other unsecured creditors; this fundamental principle laid down by the House of Lords in *Roberts Petroleum Ltd v Bernard Kenny Ltd*[73] has not been altered by *Nationwide Building Society v Wright*,[74] where it was acknowledged that a final charging order would not have been made if the court had been aware of a pending bankruptcy petition which had already been presented against the debtor in the very same court.[75] Any fair and transparent enforcement system must therefore take adequate steps to avoid priority gaining.[76] Secondly, the creditor should not be granted the most heavy handed enforcement method if a less heavy handed or otherwise more suitable one will do.[77] In other words, if there is a reasonable alternative to a charging order on its own, the creditor may have to settle for this as a more proportionate means of enforcement.[78] Thirdly, the making of a charging order should not give the creditor the right to demand immediate repayment of the entire debt. To some extent the current system recognises this insofar as the creditor must make a further application to the court for an order for possession and sale of the charged property. Yet, while the court has discretion in such matters, this discretion is likely to be exercised in favour of the creditor.[79]

This conceptual framework acts as the focal point of the procedural reforms which are proposed in this chapter.

Possible reforms

It has already been noted that the current procedure for applying for charging orders all too often fails to get the necessary information before the court, and

[73] [1983] 2 AC 192 (HL).

[74] *Wright* (n 41).

[75] Even though, as already noted, the decision in *Wright* itself was unavoidable and technically correct on a strict interpretation of the relevant statutes – see nn 41–44 and text above.

[76] Law Commission, 'Charging Orders' (Law Com No 74 Cm 6412, 1976) [43].

[77] This was the view of the Irish Law Reform Commission in its 2009 consultation paper: see Law Reform Commission of Ireland, 'Personal Debt Management and Debt Enforcement' (LRC CP 56 – 2009) [6.179–6.186].

[78] Of course, other enforcement orders are available to courts including attachment of earnings orders under CPR Sch 2, receiver orders under CPR Part 69, and third party debt orders under CPR Part 72. However, these are beyond the scope of this chapter although it is worth pointing out that the other enforcement options are not without their difficulties – for example, an attachment of earnings order imposes obligations on a third party (ie the debtor's employer) and is dependent on the debtor being in and remaining in employment, while a third party debt order is arguably more heavy-handed than a charging order.

[79] See nn 27–35 and text above.

that *Nationwide Building Society v Wright*[80] arguably provides the most graphic illustration of the consequences of this information vacuum.[81] Since full and accurate information has long been recognised as the key to a successful and balanced enforcement system,[82] the question is essentially how the necessary information is to be drawn to the court's attention.

An obvious starting point is Part 71 of CPR 1998, under which the creditor can require the debtor to attend court in order to provide information about the debtor's means or other relevant matters. However, the creditor is not compelled to make such a request. It is suggested that the order to obtain information from a judgment debtor should cease to be something the creditor *may* apply for and become something the creditor is *required* to apply for in advance of the final hearing. This order may not be fully effective in terms of revealing other creditors, but would at least be an improvement on the status quo. To the extent that a Part 71 order might be less than fully successful in revealing other creditors, it is suggested that the grant of an interim charging order should be advertised as is the current practice in a bankruptcy petition.[83] This would give other creditors whose existence was not disclosed by the debtor an opportunity to bring their interests to the attention of the court before the final charging order was made. These reforms are relatively modest in scope but they should do much to fill the information vacuum which is one obstacle preventing the substantive law of charging orders from offering the balance which is implicit in the statutory framework under the 1979 Act. In addition, this goes some way towards addressing the first qualification which was outlined in the previous section.

Turning to the second and third of these qualifications, an obvious means of addressing the defects in the current system would be to require courts to consider making an instalment order (allowing the debtor to make affordable monthly repayments) in conjunction with a charging order.[84] This could be achieved by means of a simple statutory provision inserted into the Charging Orders Act 1979. In addition, the court should use its existing powers under section 3(1) of the 1979 Act to impose conditions on the charging order in these circumstances. The relevant condition should be that, so long as the debtor pays the instalments, no application for sale will be entertained unless there has been

[80] *Wright* (n 41).

[81] See nn 41–44 and text above.

[82] One of the first places where this was stated was in the report of the Anderson Committee which led to the establishment of the Northern Ireland enforcement of judgments system – see A E Anderson (ed), *Report of the Joint Working Party on the Enforcement of Judgments, Orders and Decrees of the Courts in Northern Ireland* (HMS Office, Belfast 1965) [166]. More recently in England and Wales the conclusion to Professor Baldwin's report on the effectiveness of enforcement of undefended civil claims has made essentially the same point – see J Baldwin, *Evaluating the Effectiveness of Enforcement Procedures in Undefended Claims in the Civil Courts* (Lord Chancellor's Department, London 2003).

[83] Under current insolvency laws and practice, the Official Receiver must advertise the bankruptcy order in a newspaper and in 'The London Gazette' – Insolvency Rules 1986 (SI 1986/1925) r 6.46.

[84] Any information obtained under a Part 71 Order would also enable the court to assess the debtor's means and therefore determine what instalments the debtor might reasonably be expected to pay.

an exceptional change in circumstances.[85] Such an approach has obvious benefits for both the creditor and the debtor. An instalment order allows for structured payments to be put in place, while the attached condition ensures that both parties will have clear and reasonable expectations. The debtor has some measure of reassurance, in that adhering to the repayment plan will almost certainly mean that the charged property will not be vulnerable to an application for sale by the creditor. Again, this is particularly relevant in the context of the family home and the need to take the interests of non-debtor occupants into account as part of the balancing exercise implicit in the 1979 Act. Meanwhile, the creditor has the benefit of a steady flow of income (the debtor is making some inroads into the debt owed) yet is safe in the knowledge that, if the debtor defaults, an application for sale can be made and is likely to be looked on favourably by the court because the debtor has now missed payments on at least two occasions[86] and the creditor's expectation of repayment arguably prevails at this point. In this context, the instalment order effectively acts as a buffer between the making of a charging order and its enforcement. Section 86 of the County Courts Act 1984 currently provides that a charging order should not be made if the debtor is not in default of an instalment order.[87] However, this provision is only dealing with the situation in which an instalment order precedes the application for a charging order. By contrast, what is being suggested here is that the court should be legislatively obliged to consider making an instalment order in tandem with a charging order, with the result that the debtor would be similarly protected if he/she is adhering to the repayment plan. Of course, the debtor would not be obliged to enter into the proposed instalment order, but would at least be aware of the fact that failure to do so leaves him/her less well protected in the event of the creditor seeking sale. Again, this resonates with the need to balance the interests of all parties.[88]

[85] The Tribunals Courts and Enforcement Act 2007 s 93 contains a provision to the effect that if the debtor is making payments under an instalment order there can be no sale of property subject to a charging order in enforcement of the same debt. This section, like the rest of the enforcement provisions in this Act, has not been implemented.

[86] Namely, the original default which gave rise to the judgment debt, and the subsequent default under the instalment order.

[87] In *Ropaigealach v Allied Irish Bank Plc* [2001] EWCA Civ 1790 the Court of Appeal held that a final charging order could be made if an interim charging order was first made and the debtor offered an instalment order afterwards.

[88] All enforcement has been described as a social balancing act. For example, P A Sallmann and R T Wright, *Going to Court: A Discussion Paper on Civil Justice in Victoria* (Department of Justice, Victoria 2000) 178 observe that: 'Enforcement is a social balancing act, managing the legitimate expectations of creditors that they should be paid against the equally legitimate expectation of judgment debtors, that they should be able to carry on life in a reasonable way even though there is a judgment against them'.

The need for a more centralised system?

Thinking beyond procedural reforms, it is suggested that England and Wales might ultimately benefit from taking a closer look at the system of enforcement which currently operates in Northern Ireland under the Judgments (Enforcement) (NI) Order 1981. Under this system a judgment creditor is required to register the judgment with a central Enforcement of Judgments Office (the EJO) and surrender all enforcement action to it on payment of an enforcement fee. This fee will be recovered from the debtor in the event of successful enforcement and paid by the creditor if enforcement is unsuccessful. Moreover, the EJO will conduct an examination of the debtor's means and circumstances to determine if enforcement is likely to be successful and, if so, what the most appropriate enforcement order might be.[89] This system would prevent the kind of priority gaining which occurred in *Nationwide Building Society v Wright*,[90] and offers the possibility of a more holistic and flexible approach – for example, the EJO often combines instalment orders with orders charging land. In the insolvency context in particular, the Northern Ireland system is able, through the issue of a certificate of unenforceability, to block enforcement action where it is clear that it will not be productive. This certificate prevents the processing of all subsequent enforcement applications as well as the one which led to its issue, and as proof of the debtor's insolvency it diverts the debtor's situation into the insolvency system where it truly belongs.

While this chapter has focused largely on procedural reforms, there is an argument for a more comprehensive overhaul of the current system in England and Wales. This did not appear to be a pressing concern under the previous Labour administration given that the enforcement provisions of the Tribunals Courts and Enforcement Act 2007 (which only proposed piecemeal reforms) were never implemented.[91] However, it appears that the issue of enforcement

[89] For further discussion of this system see D Capper, 'Taking Enforcement Seriously – Lessons from Northern Ireland' (2006) 25 *CJQ* 485. See also D Capper, *The Enforcement of Judgments in Northern Ireland* (SLS Publications, Belfast 2004).

[90] Wright (n 41).

[91] In a ministerial statement issued on 17 March 2009 the then Parliamentary Under-Secretary of State for Justice, Bridget Prentice, announced that the Government would not be implementing these reforms – see Hansard HC vol 489 cols 46–47WS (March 17 2009). These reforms were the rather sparse fruit of a nearly decade long enforcement review – see Enforcement Review Consultation Paper 1, *How can the enforcement of civil courts judgments be made more effective?* (Lord Chancellor's Department, London June 1998); Consultation Paper 2, *Key principles for a new system of enforcement in the civil courts* (Lord Chancellor's Department, London May 1999); Consultation Paper 3, *Attachment of earnings orders, charging orders and garnishee orders* (Lord Chancellor's Department, London October 1999); Consultation Paper 4, *Warrants and writs, oral examinations and judgment summons* (Lord Chancellor's Department, London January 2000); *Report of the First Phase of the Enforcement Review* (Lord Chancellor's Department, London July 2000); *A single piece of bailiff law and a regulatory structure for enforcement* ('Green Paper') (Lord Chancellor's Department, London July 2001); Centre for Public Law, *Independent Review of Bailiff Law* (University of Cambridge, Cambridge June 2000); *Effective Enforcement – Improved methods*

has now returned to the forefront of the political and legislative agenda with a clear statement of intent from the new Coalition government to 'provide more protection against ... unreasonable charging orders, ensure that courts have the power to insist that repossession is always a last resort, and ban orders for sale on unsecured debts of less than £25,000.'[92] The specific details of any reform proposals are unknown at this stage, but it is suggested that a whole-scale review of the enforcements system may now be timely. In this respect policy-makers might consider following the lead of the Law Reform Commission in the Republic of Ireland and create a Debt Enforcement Office modelled on the EJO in Northern Ireland.[93] Aside from the specific benefits highlighted in the previous paragraph, a centralised Debt Enforcement Office has other advantages. For example, examination of the debtor's means and commitments, and basic decisions about whether enforcement was possible and (if it were) the most appropriate order to make would be entrusted to specialised and experienced staff. This in turn would make for a more even-handed approach between the creditor and the debtor throughout the enforcement process, while also preventing the pitfalls associated with different courts adjudicating on different stages of the process.

Of course, there are arguments against the establishment of a centralised Debt Enforcement Office in England and Wales. The relative size of the Northern Ireland jurisdiction and the proportionately lower number of enforcement claims which the EJO must process raises the obvious concern that such a system could not be effectively transplanted into a much larger jurisdiction. Yet the benefits of such a system require that it should at least be given serious consideration. Another argument which is particularly compelling in light of the current major public spending review is cost. While initial financial outlay is required to create this Office, the actual administration costs should be fairly modest given that creditors must pay enforcement fees to the Office which can then be recovered from the debtor in the event of successful enforcement. Finally, concerns might be raised that a Debt Enforcement Office, even if established, would merely be yet another quango with the potential to become bureaucratic and therefore inefficient. Aside from the fact that this has not been the experience of the EJO in Northern Ireland, such an Office would nevertheless be a considerable improvement on the status quo in England and Wales.[94]

of recovery for civil court debt and commercial rent and a single regulatory regime for warrant enforcement agents (Cm 5744) ('White Paper') (Lord Chancellor's Department, London March 2003).

[92] The Coalition: our programme for government (May 2010) <http://www.cabinetoffice.gov.uk/media/409088/pfg_coalition.pdf> accessed 4 October 2010.

[93] Law Reform Commission of Ireland, 'Personal Debt Management and Debt Enforcement' (LRC CP 56 – 2009) ch 6.

[94] These and other arguments are explored more fully in D Capper, 'Taking Enforcement Seriously – Lessons from Northern Ireland' (2006) 25 *CJQ* 485.

Conclusion

> Your home is at risk if you do not keep up repayments on a mortgage or other loan secured on it.

This standard warning attached to the grant of a mortgage or other secured loan ensures that borrowers are at least aware of the potentially dire consequences of failing to meet their repayments. Yet, when it comes to unsecured lending, most debtors might be surprised to discover that they are not necessarily immune from the same consequences. It has already been noted that the global financial crisis has exposed unprecedented levels of unsecured lending and, when looked at in conjunction with the multiple debt phenomenon, creditors are now inclined to resort to more aggressive practices when seeking to recover unpaid debts. This chapter has looked at the current charging orders system in England and Wales against this economic backdrop. However, it is not suggested that there is any causal link between the financial crisis and the existing defects in the charging orders system; merely that the economic climate and consequent increased recourse to charging orders by unsecured creditors has made these defects visible.

To reiterate, this chapter has not disputed the core rationale of the charging orders system, nor suggested that whole-scale reform is necessary. On the contrary, the legitimate expectation of creditors and wider public interest in ensuring that (so far as possible) judgment debts are paid and that creditors are provided with protection against risks means that charging orders are an essential enforcement mechanism. However, this particular legitimate expectation is subject to certain qualifications designed to prevent priority gaining (especially in insolvency) and imposing greater hardship on debtors than is necessary, while also ensuring the protection of debtors' rights in their home, provided they are taking specific steps to discharge their legal obligations.

There is little doubt that the profiles of both debtors and creditors have changed radically since the charging orders system was first enacted, as have levels of personal indebtedness. The original charging orders legislation came into effect in very different circumstances, long before the current 'credit binge'[95] culture took hold; while it has survived various mutations, it has never been adequately considered from a policy level perspective. This has allowed a judicial presumption to emerge that charging orders will be granted as a matter of course, which in turn has resulted in a number of procedural defects. Moreover, these defects undermine the need for a proportionate and balanced approach which is inherent in the 1979 Act itself. In the absence of a comprehensive review of the entire charging orders system, the modest reforms posed in this chapter would go some way towards striking a balance between the interests of creditors and debtors in this challenging area of civil justice and property law.

[95] Ramsay n 56.

5

Clash of the Titans: Article 8, Occupiers and Their Home

Sarah Nield*

Introduction

Following the enactment of the Human Rights Act 1998 (HRA) and the incorporation of the Convention for the Protection of Human Rights and Fundamental Freedoms (European Convention on Human Rights, as amended) (EHCR) into domestic law, there has been an intensifying debate about the impact of this development upon domestic property law, particularly in relation to Article 8 ECHR (Article 8). Allen, before the debate fully developed, suggested that the HRA could have two possible consequences. Either there would be little change, because human rights values are already embedded within established property rules, or the ECHR would provide an alternative set of values against which rights affecting property are to be tested and balanced, resulting in fresh approaches.[1] Some commentators have suggested 'a new form of proprietary protection'[2] or 'reservoir of entitlement'[3] but others have cautioned against upsetting the certainty of established property rules developed over the centuries.[4]

A series of decisions by the Titans of our judicial order, namely the House of Lords (now the Supreme Court) and the European Court of Human Rights (the 'Strasbourg Court'), dramatically demonstrate these contrary approaches.

* University of Southampton. The author is most grateful for the discussions with her colleagues Emma Laurie and Ed Bates which have helped to shape this chapter.

[1] T Allen, *Property and The Human Rights Act 1998* (Hart Publishing, Oxford 2005) 250.

[2] K J Gray and S F Gray, *Elements of Land Law* (5th edn OUP, Oxford 2009) [1.6.7.].

[3] A Goymour, 'Property Claims and Human Rights – "A Reservoir of Entitlement"' (2006) 65 *CLJ* 696 utilising Wilson LJ's reference in *Pirabakaran v Patel* [2006] EWCA Civ 685, [2006] 1 WLR 3112.

[4] J Howell, 'The Human Rights Act 1998: Land, Private Citizens and the Common Law' (2007) 123 *LQR* 618.

It is the purpose of this chapter to examine this clash, the central arguments of which Lord Mance has described as 'opposing armies around the forts of Verdun.'[5] It will argue that the central bone of contention is not the substance of established property rules themselves but the process by which those property rules are asserted and reconciled. The need for adequate procedural safeguards, as an essential component to the respect due for the home under Article 8, is a consistent message from the Strasbourg Court. The House of Lords is struggling to meet this procedural demand by resort to judicial review as the mechanism by which public authority decision-making can be scrutinised.

The clash is over the impact of Article 8 upon the exercise of proprietary rights to repossession of an individual's home by a public authority. Article 8 provides:

> (1) Everyone has the right to respect for his private and family life, his home and his correspondence;
> (2) There shall be no interference by a public authority with the exercise of this right except as is in accordance with the law and is necessary in a democratic society in the interests of national security, public safety or the economic well-being of the country, for the prevention of disorder or crime, for the protection of health or morals, or the protection of the rights and freedoms of others.

It has largely been fought in the context of local housing authorities' rights to possession following: termination of a licence for gypsies to occupy a mobile home site,[6] termination of a licence or non-secure tenancy of accommodation provided to those who would otherwise be homeless,[7] and termination of a joint lease by one joint tenant in pursuance of the rule in *Hammersmith and Fulham LBC v Monk*.[8] In all these cases the occupier has no legal defence to repossession under domestic law because their right to occupy the land has been lawfully terminated. There are other instances where no defence to possession may exist, for instance the notorious Ground 8,[9] as well as introductory[10] and demoted tenancies.[11] It should be noted that the majority of local authority repossession proceedings will be made on proof of statutory grounds where the court has discretion to make the possession order only if they consider it reasonable to do so and/or if suitable alternative accommodation is available.[12] However, this chapter is not directly concerned with the ECHR compatibility of statutory grounds for repossession of public authority housing[13] but will

[5] *Birmingham CC v Doherty* [2008] UKHL 57, [2009] 1 AC 367 [125].

[6] *Connors v UK* (App No 66746/01) (2005) 40 EHRR 9 and *Leeds CC v Price* [2006] UKHL 10, [2006] 2 AC 465 and *Birmingham CC v Doherty* [2008] UKHL 57, [2009] 1 AC 367.

[7] *Kay v Lambeth LBC* [2006] UKHL 10, [2006] 2 AC 465.

[8] [1992] 1 AC 478 (HL). See *Harrow LBC v Qazi* [2003] UKHL 40, [2004] 1 AC 983 and *McCann v UK* (App No 19009/04) (2008) 47 EHRR 40.

[9] Housing Act 1988 sch 2 pt 1.

[10] Housing Act 1996 pt 5.

[11] Housing Act 1985 s 82A and Housing Act 1996 pt 5.

[12] Housing Act 1985 s 84 and sch 2.

[13] These issues have been explored by others. See, for instance, E Laurie, 'The Compatibility of Introductory Tenancies and the Human Rights Act 1998' [2002] *Conv* 414; I Loveland, 'A Tale of Two Trespassers: Reconsidering the Impact of the Human Rights Act on Rights of Residence

explore the implications of the clash to repossession in the wider context of summary rights to possession.

The cases that are the subject-matter of this clash are set out below in an approximate timeline:

House of Lords	The Strasbourg Court
1. *Harrow LBC v Qazi*[14] (3:2 majority)	
	2. *Connors v UK*[15] and *Blecic v Croatia*[16]
3. *Kay v Lambeth LBC; Leeds CC v Price*[17] (4:3 majority)	
	4. *McCann v UK*[18]
5. *Birmingham CC v Doherty*[19]	
6. Court of Appeal decisions seeking to apply *Doherty*.[20]	6. *Cosic v Croatia*,[21] *Zehentner v Austria*[22] and *Paulic v Croatia*[23]
7. *Manchester CC v Pinnock* appeal to a nine panel Supreme Court.	
	8. Awaiting *Kay v UK*

This is not a seamless engagement, because decisions overlap. The clash is still raging with the Court of Appeal seeking to make sense of *Kay* and *Doherty*,[24] the Strasbourg Court's important judgment in *Kay v UK* still pending, and the Supreme Court's judgment in *Manchester CC v Pinnock*[25] awaited. Furthermore,

of Rented Housing' [2009] *EHRLR* 148 (part I) and 495 (part II); I Loveland, 'Defending Ground 8 residential possession claims through Article 8 of the European convention on Human Rights' [2009] *Conv* 396; M Davis and D Hughes, 'Gateways or Barriers? Joint Tenants, Possession Claims and Article 8' [2010] *Conv* 57.

[14] [2003] UKHL 40, [2004] 1 AC 983.
[15] (App No 66746/01) (2005) 40 EHRR 9.
[16] (App No 59532/00) (2005) 41 EHRR 13.
[17] [2006] UKHL 10, [2006] 2 AC 465.
[18] (App No 19009/04) (2008) 47 EHRR 40.
[19] [2008] UKHL 57, [2009] 1 AC 367.
[20] *Doran v Liverpool CC* [2009] EWCA Civ 146, [2009] 1 WLR 2365; *Central Bedfordshire Council v Taylor* [2009] EWCA Civ 613, [2010] 1 WLR 446; *Barber v Croydon LBC* [2010] EWCA Civ 51, [2010] HLR 26; *Salford CC v Mullen* [2010] EWCA Civ 336, [2010] BLGR 559 (a conjoined appeal with *Hounslow LBC v Powell*, *Leeds CC v Hall*, *Birmingham CC v Frisby* and *Manchester CC v Mushin*); *Brent LBC v Corcoran* [2010] EWCA Civ 774, [2010] NPC 78.
[21] (App No 3572/06).
[22] (App No 20082/02).
[23] (App No 3572/06).
[24] *Kay* (n 17) and *Doherty* (n 19).
[25] UKSC 2009/0180.

the clash has not just been between the House of Lords and the Strasbourg Court, but also within the House of Lords with their Lordships' reasoning marred by lack of unanimity and selective deafness to the consistent message being delivered by Strasbourg.

This deafness is surprising given the House of Lords' duty under the HRA section 2 to take the decisions of the Strasbourg Court 'into account'.[26] The decisions of the Strasbourg Court are not strictly binding but the expectation is that their clear and consistent tenor will be followed save in special circumstances, for instance where Strasbourg had been misinformed or misunderstood domestic law and processes.[27] Indeed the expectation is that Strasbourg jurisprudence will operate as a floor below which human rights values will not fall.[28] An unjustified failure to follow Strasbourg decisions may result in the claimant appealing to the Strasbourg Court. The Joint Committee on Human Rights has expressed concern that 'the issue of respect for people's homes in summary possession cases remains unresolved …'.[29] They suggest that the costs of pursuing *Kay v UK* would be better spent on reforming summary possession processes, a suggestion that the Government has declined to pursue, preferring to await the judgments of the Supreme Court and the Strasbourg Court.[30] The clash also raises fundamental public law concerns with the operation of the HRA being tested. The issues of precedent both within this jurisdiction and to the judgments of the Strasbourg Court and the width of judicial review have already been mentioned. Questions have been raised as to the extent of judicial deference and there is also the crucial uncertainty of horizontal application of the HRA. These issues will be merely touched upon in this chapter but it is clear that property lawyers cannot remain aloof from these wider debates and the need to enter into a dialogue with public lawyers to fully appreciate their import.

The common ground

The application of Article 8 to possession proceedings of the home is accepted by both the Strasbourg Court and the House of Lords in their interpretation both of the meaning of 'home' and the extent of respect due under Article 8.

[26] The House of Lords decided in *Kay* (n 17) [40]–[45] that the lower courts should continue to be bound by precedent even though at odds with Strasbourg jurisprudence.

[27] *R v Horncastle* [2009] UKSC 14, [2010] 2 WLR 47. See, in particular, [11].

[28] More controversial is whether Strasbourg jurisprudence operates as a restrictive ceiling on the development of human rights values see J Lewis 'The European Ceiling on Human Rights' [2007] *PL* 720.

[29] Joint Committee on Human Rights, 'Enhancing Parliament's Role in Relation to Human Rights Judgments' Fifteenth Report (2009–10) HL 85/HC 455 [71].

[30] Ibid [59]–[71]. See also: Secretary of State for Justice, 'Government Response to the Joint Committee on Human Rights' Fifteenth Report of Session 2009–10: Responding to human rights judgments' (Cm 7892, 2010).

Home

The House of Lords has accepted the earlier decisions of the Strasbourg Court in *Gillow v UK*[31] and *Buckley v UK*[32] which provide an autonomous meaning of home.[33] This meaning is not limited by proprietary rights. Thus a dwelling may be a person's home although they have no current legal right to occupy that dwelling.[34] This interpretation may come as a surprise to property lawyers whose normal area of enquiry is concerned with identifying and then reconciling competing property rights. Their interaction with the home has been dominated by discussions concerning the acquisition and quantification of interests in the home[35] and competing proprietary rights between those claiming a beneficial interest in the home and a mortgagee's right to possession.[36] However, this wider meaning of home is fundamental to the clash under discussion and to claims that Article 8 provides a 'new form of proprietary entitlement.' It opens up the respect due to the home under Article 8 to possibilities beyond the traditional boundaries of property law and forces property lawyers to look at the concept of home in a much wider context.

The autonomous meaning of home in Strasbourg jurisprudence is defined by the 'sufficient and continuing links' that the claimant has with a dwelling.[37] These links owe more to the social and psychological attachment or bond that develops with a particular dwelling and neighbourhood rather than proprietary rights. The concern is not just with the use of a dwelling as a mere shelter but also with abstract, but nevertheless powerful, ties to a particular place and locality. The concept of home is thus used in symbolic terms, rather than restricted by functionality, and as such dovetails with the similar Article 8 demand for respect for a person's 'private and family life.' A home is thus 'not just a place where one lives but also the place where one feels one belongs.'[38] It is concerned with 'identity, self-determination, physical and mental integrity ... and a settled and secure home and place in the community.'[39] In the cases under review there was little argument

[31] (App No 9063/80) (1986) 11 EHRR 336. See also *Mabey v UK* (App No 28370/95) (1996) 22 EHRR CD123.

[32] (App No 20348/92) (1997) 23 EHRR 101.

[33] See in particular *Harrow LBC v Qazi* [2003] UKHL 40, [2004] 1 AC 983.

[34] It is suggested that occupation must have been originally derived from a legal source. Thus the approach to squatters in *McPhail v Persons, Names Unknown* [1973] Ch 447 (CA) is not necessarily in issue but see contrasting comments of Lord Bingham [37] and Baroness Hale [192] in *Kay* (n 17).

[35] Most recently by *Stack v Dowden* [2007] UKHL 17, [2007] 2 AC 432.

[36] See for instance the leading cases of *Williams & Glyn's Bank v Boland* [1981] AC 487 (HL), *City of London Building Society v Flegg* [1988] AC 54 (HL) and *Abbey National Building Society v Cann* [1991] 1 AC 56 (HL).

[37] A Busye, 'Strings Attached: The Concept of Home in the Case Law of the ECHR' (2006) *EHRLR* 294.

[38] Ibid 296.

[39] *Connors* (n 6) [82].

that the property in question was the occupier's home. Only in *Leeds CC v Price*[40] were the Price family unsuccessful in establishing that the mobile home site, on which they had lived for just a few days, was their home.

Fox, in her book *Conceptualising Home: Theories, Law and Policy*, explores the meaning of home beyond its physical structure to the concept of home as 'territory', home as 'identity', home as 'social and cultural unit' as well as home as 'a financial investment.'[41] It is these intangible values of home which capture the essence of 'sufficient and continuing links' beyond a dwelling's tangible bricks and mortar. Yet lawyers and judges seem to find these home meanings challenging to accommodate, for it is this wider concept of home which underpins the conflict between domestically recognised proprietary rights and the respect due to the home under Article 8. It lies at the heart of the turmoil, both within the House of Lords and between the House of Lords and the Strasbourg Court, as the House of Lords struggles to minimise the impact of Article 8.

Respect for the home

The House of Lords, after some hesitation, has come to accept that the exercise of a legal right to possession is an interference with the respect due to the home under Article 8(1). The hesitation came in *Qazi*, notably from Lord Scott, who believed that the respect due to the home under Article 8 was limited to the protection of privacy and freedom from unwarranted State interference, and thus was not concerned with claims to possession based upon established property rights.[42] Lord Scott was alone in this restricted view, although some of his brethren showed some sympathy.[43]

The focus of attention is thus upon whether the interference with the home that possession proceedings entail is justified under Article 8(2). A right to possession will be so justified if it is in accordance with the law and if it can be demonstrated that the right addresses a pressing social need, for instance because it promotes 'the economic well being of the country' or protects 'the rights ... of others.' Domestic housing policy which confers and controls rights to possession of tenanted property provides a prime example of measures intended to address the pressing social need for adequate and appropriate accommodation. The right of a mortgagee to look to the mortgagor's home to recover its mortgage advance provides another clear example.[44] Strasbourg

[40] [2006] UKHL 10, [2006] 2 AC 465. The case was heard by the House of Lords as a conjoined appeal with *Kay v Lambeth LBC* [2006] UKHL 10, [2006] 2 AC 465.

[41] L Fox, *Conceptualising Home: Theories, Law and Policies* (Hart Publishing, Oxford 2007). See particularly ch 4.

[42] *Qazi v Harrow LBC* [2003] UKHL 43, [2004] 1 AC 983 [125].

[43] For example, ibid [108] (Lord Millett) and [48], [82] (Lord Hope).

[44] *Wood v UK* (App No 23414/02) 16 November 2004.

jurisprudence acknowledges that States, given their closer proximity to the particular domestic circumstances, enjoy a wide 'margin of appreciation' or discretion both in identifying a pressing social need and in selecting and implementing the means chosen to achieve that need. Nevertheless, States are not given a *carte blanche*. They are required to act proportionately both in terms of the substance of the interference necessary to address a given need and in the process employed to assert that interference. It this proportionality balance between the respect due to an occupier's home and the wider public interest in achieving an effective and efficient housing policy that defines the area of conflict.

This 'justification formula' is well established in Strasbourg jurisprudence and is repeated by the Strasbourg Court in every judgment. It is a mantra that must be indelibly etched on to every human rights, and now property, lawyer's mind.

No man's land: horizontal application

The question of horizontal application is not addressed by the clash. Although the judges sitting in the House of Lords (particularly in *Kay*) appear at times to have the question in the back of their minds, they have not expressed a definitive opinion.[45] All the domestic cases have been cases of vertical application. Here the meaning of public authority or a quasi-public authority, when exercising public functions,[46] is crucial to whether a body will be subject to judicial review and direct duties to act in a human rights compliant manner pursuant to the HRA section 6. The guidance of the Court of Appeal in *London & Quadrant Housing Trust v R (Weaver)*[47] suggests that housing associations may, although not necessarily will, fall within the definition of quasi-public authorities. They may do so when exercising public housing responsibilities. The issue is not settled. Although an appeal to the Supreme Court was refused in *Weaver*, it is expected that the issue may yet find its way to the Supreme Court.[48]

What also remains uncertain, yet absolutely crucial to any possible impact of Article 8 to possession proceedings brought by private landlords, mortgagees or others, is horizontal application.[49]

[45] See *Kay* (n 17) [29] (Lord Bingham), [61] (Lord Nicholls), [64] (Lord Hope).

[46] *Aston Cantlow and Wilmcote with Billesley PCC v Wallbank* [2003] UKHL 37, [2004] 1 AC 546.

[47] [2009] EWCA Civ 587, [2010] 1 WLR 363. See also *R (McIntyre) v Gentoo Group Ltd* [2010] EWHC 5 (Admin), [2010] 2 P & CR DG6.

[48] A Arden, 'Weaver and Pinnock' [2010] JHL 17. See also *Eastland Homes Partnership Ltd v Whyte* [2010] EWHC 695 (QB), where Eastland accepted they were bound by *Weaver* but reserved their position in the event of an appeal.

[49] See S Nield ,'Charges, Possession and Human Rights: A Reappraisal of s87(1) Law of Property Act 1925' in E Cooke (ed), *Modern Studies in Property Law: Volume 3* (Hart Publishing, Oxford 2005) ch 8.

There are the well known arguments in favour of indirect horizontal effect based upon the HRA section 3, which requires legislation to be interpreted in a compliant manner, and the HRA section 6 which calls for the courts (as public authorities) to act in a compliant manner in its application and development of the common law.[50] There has also been the well known example of horizontal application of Article 8 with Article 14 ECHR based upon the court's responsibilities under the HRA section 3 in *Ghaidan v Godin-Mendoza*.[51] The arguments for horizontal application are gaining acceptance and HRA-based issues between private parties have been canvassed in property cases, although with little success.[52] In other areas there has been more success. For instance, the courts have used Article 8 to facilitate the development of a new common law tort of misuse of private information.[53]

Dovetailing with issues of horizontal effect is the dual nature of a State's responsibilities under Article 8. Those responsibilities are both negative, in the sense of controls on direct State (or its public agencies) interference with the respect due to the home, and also positive in ensuring that there is a framework which prevents unjustified interference by others. Although it is clear that there is no right to a home,[54] the extent and content of a State's positive responsibilities in relation to the respect due to the home under Article 8 are undeveloped.[55] Notable examples of positive duties have concerned environmental protection.[56] *Connors* and *Zehentner* also demonstrate that particular protective measures may be necessary to safeguard those that are vulnerable before the law because of their minority cultural status as gypsies or because of some legal incapacity or disability. The consistent message from Strasbourg also calls upon States to ensure that a procedural framework is in place which allows for an independent assessment of the proportionality of

[50] J Howell, 'The Human Rights Act 1998: Land, Private Citizens, and the Common Law' (2007) 123 *LQR* 618.

[51] [2004] 2 AC 557 (HL).

[52] See for instance in relation to article 1 protocol 1 ECHR: *JA Pye (Oxford) Ltd v UK* (App No 44302/02) (2008) 46 EHRR 45 (adverse possession); *Horsham Properties Group Ltd v Clark and Others* [2008] EWHC 2327 (Ch), [2009] 1 WLR 1255 (mortgagee's power of sale); *Barca v Mears* [2004] EWHC 2170 (Ch), [2005] 2 FLR 1 (article 8); but see *Official Receiver for Northern Ireland v Rooney* [2009] 2 FLR 1437 (Ch Northern Ireland) (bankruptcy and sale); *National Westminster Bank Plc v Malhan* [2004] EWHC 847 (Ch), [2004] 2 P & CR DG9 (overreaching; articles 1 protocol 1 ECHR and article 8 ECHR); *Close Invoicing Finance Ltd v Pile* [2008] EWHC 1580 (Ch), [2009] 1 FLR 873; *C Putnam & Sons v Taylor* [2009] EWHC 317 (Ch), [2009] BPIR 769; *Foster Ketley & Co v Brent* [2009] EWHC 3441 (Ch); *National Westminster Bank Plc v Rushmer* [2010] EWHC 554 (Ch), [2010] 2 FLR 362 (charging orders and orders for sale).

[53] See *Campbell v Mirror Group Newspapers Ltd* [2004] UKHL 22, [2004] 2 AC 457; *McKennit v Ash* [2006] EWCA Civ 1714, [2008] QB 73; *Mosley v NGN Ltd* [2008] EWHC 1777 (QB), [2008] EMLR 20; *Murray v Express Newspapers Plc* [2008] EWCA Civ 446, [2009] Ch 481 discussed in T Bennett, 'Horizontality's New Horizons – re-examining horizontal effect: privacy, defamation and the Human Rights Act' [2010] *Ent L Rev* 96.

[54] *Marzari v Italy* (1999) 28 EHRR CD 175.

[55] P Kenna, 'Housing rights: positive duties and enforceable rights at the European Court of Human Rights' (2008) *EHRLR* 193.

[56] *Lopez Ostra v Spain* (App No 16798/90) (1995) 20 EHRR 277; *Hatton v UK* (App No 36022/97) 2 October 2001; *Khatun v UK* (App No 38387/97) (1998) 26 EHRR CD212.

the interference presented by possession proceedings. This need for adequate procedural safeguards does not appear confined to claims to possession from public authorities: for instance, the identity of the landlord was not significant in *McCann* and in *Zehentner*; it was Ms Zehentner's creditors who were interfering with the respect due to her home.

What is evident is that, if the HRA operates horizontally, the proportionality balance that lies at the heart of justification will need to operate differently where private rights are to be reconciled. Furthermore, there is an additional concern of reconciling competing Convention rights, particularly between protections against the deprivation of possessions; for instance a legal owner or mortgagee's property rights under Article 1 of the First Protocol to the ECHR (Article 1 Protocol 1) and the respect due to an occupier's home under Article 8.[57]

The clash of the titans: a summary

The House of Lords' opening salvo in *Qazi*

Allen's two possible approaches are exemplified by the divergent views of the House of Lords in *Qazi*, which concerned the compatibility of the rule in *Monk*. The majority comprising Lords Hope, Scott and Millett held, with varying degrees of conviction, that the exercise of a proprietary right to possession is always ECHR compliant either because it does not engage Article 8 (Lord Scott)[58] or because the right to possession is necessarily justified under Article 8(2) (Lords Hope[59] and Millett).[60]

The minority, being Lords Bingham and Steyn, called for an application of the justification formula under Article 8(2) which would require the court to consider the compatibility of the legal rules governing the claim to possession and the proportionality of their application. However, Lord Bingham acknowledged that only in exceptional circumstances would repossession in the exercise of proprietary rules be unjustified.[61] Lord Steyn was particularly robust in his criticism of the majority's approach.[62]

[57] *Nield* (n 49) 166. The balancing of competing Convention rights has received attention from commentators in other fields. See H Fenwick, 'Clashing Rights, the Welfare of the Child and the Human Rights Act' (2004) 67 *MLR* 889; S Choudhry and H Fenwick, 'Taking the Rights of Parents and Children Seriously: Confronting the Welfare Principle under the Human Rights Act' [2005] *OJLS* 453; S Harris Short, 'Family Law and the Human Rights Act 1998: judicial restraint or revolution?' [2005] *CFLQ* 329; J Fortin, 'The Effect of the HRA on Domestic Practice in Children's Cases' (2006) 69 *MLR* 300; J Herring and R Taylor, 'Relocating Relocation' [2006] *CFLQ* 517.

[58] *Qazi* (n 42) [125].

[59] Ibid [78].

[60] Ibid [109]. Lord Millett also raised the possibility of judicial review of the local authority's decision to seek possession.

[61] Ibid [25].

[62] Ibid [27].

> It would be surprising if the views of the majority on the application of European Convention on Human Rights as incorporated into our system by the Human Rights Act 1998 withstood European scrutiny. It is contrary to the purposive interpretation of article 8 read against the structure of the Convention. It is inconsistent with the general thrust of the decisions of the European Court of Human Rights ... it empties article 8(1) of any or virtually any meaningful content.

Despite Lord Steyn's comments the Strasbourg Court refused an appeal in *Qazi*, which bolstered the views of the majority when Article 8 was again considered by the House of Lords in *Kay*.

The Strasbourg Court: a consistent and robust retort

The pre-*Qazi* Strasbourg jurisprudence on Article 8 is not clearly reasoned, which at least partially explains the split in *Qazi*.[63] However, the Strasbourg Court has subsequently made its position clear in a consistent line of cases starting with *Connors*.

Connors concerned the eviction of gypsies from a local authority site. There were allegations of anti-social behaviour but the local authority chose to simply exercise their right to terminate the Connors' contractual licence without giving any reasons. The Strasbourg Court held such action to be a breach of Article 8. They applied the familiar justification formula noting, in the light of the extreme nature of the interference posed by possession proceedings, first the narrow width of a State's margin of appreciation in endorsing summary rights to possession.

> The serious interference with the applicant's rights under art 8 requires in the court's opinion particularly weighty reasons of public interest by way of justification and the margin of appreciation to be afforded to national authorities must be regarded as correspondingly narrowed.[64]

Then secondly, in measuring the proportionality of the eviction in pursuance of the council's legal rights, the Strasbourg Court emphasised the importance of an adequate process: 'The existence of procedural safeguards is ... a crucial consideration in this Court's assessment of the proportionality of the Council's decision.'[65]

The Strasbourg Court also made it clear that gypsies, as a minority group, were particularly vulnerable and a State was under a positive duty to ensure that there were measures within the regulatory framework and decision

[63] See *S v UK* (1986) 47 DR 274, *Di Palma v UK* (1986) 10 EHRR 149; *Marzari v Italy* (1999) 28 EHRR CD175; *P v UK* (App No 14751/89) (12 December 1990); *Ure v UK* (App No 28027/95) (27 November 1996); *Wood v UK* (App No 32540/96) (1997) 24 EHRR CD69; and *Larkos v Cyprus* (App No 29515/95) (1999) 30 EHRR 597.

[64] *Connors* (n 6) [86].

[65] Ibid [92].

making process to address that vulnerability and 'facilitate the gypsy way of life.'[66]

The Strasbourg Court was satisfied in *Blecic* that adequate procedural safeguards were provided where the Croatian courts had the jurisdiction to consider the merits of the relevant authority's decision to terminate Mrs Blecic's tenancy, even when the court's assessment might appear somewhat harsh. In breach of the occupational terms of her tenancy, Mrs Blecic had left her Zadar flat empty when she sought sanctuary in Italy at the height of the Balkan's conflict. It was not for the Strasbourg Court to reassess the proportionality of the court's decision on the particular facts of the case but to ensure that there was a process by which the interference with Mrs Blecic's right to respect for her home had been sufficiently considered and justified.[67] Given those circumstances, Strasbourg would intervene only where the law which resulted in that decision was 'manifestly without reasonable foundation'[68] or 'manifestly disproportionate to the legitimate aim pursued.'[69] In other words it is not within the State's margin of appreciation.

In *McCann,* the Strasbourg Court rejected the compatibility of the rule in *Monk*, which enables a single joint tenant, without the consent or even knowledge of the other joint tenant(s), to terminate the joint tenancy by notice. In the case of domestic violence some local authorities have used the rule as a simple and speedy mechanism to bring the parties' joint tenancy to an end thereby evicting the aggressor and facilitating the re-housing of the victim.[70] In *McCann* the council had followed this process by asking Mrs McCann, following her separation from her violent husband, to give notice terminating her joint tenancy, although they failed to make clear to Mrs McCann why they were asking her to do so.[71] The Strasbourg Court pointedly rejected that its call in *Connors* for adequate procedural safeguards was restricted to gypsies and reiterated its position in no uncertain terms:

> The central question in this case is therefore whether the interference was proportionate to the aim pursued and thus necessary in a democratic society. It must be recalled that this requirement under para 2 of art 8 raises questions of procedure as well as substance ... The Court is unable to accept the Government's argument that the reasoning in *Connors v UK* ... was to be confined only to cases involving the eviction of gypsies or cases where the applicant sought to challenge the law itself rather than its application in his particular cases. The loss of one's home is the most extreme form of interference with the right to respect for the home. Any person at risk of an

[66] Ibid [84].

[67] *Blecic* (n 16) [61] and [68].

[68] Ibid [65]. See also *James v UK* (App No 8795/79) (1986) 8 EHRR 123 [46] where this test was outlined.

[69] Ibid.

[70] M Davis and D Hughes, 'Gateways or Barriers? Joint Tenants, Possession Claims and Article 8' [2010] *Conv* 57.

[71] The Strasbourg Court found it immaterial whether or not Mrs McCann understood the implications of her notice: *McCann* (n 8) [55].

> interference of this magnitude should in principle be able to have the proportionality of the measure determined by an independent tribunal in the light of the relevant principles in art 8 of the Convention notwithstanding that under domestic law his right has come to an end.[72]

As Mr McCann had no legal right to remain in occupation the court had no choice but to order possession; thus Mr McCann had no opportunity to present his case against eviction. The Strasbourg Court noted that he would have had an opportunity to do so if the local authority had chosen the alternative route to recover possession based on statutory grounds.[73]

Three cases in similar vein have followed. *Cosic* and *Paulic* involved the summary recovery of possession where the occupiers had no right to remain under domestic law.[74] *Paulic* is of additional interest because the personal circumstances of the Paulic family were taken into account by the domestic courts, not in the decision to make a possession order, but in delaying enforcement of that order. This is a discretion afforded to the domestic courts in a number of instances. One example is provided by the court's discretion under the Administration of Justice Act 1970 section 36 to adjourn possession proceedings brought by a mortgagee, or to suspend or delay the execution of the possession order that they are bound to make in pursuance of the mortgagee's inherent right (as opposed to power) to possession.[75] However, the Strasbourg Court in *Paulic* held that a similar discretion:

> … [did] not satisfy the requirement of reasonableness and the proportionality of the eviction order which has to be assessed by an independent tribunal. The court notes that enforcement proceedings – which by their nature are non-contentious and whose primary purpose is to secure the effective execution of the judgment debt – are unlike civil proceedings neither designated not properly equipped with procedural tools and safeguards for the thorough and adversarial examination of such complex legal issues. Therefore the competence for carrying out the test of proportionality lies with the court conducting regular civil proceedings in which the civil claim lodged by the state and seeking the applicant's eviction is determined.[76]

The third case, *Zehentner v Austria*, represents the high point of the Strasbourg Court's insistence that Article 8 demands strict procedural safeguards. Ms Zehentner at the time in question lacked mental capacity and was absent from her flat for treatment. She had failed to pay some workmen for repairs to her

[72] Ibid [49] and [50].

[73] Ibid [52] referring to the statutory grounds conferring a right to repossession based upon the domestic violence. See Housing Act 1985 sch 2 ground 2A (secure tenancies) and Housing Act 1988 sch 2 ground 14A (registered social landlords).

[74] *Cosic* (n 21) and *Paulic* (n 23). See also *Stankova v Slovakia* (App No 7205/02) but which does not add to the debate.

[75] See also *Brent LBC v Corcoran* [2010] EWCA Civ 774, [2010] NPC 78 where the suspension a local authority's right to possession following the lawful termination of a licence to occupy was in issue.

[76] *Paulic* (n 23) [44].

flat; judgment was obtained for these costs and subsequently enforcement action was taken, with her flat sold by the Austrian equivalent of a charging order. Ms Zehentner was unable to participate in these proceedings and did not object to the sale order within the strict time limits required by Austrian law. The Strasbourg Court held that this enforcement process to recover a relatively small sum was incompatible with Article 8. The decision is noteworthy for a number of reasons. First, the dispute was between private parties, namely Ms Zehentner and her creditors, although her creditors were not solely relying upon their private contractual rights. They were also taking advantage of the judgment enforcement process sanctioned by Austrian law. Secondly, the Strasbourg Court did not doubt that the protection of creditors through the enforcement of judgement debts was a legitimate aim which could be justified under Article 8. The problem was with the proportionality of the means adopted to achieve that legitimate aim which imposed strict time limits. Thirdly, these time limits were not justified by the aims of promoting the efficiency of the enforcement process nor of protecting the bona fide purchaser who acquired the property. At least they were not justified where the victim was suffering a mental incapacity and thus was not competent to act within the required time frame, even if the court was unaware of the incapacity. In such circumstances the State had a positive duty to provide specific protection to those that were vulnerable before the law.[77]

It would be surprising, given the clarity and strength of these judgments, that the Strasbourg Court will temper its position when it delivers judgment in *Kay v UK*.[78]

The House of Lords' rearguard action

With Lords Hope and Scott providing the only continuing representatives in both the subsequent cases of *Kay* and *Doherty*, the House of Lords has moved only marginally in human rights terms. Their Lordships have instead opened what they believe to be an acceptable escape route through judicial review.

Kay concerned an unsuccessful human rights challenge to repossession brought by licensees of housing provided to homeless individuals. It was heard after the judgment of the Strasbourg Court in *Connors* and *Blecic* before a panel of seven which split in their judgment into a 4:3 majority.

The majority (being Lords Hope, Scott, Brown and Baroness Hale), although expressing different views upon whether or not *Qazi* was incompatible with *Connors*,[79] were prepared to move only marginally to accept that domestic

[77] *Zehentner* (n 22) [61] –[65].

[78] *Joint Committee on Human Rights* (n 29) and *Government Response* (n 30).

[79] *Kay* (n 17) [64] (Lord Hope), [167] (Lord Scott) thought that *Qazi* and *Connors* were not inconsistent but by contrast [179] (Baroness Hale) and [198] (Lord Brown) felt some qualification was necessary.

rights to possession in rare cases might fail to provide justification under Article 8(2) where the law itself was found to be non-compliant. They refused to accept that the personal circumstances of the occupier should be brought into an assessment of proportionality under Article 8(2).[80] Instead they decided that the decision of a local authority to repossess could be subject to judicial review on traditional *Wednesbury*[81] grounds as a decision which no reasonable authority in the particular circumstances could justify. The majority position is summarised in the judgment of Lord Hope in what has become known as Gateways (a) and (b):

> … the only situations in which it would be open to the court to refrain from proceeding to summary judgment and making the possession order are these: (a) if a seriously arguable point is raised that the law which enables the court to make the possession order is incompatible with article 8 … (b) if the defendant wishes to challenge the decision of a public authority to recover possession as an improper exercise of its powers at common law on the ground that it was a decision that no reasonable person would consider justifiable, he should be permitted to do this provided again the point is seriously arguable.[82]

It is for the occupier to make a challenge under either of these Gateways, the court being entitled to assume that the domestic law is compliant. A challenge under either Gateway can be raised in defence to possession proceedings in the county court, save where the statutory regime in question limits the county court jurisdiction.[83] In the case of a Gateway (a) challenge the case may need to be remitted to the High Court when the county court is unable to interpret the challenged law in a compliant manner, given that the county court is unable to issue a certificate of incompatibility under the HRA section 4.[84]

The minority, comprising Lords Bingham, Nicholls and Walker, considered *Qazi* was incompatible with *Connors* and *Blecic*.[85] They were prepared to accept that the occupier's personal circumstances could also form the substance of a merits review under Article 8(2) and thus that *Connors* was not confined to the circumstances of gypsies.[86] However, they did not go much further than the majority in believing that only in exceptional circumstances will domestic law be non-compliant, nor were they prepared to speculate what personal circumstances might tilt the proportionality balance:

[80] See Baroness Hale, *Kay* (n 17) [189] summarising the divergence between the majority and minority.

[81] *Associated Picture Houses Ltd v Wednesbury Corporation* [1948] 1 KB 223 (CA).

[82] *Kay* (n 17) [110].

[83] For instance a Gateway (b) challenge in the case of introductory tenancies – see the conjoined appeals in *Mullen v Salford CC* [2010] EWCA Civ 336, [2010] BLGR 559 and demoted tenancies – see *Pinnock v Manchester CC* [2009] EWCA Civ 852, [2010] 1 WLR 713 when judicial review will need to be brought before the Administrative Court.

[84] See *Kay* (n 17) [180]–[183], [188]; Baroness Hale summarising the points of agreement.

[85] Ibid [26].

[86] Ibid [35]–[36].

> The practical experience of the county court judges is likely to be the surest guide provided always that the stringency of the test is borne in mind ... I do not think however that problems and afflictions of a personal nature should avail the occupier where there are public services available to address and alleviate those problems ... .[87]

Lord Bingham explains the different conclusion of the minority:

> The two grounds are (a) that the law which requires the court to make a possession order despite the occupier's personal circumstances is Convention-incompatible and (b) that, having regard to the occupier's personal circumstances, the local authority exercise of its power to seek a possession order is an unlawful act within the meaning of section 6 (4). Deciding whether the defendant has a seriously arguable case on one or both of these grounds will not call for a full blown trial. This question should be dealt with summarily ... The procedural aim of the court must be to decide this question as expeditiously as is consistent with the defendant having a fair opportunity to present his case in this question.[88]

The House of Lords was called upon to reconsider the position in *Doherty*, which concerned a successful Gateway (a) human rights challenge where the law governing the eviction of gypsies from council-owned mobile home sites was found to be non-compliant because it discriminated between gypsies on council-owned and private sites.[89] The law was being amended and so the House of Lords saw no point in making a declaration of incompatibility. However, given the workings of the HRA the possession order made against the Doherty family was still enforceable.

Section 6(2) of the HRA provides a defence to public authorities who, in the performance of their functions, are either required,[90] or decide to act,[91] in an incompatible manner pending Parliament's amendment of the offending law.[92] The House of Lords attempted to resolve the conundrum by returning the case to the county court for a possible Gateway (b) challenge to the local authority's decision to repossess.

Doherty is difficult case for a number of reasons. First, the case was heard by a panel of five who, in their unanimous judgment, felt constrained by the panel of seven judgment in *Kay*. Secondly, the case was heard before, but judgment given just after, *McCann*. The parties were invited to make written submission for their Lordships' consideration but it is clear that the

[87] Ibid [38].

[88] Ibid [39].

[89] The Caravan Sites Act 1968 s 4 enables a court to suspend an eviction order for up to 12 months. Local authority sites were initially excluded (see s 4(6)(a)) but this exclusion was removed by Housing Act 2004 s 211(1). In addition, the Mobile Homes Act 1983 provides that a possession order of a mobile home site can only be made on specified grounds and that the court must consider the reasonableness of such an order. Local authority gypsy sites were excluded (see s 5(1)) – but this exclusion is removed by the Housing and Regeneration Act 2008 s 318, although there has been a delay in bringing this section into force.

[90] Human Rights Act 1998 s 6(2)(a).

[91] Human Rights Act 1998 s 6(2)(b).

[92] The claimant could take their claim to the Strasbourg Court.

issues raised by *McCann* were not fully canvassed. Their Lordships effectively ignored *McCann* (some more robustly than others) by distinguishing the particular facts and complaining that the Strasbourg Court did not understand the domestic conditions or provide any guidance on what procedural safeguards would be adequate.[93] They thus refused to support the minority in *Kay* regarding Gateway (a), although the Strasbourg Court in *McCann* had expressed a preference for the views of the minority.[94] Instead they attempted to further explain and modify the Gateways.[95]

Thirdly, much of their Lordships' attention was devoted to addressing the particular problems raised by the HRA section 6(2) defences referred to above which left them trying to reconcile the effect of a clearly incompatible act upon the Doherty family. A true constitutional court would have been able not only to declare the law incompatible, but also the eviction unlawful. However, the HRA preserves the supremacy of Parliament and permits the court to only declare the law incompatible.[96] Their Lordships upheld the local authority's defence under the HRA section 6(2)(b),[97] but nevertheless decided that the authority's decision to recover possession was subject to judicial review under Gateway (b).[98] In so doing they pointed out that Gateways (a) and (b) are not mutually exclusive.[99]

Lastly, although each of their Lordships tried to further explain the operation of Gateway (a) in the scheme of the HRA, and the Gateway (b) route to judicial review, they left more questions unanswered particularly in relation to a Gateway (b) challenge. In so doing their Lordships sowed the seeds of a continuing debate on the width of judicial review of a local authority's decision to seek possession which is now raging in the lower courts.[100]

There are a number of elements to this debate. First, are the personal circumstances put forward by the occupant to be considered? The unsurprising answer is yes, given the wide range of factors which may affect a local authority's

[93] *Doherty* (n 19), in particular Lord Hope [20] and Lord Scott [82]–[88].

[94] As Lord Walker, as one of the minority in *Kay*, acknowledges *Doherty* (n 19) [116].

[95] *Doherty* (n 19) [36].

[96] Human Rights Act 1998 s 4.

[97] The duty to act in a compliant manner does not apply where a public authority 'was acting to give effect to or enforce' an incompatible legislative provision – Human Rights Act 1998 s 6(2)(b). In *Doherty* (n 19), the House of Lords held that this defence applies to the exercise of a common law power which forms part of a statutory scheme – see Lord Hope [39]–[40], Lord Walker [96]–[104] and [111]–[114].

[98] Notwithstanding the Human Rights Act 1998 s 6(2) defences, see *Doherty* (n 19) Lord Mance [153]–[159].

[99] *Doherty* (n 19) Lords Hope [10] and Walker [107]–[108].

[100] See *Hillingdon LBC v Collins* [2008] EWHC 3016 (Admin); *Doran v Liverpool CC* [2009] EWCA Civ 146, [2009] 1 WLR 2365; *McGlynn v Welwyn Hatfield DC* [2009] EWCA Civ 285, [2010] HLR 10; *Taylor v Central Bedfordshire Council* [2009] EWCA Civ 613, [2010] 1 WLR 446; *Defence Estates v JL* [2009] EWHC 1049 (Admin); *Pinnock v Manchester CC* [2009] EWCA Civ 852, [2010] 1 WLR 713; *Barber v Croydon LBC* [2010] EWCA Civ 51, [2010] HLR 26; the conjoined appeals in *Mullen v Salford CC* [2010] EWCA Civ 336, [2010] BLGR 559; *Eastland Homes Partnership Ltd v Whyte* [2010] EWHC 695 (QB); and *Brent LBC v Corcorcan* [2010] EWCA Civ 774, [2010] NPC 78.

decision making process.[101] The second and more difficult issue is whether judicial review is restricted to common law irrationality or whether it has, or should be developed in the light of human rights jurisprudence, into an effective proportionality review. Some of their Lordships in *Doherty* hinted that judicial review might develop along these lines.[102] Unsurprisingly the lower courts have hesitated to take this step, constrained as they are by the precedent set by the House of Lords in *Kay* and *Doherty*. Lastly, there has been the question of which decision is under examination. Is it the original decision to seek possession or can the range of the local authority's decisions throughout the repossession process be questioned?

Definitive guidance on all these issues will hopefully be available when the Supreme Court, sitting as a panel of nine, delivers their judgment in *Pinnock*. In the meantime the Court of Appeal has expressed its views. It has refused, being constrained by *Doherty*, to hold that judicial review allows a full proportionality review which would allow the court to evaluate the merits of the decision, but there is a growing weight of opinion that judicial review is now wider than the traditional *Wednesbury* test. It seems at the moment to lie somewhere in between and has been dubbed a *Wednesbury Plus* test, although there is a lack of clarity over what that encompasses. The test (that has gained some acceptance)[103] is provided by Toulson LJ in *Doran v Liverpool CC*. An impugned decision 'was one which no reasonable person would have made' which was to be decided by 'applying public law principles as they have been developed at common law, and not through the lens of the Convention.'[104] Nevertheless Toulson LJ went onto note that:

> ... these public law principles are not frozen. Even before the enactment of the HRA, our pubic law principles were being influenced by Convention ways of thinking. Since its enactment, the process has gathered momentum. It is now well recognised fact that the Convention is influencing the shape and development of our domestic public law principles, whether one uses the metaphor of embedding, weaving into the fabric, osmosis or alignment.[105]

What is becoming evident is that a successful Gateway (b) challenge is likely only in exceptional circumstances.[106]

Lastly on the question of timing and the decision under review, the Court of Appeal has accepted that each of the decisions that a local authority makes in

[101] See *Doran v Liverpool CC* [2009] EWCA Civ 146, [2009] 1 WLR 2365 [49] and *Taylor v Central Bedfordshire Council* [2009] EWCA Civ 613, [2010] 1 WLR 446 [44].

[102] *Doherty* (n 19) [121] (Lord Walker), [161]–[163] (Lord Mance), [85] (Lord Scott). Lord Hope is more measured in his views: [55].

[103] See *Taylor* (n 100) [44], *Pinnock* (n 100) [47], *Mullen* (n 100) [61], *Corcorcan* (n 100) [11].

[104] *Doran* (n 100) [49]–[50].

[105] Ibid [52].

[106] *Mullen* (n 100). Examples of successful challenges are found in *Barber* (n 100) and *Eastland Homes Partnership Ltd v Whyte* (n 100).

the possession process is open to review.[107] It is not just the initial decision to serve a notice to quit.

The present state of play in the domestic courts in seeking to reconcile Article 8 and possession proceedings by a public authority is that there is a real prospect that a similar justification process may be achieved by the different and more tortuous route of judicial review.[108] Walker LJ in *Taylor* expressed the view that:

> ... although there is a distinction between a defence raising Article 8 rights directly for decision by the court and the question whether the council as a public authority has made a lawful decision in the light of an occupier's Article 8 rights, the distinction has, very largely become academic.[109]

Peace negotiations

Is there any way in which the divergent approaches of the House of Lords and the Strasbourg Court can be resolved? Of immediate concern is to address the substance of the clash, the heart of which centres on the procedural safeguards by which repossession rights over the home are asserted. However, the clash also demonstrates more fundamental questions that need to be resolved relating to the constitutional framework by which ECHR is incorporated into domestic law under the HRA, which affects proprietary rights as much as any other area of domestic law.

A compliant repossession process

The importance of procedural safeguards within repossession proceedings that interfere with the respect for the home under Article 8 is a loud, consistent and unmistakeable message from the Strasbourg Court. It runs through all the cases yet the House of Lords has failed to face the issue head on. Instead it has been pre-occupied, particularly in *Kay* and *Doherty*, with the speed and efficiency of county court possession proceedings.[110] The recognition that Article 8 dictates an appropriate forum and opportunity for the respect due to an occupier's home to be weighed, within the proportionality balance, against legal rights to possession is a message that the House of Lords has found difficult to swallow.[111]

[107] *Taylor* (n 100) [39]–[40], *Barber* (n 100) [18]–[22], and *Mullen* (n 100) [67]–[74] although the contrary had been suggested in *Doran* (n 100).

[108] I Loveland, 'The Latest Last Word on the Relevance of ECHR Article 8 to Possession Proceedings' [2010] *JPL* 415.

[109] *Taylor* (n 100) [38].

[110] See for instance *Kay* (n 17) [33] (Lord Bingham), [55]–[56] (Lord Nicholls). It has been suggested that an amendment to the Pre-action Protocol on Possession Claims could address some of these concerns: see N Madge, 'Article 8 – *la lutta continua*?' (2009) 12 *JHL* 43.

[111] The Irish High Court has been more willing, see *Dublin City Council v Gallagher* [2008] IEHC 354 and *Pullen v Dublin City Council* [2008] IEHC 279.

The width of the margin of appreciation: the substantive law and procedural safeguards

In matters of socio-economic policy, of which the law affecting the home forms part, it is accepted that States, given their knowledge of domestic social and economic conditions, enjoy a wide margin of appreciation. Thus their judgment will not be questioned unless it be 'manifestly without reasonable foundation' in the sense that no reasonable government would have come to a similar decision in the circumstances.[112] This wide margin of appreciation has been evident in cases concerning deprivation and controls over possessions under Article 1 Protocol 1 ECHR, for instance with respect to planning controls.[113]

The Strasbourg Court reiterated this approach to macro-level housing policy in *Connors* and *Blecic* but it also noted that the width of the margin of appreciation will vary according to the nature of the Convention right and the context of the interference with the right that is in issue. In the context of respect for the home under Article 8 and the severity of the interference that repossession presents, the margin of appreciation is much narrower. As already noted, it is not concerned with weighing competing property rights but with providing protection of an individual's identity and connections with their accommodation and place within their community. In other words, the interface between respect for the home under Article 8 and repossession goes to the heart of an individual's particular circumstances at a micro level in terms of respect for their individual 'civil (rather than proprietary) rights.' Repossession of the home is invariably the subject of court proceedings,[114] but that is not enough to demonstrate adequate respect for the home under Article 8. The court must have sufficient jurisdiction to evaluate the claim for possession against the interference with the occupier's 'sufficient and continuing links' to their home.

The distinction is evident in *Blecic*. The Strasbourg Court did not question the policy that justified repossession, but of concern was the court's ability to conduct a proper review of the manner in which that policy had been applied to Mrs Blecic which afforded her an adequate opportunity to present her circumstances and allowed the domestic court to measure those circumstances against the yardstick of the law implementing that policy.

It would be tempting to conclude that whilst on matters of the substantive content of the law implementing a particular social or economic policy, where a party is granted a right to possession against another, the State's margin of appreciation remains wide; but as a matter of the procedural operation of that policy, where the consequences dictate repossession of an individual's home, the margin is narrow. But this distinction is too simplistic. The two issues are

[112] *James v UK* (App No 8795/79) (1986) 8 EHRR 123 [46].

[113] *Buckley v UK* (App No 20348/92) (1997) 23 EHRR 101 [75].

[114] At a minimum to avoid criminal liability under Criminal Law Act 1977 s 6 and Protection from Eviction Act 1977 s 1(3).

intimately entwined because the substantive law will define the circumstances when the occupier may be heard before the court. For instance, in the cases under review (with the exception of *Blecic*) there was simply no process by which the court could consider the respect due to the occupier's home because they had no legal right to remain. As Loveland has succinctly put the issue; 'it is not what the council had done but what the court could not do'.[115]

One could take the rule in *Monk* as an example.[116] Even before Article 8 reared its head *Monk* was a controversial decision with the substance of the law open to attack.[117] Article 8 adds an additional dimension to this criticism. A law which does not afford a joint tenant even the knowledge, let alone the opportunity, to challenge the termination of their legal right to occupy their home must be devoid of respect, as the Strasbourg Court held in *McCann*.[118] To provide adequate respect one possibility would be to develop the substantive law, for instance by providing that a joint tenancy could not be terminated without the agreement of all joint tenants or by providing that the notice to quit operated to extinguish only the terminating joint tenant's interest so the remaining tenant became solely entitled to the tenancy.[119] Alternatively, there would have to be a process by which the courts could weigh the termination of the remaining joint tenant's interest against the landlord's right to repossession. For instance, there could be a mechanism that allowed the remaining joint tenant to apply for a new tenancy in their sole name which the court had discretion to consider according to defined criteria.[120] This process would inevitably colour the substance of both the landlord's and the remaining joint tenant's proprietary interests.

The other domestic cases under review challenge the ECHR compatibility of summary grounds for possession conferred by various statutory housing schemes. Whilst in determining housing policy the Government enjoys a wide margin of appreciation, the issue is whether these policies can squeeze through the narrow gap that is afforded to summary rights to possession and so justify

[115] I Loveland, 'A Tale of Two Trespassers: Reconsidering the Impact of the Human Rights Act on Rights of Residence of Rented Housing: Part II' [2009] *EHRLR* 148, 159.

[116] The rule was portrayed by Lord Browne-Wilkinson as a conflict between contract and property. See *Hammersmith and Fulham LBC v Monk* [1992] 1 AC 478 (HL) 491–93.

[117] See for instance J Dewar, 'When Joint Tenants Part' (1992) 108 *LQR* 375; J Golding, 'Service of a Notice to Quit by One Joint Tenant' [1992] *Conv* 279; L Tee, 'The Negative Nature of a Notice to Quit' [1992] *CLJ* 218; K Shorrock, 'Notice to Quit by One Joint Periodic Lessee of Residential Property' [1995] *Conv* 424; M Eaton, 'Notice to Quit Revisted' (2001) 72 *PLJ* 14. The attack continued after *Qazi*; see for instance, S Pascoe, 'Can a Joint Tenant Remain in Possession After the Other Joint Tenant Has Given Notice to Quit?' [2004] *Conv* 370 and I Loveland, 'After *Qazi*: Sole Tenant Termination of Joint Tenancies and Article 8 ECHR' [2005] *Conv* 123.

[118] Several domestic cases have challenged the compatibility of the rule. See *R (Husband) v Solihull MBC* [2009] EWHC 3673 (Admin), *Wandsworth LBC v Dixon* [2009] EWHC 27 (Admin); *Wilson v Harrow LBC* [2010] EWHC 1574 (QB); and *Poplar HRCA v Howe* [2010] EWHC 1745 (QB). All have failed because the lower courts are bound as a matter of precedent by the decision in *Qazi*. The *Joint Committee on Human Rights* (n 29 and 30) has noted this incompatibility.

[119] See *Wilson* (n 118). The effect would be similar to survivorship.

[120] See also M Davis and D Hughes, 'Gateway or Barriers? Joint Tenants, Possession Claims and Article 8' [2010] *Conv* 57.

their interference with respect for the home.[121] If horizontal application is invoked, other summary rights to possession will also need to be justified under Article 8. Primary candidates include a mortgagee's rights to possession[122] and overreaching.[123]

What about personal circumstances?

Given that an individual's home is not defined by established notions of property rights but is defined by 'sufficient and continuing links', personal circumstances must inevitably come into the equation when measuring the proportionality of a decision to interfere with the respect due to an individual's home. The circumstances of vulnerable groups are acknowledged by the House of Lords, but the Strasbourg Court has made clear that consideration of individual circumstances is not confined to any particular group. The positive duties owed by States to vulnerable groups may require them to take additional protective measures to address the vulnerability in question but others' circumstances should not be excluded from review.

The divergence between the majority and minority in *Kay* centred upon whether or not the court could bring into account the personal circumstances of the occupier in assessing the compatibility of, not just the law, but its application under Gateway (a). Following *Doherty,* the House of Lords would confine a consideration of personal circumstances to judicial review under Gateway (b), but the Strasbourg Court in *McCann* expressed a preference for the minority in *Kay*. The difference between the House of Lords and the Strasbourg Court is thus over the venue and process by which personal circumstances are considered and in particular whether judicial review is an adequate process.[124]

Judicial review

The House of Lords has tried to squeeze procedural safeguards into judicial review of the local authority's decision(s) in possession proceedings through Gateway (b). Lord Millett raised the possibility in *Qazi*,[125] and the House of

[121] Most vulnerable is perhaps Ground 8. See I Loveland, 'Defending Ground 8 Residential Possession Claims Through Article 8 of the European Convention on Human Rights' [2009] *Conv* 396, but introductory and demoted tenancies have also come under the spotlight: see *Pinnock* (n 100) (demoted tenancies), E Laurie, 'The Compatibility of Introductory Tenancies and the Human Rights Act 1998' [2002] *Conv* 414 and the conjoined appeals in *Mullen* (n 100) (introductory tenancies).

[122] B McFarlane, N Hopkins and S Nield, *Land Law: Text, Cases and Materials* (OUP, Oxford 2009) ch 31 [2.6].

[123] Ibid ch 20 [6.2].

[124] Judicial review may be brought by way of defence to a possession action (see *Wandsworth LBC v Winder* [1985] AC 461 (HL)) but whether there is jurisdiction to consider such a defence is dependent upon the statutory scheme under which possession is claimed; see *Pinnock* (n 100) and the conjoined appeals in *Mullen* (n 100).

[125] *Qazi* (n 42) [109].

Lords took up the invitation in *Kay* and *Doherty* but did not fully develop the process, with the result that the lower courts are struggling until further definitive guidance is provided by the Supreme Court.

Judicial review is somewhat of a procedural fallback which suffers from a number of difficulties as an adequate process. Most obviously, judicial review will not be available between private parties and thus would be of no assistance should Article 8 be applied horizontally. Furthermore the Strasbourg Court is so far unimpressed. They have pointed to the inadequacy of judicial review as a procedural safeguard in both *Connors*[126] and *McCann*.[127] At the forefront of their concern are the limitations of judicial review where facts are in dispute,[128] although Lord Scott in *Doherty* suggested that only a modest adjustment to judicial review procedure would be required to resolve disputed facts.[129]

Judicial review, according to *Kay* and *Doherty*, is restricted to *Wednesbury* irrationality: a test that both the House of Lords and the lower courts have tantalising hinted may be influenced by human rights and notions of proportionality. A wider basis for judicial review might meet ECHR demands for an adequate process but Loveland has pointed out the substantive and jurisdictional problems of an expanded basis for judicial review.[130] At a substantive level, a human rights-based review runs the danger of empowering the court to substitute their own decision for that of the public body, thereby turning the court into an appellate body. The jurisdictional concerns arise because judicial review is a creature of the common law but appellate jurisdiction is statutory. By developing expanded grounds for judicial review the courts could be accused of 'a judicial usurpation of legislative power.'[131] Loveland tempers these concerns by arguing that the HRA has empowered the courts to ensure compliance with the ECHR. These arguments form part of public lawyers' current debate about the width of judicial review.[132]

Although there may be little practical difference in outcome between the approach advocated by the majority in *Kay*, via Gateway (b) and expanded judicial review, and the minority, via Gateway (a) through a direct defence to possession proceedings, the question before the court is different. In judicial review it is the decision of the public authority to pursue possession which is open to scrutiny, whereas the court would be weighing the proportionality of the claim for possession where an Article 8 defence is directly in issue. The House of Lords has considered this distinction in a number of cases in other areas,

[126] *Connors* (n 6) [92].

[127] *McCann* (n 8) [53].

[128] See also the comments of Collins J in *Defence Estates v JL* [2009] EWHC 1049 (Admin) [55]–[56].

[129] *Doherty* (n 19) [68]. His Lordship's view is supported by Lord Mance [140].

[130] I Loveland, 'A Tale of Two Trespassers: Reconsidering the Impact of the Human Rights Act on Rights of Residence of Rented Housing: Part II' [2009] *EHRLR* 495, 499.

[131] Ibid 500.

[132] T Hickman, 'The Substance and Structure of Proportionality' [2008] *PL* 694 and T Poole, 'The Reformation of English Administrative Law' [2009] *CLJ* 142.

most directly in *Huang v Secretary of State for the Home Department*.[133] The view that appears to be emerging favours the court conducting a distinct human rights proportionality assessment of the public authority's decision upon the individual concerned, rather than a review of that decision making process.[134] Nevertheless, the court is not the primary adjudicator conducting a full merits review and thus should give 'appropriate weight to the judgment of a person with responsibility for a given subject matter and access to special sources of knowledge and advice.'[135]

Human rights and domestic jurisprudence

In addition to this open question on the nature of judicial review, the enactment of the HRA has opened vibrant debates upon some of the most fundamental aspects of our domestic constitutional order. Property law is not immune from these debates, although it has rarely been at the centre of study for public law experts.

There are two levels where human rights may impact upon domestic property law as the two levels of the clash demonstrate. First, there are the relations between the State and Strasbourg concerning whether domestic law is EHCR compliant. The right of an individual who has exhausted domestic rights of action to pursue their complaint against the State before the Strasbourg Court demonstrates these 'Convention rights'. In such disputes the margin of appreciation and proportionality are the governing concepts. Secondly, there are the relations between public authorities and the individual where the individual, relying upon the HRA, may challenge repossession as an act which fails to comply with ECHR. Here, it is not the margin of appreciation which is directly applicable but rather judicial deference to Parliament.

There is a fierce debate between our leading constitutional experts on the proper role and width of judicial deference.[136] At the domestic level, it is the width of judicial deference that influences the balance between Parliament and the courts in assessing the ECHR compatibility of the law in implementing policy. Judicial deference is founded upon separation of powers, in which the courts play a subordinate role to Parliament. However, presenting the relationship as a simple hierarchy is misleading in the light of the new role of

[133] [2007] UKHL 11, [2007] 2 AC 167. See also *R (Daly) v Secretary of State for the Home Department* [2001] UKHL 26, [2001] 2 AC 532; *R (Begum) v Denbigh High School Governors* [2006] UKHL 15, [2007] 1 AC 100; and *Belfast City Council v Miss Behavin' Ltd* [2007] UKHL 19, [2007] 1 WLR 1420.

[134] See M Amos, 'Separating Human Rights Adjudication from Judicial Review' [2007] *EHRLR* 679.

[135] *Huang v Secretary of State for the Home Department* [2007] UKHL 11, [2007] 2 AC 167 [16].

[136] See for example J Jowell, 'Judicial Deference' [2003] *PL* 601; T R S Allan, 'Human Rights and Judicial Review: A Critique of Due Deference' [2006] *CLJ* 671; A King, 'Institutional Approaches to Judicial Restraint' (2008) 28 *OJLS* 409 and A Kavanagh, 'Defending Deference in Public Law and Constitutional Theory' [2010] *LQR* 222.

the courts under the HRA to test the compatibility of the law they are required to apply.[137]

In assessing the proper extent of judicial deference, context is everything. *Qazi* demonstrates an extreme degree of deference in which proprietary rights to possession are not to be questioned at all – they were in fact non-justiciable![138] In *Kay* the House of Lords has shown, in both the views of the majority and minority,[139] that in relation to the regulation of housing they will show exceptional deference to the policy choices of Parliament. This is not surprising given both the degree of Parliamentary scrutiny of housing policy and the public funding underpinning that policy.[140] Similar substantial deference is to be expected in relation to proprietary rules governing possession where certainty and due balancing of the rights of third parties is necessary.[141] However, it should not mean that the ECHR compatibility of proprietary rules should be non-justiciable or even that substantial deference should be automatic. Judicial deference should be assessed on a case-by-case (or rule-by-rule) basis. The challenge is the degree of judicial deference that should pertain in respect of compatibility to Article 8 of substantive proprietary rules to possession of the home and, more significantly, the process by which such rules are asserted.

In this context, should any distinction be drawn between statutory and common law proprietary rules governing possession? Unfortunately, the HRA does not pay adequate regard to this question with section 3 and the defences under section 6(2) referring only to the interpretation of and reliance upon legislation. The question is particularly pertinent to the compatibility of proprietary rules which are derived from a patchwork of statutory and common law rules and equitable principles. Howell has pointed out that to restrict ECHR scrutiny to statutory proprietary rules would 'lead to arbitrary distinctions' given that 'whether a particular area of property law is governed by legislation is largely a matter of chance.'[142] For instance, the rights to possession in the cases under review rested upon common law rules, albeit in an area where statute has made substantial incursions. The House of Lords was prepared to extend its scrutiny to the common law; at least where the common law continues to operates alongside statute within a particularly policy scheme. The answer given in *Doherty*, so far as the HRA section 6(2) defences are concerned, is that there is no distinction between rules of common law and statute.[143] The

[137] See for instance the explanation of this role by Lord Nicholls in *Wilson v First County Trust Ltd (No 2)* [2003] UKHL 40, [2004] 1 AC 816 [61].

[138] I Loveland, 'The Impact of the Human Rights Act on Security of Tenure in Public Housing' [2004] *PL* 594.

[139] See *Kay* (n 7) for example Baroness Hale [185] and Lord Bingham [33].

[140] E Laurie notes similar substantial deference in determining rights to social security. See E Laurie, 'Judicial Responses to Bright Line Rules in Social Security: In Search of Principle' (2009) 72 *MLR* 384.

[141] J Howell, 'The Human Rights Act 1998: Land, Private Citizens, and the Common Law' (2007) 123 *LQR* 618.

[142] Ibid 628.

[143] *Doherty* (n 19) [38], [48] (Lord Hope); [67] (Lord Scott); [100]–[105] (Lord Walker).

fact that a common law rule continues to exist is to be taken to be as much a considered decision of Parliament as any legislation they may have enacted. However, where the common law operates in isolation, as in *Monk,* the question is still open. It could be argued that here the courts need display only minimal deference, and indeed Baroness Hale in *Kay* suggested that the courts will be less deferential, where Parliament may not have considered the rule or made its own assessment of compatibility.[144] The same point may be made of legislation that pre-dates the HRA. In relation to common law rules that have not been subject to Parliamentary scrutiny, the issue is as much one of precedent as deference. However, here too the House of Lords has shown a deference to their own decisions and to the prospective consideration of Parliament (or future deference) where the certainty of proprietary relations is under the spotlight.[145]

Conclusion

It is ironic that the HRA was heralded as bringing human rights home,[146] for indeed Article 8 has brought summary rights to possession of the home to the fore in the current clash between the House of Lords and the Strasbourg Court.

The wide meaning attributed to the home under Article 8 has pushed the issue beyond proprietary rights. Given the substantial interference that repossession presents, Article 8 dictates that a measure of respect for the home should be afforded to occupiers even though their legal rights to occupy have ceased. That measure turns primarily upon the nature of procedural safeguards that provide an adequate opportunity for the proportionality of the repossession to be balanced against the respect due to the occupier's home.

Where repossession is sought by a public authority, the House of Lords believes that judicial review provides the answer, although uncertainty still pervades the width of that review. The Strasbourg Court is yet to be convinced. What is certain is that judicial review will not provide the answer if the HRA applies the ECHR horizontally between private parties. Here the width of a State's margin of appreciation will be crucial to the survival of summary rights to possession of the home. If the margin remains narrow with respect to procedural safeguards, the court will need to be clothed with adequate discretion, possibly circumscribed by appropriate criteria, to show respect for the home.[147]

The clash between the House of Lords and Strasbourg Court demonstrates Allen's forecast of a fresh approach to the balancing of property values.

[144] *Kay* (n 17) [192], but see Lord Mance in *Doherty* (n 19) [129].

[145] For example *Rhone v Stephens* [1994] 2 AC 310 (HL).

[146] Secretary of State for the Home Department, 'Rights Brought Home' (Cm 3782, 1997).

[147] The Trusts of Land and Appointment of Trustees Act 1996 s 15 criteria provide a possible example.

However, the effect of this fresh approach should not be overstated. The wide margin of appreciation afforded to States in socio-economic matters and the court's deference to the legislature demonstrates that it is only in exceptional circumstances that existing property rules, or their application to an occupier's circumstances, will be incompatible. Any such 'new form of proprietary protection' is likely to spring from the entwined relationship between procedural safeguards and their impact upon substantive entitlement.

Postscript – peace in our time?

A resolution to the clash between the Strasbourg Court and our highest court has been achieved by the decisions in *Kay v UK*,[148] decided in September 2010, and *Manchester CC v Pinnock*,[149] handed down shortly thereafter in November 2010.

The decision in *Kay v UK* comes as no surprise. The Strasbourg Court once again repeated its message that repossession proceedings, which afforded no opportunity to assess before an independent tribunal the proportionality of the impact of a public authority's legal right to possession upon the targeted occupier's home, is a violation of the respect due to that home under Article 8. The possibility of judicial review of the public authority's decision to repossess on conventional *Wednesbury* grounds under the *Kay* majority's Gateway (b) was an inadequate process. The Strasbourg Court did hold out an olive branch by hinting that the expansion of conventional judicial review grounds mooted in *Doherty* might fit the bill.[150] However, at the same time it also repeated its endorsement of the *Kay* minority view that it had made in *McCann*. The Court made clear that it was for the domestic authorities to develop adequate procedural safeguards in the light of domestic conditions. A nine member Supreme Court has done so in *Pinnock*. Thankfully, at last their Lordships have spoken with one voice through Lord Neuberger.[151]

Pinnock concerns the Convention compatibility of the demoted tenancy repossession process found in Chapter 1A of Part V of the Housing Act 1996.[152] By some expansive use of its powers of statutory interpretation under section 3 of the HRA, the Supreme Court found this procedure compliant and the repossession of Mr Pinnock's demoted tenancy proportionate in the light of his

[148] *Kay v UK* (App No 37341/06).

[149] *Manchester CC v Pinnock* [2010] UKSC 45.

[150] *Kay* (n 148) [73].

[151] In contrast to *Qazi, Kay* and *Doherty,* where multiple opinions had resulted in so much confusion.

[152] Demoted tenancies are designed to address anti-social behaviour by removing secured tenancy status for one year and instituting a two stage repossession process, the first being a review by the registered provider of their decision to seek repossession, and the second being the repossession proceedings before the court in which judicial discretion is statutorily proscribed.

particular circumstances.[153] But of wider interest is their Lordships' opinion on the fundamental nature of adequate procedural safeguards in home repossession proceedings following *Kay v UK*.

Lord Neuberger acknowledges the 'unambiguous and consistent approach'[154] from Strasbourg that an Article 8 compliant repossession process must afford an opportunity for a review of the proportionality of the application of proprietary rules governing repossession on the individual personal circumstances of the occupier. Indeed, his Lordship believes that the Supreme Court would have taken into account this message even before it had been repeated in *Kay v UK*.[155] He excuses the House of Lords' deafness in *Doherty* to the difficulty of five Lords overruling the panel of seven in *Kay*.[156] Lord Neuberger refers to the court's obligation under section 2 of the HRA to 'take account' of Strasbourg jurisprudence where there is a clear and consistent line of decisions whose effect and reasoning does not misunderstand some aspect of domestic conditions, law or procedure.[157] Despite Lord Scott's reservations in *Doherty*, Lord Neuberger acknowledges that the Strasbourg Court is well versed in the domestic law governing repossession and thus there is no excuse for not falling into line with their decisions.

The mild surprise in *Pinnock* comes in the choice of a compliant process. Lord Neuberger sidelines the expanded *Doherty* Gateway (b) route in favour of the direct proportionality review advocated by the *Kay* minority. An occupier, as a possible victim within section 7 of the HRA, can thus bring a direct defence to possession proceedings by alleging that a public authority, in deciding to bring and pursue possession proceedings, has acted in breach of its obligation to act in a manner compliant with human rights under section 6 of the HRA. The success of that defence will depend upon weighing the proportionality of the public authority's legal right to possession upon the infringement of the respect due to the occupier's home under Article 8, which inevitably calls for a consideration of the effect of repossession upon the personal circumstances of the occupier. Thus not only can the law itself be challenged (the old Gateway (a)) but also its consequences upon the particular occupier. This assessment may necessitate the resolution of disputed facts for which judicial review is ill suited. This change of tack is to be welcomed as the cleaner procedural approach and provides a posthumous vindication of Lord Bingham's judgment in *Kay*.

Where does this leave judicial review under the old Gateway (b)? An occupier may of course still choose the judicial review route to challenge a public

[153] Mr Pinnock's legal advisers believe that the Supreme Court has misapplied the proportionality test and are considering an appeal to the Strasbourg Court see: J Stark, 'Housing Team Legal Bulletin: Issue 25 November 2010' <http://www.gcnchambers.co.uk/gcn/content/download/2074/13811/file/Housing%20Team%20Legal%20Bulletin-%20Nov%202010.pdf> accessed 21 November 2010.

[154] *Pinnock* (n 149) [46].

[155] Ibid [49].

[156] Ibid [47].

[157] Ibid [48].

authority's decision to repossess, but Strasbourg has made clear in *Kay v UK* that traditional review based upon *Wednesbury* unreasonableness will not do as a human rights compatible process. It has been noted, when considering judicial review in this chapter, that the *Wednesbury* standard is itself under review and that in other areas the courts have acknowledged that the scrutiny of a public authority's decision based upon human rights grounds requires a distinct approach which assesses the proportionality of the decision on the individual affected, rather than the decision making process itself.[158] These developments are not explored in *Pinnock* and merit only cursory reference.[159]

Both Strasbourg and the Supreme Court believe that a successful Article 8 challenge to the exercise of established possession rights is likely to be rare. Strasbourg and the minority in *Kay* had used the word 'exceptional'. The Supreme Court finds this guide 'unsafe and unhelpful.'[160] Instead they acknowledge the deference to be afforded to established property rules and the decisions of a public authority in the management of its housing stock which together will present a very strong case in favour of proportionality.[161]

> Therefore, in virtually every case where a residential occupier has no contractual or statutory protection and the local authority is entitled to possession as a matter of domestic law, there will be a very strong case for saying that the order for possession would be proportionate. However there may be factors which would tell the other way.[162]

What balancing factors are being referred to is left tantalising vague. As Lord Bingham before him, Lord Neuberger suggests they can be left to 'the good sense and experience'[163] of county court judges. In the meantime there is an acknowledgement that occupiers who are 'vulnerable as a result of mental illness, physical or learning disability, poor health or frailty' are likely to weigh more heavily in the proportionality balance.[164]

The fundamental conflict between the Strasbourg Court and our highest court may have been resolved but there is still much to be worked out. In no man's land remains the question on every property lawyers mind – does Article 8 with all its implications apply to possession proceedings between private parties? The Supreme Court expressly remains silent.[165] The fact that the Court alluded to a possible need to balance Conventions rights under Article 1 Protocol 1 and Article 8 and noted that Strasbourg did not mention horizontal application in considering inadmissibility in *Belchikova v Russia*,[166] (their Lordships could

[158] For a full discussion of these developments see T Hickman, *Public Law after the Human Rights Act* (Hart Publishing, Oxford 2010) particularly chs 4–9.

[159] *Pinnock* (n 149) [71]–[74].

[160] Ibid [51].

[161] Ibid [51]–[54].

[162] Ibid [54].

[163] Ibid [57].

[164] Ibid [64].

[165] Ibid [50].

[166] (App No 2408/06).

also have added *Zehentner*) suggests that the possibility has been ruled in rather than out. Whilst this uncertainty remains, whether a registered provider qualifies as a public authority remains a crucial consideration.

A further fundamental question, upon which further developments are to be expected, is the meaning of home. For instance, Lord Neuberger hints that it may be open to argument that a person's residence is their home where they have been in occupation only for a short time.[167]

The immediate concerns of public authority landlords will be first, the Article 8 compatibility of other statutory schemes and proprietary rules and secondly, the changes that they will need to make to their repossession practices to satisfy the proportionality balance even where those rules are compatible. On the first question, Lord Neuberger pointed out that the whole proceedings must be considered.[168] Here it must be borne in mind that the assessment must be made by an independent tribunal and Article 6 will be relevant. Furthermore, following *Paulic*, enforcement proceedings, in which proportionality is measured by the court's powers to suspend or delay the execution of a possession order it has already made, are inadequate. The latter point seems to have been overlooked in *Pinnock*,[169] with Lord Neuberger referring to the need to revisit section 89 of the Housing Act 1980, which limits the period for which a possession order can be postponed. His Lordship does, however, point out the need to review the compatibility of procedural provisions more generally.[170] Obvious compatibility targets are the rule in *Hammersmith and Fulham LBC v Monk* and Ground 8. The conjoined appeals in *Salford CC v Mullen* will consider the compatibility of the introductory tenancy and homeless regimes. Lord Neuberger also indicated that these appeals would be better suited to provide further general guidance.[171] On the second question, although it is for the occupier to plead a human rights defence, it will be prudent for a public authority to be forewarned of personal circumstances which might affect the compatibility of their decision to seek possession.[172]

All in all, *Pinnock* may have resolved the clash with Strasbourg but in so doing it opens the door on a wholesale reassessment of the compatibility of repossession proceedings affecting the home. As such, it is a landmark decision.

[167] *Pinnock* (n 149) [61].
[168] Ibid [45].
[169] Ibid [62]–[63].
[170] His Lordship refers to CPR 55 which governs possession actions.
[171] *Pinnock* (n 149) [59].
[172] N Madge makes a suggestion on this score, see: N Madge, 'Is the game of ping pong over' <http://nicmadge.co.uk/Art_8_-_Ping_Pong.php> accessed 21 November 2010.

II

Doctrinal Development of Property Rights

6

The Rise and Fall of the Implied Periodic Tenancy

Jill Morgan*

Introduction

Before the sixteenth century, only fixed-term leases were legally recognised and a person who was let into possession of land by the freeholder without having been granted a term certain was regarded as a tenant at will. Tenancies at will were unsatisfactory from the viewpoints of both landlords and tenants, and the implied periodic tenancy gradually emerged as a means of protecting those who had gone into possession of land and paid rent which the landlord had received and accepted. Over the past few decades, however, the development of statutory security of tenure has meant that the courts are often less willing to imply periodic tenancies. At the same time, the licence has emerged as an alternative method of allowing for the use of land. The result has been a mishmash of decisions in which the courts have found licences, tenancies at will, implied periodic tenancies, and equitable tenancies. The aim of this chapter is to consider the nature of tenancy at will and to trace the development of the implied periodic tenancy and the licence. The latter part of the chapter will focus on recent cases in which the courts have been required to decide upon the nature of transitional arrangements (referred to in this chapter as 'inchoate agreements') regarding the occupation of commercial premises which potentially fall under the umbrella of the Landlord and Tenant Act 1954, Part II.

* Reader in Property Law, Swansea University.

The tenancy at will

A tenancy at will arises if, with the consent of the owner, a person enjoys occupation of land for an indefinite period on the basis that either party is free to terminate the agreement at any time. It may be expressly created or arise by implication at common law. It has been described as the lowest estate known to the law[1] but because it is necessarily of uncertain duration, a tenancy at will does not fall within the statutory definition of a term of years absolute[2] and the tenant does not therefore have a legal estate. This means that the tenant at will cannot assign or sublet his tenancy and it will terminate on a sale of the reversion.[3] If the tenant at will becomes bankrupt, there is nothing to vest in his trustee in bankruptcy.[4] Indeed, in *Irish Shell and BP Ltd v John Costello Ltd*, McCarthy J suggested that a tenancy at will is,

> … somewhat of a misnomer if one gives to the cognate word 'tenant' the ordinary meaning rather than its limited source meaning of 'holder'. In truth a tenant at will is a person with a licence and no more than a licence to occupy.[5]

Certainly, there are commonalities between the tenant at will and the licensee, the latter merely making 'an action lawful without which it had been unlawful' but being something which 'passeth no interest, nor alters or transfers property in any thing'.[6] However, there are significant differences too. Describing the tenancy at will as occupying 'an obscurely defined no-man's land between the periodic tenancy and the mere licence',[7] Gray and Gray point out that the tenant at will has exclusive possession of the land[8] and, unlike the licensee, 'who enjoys no positive (as distinct from defensive) rights',[9] he can 'keep out trespassers'.[10] Megarry and Wade propose that the tenancy at will is probably best analysed as 'a form of tenure but one that confers no estate'. They explain that:

> Although an estate cannot exist without tenure, there seems no reason why tenure should not exist without any estate. A may hold land of B, but for no fixed period and merely for so long as B may allow. If it is remembered that tenure by itself is a purely personal relationship when unconnected with any estate or interest which can exist as a right in rem, this may explain why a tenancy at will cannot survive death or

[1] *Doe d Gray v Stanion* (1836) 1 M & W 700.

[2] Law of Property Act 1925 s 205(1)(ix).

[3] *Doe d Davies v Thomas* (1851) 6 Ex 854, 857; 155 ER 792, 794.

[4] *Re Keith G Collins Ltd and Director, Veteran's Land Act* (1987) 35 DLR (4th) 96, 101.

[5] [1984] IR 511 (Irish SC) 523. See too *Wheeler v Mercer* [1957] AC 416 (HL) 427 in which Viscount Simonds identified a tenancy at will as comprising a personal relationship between landlord and tenant.

[6] *Thomas v Sorrell* (1673) Vaugh 330, 351; 124 ER 1098, 1110.

[7] K J Gray and S F Gray, *Elements of Land Law* (4th edn OUP, Oxford 2005) [7–273].

[8] See *Lynes v Snaith* [1899] 1 QB 486 (QB) 488.

[9] *Gray and Gray* (n 7) [7.275].

[10] *Heslop v Burns* [1974] 1 WLR 1241 (CA) 1253.

alienation; and it many also explain why tenancy at will is possible despite the rule which requires every leasehold estate to be for a term certain.[11]

The imprecise nature of a tenancy at will is unlikely to have many practical consequences today and it will often make little difference to the occupier or the owner whether there is a tenancy at will or a licence, yet the nature of the arrangement may be significant where the occupier falls into arrears. Where a rent has been agreed in respect of a tenancy at will, the landlord can use the remedy of distress.[12] No such remedy is available to the licensor.[13]

The emergence of the implied periodic tenancy

The courts' insistence on a tenancy at will where the parties failed to create a term certain resulted in both landlord and tenant having an interest which was 'wholly precarious'[14] and left each party 'too much at the mercy of the other'.[15] The law relating to emblements gave a limited degree of protection to tenants at will who were ejected after sowing a crop by entitling them to enter and harvest what they had sown. At the same time, however, it was that very right to emblements which seriously reduced the value of land in the hands of landlords: while it lasted, they could neither let the land nor use it themselves.[16] Clearly a more closely defined interest was required which would place tenants in a more secure position and enable landlords to let the land at the end of the term.

Over time the courts began to 'seize upon every opportunity within their power to prevent a strict tenancy at will from arising'[17] and to 'lay hold upon any circumstances in the case'[18] which could be construed as indicating an intention of the parties that the tenancy should continue 'till a reasonable notice from either landlord or tenant that it was his election to determine it'.[19] What was meant by a reasonable notice was not at first ascertained but in due course it was accepted that half a year's notice would be required to end a yearly tenancy.[20] However, because periodic tenancies are effectively 'leases for an uncertain

[11] C Harpum, S Bridge and M Dixon, *Megarry and Wade, The Law of Real Property* (7th edn Sweet & Maxwell, London 2008) [17–078].

[12] *Anderson v Midland Railway Co* (1861) 3 El & El 614, 121 ER 573.

[13] *Interoven Stove Co Ltd v Hibberd & Painter & Shepherd* [1936] 1 All ER 263 (KB). In the absence of an express agreement for rent, the landlord may pursue a claim for damages for the tenant at will's use and occupation which will usually correspond to the open market rental value of the premises: *Lewisham LBC v Masterson* (2000) 80 P & CR 117 (CA) 122–24.

[14] A W B Simpson, *An Introduction to the History of the Land Law* (OUP, Oxford 1961) 235.

[15] J W Smith, *The Law of Landlord and Tenant: Being a Course of Lectures Delivered at the Law Institution* (William Maxwell, London 1855) 20.

[16] A L Goodhart and H G Goodhart (eds), *W S Holdsworth, A History of English Law: Vol VII* (Sweet & Maxwell, London) 243–44.

[17] *Smith* (n 15) 21.

[18] Ibid 21.

[19] Ibid.

[20] *Doe on the demise of John Shore v Porter* (1789) 3 Term Rep 13, 16–17, 100 ER 429, 432.

duration, determinable by notice'[21] and it was 'entirely optional' for each party whether and when notice should be given, 'the tenancy continued for some time to be and to be called a tenancy at will', differing from other tenancies at will in that 'reasonable notice of the determination of the will' was required to bring it to an end.[22] The advent of periodic tenancies proved 'judicially controversial' and the dispute as to their nature continued for two centuries.[23]

Holdsworth links the courts' gradual acceptance of periodic tenancies with the state's policy of encouraging agriculture 'by keeping tenants on the land'.[24] Also significant was the enactment of the Statute of Frauds in 1677. As explained by Jordan CJ in *Dockrill v Cavanagh*, (a decision of the Full Court of the New South Wales Supreme Court in which the legal history of the implied periodic tenancy was outlined) no formalities were required for the making of a lease at common law. It could be granted therefore simply by word of mouth.[25] Yet the statute provided that unless a lease was put in writing and signed by the parties creating it, it should take effect 'at will only' and would not have 'any other or greater force or effect' either at law or in equity.[26] The implied periodic tenancy developed therefore as a way not only of obviating the inconveniences associated with the tenancy at will but also of circumventing the legislative difficulty posed by the Statute of Frauds; the courts finding either implied yearly tenancies where tenants who had gone into possession paid rent which was referable to a year, or other periodic tenancies where the rent was weekly, monthly etc. In such circumstances, the tenant became entitled and subject to all the provisions of the agreement which were applicable to a tenancy from year to year,[27] there being no difference in this respect between a person who held over and one who entered into possession and paid rent on the basis of an executory agreement for a lease.[28] If it appeared that the parties intended only to create a tenancy at will, then their intention would prevail.[29] By this 'process of judicial legislation, considerable encroachments ... [were] made upon the provisions of the Statute of Frauds'.[30]

The turning point appears to have been *Leighton v Theed*,[31] in which Holt CJ adopted the approach (first advanced in the early sixteenth century) that a lease for one year and then from year-to-year as the parties pleased, at a fixed rent, was a lease for one-year followed by one-year successive terms.[32] Simpson points

[21] *Simpson* (n 14) 235.
[22] *Smith* (n 15) 21.
[23] *Simpson* (n 14) 235–37.
[24] *Goodhart and Goodhart* (n 16) 243–44.
[25] (1944) 45 SRNSW 78 (NSW SC).
[26] An exception was made for leases not exceeding a term of three years at a rack rent.
[27] *Coatsworth v Johnson* (1886) 54 LT 520.
[28] *Moore v Dimond* (1929) 43 CLR 105 (Aus HC) 119–23.
[29] *Richardson v Langridge* (1811) Taunt 128; 128 ER 277.
[30] (1944) 45 SRNSW 78 (NSW SC) 81.
[31] (1702) 1 Ld Raymond 707, 91 ER 359.
[32] See W Morrison (ed), *Blackstone's Commentaries on the Law of England* (vol 2, Routledge-Cavendish, London 2001) 145–47, quoted by Lord Bridge in *Hammersmith and Fulham LBC v Monk* [1992] 1 AC 478 (HL) 483–84. Originally, a tenant from year to year was viewed as a tenant at will to whom half a year's notice to quit possession must be given before an ejectment would lie to turn him out: *Parker d Walker v Constable* (1769) 3 Wils 25, 95 ER 913.

out that this paved the way for 'a new and important development'.[33] Now, where there was no express arrangement for a periodic tenancy, 'the courts were willing to imply one instead of a mere tenancy at will, so long as this could be justified, as it could be if rent had been paid and accepted by the year'.[34] Holdsworth notes that in the latter part of the eighteenth century the courts' predilection for implied tenancies from year to year had become so pronounced that Lord Mansfield had made the (admittedly exaggerated) observation that 'in the country, leases at will ... being found extremely inconvenient exist only notionally; and were succeeded by another species of contract which was less inconvenient'.[35] A few years later, it was said in *Richardson v Langridge*:

> Surely the distinction has been a thousand times taken, a mere general letting is a tenancy at will: if the lessor accepts yearly rent or rent accepted by any aliquot part of a year, the courts have said that it is evidence of taking for a year ... the courts have a great inclination to take any tenancy a holding from year to year if they can find any foundation for it.[36]

As indicated already, the presumption that, in the absence of express words, a periodic tenancy was impliedly created by entry into possession and the payment and acceptance of a periodic sum in the nature of rent was subject to 'the real intention of both parties'[37] and rebuttable therefore by evidence of those intentions.[38] It continued nonetheless well into the twentieth century. It was the advent of statutory protection for tenants, most notably security of tenure, which led to greater caution on the part of the courts and a weakening of the presumption in favour of implied periodic tenancies.

The impact of statutory protection

The first statutory rent controls directed specifically at the private sector were introduced by the Increase of Rent and Mortgage Interest (War Restrictions) Act 1915. So as to prevent the eviction of tenants who tried enforce their rights – eg by complaining that their rents were above the legal limit – it also provided security of tenure, thereby setting out a basic framework for the regulation of the private rented sector – rent control and security of tenure – which continued until 1988.[39] As Scarman LJ put it in *Horford Investments Ltd v Lambert*:

[33] *Simpson* (n 14) 237.

[34] Ibid.

[35] *Timmins v Rowlinson* (1765) 3 Burr 1603, 1609; 97 ER 1003, 1007.

[36] (1811) 4 Taunt 128, 132; 128 ER 277, 279.

[37] *Doe d Cheny v Batten* (1775) Cowp 243, 245; 98 ER 1066, 1068.

[38] *Doe d Bastow v Cox* (1847) 11 QB 422; 116 ER 421, where the defendant had agreed to become tenant of the demised premises at the lessor's 'will and pleasure'.

[39] Besides security of tenure, important additional protection is afforded to tenants by a number of statutes. For example, the Landlord and Tenant Act 1985 s 11 imposes repairing obligations on landlords who have granted leases for less than seven years of dwelling-houses.

> The policy of the Rent Acts was and is to protect the tenant in his home, whether the threat be to exhort a premium for the grant or renewal of his tenancy, to increase his rent, or to evict him ... The Rent Acts have throughout their history constituted an interference with contract and property rights for a specific purpose – the redress of the balance of advantage enjoyed in a world of housing shortage by the landlord over those who have to rent their homes.[40]

The protection of business tenants lagged behind and it was not until the Landlord and Tenant Act 1927 that Parliament made any serious attempt to address the problem of their exploitation. Even then, in the event that the landlord did not renew an existing business tenancy, the protection of a tenant's interest was to be achieved by the payment of compensation for authorised improvements and for any goodwill which the tenant lost by having to give up possession. Statutory security of tenure for business tenants did not materialise until the Landlord and Tenant Act 1954.[41] Where there is a tenancy to which Part II of the 1954 Act applies, the tenant has a prima facie right to the grant of a new tenancy on the expiration of the present one. In general, the Act applies to 'any tenancy where the property comprised in the tenancy is, or includes, premises which are occupied by the tenant and are so occupied for the purposes of a business carried on by him or for those and other purposes'.[42] A 'tenancy' for these purposes includes a periodic tenancy or one for a fixed term, a sub-tenancy,[43] an equitable tenancy, and a tenancy by estoppel.[44] The Act itself expressly excludes certain types of tenancy (including a tenancy granted for a term certain not exceeding six months),[45] and the precondition of a tenancy means that licences are excluded. Two reasons may be given for the courts' exclusion of tenancies at will. First, according to Lord Morton in *Wheeler v Mercer*,[46] it would be 'surprising if the legislature had intended to bring within the scope of the Act a relationship so personal and fleeting as a tenancy at will'.[47] Secondly, the Act is 'framed to regulate tenancies that can be brought to an end by notice to quit or by effluxion of time'.[48]

Not surprisingly, perhaps, the advent of statutory protection for both residential and business tenants, most particularly security of tenure, made the courts less inclined to find implied periodic tenancies in situations where previously they had been disposed to do so. Whilst before, where a tenancy came to an end, and the parties had given and received rent without expressly

[40] [1976] Ch 39 (CA) 52.

[41] M Haley, 'The Statutory Regulation of Business Premises: Private Property, Public Interest and Political Compromise' (1999) 19 *LS* 207.

[42] Landlord and Tenant Act 1954 s 23.

[43] *D'Silva v Lister House Developments Ltd* [1971] Ch 17 (Ch).

[44] *Bell v General Accident Fire and Life Assurance Corporation Ltd* [1998] 17 EG 144 (CA).

[45] Landlord and Tenant Act 1954 s 43(3).

[46] [1957] AC 416 (HL).

[47] Ibid 428.

[48] M Haley, 'Business Tenancies: Holding Over, Periodic Tenancies and Tenancies at Will' [2001] *JBL* 91.

agreeing on the creation or the terms of a new tenancy, the court's inference of the existence of a periodic tenancy was 'on the footing that this ... best fills the vacuum which the parties have left'[49] because 'that is what the parties must have intended or be taken to have intended'.[50] However, in a world in which Parliament had legislated to confer extensive protection for tenants, the implications of an implied tenancy at will could be far more serious. At common law, an implied yearly tenancy was terminable by six months' notice to quit. By contrast, the finding of an implied periodic tenancy in respect of residential premises could bring the Rent Acts into play, with the potential of providing security for the tenant and the tenant's family for 'one, two or three lives'.[51] Although in the residential sector landlords used a variety of ploys to avoid granting statutorily protected tenancies[52] and the coverage of the Rent Acts varied according to the rateable value limits at any particular time, the majority of tenancies – be they residential, commercial or agricultural – were subject to statutory protection of one sort or another. As Knox J pointed out in *Cardiothoracic Institute v Shrewdcrest Ltd*,[53] tenancies 'unaffected by statutory prolongation' were 'no longer the norm'.[54] In the words of Scarman LJ in *Heslop v Burns*, the Rent Acts had introduced 'a new dimension' to the law of landlord and tenant in order to deal with 'changed social conditions' and the change in 'the facts of society' demanded 'a more subtle investigation' of the facts of the individual case in determining the intention of the parties.[55] Suggesting that the tenancy at will now served only one legal purpose, ie 'to protect the interests of an occupier during a period of transition',[56] he identified the classic cases in which tenancies at will continue to be implied as those of 'someone who goes into possession prior to a contract of purchase, or ... someone who, with the consent of the landlord, holds over after the expiry of his lease'.[57] In each of these situations:

> ... there is a transitional period during which negotiations are being conducted touching the estate or interest in the land that has to be protected, and the tenancy at will is an apt legal mechanism to protect the occupier during such a period of transition: he is there and can keep out trespassers: he is there with the consent of the landlord and can keep out the landlord as long as that consent is maintained.[58]

The presumption of a periodic tenancy from entry into, or retention of, possession and payment of rent lost its force. Now, the consequences of giving and accepting rent were to be determined by the 'intentions of the parties in all

[49] *Cardiothoracic Institute v Shrewdcrest Ltd* [1986] 1 WLR 368 (CA) 378.
[50] Ibid.
[51] T Honore, *The Quest for Security: Employees, Tenants, Wives* (Stevens, London 1982) 59.
[52] See J Morgan, *Aspects of Housing Law* (Cavendish, London 2007) 261–3.
[53] [1986] 1 WLR 368 (Ch).
[54] Ibid 378.
[55] [1974] 1 WLR 1241 (CA) 1252.
[56] Ibid 1253.
[57] Ibid.
[58] Ibid.

the circumstances'[59] and the existence of statutory protection was a significant factor in evaluating those intentions. The 'high water mark' of such reasoning can be found in *Longrigg, Burrough & Trounson v Smith*, where Ormrod LJ said that, although

> ... the old common law presumption of a tenancy from the payment and acceptance of a sum in the nature of rent dies very hard ... the authorities make it quite clear that in these days of statutory controls over the landlord's right of possession, this presumption is unsound and no longer holds. The question now is a purely open question; it is simply: is it right and proper to infer from all the circumstances of the case, including the payments, that the parties had reached an agreement for a tenancy? I think it does not now go any further than that.[60]

Accordingly, where a property owner allows another into possession of the owner's land in return for rent without the parties coming to an express agreement as to the nature of the transaction, a periodic tenancy will not be presumed if the relevant circumstances indicate that the parties had no intention to create such a tenancy. An important case in this regard is *Javad v Aqil*,[61] where the owner allowed the defendant into possession of business premises pending negotiation of a ten-year lease. The tenant paid £2,500 which was expressed in a receipt signed by the landlord as being 'rent for 3 months in advance'.[62] Almost a year later, a lease had not been granted and the landlord wanted possession. The defendant argued that he had a periodic tenancy protected by the Landlord and Tenant Act 1954, Part II. The Court of Appeal disagreed, holding that the true inference to be drawn from all the circumstances was that the parties did not intend to create such a tenancy and that the defendant was merely in possession as a tenant at will. The court considered it particularly significant that the occupier had been allowed into possession in anticipation of terms being agreed, such agreement in fact never having been concluded.

As Nicholls LJ advised:

> Of course, when one party permits another to enter or remain on his land on payment of a sum of money, and that other has no statutory entitlement to be there, almost inevitably there will be some consensual relationship between them. It may be no more than a licence determinable at any time, or a tenancy at will. But when and so long as the parties are in the throes of negotiating larger terms, caution must be exercised before inferring or imputing to the parties an intention to give to the occupant more than a very limited interest, be it licence or tenancy. Otherwise the court would be in danger of inferring or imputing from conduct, such as the payment of rent and the carrying out of repairs, whose explanation lies in the parties' expectation that they will be able to reach agreement on the larger terms, an intention to grant a lesser interest, such as a periodic tenancy, which the parties never had in contemplation at all.[63]

[59] *Cardiothoracic Institute v Shrewdcrest Ltd* [1986] 1 WLR 368 (CA) 378.
[60] (1979) 251 EG 847 (CA) 849.
[61] [1991] 1 WLR 1007 (CA).
[62] Ibid 1009–10.
[63] Ibid 1013.

The same principles have been applied where a tenant has remained in occupation following the expiry of its lease.[64]

The development of the licence

As indicated earlier, before the emergence of statutory protection for tenants, exclusive possession with the landlord's consent but without more was likely to be construed as a tenancy at will. At this juncture, there was no possibility of such an occupier having a licence, this being the domain of an occupier *without* exclusive possession.[65] However, at the same time as Parliament was legislating to protect tenants – and perhaps as a response to that legislation – the courts were developing the licence to occupy to become 'a possible mode of land-holding ... which had certainly not been developed into anything like its current maturity in the nineteenth century'.[66] Thus the courts came to declare that, even an occupier with exclusive possession would nonetheless be only a licensee 'if the circumstances and conduct of the parties show that all that was intended was that the occupier should be granted a personal privilege, with no interest in the land',[67] or the exclusive possession was referable to a legal relationship other than a tenancy. Examples of the latter included a purchaser allowed into possession before completion. In *Essex Plan Ltd v Broadminster*,[68] this was extended by analogy to include an occupier who had gone into possession as a licensee for a one-year trial period with an option to take a 30-year lease from the commencement of the licence term.[69] In each case, the occupier was regarded as having an immediate equitable interest in the land to which his possession was ancillary. Given that the situation in the *Essex Plan* case involved, as referred to in *Heslop v Burns*, 'a transitional period during which negotiations are being conducted',[70] and that it had already been held in *Francis Jackson Developments v Stemp*[71] that the purchaser/occupier would have a tenancy at will, it is hard to see why the court opted for a licence.

The development and increased use of the licence can be linked to two significant factors relating to the Rent Acts: judicial recognition that a tenant at will is entitled to the protection of the Acts[72] and the inability of the parties to contract out of them. Contracting out is forbidden not only because it would

[64] *Dreamgate Properties Ltd v Arnot* (1998) 76 P & CR 25 (CA).

[65] *Peakin v Peakin* [1895] 2 IR 359; cf *Doe d Tomes v Chamberlaine* (1839) 5 M & W 14, 151 ER 7 and *Lynes v Snaith* [1899] 1 QB 486 (QB) 488.

[66] *Heslop v Burns* [1974] 1 WLR 1241 (CA) 1252.

[67] See *Errington v Errington* [1952] 1 TLR 231 (CA) 235–6.

[68] (1988) 56 P & CR 353 (Ch) 356.

[69] Provision was made for the payment by Essex Plan of a licence fee, rates, taxes and other outgoings.

[70] [1974] 1 WLR 1241 (CA) 1253.

[71] [1943] 2 All ER 601 (CA).

[72] *Francis Jackson Developments v Stemp* [1943] 2 All ER 601 (CA) 603–4.

entail ousting the jurisdiction of the court but it would also mean that, by asking the court to sanction such an agreement, the parties would be giving the courts 'jurisdiction which the legislature has enacted they are not to have'.[73] Moreover, as Lord Templeman explained in *AG Securities v Vaughan*, 'the Acts would be a dead letter'[74] if the parties could contract out of them, given that 'in a state of housing shortage a person seeking residential accommodation may agree to anything to obtain shelter'.[75] The Housing Act 1988 (as amended) expressly provides that any surrender, notice to quit or other document executed, signed or given by the tenant, before or at the time the tenancy is entered into, to bring the tenancy to an end in the future, will be of no effect.[76] Any attempt to contract out after the date of the tenancy will probably be unenforceable by the landlord, the same rules applying to attempts by the parties to oust the jurisdiction of the court as those which apply in relation to the Rent Act 1977. By contrast, the parties to a business tenancy which, by section 38A of the 1954 Act, is for a 'term certain exceeding one year', can agree to exclude the renewal provisions provided that the appropriate procedure is correctly followed. The difference in approach is explained by the propositions that the 1954 Act concerns 'purely commercial relationships' and that 'the degree of protection, and the need to redress inequality, is less than ... with the housing market'.[77] Nonetheless the combination of a prohibition against contracting-out and the acceptance that tenancies at will are caught by the Rent Acts compelled lawyers – and the courts – to look elsewhere to find arrangements which would redress the balance in favour of landlords. The licence seems to have been an obvious solution. The result of such judicial creativity has been a further blurring of the boundaries between the different types of occupation status – a problem which, as we shall see, has become particularly pronounced in relation to certain situations in which the Landlord and Tenant Act 1954 potentially applies.

The Landlord and Tenant Act 1954, Part II

Landlords of commercial properties will be anxious to achieve as few voids as possible – particularly in a difficult economic climate. Keen for its income stream to start – or continue – flowing, a landlord may be tempted to allow a prospective tenant into occupation while the details of a formal lease are being finalised or to allow an existing tenant to hold over after the end of its lease,

[73] *Barton v Fincham* [1921] 2 KB 291 (CA) 299. See also *R v Bloomsbury & Marylebone County Court ex p Blackburne* (1984) 14 HLR 56 (QB), *R v Newcastle upon Tyne County Court ex p Thompson* (1988) 20 HLR 430 (QB), *Appleton v Aspin* [1988] 1 WLR 410 (CA).

[74] [1990] 1 AC 417 (HL) 458.

[75] Ibid 458.

[76] Housing Act 1988 s 5(5).

[77] M Haley, 'Business Tenancies and Interventionism: The Relegation of Policy' (1993) 13 *LS* 225, 225.

perhaps while the parties are negotiating a new one. It can be difficult in such situations – which for the sake of brevity will from now on be referred to as 'inchoate agreements' – to determine whether there is a tenancy to which the Act applies. Generally, speaking, this is not an issue for tenancies which have security of tenure under the Landlord and Tenant Act 1954, Part II. Unless and until brought to an end by one of the methods specified in the Act, the tenancy will automatically continue under section 24. However, where the former tenancy was contracted out of the Act but the tenant is holding over, the situation potentially becomes more problematic, and a landlord who demands and accepts rent may find that it has unwittingly created a new periodic tenancy with 1954 Act protection. Where, however, the tenant is allowed to remain in occupation while the parties are negotiating a new lease, a different inference may be drawn. The possibilities include a tenancy at will, a licence, an implied periodic tenancy and/or an equitable lease – and perhaps even a non-proprietary lease as advocated by the House of Lords in *Bruton v London and Quadrant Housing Trust*.[78] The boundaries of these possibilities are unclear and, it would appear, capable of overlapping.

It may be thought that *Street v Mountford*[79] – the seminal decision on the issue of the lease/licence distinction – might have revived the implied periodic tenancy and reduced the significance of the licence, given Lord Templeman's downplaying of the role of the parties' intentions and his Lordship's emphasis on the importance of exclusive possession. The presence of statutory protection (which formerly would have been regarded by the courts as underpinning the parties' intentions) seemingly loses its significance. However, as Bright argues, although *Street v Mountford* suggests that 'the parties' intentions are relevant only to show an intention to create legal relations and an intention to confer exclusive possession',[80] it overlooks the fact that in many modern cases the courts still seek to give effect to the agreement in the way which the parties intend. Bright observes that establishing the intention of the parties can be problematic, particularly where the agreement is undocumented and the occupier simply moves in and starts paying rent on a regular basis, there having been little or no discussion of other terms. Similar uncertainty can arise where the occupier stays in possession after the tenancy has ended (even though there is no new agreement) paying a periodic rent to the owner. In such cases, the absence of any documentation setting out what the parties have agreed means that the statutory regime which will apply to the arrangement is still crucial in determining the nature of the occupation, especially if 'it is clear from the context that the arrangement is only intended to be a temporary or interim one'.[81] Bright suggests that a doctrinal solution to this inconsistency with *Street*

[78] [2000] 1 AC 406 (HL).

[79] [1985] 1 AC 809 (HL).

[80] S Bright, 'Street v Mountford Revisited' in S Bright (ed), *Landlord and Tenant Law: Past, Present and Future* (Hart Publishing, Oxford 2006) 20.

[81] Ibid 22–3.

v Mountford lies in the requirement that a lease can only exist where there is certainty of term.[82] In most of the 'moving in' cases where the occupier has been held to be only a licensee or a tenant at will, the parties are still trying to finalise the agreement. Although some kind of discussion is likely to have preceded the occupier's entry into possession, the fact that the parties have not yet reached a settled agreement and only intend the present arrangement to be temporary, supports the idea that there is no term certain:

> The owner has not accepted the idea that the occupier can stay for any fixed period; and, it is understood by the parties that if they do not reach an agreement the occupier will have to leave. This cannot be a 'term of years'.[83]

As Stephenson LJ indicated in *Sopwith v Stuchbury*, a periodic tenancy might be implied only if the occupiers had gone into occupation 'as it were awaiting a tenancy ... [if] the terms of that tenancy were fully agreed during the waiting period'.[84]

Bright maintains that the 'staying on' cases are potentially more complex. Here, where the tenant (or an assignee) holds over at the end of the term, he may simply continue what he was doing during the currency of the tenancy and there are 'no new discussions to draw on'.[85] However, staying on while the parties negotiate future arrangements can also be explained on the basis that there is no agreed term – even though, in practice, 'the judicial language used to explain the result is in terms of the parties not intending to create a periodic tenancy, rather than focusing upon the absence of the term'.[86]

Given that 'undocumented occupation often leads to unwanted rights',[87] expressing as a licence the basis of occupation under an inchoate agreement may assist in avoiding a successful claim that the occupier is entitled to statutory protection. It was pointed out in *Dresden Estates Ltd v Collinson*,[88] that 'the attributes of residential premises and business premises are often quite different' and 'the indicia, which may make it more apparent in the case of a residential occupier that he is indeed a tenant, may be less applicable or be less likely to have that effect in the case of some business tenancies'.[89] Even so, the multiplicity of uses to which commercial premises may be put mean that the opportunities for creating a genuine licence (where, for example, the occupier has no exclusive possession) appear greater in the commercial context than in the residential sector. The attractions of a licence lie in its flexibility: it can be of fixed duration or periodic, provision can be made for contractual payment and,

[82] *Lace v Chantler* [1944] KB 368 (CA); *Prudential Assurance Co Ltd v London Residuary Body* [1992] 2 AC 386 (HL).
[83] *Bright* (n 80) 24–25.
[84] (1983) 17 HLR 50 (CA), 73.
[85] *Bright* (n 80) 25.
[86] Ibid 27.
[87] R Webber, 'The Guest Who Just Won't Leave' (2009) 227 *PLJ* 2.
[88] (1987) 55 P & CR 47 (CA).
[89] Ibid 52.

as we have seen, it is not protected by the Landlord and Tenant Act 1954. As such, it will usually be preferable to a tenancy at will which (although similarly unprotected) is, by definition, of indefinite duration. Murdoch warns that 'the risk of the licence approach is that, under the rule in *Street v Mountford*, the courts may treat the occupation as a lease and the occupier will then have a (protected) tenancy'[90] but it seems more likely that what the courts choose to regard as the intentions of parties may prevail. In *Cameron Ltd v Rolls Royce plc*,[91] Rolls-Royce held over on expiry of two contracted-out subleases under which it occupied certain premises. It subsequently entered into agreements for two new contracted-out subleases, the agreements stating that until such time as the court's approval of the contracting out and the head landlord's consent were obtained, Rolls-Royce would be licensee of the premises on the same terms as the expired leases. The licences were drafted in such a way that, if either the court did not sanction the contracting-out or the landlord failed to give consent, they could operate effectively and independently for the full period of the intended subleases. The court orders were obtained and the landlord gave its consent but Rolls-Royce refused to enter into the agreed leases, arguing that its so-called licences were, in reality, tenancies protected by the 1954 Act.

It was held that the parties could not have intended the grant of a tenancy to which the Act applied. The ostensible purpose of the agreements was to bring about a situation in which Rolls Royce occupied the premises with the benefit of a tenancy but without the protection of the 1954 Act. Moreover, the agreements were expressly stated to be licences. Whilst labels and apparent intentions were not determinative, and what mattered was the interest which the parties had actually created; the *Street v Mountford* criteria were only a starting point. One situation which was clearly analogous to the instant case – in which exclusive possession was consistent only with a licence – was where a person was in occupation of land pending its sale.[92]

The court also felt that a distinction should be drawn between cases where the licence (or purported licence) and some other transaction were entirely independent (making the licence a stand-alone transaction), and those where the occupation under the licence (and the licence itself) was part of a bigger picture. It concluded that in the instant case the licences were not stand-alone arrangements but part of an overall scheme under which Rolls Royce would effectively move from one contracted-out lease to another. Rolls Royce was therefore a mere licensee and was consequently obliged under its agreement to take the contracted-out leases. As Murdoch observes, this distinction is questionable. She explains that although the overall scheme in the present case was clear, it was equally apparent that the licences were drafted so that they could, if necessary, operate effectively and independently for the full period of

[90] S Murdoch, 'Not as Straightforward as It May Seem' (2008) 808 *EG* 155, 155.
[91] [2007] EWHC 546 (Ch), [2008] L & TR 22.
[92] *Essex Plan Ltd v Broadminster* (1988) 56 P & CR 353 (Ch).

the intended leases. In such an event, they were meant to replicate those intended leases. They contained the same terms as the lease and the landlord had even purported to give itself the remedy of distress. She concludes that, in reality:

> … these arrangements had the word 'tenancy' written all over them. What the parties (possibly just the landlord) really sought to avoid was not a tenancy but statutory protection, by dressing up a tenancy as a licence.[93]

The court described the stance of Rolls Royce as 'unattractive and even dishonourable'[94] and Murdoch speculates as to whether the outcome would have been the same if the merits were not so obviously with the landlord. This brings us back to the unsatisfactory nature of seeking to determine the status of the agreement on the basis of the parties' intentions. Murdoch's observation that it was 'possibly just the landlord' who sought to avoid statutory protection raises the point that it may not truly be the common or shared intention of 'the parties' which the court claims to have identified. There is a related issue of whether both parties are actually in a position to share any intention. As mentioned already, the 1954 Act is predicated on the assumption that the parties are of equal bargaining strength and will have sufficient business acumen and access to professional advice to have a genuine understanding of what the agreement entails. This assumption, together with the emphasis on the significance of the parties' intention, overlooks the 'tendency for secondary property to be subject to unnecessarily complex leases' and the fact that smaller business tenants are often 'left bewildered by lease documentation that they can neither understand nor afford to have properly explained to them'.[95] This informational asymmetry between the parties is subsumed within the rhetoric of the parties' intention. Bright's analysis which focuses on the presence (or absence) of a term certain leads to a more logical and consistent outcome. In contrast to many inchoate agreements, where the parties are still 'feeling their way' to a final agreement, the interim 'licences' in the *Rolls Royce* case[96] were for term certain and could stand in as substitutes if it became impossible for the new contracted-out subleases to be granted. The labels attached to them therefore fell foul of the narrow ratio of *Street v Mountford*, ie that the parties cannot label as a licence an agreement which possesses the hallmarks of a tenancy.

In *Newham LBC v Thomas-Van Staden*,[97] it was the landlord's attempt to safeguard its position by documenting the transitional period which proved its downfall. Because of its regeneration plans for the area it had been willing to grant the tenant a contracted-out lease only. The necessary court order was obtained and the lease was granted. The term was stated to expire on 28

[93] *Murdoch* (n 90) 155.

[94] [2007] EWHC 546 (Ch), [2008] L & TR 22 [7].

[95] S Murdoch, 'Commercial Leases: Future Directions' in S Bright (ed), *Landlord and Tenant Law: Past, Present and Future* (Hart Publishing, Oxford 2006) 90.

[96] [2007] EWHC 546 (Ch), [2008] L & TR 22.

[97] [2008] EWCA Civ 1414, [2009] 5 EG 108.

September 2004 but was then defined expressly to include 'any period of holding over or extension of it whether by statute or at common law or by agreement'.[98] After the end of the term, the tenant remained in occupation, continuing to pay rent. She argued that following the expiry of the initial fixed (and contracted-out) term, she had acquired a periodic tenancy with security of tenure under the 1954 Act. The judge at first instance agreed with the landlord that when the lease expired the tenant had not entered into any new periodic tenancy but had merely held over on the same terms; as the original tenancy was not a protected tenancy it was not protected when it was held over. The landlord's notice to quit served after the expiry of the fixed term brought the tenancy to an end.

The tenant appealed, claiming that a lease containing a holding over clause was inconsistent with the nature of a contracted-out lease. The council argued that if – as the judge had found – no new tenancy had been entered into and the tenant had merely held over, the tenant must, at most, have been holding over as a tenant at will. The Court of Appeal allowed the tenant's appeal, holding that the words of extension used when defining the term meant that it could not be regarded as being for a 'term of years certain' as required by section 38A, and the contracting-out was therefore void. There was no need therefore to determine whether, assuming that only the initial fixed term was contracted out, the tenant continued in occupation as a monthly tenant or a tenant at will. However, Rimer LJ (who delivered the only substantive judgment on behalf of the Court of Appeal) intimated that the argument supporting a tenancy at will appeared 'unpromising'.[99] At the very least, it was said, the words of extension must have meant that the tenant held over on the terms of the lease so far as applicable. One of those terms was that the tenant was entitled to 21 days' notice terminating her occupation. This meant that the tenant could not have been a tenant at will 'because it is the essence of such a tenancy that the tenant can be removed at will'.[100] This suggests that even if the parties had been negotiating a further term and 'feeling their way' towards a new agreement, the importation of the notice clause from the earlier agreement would have imported with it certainty of term.

Rimer LJ also raised the point – without deciding it – that the initial term of years certain plus, by the words of extension, a subsequent indefinite period, could have rendered the lease void for uncertainty.[101] If this were to be so then, in line with *Prudential Assurance Co Ltd v London Residuary Body*,[102] a periodic tenancy could have been implied in place of a lease for an uncertain term.

[98] Ibid [10]. Since the decision in *City of London Corporation v Fell* [1993] QB 589 (CA), commercial leases have often contained extended definitions of 'the term' so as to ensure that former tenants or guarantors remain bound if the tenant remains in occupation after the lease reaches its contractual expiry date.

[99] [2008] EWCA Civ 1414, [2009] 5 EG 108 [24].

[100] Ibid [24].

[101] Ibid [23].

[102] [1992] 2 AC 386 (HL).

However, while this might have saved the lease from being declared void for uncertainty, the discovery of an implied periodic tenancy would not have assisted the landlord because the contracting-out provisions of the 1954 Act apply only to leases 'granted for a term of years certain'.[103] The court would therefore have been obliged to hold that the parties had created a periodic tenancy within the Act and that the contracting-out order was a nullity.[104]

Conclusion

Dixon has recently observed that 'clarity, conceptual certainty and a liking for bright-line distinctions'[105] seem to characterise what property lawyers do and how they think. This reflects the fact that

> ... land ... is best managed by principles that do not change with the seasons and which establish a *system* that is predictable. Property lawyers are, perhaps more than most, concerned to ensure that the substance and the language of the law of real property is regular and, within its own terms, conceptually orthodox.[106]

In *Shell-Mex v Manchester Garages*,[107] Lord Denning said it was 'no bad thing' that 'the parties can by agreeing on a licence get out of the Act', especially as they 'can now with the authority of the court contract out of the Act even in regard to tenancies'.[108] Seemingly, the state-sanctioned ability to exclude the operation of the 1954 Act by formal mechanism had, in his Lordship's view, liberated the parties to use whatever contractual means they could find to achieve the same outcome. In consequence, there is no clear-cut model for establishing the nature of occupation under an inchoate agreement. As we have seen, the tenancy at will was largely replaced by the implied periodic tenancy but the advent of statutory protection led to the relegation of the latter and the promotion of the licence. Unfortunately, these developments have inclined the courts to focus upon what they regard as the parties intentions, thereby detracting from a meaningful analysis of the doctrinal basis of the arrangement. The problem could, perhaps, be ameliorated by amending the 1954 Act to the effect that once a contracted-out lease always a contracted-out lease but unless and until such legislative intervention takes place, owners and occupiers, their legal advisers, and the courts are left with the problem of trying to disentangle the conceptual basis of inchoate agreements. There is a tendency to speak of tenancies at will and licences almost in one breath as though they were interchangeable concepts.

[103] Landlord and Tenant Act 1954 s 38A.

[104] Although landlords and tenants can now enter into agreements to exclude business leases from the 1954 Act without having to obtain an order from the court, the position would be the same.

[105] M Dixon, 'A matter of clarity' [2009] *Conv* 1, 1.

[106] Ibid.

[107] [1971] 1 WLR 612 (CA).

[108] Ibid 616.

Given that neither enjoys the protection of the Landlord and Tenant Act 1954, Part II, such grouping is perhaps understandable and the practical outcomes will be virtually the same, whether the occupier is a tenant at will or a (genuine) licensee. However, even though the collateral damage here may not be not great, the result is a lack of conceptual clarity. Generally, such uncertainty can – as Bright suggests – be cured by considering whether the arrangement as a whole gives rise to a term certain. But, as demonstrated by *Newham v Thomas-Van Staden*, the implied periodic tenancy cannot be discounted.

7

A Longitudinal Analysis of the Mortgage Repossession Process 1995–2010: Stability, Regulation and Reform

Lisa Whitehouse*

Introduction

The English law of mortgage[1] is remarkable. Its complexity rivals that of Euler's equation and could, in the same manner, be described as 'beautiful'.[2] Its stubborn retention of archaic terms and concepts operates in sharp contrast to the ever changing world of finance which it inhabits. Most impressive of all, however, is its capacity for stability in the face of fundamental shifts in the socio-economic context in which it operates. It has proven possible, for example, since the late nineteenth century, to put the legal device of the mortgage to new uses without the need to alter its fundamental doctrinal characteristics.[3] The stability apparent within the law of mortgage, it will be argued, derives from a concern to establish requirements as to formality and procedure, leaving much of the substance of the mortgage relationship to be

* School of Law, University of Hull. The author would like to thank the respondents who participated in the empirical research projects; Daniel Metcalfe, Research Assistant at the Law School of the University of Hull; the Socio-Legal Studies Association and the Faculty of Arts and Social Sciences at the University of Hull for funding aspects of this research.

[1] By this, I mean the body of English case law and legislation related directly to first legal mortgages in respect of residential property.

[2] See, for example, J Rehmeyer, 'Euler's Beautiful Equation' *Science News* (April 2007) <http://www.sciencenews.org/view/generic/id/8406/title/Math_Trek_Eulers_Beautiful_Equation> accessed 5 October 2010.

[3] For example, despite the rapid growth during the twentieth century in the use made of the mortgage as a means of purchasing residential property, the definition of it remains as it did in 1899; see *Santley v Wilde* [1899] 2 Ch 474 (CA).

'regulated'[4] through more malleable processes such as contractual 'negotiation',[5] 'discretion'[6] and 'soft law'.[7] While we may marvel at its resilience, however, this chapter will reveal, through an analysis of qualitative data obtained during interviews conducted in 1995 and 2008,[8] that the 'bare bones' approach adopted within the law of mortgage gives rise to two significant implications.

First, in terms of developing our understanding of the law of mortgage, it implies that a 'positivist account'[9] of it has the potential to misrepresent its social significance. Such an account would, for example, reveal that the mortgage is a disposition of some ownership interest in property, 'as a security for the payment of a debt or the discharge of some other obligation for which it is given'[10] which must, if it is to be legal, be created by a 'charge by deed expressed to be by way of legal mortgage'.[11] Beyond this it would reveal little if anything about the type of individual who has sought to make use of the mortgage, the purposes served by mortgage finance or its social, economic or political significance. A true understanding of the law of mortgage can, therefore, arise only through knowledge of it 'in action' rather than 'in books'.[12]

Second, the preservation of an ossified legal framework supplemented by an array of various regulatory mechanisms, overseen by statutory bodies such as the Financial Services Authority (FSA),[13] has resulted in a regulatory framework

[4] This chapter adopts a 'decentred' view of regulation which conceives of law as one method among many that may be used by various actors in seeking to regulate behaviour so as to achieve pre-determined goals. See, for example, J Black, 'Critical Reflections on Regulation' (2002) 27 *Australian Journal of Legal Philosophy* 1; B Morgan and K Yeung, *An Introduction to Law and Regulation* (CUP, Cambridge 2007) 5.

[5] This chapter will question, given the power enjoyed by mortgagees, whether the parties engage in meaningful negotiation. See text to n 40.

[6] A contested concept, particularly between 'positivists' and 'naturalists'. For more on the debate see R Dworkin, *Taking Rights Seriously* (Duckworth, London 1991); H L A Hart, *The Concept of Law* (Clarendon Press, Oxford 1961). For an alternative view see L Wolcher, *Law's Task* (Ashgate, Burlington 2008).

[7] For a definition see, for example, A McHarg, 'Reforming the United Kingdom Constitution: Law, Convention, Soft Law' (2008) 71 *MLR* 853; SC Kuruvilla and A Verma, 'International Labour Standards, Soft Regulation, and National Government Roles' (2006) 48 *JIR* 41.

[8] The qualitative data used in this chapter was obtained during two empirical research projects. The first was conducted between May–October 1995 and involved a series of semi-structured interviews with representatives of thirteen mortgagees, six district judges, a representative of the CML, two officers of the Building Society Ombudsman and two lawyers who undertook repossession work for two of the mortgagees. The second project, conducted between February–July 2008, involved representatives of five mortgagees, eight district judges, the Financial Ombudsman Service, the Building Societies Association, the Financial Services Consumer Panel, National Debtline, the Financial Inclusion Centre, the National Consumer Council and Shelter. Due to the economic and political sensitivity of repossession, the individual respondents have been granted anonymity.

[9] An account concerned solely with legal doctrine and primary sources of law.

[10] *Santley v Wilde* [1899] 2 Ch 474 (CA).

[11] Law of Property Act 1925 ss 85(1) and 86(1) as amended by Land Registration Act 2002 s 23(1)(a).

[12] Terminology used by, for example, *Black* (n 4) 26.

[13] The FSA is an independent non-governmental body given statutory powers by the Financial Services and Markets Act 2000.

that, according to the FSA and others,[14] has failed to control effectively the behaviour of some mortgagees leading, on occasion, to the inconsistent and inequitable treatment of mortgagors.[15] In response, the FSA implemented in June 2010 a number of changes to the regulatory framework.[16] While the more interventionist approach adopted by the FSA is to be welcomed, this chapter will argue that, in order to achieve a greater degree of consistency and equity in the treatment of mortgagors, more broad based and systematic regulatory techniques are required. In particular, given the failure of non-juridical mechanisms to regulate effectively the behaviour of some mortgagees,[17] it will be necessary to employ a 'command and control'[18] approach. This will involve the use of legal rules, supported by effective sanctions that apply equally to all mortgagees in pursuit of normative objectives.[19] In assessing the potential for the command and control approach to be achieved in practice, reference will be had to the Home Owner and Debtor Protection (Scotland) Act 2010 (the Scottish Act).[20] While the Scottish property system differs significantly from that employed in England, the measures contained within it serve to illustrate that the executive is, on occasion, willing to forsake administrative control in favour of a more proactive and prescriptive legislative approach in regulating the mortgage relationship.[21]

In seeking to justify these propositions, this chapter will begin by offering evidence in support of the claim that the law of mortgage has indicated a capacity to remain relatively unchanged despite a radical transition in the context in which it operates. This is followed by an account of the reasons for

[14] Citizens Advice, 'Set Up To Fail: CAB Clients' Experience of Mortgage and Secured Loan Arrears Problems' (12 December 2007) <http://www.citizensadvice.org.uk/set_up_to_fail-2> accessed 5 October 2010; FSA, 'Mortgage Effectiveness Review: Arrears Findings' (ResearchReport Project No 30895, Illuminas, London August 2008) <http://www.fsa.gov.uk/pubs/other/mer_report.pdf> accessed 5 October 2010; House of Commons Treasury Committee, 'Mortgage Arrears and Access to Mortgage Finance' HC (2008–09) 767, 3.

[15] Shelter, for example, offers evidence of sub-prime lenders flouting current rules by imposing disproportionate charges upon mortgagors in arrears, see, B Rashleigh and T Marshall, 'Charged Out' *Roof* (March/April 2010) 24. The House of Commons Treasury Committee was also highly critical of the FSA's principles-based approach and offered substantial evidence of its failure to ensure that mortgagors were treated consistently and fairly: see *House of Commons Treasury Committee* (n 14) [47].

[16] FSA, 'Mortgage Market Review: Arrears and Approved Persons. Feedback to CP10/2 and Final Policy' Policy Statement (June 2010) <http://www.fsa.gov.uk/pubs/policy/ps10_09.pdf> accessed 5 October 2010.

[17] *House of Commons Treasury Committee* (n 14) [47].

[18] See, for example, *Black* (n 4) 2.

[19] See, for example, R Baldwin and M Cave, *Understanding Regulation* (OUP, Oxford 1999) 35–39.

[20] For a copy of the Act, see: <http://www.legislation.gov.uk/asp/2010/6/pdfs/asp_20100006_en.pdf> accessed 5 October 2010. See also A McIntosh, 'Homeowner and Debtor Protection (Scotland) Bill' *SCOLAG Journal* (November 2009) 272.

[21] A similar move has also been made by the Parliament of Ireland; see the Land and Conveyancing Law Reform Act 2009 Part 10 which came into effect in December 2009.

this stability and the implications that arise from it in respect of developing our understanding of the law of mortgage and the likelihood of legislative reform being undertaken. Despite a bleak prognosis in respect of the latter, the final section offers an account of the Scottish Act as an example of the type of reform that could be achieved in practice. The chapter concludes by suggesting that, despite the apparent unwillingness of successive governments to undertake legal reform, the regulation of the mortgage relationship appears to be undergoing a process, the natural culmination of which will be regulation enforced through mandatory sanctions.[22] What this chapter is calling for is an acceleration of that process so as to ensure due process, transparency and consistency within the mortgage relationship.

The law of mortgage: continuity and change

The doctrinal content of the English law of mortgage has indicated a remarkable capacity for stability. The classic definition of the legal device of the mortgage, for example, pronounced by Lindley LJ as the transfer of an interest in property as, 'a security for the payment of a debt or the discharge of some other obligation for which it is given',[23] was enunciated in 1899 and yet continues to offer an accurate definition of the mortgage as it operates today. The enduring quality of this pronouncement is mirrored by other aspects of the law of mortgage. The mortgagee's inherent right to possession, for example, has been in evidence since the sixteenth century[24] while the methods by which a mortgage is created, coupled with other rights and remedies afforded to both the mortgagor and the mortgagee, are governed by the Law of Property 1925 (LPA 1925). The most recent substantive reform took place in 1970 with the introduction of the Administration of Justice Act 1970 (AJA 1970).[25]

The continued reliance upon legal rules established over forty or more years ago may, at first glance, be considered unremarkable and could be accounted for on the basis of, for example, perfection in their drafting.[26] The significance of this stability, however, becomes apparent when one considers the fundamental change that has been achieved in the function served by mortgage finance and the context within which it operates. Most notably, the mortgage has, since the twentieth century, come to serve as the means by which millions of households within England and Wales have gained access to the home-ownership sector.

[22] See the 'pyramid strategy' discussed in I Ayres and J Braithwaite, *Responsive Regulation: Transcending the Deregulation Debate* (OUP, Oxford 1992) 35–53.

[23] *Santley* (n 10).

[24] See, for example, F W Maitland, *Equity: A Course of Lectures* (CUP, Cambridge 1936); A W B Simpson, *An Introduction to the History of the Land Law* (OUP, Oxford 1964).

[25] Amended by the Administration of Justice Act 1973.

[26] Alternative responses have been offered, see, for example, A Stewart, *Rethinking Housing Law* (Sweet & Maxwell, London 1996).

Prior to this, it had served primarily as a means by which landowners had obtained funds to assist in the alleviation of financial difficulties.[27]

While this transition in the use made of the mortgage owes much to the willingness of building societies to offer mortgage finance for the purpose of purchasing residential property,[28] it was the housing policies of post-war governments and in particular, the Conservative governments of 1979–1997, which increased its momentum.[29] The pursuit of a mass home ownership market through policies such as the 'right to buy',[30] the 'residualisation'[31] of the public rented sector and the deregulation of the mortgage market[32] contributed to the steady growth in the number of owner occupied properties within England and Wales, with a ten per cent increase in home-ownership during the 1980s alone.[33] Perhaps more significantly, however, these initiatives transformed fundamentally the mortgage finance industry, perceptions as to what qualified as 'decent' housing and the quantity, quality and provision of housing in each sector.[34] To this extent, therefore, the function served by the law of mortgage and the environment in which it operated experienced a radical transformation. What is most significant about this period for our purposes, however, is that the Conservative governments did not consider it helpful or necessary, in pursuit of their housing policy objectives, to alter the norms which constituted the law of mortgage. As AdviceUK, Citizens Advice and Shelter note, 'current residential mortgage law has not been updated since the 1970s, when less than half of the homes in the UK were owner occupied.'[35]

In accounting for this phenomenon, this chapter argues that the stability apparent over decades, if not centuries, within the law of mortgage derives from its adoption of a largely peripheral role in the regulation of the mortgage

[27] B Rudden, 'The Mortgagee's Right to Possession' [1961] *Conv* 278.

[28] See, for example, M Boddy, *The Building Societies* (London, Macmillan Press 1980); E J Cleary, *The Building Society Movement* (London, Elek Books 1965); A Murie, 'Secure and Contented Citizens? Home-ownership in Britain' in A Marsh and D Mullins (eds), *Housing and Public Policy* (Open University Press, Buckingham, 1998) 79.

[29] See, for example, D Cowan and M McDermont, *Regulating Social Housing: Governing Decline* (Routledge-Cavendish, Oxford 2006); J Kemeny, *The Myth of Home-Ownership* (Routledge & Kegan Paul, London 1981); L Whitehouse, 'The Impact of Consumerism on the Home-Owner' in D Cowan (ed), *Housing: Participation and Exclusion* (Ashgate Publishing, Aldershot 1998) 126.

[30] See, for example, C Jones and A Murie, *The Right to Buy: Analysis and Evaluation of a Housing Policy* (Blackwell, Oxford 2006).

[31] See R Forrest and A Murie, *Right to Buy? Issues of Need, Equity and Polarisation in the Sale of Council Houses* (School for Advanced Urban Studies, Bristol 1984); R Forrest and A Murie, *Residualisation and Council Housing: A Statistical Update* (School for Advanced Urban Studies, Bristol 1990); P Malpass and A Murie, *Housing Policy and Practice* (MacMillan, London 1994).

[32] See, for example, M P Kleinman and C M E Whitehead, 'British Housing since 1979: Has the System Changed?' (1988) 3 *Housing Studies* 3–19.

[33] S Wilcox, *Housing Finance Review 1994/95* (Joseph Rowntree Foundation, York 1994) 111 Table 15d.

[34] See the literature cited in n 29.

[35] AdviceUK, Citizens Advice and Shelter, 'Turning the Tide?' (15 December 2009) 17 <http://www.citizensadvice.org.uk/index/campaigns/policy_campaign_publications/evidence_reports/er_consumerandebt/turning_the_tide_.htm> accessed 5 October 2010.

relationship. In essence, the law of mortgage seeks principally to protect the security of the mortgagee while allowing the mortgagor an unfettered right to redeem.[36] Beyond this, it imposes few if any substantive requirements upon the parties to the mortgage, leaving much of the substance of the mortgage relationship to be filled in by alternative regulatory techniques. A change in the use to which mortgage funds are put, therefore, can be achieved without the need to alter the legislative content of the law of mortgage. In offering evidence in support of this contention, the following three sections focus on the law of mortgage and the non-juridical regulatory techniques used to fill the gaps left by it, namely contractual negotiation, the exercise of discretion and soft law.

Contractual negotiation

A feature characteristic of English land law is the reliance on formality as the means of creating certainty in dealings with land. The imposition of formal rules ensures that the parties to, and the subject of, the agreement or dispute concerning land can be identified. It is perhaps unsurprising therefore that the law of mortgage establishes formalities in respect of the creation of a mortgage.[37] Other than this, the law of mortgage is notable for what it fails to prescribe including matters such as; the method of repayment of the loan, the length over which repayment should be made or the rate of interest to be charged. In leaving such matters to be determined through contractual negotiation, the law of mortgage invests the mortgage relationship with a substantial degree of flexibility. In order to enable households within England and Wales to purchase a home, for example, mortgagees have been able to increase the length of repayment to an average of twenty-five years and to offer a wide range of mortgage products.[38]

This reliance upon contractual negotiation as the means by which to construct the substance of the mortgage relationship is not unusual within land law, as Gray and Gray note, 'like so many phenomena of land law, the mortgage or charge represents a conjunction of the *contractual* and the *proprietary*.'[39] It derives in part from the assumption that the mortgagor and mortgagee enjoy equality in bargaining power. This necessarily leaves open the question as to whether such equality exists and the extent to which mortgage contracts are the product of negotiations that lead to the construction of mutually acceptable terms. These contracts are, of course, subject to general contractual principles,

[36] K J Gray and S F Gray, *Elements of Land Law* (OUP, Oxford 2009) 715–46.

[37] See the Law of Property Act 1925 ss 85(1) and 86(1) as amended by Land Registration Act 2002 s 23(1)(a).

[38] See for example, D Maclennan and others, *Fixed Commitments, Uncertain Incomes: Sustainable Owner-Occupation and the Economy* (Joseph Rowntree Foundation, York 1997); M P Thompson, *Modern Land Law* (OUP, Oxford 2009) 427–28.

[39] *Gray and Gray* (n 36) 694.

consumer legislation and judicial oversight,[40] but an examination of the terms contained within the typical mortgage contract suggests that the mortgagee has considerable influence in respect of its content. As Stewart suggests, 'noticeably absent from the document is any reference to the mortgagor's rights although the mortgagee's rights are set out in some detail.'[41] A mortgagee is, for example, entitled to be indemnified for all charges and expenses reasonably incurred in enforcing or preserving the security.[42] In order to supplement this general legal principle, however, mortgagees tend to incorporate terms within the contract which impose liability for costs upon the mortgagor. The importance of this term within the repossession process will be explored in more detail below.[43] For the time being, however, it is perhaps worth noting that the initial stages of the mortgage relationship appear to be of little if any concern to the law of mortgage, with the decision as to whom and on what terms to lend mortgage monies left almost entirely at the discretion of the mortgagee.[44] It is not only in relation to decisions of this type, however, that the law of mortgage presents mortgagees and others with significant decision-making power.

Discretion

In its concern to establish form and procedure, the law of mortgage, either implicitly or explicitly, relies heavily upon the exercise of discretion by various parties within the mortgage relationship as a means of adding substance to it. Discretion is a contested concept and one that deserves greater attention than is possible to provide here. Suffice to say for present purposes, however, that the law of mortgage tends, to borrow Dworkin's taxonomy, to allow mortgagees to exercise discretion in the 'strong sense'[45] and district judges to exercise it in the 'weak sense'.[46] The latter relates to a situation where, 'for some reason the standards an official must apply cannot be applied mechanically but demand the use of judgment.'[47] By virtue of the AJA 1970 section 36, where a mortgagee

[40] See, for example, the Consumer Credit Act 1974, as amended by the Consumer Credit Act 2006, in respect of second mortgages; the Unfair Terms in Consumer Contracts Regulations 1999 in respect of which see S Bright 'Winning the Battle Against Unfair Contract Terms' (2000) 20 LS 331 and the 'no clogs or fetters' on the equity of redemption case law, including *Fairclough v Swan Brewery Ltd* [1912] AC 565 (HL).

[41] *Stewart* (n 26) 46.

[42] *Detillin v Gale* (1802) 7 Ves 583, 32 ER 234; *Re Wallis* (1890) 25 QBD 176 (CA).

[43] Text to n 87.

[44] The FSA regulates lending decisions to some extent by requiring mortgagees to take account of the customer's ability to repay; Mortgages and Home Finance: Conduct of Business Sourcebook (MCOB) 11.3.1R (see <http://fsahandbook.info/FSA/html/handbook/MCOB> accessed 5 October 2010). They are also consulting on changes to affordability assessments, see FSA, 'Mortgage Market Review: Responsible Lending' Consultation Paper 10/16 (July 2010) [1.19]–[1.25] <http://www.fsa.gov.uk/pubs/cp/cp10_16.pdf> accessed 5 October 2010.

[45] *Dworkin* (n 6) 32.

[46] Ibid 31.

[47] Ibid.

initiates proceedings in the county court for possession,[48] the district judge is given a discretion to suspend an order for possession upon specified payment terms if, 'it appears to the court that in the event of its exercising the power the borrower is likely to be able within a reasonable period to pay any sums due under the mortgage'.[49] The criteria to be employed in exercising this discretion are not specified by the AJA 1970, hence its categorisation in the 'weak sense'.

Guidance has, however, been offered by the Court of Appeal in *Cheltenham and Gloucester Building Society v Norgan*.[50] In relation to the meaning to be attributed to the 'reasonable period' under the AJA 1970 section 36, for example, Waite LJ suggested that 'the court should take as its starting point the full term of the mortgage and pose at the outset the question: would it be possible for the mortgagor to maintain payment-off of the arrears by instalments over that period?'[51] The extent to which this guidance has impacted upon the exercise of judicial discretion will be explored further below.[52] While the discretion afforded to district judges appears to operate within clearly defined boundaries,[53] however, the discretion enjoyed by mortgagees is largely of an 'open texture' in that a significant gap exists between standards that might seek to structure it and the manner in which it is exercised. This is particularly true in respect of the decision as to when and how to seek possession of the secured property.

In strict terms, an action for possession by a legal mortgagee is a 'right' which derives from the mortgagee's legal estate in the secured property.[54] A legal mortgagee[55] may therefore go into possession of the property 'before the ink is dry on the mortgage unless there is something in the contract, express or by implication, whereby he has contracted himself out of that right.'[56] In

[48] Despite claims that the Administration of Justice Act 1970 imposes a requirement of due process upon a mortgagee seeking possession, the inherent right to possession remains and an order from the court is not necessary; confirmed in *Ropaigealach v Barclays Bank Plc* [2000] QB 263 (CA). See also, A Clarke, 'Further Implications of Section 36 of the Administration of Justice Act 1970' [1983] Conv 293.

[49] The term 'any sums due' applies only to the arrears outstanding at the time in addition to normal contractual payments, Administration of Justice Act 1973 s 8.

[50] [1996] 1 WLR 343 (CA).

[51] Ibid 458.

[52] Text to n 86.

[53] The district judge must be convinced that the mortgagor can pay the agreed instalments plus the arrears outstanding within a reasonable period. The factors are, therefore, entirely financial. For a discussion on how we might include 'social' considerations in this decision-making process, see S Bright, 'Dispossession for Arrears: The Weight of Home' (2009) Oxford Legal Studies Research Paper No 25/2009 <http://ssrn.com/abstract=1435326> accessed 5 October 2010.

[54] The charge by deed does not create a term in the mortgagee, but the mortgagee is given the same powers, protection and remedies as if the mortgagee had a term of 3,000 years, including the right to possess the land; Law of Property Act 1925 s 87(1). See R J Smith, 'The Mortgagee's Right to Possession – The Modern Law' [1979] *Conv* 266.

[55] The inherent right to possession derives from the legal estate granted to the mortgagee. An equitable mortgagee, therefore, does not have such a right. In order to gain possession, an equitable mortgagee must make specific provision in the mortgage deed or seek an order for possession in the courts.

[56] *Four-Maids Ltd v Dudley Marshall (Properties) Ltd* [1957] Ch 317 (Ch) 320.

relation to mortgage monies utilised for the purpose of purchasing residential property, a mortgagee rarely wishes to gain possession as a remedy per se but as a 'preliminary to the exercise of the mortgagee's power of sale'.[57] The majority of mortgage contracts reflect this by incorporating an express term that states that the mortgagee will not seek possession until the mortgagor is in default, highlighting again the important role played by contractual, if non-negotiable, terms within the mortgage relationship.

Mortgagees have, therefore, considered it to be in their self-interest to restrict the wide discretion given to them by the law of mortgage. Upon default by the mortgagor, however, a legal mortgagee may decide to take physical possession of the secured property, bring an action for possession in the county court or sell the property without first having obtained possession.[58] In respect of the latter approach, the Council of Mortgage Lenders (CML)[59] issued a voluntary statement indicating that, 'members will not seek to sell a mortgaged property when the borrower is in default without first obtaining a court order for possession', although this does not apply to buy-to-let properties.[60] While in practice, the majority of mortgagees tend to seek an order from the courts,[61] the question as to when and how to seek possession rests ultimately with the mortgagee, thereby affording them discretion in the 'strong' sense:

> We use 'discretion' sometimes not merely to say that an official must use judgment in applying the standards set him by authority, or that no one will review that exercise of judgment, but to say that on some issue he is simply not bound by standards set by the authority in question.[62]

Given the significant degree of discretion enjoyed by both mortgagees and district judges within the repossession process, it is perhaps surprising that standards or further guidance on how best to exercise it has not been offered through legislative means. This omission has, however, been remedied in large part through the use of alternative regulatory mechanisms.

[57] *Gray and Gray* (n 36) 768.

[58] Possession is not a pre-requisite for the exercise of the mortgagee's power of sale under the Law of Property Act 1925 s 101, see *Horsham Properties Group Ltd v Clark & Others* [2008] EWHC 2327 (Ch), [2009] 1 WLR 1255. Following this case, the MOJ initiated a review of the mortgagee's power of sale, see MOJ, 'Mortgages: Power of Sale and residential Property' Consultation Paper CP55/09 (December 2009).

[59] The trade association for the majority of first charge mortgage lenders. Its members hold over ninety eight per cent of the assets of the UK mortgage market.

[60] CML, 'CML voluntary statement on s 101 of the Law of Property Act 1925 following the Horsham Properties v Clark and Beech case' (15 December 2008) <http://www.cml.org.uk/cml/policy/issues/4707> accessed 5 October 2010.

[61] This is partly in response to the imposition of duties and liabilities upon a mortgagee in possession. See, for example, *White v City of London Brewery Co* (1889) 42 Ch D 237 (CA), the Criminal Law Act 1977 s 6 and the Protection from Eviction Act 1977.

[62] *Dworkin* (n 6) 32.

Soft law

Soft law refers to regulatory mechanisms that have some of the features of law but which do not have the 'force of law (most often because they do not comply with relevant formalities or for other reasons are not regarded as legally binding), but nonetheless affect the behavior of others …'.[63] There exists a rather complex set of soft law mechanisms which seek to offer mortgagees guidance on how best to exercise their rights and remedies. The complexity of the system relates, in part, to the different regimes that operate, with 'regulated mortgages';[64] namely first legal mortgages on residential property taken out after October 2004, subject currently to regulation by the FSA while second mortgages are subject to regulation by the Office of Fair Trading (OFT) under the Consumer Credit Act 1974 (CCA 1974).[65] The Coalition government's proposals to reform substantially the regulation of the financial services industry, including transferring the responsibilities of the FSA to the Bank of England, are currently under consideration with a view to securing their implementation by 2012.[66] For the time being, however, the FSA continues in its role. Given that this chapter is concerned with first legal mortgages in respect of residential property it will focus upon attempts by the FSA to regulate the mortgage industry.

The main regulatory instrument used by the FSA is the Mortgages and Home Finance: Conduct of Business Sourcebook (MCOB);[67] a set of provisions that, prior to June 2010,[68] ranged in nature from 'rules', to 'evidential provisions' and 'guidance'.[69] In relation to the repossession process, for example, MCOB states that repossession should be undertaken only 'where all other reasonable attempts to resolve the position have failed'[70] and that the equivalent of at least two months' arrears must have accumulated before court proceedings should be initiated.[71] The enforcement powers granted to the FSA under the Financial Services and Markets Act 2000 include withdrawing a firm's authorisation, imposing penalties for market abuse and prosecuting various offences. The extent to which regulated mortgagees

[63] E A Posner and J E Gersen, 'Soft Law Lessons From Congressional Practice' (2008) 61 *Stan LRev* 573, 577.

[64] For a definition, see: Financial Services and Markets Act 2000 (Regulated Activities) Order 2001 s 63(1).

[65] The Consumer Credit Act 1974 was amended by the Consumer Credit Act 2006 so that all second mortgages are now covered by the Act.

[66] HM Treasury, 'A New Approach to Financial Regulation: Judgement, Focus and Stability' (Cm 7874, 2010).

[67] See <http://fsahandbook.info/FSA/html/handbook/MCOB> accessed 5 October 2010.

[68] The FSA implemented changes to MCOB by virtue of the Mortgage Arrears Instrument 2010, see *FSA* (n 16) Part 1, Appendix 1.

[69] A definition of these terms is provided in the glossary to MCOB: <http://fsahandbook.info/FSA/html/handbook/Glossary/> accessed 23 February 2010.

[70] MCOB 13.3.2AR(6).

[71] MCOB defines 'arrears' as a shortfall (equivalent to two or more regular payments) in the accumulated total payments actually made by the borrower (n 69).

comply with MCOB has been the subject of significant recent research which is explored in greater detail below.[72]

In addition to the now familiar use of a regulatory agency to monitor the activities of private business, soft law of more doubtful provenance has also been utilised. Reflecting provisions contained within MCOB, the *Pre-Action Protocol for Possession Claims Based on Mortgage or Home Purchase Plan Arrears in Respect of Residential Property* (the Protocol) was drafted by the Civil Justice Council (CJC) and introduced in November 2008 by the Civil Procedure Rules Committee.[73] Despite questions being raised regarding the authority of the CJC,[74] the Protocol was introduced with the objective of encouraging increased pre-action communication between the parties to the mortgage while ensuring that they 'act fairly and reasonably' with each other in addressing any concerns relating to the mortgage.[75] Although similar in content to MCOB, the Protocol applies equally to all residential mortgages, regardless of whether they are regulated by the FSA, the OFT or remain unregulated.[76]

Under the Protocol, no sanctions of any kind exist; rather, the 'parties should be able, if requested by the court, to explain the actions that they have taken to comply with this protocol.'[77] In order to assist district judges in this respect, mortgagees are required to complete, prior to the hearing, two copies of a checklist indicating the extent to which they have complied with the Protocol.[78] Failure to provide the required information can lead to an adjournment of the case but the Protocol is silent in respect of the situation where the mortgagee's 'explanation' is considered unsatisfactory. Given the lack of any meaningful sanctions, it must be assumed that the Protocol supplements the criteria which district judges should take into account when deciding whether to adjourn claims for possession under the AJA 1970, although whether this is proving to be the case will be explored further below.[79]

Implications and assertions

The account of the law of mortgage offered above reveals a skeletal framework of rules and procedures that facilitates those who are party to the mortgage

[72] Text to n 95.

[73] See <http://www.justice.gov.uk/civil/procrules_fin/contents/protocols/prot_mha.htm> accessed 5 October 2010. For more on the Protocol see L Whitehouse, 'The Mortgage Arrears Pre-Action Protocol: An Opportunity Lost' (2009) 72 *MLR* 793.

[74] CML, 'Mortgage Arrears Protocol: Response by the Council of Mortgage Lenders to the Consultation by the Civil Justice Council' (May 2008) [19] <http://www.cml.org.uk/cml/policy/responses?keyword=&key_area=0&date=0&page=8> accessed 5 October 2010.

[75] The *Protocol* (n 73) [2.1].

[76] Ibid [3]. The Protocol does not cover 'buy-to-let' loans as these are regarded as commercial transactions.

[77] Ibid [9.1].

[78] CPR PD 55A, 55.8, 5.5 (possession claims), Prescribed Form N123.

[79] Text to n 124.

in placing the flesh on its bones. It is this which accounts for the stability apparent in the doctrinal content of the law but which leaves unanswered a number of questions. For example, how do mortgagees decide when and how to seek possession? What criteria do district judges employ in exercising their discretion under the AJA 1970? What impact has soft law had within the mortgage relationship? In seeking an answer to these questions, two empirical research projects were conducted in 1995 and 2008 which involved semi-structured interviews with a sample of mortgagees, district judges, regulators and consumer advice agencies.[80]

An analysis of the data obtained as a result of those two projects coupled with the observations made in respect of the nature and operation of the law of mortgage gives rise to two fundamental assertions. The first is that, given the 'bare bones' nature of the law of mortgage, positivist accounts of it have the potential to misrepresent its operation and significance within the social context. The second is that successive governments, in seeking to achieve policy objectives through predominately 'administrative' rather than legal means,[81] have created a regulatory framework that, according to the FSA and others, has left mortgagors vulnerable to the exercise of unstructured and unaccountable power by mortgagees. The following two sections examine these contentions in greater detail, beginning with the implications for those undertaking research into the law of mortgage.

Positivism vs practice

The contention that a positivist analysis of law will fail to offer sufficient insight into its practical significance is a familiar one, not least to those affiliated with the socio-legal tradition.[82] The aim of this section, however, is not to repeat that debate but to offer an example from the law of mortgage in support of it. A purely juridical analysis of the decision in *Norgan*,[83] for example, would suggest that district judges, when deciding whether to suspend an order for possession, will begin by asking whether the mortgagor can repay the arrears over the remaining term of the mortgage. Given that the typical length of most first acquisition mortgages is twenty-five years and that the majority of cases that come before the courts are in the early stages of the mortgage,[84] it can

[80] See n 8 above.

[81] See, for example, G Majone, 'The Rise of the Regulatory State in Europe' in R Baldwin, C Scott and C Hood (eds), *A Reader on Regulation* (OUP, Oxford 1998) 198; P McAuslan, 'Mortgage Arrears: The Repossession Crunch' (2009) 3 *Journal of International Banking and Finance Law* 137; *Stewart* (n 26).

[82] For an early account of socio-legal research see, CM Campbell and P Wiles, 'The Study of Law in Society in Britain' (1976) 10 *Law and Society Review* 547.

[83] [1996] 1 WLR 343 (CA).

[84] Research suggests that repossession is more likely in the first few years of the mortgage due to the lack of equity in the home and payments tending to be at the margins of affordability, see *AdviceUK* (n 35) 9.

be assumed that most mortgagors (capable of meeting their normal monthly payments) will be able to show an ability to clear their arrears over this period. As Thompson suggests:

> ... it will clearly be easier to meet the additional payments necessary to clear the arrears and meet the ongoing payments if such payments are spread out over the whole period of the loan rather than having to be made within a set, and somewhat arbitrary, period.[85]

The qualitative data, however, reveals that the decision in *Norgan* has had little, if any, impact upon the exercise of judicial discretion. District judges interviewed in 1995, for example, set different limitations on the reasonable period but tended not to extend the period beyond five years.[86] Following the decision in *Norgan*, it would seem reasonable to assume that this time period would have extended beyond the typical maximum evident in 1995. The data provided by district judges in 2008, however, suggests that this has not proven to be the case. Despite acknowledging the decision in *Norgan* and its implications for determining the reasonable period, the period for suspension remained typically between one to five years.

The reason offered by district judges as to why *Norgan* appears to have failed to impact significantly upon the exercise of their discretion is that they are concerned to ensure that mortgagors are not subjected to years of ever increasing financial debt. The basis for this argument relates to the liability imposed upon a mortgagor for the costs of any legal proceedings undertaken in relation to the mortgage and additional charges while they remain in arrears.[87] If a district judge were to suspend a possession order for twenty years, for example, the mortgagor would remain in arrears for this period and would be required to pay interest on them. Although the mortgagor would be making payments in respect of clearing the arrears as they stand at the time of the hearing, the interest payments would continue to accumulate leading to an increasing financial debt.[88] District judges, therefore, believe that a period shorter than that of the remaining term of the mortgage is in the best interests of the mortgagor.

In addition, the majority of district judges believed that they had little if any power to intervene in the issue of costs. Despite the apparent unfettered right of mortgagees to impose the costs of legal proceedings upon the mortgagor, a district judge does have the power to prevent a mortgagee from adding its costs to the security, albeit one that is, in reality, rather limited.[89] According to the Practice Direction About Costs, '[w]here there is a contractual right

[85] *Thompson* (n 38) 478.

[86] L Whitehouse, 'The Right to Possession. The Need for Substantive Reform' in P Jackson and DC Wilde (eds), *The Reform of Property Law* (Ashgate, Aldershot 1997).

[87] Text to n 43.

[88] The FSA has sought to restrict the ability of mortgagees to impose interest and charges on mortgagors in arrears where a repayment agreement is in operation, see *FSA* (n 16) [3.1]–[3.3] and MCOB 12.4.1AE.

[89] CPR PD 50.3 (costs: directions relating to Part 48).

to the costs the discretion should ordinarily be exercised so as to reflect that contractual right.'[90] For this reason, district judges feel unable to invoke this sanction given that the issue of costs has been contractually agreed.[91] What this approach does not take into account, however, is the imbalance in the strength of the bargaining positions of the respective parties. Mortgagors are not free to negotiate the terms of their mortgage contract but must accept standard terms which make them liable for all costs incurred in the enforcement of the mortgagee's rights under that contract. The mortgage market is therefore failing to operate effectively on the basis of choice and competition, but district judges do not have or are unwilling to exercise the power to intervene in the contractual relationship between the mortgagor and mortgagee to redress this imbalance.

It seems evident, therefore, that positivist accounts of the law of mortgage, which would suggest that *Norgan* offers mortgagors substantial assistance in avoiding repossession, have the potential to misrepresent the true nature of such decisions. It is essential, therefore, in order to gain a true understanding of the law of mortgage that further socio-legal, and in particular empirical research, is conducted. The value of employing these methodological techniques is made more evident by the existence of and the need to know more about the use of non-juridical mechanisms in the regulation of the mortgage relationship.

An ineffective regulatory regime

It would seem evident that despite attempts by the FSA to regulate the activities of some mortgagees, the regulatory framework has failed to achieve its objective of ensuring that mortgagors are treated 'fairly'.[92] Evidence arising out of the empirical study undertaken in 1995, for example, revealed that some mortgagees instigated court action at a much earlier stage than others and did so regardless of an agreement having been reached with the mortgagor for the repayment of the arrears.[93] The impact of such action was significant for the reason that the costs of the court proceedings were borne by a mortgagor who was already experiencing financial difficulties and had to convince the court that they could pay their normal contractual payments plus an amount off the arrears within a 'reasonable period'. Compared with mortgagors who were

[90] Ibid 50.3(2).

[91] L Whitehouse 'The Home Owner: Citizen or Consumer?' in S Bright and J Dewar (eds), *Land Law: Themes and Perspectives* (OUP, Oxford 1998) 194.

[92] See, for example, FSA, 'Treating Customers Fairly – Towards Fair Outcomes for Consumers' (July 2006) <http://www.fsa.gov.uk/pubs/other/tcf_towards.pdf> accessed 5 October 2010; FSA, 'Mortgage Market Review: Arrears and Approved Persons' Consultation Paper 10/2 (January 2010) [3.2] <http://www.fsa.gov.uk/pubs/cp/cp10_02.pdf> accessed 5 October 2010.

[93] *Whitehouse* (n 91) 192.

allowed by their mortgagee to repay their arrears without recourse to the court, these mortgagors were placed at a significant disadvantage.

Since then, the FSA has taken over responsibility for regulation of first charge mortgages taken out after October 2004. Unfortunately, the empirical data obtained in 2008 reveals that the introduction of MCOB has had little if any impact on the inconsistent application of arrears management practices by mortgagees. As was the case in 1995, some mortgagees continue to seek possession automatically upon two months' arrears regardless of an agreement having been reached with the mortgagor, while other mortgagees indicated that they would avoid court action if at all possible. These findings are supported by research undertaken by Citizens Advice[94] and the FSA's own review of the regulation of the mortgage market,[95] which have found inconsistent compliance with MCOB, particularly within the 'sub-prime'[96] and second charge sectors, resulting in 'excessive costs, stress and worry for borrowers which could have been avoided if lenders had acted in accordance with the rules that govern arrears management conduct.'[97]

In response to the criticisms levelled at mortgagees by the FSA, the CML published new industry guidance on arrears and possessions practices which reiterates the requirements of MCOB but in so doing, offers examples of good practice including, 'court action should not be taken where an agreement is in place and is being adhered to.'[98] This guidance applies only to regulated mortgages and, as the CML is keen to point out, it 'is not a definitive statement of what lenders "should" do in each case but rather a reference point to support lenders' self-assessment of their own policies and procedures.'[99] Compliance with it, therefore, remains entirely voluntary and could be viewed as an attempt by the industry to avoid more stringent regulation.[100]

The permissive approach adopted within the regulatory framework, however, appears to be under threat by virtue of the FSA's commitment to regulate more closely the arrears management practices of first charge mortgagees, with the

[94] *Citizens Advice* (n 14).

[95] *FSA* (n 14); FSA, 'Mortgage Market Review' Discussion Paper 09/3 (October 2009) <http://www.fsa.gov.uk/pubs/discussion/dp09_03.pdf> accessed 5 October 2010.

[96] For a definition of 'sub-prime', see M Stephens and D Quilgars, 'Managing Arrears and Possessions' (2007) 5 *Housing Finance* 1, 3–4. See also, M Munro and others, *Lending to Higher Risk Borrowers: Sub-Prime Credit and Sustainable Home-Ownership* (Joseph Rowntree Foundation, York 2005) 1–3.

[97] Citizens Advice, 'Mortgage Arrears Protocol: Response by Citizens Advice to the Civil Justice Council' (May 2008) 4–5 <http://www.citizensadvice.org.uk/mortgage_arrears_protocol_-_a_response_to_the_cjc.pdf> accessed 5 October 2010. See also *House of Commons Treasury Committee* (n 14) [26].

[98] CML, 'Industry Guidance on Arrears and Possessions to Help Lenders Comply with MCOB 13 and TCF Principles' (October 2008) 1.1 <http://www.cml.org.uk/cml/media/press/1965> accessed 5 October 2010.

[99] CML, 'CML Issues New Arrears Guidance and Responds to Government Announcements Today' (October 2008) <http://www.cml.org.uk/cml/media/press/1965> accessed 5 October 2010.

[100] Baldwin and Cave make the point that self-regulation is often used to hold legislative controls 'at bay': *Baldwin and Cave* (n 19) 39.

'light touch' of previous years to be replaced by 'an aggressive and proactive approach to monitoring and enforcement.'[101] That commitment has been made manifest by virtue of a number of amendments to MCOB including ensuring that charges imposed on mortgagors in arrears cover the cost of administering them rather than being treated as a source of profit.[102] In particular, these charges should not be imposed on a mortgagor who has reached and is keeping to an agreement for repaying the arrears.[103] Another major reform has been to enhance the regulatory force of MCOB 13 so as to convert it into rules rather than a mixture of rules, guidance and evidential provisions.[104] This includes the insistence that mortgagees do not repossess the property unless all other reasonable attempts to the resolve the position have failed.[105] The outcome of this more 'aggressive' approach was illustrated recently when the FSA fined GMAC-RFC, the eleventh largest mortgagee in the UK,[106] £2.8 million for failing to treat customers fairly; including imposing costs that did not reflect administration costs and issuing repossession proceedings without considering alternative measures.[107] As Margaret Cole, director of Enforcement and Financial Crime at the FSA, suggests 'this case shows credible deterrence in action. It is an excellent example of what the FSA's more intrusive approach can achieve for consumers …'.[108]

While these reforms are welcome, questions remain over their potential coverage and efficacy. The first point to note is that they apply only to first charge mortgages taken out after October 2004. Research by advice agencies, however, suggests that first charge mortgagees are more likely to seek possession only as a last resort so that 'some major high street mortgage lenders hardly appeared in the court lists',[109] while 'sub-prime' lenders constituted a disproportionate share of the court hearings to the extent that their court action 'appears nine times more than proportionate to their combined market share.'[110]

The second note of concern relates to their potential enforcement. As Citizens Advice suggest, the difficulty faced by regulators in monitoring

[101] FSA, 'Mortgage Market Review' Discussion Paper 09/3 (October 2009) 3 <http://www.fsa.gov.uk/pubs/discussion/dp09_03.pdf> accessed 5 October 2010.

[102] See, for example, FSA, 'Treating Customers Fairly – Towards Fair Outcomes for Consumers' (July 2006) [4.2] <http://www.fsa.gov.uk/pubs/other/tcf_towards.pdf> accessed 5 October 2010. See also *House of Commons Treasury Committee* (n 14) [33]–[40].

[103] MCOB 12.4.1AE.

[104] *FSA* (n 16) [3.4]–[3.7].

[105] MCOB 13.3.2AR(6).

[106] According to GMAC-RFC, see <http://www.gmacrfc.co.uk/about_us/who_we_are> accessed 5 October 2010.

[107] FSA, 'GMAC-RFC Limited fined £2.8million for unfair treatment of customers in arrears and repossessions and will pay up to £7.7m customer redress' Press Release FSA/PN/147/2009 (October 2009) <http://www.fsa.gov.uk/pages/Library/Communication/PR/2009/147.shtml> accessed 5 October 2010.

[108] Ibid.

[109] *AdviceUK* (n 35) 10.

[110] Ibid.

compliance within the mortgage market 'is that the regulator, whether OFT or FSA, is always at a distance and is only likely to pick up problems after they have occurred.'[111] Given the FSA's failure to regulate MCOB effectively in recent years,[112] significant improvements will have to be made in enforcement procedures. While the changes proposed to the regulatory framework by the Coalition government are awaited, a more effective enforcement outcome could be achieved by transferring responsibility for monitoring compliance with MCOB away from the FSA and towards district judges so that adherence would be checked in each and every case. This approach was mooted during the consultation stage in respect of the Protocol but was eventually rejected and it does not feature as part of the current proposals.[113] It must be assumed, therefore, that district judges will continue to rely on the less stringent requirements established under the Protocol. It should also be noted that the inherent right to possession remains intact so that mortgagees will remain entitled to seek possession without a court order.

In addition to the proposals put forward by the FSA and in keeping with the apparent preference of successive governments, the previous Labour government relied almost exclusively on non-statutory means to achieve its aim of regulating the mortgage relationship and in particular, reducing the number of repossessions. Measures introduced in response to recent financial circumstances included the introduction of a mortgage rescue scheme (MRS),[114] the long awaited (if temporary) change to the payment of support for mortgage interest, [115] a scheme that allowed some mortgagors to defer part of their payments for up to two years,[116] and the expansion of free legal advice in county courts.[117] Recent research reveals that these measures may well have assisted some mortgagors in their efforts to avoid repossession.[118] Statistics published by the Ministry of Justice (MOJ), for example, suggest that in the fourth quarter of 2009, the number of possession claims issued

[111] *Citizens Advice* (n 97) 7.

[112] *House of Commons Treasury Committee* (n 14) 3.

[113] *Whitehouse* (n 73).

[114] See 'The Mortgage Rescue Scheme' <http://webarchive.nationalarchives.gov.uk/+/http://www.communities.gov.uk/housing/buyingselling/mortgagerescuemeasures/> accessed 8 October 2010.

[115] See<http://www.direct.gov.uk/en/MoneyTaxandBenefits/BenefitsTaxCreditsandOtherSupport/On_a_low_income/DG_180321> accessed 5 October 2010.

[116] See Communities and Local Government, 'Real help for the housing market' <http://www.communities.gov.uk/documents/housing/pdf/1153110.pdf> accessed 25 February 2010.

[117] Ibid. For an account of these measures see *House of Commons Treasury Committee* (n 14) ch 4.

[118] See, for example, *AdviceUK* (n 35) and MOJ, 'People at risk of home repossession and eviction in Newcastle and Gateshead offered a lifeline' (3 December 2010) <http://www.justice.gov.uk/news/newsrelease031209c.htm> accessed 5 October 2010. Recent research suggests that in combination, income support and lenders' forbearance policies have reduced the number of repossessions, see J Aron and J Muellbauer, 'Modelling and Forecasting UK Mortgage Arrears and Possessions' Communities and Local Government Report (July 2010) 33 <http://www.communities.gov.uk/documents/housing/pdf/1643676.pdf> accessed 5 October 2010.

in the county courts fell by twenty-six per cent compared with the fourth quarter of 2008.[119]

The extent to which these initiatives have played a role in this reduction has been explored in research undertaken by AdviceUK and others. Based on data obtained from 452 cases in which mortgagors attended the court hearing and sought advice at the court, the research found that eleven of those cases were adjourned or the possession order suspended in order to allow the mortgagor time to pursue an application under the MRS.[120] Unfortunately, there were also thirteen cases where the advisers considered that the mortgagor may have been eligible for the MRS but an immediate possession order was granted.[121] The Coalition government has maintained the MRS, albeit with a reduction in the funding paid to housing associations, but its long term future seems uncertain given the government's commitment to a reduction in spending.[122] While the fall in the number of repossessions may have been due to the measures introduced by the previous government, the MOJ suggests that a further possible cause may have been the introduction of the Protocol.[123]

In relation to its impact upon judicial decision making, early research indicates that the Protocol is being relied upon by some district judges to adjourn claims for possession. However, it would appear that it is being applied inconsistently, with some courts being 'scrupulous about implementing the recommendations,'[124] while in other cases 'the protocol is being ignored not only by the courts, but also by the lenders bringing the actions – some of which have had billions of pounds of public money – and the solicitors acting on their behalf.'[125] Research by AdviceUK and others indicates that in a third of 300 repossession cases examined in July 2009, the mortgagee had not complied with the Protocol but in only six cases were sanctions applied for non-compliance.[126] Specific data suggests that in eleven per cent of the cases examined, no contact had been made between the mortgagor and mortgagee and that in seventy-one per cent of cases, the mortgagee had offered no alternatives to possession.[127] The advice agencies have called for greater clarity in relation to the sanctions and, in particular, the ability of district judges to prevent mortgagees adding the

[119] MOJ, 'Statistics on Mortgage and Landlord possession Actions in the County Courts – Fourth Quarter 2009' (February 2010) <http://www.justice.gov.uk/publications/mortgatelandlordpossession.htm> accessed 5 October 2010.

[120] *AdviceUK* (n 35) 8.

[121] Ibid.

[122] Communities and Local Government, 'Grant Shapps Outlines Government Support for Struggling Homeowners' (20 July 2010) <http://www.communities.gov.uk/news/corporate/1643931> accessed 5 October 2010.

[123] *MOJ* (n 119) 4.

[124] T Marshall, 'Anger in Court' *Roof* (May/June 2009) 28.

[125] Ibid. See also *House of Commons Treasury Committee* (n 14) [62]; T Marshall, 'Under the Heel: Loophole Leaves Courts Powerless to Help Borrowers in Arrears' *Roof* (May/June 2010) 19.

[126] *AdviceUK* (n 35) 1.

[127] Ibid 12.

costs of the hearing to the mortgagor's account where non-compliance with the Protocol is found.[128]

Despite repossession figures proving to be significantly lower in 2009 than originally predicted by the CML,[129] advice agencies have warned that 'the tide of mortgage repossessions has not yet turned'[130] and that unemployment and rising interest rates could lead to an increase in repossessions. Given that the CML are predicting 39,000 repossessions in 2010,[131] it is essential that reform is undertaken, not least to counteract some of the problems identified in respect of the permissive approach adopted in the regulation of the mortgage relationship. The attempts by the FSA in this respect are commendable but they do not of course extend beyond the remit of the FSA's powers, with the result that the proposals deal only with MCOB 13 and apply only to regulated mortgages. The regulation of the mortgage relationship will, therefore, continue to rely upon legal rules, contractual negotiation, discretion and soft law. It seems evident that in order to enhance due process and to ensure consistent and equitable treatment for mortgagors, a more prescriptive and systematic approach is required. Given the apparent preference for administrative regulation by successive governments, it would seem somewhat unlikely that any government will choose to limit its capacity for implementing flexible and timely measures in favour of rigid and time consuming legislative reforms. There is precedent for such a move, however, in the form of the Scottish Act.

The Home Owner and Debtor Protection (Scotland) Act 2010: a prescription for success?

Passed unanimously by MSPs in February 2010 and having received Royal Assent on 18 March 2010, the Scottish Act is intended to 'protect home owners and debtors during a period of recession, and in particular to reduce the risk of homelessness as a result of insolvency.'[132] Arising out of reports published by

[128] Ibid 17.

[129] At the start of 2009, the CML predicted that 75,000 homes would be repossessed during the year. The actual total was 46,000 but this was still 15 per cent higher than in 2008, see CML, 'Mortgage arrears and possessions declined in fourth quarter of 2009' (11 February 2010) <http://www.cml.org.uk/cml/media/press/2541> accessed 5 October 2010.

[130] *AdviceUK* (n 35) 2.

[131] This figure was revised down from a forecast earlier in 2010 of 53,000 repossessions but the CML have suggested that 'there is no room for complacency looking further ahead': CML, 'CML Reports Decline in Arrears and Repossessions' (12 August 2010) <http://www.cml.org.uk/cml/media/press/2680> accessed 5 October 2010.

[132] Scottish Parliamentary Corporate Body, 'Home Owner and Debtor Protection (Scotland) Bill: Policy Memorandum' (October 2009) [2] <http://www.parlamaid-alba.org/s3/bills/32-homeOwner/b32s3-introd-pm.pdf> accessed 5 October 2010.

the Debt Action Forum,[133] and its sub-group the Repossessions Group,[134] the Act seeks to enhance due process and consistency within the repossession process by requiring court authorisation prior to the exercise of the mortgagee's remedies. The significance of this Act should not be underestimated for it effectively removes the mortgagee's inherent right to possession by making it conditional upon the award of an order from the court.

Under previous rules, mortgagees could, by virtue of the Conveyancing and Feudal Reform (Scotland) Act 1970 (CFRA 1970), take possession without a court order through the service of a notice of default (where the mortgagor is in breach of the agreement) or a calling up notice (where mortgagor is required to pay the outstanding mortgage debt). Added to this was the Mortgage Rights (Scotland) Act 2001 (MRA 2001) which entitled the mortgagor to request that the court suspend the exercise of the rights which the mortgagee has to such extent, for such period, and subject to such conditions, as the court thinks fit.[135] In effect, mortgagees were not obliged to seek an order from the court but the mortgagor could apply to the court for the exercise of the mortgagee's rights to be suspended. While the Repossessions Group noted that in practice, most mortgagees did seek a court order under the CFRA 1970 section 24, the vast majority of mortgagors did not take advantage of the MRA 2001.[136]

In an effort to improve the protection afforded to mortgagors, the Repossessions Group recommended that all cases should come before the court and that the mortgagor should be entitled to attend or be represented.[137] In seeking to implement these proposals, the Scottish Act amends the CFRA 1970, so as to make a mortgagee's entitlement to the rights[138] under the security, where the mortgagor is in 'default',[139] conditional upon the grant of a warrant from the court.[140] Prior to seeking a warrant from the court, the mortgagee is required to comply with the pre-action requirements set out in the new CFRA 1970 section 24A.[141] The mortgagee must, for example, provide the mortgagor with clear

[133] A group of stakeholders invited in January 2009 by Scottish Ministers to report on measures that might help to protect mortgagors during recession, see: Debt Action Forum, 'Final Report' (June 2009) <http://www.aib.gov.uk/About/DAF/DebtActionForumFinalRepo> accessed 5 October 2010.

[134] Repossessions Group, 'Final Report' (June 2009) <http://www.scotland.gov.uk/Publications/2009/06/08164837/0> accessed 5 October 2010.

[135] Mortgage Rights (Scotland) Act 2001 s 2(1).

[136] The Repossessions Group does not have accurate figures but estimates that applications under the Mortgage Rights (Scotland) Act 2001 were made in only five to ten per cent of cases: *Repossessions Group* (n 134) [6.32].

[137] Ibid [6.34].

[138] These can be found in Conveyancing and Feudal Reform (Scotland) Act 1970 sch 3 standard condition 10.

[139] Conveyancing and Feudal Reform (Scotland) Act 1970 sch 3 standard condition 9 defines 'default' so as to include (a) where a calling-up notice in respect of the security has been served and has not been complied with; and (b) where there has been a failure to comply with any other requirement arising out of the security.

[140] Home Owner and Debtor Protection (Scotland) Act 2010 (HODP Act 2010) s 1 inserts a new Conveyancing and Feudal Reform (Scotland) Act 1970 (CFRA 1970) s 20(2A) and s 23(4).

[141] HODP Act 2010 s 2(2) inserts a new CFRA 1970 s 24(1C). See also, Home Owner and Debtor Protection (Scotland) Act 2010: Guidance on Pre-Action Requirements for Creditors.

information about any arrears and charges in respect of late payments and sources of debt advice.[142] In addition, the mortgagee must not seek to enforce its rights if the mortgagor is taking steps which are likely to result in the payment, within a reasonable time, of any arrears, or the whole amount, due.[143]

In determining whether to grant the warrant, the court must be satisfied initially that the mortgagee has complied with the pre-action requirements and that it is reasonable in the circumstances of the case to do so.[144] If those two requirements are met, the court may, where the mortgagor appears or is represented,[145] have regard to matters such as, the nature of and reasons for the default, the ability of the mortgagor to fulfil within a reasonable time the obligations under the mortgage and the ability of the mortgagor to secure reasonable alternative accommodation.[146] This process does not apply if the mortgagor has voluntarily abandoned the property provided that the mortgagor and any spouse or civil partner has certified in writing that they no longer occupy the property and that they consent to the mortgagee exercising their rights provided consent is given freely and without coercion.[147]

It seems clear that the provisions contained within the Scottish Act are intended to offer greater protection to mortgagors in their efforts to avoid repossession. In particular, it removes the obligation, previously imposed upon mortgagors, to seek suspension of the order for possession, and instead requires mortgagees to seek an order from the court having first complied with a series of pre-action requirements. It would seem that the mortgagor is still expected to attend, for it is only where the mortgagor is in attendance or represented that the court may consider additional factors such as the reasons for the default or the mortgagor's ability to find alternative accommodation. As the Repossessions Group note, however, their proposals were intended to suggest ways 'to improve borrower representation in actions for possession'.[148]

One issue that has garnered a degree of criticism relates to the award of costs and in particular, the question as to who pays for the legal fees if a mortgagee's request for a warrant is denied.[149] It would seem that the mortgagee will not be entitled to 'charge expenses' to the mortgagor's account if the application is denied due to their failure to comply with the pre-action requirements. Shelter, however, has called for more stringent rules which would prevent a mortgagee from claiming legal fees where the case is refused for whatever reason.[150]

[142] HODP Act 2010 s 4(1) inserts a new CFRA 1970 s 24A(2) and (5).

[143] HODP Act 2010 s 4(1) inserts a new CFRA 1970 s 24A(3) and (4).

[144] HODP Act 2010 s 2(5) inserts a new CFRA 1970 s 24(5).

[145] 'Entitled residents' may also apply to the court – these include spouses, civil partners and 'common law' spouses; see HODP Act 2010 s 5 which inserts new CFRA 1970 ss 24B and 24C.

[146] HODP Act 2010 s 2(5) inserts a new CFRA 1970 s 24(7).

[147] HODP Act 2010 s 1(3) inserts a new CFRA 1970 s 23A.

[148] *Repossessions Group* (n 134) [6.34].

[149] See, for example, Shelter Scotland, 'Home Owner and Debtor Protection (Scotland) Bill Briefing for Stage 3 Debate' (February 2010) <http://scotland.shelter.org.uk/__data/assets/pdf_file/0006/253671/HODPB_Stage_3_briefing.pdf> accessed 5 October 2010.

[150] Ibid 2.

It is, of course, difficult at this early stage to assess the impact of the Scottish Act; as McIntosh notes, 'much will depend on the approach of sheriffs and their interpretation of what constitutes "reasonable".'[151] While the provisions contained in the Act are similar to those contained in MCOB and the Protocol, however, the rationale which underpins it is very different, namely, that the Scottish Parliament is prepared to implement legal rules in pursuit of improvements to the treatment of mortgagors in arrears. Unlike the Protocol, for example, which asks mortgagees to *consider* not starting a possession claim in specified circumstances,[152] the Scottish Act *requires* mortgagees to delay court action if an agreement has been reached with the mortgagor. In addition to going further than the soft law mechanisms employed in England and Wales, the statutory force of these provisions means that they will apply equally to all mortgagees and will be enforced in each and every case. If provisions similar to those contained in the Scottish Act were to be implemented in England and Wales, therefore, problems in terms of the coverage and enforcement capabilities of the FSA would be removed. By making possession conditional on the award of an order from the court, thereby effectively removing the mortgagee's inherent right to possession, they would constitute also one of the most radical reforms of the law of mortgage for decades, if not centuries. The effective demotion of the mortgagee's claim for possession from a right to a remedy is a move that has been called for on several occasions by numerous parties but which has not been taken forward by previous governments.[153] Perhaps the radical step taken by MSPs will encourage the Coalition government to consider such a move.

Conclusions

The English law of mortgage has demonstrated a remarkable capacity for stability. Admittedly, there have been new developments within the case law but even judicial pronouncements have indicated a capacity to persist over several decades.[154] While the law of mortgage has continued largely undisturbed over the last forty years or so, however, the social context has witnessed fundamental changes. In accounting for this phenomenon, it is possible to point to the minimalist nature of the law of mortgage which sketches out the boundaries of

[151] *McIntosh* (n 20) 273.

[152] See, for example, the *Protocol* (n 73) [6.1].

[153] See, for example, M Dixon, 'Sorry, We've Sold Your Home: Lenders and Their Possessory Rights' (1999) 58 *CLJ* 281; J Howell, 'The Human Rights Act 1998: Land, Private Citizens, and the Common Law' (2007) 123 *LQR* 618; Law Commission, 'Transfer of Land – Land Mortgages' (Law Com No 204 HC 5, 1991); *McAuslan* (n 81).

[154] See, for example, the definition of the mortgage in *Santley v Wilde* [1899] 2 Ch 474 (CA) and confirmation of the inherent right to possession in *Four-Maids Ltd v Dudley Marshall (Properties) Ltd* [1957] Ch 317 (Ch).

the mortgage relationship while leaving the 'colour' to be added in by alternative regulatory techniques. The implication of this, in terms of developing our understanding of the law of mortgage, is significant in that it must follow that positivist accounts of the law of mortgage will fail to offer sufficient insight into the substance of the mortgage relationship. It is imperative, therefore, that further socio-legal research is conducted in order to offer fully informed accounts of the mortgage relationship.

Whatever the reasons are for the stability apparent within the law of mortgage, it is clear that the outcome for mortgagors is a relationship in which they are vulnerable to the exercise of unregulated and unaccountable decision-making power and a repossession process in which like cases are not always treated alike. In order to invest the mortgage relationship, and in particular, the repossession process with a greater degree of due process and transparency, it is essential that reform is undertaken. What this chapter has sought to argue is that alternative regulatory measures have been tried and have failed to prove effective. As the Treasury Committee noted in its detailed and highly critical report on mortgage arrears, 'industry guidelines are not a substitute for more robust rules – they are voluntary not binding, there is often little monitoring or supervision and there are no sanctions for non-compliance.'[155] For this reason, it is essential that the government regains control of the regulatory enterprise and gives equal voice to the concerns of the mortgagor and mortgagee. While this seems unlikely given the apparent reluctance on the part of successive governments to undertake legal reform, there is evidence to suggest that command and control regulation is the next natural step. The progression from self-regulatory schemes implemented by industry representatives,[156] to 'enforced self-regulation'[157] monitored by the FSA and now regulation supplemented by discretionary punishment enforced by the FSA,[158] appears to be consistent with Ayres' and Braithwaite's 'pyramid strategy'.[159] If this is the case, then the next step in that process will be command regulation with 'nondiscretionary punishment'.[160] As Ayres and Braithwaite note:

> … given that an industry will be tempted to exploit the privilege of self-regulation by socially suboptimal compliance with regulatory goals, the state must also communicate its willingness to escalate its regulatory strategy up another pyramid of interventionism.[161]

In arguing that such a step should be taken sooner rather than later, this chapter has offered an account of the Scottish Act which seeks to make mandatory

[155] *House of Commons Treasury Committee* (n 14) [47].

[156] During the 1990s, the CML *Statement of Practice* encouraged its members to adopt more efficient methods of communication with their borrowers and more flexible arrangements for assisting them in clearing their arrears; see *Whitehouse* (n 29).

[157] See, for example, *Baldwin and Cave* (n 19) 39–41.

[158] *FSA* (n 16).

[159] *Ayres and Braithwaite* (n 22).

[160] Ibid 38.

[161] Ibid.

provisions similar to those contained in MCOB and the Protocol. It seems unlikely, given the potential for legislation of this kind to shake one of the central pillars of the English law of mortgage; namely, the mortgagee's inherent right to possession, that it will be before Parliament any time soon. What the Scottish Act will do, however, is give further credence and momentum to the claim that legal reform is well overdue.[162]

[162] See the authors cited in n 153.

8

Proprietary Estoppel, Promises and Mistaken Belief

John Mee*

Introduction

The decision of the House of Lords in *Yeoman's Row Management Ltd v Cobbe*[1] represents a curious turn in the development of the law of proprietary estoppel. Taking its first opportunity to pronounce upon the doctrine of proprietary estoppel since the seminal decision in *Ramsden v Dyson* in 1866,[2] the House of Lords in *Cobbe* put forward an unexpectedly restrictive view of the scope of the doctrine. The case involved an experienced property developer, Cobbe, who had reached an agreement in principle with the owner of certain land under which Cobbe would pursue an application for planning permission in respect of the land and, if the planning permission were obtained, the land would be sold to Cobbe at an agreed price as part of an arrangement whereby he would develop the land and sell it on (although not all the details of the arrangement had been worked out). Both parties were aware that the agreement was binding only 'in honour'. As it turned out, once the planning permission had been obtained through Cobbe's extensive work, the land-owner sought to raise substantially the price Cobbe would have to pay for the land, ultimately triggering litigation between the parties. Cobbe's proprietary estoppel claim failed in the House of Lords, although he did succeed in obtaining remuneration for his time and effort under restitutionary principles.

While the actual result in *Cobbe* was regarded with approval by most commentators, the reasoning of both Lord Scott and Lord Walker (who gave the

* Law Faculty, University College Cork. I am grateful to Dr Mary Donnelly, and to the anonymous referee, for their comments on an earlier draft. Any remaining errors are solely my responsibility.

[1] [2008] UKHL 55, [2008] 1 WLR 1752.

[2] (1866) LR 1 HL 129 (HL).

only substantive judgments) has been the source of controversy. The approach of both of their Lordships was seriously at odds with previous authority and, if taken seriously, would have resulted in a far less potent doctrine of proprietary estoppel.[3] As it happened, *Cobbe* was swiftly followed by another House of Lords decision. In *Thorner v Major*,[4] the factual background was rather different. David Thorner had worked without pay for many years on the farm of his father's cousin, Peter Thorner, on the basis of oblique indications that he would inherit the farm on Peter's death. When Peter died intestate, David succeeded in establishing a claim to the farm on the basis of proprietary estoppel. In *Thorner*, Lord Walker described the proposition that *Cobbe* had 'severely curtailed, or even virtually extinguished, the doctrine of proprietary estoppel' as 'a rather apocalyptic view',[5] giving the impression, without actually committing himself, that he regarded this proposition as mistaken. There seem to be clear inconsistencies between *Cobbe* and *Thorner* and, following the two decisions, aspects of the law of proprietary estoppel are left in some doubt.

Although Lord Scott and Lord Walker approached the question from different angles, the view taken in each of their speeches in *Cobbe* appears to have been that the claimant (C) could not succeed in a proprietary estoppel claim unless he acted in the belief that he had a legally enforceable right against the defendant (D). In other words, there could be no remedy under proprietary estoppel in a case where C simply trusted in D's promise, rather than mistakenly believing that he was taking no risk because he was protected by a legal entitlement. This chapter argues that the result of accepting the approach in *Cobbe* would effectively be that the law would no longer recognise the principle expressed in Lord Kingsdown's speech in *Ramsden v Dyson*, which (although often described as representing the 'expectation' limb of proprietary estoppel) essentially turns on the making of a promise by D. While, in fact, a case could be made for taking the dramatic step of discarding this principle, which it will be suggested is one of a number of distinct principles subsumed by proprietary estoppel, the House of Lords in *Cobbe* did not appear to grasp the significance of the question and, therefore, addressed neither the weight of contrary authority nor the key issues of principle. Therefore, it is probably best that the unorthodox views expressed in the case should be forgotten or, at least, shelved until they can be revisited by the Supreme Court with the benefit of an awareness of the extent to which they run counter to the current of authority since the 1960s. The contrasting outcomes in *Cobbe* and *Thorner v Major*, and an extra-judicial

[3] See eg B McFarlane and A Robertson, 'The Death of Proprietary Estoppel' [2008] *LMCLQ* 449; T Etherton, 'Constructive Trusts and Proprietary Estoppel: The Search for Clarity and Principle' [2009] *Conv* 104, 116–20.

[4] [2009] UKHL 18, [2009] 1 WLR 776. See eg B McFarlane and A Robertson, 'Apocalypse Averted: Proprietary Estoppel in the House of Lords' (2009) 125 *LQR* 535; N Piska, 'Hopes, Expectations and Revocable Promises in Proprietary Estoppel' (2009) 72 *MLR* 998; J Mee, 'The Limits of Proprietary Estoppel: *Thorner v Major*' (2009) 21 *CFLQ* 367.

[5] [2009] UKHL 18, [2009] 1 WLR 776 [31].

contribution by Lord Neuberger,[6] raise the possibility that the requirement of belief in a legal entitlement could be applied in the commercial context but not in the 'domestic' context. This possibility is also considered in this chapter and it is concluded that, despite its superficial plausibility, it would not represent a desirable development for the law. This is, in part, because it seems to be an oversimplification to assume that more intrusive equitable intervention is appropriate in the domestic, as compared to the commercial, context.

Cobbe and mistaken belief

The approach in *Cobbe*

The view that C cannot succeed unless C believed that he or she had a legal entitlement to an interest in D's land emerges with particular clarity from the speech of Lord Walker. The views of Lord Walker did not receive majority support in *Cobbe*, given that Lord Mance and Lord Hoffmann agreed instead with Lord Scott, with Lord Brown agreeing with both Lord Scott and Lord Walker. Lord Walker commented that the type of case at issue often has 'at least a flavour of mistake, or at any rate what restitution lawyers call misprediction (Mr Cobbe predicted, wrongly, that Mrs Lisle-Mainwaring [the defendant] would not withdraw from the non-binding arrangement)'. He then asked himself: 'Was it also necessary for Mr Cobbe to believe, wrongly, that Mrs Lisle-Mainwaring had no legal right to withdraw from it?'[7] Lord Walker concluded that it was indeed necessary that the claimant should have believed that he had a legally enforceable right. Lord Walker emphasised the view of Lords Cranworth and Wensleydale in *Ramsden* that an agreement which was known to be binding only in honour could not form the basis of a valid claim.[8] Although, according to his Lordship, the language of Lord Kingsdown's key statement of principle in his dissenting speech in *Ramsden v Dyson* was 'not without ambiguity' on the point, the rest of his speech indicated that 'Lord Kingsdown's reading of the facts was that the tenants believed (wrongly) that they had a legal right to a long lease, and that that was of critical importance'.[9] Lord Walker felt that, in *Plimmer v Mayor of Wellington*, this requirement had also been applied and found to be satisfied.[10]

His Lordship conceded that the relevant point had been made less frequently in the context of 'cases with more of a domestic or family flavour'[11] but he

[6] Lord Neuberger, 'The Stuffing of Minerva's Owl? Taxonomy and Taxidermy in Equity' (2009) 68 *CLJ* 537.

[7] *Yeoman's Row Management Ltd v Cobbe* [2008] UKHL 55, [2008] 1 WLR 1752 [63].

[8] Ibid [53].

[9] Ibid [64].

[10] Ibid [65], referring to *Plimmer v Mayor of Wellington* (1884) 9 App Cas 699 (PC) 712.

[11] Ibid [66].

felt that the requirement was also applicable in such cases. He insisted that 'in those cases in which an estoppel was established, the claimant believed that the assurance on which he or she relied was binding'.[12] Lord Walker was willing to accept that some of the domestic cases might have been decided differently 'if the nature of the claimant's belief had been an issue vigorously investigated in cross-examination'.[13] However, Lord Walker believed that it was not a coincidence that the matter cropped up more frequently in the commercial context than in the family context. He explained that '[t]he typical domestic claimant does not stop to reflect (until disappointed expectations lead to litigation) whether some further legal transaction (such as a grant by deed, or the making of a will or codicil) is necessary to complete the promised title'.[14]

In his speech in *Cobbe*, Lord Scott did not address the point as directly as Lord Walker. However, a requirement that C believed that he was legally entitled to an interest in D's land appears to follow logically from Lord Scott's overall analysis of proprietary estoppel. Departing from pre-existing orthodoxy, Lord Scott took literally the phrase 'proprietary *estoppel*'.[15] He insisted that, like other estoppels, a proprietary estoppel 'bars the object of it from asserting some fact or facts, or, sometimes, something that is a mixture of fact and law, that stands in the way of some right claimed by the person entitled to the benefit of the estoppel'.[16] Lord Scott's notion that proprietary estoppel is a true estoppel seems to lead, as a matter of principle, to a requirement that C have believed in the assertion of fact (or of fact mixed with law) by D which is alleged to form the basis of the estoppel. If D's representation was not believed by C, and acted upon, it would not be reasonable to regard D as having been estopped by virtue of having made it. This suggests that, for a proprietary estoppel claim to succeed, C must have believed that he was legally entitled to the interest in D's land which was the subject of D's representation. From various comments made in the course of his speech, it seems clear that Lord Scott did indeed believe that a proprietary estoppel claim could not be based on a promise which C knew to be legally unenforceable.[17] It should be noted, however, that his Lordship did approve of cases such as *Inwards v Baker*[18] and *Plimmer v Mayor of Wellington*[19]

[12] Ibid.

[13] Ibid [67]. Lord Walker suggested that such cross-examination had taken place in *Gillett v Holt* [2001] Ch 210 (CA) 229. In fact, however, this cross-examination seems clearly to have been directed to the question of whether D's representations were 'binding' in the sense of amounting to a promise (as opposed to a statement of current testamentary intentions), rather than to the distinct question of whether this promise was believed by the claimant to be legally binding. Unfortunately, these two questions have not always been clearly distinguished. See further *Mee* (n 4) 370–372 (discussing ambiguity in *Gillett* in respect of the idea of irrevocability). See also (n 42).

[14] Ibid [68].

[15] Contrast C Harpum, S Bridge and M Dixon, *Megarry and Wade, The Law of Real Property* (7th edn Sweet & Maxwell, London 2008) 699.

[16] *Cobbe* (n 7) [14].

[17] See ibid [15]; [27], [37].

[18] [1965] 2 QB 29 (CA).

[19] (1884) 9 App Cas 699 (PC).

which might be seen as based on a promise by D; his Lordship's reasoning was that, where D has stated that C's license to occupy D's land is irrevocable, D can be estopped from denying that this is so.[20]

Lord Walker, *Ramsden v Dyson* and the *probanda*

Upon closer inspection, it seems that Lord Walker's approach in *Cobbe* may have been unwittingly influenced by the same thinking which inspired the discredited *probanda* stated by Fry J in *Willmott v Barber*.[21] The first of the five *probanda* requires that 'the plaintiff must have made a mistake as to his legal rights', (the other *probanda* being (2) that C has acted on the faith of his mistaken belief; (3) that D knew of the existence of his own inconsistent right; (4) that D knew of C's mistaken belief; (5) that D encouraged C's detrimental action, either directly or by abstaining from asserting his right).[22] Although, in *Cobbe*, Lord Walker indicated no support for any aspect of the *probanda*, and in fact went out of his way to comment negatively on their influence,[23] he did rely on the majority judgments in *Ramsden v Dyson*. However, it appears that Fry J derived his *probanda* from those majority judgments, which are actually the source of the idea, inconsistent with the thrust of modern proprietary estoppel jurisprudence, that a mistake on C's part is a prerequisite to any remedy in (what is now known as) proprietary estoppel.

It is well known that the majority in *Ramsden v Dyson* stated the principle behind the 'mistake limb' of proprietary estoppel, which applies '[i]f a stranger begins to build on my land supposing it to be his own, and I, perceiving his mistake, abstain from setting him right, and leave him to persevere in his error'.[24] On the face of it, there was no possibility that the claimant in *Ramsden* could succeed on the basis of this principle because he had not been mistaken as to the ownership of the land. He knew that he was a tenant at will but his case was based on the proposition that he had been led to expect that he would be able to obtain a more substantial lease. What is interesting is that both Lord Cranworth and Lord Wensleydale[25] envisaged a means whereby a claimant who had not made a mistake in an obvious sense, but who had been led by D's promise to

[20] *Cobbe* (n 7) [22] and note also his Lordship's rationalisation of the decision in *Crabb v Arun DC* [1976] Ch 179 (CA).

[21] (1880) 15 Ch D 96 (Ch). For discussion of the demise of the *probanda*, signalled by *Taylor Fashions v London Victoria Trustees Ltd* [1982] QB 133n (Ch), see K J Gray and S F Gray, *Elements of Land Law* (5th edn OUP, Oxford 2009) 1207–10. Note also the discussion of the *probanda* by Patten LJ in *Lester v Woodgate* [2010] EWCA Civ 199 [27]–[39].

[22] (1880) 15 Ch D 96 (Ch) 105–6.

[23] *Cobbe* (n 7) [56]–[58].

[24] *Ramsden v Dyson* (1866) LR 1 HL 129 (HL) 140–41 (Lord Cranworth). Note the very similar formulation by Lord Wensleydale at 168.

[25] Lord Westbury agreed with Lord Cranworth, as did the fifth judge, Lord Brougham (who was not present to give a speech).

believe that he had a legal right to the land, could succeed by analogy with the principle applicable in cases of mistake. Lord Cranworth explained that the trial judge (who had upheld C's claim) had concluded that C had built his house 'in the belief, created or encouraged'[26] by D that C was at any time entitled to call for a new lease. If Lord Cranworth had accepted Lord Kingsdown's principle, it would have been obvious why this interpretation of the facts would have led to a remedy for C. However, Lord Cranworth felt it necessary to explain that the trial judge must have considered that, on this interpretation of the facts, the case fell within the mistake principle because D had been aware of C's mistaken belief in a legal entitlement and had failed to intervene.[27] Lord Wensleydale reasoned in a similar way.[28] In the end, however, since both judges believed that C had not been mistaken as to his rights and that D had not known or believed that C was acting on the basis of a mistake, they refused any remedy to C.

Thus, for the majority judges, a contractually unenforceable promise by D was not significant in itself but mattered only insofar as it might have created a mistaken belief in a legal entitlement on the part of C.[29] This is because, on the majority's view, even if D had created or encouraged C's belief by making a promise, it was necessary (i) that C believed wrongly that he had a legal entitlement and (ii) that D knew that C did not have a legal entitlement. This makes it very unlikely that the difference between Lord Kingsdown and the other four members of the House of Lords was simply on the correct interpretation of the facts. It would have made no sense for Lords Cranworth and Wensleydale to explain that C could succeed if the above two conditions were satisfied if they thought that, in addition, C could succeed where neither condition was satisfied.

Interestingly, when Lord Walker suggested in *Cobbe* that the difference in *Ramsden* between Lord Kingsdown and the majority judges was on the correct reading of the facts and not on the law,[30] he was doing so on the opposite basis to judges in earlier cases such as *Crabb v Arun District Council*.[31] In those previous cases, the assumption was that the majority judges in *Ramsden* would have had no objection in principle to the broad expectation principle expressed by Lord Kingsdown, whereas Lord Walker's conclusion was that Lord Kingsdown shared the majority judges' view that, in all cases including those involving a promise, C must have acted on the basis of a mistaken belief in a legal entitlement. In the current author's view, both attempts to downplay the differences between Lord Kingsdown and the majority judges in *Ramsden* are misguided. The

[26] *Ramsden* (n 24) 142.

[27] Ibid.

[28] Ibid 169.

[29] This same strategy of trying to explain promises in terms of mistakes is evident in certain cases where an attempt was made to apply the *probanda* in cases involving promises. See *Griffith v Williams* (1978) 248 EG 947 (CA) 949; *Coombes v Smith* [1986] 1 WLR 808 (Ch) 818; *Stilwell v Simpson* (1983) 133 NLJ 894; *Matharu v Matharu* (1994) 68 P & CR 93 (CA) 102–103. Note also *Crabb* (n 20) 192.

[30] *Cobbe* (n 7) [52].

[31] *Crabb* (n 20) 194. See also *Plimmer v Mayor of Wellington* (1884) 9 App Cas 699 (PC) 711.

consequences of Lord Walker's approach, however, seem to be more serious. The pre-*Cobbe* rationalisation of *Ramsden* simply involved airbrushing out of the picture some early support for the universal applicability of the *probanda*, thus making the conventional modern understanding of proprietary estoppel seem to have a firmer historical basis. However, Lord Walker's reading of *Ramsden* led him, at the same time as rejecting the *probanda* out of hand, to try to reintroduce an important aspect of them in the form of a requirement of mistaken belief.

It will be necessary shortly to consider the status of the approach in *Cobbe* as a matter of authority and principle. Prior to this, however, it is necessary to prepare the ground by sketching out a taxonomy that would identify the different principles subsumed under 'proprietary estoppel'. This will allow for a better understanding of the limitation on the scope of proprietary estoppel which would result from an acceptance of the approach in *Cobbe*.

A taxonomy of proprietary estoppel

This section attempts briefly to map out what appear to be the three principles within the territory which proprietary estoppel covers (although no attempt is made to state all the requirements of a successful claim under each principle, whether as a matter of principle or of current law). As will be seen, the three principles are based respectively on acquiescence, representation and promise. Each principle provides a distinct basis for legal intervention, although it is possible that more than one principle could be triggered by a given set of facts. It could also be argued, on the basis of an expansive vision of unconscionability not shared by the current author, that a remedy may be available in certain cases that fall outside the scope of the three principles identified here.[32] However, the possible existence of such cases, which would probably be comparatively rare in any case, does not affect the substance of the arguments put forward in this chapter.

The taxonomy presented here differs to some extent from Gray and Gray's commonly cited three-fold classification (adopted by Lord Walker in *Cobbe*),[33] which divides the doctrine into (1) the 'imperfect gift' cases, (2) the 'common expectation' cases, and (3) the 'unilateral mistake' cases. According to Gray and Gray, '[t]hese cases alike present the essential characteristics of proprietary estoppel, but each class of case in its turn gives a heightened emphasis to one or other of the constituent elements of representation, reliance and unconscionable

[32] Perhaps in certain circumstances where C has made a mistake to which D has not contributed and D was not aware of his own rights (so that neither the representation principle nor the acquiescence principle would apply). See also n 42 in respect of whether a claim could arise in respect of something falling short of a promise.

[33] *Cobbe* (n 7) [48] and following.

disadvantage'.[34] The current author's view is that the overall category of 'proprietary estoppel' is not a helpful one and that it is questionable whether the three distinct principles described below in fact share 'essential characteristics'.

Acquiescence

C acts to his detriment in the mistaken belief that he has an interest in land which in fact belongs to D. D realises what is happening and does not correct C's mistake.

The acquiescence scenario is clearly covered by the fundamental statements of principle by the majority in *Ramsden v Dyson*.[35] This category, which the older cases also refer to in terms of 'lying by', has also been recognised in cases arising outside the context of disputes over land.[36] In the view of the current author, the tendency to treat D's failure to act as a representation by silence due to the fact that he was under a duty to speak[37] (so that this category could be subsumed within the representation principle, discussed below) serves only to confuse the matter. In principle, nothing which can be construed as a representation needs to be communicated from D to C, so that the principle can apply in a case where C was unaware that D was observing events and C could not, therefore, have read anything into D's failure to intervene.[38] The reason for equitable intervention is not the fact that D has led C to act to his detriment by means of a representation or promise but rather that D has failed to act when he was aware that C was acting to C's detriment on the basis of a mistake concerning D's rights (although the precise scope of the principle is in need of further analysis).[39]

Representing

D makes a representation to C to the effect that C has an interest in D's land. C acts to his detriment on the basis of this representation.

In this scenario, D is responsible for C's belief that C has rights over D's land. This means that, unlike in the previous category of case, it is not crucial that D have been aware of his own rights. The basis for legal intervention in this second scenario is that, having made a representation as to the facts or as to the state of

[34] *Gray and Gray* (n 21) 1202.

[35] *Ramsden* (n 24) 140–41 (Lord Cranworth); 168 (Lord Wensleydale).

[36] See eg *Proctor v Bennis* (1887) 36 Ch D 740 (CA) 759–761 (Cotton LJ); 761–62 (Bowen LJ); 765–66 (Fry LJ).

[37] *De Bussche v Alt* (1878) 8 Ch D 286 (CA) 314.

[38] Note *Blue Haven Enterprises Ltd v Tully* [2006] UKPC 17 [24].

[39] The current author disagrees with the proposition that this category is 'an extension of, though not different in principle from, the positive statement estoppels': P Matthews, 'The Words Which Are Not There: A Partial History of the Constructive Trust' in C Mitchell (ed), *Constructive and Resulting Trusts* (OUP, Oxford 2010) 27 (citing A K Turner (ed), *G Spencer Bower: The Law Relating to Estoppel by Representation* (3rd edn Butterworths, London 1977) [290]).

D's own rights, D should not be permitted to resile freely from that representation if C has acted to his detriment on the basis of it. There is a clear overlap here with the legal doctrine of estoppel by representation. However, cases of this nature have sometimes been classified under the heading proprietary estoppel, notably in *Taylor Fashions v London Victoria Trustees Ltd*.[40] Possible limitations on the scope of estoppel by representation, eg in terms of whether it applies to representations of law rather than of fact, can effectively be sidelined if a case is analysed under the vaguer rubric of proprietary estoppel. It is not possible within the scope of this chapter to address the difficult issues which arise concerning the borderline between estoppel by representation and proprietary estoppel. It is intended only to note that the representation principle is clearly distinct, in principle, from acquiescence and promising, and that some, even if not all, examples of it have been regarded by the courts as falling within the ambit of 'proprietary estoppel'.

Promising

D promises C that C will acquire an interest in D's land and C acts to his detriment on the basis of this promise.

This is Lord Kingsdown's principle from *Ramsden v Dyson*. The grounds for equitable intervention in this situation must be seen as the proposition that, once C has relied to his detriment on a promise, D should not be able to resile freely from it. Significantly, traditional equitable discourse has not tended to acknowledge openly the role of promise in proprietary estoppel. Gray and Gray's third category, 'common expectation', appears to correspond to the current sub-heading. However, instead of discussing the idea of a promise by D, Gray and Gray explain the relevant principle as applying to 'the situation where … [D] and [C] have consistently dealt with each other in such a way as reasonably to cause … [C] to rely on a shared supposition that he would acquire rights of some kind in … [D]'s land'.[41] Taking it that Gray and Gray are accurately reflecting the language in the cases, this shows equity favouring a curiously indirect way of describing the relevant type of case, which generally involves D simply making a promise or promises to C. The supposition on C's part that he will acquire rights in D's land has normally been created by D's promise and whether D 'shares' this supposition (or, instead, plans to break his promise) does not seem relevant.[42]

[40] [1982] QB 133n (Ch). Note also Judge Nugee QC's frequently quoted definition of proprietary estoppel: *Re Basham* [1986] 1 WLR 1498 (Ch) 1503.

[41] *Gray and Gray* (n 21) 1204.

[42] A possible reason for not speaking in terms of 'promise' is the idea that a claim in proprietary estoppel could successfully be founded on something less than a promise (as well as on a promise). For discussion of some of the relevant issues, see S Nield, 'Estoppel and Reliance' in E Cooke (ed), *Modern Studies in Property Law: Volume 1* (OUP, Oxford 2003) 84–86, 88–89; *Mee* (n 4) 370–72. Although it is not possible or necessary to pursue the point in detail in the present chapter, the current author's view is, to the contrary, that it is wrong in principle to suggest that a mere expression of current intention, which does not contain an implied promise to give effect to the relevant intention, could form the basis of a claim in proprietary estoppel.

How the approach in *Cobbe* fits into the taxonomy

In terms of the taxonomy which has just been sketched out, the impact of taking *Cobbe* seriously would seem to be that the last of the three principles, Lord Kingsdown's promise principle, would effectively be eliminated from the law. It will be recalled that Lord Scott's view was that, like other estoppels, proprietary estoppel bars the object of it from asserting something that stands in the way of a right claimed by the person relying on the estoppel.[43] This shows that he was thinking only in terms of the representation principle (presumably regarding the acquiescence principle as a subset for this). Lord Scott's formulation leaves no room for proprietary estoppel to operate on the basis of a promise, rather than a representation or assertion, by D. This is not to say that C could never succeed in a case involving a promise by D. If D's promise to C reasonably gave C the impression that he had an entitlement to rights over D's land, then D could be regarded as having made a representation to C to this effect, so that the case would fall within the representation principle.[44]

In relation to Lord Walker's presentation of the matter, the introduction of a requirement of a mistaken belief on the part of C appears to have much the same effect in terms of eliminating any independent significance for a promise by D. There does, however, seem to be some degree of difference between the two approaches. Consider a situation where D makes a promise to C in respect of D's land and, although D cannot (on a reasonable interpretation of his words and conduct) be regarded as having made any representation to this effect, C forms the view that the promise is legally binding and acts to his detriment on this basis. No claim would appear to lie under Lord Scott's approach, since D cannot be regarded as having made a representation of fact or law, the truth of which he could be estopped from subsequently denying. Under Lord Walker's approach, however, it appears that C could make a successful claim, given that he has satisfied the requirement of having a mistaken belief in a legal entitlement. Thus, while Lord Walker's approach comes close to eliminating Lord Kingsdown's principle from the law (except insofar as it overlaps with the other two principles), it does not appear to do so entirely.

The position as a matter of authority

The view that Lord Kingsdown's principle does not form part of the law is not a novel one. The conventional wisdom on the acceptance of Lord Kingsdown's principle into the law of proprietary estoppel blames confusion generated by the *probanda* for any opposition to the principle. In an influential account,

[43] *Cobbe* (n 7) [14].

[44] Moreover, Lord Scott would presumably also have accepted that C could, in suitable circumstances, obtain a defensive remedy under promissory estoppel on the basis of a promise by D.

Gray and Gray suggest that for 'the 100 years following *Willmott v Barber*, Fry J's five probanda were to impose a strait-jacket on the development of proprietary estoppel',[45] given that they 'came to be applied indiscriminately to all forms of estoppel claim ... thereby dramatically curtailing the availability of estoppel-based remedies'.[46] This '[d]ogmatic insistence on the five probanda'[47] finally fell from favour after the 'watershed'[48] represented by *Taylor Fashions*. The assumption in this account is that Lord Kingsdown's principle was recognised by the law in the nineteenth century, as indicated by *Plimmer v Mayor of Wellington*,[49] but that Fry J 'without making explicit reference to any existing case law',[50] had confused matters with his overly strict approach. It may be, however, that this account puts too much emphasis on the *probanda* and overstates the ineluctability of the acceptance of Lord Kingsdown's principle.

An alternative narrative is as follows. In his dissenting speech in *Ramsden*, Lord Kingsdown briefly articulated a principle which seems to correlate to the modern 'expectation limb' of estoppel. Because he had the support of none of his colleagues, Lord Kingsdown explained that he would not deliver the 'very full' statement that he had prepared of the grounds for his conclusions. Instead, he gave a truncated statement of his views, setting out 'in a very few words what I understand to be the law upon the subject, and the effect generally which the evidence has produced on my mind'.[51] Thus, it is difficult to be sure what precisely his Lordship had in mind (and whether, for example, he intended his principle to have the broad scope subsequently attributed to it or, instead, envisaged some limitation upon it). It is possible to speculate that, if Lord Kingsdown had stated his views at length and attempted to defend them by reference to principle and existing authority, the doctrine of proprietary estoppel might have developed very differently. The one authority relied upon by Lord Kingsdown was the part performance case of *Gregory v Mighell*.[52] Subsequently, in *Plimmer*, Lord Kingsdown's principle was applied by the Privy Council but it seems to be stretching the point to see this one decision as entrenching the principle in the law, in the face of the lack of support from the majority of the House of Lords in *Ramsden*, especially as the principle does not appear to have been applied again for another 80 years.[53]

It is possible that the *probanda* constrained the development of the law on proprietary estoppel in an indirect way, as a result of the emphasis placed on

[45] *Gray and Gray* (n 21) 1207.
[46] Ibid.
[47] Ibid.
[48] Ibid 1209.
[49] (1884) 9 App Cas 699 (PC).
[50] *Gray and Gray* (n 21) 1207.
[51] *Ramsden* (n 24) 170.
[52] (1811) 18 Ves 328.
[53] An earlier authority, using the language of contract and consideration in the context of an imperfect gift, is *Dillwyn v Llewelyn* (1862) 4 De GF & J 517. See *Matthews* (n 39) 30–40 for an argument that Lord Kingsdown's approach finds support in the earlier case law.

them by Spencer Bower in his well-known work on *Estoppel by Representation*.[54] However, for many decades, there does not appear to be any indication in the case law that the reason why Lord Kingsdown's principle was not being applied was as a result of a misunderstanding created by the *probanda*. Even in more modern times, there is not a large number of cases where the *probanda* were 'dogmatically' applied to exclude the 'expectation limb' of proprietary estoppel, so as to defeat a claim.[55] Some of the pre-*Taylor Fashions* cases which mention the *probanda* doubt their strict applicability.[56] It may be that the reason why the courts did not apply Lord Kingsdown's principle lay more in their view of the acceptability of that principle than in any confusion caused by the *probanda*.

The final acceptance of Lord Kingsdown's principle occurred only in a series of modern cases beginning with *Inwards v Baker*[57] where it was adopted, with limited analysis, by Lord Denning's Court of Appeal. There subsequently developed a very substantial body of case law, albeit never at House of Lords level, applying the principle. In *Taylor Fashions*, the universal application of the *probanda* was rejected by Oliver J. In terms of the facts of the case, the important point to establish was that the representation principle, the second in the tripartite classification suggested above, could apply even though not all the *probanda* were satisfied because D was not aware of C's mistake or of his own rights. However, Oliver J's comments were clearly also directed against the idea of insisting that C must always be mistaken as to his rights (this being the first of the *probanda*, which was actually satisfied on the facts of *Taylor Fashions*). In a famous statement of principle, Oliver J argued that:

> ... the more recent cases indicate, in my judgment, that the application of the *Ramsden v. Dyson* ... principle – whether you call it proprietary estoppel, estoppel by acquiescence or estoppel by encouragement is really immaterial – requires a very much broader approach which is directed rather at ascertaining whether, in particular individual circumstances, it would be unconscionable for a party to be permitted to deny that which, knowingly, or unknowingly, he has allowed or encouraged another to assume to his detriment than to inquiring whether the circumstances can be fitted within the confines of some preconceived formula serving as a universal yardstick for every form of unconscionable behaviour.[58]

Although Oliver J's formulation of principle in *Taylor Fashions* has been widely praised, it appears in fact to be distinctly unhelpful in terms of facilitating the

[54] See eg G Spencer Bower, *The Law Relating to Estoppel by Representation* (1st edn, London 1923) 351–59 (discussing estoppel by acquiescence/encouragement in the context of land).

[55] See *E & L Berg Homes Ltd v Grey* [1980] 1 EGLR 103 (CA); *Stilwell v Simpson* (1983) 133 NLJ 894; *Coombes v Smith* [1986] 1 WLR 808 (Ch) (cases in which the claim would arguably have failed for other reasons). Note also *Kammins Ballrooms Co Ltd v Zenith Investments (Torquay) Ltd* [1971] AC 850 (HL) 884–85.

[56] See eg *Electrolux Ltd v Electrix* (1954) 71 RPC 23 (CA); *Shaw v Applegate* [1977] 1 WLR 970 (CA).

[57] [1965] 2 QB 29 (CA).

[58] [1982] QB 133n (Ch) 151–52.

coherent development of the law in this area. The obvious criticism of the *probanda*, or rather of the idea of applying them to all 'proprietary estoppel' cases, is that the *probanda* do not make sense when applied to a claim based on representation or promise rather than on acquiescence. Oliver J's response to the confusion between the different principles indicated by the inappropriate application of the *probanda* was, unfortunately, not to separate out the distinct principles but instead to state an 'unconscionability' test which was pitched at a sufficiently high level of generality that it could cover all three principles. Thus, he unified the different principles under the heading of 'the *Ramsden v Dyson* ... principle'. But why should they be considered as one? It is true that the acquiescence principle and Lord Kingsdown's promise principle both happen to emanate from different speeches in the same case (*Ramsden v Dyson*) but this is truly 'immaterial' in analytical terms. The confusing term 'proprietary estoppel', which clearly misled Lord Scott in *Yeoman's Row v Cobbe*,[59] enshrines no coherent principle and so, in itself, appears to offer no theoretical justification for unifying a number of distinct principles.

To conclude this sketch of the reception of Lord Kingsdown's principle, following *Taylor Fashions* the principle was applied with increasing frequency in the High Court and in the Court of Appeal in cases such as *Wayling v Jones*,[60] *Yaxley v Gotts*,[61] *Gillett v Holt*,[62] *Campbell v Griffin*,[63] *Jennings v Rice*,[64] *Ottey v Grundy*[65] and *Powell v Benney*.[66] This substantial body of case law indicates that, up until *Cobbe*, the standard case falling under the 'expectation limb' of proprietary estoppel involved the making of a promise to C, upon which C relied to his or her detriment. Despite Lord Walker's view in *Cobbe*, it is really quite untenable to suggest that in these cases the courts were silently insisting upon (and, implausibly in many cases, finding to be satisfied) a requirement that C had believed in the existence of a legal entitlement. The courts did tend to speak in terms of a 'belief' on the part of C but this was a belief 'that he either has or is going to be given a right in or over B's property' rather than necessarily a belief in a legal entitlement to the right.[67] The assumption of the courts, as encapsulated in a comment by Goff J in *Holiday Inns Inc v Broadhead*, was that 'mistake is not an essential element'.[68]

Only a year after *Cobbe*, the House of Lords decided *Thorner v Major*,[69] where a claim, in the 'domestic' context, was unanimously upheld on

[59] *Cobbe* (n 7) [16].
[60] (1993) 69 P & CR 170 (CA).
[61] [2000] Ch 162 (CA).
[62] [2001] Ch 210 (CA).
[63] [2001] EWCA Civ 990.
[64] [2002] EWCA Civ 159, [2003] 1 P & CR 100.
[65] [2003] EWCA Civ 1176.
[66] [2007] EWCA Civ 1283.
[67] *Re Basham* [1986] 1 WLR 1498 (Ch) 1503.
[68] (1974) 232 EG 951 (Ch) 1087.
[69] [2009] UKHL 18, [2009] 1 WLR 776.

the basis of (oblique) promises by D. In his speech in *Thorner*, with which Lords Rodger and Neuberger expressed agreement, Lord Walker did not restate his views in *Cobbe* as to the need for a belief on the part of C that he was legally entitled to an interest in D's land (although neither did he explicitly resile from them). Similarly, the speeches of the other Law Lords in *Thorner* appeared to take the conventional pre-*Cobbe* view, which makes no requirement of a belief in legal entitlement on the part of C but is satisfied with a promise on the part of D upon which C relies.[70] While focusing his remarks on the narrow questions at issue in *Thorner*, Lord Neuberger remarked that 'much of the reasoning in *Cobbe* ... was directed to the unusual facts of that case'.[71] Even Lord Scott appeared to retreat significantly from the view as to the nature of estoppel which he had expressed in *Cobbe*. He did not dissent from the conclusion of his brethren that the claimant was entitled to succeed on the basis of proprietary estoppel but merely found it 'easier and more comfortable' to regard the claimant's remedy as arising via a constructive trust (an approach betraying an unconventional understanding of the law of constructive trusts).[72]

Overall, the better view seems to be that there is no requirement, as the law currently stands, that C must have a belief in a legal entitlement. However, the position will continue to be complicated by what was said by the House of Lords in *Cobbe*, and never overtly retracted,[73] and it is possible that future cases will take up the approach favoured in *Cobbe*. Given this possibility, it is important to assess, as a matter of principle, the attractiveness or otherwise of that approach.

The place of Lord Kingsdown's principle in the legal system

The question of whether Lord Kingsdown's principle should be excised from the law is a very large one, which can only be touched upon in the current chapter. It is not difficult to identify why the acceptance of the promise principle might create difficulties for the legal system. The principle enters territory covered by the law of contract, arguably undermining the doctrine of consideration. While it is true that the remedy provided by proprietary estoppel does not invariably take the form of enforcing the promise, this is only a partial response to the relevant concern (and the cases still show a questionable bias in favour

[70] See eg *Thorner* (ibid) [2] C must prove 'a promise or assurance' (Lord Hoffmann).

[71] Ibid [99].

[72] Ibid [14]. For discussion of Lord Scott's views in *Thorner* on what he termed 'the remedial constructive trust' arising under the principle in *Gissing v Gissing* [1971] AC 886 (HL), see *Mee* (n 4) 378–81.

[73] See eg *Capron v Government of Turks and Caicos Islands* [2010] UKPC 2 [33], where Lord Kerr quoted a heretical passage from Lord Scott's speech in *Cobbe* (n 7) [14], describing it as 'a succinct summary of the principle'.

of awarding an expectation remedy).[74] There is also the major question of why this principle, with the potential to be used as a cause of action, should be recognised in respect of promises involving land (and, according to recent cases, other forms of property)[75] but not in respect of other promises, where only the defensive doctrine of promissory estoppel is available.

It does seem that in the future, if the law in this area is to be made defensible as a matter of principle, it will be necessary either to go forward or turn back; in other words, either the courts should follow the Australian approach of collapsing the distinction between proprietary and promissory estoppel, thus creating a doctrine which would not discriminate arbitrarily between promises involving land/property and other promises,[76] or else the courts should (which is perhaps difficult to imagine) row back from the jurisprudence of the last forty years or so and decisively eliminate Lord Kingsdown's principle from the law. In the meantime, a desirable development would be to move towards a more open recognition of the fact that this aspect of 'proprietary estoppel' is promise-based. This reality is somewhat obscured by the language conventionally used in discourse on equity, eg by the tendency to speak in terms of 'common expectation' and to describe D's promise as a 'representation' or an 'assurance'. The lack of clarity is exacerbated by the fact that three distinct principles, based respectively on acquiescence, representation and promise, form part of proprietary estoppel and a virtue is made of the fact that all three can be blurred together under the 'flexible' unconscionability slogan.

Rather than pursuing any further the very general question of whether Lord Kingsdown's principle should remain part of our legal system, it is proposed to narrow the focus and turn to a consideration of the possibility, raised by *Cobbe*, that perhaps proprietary estoppel goes too far in an obviously objectionable way and so, to avoid clearly undesirable outcomes, needs to be restricted. In *Cobbe*, Lord Scott appears to have been influenced by the fact that it does not seem right that C should succeed where he knew that D's promise was binding in honour only.[77] Lord Walker also insisted in *Cobbe* that '[i]t is not enough to hope, or even to have a confident expectation, that the person who has given the assurances will eventually do the proper thing ... [H]opes by themselves are not enough'.[78] These views highlight a potential difficulty for the orthodox theory of proprietary estoppel. Prior to *Cobbe*, most commentators would have rejected the idea of a requirement that C must believe in the legal enforceability of D's promise. However, at the same time, it does not seem right that C should be able to obtain a remedy on the basis of a mere hope that D would behave in a certain way. If one emphasises the proposition that D's promise is, to C's

[74] See generally J Mee, 'The Role of Expectation in the Determination of Proprietary Estoppel Remedies' in M Dixon (ed), *Modern Studies in Property Law: Volume 5* (OUP, Oxford 2009).

[75] See eg *Cobbe* (n 7) [14] (Lord Scott); *Thorner* (n 69) [61] (Lord Walker).

[76] The leading case is *Waltons Stores (Interstate) v Maher* (1988) 164 CLR 387 (Aus HC).

[77] *Cobbe* (n 7) [27].

[78] Ibid [65]–[66].

knowledge, not legally binding, it begins to look overly generous to provide C with a remedy if C chooses to take the risk of relying on that promise – particularly if the promise is made in a 'commercial context' (although, in fact, it is difficult to see why, if the force of this point were accepted, it would not also be relevant in the domestic context).

It seems, however, that there is a solution to this apparent problem. It appears that, even on an understanding of proprietary estoppel which does not require that C believes that he has a legally enforceable right, it would not be appropriate to provide a remedy against D where it is clear that D's promise is not one which will have any legal consequences. The point is that it is possible to qualify a promise in a way which changes the intended consequences of a breach. Imagine that I promise you that I will do something for you and, seeing you look doubtful, I add the words, 'I am serious about this promise, so much so that I am giving this crisp five pound note to our friend, Bill, telling him to give it to you if I should fail to perform'. These added words qualify the promise, in the sense that we now have a different understanding of the consequences of my not fulfilling it. It is similar if I promise you 'on my honour' or describe our agreement as 'a gentleman's agreement'. The implication here is that, if I do not perform, you are entitled to regard me as dishonourable or, in the latter case, as not a gentleman at all but rather as a bounder and a cad. The disincentive to my non-performance is the possibility that you, and anyone who hears of the matter, will think less of me. In a case where we might otherwise have imagined that legal consequences would attach to my promise, it may now be clear that the consequences of non-performance will relate only to my reputation. If, however, I make an unqualified promise, I do not restrict the consequences of the non-fulfilment of my promise and it remains possible, in principle, that legal consequences (in the realm of proprietary estoppel) could attach to that promise.[79] Thus, the fact that the promise itself is qualified by reference to the promisor's honour (or in some parallel way) may provide a reason, independent of a possible requirement that C must believe that he has a legal entitlement, why no estoppel remedy should be available.

It is also possible to see similar issues arising in the context of a promise which is made, explicitly or implicitly, subject to contract. If one business person makes an apparent promise to another business person in circumstances where both parties are aware that no binding contract can arise unless it is reduced to writing, it will often be the case that the promise in question has the same status as a promise 'in honour',[80] in that the parties understand that the consequence of a breach of the promise will lie at the level of damage to

[79] At a more general level, it seems that part of the conceptual complexity which arises in this area concerns the difficult relationship between the moral concept of promise and the legal concept of contract. See generally eg D Kimel, *From Promise to Contract: Towards a Liberal Theory of Contract* (Hart Publishing, Oxford 2003); S Shiffrin, 'The Divergence of Contract and Promise' (2007) 120 *Harv L Rev* 708; M Pratt, 'Contract not Promise' (2007–08) 35 *Fla St U L Rev* 801.

[80] See Lord Neuberger, 'The Stuffing of Minerva's Owl? Taxonomy and Taxidermy in Equity' (2009) 68 *CLJ* 537, 541.

the business or personal relationship between the parties. If such is the nature of the relevant 'promise' then, like a promise upon D's honour, it is not the kind which could trigger a proprietary estoppel claim. On the other hand, it is not difficult to envisage examples, in the commercial as well as the domestic sphere, where the promise is not qualified in the manner under discussion. An example is provided by the facts of the leading Australian case of *Waltons Stores (Interstate) v Maher*,[81] where Maher acted to his detriment on the basis of an assurance from Waltons Stores that the promised deal would proceed and that the exchange of contracts required to create a binding contract would occur as a matter of course.[82]

The fact that some apparent promises are, in fact, qualified in such a way as to preclude a remedy in proprietary estoppel seems to undercut the plausibility of the suggestion that there must be a requirement of mistaken belief in a legal entitlement in order to prevent a person obtaining a remedy on the basis of 'mere hopes'. What seems to be required is simply a promise which, in the sense under discussion, is unqualified. It certainly seems to be true that the restrictive approach put forward in the speeches in *Cobbe* was not necessary to a satisfactory resolution of the case. Depending on the true interpretation of the facts, the case could have been resolved on the basis (i) that the parties understood that D's promise was effectively subject to contract or (ii) that, even if D's promise was an unqualified one, it was essentially that C would acquire the land on reasonable terms, in circumstances where the court would be unable to devise reasonable terms by reference to past dealings between the parties[83] or (iii) that the result actually reached in *Cobbe* should have been justified on the basis of upholding D's proprietary estoppel claim and granting a detriment-based remedy as the minimum equity required to do justice (it being difficult to understand how C could have been entitled to the restitutionary remedy he actually received from the House of Lords if he could obtain no estoppel remedy because he had assumed the risk of obtaining no recompense in the event that the deal fell through).[84]

The remainder of this chapter will be given over to a consideration of another comparatively narrow issue, as to whether it might be appropriate to draw a

[81] *Waltons Stores (Interstate)* (n 76). It is not relevant for present purposes that, on the facts of the case itself, the expectation induced in C was not that he would acquire an interest in D's land but rather that D would take a lease of C's land.

[82] Compare Dixon's argument that gives central place to formal requirements, and an implicit or explicit secondary agreement to disregard them, in the rationale for upholding proprietary estoppel claims: M Dixon, 'Confining and Defining Proprietary Estoppel: the Role of Unconscionability' (2010) 30 *LS* 408; M Dixon, 'Proprietary Estoppel and Formalities in Land Law and the Land Registration Act 2002: A Theory of Unconscionability' in E Cooke (ed), *Modern Studies in Property Law: Volume 2* (Hart Publishing, Oxford 2003). Space does not permit a detailed engagement with Dixon's interesting argument. The current author does not, however, accept Dixon's thesis, preferring to emphasise the need for a promise which is not limited in the manner discussed in the text.

[83] See *Cobbe* (n 7) [23].

[84] For criticism of the restitution law aspects of the decision, see J Getzler, 'Quantum Meruit, Estoppel, and the Primacy of Contract' (2009) 125 *LQR* 196.

distinction between the commercial and the domestic contexts in terms of the application of a requirement of mistaken belief in legal entitlement (or, which is close to the same thing, whether such a distinction should be drawn in terms of applying Lord Kingsdown's principle).

A possible distinction between domestic and commercial cases

The contrast between the actual results in *Cobbe* and *Thorner v Major* suggests the possibility of drawing a distinction between the commercial and the domestic spheres, with a requirement of mistaken belief being applied only in the commercial context. This approach might involve the concession that certain cases, eg *Crabb v Arun DC*,[85] were wrongly decided but it would leave untouched the larger number of modern cases in the domestic context. In a recent extra-judicial contribution, Lord Neuberger has supported the idea of drawing this kind of distinction.[86] Lord Neuberger noted that:

> Ben Macfarlane and Andrew Robertson have suggested that *Cobbe* represented 'the death of proprietary estoppel,' not so much because the decision was wrong but because the reasoning precluded a proprietary estoppel claim unless the claimant believed that he had a legally enforceable claim.[87] I agree – and, at least in a commercial context, what's wrong with it?[88]

Lord Neuberger felt, however, that 'at least in many domestic cases, it would be inappropriate to require strict adherence to a rule that the claimant must have believed that he had a legally enforceable right'.[89] Lord Neuberger's logic appears to be that claimants in the family situation may often face an 'emotional or social impediment to insisting on some form of legally binding protection', they may not have easy access to legal advice, and often it would be 'somewhat unreal' to expect them to insist upon a commitment in writing.[90] It is not entirely clear whether Lord Neuberger would apply the requirement at all in the context of 'domestic' cases or whether he would apply it but (in some unexplained way) not 'strictly'. Lord Neuberger's distinction between the commercial sphere and the domestic context has some echoes of certain remarks of Baroness Hale in *Stack v Dowden*,[91] a case where Lord Neuberger, in fact, showed less enthusiasm

[85] *Crabb* (n 20).

[86] *Neuberger* (n 80). Note also Lord Neuberger's remarks in *Thorner* (n 69) [96]–[100], which strongly emphasise the importance of context but which are, on the face of them, limited to the issue of certainty as to the property which is the subject of D's representation.

[87] *McFarlane and Robertson* (n 3).

[88] *Neuberger* (n 80) 543.

[89] Ibid 544.

[90] Ibid 542.

[91] [2007] UKHL 17, [2007] 2 AC 432 [42], [69]. On *Stack* and the idea of 'context', see N Hopkins, 'Regulating Trusts of the Home: Private Law and Social Policy' (2009) 125 *LQR* 310; B Sloan

for drawing a distinction between the two spheres.[92] On balance, for reasons which will now be explored, the current author feels that Lord Neuberger's suggestion is not a felicitous one.

The first point relates to Lord Neuberger's justification for his suggested approach. He explained that:

> In the original cases such as *Dann* v. *Spurrier*,[93] *Ramsden* v. *Dyson* and *Rochdale Canal Co* v. *King*,[94] the basis of the estoppel claim was the plaintiff's mistaken belief that he was legally entitled to a property interest. Why should it be any different where the claimant believes he will receive a property interest?[95]

At this point, his Lordship seems to fall into the trap of confounding the different principles subsumed under the banner of proprietary estoppel. The 'original cases' to which he refers applied the acquiescence principle. Seeking to extend the mistake requirement appropriate in the acquiescence context to cases involving a promise by D, rather than a mistake by C, is redolent of the tendency in some earlier cases to apply the *probanda* to any possible case of proprietary estoppel. The answer to the question 'why should it be any different?' in the promise context as compared to the acquiescence context is that there are two different principles at issue and that, in terms of the logic of the promise principle, there is no obvious justification for the imposition of a mistaken belief requirement.[96]

The second problem relates to Lord Neuberger's emphasis on the question of ease of access to legal advice. Lord Walker had referred in *Cobbe* to this issue[97] but only to explain why the requirement of a mistaken belief was more likely to be satisfied in the domestic context. As a matter of logic, it is difficult to see how the fact that commercial claimants are less likely to satisfy a requirement of mistaken belief would serve to justify imposing such a requirement on them. In respect of the promise principle, what is crucial is that C has trusted D to keep his promise, something to which the availability of legal advice is not directly relevant. It might be argued that a different type of restriction should be imposed, to the effect that C could not obtain a remedy unless it was reasonable for him to have trusted D to keep his promise. This could conceivably lead to different results in the commercial context as compared to the domestic context, since it might be seen as reasonable to trust a friend or relation but not

'Proprietary Estoppel: Recent Developments in England and Wales' (2009) 22 *Singapore Academy of Law Journal* 110, 123–128.

[92] *Stack* (ibid) [107].
[93] (1802) 7 Ves 231.
[94] (1853) 16 Beav 630.
[95] *Neuberger* (n 80) 543.
[96] In the context of promissory estoppel, which is also based on a promise by D (not to enforce his or her strict legal rights), there is no indication that a similar requirement applies in the commercial context.
[97] *Cobbe* (n 7) [66] and [68].

a business associate. However, this seems highly speculative – it might actually be objectively less reasonable to trust an unreliable or vindictive relative than to trust a fair-minded business partner (and, in general, the question of whether it is 'reasonable' to trust someone seems very difficult to assess). It seems more plausible that equity would simply make it a requirement that C actually did trust D (since otherwise there would be no reliance on D's promise), with this being seen as less likely, as a factual matter, to have happened in the business context where C may well have understood that D's apparent promise was effectively 'subject to contract'.

A third issue is that, in fact, the superficially plausible distinction between the commercial and the domestic contexts is not a reliable one. The two often blur together, as for example in a case like *Yaxley v Gotts*[98] where the parties entering into a business arrangement were 'friends of long-standing'. Similarly, into which category would one have placed *Cobbe* if the parties had been, say, cousins or siblings? In reality, the parties are more likely to trust each other if they are friends or relations or if they have built up a personal relationship over a series of business dealings over a long period. To talk of a reluctance to apply estoppel principles in 'a commercial arm's length context'[99] is not very helpful because, to the extent that one party has genuinely trusted the other, the parties cannot be said to have been dealing at arm's length.

A fourth point relates to Lord Neuberger's argument that 'certainty and clarity are particularly important' in the business context, so that it is 'probably all to the good' that proprietary estoppel will not often assist a claimant in the commercial context where 'judges should be slow to encourage the introduction of uncertainties based on their views of the ethical acceptability of the behaviour of one of the parties'.[100] There is obviously force in the point that certainty is important in a commercial context. However, a number of counter-arguments may be made against Lord Neuberger's position. His argument, reflecting that of Lord Scott in *Cobbe*, assumes that the doctrine of proprietary estoppel would, unless restricted in the manner under discussion, allow judges, unconstrained by principle, to give expression to idiosyncratic views as to what is unconscionable or unethical.[101] However, it is not really true that beyond the acquiescence and representation principles lies only an uncharted wasteland ruled by judicial moral indignation. What is at issue is whether a specific principle, Lord Kingsdown's promise principle, should be recognised alongside the acquiescence and representation principles (or, at least, recognised without being eviscerated by a requirement of mistaken belief). While the promise principle is by no means devoid of uncertainty, it has been applied by the courts for the past forty years and

[98] [2000] Ch 162 (CA).
[99] *Neuberger* (n 80) 542.
[100] Ibid 543.
[101] *Cobbe* (n 7) [17].

cannot be said to leave judges entirely free to indulge their idiosyncratic ethical preferences. Moreover, it must be asked whether certainty, in the sense of freedom from legal liability imposed by judges based on their personal ethical views, is not equally important in the domestic context. An actor in the commercial context is, after all, in the business of assuming legal liabilities (including on the basis of the making of promises) and may reasonably expect, depending on the extent of his or her commercial activities, at times to become involved in litigation. However, an individual acting in a private capacity will normally not expect to become tangled up in acrimonious litigation.[102]

The preceding argument has links to a fifth and final point. This is the argument that, as well as the fact that the boundary between the commercial and the domestic contexts is not a clear one, it is dangerous to assume glibly that greater equitable intervention is appropriate in the domestic context, as compared to the commercial context. Lord Neuberger suggested that, in the commercial context of *Cobbe*, 'it is not for the courts to go galumphing in, wielding some Denningesque sword of justice'.[103] However, it is not just because it is a commercial premises that you do not want a bull in your china shop. Even in the context of domestic relationships, there are fragile and valuable items that one would like to shield from equity's clumsiness. One of these is trust. In this context, it is interesting to consider Dori Kimel's arguments concerning the relationship between contract and promise.[104] Kimel argues that 'at times, the law best supports valuable social practices by refraining from absorbing their constitutive norms'.[105] In Kimel's view, one of the functions of the law of contract is to allow people to deal with each other without needing to repose personal trust in each other. The enforceability of contracts allows one to preserve a degree of 'personal detachment'. On the other hand, a strength of the concept of a (non-legally binding) promise is that it can foster trust between people. If I promise you that I will do something and, not being forced to do it by the threat of legal sanctions, I complete the 'circle of trust' by living up to my word, you are more likely to trust me in future and our personal relationship is likely to be enhanced generally.

Consider the facts of *Thorner v Major*[106] where, it will be recalled, David Thorner worked without pay for many years on the farm of his father's cousin, Peter Thorner, on the basis of oblique suggestions that he would inherit the farm. Lord Neuberger pointed out that for David to have sought to formalise

[102] Contrast *Neuberger* (n 80) 544, arguing that, unlike in the commercial context, 'equity should [not] fear to tread … where the relationship between the parties is such that they cannot be expected to have recourse to contracts'.

[103] Ibid 541.

[104] *Kimel* (n 79). See also S Shiffrin, 'Promising, Conventialism and Intimate Relationships' (2008) 117 *Phil Rev* 481.

[105] D Kimel, 'The Choice of Paradigm for Theory of Contract: Reflections on the Relational Model' (2007) 27 *OJLS* 233, 233.

[106] *Thorner* (n 69).

the arrangement in a contract 'would have risked harming the relationship with Peter'.[107] It is not clear, furthermore, how a contract could have been drafted which would have addressed the various possible contingencies, eg whereby Peter might become ill and need to fund nursing home care or David might decide to get married and move away from the farm after a dozen years of work. The parties might have felt that, if policed by a contract, they could not have successfully shared the difficult life on the farm. Perhaps an arrangement depending on trust, without the possibility of legal sanctions against either party, represented the most appropriate way of allowing these people to achieve what they wanted. Obviously, an arrangement based on trust carries risks but then so too would any attempt to regulate the parties' dealings by reference to legal concepts.

A possible riposte to the argument that equity's intervention may serve to destroy trust in personal relationships is that the parties are unlikely to be aware of the law of proprietary estoppel at the time they deal with each other, so that equity's intervention comes only after the event – in other words, after a dispute has arisen and trust between the parties has, in any case, already broken down. One gets the impression (particularly in the domestic context) that the courts would prefer to see the principles of proprietary estoppel as 'decision' rules which allow judges to provide relief for a claimant who has acted in ignorance of the existence of the law. One indication of this is the emphasis on a retrospective assessment of unconscionability, summed up cryptically by Lord Hoffmann in *Thorner* when he remarked that '[t]he owl of Minerva spreads its wings only with the falling of the dusk'.[108]

So, perhaps equity's approach depends to some extent on the proposition that, until a dispute has arisen and legal advice has been obtained, C will not be aware of the possibility of a remedy based on proprietary estoppel. This is reminiscent of an idea put forward by Meir Dan-Cohen in a different context; that of 'acoustic separation'.[109] Dan-Cohen reflected on the possibility of a system whereby there was selective transmission of legal rules to citizens, discussing an imaginary system in which only 'conduct rules' were transmitted to ordinary citizens, so that the decision rules were known only to the decision-makers. It is an interesting question as to whether, as a factual matter in the estoppel context, there truly is complete 'acoustic separation', so that a claimant can be assumed not to be aware of the possibility that equity will intervene to rescue the situation after the event. While it is obvious that most claimants will not know the law, it may be naïve to assume that no claimant will be aware of the law. Leading cases on estoppel, and the common intention constructive trust, are reported in newspapers and even small towns have solicitors who dispense legal advice to claimants or to friends or acquaintances of potential

[107] *Neuberger* (n 80) 542.

[108] *Thorner* (n 69) [8].

[109] M Dan-Cohen, 'Decision Rules and Conduct Rules: On Acoustic Separation in Criminal Law' (1984) 97 *Harv L Rev* 625.

claimants, thus providing a (not entirely reliable) means whereby legal rules can conceivably be transmitted even to claimants who are not schooled in the law. If this seems implausible, it can be pointed out any faithful reader of the Daily Mail would have seen detailed coverage of David Thorner's success at first instance and in the House of Lords (with pictures of the claimant and the farm).[110] While recognising the significance of the phenomenon of 'acoustic separation', the importance of preserving trust in intimate relationships does appear to point in favour of some degree of restraint in terms of the level of equitable intrusion in the domestic context.

Overall, in the current author's view, the distinction between the domestic and commercial contexts is essentially a crude heuristic; a short cut that cannot be depended upon to give reliable results. There may a tendency to infantalise claimants in the so-called domestic sphere, assuming that nothing can be expected of them in terms of safeguarding their own interests, while exaggerating the extent to which actors in the 'commercial sphere' are immune to the human tendency to repose trust in people with whom they have had frequent dealings. It is easy to imagine an individual who is engaged in a business enterprise as a sole trader but is vulnerable to being taken advantage of by a defendant who is able to induce the claimant to trust him or her. It seems that what is important is not whether the context is domestic or commercial but rather how the particular facts match up with the specific requirements of the aspect of proprietary estoppel at issue.

Conclusion

This chapter has considered the restrictive vision of proprietary estoppel which was put forward by Lord Scott and Lord Walker in *Cobbe*. It has explained that the impact of taking their arguments seriously would be the elimination (or, at least, the severe restriction) of one of the three distinct principles subsumed within proprietary estoppel, ie the promise principle stated by Lord Kingsdown in *Ramsden v Dyson*. The chapter has suggested that, although the approach in *Cobbe* runs counter to the current of equitable development over the last forty years, it does highlight important issues of principle surrounding the scope of proprietary estoppel. Despite the tendency to downplay the role of promise within the doctrine, the pre-*Cobbe* version of proprietary estoppel ventures into the territory of the law of contract, doing so only in respect of promises related

[110] See L Salkeld, 'Farm labourer inherits £2.3m farm he worked on for 25 years after two-year legal battle over will' *Daily Mail* (London 7 November 2007) <http://www.dailymail.co.uk/news/article-492024/Farm-labourer-inherits-2-3m-farm-worked-25-years-year-legal-battle-will.html> accessed 8 October 2010; – 'Labourer is handed £2.3 million farm where he worked unpaid for 25 years' *Daily Mail* (London 25 March 2009) <http://www.dailymail.co.uk/news/article-1164810/Labourer-handed-2-3million-farm-worked-unpaid-25-years.html> accessed 8 October 2010.

to land/property (without any convincing justification as a matter of principle for this restriction). Rather than seek to deal comprehensively with the very large question as to the merits or otherwise of Lord Kingsdown's promise principle, this chapter has sought to address a more modest set of questions. First, it has pointed out that the particular concern which seems to have animated the judges in *Cobbe* – that it is wrong to allow C to succeed on the basis of a promise which C knows is binding only in honour – can be accommodated within the conventional modern understanding of proprietary estoppel, without any need to eliminate or severely curtail Lord Kingsdown's principle. Secondly, the chapter addresses the seductive suggestion that a distinction should be drawn between the commercial and the domestic contexts, with the restriction upon proprietary estoppel suggested in *Cobbe* applying only in the commercial context. It is concluded, on the basis of a number of different arguments, that this suggestion does not represent a desirable avenue of development for the law. One of the points made against any application of a mistake requirement in the context of the promise principle is that this requirement makes sense only in the context of the acquiescence principle; the suggestion that it should be applied more broadly appears reminiscent of attempts in the past to apply the *probanda* to all proprietary estoppel cases.

We are all familiar with the adage that 'hard cases make bad law'. At one level, it might be best if *Cobbe* were simply written off as a case where a 'soft' or 'easy' case made bad law – it was obvious that the Court of Appeal's decision to make an expectation award in the favour of Cobbe was too generous but, unfortunately, the House of Lords did not focus with sufficient care on what was wrong with such an award under the orthodox doctrine of proprietary estoppel. The subsequent decision in *Thorner v Major*[111] may represent the beginning of a process of (in effect) pretending that *Cobbe* did not happen. Nonetheless, it is difficult to see how confusion will not be caused in the lower courts by the speeches in *Cobbe*. It is surely a testament to the obscurity which has surrounded the role of promise within proprietary estoppel that the House of Lords could take a view of that role in *Cobbe* which was so much at odds with the pre-existing case law. In terms of the future development of the law of estoppel, what is needed is a willingness to separate out for analysis the distinct principles which have, for historical reasons, been grouped together under the heading of proprietary estoppel. The emphasis on 'unconscionability' and 'synthesis', encouraged by the overrated judgment of Oliver J in *Taylor Fashions*, have contributed to the current confused state of the law. Following the debacle represented by *Cobbe*, it is time for a somewhat more reflective approach.

[111] *Thorner* (n 69).

III

Easements, Covenants and Public Rights of Way: Scope and Reform

9

The Genetics of Appurtenant Interests

Elizabeth Cooke*

At the conference that preceded this volume, in March 2010, I gave one paper in two parts. The first was about the nature of appurtenant interests, and the second was a response to the points raised in Lu Xu's paper. There are connections between the two parts, as will be seen; but they are presented here as two short chapters so that readers can consume both halves of the sandwich or just one, as they prefer.

The heart of the matter: the genetics of easements

The Law Commission's project *Easements, Covenants and Profits à Prendre*, on which we consulted in March 2008,[1] is only the latest – and really must be the last – episode in a story that has been going on for several decades. The story is largely about freehold covenants and the desire of many to make it possible to burden land with positive obligations without using a lease, as is possible in a number of other jurisdictions; but it also concerns easements and the need to modernise the law, particularly in the areas of prescription and implication where there seems to be too much complexity and far too many ways of achieving the same end.

In this chapter I would like to focus on easements, and on the light that easements shed upon a bigger question: what is an appurtenant interest? It has been important in the course of the Law Commission's project to ask that question, not only for the entertainment of a fascinating puzzle, but also because it has a bearing on the way that we reform the law of freehold covenants. If it is

* Professor of Law, University of Reading; Law Commissioner for England and Wales.

[1] Law Commission, 'Easements, Covenants and Profits à Prendre' (Law Com Cp No 186, 2008), hereinafter 'the Consultation Paper'. I acknowledge gratefully the work on this project of the other members of the property law team at the Law Commission: Matthew Jolley, Julia Jarzabkowski and Colin Oakley.

going to be possible to burden land with positive as well as negative obligations, do we want simply to extend the law relating to restrictive covenants so as to include positive ones as well, or do we want to transform the law relating to covenants so that the benefit of an obligation becomes an appurtenant interest?

I discuss that question in my second chapter.[2] This chapter looks just at easements and the nature of appurtenant interests as the law stands. Not only is this a necessary preliminary to the examination of freehold covenants, but also one of the questions asked in our consultation paper in 2008 goes to the very heart of this issue. That was the question about the Court of Appeal's decision in *Wall v Collins*.[3]

The problem: the implications of appurtenance

Not all the interests under consideration in our project are appurtenant ones. As we all know, a profit à prendre may exist in gross,[4] which means that it may be owned independently of an estate in land and registered with an independent title.[5] But an easement must have a dominant as well as a servient tenement, and it must accommodate and serve that dominant land.[6] A profit à prendre may be appurtenant rather than held in gross, and appurtenant profits are generally governed by the same body of law as are easements.[7] Accordingly, for simplicity I refer only to easements in this chapter.

In order to take effect at law, an 'easement, right or privilege' must be 'for an interest equivalent to an estate in fee simple absolute in possession or a term of years absolute'.[8] An easement or a profit can be granted to a leaseholder by a third party (a neighbour, say, who is not the landlord), or by a leaseholder to a third party. Such interests exist, obviously, for the duration of the lease and no longer, and so would be for a term 'equivalent to ... a term of years absolute'.[9]

Whether granted by a leaseholder or a freeholder: to what is an easement appurtenant? As a registrable interest it is to be found in the property register of a registered freehold or lease, and as land lawyers we deal with estates rather than tangible things and so we think of it as being appurtenant to, or attached to, an estate in land. But the language of attachment is a metaphor, and the word 'appurtenance' is not much better. We are speaking the language of reification

[2] See Chapter 11 'The Consequences of Genetic Engineering: a Comment on Lu Xu's Chapter'.

[3] [2007] EWCA Civ 444, [2007] Ch 390.

[4] J Gaunt and P Morgan (eds), *Gale on Easements* (18th rev edn Sweet & Maxwell, London 2008) [1–143].

[5] Land Registration Rules 2003 SI 2003/1417 Rule 2(2).

[6] *Re Ellenborough Park* [1955] 2 All ER 38 (Ch).

[7] See the *Consultation Paper* (n 1) [6.7] and [6.14].

[8] Law of Property Act 1925 s 1(2)(a).

[9] There is, of course, nothing to prevent a freeholder from granting an easement for a term of years.

here, and there is a temptation to think of an easement as a thing glued to another thing. So if we say that an easement is appurtenant to a particular estate, what does or should that mean?

The idea of appurtenance seems to involve not only sharing duration, but also two further features:

1. An easement appurtenant to a lease can be enjoyed by those who benefit from that lease and not – absent express arrangement – those who hold any superior estates.
2. An easement appurtenant to a lease will not only be doomed from its beginning to come to an end when the lease expires by effluxion of time; it will also – or so we have until recently supposed! – come to an end if the lease comes to an early end.

As we all know, that latter proposition was denied by the Court of Appeal in *Wall v Collins*, in terms that cast the whole meaning of appurtenance into doubt and prompts us to ask afresh: to what is an easement appurtenant? In *Re Ellenborough Park*, Danckwerts J said:

> An easement must accommodate the dominant tenement, ie, be connected with its enjoyment and for its benefit.[10]

The question I have posed about the meaning of appurtenance was not in issue in *Re Ellenborough Park*; indeed, it does not seem to have troubled the English courts until *Wall v Collins* came to be decided by the Court of Appeal.

The question at issue in *Wall v Collins* was, broadly stated: What is the effect on the easement or other interest, should the estate to which it is attached cease to exist other than by effluxion of time? This could happen in a number of ways. The estate could be terminated by notice to quit (whether given by landlord or tenant), it could be forfeited for breach of condition or covenant, disclaimed on an insolvency, surrendered to the landlord, or merged. Merger takes place where a tenant acquires the landlord's reversion if, in accordance with equitable principles, there is an intention that there be a merger.[11] The ratio of *Wall v Collins* concerned only merger, but we shall have to examine how far it takes us into the wider question of other forms of termination.

As a matter of principle, one would assume that on termination of the dominant estate by any of these means, the appurtenant interest would be automatically extinguished.[12] There would no longer be an estate to which it could be said to be attached, and the interest would therefore cease to exist. Applying the metaphor commonly used in relation to the effect of forfeiture

[10] [1955] 2 All ER 38 (Ch) 43.
[11] Law of Property Act 1925 s 185.
[12] This is a very different situation from that which arises when a dominant owner, in respect of an easement, purchases the servient tenement and thus owns both; we discuss that in the *Consultation Paper* (n 1) [3.56]–[3.66].

of a head lease on those interests (such as sub-leases or mortgages) derived out of it, the branch would fall with the tree.[13] This would, I suggest, have been regarded as beyond dispute in the major texts prior to *Wall v Collins*.

It must be added that even on that view an easement or other interest benefiting a lease would not be automatically extinguished whenever a tenant acquires the freehold since this need not necessarily lead to merger and consequent termination of the leasehold estate. However, if there is a merger the orthodox view has been that the easement, appurtenant to the lease, comes to an end. Naturally, if the leaseholder had the benefit of an easement attached to his lease, which he did not want to lose, he would choose not to merge the two estates but to continue to own both.

However, the Court of Appeal took a very different view in *Wall v Collins*.[14]

Wall v Collins: the facts and decision

The claimant sought to enforce a right of way which, the parties agreed, had been expressly granted in 1911 in favour of the leaseholder of the property of which he was now the freehold owner. At the time of the grant, the then dominant owner held a 999 year lease of the dominant land, granted in 1910. Later, the tenant under that lease acquired the freehold estate in the dominant land. At first, the freehold estate was expressed to be subject to the 1910 lease and an entry was made in the charges register of the freehold title noting the lease; that meant that the lease did not merge with the freehold and was no doubt a deliberate move to avoid destroying the easement. However, in 1999, when the claimant bought the property, the entry in the charges register was removed on the express instruction of his solicitor. There seems little doubt that at that moment the freehold and leasehold estates merged, and the leasehold estate ceased to exist.[15]

The question for the court was the effect of that merger upon the claimant's easement. The judge at first instance had held that as the right of way was attached to the lease, the right was lost when the lease was extinguished by merger. While accepting that the easement could not benefit the freehold in 1911, and accepting that the easement could last only as long as the lease would have lasted, the Court of Appeal nevertheless denied that an easement is attached to an estate as such, and asserted that, whatever its legal source (whether a conveyance, a lease, or a separate grant), the easement is attached to the land it

[13] C Harpum, S Bridge and M Dixon, *Megarry and Wade, The Law of Real Property* (7th edn Sweet & Maxwell, London 2008) [18-031], which cites *Great Western Railway Company v Smith* (1875–1876) LR 2 Ch D 235 (CA) 253 and *Viscount Chelsea v Hutchinson* [1994] 2 EGLR 61 (CA) 62 as authorities for the principle.

[14] [2007] EWCA Civ 444, [2007] Ch 390; see also T Ward, '*Wall v Collins* – the effect of mergers of a lease on appurtenant easements' [2007] *Conv* 465.

[15] See [2007] EWCA Civ 444, [2007] Ch 390 [12].

is intended to benefit (the dominant tenement). Accordingly, the merger of the leasehold with the freehold did not effect an extinguishment of the right of way.

Lord Justice Carnwath stated:

> Equally, as a matter of common sense, it is difficult to see why a lessee should be worse off, so far as concerns an easement annexed to the land, merely because he has acquired a larger interest in the dominant tenement.[16]

The practical implications of the decision in *Wall v Collins*

The decision in *Wall v Collins* is patently intended to make life easier for dominant owners in this situation. Of course, on the orthodox view a lessee will only lose an easement appurtenant to his lease if he intends that a merger should take place. Such an intention was established in *Wall v Collins* by reference to the application of the claimant's solicitor to remove the entry in the charges register. Where no merger can be established, the leasehold estate to which the easement is attached would not be terminated. One downside of that obvious way to rescue an easement is that it may be missed through inadvertence, as must have happened in *Wall v Collins*: a further and more important downside is that when it is employed, it then leads to a title cluttered up with an appendant lease that no-one wants, and to the need to transfer both the lease and the freehold when the land changes hands. So the decision in the Court of Appeal was responding to a real problem.[17]

Wall v Collins has caused Land Registry to change its practice. Land Registry Practice Guide 26 formerly stated that 'on determination of a lease any beneficial easements granted by the lease come to an end'.[18] It has since published an addendum to this Practice Guide, noting that in light of *Wall v Collins* the information previously given is no longer accurate:

> The Court of Appeal held in this case that an easement must be appurtenant to a dominant tenement, but not necessarily to a particular interest in that dominant tenement. So when a lease is extinguished on merger, the tenant does not automatically lose any easements granted to him or her or to previous tenants; these easements

[16] [2007] EWCA Civ 444, [2007] Ch 390 [18].

[17] That may be why the Court of Appeal did not decide the case purely on the basis of s 62 of the Law of Property Act 1925, which would have resolved the claimant's problem without disturbing the wider law.

[18] Land Registry, 'Practice Guide 26 Leases – determination' (10 November 2008) <http://www1.landregistry.gov.uk/assets/library/documents/lrpg026.pdf> accessed 24 August 2010 [4.4]. It seems that, when the Land Registry Practice Guide refers to 'easements granted by the lease', it is referring to easements granted by the landlord over land not comprised in the demise, in other words, where the leasehold estate benefits from an easement. The effect of *Wall v Collins* would equally apply where a third party landowner granted an easement over their property to benefit a leasehold estate without also granting the same to the reversionary interest.

continue to exist and to be exercisable by the occupier of the dominant tenement for the period for which they were granted.[19]

Responding to *Wall v Collins*

The Law Commission took the view in the Consultation Paper that as a matter of principle an easement is attached to an estate in the land (either freehold or leasehold), and that it follows as a matter of logic that termination of that estate must extinguish the easement. This approach, conceptually, is required for consistency with the doctrine of estates, which is a fundamental principle of our land law. Moreover, the fact that appurtenant interests are appurtenant to estates is at the heart of the system of registration of title and of the Land Registration Act 2002; title registration is structured on the basis of estates, not of physical land.

It is of course common to speak of interests being appurtenant to land. But until the decision in *Wall v Collins* it was axiomatic that when precision was required, we had to speak of the interest being attached, not to land, but to an estate – just as we speak colloquially, even in legal writing, of owning land, whereas in English law what is owned is not land but an estate.

Accordingly, the Law Commission provisionally proposed that where an easement is attached to a leasehold estate, the easement should be automatically extinguished on termination of that estate, thus reversing *Wall v Collins*.[20]

There was considerable support for the Consultation Paper's proposal. But a significant proportion of consultees disagreed with it. The disagreement was not with the Commission's analysis of the law, but rather with the effect of our proposal. Many consultees believed that *Wall v Collins* created a just result, and that the effect of reform would be to unravel this. Consultees found persuasive the idea that, just because a tenant acquires a greater interest, he should not lose the benefits attached to the lease. They were unhappy that, without *Wall v Collins*, merger would have to be avoided, and therefore leases preserved (and registered titles kept open) when title could otherwise be cleaned up. The sentiment was summed up by one consultee:

> I take the points made in the paper, but I have sympathy for the plight of a dominant owner who loses a valuable right through inadvertence to the consequences of merger, even if the merger has been expressly declared or sought. I would favour some saving provision for that situation, which the Court of Appeal appears to have afforded in an unsatisfactory analysis of the law.[21]

[19] Land Registry, 'Addendum to Practice Guide 26 Leases – determination' <http://www1.landregistry.gov.uk/assets/library/documents/lrpg026_addendum2.pdf> accessed 24 August 2010.

[20] See the *Consultation Paper* (n 1) [5.86].

[21] When we publish our Report at the end of the project we shall also produce an analysis of responses, where responses will be attributed to consultees by name; it seems better at this stage to reproduce consultee comments anonymously.

These practical concerns have to be taken seriously. If *Wall v Collins* is reversed without replacement, then there is a potential for unfair results due to inadvertent loss of rights.

If *Wall v Collins* were to be reversed, a tenant acquiring a freehold would have to ensure that the estates did not merge, in order to enable a right attached to the inferior estate to survive.[22] If that were the case then, for the duration of the surviving right (and estate), unnecessary costs might well be incurred on dispositions of the land. All future conveyances and mortgages would involve dealing with two estates where ordinarily there would be one, with attendant costs in advisers explaining the position to purchasers and banks, and a greater potential for errors in the conveyancing and registration formalities.

Moreover, it is hard to see any detriment to a third party servient estate owner arising from the effect achieved by *Wall v Collins*. A servient estate owner will, at the time of the grant, expect to be bound for the duration of the grant. If the dominant and servient estates are both freehold, and the grant equivalent, then the appurtenant interest would be for a term equivalent to a fee simple. If one or other of the estates were a 25-year lease, then the interest would be expected to last for the unexpired residue of the term at the time of grant. It is hard to envisage a circumstance where a servient owner could legitimately claim to be prejudiced in the event that a right, benefiting a dominant estate, was to remain enforceable despite the termination of the estate to which it was originally annexed.

So what is wanted is a reform that will re-establish the orthodoxy that appurtenant interests are appurtenant to estates, while allowing an interest appurtenant to a lease to survive the termination of the lease in certain special cases so as to meet the practical concerns of our consultees.

Technical issues

Can it be done? In order to answer that question we have to ask how far *Wall v Collins* goes.

Let us look at a different form of early termination of a lease, namely forfeiture. On forfeiture, the lease disappears altogether and any benefits and burdens attaching to it come to an end;[23] by contrast, on surrender or merger any burdens attached to the lease in favour of third parties will survive.[24] The same is true when a lease is disclaimed.[25] The decision in *Wall v Collins* is about

[22] It is worth noting that the earlier version of the Land Registry Practice Guide specifically informed parties that this is what they should do.

[23] See *Harpum, Bridge and Dixon* (n 13).

[24] Mr Justice Lewison and others, *Woodfall's Law of Landlord and Tenant* (vol 1, Sweet & Maxwell, London 2010) [17.044] and following, citing *Mellor v Watkins* (1873–74) LR 9 QB 400 (QB) and *Barrett v Morgan* [2000] 2 AC 264 (HL), among other cases, as authorities for the principle.

[25] A lease may be disclaimed by the trustee in bankruptcy of an individual tenant, or by the Treasury Solicitor when the lease becomes *bona vacantia* on liquidation of a company; in these

the other side of the coin: do any benefits, vis-à-vis third parties, survive all these events? Or does the decision apply only to merger?

As a matter of logic, perhaps all these events should have the same effect. Do we have to say that on termination of the dominant estate by any of these means, the appurtenant interest – which we would have supposed before *Wall v Collins* would have been automatically extinguished – will nevertheless survive to benefit the superior estate, for as long as the lease would otherwise have continued?

So far as I am aware there has been no suggestion in legal writing since *Wall v Collins* that its ratio extends beyond merger. But the point may be argued in the future. Certainly the idea that it might apply on forfeiture is extremely counter-intuitive. But can we distinguish these other methods of termination?

A useful distinction that we can make, and that a number of consultees pointed out, is that merger and surrender can be distinguished from forfeiture because they are consensual transactions, while forfeiture is not. The axiom that forfeiture brings every aspect of a lease to an end is so well-embedded in the law that it is probably implausible that any court would extend the ratio of *Wall v Collins* to forfeiture – not only for that theoretical reason, but also because it would be highly controversial to make a decision that, in effect, might give landlords an incentive to forfeit (since they would thereby obtain benefits, perhaps valuable ones, attached to the lease).

It is also likely that any claim that appurtenant benefits survived disclaimer might be regarded as too far at odds with the orthodox view of what happens when a lease comes to an end on disclaimer – although we note that burdens do survive.[26] Disclaimer is closer to forfeiture than to merger and surrender in that it is not a consensual transaction.

Finally, whether or not *Wall v Collins* extends to surrender is unknown. Land Registry guidance does not express the view that it does. We can see that, on one logic, it should: if the benefit attaches to the land, that is as true for surrender as for merger.[27] But whereas in merger it is the tenant who acquires the freehold and there is therefore an unfairness if he or she loses a benefit he held as tenant,[28] on surrender the landlord acquires the lease and, arguably, the same unfairness does not arise. On the other hand, surrender can be analysed as a transfer,[29] and that would seem to indicate that benefits might survive. Moreover, there are occasions when the tenant remains in possession of the land after surrender. It

circumstances, and in the absence of a vesting order in favour of another interested party, the lease comes to an end – whereas a freehold, in these circumstances, escheats (see *Lewison* (n 24) [16.118] and following and [17.271]–[17.275]).

[26] Land Registry practice is to transfer easements and restrictive covenants upwards to the superior title on merger, surrender and disclaimer.

[27] But unfortunately equally true for forfeiture.

[28] See quote accompanying n 16 above, from *Wall v Collins* [2007] EWCA Civ 444, [2007] Ch 390 [18].

[29] See N Hopkins, 'Surrender as an Assignment and the Protection of Third Parties' [1996] *Conv* 284.

is clear law that when the landlord and tenant agree an extension of the term of the lease, that transaction operates as a surrender and a re-grant. In those circumstances, precisely the same unfairness – and considerable inconvenience – arises if the benefits attached to the surrendered lease disappear.

Accordingly, while it is relatively clear that the decision in *Wall v Collins* does not extend to forfeiture and disclaimer, and that attempts to argue that it does would fail, it seems to be an open question whether or not the decision could be invoked to argue that benefits appurtenant to a lease might survive surrender.

What matters is the practical result. A number of consultees felt that surrender and merger were very similar transactions and that benefits *should* survive both. It would be possible to make provision to reverse *Wall v Collins* so that an appurtenant benefit does indeed – as orthodoxy dictates – come to an end with the ending of the estate that it benefits while enabling the holder of the superior estate,[30] on surrender or merger, to elect to keep those appurtenant benefits. I make no comment here about how that would be drafted, which is a matter for Parliamentary Counsel.

Conclusion

That has been something of a gallop through a practical problem caused by a theoretical position. Land law, as we all know, does not work if inconsistencies are introduced; yet in the *Wall v Collins* problem we encountered an instance where inconsistency with the theory of appurtenance actually seemed to solve a practical problem. The correct solution seems to be to restore orthodoxy while facilitating convenience.

When we turn to the reform of the law of positive covenants we have a number of orthodoxies and practical positions to work with. These include: the views of the many who want to make it possible to bind land with positive obligations, the current law of restrictive covenants which confines them to a hybrid status as equitable interests rather than allowing them the full status of legal burdens giving rise to legal rights; the different ways in which other jurisdictions have reformed the law in order to allow positive obligations to attach to land; the importance that the land law of England and Wales places upon the registration and therefore publicity of interests; and the logic of appurtenant interests, which we have just explored in the context of the decision in *Wall v Collins*. All those ideas and more have to have their place in devising reform.

[30] Generally; but the leaseholder where there is a deemed surrender and re-grant by operation of law.

10

Framework for Land Obligations: What Can be Learnt from the Scots Law of Real Burdens?

Lu Xu*

Introduction

The Law Commission's Consultation Paper (No 186, 2008) on *Easements, Covenants and Profits à Prendre* has reinvigorated the quest for introducing a new type of interest into English land law, namely Land Obligations. It brings a new hope that English law will finally be able to facilitate the imposition of positive obligations on land ownership, after more than forty years of unequivocal statements to such effect from parliamentary commissions, senior judges, practitioners and academics. Better late than never.

Interestingly, such procrastination might have bestowed advantages upon the current reform, such as, inter alia, a better system of land registration and the possibility to leave out issues already dealt with by the new commonhold structure. Amongst the advantages, it is submitted, is the unique opportunity to learn from the Scottish law of real burdens and its recent reform. This is probably the least expected implication from a delay in the reform of English law, given the fundamental differences between the two jurisdictions on property law principles and traditions. However, the recent Scottish reform presented many valuable ideas and experience which may be of interest to the ongoing English reform. To its great credit, the Law Commission has already paid considerable attention to numerous comparative aspects of the law in the Consultation Paper.

This chapter explores further angles for such comparative exercise which have not been previously considered. In the light of the Scottish reform, it is submitted that a statutory codification presents the ideal time for a stricter approach to the use of labels and terminology. The English reform should be

* Lecturer in Property Law, Norwich Law School, University of East Anglia.

prepared to take on the challenge of finding, or creating, theoretical coherence in the system, and not to be afraid of breaching established boundaries in the process. Finally it draws attention to the rather unforeseen difficulty of the Scots law in defining the necessary 'interest to enforce' an obligation, which might prompt the English reform to adopt an alternative strategy.

Background and timing of the reform

The 2008 Consultation Paper was a renewal of the involvement by the Law Commission for England and Wales on the matter of reforming the law of restrictive covenants. As explained in the paper, an earlier report, which emerged more than twenty years ago in 1984 with the Law Commission making similar recommendations, was abandoned by the government. The main reason given was not anything against the principle of the proposal, but the need to consider the effect of future developments in property law and 'in particular the introduction of a commonhold system'.[1]

Blessed with hindsight, it seems that this decision is questionable at least in terms of proportionality. Statistics supplied by the Land Registry indicate that there were more than thirteen million registered freehold titles affected by restrictive covenants by the end of 2005, while more than a quarter of a million covenants were being registered every year.[2] Given strong criticism against the existing system of covenants has been well known from as early as the Wilberforce Committee in 1965,[3] it is intriguing that the decision was taken to halt its reform for what turned out to be more than twenty years, in anticipation of developments on the commonhold frontier, which could not ever possibly have a comparable influence due to the almost negligible number of commonhold schemes in England. More than five years after the commencement of the commonhold mechanism in September 2004, the total number of schemes so registered in England is still fewer than twenty. It seems logical to argue that if any reform should have been concerned with consistency of the law or compatibility with concurrent reforms, it is the commonhold concept which should have accommodated the reform of covenants. The implication of this significant delay in reform is unsurprising, most clearly reflected in the disappointment voiced by Lord Templeman at the situation that 'nothing has been done' to change the 'illogical, uncertain, incomplete and inflexible' law.[4]

On the other hand, every cloud has a silver lining. After decades of doing nothing, the current project of reform is operating on a very different stage

[1] Law Commission, 'Easements, Covenants and Profits à Prendre' (Law Com Cp No 186, 2008) [1.15].

[2] Ibid Appendix A.

[3] Wilberforce Committee, 'Report of the Committee on Positive Covenants Affecting Land' (Cmnd 2719, 1965).

[4] *Rhone v Stephens* [1994] 2 AC 310 (HL) 321.

as compared to the original proposal in 1984.[5] English land law and, as to be discussed below, Scottish land law are now very different from that in the 1980s. By appreciating and harnessing such differences, the current reform is therefore capable of achieving more than the original, if only late by thirty years.

Some of the differences are reasonably obvious. With the inception of the commonhold, however minuscule its number is in practice, the current reform can finally concentrate on what was formerly known as 'neighbour obligations'. The awkward position of the 1984 report was that on various issues 'development obligations' had to be supplemented by many independent rules and exceptions, in order for them to be fitted somewhere uncomfortably alongside these neighbour obligations, which for all purposes correspond much closer to existing covenants, the subject matter of the reform. Furthermore, given the expanded scope of compulsory registration of titles to land and the time elapsed since such expansion, the current reform can possibly afford to avoid, or minimise, substantial changes to the law pertaining to unregistered land.[6] This again simplifies things significantly and may contribute to a clearer and more focused reform. For registered land, it may be generally accepted that the Land Registration Act 2002 is an improvement on its 1925 predecessor by providing a better system of title registration, which can only help the reform. Furthermore, there has been a significant change in the perception of the role and capability of land registration. In the 1984 report, for instance, the reform seemed ready to give in to the Land Registry's 'misgiving about the impact upon their workload' if a land obligation were to be entered against not only the servient land but also the benefited land, despite this being identified as the preferred approach.[7] Such sympathy or compromise seems unlikely today in the light of the objective for land registration overall that it is to accurately reflect the state of the title of the land at any given time with 'the absolute minimum of additional inquiries and inspections'.[8] Other initiatives, such as the move towards electronic conveyancing, also add weight to the support for the rigorous approach of dual registration of benefits and burdens, which again would not have been contemplated back in 1984. All these elements of change in the last twenty or thirty years help to construe a more convenient and effective platform to launch the long-awaited reform.

Meanwhile, changes outside of England and Wales may not be as important or influential to a land law reform at first sight. However, it is submitted that for the current initiative to introduce Land Obligations into English law, some

[5] Law Commission, 'Transfer of Land: The Law of Positive and Restrictive Covenants' (Law Com No 127, 1984).

[6] Law Commission, 'Easements, Covenants and Profits à Prendre' (Law Com Cp No 186, 2008) [8.31].

[7] Law Commission, 'Transfer of Land: The Law of Positive and Restrictive Covenants' (Law Com No 127, 1984) [9.25].

[8] The Stationary Office, *Explanatory Notes to the Land Registration Act 2002*, (TSO, London 2002) para 10.

attention should be paid to the development of the Scottish counterpart: the law of real burdens. The two concepts are too similar, and the latter far more experienced in terms of established law and practice, for English law to forego the opportunity of learning from its northern neighbour during this major reform.

The Scottish law of real burdens

The influence of Scots law in general is obvious in the Consultation Paper produced by the Law Commission. On a cursory count of the whole document, more reference to Scots law or the Scottish reform is made than those to all other jurisdictions, such as Australia or the United States, put together. This in itself may be of some interest to property lawyers. Despite the geographical and political proximity of these two jurisdictions, Scots property law is mostly regarded as one of the most distinguishable areas in its mixed legal system which resisted English judicial influences. As famously claimed by Professor Reid during the *Sharp v Thomson*[9] saga, which was widely criticised as an example of the House of Lords permitting concepts of English property law to threaten the foundation of Scots law, property law in Scotland is 'nine part Roman to one part feudal'.[10]

Within this Roman and feudal mixture, the system of real burdens is however largely home-grown and native to Scotland, independent of the *numerus clausus* principle typically treasured by a civilian system. It has been developed since the leading case of *Tailors of Aberdeen v Coutts*,[11] reported in 1840, notably only a few years ahead of English law's 1848 landmark decision of *Tulk v Moxhay*.[12] However, unlike English law which dwelled on the distinction between law and equity for the next 150 years, Scottish courts immediately allowed the ascendency of real burdens to the status of proprietary interests (real rights as in Scots law) if they comply with all the requirements prescribed in case law since *Coutts*. A real burden can be either affirmative, by requiring the owner of land to perform certain actions for the benefit of neighbouring land, or negative, by restricting the owner from using his land in certain ways for the benefit of neighbouring land. It seems fair to argue that real burdens enjoyed many advantages over English restrictive covenants since the mid-nineteenth century. Armed with the capability of imposing positive obligations such as building maintenance on successive landowners, Scots law has enabled the outright ownership of flats within buildings, without resorting to long leases and without legislative

[9] 1997 SC (HL Sc) 66.
[10] K G C Reid, '*Sharp v Thomson*: A Civilian Perspective' (1995) *SLT (News)* 75.
[11] (1840) 1 Rob 296.
[12] (1848) 47 ER 1345.

intervention throughout the twentieth century.[13] Helped by a compulsory register of all deeds relating to land since 1617, the Register of Sasines, the mechanism of real burdens operated at a level of formality, publicity and certainty unrivalled by English covenants or easements until at least 1925, arguably even today in many regards.[14]

The perception of real burdens in Scots law is highly positive. The Scottish Law Commission stated that 'strictly, the real burden is unique to Scotland', despite the existence of similar devices elsewhere, such as restrictive covenants in Anglo-American systems and servitudes in Continental Europe.[15] The reform and codification of the law of real burdens was one of the centrepieces in the revolution of Scots land law between 2000 and 2004. In that respect, the Title Conditions (Scotland) Act 2003 which is now the governing statute provides a valuable and convenient platform for understanding Scots law, which may partly explain the willingness of the Law Commission to engage in comparative studies. In contrast, the 1984 report on covenants hardly ever mentioned Scotland. As Scots law has made itself accessible by codification, the English reform can benefit by looking at a reasonably mature system in this context.

If it can be generally accepted that a similar concept with more than 170 years worth of case law and conveyancing experience behind it is valuable in comparative studies for the new Land Obligations, the question is then what can be learnt from the law of real burdens that may help the formulation of a better framework for Land Obligations. The Law Commission has already alluded to the position under Scots law on many important issues in the Consultation Paper. It is submitted that there are several other noteworthy issues which have arisen from Scots law before and after its codification which may shed some light on where the difficulties or even solutions may be for the English reform.

The label of 'Land Obligations'

It is sometimes human nature to start judging a book by its cover or a thing by its name. In that regard the current project to reform 'easements, covenants and profits à prendre' makes itself appear difficult or complicated. As noted by the Law Commission, these terms are not widely used or understood in the twenty-first century.[16] If that is not unusual for legal terminology with some history behind it, the fact that we do not even have a universally accepted name

[13] The Tenements (Scotland) Act 2004 was the first statute on the subject matter. Even the statutory scheme is subject to variation by real burdens in individual developments.

[14] In unregistered land there is still no record of covenants created before 1926, even if they are effective. By contrast, all real burdens always have to be recorded either on the Register of Sasines or the Land Register for Scotland in order to be effective.

[15] Scottish Law Commission, 'Report on Real Burdens' (Scot Law Com No 181, 2000) [1.5].

[16] Law Commission, 'Easements, Covenants and Profits à Prendre' (Law Com Cp No 186, 2008) [1.11].

for 'covenants' is certainly an indication of some of the inherent difficulties of the concept. A glance at several popular student textbooks reveals an impressive array of names for essentially the same subject, such as 'covenants between freeholders',[17] 'covenants relating to freehold land',[18] 'freehold covenants',[19] and 'restrictive covenants'.[20] Strictly speaking each label carries a slightly different meaning and none of them seems more appropriate than the rest. Some of these labels may even be misleading without further clarification. For instance, as explained by Professor Cooke, the Law Commissioner currently in charge of this reform project, freehold covenants do not exclude covenants between two leaseholders as long as they are not made between a landlord and his tenant.[21]

This difficulty of finding an appropriate label is possibly attributable to the fact that this whole branch of the law on covenants was developed in a piecemeal fashion by the courts over many decades without an overall scheme or schedule in terms of what will be covered and what will not be. It may be reasonable to argue that *Tulk v Moxhay* did not envisage *Austerberry v Corporation of Oldham*[22] narrowing it down to 'restrictive' covenants some forty years later. Given the notion that judges are not meant to make new laws, it may indeed be odd if the court suddenly steps up and names a new concept once and for all, even if the concept has in fact developed entirely through case law over the last 170 years or so.

The same difficulty and confusion was seen in Scots law regarding real burdens and related concepts. Before the recent reform, real burdens had many alternative names such as 'real obligations', 'real conditions' or 'conditions of the right'; it can also be used in the sense of a particular right in security for the payment of money.[23] Furthermore, the leading academic works were in constant dispute as to whether real burdens were a branch of real conditions, or an independent, lesser form of conditions running with land.[24] The relationship between real burdens and servitudes, the Scottish counterpart of easements in English law, was no easier to explain or theorise without dispute as to whether there were more similarities or differences between the two. Not surprisingly, there was not a universally accepted name to include both concepts. Then there came the Title Conditions (Scotland) Act 2003 which swept away all such uncertainties, with the new statutory term 'title conditions' to include both real burdens and servitudes.[25] The term was chosen because it had never been used by anyone. It had no history or basis nor was it necessarily better or worse than any

[17] M Thompson, *Modern Land Law* (4th edn OUP, Oxford 2009).

[18] J MacKenzie and M Phillips, *Textbook on Land Law* (12th edn OUP, Oxford 2008).

[19] A Stroud, *Making Sense of Land Law* (2nd edn Palgrave Macmillan, Basingstoke 2008).

[20] D Chappelle, *Land Law* (8th edn Pearson Longman, Essex 2008).

[21] E Cooke, 'To Restate or not to Restate? Old wine, New Wineskins, Old Covenants, New Ideas' [2009] *Conv* 448, 453.

[22] (1885) LR 29 Ch D 750 (CA).

[23] Scottish Law Commission, 'Real Burdens' (Scot Law Com Dp No 106, 1998) [1.1].

[24] G L Gretton and K G C Reid, *Conveyancing* (2nd edn W Green/Sweet & Maxwell, Edinburgh 1999) [13.01]. Cf A J McDonald and others, *Professor McDonalds' Conveyancing Manual* (6th edn T&T Clark, Edinburgh 1997) [10.4].

[25] Title Conditions (Scotland) Act 2003 s 122. Interestingly while 'real burdens' are defined by s 1, 'servitudes' are not defined by the Act.

other alternatives. However, it is unlikely that anyone will use a term different from the statute when referring to these concepts in future. With a statutory reform, any term to describe the subject is possibly better than not having one.

A similar opportunity is afforded to the current reform of English law. It may be reasonable to consider whether there should be a formal name for what we now refer to as 'easements, covenants and profits', such as 'appurtenant rights' first used by the Law Commission back in the 1970s.[26] Admittedly such a label is not a perfect description of its contents, in particular given the concern that profits may exist 'in gross' rather than as an appurtenant right. However, any such term, once adopted by legislation, still seems to be a much easier and much more certain expression than the 'technically correct' phrase of 'easements, covenants relating to land other than those made between landlord and tenant, and profits other than profits in gross'.

Mandatory use of the label

More important than appearances is that the use of a label may also have a significant impact on the content, especially in the case of a Land Obligation or a covenant. The Consultation Paper was minded to prescribe the mandatory use of the label 'Land Obligation' for the creation of any Land Obligation, which mirrored the previous position under the 1984 report.[27] However, new information seems to suggest a possible retreat in that regard,[28] permitting the customary use of non-specific terms such as 'to promise' or 'to covenant'. An explanation offered is that a stringent formal requirement will be 'an unnecessary trap for the unwary and would create too many hard cases'.[29]

Nevertheless, it is worth noting that the Scottish Law Commission faced similar objection from some of its consultees when proposing a similar rule of compulsory use of exact terminology for the creation of real burdens.[30] In the views of the Scottish Law Commission, the leniency as to terminology was understandable while real burdens were new and being developed by common law. However, with the development now formalised and codified by statute, certainty must prevail over the previous situation of flexibility. The example given by the Scots Law Commission in support of this decision is that in order to create a standard security, the Scottish equivalent of a mortgage or charge in English law, parties must use the precise term 'standard security'.[31]

[26] Law Commission, 'Transfer of Land: Appurtenant Rights' (Law Com Working Paper No 36, 1971).

[27] Law Commission, 'Easements, Covenants and Profits à Prendre' (Law Com Cp No 186, 2008) [8.25].

[28] *Cooke* (n 21) 464.

[29] Ibid.

[30] Scottish Law Commission, 'Report on Real Burdens' (Scot Law Com No 181, 2000) [3.29].

[31] Ibid.

A virtually identical argument can be raised under English law. In order to create a 'legal charge' introduced by the Law of Property Act 1925, the deed must contain a statement with the exact words that the charge is 'by way of legal mortgage'.[32] There is no alternative. And it seems that this has never been a trap for the unwary in the last eighty-odd years. There is no reported incident of any conveyancer attempting to create a legal charge in an innovative way by using his own choice of words. Thus it is very difficult to see where those 'too many hard cases' will come from, if the statute establishing the concept of Land Obligations prescribes this unequivocal rule that in order to create a Land Obligation one has to use these two words 'Land Obligation'. Two imaginary tales of possible misfortune come to mind. Maybe parties with no knowledge of the law will attempt to create Land Obligations without the advice and help of a qualified conveyancer and somehow manage to satisfy all other necessary legal requirements, including dual registration at the Land Registry, but fail this one last hurdle of using the correct statutory wording 'Land Obligation'. Alternatively, a conveyancer may somehow be unaware of the absolute need to employ such words when instructed to create Land Obligations, despite the unambiguous statutory provision which gave birth to the interest in the first place. Neither scenario seems to be credible, nor 'hard' enough to justify the compromise of the whole system which can otherwise be very principled on this point.

It is important to always bear in mind that Land Obligations will have to be created expressly by deed and specifically registered. How likely is it for anyone to understand and comply with both requirements but then fail to appreciate the mandatory use of the technical term 'Land Obligation'? It would seem that this is a principle which the current law reform should hold firm even if there are contrary opinions. With important movements such as electronic conveyancing looming large, it is plainly odd to allow parties the complete freedom to choose what name they want to call an interest by, when they are clearly trying to create a Land Obligation.

Difficulty in categorisation of easements and Land Obligations

Another argument raised against the use of a mandatory term is that to resist the imposition of a new label will signal the continuity of the old law, making it clear that the old case-law continues to be relevant.[33] It firstly sounds surprising that a new label will necessarily sever the link with old case law. In a common law system, it is arguably unlikely to deter any reference to old cases, as seen in

[32] Law of Property Act 1925 s 87(1).
[33] *Cooke* (n 21) 464.

the rebranding of 'overriding interests' as 'interests that override' by the Land Registration Act 2002. Furthermore, given the nature and potential scope of the current reform, it is questionable whether the continuity of case law is really useful or preferable.

One example of possible difficulty in the current law is the requirement of 'accommodate and serve' test for easements and 'touch and concern' test for covenants. As pointed out by Professor Cooke, there is no fundamental difference between the two. They are traditionally treated separately because they have traditionally been in different streams of case law dealing with two separate concepts, namely easements and covenants.[34] However, if there is to be a possible restructuring of this area of law which straddles both streams, it may be useful to abolish such subtlety in favour of coherence and consistency of the law.

As noted by the Consultation Paper, the requirement of 'relating to land' is seen in other civil law jurisdictions, and Scotland.[35] However, although this was always known as the 'praedial rule' in Scots law, this apparently aged term was not imported into the statute. Instead, the legislation opted in favour of much plainer English, stating that 'a real burden must relate in some way to the burdened property'[36] and 'the relationship may be direct or indirect but shall not merely be that the obligated person is the owner of the burdened property'.[37] It would seem that a simple 'relate to' test is preferable to two 'similar-but-different' tests of 'accommodate and serve' and 'touch and concern', especially for a statute in the twenty-first century.

The more important concern is of course whether the traditional boundary between easements and covenants shall be re-drawn in the new easements and Land Obligations era. The most out of place interest in the overall framework is a negative easement, which is largely equivalent in practical effect to a restrictive covenant, but is accepted as an easement in terms of creation, formality and enforceability. As explained by Professor Cooke, negative easements are now too commercially important in practice to be meddled with by the current reform of legal principles.[38] Consequently, this view that the current English reform cannot mirror the law in Scotland or the United States, leading to the inevitable lack of 'neatness' in the categorisation of interests, is fundamentally convincing and largely conclusive.

In the meantime, it seems reasonable to discuss whether the unavoidable continuation of negative easements is necessarily the stumbling block to a principled categorisation of interests under English law. Borrowing the analysis by the Scots Law Commission, there are essentially three different types of obligation which run with land:

[34] *Cooke* (n 21) 468.

[35] Law Commission, 'Easements, Covenants and Profits à Prendre' (Law Com Cp No 186, 2008) [8.72].

[36] Title Conditions (Scotland) Act 2003 s 3(1).

[37] Ibid s 3(2).

[38] *Cooke* (n 21) 470–471.

(i) an obligation on the burdened owner to do something, such as to use the property for a particular purpose, or to maintain the building;
(ii) an obligation not to do something, such as to build on the property, or to use it for commercial purposes; and
(iii) an obligation to allow the benefited owner some limited use of the property, such as to walk or drive over part of it, or to run a pipe through it.[39]

Under the current English law, there is no reliable means to create anything under (i), which is the most pressing reason for the current reform anyway. Once introduced, a positive Land Obligation will facilitate the positive obligation to do something that will 'run with the land'. However, there are two competitors under (ii), namely restrictive covenants and negative easements. Obligations under (iii) are exclusively positive easements. If it is accepted that negative easements will reserve a place under (ii), then unless we throw out restrictive covenants or their successors Land Obligations from (ii), which is most unlikely, then logically the system will never be 'neat'.

Redefining the boundaries

However, the awkward position of negative easements may not preclude all possibility of achieving a coherent and principled structure, if there can be a dividing line between easements and Land Obligations that is construed differently from this functional approach. One fundamental difference between easements and covenants, or easements and Land Obligations to come, is that easements can be acquired by prescription or implication, while covenants and Land Obligations must be explicitly created by deed. Notably this is also the main reason why negative easements are so commercially valuable, because most of them, especially most of the right to light, would have been created by prescription rather than grant. Therefore, arguably we can then build on the functional analysis, which is insufficient in the attempt to achieve coherence, and use in addition to it the formality requirement as the division between easements and Land Obligations.

In other words, all obligations relating to land under (i), (ii) or (iii) created explicitly after the reform should be Land Obligations, including those under (iii) which would previously be known as positive easements. No obligation may arise under (i) without express grant. Obligations under (ii) or (iii) may be acquired through prescription or implication after the reform and known respectively as negative easements and positive easements. All Land Obligations, whether under (i), (ii) or (iii), will be registered. Borrowing from the Scots Law Commission analysis again, these can be categorised as 'positive' Land

[39] Scottish Law Commission, 'Report on Real Burdens' (Scot Law Com No 181, 2000) [12.2].

Obligations, 'restrictive' Land Obligations and 'passive' Land Obligations. In contrast, all easements under the new system, whether under (ii) or (iii), will not initially be registered because they arise from prescription or implication. However, if any of them become registered afterwards, it is converted into a Land Obligation on registration and ceases to be an easement.

The advantages of such an admittedly audacious approach are noticeable. The system will be coherent with no gap and no overlap between easements and Land Obligations. It is certain and easy to tell whether any interest is an easement or a Land Obligation, depending on whether it is expressed and registered or not. Easements presumably will continue to operate as 'interests that override' in land registration, but now without the trap for the unwary (unwary law students at least) that an expressly granted easement in registered land is in fact not a legal easement capable of overriding registration because of the requirement of registration.[40] The new principle will be streamlined and easy to impress on conveyancers or even laypersons: if you need to put it on paper, it is a Land Obligation and you need registration.

The disadvantages and challenges of this approach are also numerous. Such a concept of Land Obligation will be taking on responsibilities which are not previously envisaged and traditionally entrusted to positive easements. If this is not a huge problem for a brand new concept, the fact that such a restructuring will essentially sever a major branch, namely all express easements, from the established institution of easements is certainly drastic to the sentiments of property lawyers.

What can be said in support is that the current reform is on course to change some of the fundamental principles in the law of easements and covenants anyway. For example, one of the four fundamental rules in *Re Ellenborough Park*,[41] that the dominant and servient tenements must be owned by different persons, may be circumvented with registration, following the Scottish position on the same issue.[42] It is arguably worth reshaping the traditional definition of an easement, if the end result is a more coherent system of proprietary interests overall. In terms of conveyancing practice, the impact of such a drastic theoretical reform may not be as significant as it first appears. For instance, a typical drafting of a 'right of way' would not need to refer to the term 'easement' in the first place. Consequently many of the transitions in this regard can be almost seamless, using the same terms for the creation of a pre-reform easement for the creation of a post-reform 'passive Land Obligation', subject to the additional statutory requirements of mandatory label and dual registration.

Furthermore, the fact that the current law does not distinguish between easements which are expressly created and those which are implied on subdivision of land or arise out of prescription is not necessarily a desirable situation to be

[40] Land Registration Act 2002 s 27 and sch 3 para 3.

[41] [1956] Ch 131 (CA).

[42] Law Commission, 'Easements, Covenants and Profits à Prendre' (Law Com Cp No 186, 2008) [3.56]–[3.66].

in. Introducing such differences by rebranding the former as Land Obligations may become important and convenient in recognising the inherently different circumstances and expectations of these interests. For example, in the context of the 'ouster principle' surrounding cases such as the right of parking vehicles, it may be much easier as a matter of principle for the law to endorse the validity of an expressly granted right than one which is acquired through prescriptive use or by implication. Instead of the Law Commission's provisional proposal to completely abolish the ouster principle,[43] hence risking controversies which cases such as *Copeland v Greenhalf*[44] sought to avoid, it may be sensible and justifiable to recast the law to the effect that Land Obligations will not trigger the ouster principle. This reflects the unequivocal nature of express agreement between parties and registered interests in land. Meanwhile, positive easements, all of which will be unwritten post-reform, will continue to be limited by the ouster principle, reflecting the characteristics of easements as non-possessory, non-exclusive interests.

Against legal tradition and established understanding, the Scottish reform in this area converted all negative servitudes into negative real burdens, in order to achieve a framework with no overlap of the two concepts. Although such a conversion cannot be simply emulated by the English reform because of the existing commercial concerns in implied and prescriptive negative easements, the 'neatness' in principle is not beyond the reach of English law, if it is willing to construct a new boundary between easements and Land Obligations on the basis of formality required for their creation.

Interest to enforce Land Obligations

It may be argued on the basis of some of the issues discussed above that the Scottish reform took a very principled and non-compromising approach. The resulting law is generally welcomed by all and so far there has been very little criticism levelled against it. However, the reform has also encountered some rather unexpected difficulties in case law on the issue of 'interest to enforce' an obligation. It is submitted that the English reform may learn from this experience by considering the issue sooner rather than later.

In order to enforce a real burden under Scots law, a person must have both the title to enforce and the interest to enforce.[45] The title to enforce was a big problem prior to the reform, as much of it was dependent on the position of a common feudal superior, comparable to the concept of a 'scheme of development' in the English law on restrictive covenants. However, since the statutory reform and the complete abolition of feudal structure, it is now usually straightforward to

[43] Ibid [3.34]–[3.55].

[44] [1952] Ch 488 (Ch).

[45] Title Conditions (Scotland) Act 2003 s 8(1).

establish a title to enforce a particular real burden, such as by being the owner of a plot of land registered as the benefited property of the said burden.

The interest to enforce a real burden under the common law was also noticeably obscure, often only described as having a 'patrimonial' or 'praedial' interest. In general, before the statutory reform, the person seeking to enforce a real burden had to prove that his property had been injured by the breach of the burden.[46] As noted by the Scottish Law Commission, there were only a few cases on the issue of interest to enforce,[47] despite this being a key requirement of the law on enforcement. Essentially, the aim of the rule on title and interest to enforce is to filter out frivolous law suits by people who are not really related to the land or not really affected by a particular breach.

English law traditionally takes a very different approach in this regard. The Law Commission addressed the issue in its 1984 report:

> Under the present law of restrictive covenants, several rules combine to ensure that the benefit of a covenant normally does not pass to someone who acquires part of the 'dominant' land which is not in fact capable of benefiting from it. Inevitably therefore, such a person is debarred from enforcing the covenant.[48]

However, the land obligation concept proposed at that time, similar to the current Land Obligation being considered now, would be different from the common law covenants in terms of the passing of 'benefit' to enforce, to the extent that some people may end up holding benefited land while not capable of actually benefiting from a land obligation. The Law Commission acknowledged the impact of this change and instead of the benefit rule proposed the rule that 'no one should be entitled to any remedy for a contravention unless he has been materially prejudiced by it'.[49]

It is submitted however that the Law Commission inadvertently mixed two related but different rules, without distinguishing them. The subtlety between a general rule, such as the benefit rule under English law or the praedial rule under Scots law, and a specific rule on the interest to enforce, is appreciated and explained more clearly by the Scottish Law Commission in its 1998 report:

> [The two rules] ... operate at different levels of generality. The praedial rule is concerned with the general question of whether a burden is by its nature capable of conferring benefit on the benefited property or properties. The interest to enforce rule is concerned with a specific breach by a specific burdened owner at a specific time, and by the attempt to found on that breach by a specific person. The specificity makes all the difference. On the particular facts, the benefited and burdened properties may be too far apart for enforcement to be permitted; or the breach may be too trivial to impact on the benefited property; or the enforcer's right in that property may

[46] Scottish Law Commission, 'Report on Real Burdens' (Scot Law Com No 181, 2000) [4.16].

[47] Ibid [4.17].

[48] Law Commission, 'Transfer of Land: The Law of Positive and Restrictive Covenants' (Law Com No 127, 1984) [13.22].

[49] Ibid [13.21].

> be too slight or temporary; or the neighbourhood may have changed in such a way that praedial benefit, present at the time of original constitution, has now largely disappeared. It follows that a burden which easily satisfied the praedial rule might turn out to be unenforceable in particular cases because of lack of interest to enforce. But probably it would not be unenforceable in all cases. The next breach might be more serious; or the dispute might lie between two properties which are closer together. For community burdens, in particular, proximity is often a decisive factor. Burdens can be enforced against the house next door, but not, usually, against the house at the opposite end of the estate.[50]

In the light of this analysis, it would seem that the 1984 report by the Law Commission was attempting to replace the general rule of passing of the benefit with a specific rule of enforcement, the differences between which have probably never been formally recognised by English law. Nevertheless, when the Scottish Law Commission came to formulate a statutory statement of the rule of enforcement, the end product appeared remarkably similar to the idea of a 'material prejudice' test presented by the Law Commission for England and Wales earlier in 1984.[51] For burdens other than an affirmative burden relating to financial contribution, a person will only have the interest to enforce if 'in the circumstances of any case, failure to comply with the real burden is resulting in, or will result in, material detriment to the value or enjoyment of the person's ownership of, or right in, the benefited property'.[52]

Although there is no evidence or indication of any comparative input or influence on this point, the fact that both reports produced fourteen years apart in different jurisdictions converged on a similar rule seem to illustrate a consensus of its importance. In the words of the 1984 report, this recommendation seemed 'self-evidently right'.[53] It is then even more remarkable that consideration of this issue appears to be omitted in the Consultation Paper for the current reform. In order to enforce a Land Obligation, the Consultation Paper only expects the benefit rule to be satisfied and the fact that 'there is a breach of the Land Obligation'.[54] However, using the example provided by the Scottish Law Commission, building rabbit hutches would constitute a breach of the obligation not to build, just as the construction of a five-storey block of flats would.[55] But it is unreasonable to allow enforcement against such a breach, where the immediate neighbours have no objection to a harmless contravention, while the owner of a house at the opposite end of the estate 200 yards away has.

It would appear that the 'material prejudice' test suggested by the Law Commission in 1984 and the 'material detriment' test adopted by the Title

[50] Scottish Law Commission, 'Report on Real Burdens' (Scot Law Com No 181, 2000) [4.16].

[51] Text to n 49.

[52] Title Conditions (Scotland) Act 2003 s 8(3)(a).

[53] Law Commission, 'Transfer of Land: The Law of Positive and Restrictive Covenants' (Law Com No 127, 1984) [13.22].

[54] Law Commission, 'Easements, Covenants and Profits à Prendre' (Law Com Cp No 186, 2008) [9.6].

[55] Scottish Law Commission, 'Report on Real Burdens' (Scot Law Com No 181, 2000) [4.17].

Conditions (Scotland) Act 2003 would provide help and useful guidance when faced with such cases. An owner living 200 yards away will not suffer material detriment or prejudice if rabbit hutches were built on the burdened land. However, he is more than likely to have the interest to enforce if the construction is actually a five-storey building. As quoted above, 'the specificity makes all the difference'.[56] But as things stand the current English reform seemingly has not paid sufficient attention to the issue, at least not in the form of any clearly formulated rule.

Incidentally the concern may not be that Land Obligations will not be widely used, but that they will be popular and readily adopted in developments of all sizes and varieties except for commonhold schemes. It will be much easier and more certain to identify the benefit and burden of a Land Obligation and these will be passed on. Without any threshold for enforceability, there would be nothing to stop an owner bringing litigation to prevent the building of rabbit hutches while living in houses 200 yards away from the property in question.

The detriment of 'material detriment'

Furthermore, it soon turned out that simply having a statutory statement of 'material detriment' in Scots law did not necessarily help the clarification of the interest to enforce, which was previously vague before codification. It may be argued that the Scottish Law Commission did not really expect too much difficulty in its choice of the word 'material', to the extent that in the relevant part of its report no explanation or reasoning was directed at this seemingly self-explanatory word.[57] The first case to ponder the meaning of this new test, *Barker v Lewis*,[58] came before the court in 2007.

The development in the case was in a rather reclusive area near St Andrews. It comprised five detached houses of two to five bedrooms located in close proximity to each other and served only by a private road. In 2003 and 2004, the parties purchased the properties from the same developer who renovated these buildings previously used as an old farm. Each individual title was duly bound by the same deed of conditions setting out the real burdens applicable to all of them. The most relevant of these burdens in this case restricted the use of the property in the following manner:

The dwellinghouse and garage erected or to be erected on each individual plot shall be used and occupied by the proprietors as a domestic dwellinghouse with relative offices only and for use by one family only and no other purpose whatsoever.[59]

[56] Text to n 50.

[57] Scottish Law Commission, 'Report on Real Burdens' (Scot Law Com No 181, 2000) [4.20]–[4.24].

[58] 2007 SLT (Sh Ct) 48.

[59] Ibid 49.

Despite such restriction, in 2005 the defender opened up her property as a bed and breakfast. The business was advertised online and soon became very successful. The steady flow of guests caused a series of unpleasant incidents for the neighbours. Guests were driving or parking where they shouldn't have. They came to the wrong properties and attempted to enter them. They took photos of the other properties, walked around them or paid too much attention to the activities of the neighbours, probably as to be expected from tourists mostly from foreign countries. Many of the guests arrived late at night or left early in the morning, with considerably increased levels of noise in this otherwise peaceful and quiet rural residential development. After more than a year of unsuccessful discussion amongst the owners, three out of four neighbours eventually took the owner of the bed and breakfast to court for breaching the aforementioned real burden.

There was no question that the defender in the case was the owner of a burdened property and the pursuers were the owners of benefited properties. Running a bed and breakfast business was not using the property as a domestic dwellinghouse by one family. In other words, everyone accepted that there was a clear breach of the restriction. The only question in this case was whether the breach resulted in material detriment to the value or enjoyment of the neighbouring properties to enable the neighbours to enforce against it.

To the surprise of many, the sheriff concluded that there was no material detriment in the case, as long as the number of guests taken does not exceed the then level of about 250 per year. However, the reasoning by the sheriff in reaching the conclusion was strongly criticised by Professor Reid.[60] The sheriff concluded that the 'plain meaning of the word' dictates that 'material' detriment should be interpreted as 'substantial' detriment.[61] Professor Reid, who was the Scottish Law Commissioner in charge throughout the series of property law reform, pointed to the careful hierarchy of usage of these two different words in the statutes, arguing that they clearly meant different things. To replace one with another is altering the statute and the Scottish Parliament's intention. The sheriff also drew help from the law on nuisance in the particular case, holding the view that the breach may not necessarily be a nuisance under the common law. In response, Professor Reid argued that this was exactly the reason why specific real burdens were introduced to supplement the general law of nuisance where it would not be sufficient to control the behaviour of parties. Such an understanding seems to echo quite well with the English law on restrictive covenants, as seen in the recent Court of Appeal decision of *Davies v Dennis*,[62] where 'nuisance and annoyance' in a private deed was confirmed as a wider notion than the general notion of 'nuisance'.

[60] K G C Reid, 'Interest to Enforce Real Burdens: How Material is "Material"?' (2007) *Edin L Rev* 440.

[61] *Barker* (n 58) 55.

[62] [2009] EWCA Civ 1081, [2010] 1 P & CR DG13.

Given the lack of other sources on this new statutory term, Professor Reid's article became the key to the litigation when *Barker* was appealed to the sheriff principal. In short, the sheriff principal agreed with everything Professor Reid said in principle, to the conclusion that the sheriff approached the interpretation of 'material detriment' on an erroneous basis. Remarkably however, the sheriff principal then refused to overturn the original decision or to attempt to his own assessment on the facts of the case. In other words the first instance judge came to the right decision after all despite having all the wrong understandings of the principles involved.

It may be fair to say that the decision and the appeal were not received with enthusiasm by academics and conveyancers in Scotland. The traditional view had always been that despite the uncertainty associated with the common law idea of interest to enforce, the immediate neighbours would have such interest in almost all cases where there was a breach. According to leading practitioners such as Professor Rennie, *Barker* not only failed to take the law any further forward by not providing any helpful guidance on a new statutory threshold, but in fact removed this only shred of certainty inherited from the pre-2004 era.[63]

Unfortunately, a decision which did not take the law forward might have more negative influence than a missed opportunity. It did not take long for the impact of *Barker* to be felt in other cases, particularly those under the Lands Tribunal for Scotland regarding variation or discharge of real burdens.

In *Smith v Lawrence*,[64] only a few months after *Barker*, it would seem that the parties and the tribunal were largely oblivious to the weight of the decision. The property concerned was in the town of Musselburgh, right next to the campus of Queen Margaret University. The title of the five bedroom house was subject to the real burden, very similar to that in *Barker*, that the property shall be used solely as private dwellinghouse and not sub-divided or occupied by more than one family at a time. The owner wanted to rent it out to a group of students studying at the university. He applied to the Lands Tribunal for the burden to be varied or discharged. Some of the neighbours objected to the application and the Tribunal decided in their favour. Viewed together with *Barker* and given the drastic contrast between the settings of these two properties, it seems logical to question whether the neighbours living in urban areas of a populous town could possibly prove a more 'material' detriment than those in a reclusive rural location for breach of a similar burden. *Barker* was, however, never mentioned by either party.

Things changed rather quickly in 2009. In *Fleeman v Lyon*,[65] the burdened owner sought discharge of a restriction on building in order to construct an additional house in his garden. *Barker* was cited in support for the contention that this would not cause enough material detriment to those neighbours

[63] R Rennie, '*Barker v. Lewis* on appeal' (2008) *SLT (News)* 77.
[64] 2009 GWD 6-104.
[65] 2009 GWD 32-539.

who objected to the proposal. The counter-argument submitted that *Barker* concerned transient breaches of a burden while the subject matter of the case was a permanent contravention in the form of a substantial building. The Tribunal itself did not express any view on the applicability of *Barker* in the case.

It may be argued that the principle involved here is as explained by the Scottish Law Commission as quoted above.[66] One is a question of specificity of whether one particular breach is material enough, while a permanent discharge is a general question of whether a breach will ever be material enough.

Unsurprisingly such a principled stance did not hold out for long given the close relationship between these two questions in practice. Soon enough, *Clarke v Grantham*[67] crossed the boundary, with the Lands Tribunal citing *Barker* in approval. The original owner in the case sold part of a historic building and half of the courtyard attached to the property to the first disponee, while still retaining the other half of it. The title of the first disponee to the courtyard was subject to the real burden that it should not be used for parking except for 'setting down temporarily'. The second half of the courtyard and the remainder of the building were then sold to the second disponee, but without such burden attached. The second disponee used her half of the courtyard for parking as it was not restricted in any way. The first disponee then sought to discharge the real burden on his half of the courtyard, contending that it would not cause material detriment to the property such as in terms of amenity. The Lands Tribunal cited *Barker* and duly granted the discharge in the case on its facts.

It would appear that the fine line between specificity and generality has finally been breached in this case, less than two years after the appeal in *Barker*. The view that parking a car in a courtyard which already has cars parked on the other half of it does not result in material detriment seems to be fair enough. It may nevertheless be a completely different detriment where the vehicle parked later on turns out to be a permanently settled caravan or a twenty-ton lorry. Once a real burden is discharged, however, it apparently cannot be revived against even the lorry. It remains to be seen how Scots law will continue to develop and define this novelty of 'material detriment', which has arguably been the most problematic issue since the commencement of Title Conditions (Scotland) Act 2003.

In the meantime, it appears that the current English reform can neither afford to ignore this rule proposed by its predecessor and its Scottish counterpart, nor rely too much on the experience of the latter on this, which has turned out to be unexpectedly troublesome. If there is to be a rule along the lines of interest to enforce, it is important to consider whether there should be a rule of generality or specificity, or both. Judging by the Scottish experience so far, it will be a challenge to work out the appropriate statutory wording and criteria, in an

[66] Text to n 50.
[67] 2009 GWD 38-645.

area with very little established knowledge but considerable potential impact in practice. After all, no one wants to see an owner having words about rabbit hutches 200 yards away from his property. The question is how and by what criteria the law of Land Obligations can distinguish between this contravention and that of the construction of a five-storey building next door. How much guidance should the statute provide for the court in favour of certainty of the law? The lesson from Scotland so far seems to suggest that even one questionable decision in the lower courts can cause a lot of problems for a novel concept for many years.

Conclusion

The Scottish law of real burdens is a valuable source of comparative law for the ongoing discussion of Land Obligations in English law. It represents a system with more experience and heavier reliance on the concept for more than a century. It has also undergone its own reform very recently, with the added bonus of a codified and principled statute for the interested lawyers from elsewhere.

The Scottish reform has been very firm on formality, especially the mandatory use of the correct terminology. This was deliberately inconsistent with the traditional common law approach. However, once forced through by statutes, there has never been any suggestion of injustice or harshness because of this approach. Furthermore, the reform was not afraid to redefine the well-established boundaries between servitudes and real burdens in order to achieve coherence and consistency in the law. While English law has its own peculiarities in this regard, it would seem unsatisfactory if the reform simply gives up the hope of making sense of the array of interests on the grounds of historical reasons alone. Where an analysis based on functionality could not produce the desired coherence, it may worth looking for another criterion, such as that of formality suggested in this chapter.

However, the Scottish reform has encountered arguably unexpected difficulties and undesirable consequences of its own, as seen in the continuing search for the meaning of 'material detriment' in relation to the enforcement of real burdens. So far the current English reform has paid little attention to this important issue. The hope is that with the necessary attention and by learning from the Scottish experience, the incoming framework of Land Obligations can provide a better solution to the problem than its predecessor and its neighbour.

11

The Consequences of Genetic Engineering: a Comment on Lu Xu's Chapter

Elizabeth Cooke*

Lu Xu very kindly allowed me to see a copy of his paper some weeks before the conference in Oxford that preceded this volume. The editor kindly allowed me to present a response to it at the conference, and that response is reproduced as a separate chapter here.[1]

I would like to respond to two issues that Lu Xu raises. One is about labelling, and the other is about enforcement.

Labels, species and function

I begin by deploring a deficiency in the English language: we have no single term that defines the interests under consideration in the Law Commission's current project, clumpily labelled *Easements, Covenants and Profits à Prendre*. As Lu Xu observes, we cannot call them appurtenant rights because profits need not be appurtenant. They can be grouped together as non-ownership, non-security rights in land. We cannot do as the North Americans do and call them all servitudes[2] because Scots and continental European usage reserves that term for easements. So if a common label is wanted, we are in some difficulties.

That begs a question – is a common label wanted? I would like to explain why a common label for this group of interests in land, following the reforms that the Law Commission is going to recommend, is both desirable and misleading.

* Professor of Law, University of Reading; Law Commissioner for England and Wales.

[1] As in my first chapter, chapter 9 above, I make reference to Law Commission, 'Easements, Covenants and Profits à Prendre' (Law Com Cp No 186, 2008), hereinafter 'the Consultation Paper'. I acknowledge gratefully the work on this project of the other members of the property law team at the Law Commission: Matthew Jolley, Julia Jarzabkowski and Colin Oakley.

[2] See American Law Institute, *Restatement of the Law Third, Property (Servitudes)* (Philadelphia, PA 2000).

It may be tempting to dismiss out of hand the idea that all the rights we are looking at, if created expressly, should be labelled Land Obligations, for the simple reason that whatever its academic merits it would just never sell in the real world of legal practice. But I would like to take the opportunity that Lu Xu's suggestion provides to explain something of my thinking about labelling.

To do that, we have to re-trace our steps and look at the most fundamental question that this project has to answer.

The big issue and its consequences

The most profound question that the Law Commission has to answer, whatever else it does or does not achieve in this project, is whether positive obligations should be able to run with land.[3] That question is woven into the Commission's own roots. In *Law Reform Now*,[4] in making their case for the establishment of a Law Commission, Gerald Gardiner and Andrew Martin gathered together articles by leading scholars. Gerald Dworkin's chapter on land law identified as one of the major issues crying out for reform the fact that positive covenants do not run with land. And Lu Xu has traced the history of the Commission's work on covenants, through the 1984 Report *Transfer of Land, The Law of Positive and Restrictive Covenants*,[5] and the journey to commonhold. We have the opportunity, with commonhold invented (albeit in need of some reinvention) and land registration modernised, to deal with this problem once and for all.

For reasons explained elsewhere,[6] in the light both of the responses of consultees and of arguments pragmatic[7] and theoretical,[8] we are taking the answer

[3] The *Consultation Paper* (n 1) listed, [7.36]–[7.45], the problems associated with the law of freehold covenants as follows:

1. It is difficult to identify who has the benefit of a restrictive covenant, first because there is no requirement that the instrument creating it should describe and identify the dominant estate in detail, but second because there is no requirement or power for Land Registry to enter the benefit on the title to the dominant land.
2. There are differing and complicated rules for the running of the benefit and burden of restrictive covenants.
3. The contractual liability between the original parties to a covenant persists despite changes in the ownership of the land. As a result, sellers often go to the expense and trouble of entering into indemnity agreements or taking out indemnity insurance.
4. Whereas the benefit of a positive covenant can run at law, the burden of a positive covenant does not run so as to bind successors in title, either at law or in equity. Devices which have been developed to circumvent this rule are complex and insufficiently comprehensive.

[4] G Gardiner and A Martin (eds), *Law Reform Now* (Victor Gollancz Ltd, London 1963).

[5] Law Commission, 'Transfer of Land: The Law of Positive and Restrictive Covenants' (Law Com No 127, 1984).

[6] See E Cooke, 'To Restate or not to Restate? Old Wine, New Wineskins, Old Covenants, New Ideas' [2009] *Conv* 448; E Cooke, 'Is the *Numerus* Really *Clausus*? Servitudes, Covenants and the Problem of Positive Obligations' in M Habdas and A Wudarski (eds), *Festschrift für Stanislawa Kalus – Ius est ars boni et aequi* (Peter Lang Verlag, Frankfurt am Mein 2010).

[7] One of the arguments in favour of change is that there is already a multitude of ways to attach positive obligations to land, namely through estate rentcharges, chains of indemnity, the benefit and

to that big issue to be yes. Without going into all the detail of the argument here, we conclude that it should be possible to burden land with an obligation to do something, so that that burden is enforceable by the successors in title to the benefited land[9] and against the successors in title to the burdened land.[10]

Having made that decision, we have to address the question of how to do it. There are a number of options. Note that my intention here is not to criticise any particular reform model; it is simply to point out different ways of doing things.

One option is just to extend the existing law relating to restrictive covenants. *Tulk v Moxhay*[11] can be stretched so that it does for positive covenants what it already does for restrictive ones. But that leaves in place the irksome rules for the running of the benefit and burden of covenants, which is one of the elements of the current law that our Consultation Paper deplores.

A step further gets rid of those rules and sets out in statute that is bound by freehold covenants. This is what the New Zealand legislation does, in the Property Law Act 2007.[12] Section 303 provides:

> *Legal effect of covenants running with land*
>
> **303** (1) This section applies to a restrictive covenant, and also to a positive covenant coming into operation on or after 1 January 1987 ... in either case whether expressed in an instrument or implied by this Act or any other enactment in an instrument, if—
>
> (a) the covenant burdens land of the covenantor and is intended to benefit the owner for the time being of the covenantee's land; and
>
> (b) there is no privity of estate between the covenantor and the covenantee.
>
> (2) Every covenant to which this section applies, unless a contrary intention appears, is binding in equity on—
>
> (a) every person who becomes the owner of the burdened land (whether by acquisition from the covenantor or from any of the covenantor's successors in title, and whether or not for valuable consideration, and whether by operation of law or otherwise); and

burden principle in *Halsall v Brizell* [1957] Ch 169 (Ch), and of course leasehold; reform of the law relating to positive covenants is arguably just a simplification of something that can already by done by various workarounds.

[8] Does the *numerus clausus* really stand in the way of this reform? Bernard Rudden's discussion at 'Economic Theory vs Property Law: The *Numerus Clausus* Problem' in J Eekelaar and J Bell (eds), *Oxford Essays in Jurisprudence* (3rd series, Clarendon Press, Oxford 1987) 239, remains a primary reference point here, and his conclusion is that it does not. See further the discussion in the two papers cited above: *Cooke* (n 6).

[9] We have rejected the possibility of introducing covenants, or easements, that can be held in gross as can profits.

[10] Inevitably, the class of those bound by a positive obligation is narrower than those bound by a negative one; the positive obligation can only be imposed on successors in title, and subject even then to some practical limitations, whereas even occupiers of the land can be bound by a restrictive covenant and can be restrained from obstructing an easement.

[11] (1848) 47 ER 1345.

[12] Reform was effected by the Property Law Amendment Act 1986, amending the Property Law Act 1952.

> (b) every person who is for the time being the occupier of the burdened land.
>
> (3) Every covenant to which this section applies, unless a contrary intention appears, ceases to be binding on a person referred to in subsection (2) when that person ceases to be the owner or the occupier of the burdened land but without prejudice to that person's liability for any breach of the covenant arising before that person ceased to be the owner or occupier of the land.

New Zealand freehold covenants are still equitable interests, living in the world of both contract and property law; they are like a duck-billed platypus, with features of both mammals and reptiles. But they are looking much tidier; enforceability is governed by statute.

Sub-section (3) tackles another of the problems that the Law Commission set out to solve.[13] Under the current law, a restrictive-covenantor is liable on the covenant for ever – hence the chains of indemnity covenants that clutter up titles. If we extend that principle to positive obligations, so that once you have covenanted to maintain an estate road, say, you remain liable on that covenant forever, then we have created bad law. We would then have in freehold land the sort of problem that had to be solved, but could only be partially solved, in leasehold land by the Landlord and Tenant (Covenants) Act 1995. So whatever the form in which positive covenants are introduced as interests in land, we do need to make provision for original covenantors to lose their liability once they part with the land, except of course as regards breaches that took place during their ownership.

However, if we were to translate the New Zealand approach direct to this jurisdiction, the major difficulty would be that the benefit of a positive covenant would remain outside the registration system. One of the most significant arguments against reform of the law relating to positive covenants is that it is undesirable to have no public record of the benefited land, because that makes it practically impossible to work out how to negotiate (or litigate) a release, and then land becomes clogged with burdens that cannot be lifted. That is already a problem with restrictive covenants and we must not create that problem for positive obligations.

It would not be impossible to expand the scope of title registration under the Land Registration Act 2002 to include the title to equitable interests in land.[14] But doing so would be extremely counter-intuitive and would produce a strange knot in the smooth texture of that statute. Far better to give positive obligations, and indeed negative ones too, the status of legal interests in land; the way then lies clear for the benefit of those obligations to be a registrable estate, where title to land is registered.[15]

[13] See the list at n 3 above.

[14] So that it would become one of the registrable interests listed in the Land Registration Act 2002 s 2.

[15] The benefit of a covenant cannot be registered in unregistered land. The burden can; currently restrictive covenants fall within the Land Charges Act 1972, and amendments can be made to that statute to incorporate the burden of the new legal interest.

Let us examine what the Irish legislation does. The Land and Conveyancing Law Reform Act 2009 provides at section 11 that freehold covenants are among the available legal interests in land. It then goes on to say in section 49:

> **49.**—(1) Subject to *subsection (6)*, the rules of common law and equity (including the rule known as the rule in *Tulk v. Moxhay*) are abolished to the extent that they relate to the enforceability of a freehold covenant.
>
> (2) Subject to *subsections (3)* to *(6)*, any freehold covenant which imposes in respect of servient land an obligation to do or to refrain from doing any act or thing is enforceable—
>
> (*a*) by—
>
> (i) the dominant owner[16] for the time being, or
>
> (ii) a person who has ceased to be that owner but only in respect of any breach of covenant occurring during the period when that person was such owner,
>
> (*b*) against—
>
> (i) the servient owner for the time being in respect of any breach of covenant by that owner or which occurred before and continued unremedied after that person became the servient owner, or
>
> (ii) a person who has ceased to be that owner, but only in respect of a breach of covenant which occurred during the period when that person was such owner.

How much has changed here? *Tulk v Moxhay* has gone,[17] and the rules about enforceability are set out in the statute instead; and they apply to both positive and negative covenants. The benefit of a covenant is a legal interest in land and it binds and benefits the successors in title to the original parties by virtue of the statute. To make a contractual promise that is going to fall within these sections must therefore be to make a grant.[18]

It is not yet possible to say what will be the shape of the relevant provision in the draft Bill to be attached to the Report that the Law Commission for England and Wales will be publishing in a year's time. They will not be modelled on the Irish Bill, and our Bill is likely to look quite different – there are a number of different ways of achieving the same or a similar effect. But the important thing to note is that by transforming a covenant into a legal interest in land, we have gone beyond cosmetics and on to genetic engineering. There will be a new interest in land that arises from the provisions of the statute and so will not depend on the creation of an obligation by contract. It binds all parties, original and successors, by virtue of statutory provision and not as a contract. The covenant has moved out of its twilight world and into the sunshine, out of contract and into the world of interests in land.

[16] This and other terms are defined at s 48 of the Land and Conveyancing Law Reform Act 2009.

[17] For freehold covenants; it is still needed to make the covenants in a headlease enforceable against a sub-lessee and others.

[18] Even though the character of the obligation as contractual appears to be preserved, in the Irish statute, by s 49(6)(a)(i).

So far I have talked only about covenants, and in order to make this reform as useful as possible it is desirable to ensure that the new interests can continue to be drafted as covenants. But once it is admitted that the new interest takes effect through the statute and not through the law of contract, then there is no reason why it should not arise from an instrument that does not take the form of a covenant; the new interest can be defined simply as an obligation to do or not do something on land.[19]

Labelling

Once that metamorphosis has taken place, we have a new creation, and one that looks very much indeed like an easement or a profit. Moving into the statutory language of England and Wales, we can say that as a right in land it is encompassed within the term 'easement, right or privilege' in section 1(2)(a) of the Law of Property Act 1925 and therefore automatically takes its place among the legal interests the title to which is registrable under the Land Registration Act 2002. Section 52 of the Law of Property Act 1925 will govern its creation without further provision.[20]

At this point the lack of a common label becomes more of a trouble than it already is because now instead of easements, profits and freehold covenants looking like a mouse, a hamster and a duck-billed platypus, we have something more like a mouse, a hamster and a gerbil and it would be very convenient to call them all rodents. Or land obligations, or servitudes or what you will. Which brings us to Lu Xu's suggestion and the wisdom that it embodies: we could indeed have one name for these three things.

On the other hand we still have to distinguish the three creatures. For one thing, easements can be created by prescription and implication, whereas our recommendation will be that it shall not be possible to create either profits or the new obligations otherwise than expressly. But we cannot use that as the major subdivision, as Lu Xu suggests, because there are other more radical subdivisions. Profits can exist in gross and the other interests cannot. The new obligations will have to have a very separate range of remedies from those for easements and profits; the latter are protected by the law of nuisance, whereas we need something that, albeit statutory, will look much more like breach of contract for breach of an obligation whether positive or negative. And positive obligations need very special provisions about liability, because the general law

[19] There will be a number of adjustments to be made to that functional definition to ensure that it does not extend too widely; we want to ensure, for example, that a covenant to work in the neighbouring shop five days a week cannot be an interest in land, nor an overage covenant. But an obligation to do or not do something on land is certainly at the heart of the definition.

[20] The *Consultation Paper* (n 1) proposed additional formalities requirements including the precise use of the term 'Land Obligations'; we do not propose to pursue that suggestion, preferring to adopt a functional definition to distinguish the new interest from easements.

will ensure that all estates derived from the burdened estate will take the burden and so we need special provision (which easements and restrictive covenants do not) to ensure:

a) that those with a very limited estate do not bear disproportionate burdens; we do not want the weekly tenant to have to undertake major works; and
b) that there is some default arrangement for apportionment of burdens where there is a disposition of part.

Those are both points for discussion in our Report; my point here is that we are still going to have to distinguish between different species of right for very practical reasons, even though these three interests now have so much in common that they can be regarded as three instances of the same sort of thing in much the same way that easements and profits are akin at present.

And for that reason the lack of a common denominator label is not as important as is the need for functional definitions of the different interests,[21] so as to enable us to retain the distinctions that have to remain. And that is why, desirable though it might be to have a single label for these interests, it is in practical terms essential to keep them separate.

Enforcement

Lu Xu's chapter discusses the Scots law of real burdens and the distinction made there between 'title to enforce' and 'interest to enforce'. The idea in Scots law is that not everyone who has title to enforce a breach of an obligation (for example, not to build) because he holds an estate that has the benefit of it should actually be able to sue upon it. Instead, only someone who suffers material detriment as a result of the breach can sue.

Scots law does not allow the level of vertical fragmentation that English law permits, owing to the absence of long leases and the far more restricted use of trusts. The Scottish legislation sets out those who have title to enforce the real burden – as it must do, since the Scots cannot use the concept of a derivative estate to which the benefit passes automatically;[22] but it also requires that on any one occasion the only people entitled to enforce an individual breach are those who also have an 'interest to enforce' it. A person has an interest to enforce if:

(a) in the circumstances of any case, failure to comply with the real burden is resulting in, or will result in, material detriment to the value or enjoyment of the person's ownership of, or right in, the benefited property; or

[21] Negative easements are a problem; they could certainly be expressed as new obligations (an obligation not to build, for example, or not to withdraw support or block the light to a window). But to cease to treat them as easements is probably too much of a disturbance to existing law.

[22] Title Conditions (Scotland) Act 2003 s 8(2).

(b) the real burden being an affirmative burden created as an obligation to defray, or contribute towards, some cost, that person seeks (and has grounds to seek) payment of, or as respects, that cost.[23]

We do not think that in general, leaving aside obligations to pay money, there will be a problem arising from having a number of people entitled to enforce a positive obligation. An obligation to mend a fence is a task that has to be done, and it does not particularly matter whether one or ten people are able to remind the servient owner to do it, or even to sue him for failing to do so. He only has to do it once. In Scotland, in the absence of a concept of estates, and in the absence of long leases, far fewer people will satisfy condition (a) above than will do so in English law; here, freeholders, equitable owners and leaseholders alike may have a valuable interest in having the boundary maintained or the roof mended, or even the grass cut. Accordingly, we think that condition (a) above would not be particularly effective even if we accepted that a control on the numbers able to enforce were necessary.

However, where there may be a problem arising from the ability of a number of people to enforce is in the case of money obligations. If the obligation is to pay for the upkeep of a shared road, obviously we have to ensure that only one of those who hold estates that benefit from it can require payment. We do need a provision that ties a money payment to the performance of a reciprocal obligation – so it can be a service charge, or a payment for the upkeep of a shared driveway, say, which the other party has himself covenanted to maintain. In the Consultation Paper we called that money obligation a 'reciprocal payment obligation',[24] and while that does not have to be used as a term of art it is a useful description of what is happening here. Accordingly, it follows that of those who hold an estate that benefits from an obligation to pay, say, towards maintenance of a driveway, the only ones entitled to recover payment are those who have incurred expenditure in providing a service.

So that is why we have not followed the Scots provisions about interest to enforce: we see no need to limit the numbers entitled to enforce an obligation to do things, and the enforcement of a payment obligation can be controlled by ensuring that it is only valid when it is reciprocal to another obligation.

We have been aware of the Scots law in this context, but have decided not to follow it – even though the same sort of condition for enforcement was proposed in the 1984 Report, as Lu Xu points out. But what that Report and the Scots scheme have in common is that they encompass the use of obligations in extended developments where it is quite possible that a covenant that is really important to my immediate neighbour may be of no concern to someone four streets away. That sort of problem does not really arise when we are looking essentially at what the 1984 Report called neighbour burdens – an obligation not to build, for the benefit of next door, for example.

[23] Title Conditions (Scotland) Act 2003 s 8(3).

[24] The *Consultation Paper* (n 1) [9.11] and following.

That said, our scheme will enable the mutual enforceability of obligations between a number of neighbours, as under the current law relating to building schemes;[25] and we have commonhold as a purpose-built vehicle for obligations within interdependent properties. So why do commonhold, and the current law relating to building schemes,[26] contain no control mechanism comparable to the 'interest to enforce' idea?

I suggest there are two reasons why we do not have this concept and do not want to take it on. The first is that in Scots law, precisely as Lu Xu points out, the 'interest to enforce' idea presents an additional layer of uncertainty that has not been an effective control mechanism at all. *Barker v Lewis*[27] is no advertisement for the concept of interest to enforce. The second is that the idea behind interest to enforce seems to be to ensure that people *are* allowed to break those obligations provided that the breach is not too serious. That has drafting implications. It leads inevitably to a culture where precision in drafting does not matter, and where it is acceptable to draft a covenant that is intended to prevent the construction of a block of flats in terms so wide that it prevents the building of rabbit hutches. We simply would not want to introduce the idea that the terms of an obligation do not matter because you can be statutorily 'let off' if your breach does not in fact harm your neighbour.[28]

Where we have followed the Scottish experience[29] is in two different aspects of the enforceability of positive obligations. This is an area that we have to distinguish carefully, as discussed under the topic of 'labelling', because we have to make special provisions that do not apply to negative obligations, nor to easements or profits. The difficulties arise when burdened land is subdivided, either by the creation of derived estates (legal or equitable), or by dispositions of part. Here are just two of the practical problems that arise.

One is where a number of estates are concurrently liable for the same positive obligation over the same land – for example, freeholder, tenant and sub-tenant. They all have to be liable to the dominant owner if the dominant owner chooses to enforce.[30] But as between themselves, if there is no explicit provision made

[25] To explain why would be beyond the scope of this chapter; see the *Consultation Paper* (n 1) [3.56] and following, where we explain that we propose to modify the rule relating to unity of seisin so as to make it possible for a developer to set up easements and obligations between defined plots within his own land prior to their sale. That will mean that he can define the area benefiting from a covenant as the whole of the rest of the estate.

[26] *Elliston v Reacher* [1908] 2 Ch 665 (CA).

[27] 2007 SLT (Sh Ct) 48.

[28] And in general people do not enforce breaches of covenant that do not bother them. Even if a restriction on building is so badly drafted as to preclude the owner from building rabbit hutches, the likelihood of anyone having words about rabbit hutches 200 yards away is too small to merit provisions to prevent it.

[29] We have drawn not only upon the provisions of the Title Conditions (Scotland) Act 2003 but also upon very helpful discussion with Professor Kenneth Reid.

[30] If only the freeholder is liable (option 2 of those suggested at [9.20] of the *Consultation Paper* (n 1)) then it would be possible to escape liability for a covenant altogether: A enters into a positive covenant with B, and then A grants a 999-year lease of the land to a company that he controls and sells the freehold to a 'man of straw' (whether a natural person or another company).

between them, the law has to provide a default position for liability, and the default that makes most sense is for the freeholder to take responsibility.

The other is where land that is burdened by a positive obligation is divided up, usually by a sale of part.

Again, as with 'vertical' subdivision of the burdened estate, this sort of disposition cannot be allowed to dilute the dominant owner's interest. So if B covenants with A that he will mend the fence between their two properties, and B then sells part of his property to C, C must share joint and several liability to A with B. Of course, B and C ought to make an explicit apportionment agreement between themselves;[31] but if they do not, then again the law must provide a default solution, and we have adopted the Scots solution, which is to apportion by area.[32] That solution is not appropriate in all possible situations; B and C may be prepared to stick with the default apportionment, or they may agree a different apportionment. They may even be able to agree with A to exonerate C's land altogether, or they may apply to the Lands Tribunal for an order modifying the obligation so as to exonerate C's land.

Conclusion

My two chapters in this volume have examined a number of different aspects of appurtenant interests. My first chapter, 'The genetics of appurtenant interests', began with the existing law and the effect of the decision in *Wall v Collins*,[33] where reform is needed to restore orthodoxy. With orthodoxy restored we can go on to look in this chapter at obligations as a new form of appurtenant interest. I agree with Lu Xu that labels are important, and the addition of a new appurtenant interest alongside those that are already possible makes us think about what these interests should be called. I have suggested that there are distinctions that Lu Xu does not take into account in his suggested re-packaging of the genus of 'non-ownership, non-security real rights', and that we have to make explicit by what we call the various interests. Finally, Lu Xu and I have discussed the enforceability of these appurtenant interests, focusing now on obligations. And I agree that the Scots experience of real burdens is particularly valuable. I am unpersuaded of the virtues of the concept of 'interest to enforce', but I take on board some of the other lessons we can learn from the Title Conditions (Scotland) Act 2003 in the formulation of a solution to a very difficult set of practical challenges.

[31] Which must itself qualify as a new proprietary obligation; we do not want such arrangements to have to depend upon personal covenants and chains of indemnity.

[32] Title Conditions (Scotland) Act 2003 s 11(1)(b).

[33] [2007] EWCA Civ 444, [2007] Ch 390.

12

Prescription and User 'As of Right': Ripe for Wholesale Reform?

Rowena Meager*

Introduction

The doctrine of prescription is one which has, in one form or another, facilitated the creation of rights in or over property for centuries. Its origins are firmly entrenched in Roman law, under which jurisdiction prescription enabled both the creation and destruction of titles to property, real and personal, as a consequence of acts of qualifying user[1] coupled with the lapse of time. Two distinct modes of prescription were therein established,[2] *usucapio*[3] and *longi temporis praescriptio*,[4] these two modes, later, essentially becoming fused.[5]

As is already apparent from the foregoing, the Roman law doctrine of prescription had a far more extensive reach than the model of prescription which operates in English law today. One of the key distinctions between the

* Barrister (No 5 Chambers).

[1] In respect of *usucapio* (see also n 3). 'The person claiming to *usucapt* must have uninterrupted possession for the requisite period; the possession must have been acquired both *ex iusta causa* and in good faith; the thing must be capable of being owned (not, for example, a free man believed to be a slave); and it must not at any time have been stolen or taken by force': B Nicholas, *An Introduction to Roman Law* (OUP, Oxford 1962) 122. For *longi temporis praescriptio* the rules for qualifying use in relation to *usucapio* were mostly applicable here too. However, one key difference was that under *longi temporis praescriptio* a possessor could add his predecessor's period of possession to his own.

[2] A third method of prescriptive acquisition was later introduced in the fourth century AD, *longissimi temporis praescriptio*, further discussion of which is beyond the scope of this chapter.

[3] *Usucapio*, a system of acquisitive prescription which applied only to things which were capable of private ownership in Roman law; this did not include provincial land.

[4] *Longi temporis praescriptio* emerged, initially functioning as a rule of limitation but eventually taking on an acquisitive role, filling the gap in relation to provincial land.

[5] Under Justinian the rules of *usucapio* and *longi temporis praescriptio* became moreorless indistinguishable, save for the lapse of time requirement which was much longer in relation to land than in relation to movables.

English model and its historic predecessor is that, in English law, prescription facilitates only the acquisition of rights in or over real property belonging to another, not the acquisition of title to property which results in a transfer of ownership.[6] Whilst the English law of prescription operates in a substantially more limited way than its Roman counterpart it does, nevertheless, make a very significant contribution to the law governing the establishment of rights in property. The doctrine operates to facilitate the creation of a diverse array of private and public rights over another's land. Such rights include easements, profits à prendre, public rights of way and the recreational rights which arise upon the registration of new town and village greens.[7]

The fact that so many rights are capable of creation by prescription is indicative of the importance of the doctrine in the contemporary English legal landscape, illustrating that it continues to perform a useful and desirable function. This view is reinforced by the fact that even very recently enacted legislation has continued to utilise rules of prescription as a method of acquiring rights over property.[8] It is further supported by provisional proposals made by the Law Commission[9] in 2008 which favour the retention of the doctrine as a method of creating easements, albeit in a substantially revised form. This clear inclination to continue to utilise rules of prescription is consistent with the sentiments expressed by Lord Hoffmann in *R v Oxfordshire County Council, ex p Sunningwell Parish Council*[10] (*Sunningwell*), where he stated:

> Any legal system must have rules of prescription which prevent the disturbance of long-established *de facto* enjoyment.

With this in mind, the purpose of this chapter is to consider, in light of the fact that quite significant reform of the rules of prescription has now been provisionally proposed by the Law Commission (at least as they apply to the creation of easements and profits à prendre), whether this might not be an opportune time to engage in a more holistic review of the doctrine and its operation. In particular, this chapter will consider whether more widespread doctrinal reform

[6] The acquisition of title to property in English law is governed by the doctrine of adverse possession which operates under two separate sets of rules depending upon whether the land concerned is registered or unregistered. For registered land the provisions of the Land Registration Act 2002 apply and for unregistered land the provisions of the Limitation Act 1980 apply.

[7] It is perhaps worth noting that not all of these rights would be classed as property rights in the hands of those who enjoy the benefit of them, notwithstanding the fact that they are all rights over property. Only in respect of easements and some profits à prendre (those created under the Prescription Act 1832) is it necessary for the rights acquired to be attached to property; in other words, for there to be a dominant tenement. Profits à prendre created other than under the Prescription Act 1832 (under the common law rules or the doctrine of lost modern grant) are capable of existing in gross, and public rights of way or rights of recreation referable to a newly registered town or village green quite logically, given the nature of the rights concerned, have no requirement for there to be a dominant tenement to which the right claimed is or can be annexed.

[8] The Highways Act 1980 and the Commons Act 2006.

[9] Law Commission, 'Easements, Covenants and Profits à Prendre' (Law Com Cp No 186, 2008) [4.183].

[10] [2000] 1 AC 335 (HL) 349.

might be appropriate; applicable in all of the specific circumstances in which rules of prescription are capable of creating new rights. This is not a radical suggestion by any means. It was noted some years ago that:

> The developing law of village greens, and in particular the difficulties being experienced in relation to the necessary elements of prescriptive acquisition, do send a warning for those looking for the appropriate means of reforming analogous areas.[11]

In order to assess whether there are aspects of the rules of prescription which would benefit from some wholesale reform, but which are outside the ambit of the Law Commission's current parameters of review, it is first useful to understand why we retain and utilise the doctrine of prescription at all. Such understanding will assist in determining whether the rules of prescription are currently achieving their intended aim or whether some legislative intervention might be desirable to ensure that the doctrine's operation continues to produce outcomes which are consistent with its purpose. This chapter will consider both the justification for the doctrine and the theoretical basis upon which the rules of prescription operate. It will then consider the way in which the rules of prescription have operated in practice, with particular emphasis being placed on examining the way the user 'as of right' test, which is central to successfully establishing a prescriptive claim, has been interpreted and applied. Finally, the chapter will conclude by reflecting upon whether there is any real need for more extensive reform of the doctrine than that which is provisionally proposed by the Law Commission within the narrower confines of their current project concerning easements and profits à prendre. It is helpful, however, in order to place the doctrine within its proper context, to begin by setting out in a little more detail the various species of rights which the rules of prescription currently operate to create, including a brief overview of the variety of methods of prescription which apply in respect of each of them.

Easements and profits à prendre

Easements and profits à prendre are part of the staple diet of every undergraduate land law student and thus require very little by way of introduction. It suffices to say that each of these species of right constitutes a private right to do something on or to take something from land which belongs to another.[12]

[11] S Bridge, 'Prescriptive Acquisition of Easements: Abolition or Reform?' in E Cooke (ed), *Modern Studies in Property Law: Volume 3* (Hart Publishing, Oxford 2005) 3–21, 8.

[12] Rights of common are included in the category of interests known as profits à prendre, the latter being the generic term used to identify a right which permits the taking of something from somebody else's land, for example, turf or timber. A right of common is a private right but may be exercised 'in common' with the landowner or other persons to whom the same right has been granted.

There are currently three methods of prescription which operate to create easements and profits à prendre: prescription at common law,[13] the doctrine of lost modern grant,[14] and prescription under the Prescription Act 1832.[15] For an easement to be created under any of these methods of prescription twenty years' qualifying use is required.[16] The same is true of profits à prendre which are claimed under the common law rules. However, the Prescription Act 1832 requires thirty years' use for the establishment of such a right.[17]

The Law Commission has identified that 'there is no discernable need for three concurrent systems of prescriptive acquisition' in relation to easements which 'leads inevitably to complicated proceedings as claimants argue their case in the alternative to maximise their chances of success'.[18] It has provisionally proposed that the three existing methods of prescription be abolished with prospective effect[19] and replaced with a single statutory scheme which is dependant only upon the establishment of long, qualifying use.[20] The Law Commission's provisional proposals relating to profits à prendre, if introduced, would render it impossible, in the future, to acquire such rights by prescription.[21]

Public rights of way

A public right of way is a way over which members of the public have a right to pass and repass. There are numerous categories of public right of way including footpaths,[22] bridleways[23] and carriageways.[24] Public rights of way can be created

[13] This method of prescriptive acquisition is more or less obsolete given that proof that the right claimed could not have existed or has ceased to exist (even temporarily, but sufficient to interrupt the use of the right claimed) at some time since 1189 will be sufficient to defeat such a claim.

[14] This was an invention of the courts to circumvent the difficulties posed by the common law rules. This doctrine presumed, on the evidence of long user, that there had once been a grant that had subsequently been lost. However, even proof that there had never been a grant will not defeat the operation of the doctrine.

[15] It is to be noted that profits in gross can be created by operation of the doctrine of lost modern grant and, apparently, by prescription at common law. However, they cannot be created under the Prescription Act 1832; only profits appurtenant.

[16] There are subtle differences in the detail of the various rules. For example, the doctrine of lost modern grant does not require that user continue until the time of the action in which the right is claimed whereas an application under the Prescription Act 1832 requires the user relied upon to have been enjoyed during the period 'next before action'. Furthermore, under the Prescription Act 1832 s 2, forty years user of the claimed right without interruption makes the right absolute and indefeasible unless it can be established that the right was enjoyed by written consent.

[17] The Prescription Act s 1 also prescribes that sixty years user will cause the claimed right to be deemed absolute and indefeasible in the absence of written consent.

[18] Law Commission, 'Easements, Covenants and Profits à Prendre' (Law Com Cp No 186, 2008) [4.168].

[19] Ibid [4.174].

[20] Ibid [4.194]–[4.196] and [4.202]–[4.210].

[21] Ibid [6.28].

[22] A right of way on foot only.

[23] A right of way on foot and '...riding on or accompanied by a beast of burden': *Suffolk County Council v Mason* [1979] AC 705 (HL) 710.

by rules of prescription at common law[25] and under the Highways Act 1980 section 31. Section 31(1) of the 1980 Act provides:

> Where a way over any land, other than a way of such character that use of it by the public could not give rise at common law to any presumption of dedication, has been actually enjoyed by the public as of right and without interruption for a full period of 20 years, the way is to be deemed to have been dedicated as a highway unless there is sufficient evidence that there was no intention during that period to dedicate it.

As can be seen from the foregoing, section 31 of the Highways Act 1980 requires there to be twenty years' qualifying user which is largely consistent with the temporal requirements of the rules of prescription as they apply in other contexts.[26]

In contrast, prescription at common law requires the claimed users to demonstrate qualifying use over a period of time which is simply sufficient to give rise to an inference of an intention to dedicate the way as a public right of way.[27] Unlike all other incarnations of the rules of prescription, the common law rules in this context dictate no minimum period of use. The length of use will depend upon the circumstances of each case. For example, 'in some cases, because of particular circumstances (eg heavy use), relatively low periods [have been] accepted as sufficient'.[28] The common law rules are, therefore, a useful alternative to claiming a prescriptive right under the statute for those who are unable to establish use for the full twenty year period. However, the difficulty with relying on the common law rules will always be in predicting whether a shorter period is likely to be sufficient to meet the requisite test on the particular facts of each case, lending a degree of uncertainty to any such claim.

The registration of new town & village greens

Land is susceptible to registration as a new town or village green if it can be established that the relevant prescriptive criteria are met. One very obvious distinction between, on the one hand, the registration of new greens and, on the other, the creation of private and public rights of way is immediately apparent. Whereas the creation of private and public rights of way explicitly concerns the creation of 'rights' of continuing use, the registration of new greens simply facilitates land acquiring a new 'status'; that of town or village green. The significance of this distinction is material and will be explored shortly.

[24] A right of way over which there are footpath and bridleway rights and, in addition, the right to pass and repass in or on a vehicle.

[25] Which method of acquisition is expressly preserved by the Highways Act 1980 s 31(9), and is generally resorted to where the statutory alternative cannot be relied upon.

[26] For example, easements and the registration of new town and village greens.

[27] *Folkestone Corporation v Brockman* [1914] AC 338 (HL).

[28] J Riddall and J Trevelyan, *Rights of Way: A Guide to Law and Practice* (4th edn Ramblers' Association and Open Spaces Society, 2007) 41, citing cases such as *R v Petrie* (1855), eight years' use, *Rugby Charity Trustees v Merryweather* (1790), six years' use, and *Rowley v Tottenham Urban District Council* (1914), three years' use, as examples.

The only method of prescription operating to enable the registration of new town and village greens is statutory, it being contained in the Commons Act 2006 section 15 (previously the Commons Registration Act 1965 section 22(1A), as amended by the Countryside and Rights of Way Act 2000 section 98). There is no common law alternative. The statutory test in section 15 of the 2006 Act allows any person to apply to the commons registration authority to register land as a town or village green where:

> … a significant number of the inhabitants of any locality, or of any neighbourhood within a locality, have indulged as of right in lawful sports and pastimes on the land for a period of at least 20 years… .

The oddity which arises in relation to the registration of new town and village greens, alluded to above, is that whilst the rules of prescription clearly operate to qualify land for registration, the statute does not specifically confer any continuing right of use upon those claiming registration once registration has actually taken place. It is uncontroversial that, once an easement or a public right of way has been created, a right of continuing use is established. However, it has only recently been determined that the registration of a new town or village green confers rights of continuing use following its registration.[29] The continuing rights of use are not necessarily limited to those activities (the particular 'lawful sports and pastimes' relied upon in the application) which formed the basis of the application for registration and which may, as a matter of fact, have been relatively limited. The rights of continuing use arising upon the registration of a new green are rights to indulge in lawful sports and pastimes generally,[30] although it is thought that there must be some measure of equivalence between the extent of the use before and after registration.[31]

Justification for the rules of prescription

Having briefly explored and summarised the various contexts in which the doctrine of prescription operates and the different rules which currently exist, it is now useful to consider the reason why English law permits the acquisition of rights over another's land in this way. This inquiry is particularly pertinent given that those who are able to establish that rights have been created in this way

[29] This was a criticism levelled at the law relating to the registration of new greens some 35 years ago by Lord Denning MR in *New Windsor Corp v Mellor* [1975] Ch 380 (CA) 392. However, the issue was finally resolved by Lord Hoffmann in *Oxfordshire County Council v Oxford City Council* (*Oxfordshire*) [2006] UKHL 25, [2006] 2 AC 674 [50] and more recently reaffirmed and discussed in *R (Kevin Lewis) v Redcar & Cleveland Borough Council & Anor* (*Redcar*) [2010] UKSC 11, [2010] 2 WLR 653 (all references to *Redcar* following are references to the judgment of the Supreme Court unless specifically stated otherwise).

[30] *Oxfordshire* (n 29) and *Redcar* (n 29).

[31] *Redcar* (n 29) [71].

will have given no consideration in respect of them.[32] This inevitably gives rise to the need for there to be some convincing justificatory basis for the retention of a doctrine which might otherwise be regarded as offensive to any normative understanding of the significance of property ownership, particularly in relation to land which is registered. And perhaps more importantly, for present purposes at least, the underlying justification for retaining rules of prescription may help to inform the appropriate approach to interpreting the qualifying use tests which will constitute a central aspect of this chapter's discussion.

Not surprisingly, any rule of law which allows for the informal creation of rights, particularly rights which attach to property and can then endure changes of ownership, is likely to attract significant scrutiny. Innumerable judges and scholars alike have sought to identify the justification for the acquisition of rights by virtue of the operation of rules of prescription. The answer which has generally emanated from such an inquiry, in one form or another, is that prescription is essentially a doctrine of expediency.

> The doctrine of prescription is based, not on natural justice, but on the convenience of the community. (See the words of Vaughan Williams, LJ, *Union Co v Dock Co* [1902] 2 Ch 569, and of Lord Blackburn in *Dalton v Angus* (1880-81) 6 AC 818). And this convenience has been carried far. 'The Court', said Collins MR, 'is endowed with a great power of imagination for the purpose of supporting ancient user' (*Neaverson v Peterborough Council* [1902] 1 Ch 573).[33]

The justification for retaining rules of prescription has recently been considered by the Law Commission. It was concluded that a landowner's failure to object to use of their land might make it 'unconscionable'[34] for that landowner to then prevent the user (or their successors in title) from continuing to enjoy the benefit of the claimed right. It has also been suggested that it may simply be 'just and reasonable'[35] for the courts to recognise rights which have been exercised for a considerable time on the basis that rights exist and may be exercised. Perhaps most importantly, however, the Law Commission observed that 'land is a social resource', long use of which should arguably be clothed with a legal right.[36] This stance echoes the sentiments expressed by Fry J in *Moody v Steggles*,[37] where he stated:

[32] The presence of consideration would suggest an agreement and, as will be discussed later in this chapter, an agreement would undoubtedly confer some kind of permission which would be fatal to the qualifying user test.

[33] T H Carson, *Prescription and Custom: Six Lectures* (Sweet & Maxwell, London 1907) 14. The extract recited above is referable to the court's ability to presume that long user is attributable to some earlier grant which, it is acknowledged, is a pure fiction, there having never been such a grant. This illustrates the significant power of the doctrine of prescription which operates to preserve long established use despite there having been no legal right vested in the user which permitted or authorised such use.

[34] Law Commission, 'Easements, Covenants and Profits à Prendre' (Law Com Cp No 186, 2008) [4.179].

[35] Ibid [4.180].

[36] Ibid [4.182].

[37] (1879) 12 Ch D 261 (Ch) 265.

> Where there has been a long enjoyment of property in a particular manner it is the habit, and, in my view, the duty, of the Court, so far as it lawfully can, to clothe the fact with right.

Notwithstanding the many judicial statements which point to expediency being the real explanation for the utilisation of the doctrine of prescription, it is not the only purported justification for the continuing acceptance of it. It has recently been suggested[38] that we should look to Article 13 of the Universal Declaration of Human Rights which enshrines the right to freedom of movement.[39] However, notwithstanding this notion that continuing employment of the doctrine of prescription might be justified on the basis of a human rights argument, a suggestion which is not reflected in any of the case law, it is clear that the rules of prescription operate to preserve the long established status quo, on the basis that this produces the most acceptable outcome, despite the fact that the effect of their operation may be to deprive a landowner of some aspect of the enjoyment of his ownership of land. The rules of prescription are, to all intents and purposes, a manifestation of some relatively loosely articulated policy which recognises the desirability of sanctioning the continuing enjoyment of a right, prior use of which has endured for a significant time. This policy is clearly broad in its scope given that the rules which give effect to it facilitate the creation of so many varieties of rights, both private and public.

The notion that long enjoyment, in a qualifying manner, is sufficient to justify the adjustment or reallocation of property rights may appear to conflict with the purpose of a system of land registration which is designed to identify and be determinative of all rights and interests in any given piece of land (subject to the limited interests which are permitted to exist off register). To this end parallels have been drawn between the doctrines of prescription and adverse possession, the latter having been severely curtailed under the Land Registration Act 2002 precisely because its operation appeared to be totally at odds with a system of land ownership based upon principles of registration. However, it has been recognised that 'prescription does not have the same Draconian quality as adverse possession',[40] because it does not cause title to be lost, thereby depriving the title owner of something which he previously enjoyed. Prescription simply legitimises existing use (as distinct from facilitating a claim to ownership) which has been enjoyed over a number of years and is, therefore, defensible for the reasons identified above.

However, there are, arguably, shades of the Draconian about the effect of the prescriptive rules in at least one context in which they operate. It is quite possibly for this reason that the courts appear to have been inclined to adopt

[38] See C Sara, 'Prescription – What Is It For?' [2004] *Conv* 13, 17.

[39] The right to freedom of movement is to be found in Protocol 4, Article 2 of the Convention for the Protection of Human Rights and Fundamental Freedoms (European Convention on Human Rights, as amended). However, rights under Protocol 4 are not incorporated into English Law under the Human Rights Act 1998 s 1(1).

[40] *Bridge* (n 11) 3–21, 16.

a more restrictive approach to the interpretation of the rules of prescription as they apply to applications for the registration of new greens. This is because, once registered, greens are subject to the provisions of the Inclosure Act 1857 and the Commons Act 1876[41] which, between them, prevent encroachment, enclosure, development or interference with a green. Whilst it has been judicially acknowledged that registration of a new green is unlikely to prevent the landowner from carrying on activities consistent with those he had indulged in during the period of qualifying use, it is certainly the case that he might be prevented from making an alternative use of his land thereafter if that use is inconsistent with the rights arising upon registration for the local inhabitants to indulge in lawful sports and pastimes on the newly registered green. He will, most certainly, be prevented from developing the land.

The sort of land which is generally, although not exclusively, the subject of a new green application is land which has been rarely or intermittently used by the land owner; the absence of regular use being what attracts local inhabitants to make use of the land themselves. It is not unusual for land which has been earmarked for future development, subject to acquiring the requisite planning permission, to become the subject of an application for registration as a new green. This is because, until such time as any intended development can be progressed, the land may be of little immediate interest to its owner and may well have been neglected. It is, therefore, quite obvious that any recognition that the owner of a newly registered green can continue to use his land in the same way as he has used it during the qualifying period is unlikely to provide much in the way of comfort.

Theoretical basis underpinning the rules of prescription

The majority of the variants of the rules of prescription are based upon the fictitious notion of a presumed grant,[42] although in the context of public rights of way they are predicated upon the distinct but similar presumption (or inference) of dedication. The exception to this general rule concerns the registration of new town and village greens; 'there is no question here of adopting a fiction that the use must be ascribed to an original grant of the right by the owner'.[43] The registration of new greens is simply based upon long, qualifying use, and nothing more.

The fact that most forms of prescription are predicated upon the spurious notion that qualifying use coupled with the lapse of time is somehow evidence of a prior express conferment of the right claimed, by the landowner, may be

[41] This was confirmed in *Oxfordshire County Council v Oxford City Council* [2006] UKHL 25, [2006] 2 AC 674.

[42] *Dalton v Angus* (1881) 6 App Cas 740 (HL) 773–74.

[43] Alison Clarke, 'Use, Time, and Entitlement' [2004] 57 *CLP* 239–75, 263.

conceptually unpalatable. However, it is no more sinister than that. Current Law Commission proposals for the reform of the doctrine of prescription, as it relates to easements and profits à prendre, would explicitly discard these specious presumptions. This move is to be welcomed if for no other reason than the promotion of conceptual integrity. Given that the registration of new greens is not underpinned by any bogus presumptions this would leave only the prescriptive acquisition of public rights of way being dependant upon some underlying fiction; that of presumed dedication. However, that fiction is less easily abandoned given that a contrary intention expressed by the landowner is sufficient to rebut the presumption of dedication of a public right of way,[44] thereby defeating what could otherwise constitute a legitimate prescriptive claim. It is, therefore, clearly not possible to divorce the prescriptive acquisition of public rights of way from the underlying fictitious inference of dedication

The operation of the rules of prescription

The lapse of time

All methods of prescription require the right claimed to have been exercised over a lengthy period of time; usually, but not exclusively,[45] for a period of twenty years. However, the lapse of time, without something more, is insufficient by itself to create rights; the long use relied upon must be use of a qualifying nature.

Qualifying use

Qualifying use is referable to the nature and quality of the use which is relied upon as substantiating the claim. What constitutes qualifying use will vary depending upon the context in which the rules operate. In relation to a claimed easement, for example, the right claimed must be referable to a dominant tenement; an easement cannot exist in gross. In contrast, in an application for the registration of a new town or village green, the users (upon whose use the prescriptive claim is based) do not need to identify any dominant tenement

[44] The Highways Act 1980 s 31, reproduced earlier in the main text of this chapter under 'Public rights of way', contains a proviso which prevents the dedication of a highway being deemed to have occurred where '…there is sufficient evidence that there was no intention during that period to dedicate it'.

[45] Under the Prescription Act 1832 s 1, a claimed profit à prendre must have been enjoyed without interruption for a period of thirty years notwithstanding that under the common law doctrine and lost modern grant a period of only twenty years is necessary. The common law rules for the prescriptive creation of public rights of way do not specify any particular period of user.

but they do need to have indulged in lawful sports and pastimes[46] on the land concerned. It must also be demonstrated that such use has been indulged in by a significant number of the inhabitants of a locality,[47] or a neighbourhood within a locality.[48] This illustrates that the qualifying use test varies, as it logically must, depending upon the species of right being claimed.

However, notwithstanding the fact that the rules of prescription can require different criteria to be met depending upon the nature of the right that the rules are claimed to have created, one aspect of the rules which is common to all forms of prescriptive acquisition is that the use relied upon must have been user 'as of right'. In the recent decision of the House of Lords in *R (Beresford) v Sunderland City Council*,[49] (*Beresford*) it was said that user as of right did not mean user 'of right' but was more accurately characterised by the concept of user 'as if of right'.[50] So what, then, constitutes user as of right? It is uncontroversial that it must be *nec vi, nec clam, nec precario*; that is without force, without stealth, and without permission. There are, however, further components to the as of right test which have been acknowledged as necessary by the courts; many of which have been subsequently discarded. Each, including the traditionally recognised tripartite criteria, will be considered in turn in order to identify any divergence between the necessary components of the user as of right test as it applies in the various contexts in which it operates.

Nec vi

User which is *vi* (by force) is not restricted to use by physical force alone; it is any user which may be regarded as contentious. In the recent decision of *Smith v Brudenell-Bruce*, Pumfrey J said :

> The requirement that user not be forcible requires that it be peaceable. Included is the requirement that the user not be 'contentious'... It seems to me that user ceases to be user 'as of right' if the circumstances are such as to indicate to the dominant owner, or to a reasonable man with the dominant owner's knowledge of the circumstances, that the servient owner actually objects and continues to object and will back his objection either by physical obstruction or by legal action. A user is contentious when

[46] Such activities as walking dogs or children playing qualify as lawful sports and pastimes, *R v Oxfordshire County Council, ex p Sunningwell Parish Council* (*Sunningwell*) [2000] 1 AC 335 (HL) 357.

[47] What constitutes a significant number was discussed in *R (Alfred McAlpine Homes Ltd) v Staffordshire County Council* [2002] EWHC 76 (Admin), [2002] 2 PLR 1, 17. It does not mean a considerable or substantial number. Use by a sufficient number of users to indicate general use by the local community is all that is required.

[48] In the recent case of *R (Oxfordshire & Buckinghamshire Mental Health NHS Foundation Trust & Another) v Oxfordshire County Council & Others* [2010] EWHC 530 (Admin), [2010] LGR 631 the use of a single residential road as constituting a 'neighbourhood within a locality' was not challenged.

[49] [2003] UKHL 60, [2004] 1 AC 889.

[50] Ibid [72].

> the servient owner is doing everything, consistent with his means and proportionately to the user, to context and to endeavour to interrupt the user.[51]

However, determining whether user is contentious is not necessarily a straightforward inquiry. Clearly, user which has indulged in the breaking down of fences or the forcing of locked gates is *vi* and such use cannot form the basis of a prescriptive claim. *Smith v Brudenell-Bruce* concerned a successful claim to an easement under the doctrine of lost modern grant, notwithstanding some limited objection to the claimant's use having allegedly been expressed by the landowner. The dicta of Pumfrey J, recited above, does illustrate that whilst sustained objection will render user *vi*, objection must be continuing and followed up with action if necessary in order to have such an effect.

The erection of prohibitory signs, for example, may render user contentious, and therefore *vi*, if those signs convey the message that the use being indulged in is objected to and continues to be objected to. Difficulties can arise, however, where signs are erected and are then either torn down and not replaced or are simply ignored by those at whom they are directed. It was acknowledged by Lord Walker in *Beresford*[52] that 'a landowner who puts up a notice stating "private land – keep out" is in a less strong position, if his notice is ignored by the public, than a landowner whose notice is in friendlier terms'.[53] This is an explicit recognition that a prohibitory notice, without more, may not provide adequate protection for the landowner. The observation by Lord Walker in *Beresford* is further supported by the dicta of Lord Hoffmann in *R (Godmanchester Town Council) v Secretary of State for Environment, Food and Rural Affairs*[54] (*Godmanchester*), a case concerning a claimed public right of way, where he acknowledged that a 'trespassers will be prosecuted' sign, if ignored, would not prevent use being as of right, although in an application for the prescriptive acquisition of a public right of way it would clearly satisfy the proviso contained within the Highways Act 1980 section 31(1) (ie sufficient evidence of contrary intention to dedicate), thereby defeating a prescriptive claim on that basis.

Nec clam

User which is *clam* (by stealth) will not found the basis of a prescriptive claim. The servient owner must be able to ascertain that qualifying use is being indulged in upon his land. In *Sturges v Bridgman*, Thesiger LJ stated:

> ... consent or acquiescence of the owner of the servient tenement lies at the root of prescription ... a man cannot, as a general rule, be said to consent to or acquiesce in the acquisition by his neighbour of an easement through an enjoyment of which he has no knowledge, actual or constructive... .[55]

[51] (2002) 2 P & CR 4 (Ch) [11] and [12].
[52] *Beresford* (n 49) [72].
[53] By which he meant permissive notices which would have rendered user *precario*.
[54] [2007] UKHL 28, [2008] AC 221 [24].
[55] (1879) 11 Ch D 852 (CA) 863.

Actual knowledge of the use upon which the claim is predicated or, in the case of the landowner who is either absent or unobservant, use which would have come to the attention of a reasonable landowner is required in order for the use to satisfy the *nec clam* criterion. After all, 'the English theory of prescription is concerned with how the matter would have appeared to the owner of the land (or if there was an absentee owner, to a reasonable owner who was on the spot)'.[56]

Nec Precario

User which is *precario* (by permission) will be fatal to a prescriptive claim. If user is permissive then it is attributable to some kind of licence from the landowner. In *Gardner v Hodgson's Kingston Brewery Company Limited*,[57] Lord Lindley said 'the common law doctrine is that all prescription presupposes a grant. But if the grant is proved and its terms are known, prescription has no place'.

It is, of course, possible that a licence may be implied. In *Beresford* Lord Walker stated that:

> ... as a general proposition [implied permission could defeat a claim to user as of right] provided that the permission is implied by (or inferred from) overt conduct of the landowner, such as making a charge for admission, or asserting his title by the occasional closure of the land to all comers.[58]

In this case it was established that providing benches and mowing the grass, thereby facilitating the recreational use of the land, did not amount to the grant of an implied licence, demonstrating that the threshold for establishing an implied licence will not be an easy one to meet.

Acquiescence

Acquiescence has consistently been regarded as being at the heart of the concept of user as of right. This is illustrated by the frequently cited passage of Fry J in *Dalton v Angus & Co*, in which he states 'the whole law of prescription and the whole law which governs the presumption or inference of a grant or covenant rest upon acquiescence'.[59] Of course, unlike in relation to other rights, the prescriptive rules which apply to the registration of new greens are not dependant upon any presumption of grant or dedication. It is, nevertheless, accepted that acquiescence is as important to the operation of the rules in that context as in any and every other. For example, in *Beresford*, a case which concerned an application to register a new green, Lord Walker

[56] *Redcar* (n 29) [36].
[57] [1903] AC 229 (HL) 239.
[58] *Beresford* (n 49) [83].
[59] (1881) 6 App Cas 740 (HL) 773–74.

stated that 'a landowner who wishes to stop the acquisition of prescriptive rights over his land must not acquiesce and suffer in silence',[60] clearly indicating that, in order to prevent prescriptive user from acquiring rights, it is necessary for the landowner to take some positive action to bring user as of right to an end.

Notwithstanding the apparent importance of acquiescence and its role in establishing that user has been as of right, it does not appear to be an added component of the as of right test. Its role is simply confined to a recognition that, in the face of user which is *nec vi*, *nec clam*, *nec precario*, it is necessary for the landowner to do something, to take some positive steps, to bring that user to an end; acquiescence, as a matter of fact, in the face of such user, will be determinative that user as of right is continuing.

The Law Commission has provisionally proposed that the rules of prescription, as they apply to easements, should no longer be underpinned by acquiescence but should be limited to long, qualifying use only; that being use which is *nec vi*, *nec clam*, *nec precario*.[61] If acquiescence is not a component of the legal test, as suggested above, then it is perhaps unnecessary to explicitly divorce the rules of prescription from acquiescence. Even if it is determined that acquiescence will have no relevance in the future to the prescriptive acquisition of easements, unless there is some more far-reaching reform of prescription as it applies to both public rights of way and the registration of greens as well, it will be impossible to now depart from the many judicial statements which recognise the central importance of acquiescence in those contexts. Moreover, if acquiescence is simply an issue of fact rather than law, even an express departure from acquiescence cannot sever the link between acquiescence and user as of right. As long as a landowner retains the right to object, any lack of objection is tantamount to acquiescence. If the Law Commission's provisional proposals are adopted and the user as of right test is determined to be simply use which is *nec vi*, *nec clam*, *nec precario*, if that test is met then it will be by virtue of the landowner having done nothing to bring that use to an end, having acquiesced in that use for the duration of the qualifying period.

User must be trespassory

One might logically conclude that user which is *nec precario* is necessarily trespassory. In the majority of cases that will be so, given that the use relied upon will have been without the permission of the landowner. However, in *Beresford* the House of Lords considered that if the public had used land pursuant to a legal right to do so which might have been conferred upon them, say, by statute, then notwithstanding the absence of permission by the actual landowner such

[60] *Beresford* (n 49) [77].

[61] Law Commission, 'Easements, Covenants and Profits à Prendre' (Law Com Cp No 186, 2008) [4.202]–[4.204].

use would not be trespassory and would, therefore, not be as of right.[62] It should be noted that the House of Lords in *Beresford* made no ruling on this point; it was a subsidiary issue. Such an issue is, in reality, only likely to arise where the land concerned is in public, rather than private, ownership. This is because it is only likely to be in the context of publicly owned land that general public rights of use might be conferred by statute. It is, therefore, probable that in the majority of cases user which is *nec precario* will also be trespassory. It is worth noting, however, that in some very limited circumstances, as identified above, the *nec precario* limb of the tripartite test cannot be assumed to have been met in every case in which the landowner has not given permission for the use of his land.

Users' belief in right to use

In the case of *R v Suffolk County Council, ex p Steed* (*Steed*),[63] the Court of Appeal said that in order to succeed in an application for the registration of land as a new green it was necessary, in addition to meeting the *nec vi*, *nec clam*, *nec precario* test, for the users to have an honest belief that the inhabitants of the locality had a legal right to use the land for recreation. This new criterion was described as a 'virus [which] infected the law, one that corrupted and distorted the logic on which the law has rested since Roman times'.[64] Mercifully, the House of Lords in *Sunningwell* determined that *Steed* was wrongly decided on that point; Lord Hoffmann stating that the 'new and additional requirement of subjective belief ... [has] no previous authority and ... [is] contrary to the principles of English prescription'.[65]

Deference

The most recent attack on the orthodox simplicity of the as of right test arose, once again, in relation to the rules of prescription as they apply to new green registration. In *R (Laing Homes Ltd) v Buckinghamshire County Council*,[66] (*Laing Homes*) Sullivan J determined that where there were competing uses between the landowner and the recreational users, user could not be as of right where local inhabitants gave the impression of deferring to the landowner's right to use his land. Lord Hoffmann in *Oxfordshire*, referring to the judgment of Sullivan J in *Laing Homes*, made an obiter remark that 'use by the landowner

[62] *Beresford* (n 49). See, in particular, the speech of Lord Scott of Foscote at [24]–[31] and [52] in which a number of statutory provisions are identified which might have the effect of conferring a right to use upon members of the public. These provisions include those contained in the Open Spaces Act 1906, the Local Government Act 1972 and the New Towns Act 1981.

[63] (1995) 70 P & CR 487 (QB); (1998) 75 P & CR 102 (CA).

[64] *Riddall and Trevelyan* (n 28) 49.

[65] *Sunningwell* (n 46) 355.

[66] [2003] EWHC 1578 (Admin), (2004) 1 P & CR 36 [85].

may be relevant to the question of whether he would have regarded persons using it for sports and pastimes as doing so as of right'.[67]

In the more recent case of *R (Kevin Lewis) v Redcar & Cleveland Borough Council*,[68] (*Redcar*) the relevance of deference to the establishment of user as of right was revisited. At first instance Sullivan J (who, it will be noted from the passage above, was responsible for the introduction of the concept of deference in *Laing Homes*) determined that the deference of the recreational users to the landowner's use of the land was fatal to their claim for registration, notwithstanding the fact that the recreational users had made extensive use of the land concerned for lawful sports and pastimes. The Court of Appeal upheld the judgment of Sullivan J, finding that in addition to establishing that user must be *nec vi, nec clam, nec precario* it was *also* necessary to 'show that the user relied upon was such as to give the outward impression to the reasonable landowner that the user is being asserted and claimed as of right'.[69] The deference by the recreational users to the landowner's own use of the land, said Dyson LJ (delivering the leading judgment of the Court of Appeal), meant that the outward impression created was not one of an assertion of a right. The remark by Lord Hoffmann in *Oxfordshire*, recited above, was interpreted as being an endorsement of this approach which had first been adopted by Sullivan J in *Laing Homes*.

The UK Supreme Court reversed the decision of the Court of Appeal and ordered that the land with which the application for registration was concerned be registered as a green. Lord Walker, delivering the leading judgment in the Supreme Court, said he had:

> ... no difficulty in accepting that Lord Hoffmann was absolutely right in *Sunningwell* to say that the English theory of prescription is concerned with 'how the matter would have appeared to the owner of the land' ... but [he had] great difficulty in seeing how a reasonable owner would have concluded that the residents were not asserting a right to take recreation on the disputed land, simply because they normally showed civility (or, in the inspector's word, deference) ... .[70]

The fact that deference by the users has no part to play in the meeting of the user as of right test was, here, finally resolved, six years after it was first introduced by Sullivan J in *Laing Homes*.

Conclusion

The approach of the courts to the proper interpretation of the as of right test, as it applies to the acquisition of easements, profits à prendre and public rights

[67] [2006] UKHL 25, [2006] 2 AC 674 [57].

[68] [2010] UKSC 11, [2010] 2 WLR 653.

[69] *R (Kevin Lewis) v Redcar & Cleveland Borough Council* [2009] EWCA Civ 3, [2009] 1 WLR 1461 [35].

[70] *Redcar* (n 68) [36].

of way, has been relatively consistent in the sense that it does not appear to suffer from the frequent addition of extra components such as deference and the need for users to have a subjective belief in a right to use, for example, which has become ever more commonplace in the context of new green registration cases. Where applications for the registration of new greens are concerned, the way in which the user as of right test has been interpreted and applied has been, as the foregoing illustrates only too clearly, anything but stable and consistent. As much is evident from the relatively extensive body of case law which has developed in the last decade or so and, in particular, the fact that four new green registration cases have been heard at the highest judicial level throughout a period of just eleven years.

There is a growing perception that new green registration applications are being used as a means of circumventing normal planning processes. When the conventional methods of objecting to development on sites which have been openly enjoyed by local inhabitants for informal recreation for over twenty years have been exhausted, the possibility of having the land registered as a new green inevitably raises its ugly (or, to some, rather attractive) head. As Lord Walker noted in *Redcar*:

> Disparaging references are sometimes made to the 'village green industry' and to applications for registration being used as a weapon of guerrilla warfare against development of open land ... However, in the Commons Act 2006 Parliament has made it easier, rather than more difficult, to register a green.[71]

In light of these observations, together with the substantive implications of the decision in *Redcar* (which has now removed what represented a very real potential threat to the likely prospects of success in applications for the registration of new greens), there is no reason to suppose that the new green registration applications will not just keep on flooding in. There is certainly 'no sign that the enthusiasm of those claiming rights to town or village greens is on the wane'.[72] Any lack of consistency in the application of the relevant legal test or any inclination to interpret and apply the test particularly restrictively (perhaps because of some underlying judicial discomfort regarding the effect of the new green registration legislation) is likely to precipitate further litigation. This is not a state of affairs which can be met with any enthusiasm.

It can be seen that, in the context of applications for the registration of new greens, the courts have tended to adopt a much more complex approach to the user as of right test. To some extent this may be unavoidable when one recognises that the circumstances surrounding such applications do potentially give rise to issues which are simply not going to arise in prescriptive claims to other types of right, especially private rights. For example, no court considering a claim to an easement by prescription is ever likely to be troubled by issues

[71] *Redcar* (n 68) [48].
[72] *Bridge* (n 11) 3–21, 8.

concerning whether or not there are public rights of access conferred by statute upon those claiming the right, as was discussed in the *Beresford* case. However, recent case law in the new green context has also seen the introduction (albeit temporarily) of various new elements to the user as of right test, such as the need for subjective belief of a right to use by those claiming rights and the need to give the outward appearance to the landowner of the assertion of a right of use, in addition to the traditional test that user be *nec vi, nec clam, nec precario*. Even though these 'add-ons' have come and now gone again, there is always scope for more of them to be invented[73] as and when the opportunity arises, potentially complicating the as of right test further. This is particularly likely if there is judicial reluctance in accepting the idea that large parcels of land (sometimes land which bears little resemblance to the archetypal 'village green') can effectively be sterilised, at least as far as the landowner is concerned, as a result of new green registration.

Moreover, the lower courts' very restrictive approach[74] to the as of right test in the new green registration context is arguably inconsistent with the policy underpinning the legislation which clearly regards long use and enjoyment of land as being worthy of legal protection. This is a particularly compelling observation when one considers that the statutory provisions which currently govern new green registration are more recent than any of the other statutory or common law rules of prescription, and were introduced specifically, as Lord Walker in *Redcar* recognised, to make it 'easier, rather than more difficult, to register a green'.[75] If, on reflection, having had the opportunity to assess the results that the statutory provisions are bringing about, Parliament determines that the legislation is being abused, misused or simply operating in a way which it considers to be unacceptable or unjustifiable, then that would surely be a matter for Parliament,[76] not the courts.

It is, of course, possible, and indeed probable, that the introduction of any further qualifications or complexities to the as of right test in the future would be applied only in relation to applications for the registration of new greens. Whilst the new green registration case law has borrowed extensively from the case law concerning the prescriptive acquisition of both easements and public rights of way in determining the proper approach to interpreting and applying the as of right test, there is no sign that any future requirements which might

[73] The term 'invented' is used because Sullivan J explicitly acknowledged that 'deference' was '…judge made law, judge-made by me', see *Redcar* (n 68) [15].

[74] On each of the four occasions that a new green registration case has come before the House of Lords / Supreme Court, the appeals have been allowed and the applications for registration have, consequently, been successful.

[75] *Redcar* (n 68) [48].

[76] In 2009 Defra commissioned the Countryside and Community Research Institute to undertake a study to examine successful and unsuccessful green applications, including identifying whether any of the sites had been earmarked for development. As a result of those findings Defra is now undertaking a review of the town and village green registration system. For more information see <http://www.defra.gov.uk/rural/protected/commonland/tvg.htm> accessed 4 October 2010.

be grafted onto the as of right test in the new green context would then be applied the other way, to claims of easements or public rights of way. Indeed, if the Law Commission's current proposals are eventually introduced, thereby significantly reforming the rules of prescription as they apply to easements, it is quite clear that the only requirement for meeting the as of right test in that context will be that user be *nec vi, nec clam, nec precario*; nothing more. What is not presently clear is whether any new statutory provision providing for the prescriptive acquisition of easements would simply refer to user needing to be user as of right or whether it would specifically spell out that qualifying user must be user which is, and perhaps is limited to, user which is *nec vi, nec clam, nec precario*. The latter approach would safeguard the law from any prospect that additional requirements which might be judicially grafted onto the as of right test in other contexts could then be imported into the as of right test as it applies to easements. Such an approach would also be consistent with that which has recently been adopted in Ireland[77] under the new Land and Conveyancing Law Reform Act 2009, which reforms the law on the prescriptive acquisition of easements and profits à prendre, amongst other things. Section 33 of that Act provides a definition of 'user as of right' in the following terms:

> 'user as of right' means use or enjoyment without force, without secrecy and without the oral or written consent of the servient owner.

Whilst it seems unlikely that any difficulty will be caused to analogous areas of the law, in the event that the as of right test is tinkered with yet further in the new green registration context, it might be preferable, now that the rules of prescription have been brought under the spotlight once again within the auspices of the Law Commission's current review of easements and profits à prendre, to consider whether the user as of right test would not benefit from more extensive intervention and reform. Simple codification of the test, to apply in all the contexts in which the user as of right test is employed, would alleviate the difficulties being experienced in the new green registration cases.

It is clear that the rules of prescription, in their entirety, cannot be universally codified to meet the requirements of all circumstances in which they apply. In the creation of public rights of way the rules can be defeated by the demonstration of contrary intention and in new green registration applications there are specific locality requirements which apply to the users and the use must have been in the nature of lawful sports and pastimes. However, the user as of right test is susceptible to uniform codification and, for the sake of consistency and certainty in the way in which the law is to be applied, such codification would no doubt be helpful. The adoption of this suggestion would inhibit the courts' ability to interpret the rules of prescription as restrictively as has been their inclination in the new green registration context. If this resulted in an unacceptable number of new green registration applications succeeding

[77] Following the broad recommendations of the Irish Law Reform Commission: see Law Reform Commission of Ireland, 'Report on the Acquisition of Easements and Profits à Prendre by Prescription' (LRC 66 - 2002) [3.32].

because the user as of right test was too easily met, that would be a matter for Parliament to revisit the desirability of having legislation which is capable of producing such an effect. This would require the underlying policy which justifies the rules of prescription operating in that context to be revisited and, if necessary, reconsidered. This would be far more appropriate than having the rules of prescription inconsistently judicially interpreted in the overly complex and technical manner which has become the recent norm.

IV

Land Registration

13

Morality and the Mirror: The Normative Limits of the 'Principles of Land Registration'

Aruna Nair*

Introduction

It has frequently been asserted that, in resolving disputes involving registered land,[1] the courts should be careful to avoid drawing on the principles applicable to unregistered land.[2] In one sense, the truth of this claim is obvious. The registration rules were introduced to cure problems that arose under certain rules that remain broadly applicable[3] to unregistered land; that objective would clearly be undermined if the courts smuggled the very rules generating those problems back into the context of registered land. For example, one aim of the introduction of the land registration legislation was to avoid the conveyancing problems which arose out of the doctrine of notice as it applied to purchasers of land from trustees;[4] given this, it would clearly defeat one of the

* DPhil Candidate, University of Oxford.

[1] The Land Registration Act 2002 ('the LRA 2002') defines 'registered land' for the purposes of the statute as a 'registered estate' or a 'registered charge', where a registered estate or charge is an estate or charge the title to which is entered in the register of title governed by that Act: LRA 2002 s 132. This chapter follows the statutory definition. So, for example, if a leasehold title to a given plot of land has been registered and a fee simple title to the same plot has not, a dispute affecting the rights of the leaseholder is a dispute concerning 'registered land', while a dispute affecting the rights of the freeholder is a dispute concerning 'unregistered land'.

[2] See, for example, Law Commission and HM Land Registry, 'Land Registration for the Twenty-First Century: A Consultative Document' (Law Com No 254, 1998) [1.5]–[1.6]; D Jackson, 'Security of Title in Unregistered Land' (1978) 94 *LQR* 239; E Cooke, *The New Law of Land Registration* (Hart Publishing, Oxford 2003) 129; D Fox, 'Forgery of the Register under the Land Registration Act 2002' in E Cooke (ed), *Modern Studies in Property Law: Volume 3* (Hart Publishing, Oxford 2005) 29.

[3] Subject to certain limited reforms, such as the provisions of the Land Charges Act 1972.

[4] See J S Anderson, *Lawyers and the Making of English Land Law 1832 – 1940* (Clarendon Press, Oxford 1992) 266–71.

purposes of reform if the courts interpreted the provisions of that legislation in such a way as to subject such purchasers to the doctrine of notice.[5]

However, once the validity of the distinction between unregistered and registered land is accepted, we are left with the question of its scope. At one extreme, some of the arguments invoking the distinction can be taken to suggest that there exist two distinct 'systems' of law applicable to land in England and Wales: one system is relevant to unregistered land, the other is relevant to registered land, and it is always an error to reason from the principles applicable to unregistered land when one is dealing with registered land. At the other extreme, they can be confined to the trite proposition that, where the statute expressly provides for a result different from that yielded by the pre-existing common law rules, the courts should give effect to those provisions. Neither of these views is a plausible account of what is being argued when the courts are urged to be mindful of the difference 'in principle' between registered and unregistered land. The purpose of this chapter is to clarify the scope of that argument, given that it must be intermediate between these two extremes, and to reject an over-broad conception of what it demands. The issues at stake are illustrated by reference to the dispute over the proper interpretation of certain provisions of the LRA 2002 schedule 4, which governs when the register of title can be altered.

The argument is in three parts. The first sets out the question that the chapter is intended to address and explains its practical significance. It briefly considers the two extreme formulations set out above and dismisses both as implausible accounts of the current law and of the views of the writers who put forward the claim under discussion. It concludes that, although the importance of the distinction between registered and unregistered land is frequently stressed, the principled basis of that distinction has not been fully explained. It then goes on to demonstrate the practical implications of this problem, with reference to one of the areas of law where the distinction has been recently invoked: the jurisdiction of the court or registrar to alter or rectify the register in circumstances where there has been a mistake.

The second part considers the view that the fundamental 'principles of land registration', set out in the joint Report of the Law Commission and HM Land Registry which preceded the LRA 2002,[6] represent special principles applicable only to registered land and can thus be drawn upon to indicate the circumstances in which the principles applicable to unregistered land are displaced. It rejects this view on the basis that the so-called 'principles' in fact represent competing policy goals, which are indeterminate between different outcomes, and argues

[5] A point made by Lord Wilberforce in *Williams & Glyn's Bank v Boland* [1981] AC 487 (HL) 504: '[to] have regard to and limit the application of … [section 70(1)(g) of the Land Registration Act 1925] in the light of the doctrine of notice … would run counter to the whole purpose of the Act'.

[6] Law Commission and HM Land Registry, 'Land Registration for the Twenty-First Century: A Conveyancing Revolution' (Law Com No 271, 2001).

that a better model of the normative principles underlying the statute can be derived from an account that focuses on its regulation of individual rights and liabilities. It is suggested that an event-oriented analysis of the provisions of the statute would provide the best such account.

The third part applies such an analysis to the transfer of title to registered land. It considers the response of English law to two fact situations that would give rise to property rights in the context of unregistered land and explores the effect of the parties' dealings with the Land Registry, or failures to deal with the Land Registry, on that response. Those fact situations are express declarations of intention by a person who is already a right-holder in respect of land and the act of taking physical possession of land. After this, it considers the situation where none of the events which give rise to property rights in unregistered land have actually taken place but registration occurs anyway.

Finally, part four summarises the conclusions reached. It concludes that the language of separate systems seriously overstates the differences between the rules that govern registered land and those that apply to other forms of tangible property, and that it is preferable to see the provisions of the LRA 2002 as underpinned by principles that are on the same basic continuum as those that apply throughout the English law of property. For this reason, it argues that rhetoric which suggests that registered land is simply different to unregistered land is unhelpful and should not, without more, be relied upon by the courts as a guide to the interpretation of the LRA 2002. It then applies this conclusion to put forward a preferred interpretation of the disputed provisions of the LRA 2002 schedule 4.

Defining the question

Since the first introduction of land registration legislation in England,[7] the extent to which that legislation alters and is intended to alter previously settled law on the substantive rights and liabilities of individuals has a been a live question.[8] Early writers often drew a distinction between the 'machinery' of land transfer and the 'substantive law', to which it was subordinate.[9] Thus, for example, in a pamphlet recommending the introduction of title registration in England, Robert Wilson presented it as a merit of the proposed system that, 'it only *professes to facilitate the practical workings of the law as it stands*; to expand the principles and improve the machinery of our existing institutions'; he contrasted this modest aim with the more radical project of 'the substitution

[7] The Land Transfer Act 1862.

[8] See *Anderson* (n 4) 85–136.

[9] An echo of this language is found in the First Report of the Real Property Commissioners in 1829, which stated that, although the law relating to land transfer was very defective, the substantive law approached perfection: First Report of the Real Property Commissioners, (1829) House of Commons Papers x, 7.

of a new system of real property for the immense compound of traditionary customs, legislative enactments, and judicial expositions, which our ancestors have transmitted to us.'[10] In a similar vein, Hargreaves, writing in 1949, drew conclusions on the proper interpretation of the Land Registration Act 1925 on the basis that it was 'essentially a conveyancing Act and that in consequence there … [was] a very strong presumption against any interpretation of it which would involve a change in the substantive law of the land.'[11]

Whatever the position under the old law, it is clear that the LRA 2002 is intended to represent a decisive shift away from this minimalist notion of the function and impact of the land registration legislation. In the Consultative Document preceding the Act, the Law Commission stated that the new Act is not intended to be 'mere machinery for translating … [the principles applicable to unregistered land] into a registered format',[12] denying the contrast between the 'machinery' of land registration and the 'substantive law of the land' drawn by earlier commentators. In the light of this and similar statements made both in the Consultative Document and the Report, it is highly implausible to argue that the proper interpretation of the LRA 2002 is one which treats minimising the difference between registered and unregistered land as a positive objective.

On the other hand, it is not clear how far the presumption goes the other way. It has been argued that, in dealing with disputes concerning registered land, the courts ought to be 'registration-minded', 'start[ing] with the statutory framework instead of continuously looking for analogies with a system which is distinct in its fundamentals.'[13] This idea of separate systems can also been seen as implicit in the Scottish Law Commission's characterisation of the English rules as belonging to a class of title registration schemes that are 'bijural' by nature:

> … a positive system has no choice but to work with two different laws of property. In the first instance the position is governed by the special rules of the positive system … But in the event of a dispute the position must then be re-analysed using the ordinary rules of property law … A system which operates with two different laws of property may be described as 'bijural'.[14]

This suggests that the 'special rules of the positive [registration] system' constitute a distinct 'law of property', distinguishable from 'the ordinary rules of property law' in some systematic sense. This idea – that the land registration

[10] R Wilson, *Outlines of a Plan for Adapting the Machinery of the Public Funds to the Transfer of Real Property* (Thomas Blenkarn, London 1844) 59. For the context and impact of Wilson's pamphlet, which he presented to the Real Property Committee of the Law Amendment Society in 1844 and which it considered in 1846, see *Anderson* (n 4) 63–71.

[11] A D Hargreaves, 'Registered Conveyancing and the Land Law – A Reply' (1949) 12 *MLR* 139, 142.

[12] *Law Commission and HM Land Registry* (n 2) [1.5].

[13] *Jackson* (n 2) 254.

[14] Scottish Law Commission, 'Land Registration: Void and Voidable Titles' (Scot Law Com Dp No 125) [1.11].

rules constitute an alternative or a competing system of property law – can be taken to suggest that the provisions of the LRA 2002 (including the rules which are made under it)[15] have created a self-contained set of principles, capable of resolving disputes in terms that are entirely unconnected to any principles that are applicable to unregistered land (or to other forms of tangible property). This follows from the standard understanding of a 'system' as something that is both internally consistent and independent of any external influence.[16]

However, it is apparent from its language that the LRA 2002 is not intended to and does not create a free-standing code that governs every dispute that may arise between parties with regard to registered land. Thus, for example, section 2 provides:

> This Act makes provision about the registration of title to –
> (a) unregistered legal estates which are interests of any of the following kinds–
> (i) an estate in land,
> (ii) a rentcharge,
> (iii) a franchise,
> (iv) a profit a prendre in gross, and
> (v) any other interest or charge which subsists for the benefit of, or is a charge on, an interest the title to which is registered; and
> (b) interests capable of subsisting at law which are created by a disposition of an interest the title to which is registered.

Of the terms used in this section, only 'land', 'legal estate' and 'charge' are defined by the Act itself, and the definitions of 'legal estate' and 'charge' provided refer to concepts defined elsewhere in the law.[17] So, where there is a dispute between parties as to whether a given right qualifies as one of these categories of interests in land and is suitable for registration, the LRA 2002 gives no guidance; it is generally accepted that the resolution of disputes of this type must depend on rules found in other sources.[18] For this reason, the argument

[15] Such as the Land Registration Rules 2003 ('the LRR 2003').

[16] The Oxford English dictionary defines a system as 'a set or assemblage of things connected, associated, or interdependent, to as to form a complex unity'. More narrowly, in the context of principles etc, it states that a system consists in 'the set of correlated principles, ideas, or statements belonging to some department of knowledge or belief ... a connected and regularly arranged scheme of the whole of some subject; a comprehensive body of doctrines, conclusions, speculations, or theses'. The implication is that a system of rules consists of a body of doctrines or principles that are (a) internally connected to each other in some orderly fashion and (b) comprehensive, covering the whole of the subject-matter that they refer to.

[17] Both refer to the Law of Property Act 1925, which defines the relevant terms at s 205(1)(x) and s 205(1)(xvi) respectively.

[18] R Smith, 'The Role of Registration in Modern Land Law' in L Tee (ed), *Land Law: Issues, Debates, Policy* (Willan Publishing, Devon 2002) 29, 30: 'the great majority of land law is unaffected by land registration: the definition of a lease or easement, for example.' In *Polo Woods Foundation v Shelton-Agar* [2009] EWHC 1361 (Ch), [2009] 1 P & CR 12, for example, the claimant had applied to the Land Registry to be registered as the proprietor of a profit appurtenant subsisting for the benefit of its registered estate (see the LRA 2002, s 13) and for the noting of the burden of the same profit on the defendants' title (see the LRA 2002, s 34). The defendants contended that the right claimed (the right to graze ponies on part of their farm) did not qualify as a profit appurtenant

cannot be that the LRA 2002 displaces all the pre-existing rules applicable to land and replaces them with a new statutory code that the courts ought to apply without regard to the old law.

Nor, however, can it be said that the assertion is simply to do with the primacy of statute over pre-existing and inconsistent common law rules. This can be shown by the use that has been made of it.[19] The distinction between 'land registration principles' and 'unregistered land principles' has been relied upon as one that the courts ought to actively rely upon as a guide to the interpretation of the statute where more than one view on the effect of a given provision is available or even in determining issues on which the statute is silent.[20] It has also been seen as a principle capable of generating fundamental reforms of the law, such as the abandonment of the principle of a limited numerus clausus of property rights.[21]

The distinction has most recently been invoked as a guide to the proper interpretation of the concept of a 'mistake' in the LRA 2002 schedule 4. That schedule governs the situations in which the register may be altered. It operates as follows. Under paragraph 2(a), the court is empowered to make an order for the alteration of the register for the purpose of 'correcting a mistake'; the effect of such an order is to place the registrar under a duty to comply with it. Paragraph 5(a) directly empowers the registrar to alter the register for the same purpose, without the necessity for a court order. Where an alteration for the purpose of correcting a mistake would prejudice the title of a registered proprietor, it is known as a rectification.[22] In relation to land in the registered proprietor's possession, a rectification may be ordered (by the court) or made in the absence of a court order (by the registrar) only if the proprietor consents or if the conditions in paragraph 3(2) (in relation to court orders) or 6(2) (in relation to rectification absent a court order) are met. These conditions are essentially in identical terms; they permit rectification, in the absence of the registered proprietor's consent, only where he has by his own fraud or lack of proper care caused or substantially contributed to the mistake or where it would for any other reason be unjust to deny rectification.

because it did not accommodate and serve the claimant's land. The resolution of the dispute turned on the Deputy Adjudicator and the High Court's interpretation of *Re Ellenborough Park* [1956] Ch 131 (Ch) and other common law authorities on the characteristics of an appurtenant right.

[19] The difference between this sort of argument and the argument from principle is clearly demonstrated by E Cooke and P O'Connor in their criticism of the decision in *Peffer v Rigg* [1977] 1 WLR 285 (Ch). They criticise that decision on two distinct grounds: first, because it ignores a specific provision of the Land Registration Act 1925 and 'secondly, [because] … it ignores one of the principles of English title registration, namely, that a purchaser is not to be adversely affected by notice of an unregistered interest: 'Purchaser liability to third parties in the English land registration system: a comparative perspective' (2004) 120 *LQR* 640, 653.

[20] Such as the elements of a personal claim in knowing receipt against a registered proprietor: *Fox* (n 2) 40–41.

[21] *Smith* (n 18) 57–62.

[22] LRA 2002 sch 4 para 1.

Thus, the notion of a 'mistake' is of critical significance to the scope of the jurisdiction of the court and the registrar to alter the register (and thus alter substantive rights, given the dispositive consequences of title registration). If it is found that there is a mistake on the register that is capable of correction, the relevant officials are entitled to exercise the complex, structured discretion to alter or rectify the register given to them by the schedule. If they decide not to rectify the register, the person who suffers loss as a result of the decision may claim an indemnity from the Land Registry under schedule 8.[23] If there is no mistake, then (assuming that none of the other, more limited grounds for alteration of the register apply[24]) the question does not arise for decision; no change can be made and no indemnity is available.

Unfortunately, however, there is little guidance on what constitutes a 'mistake' for the purposes of the schedule. In the explanatory notes to the draft Bill which became the LRA 2002, it is suggested that a mistake will have occurred '[where] X has forged Y's signature on a certificate of transfer and has been registered as the proprietor of Whiteacre ...'.[25] More broadly, the natural meaning of the word means that it is likely to cover other situations where the Land Registry would not have registered X as proprietor if it had not interpreted X's application to register on the basis of some false view of the facts or of the law. An example of such a situation is where X applies to be registered as proprietor of Blackacre under the LRA 2002 schedule 6 (dealing with adverse possession) and an official at the Land Registry registers him as such although, in fact, X's occupation of Blackacre is incapable of constituting adverse possession in law.[26]

However, the relevance of the schedule to the situation where there was a flaw in some registered transaction prior to X's application to register is less clear. Where a transfer to Y was voidable, but Y, having become registered proprietor, goes on to transfer title to X, it is generally accepted that the completion of this second transfer by registration is not a mistake for the purposes of the schedule.[27] However, the question of whether this reasoning applies where the purported 'transfer' to Y was not merely voidable but void[28] is not resolved.

[23] LRA 2002, sch 8 para 1(1).

[24] These are to update the register and to give effect to a right excepted from the effect of registration; the registrar also has an additional power to remove superfluous entries.

[25] *Law Commission and HM Land Registry* (n 6) Explanatory Notes to the Draft Bill [630].

[26] See, for example, *Baxter v Mannion* [2010] EWHC 573 (Ch), [2010] 1 WLR 1965.

[27] *Norwich Building Society v Steed* [1993] Ch 116 (CA); *Barclays Bank plc v Guy* [2008] EWHC 893 (Ch). See, however, the criticisms of this conventional analysis, put forward by T Weekes and S Wortley: 'Ambiguity Prevails' (2009) 38 *EG* 104.

[28] This question only arises on the assumption that, in the absence of a successful claim for rectification or alteration, the registered proprietor will have a good title vested in him by the LRA 2002 s 58 and will have various unfettered powers of disposition vested in him by the LRA 2002 s 23. This ignores the view that, following cases such as *Epps v Esso Petroleum Co Ltd* [1973] 1 WLR 1071 (Ch) and *Malory Enterprises Ltd v Cheshire Homes (UK) Ltd* [2002] EWCA Civ 151, [2002] Ch 216, the registered proprietor holds his title and powers on trust for the former registered proprietor in every case where there has been a forgery. The reasoning in those cases depends on the 'retention of the equitable interest' theory of the creation of trusts, rejected by

The authors of Ruoff and Roper have argued that, under the LRA 2002, it does apply to a case where the transfer is void.[29] Similar views have been put forward by others.[30]

However, whether this argument will be accepted by the courts is not yet clear. In *Odogwu v Vastguide Ltd*,[31] the claimant was the registered proprietor of a house in London. An unknown fraudster impersonated him and purported to grant a charge of the registered estate to a third party (Credit & Mercantile Ltd), which was then registered as proprietor of that charge. Credit & Mercantile exercised its power to appoint a receiver and was in the process of selling the property when the claimant's solicitor discovered the fraud and reported it to the police. At this stage, the first defendant, Vastguide Ltd, had already lodged a priority search with the Land Registry, precluding the claimant's solicitor from entering a unilateral notice. Instead, having been informed of the search by the Land Registry, the solicitor personally informed both Credit & Mercantile and the defendant of the fraud and supplied the defendant's solicitor with evidence that the fraud had taken place (in the form of a letter of confirmation from the police). The defendant sought legal advice and was told that, under the LRA 2002 section 58, there would be no mistake on the facts and therefore rectification against it would not be available once registration had occurred. Credit & Mercantile went ahead with the sale to the defendant, which was duly registered as proprietor of the house and took possession. The charge obtained by forgery was deleted from the register.

The claimant sought rectification, on the grounds that the registration of Vastguide as proprietor was a 'mistake' within the meaning of schedule 4(a) 'because it ... [was] an entry which would not have been made on the register were it not for the forgery committed by the fraudster.' The claimant also contended that, although Vastguide was a registered proprietor in possession, it had caused the mistake by its own fraud or lack of proper care.

Vastguide initially argued that there was no mistake on the facts and contended that the court had no jurisdiction to entertain the application. However, after seeking advice from the Land Registry, it abandoned this line of argument. The case was decided on the footing that, as a result of this concession, the defendant was estopped from denying that there was a mistake on the facts. As a result it is not authority for that view of the law. However, it is apparently

Lord Browne-Wilkinson in *Westdeutsche Landesbank Girozentrale v Islington LBC* [1996] AC 669 (HL) 706, and their correctness is therefore controversial for reasons that do not depend on the distinction between registered and unregistered land. For this reason, it is assumed for the purposes of this chapter, in accordance with the view taken by Ruoff & Roper, that the *Malory* reasoning is unsound as an interpretation of the new Act and that the controversy examined in the text does arise.

[29] D Cavill and others, *Ruoff & Roper on the Law and Practice of Registered Conveyancing* (7th edn, Sweet & Maxwell, London 2003) [46.030].

[30] *Cooke* (n 22), *Fox* (n 2).

[31] [2009] EWHC 3565 (Ch).

evidence that the Land Registry has taken the view that the interpretation of the statute in Ruoff 'take[s] too narrow a view and do[es] not reflect a correct interpretation of the statute.'[32]

For present purposes, the crucial point about this unresolved debate is that it turns on the extent to which the LRA 2002 operates as a self-contained system within which the idea of a 'mistake' takes its meaning. This can be seen in the Ruoff argument about the application of the schedule in the *Odogwu*-type situation. The authors argue that:

> Any other result would undermine the general aim of the Act that the register should indicate accurately and comprehensively the state of the registered proprietor's title. A registered proprietor cannot be deemed to lack powers of disposition which the fact of registration indicates that he actually has. Secondly, the 2002 Act has narrowed the grounds of rectification provided in the 1925 Act so that it no longer allows rectification where the proprietor of a legal estate would not have been the estate owner if the land had been unregistered. The applicant for rectification must prove some error in registration.[33]

There are two elements to this argument. The first is that, as a matter of principle, protecting the conclusiveness of the register ought to be an overriding objective in the interpretation of the LRA 2002 and that the availability of the jurisdiction to rectify on these facts would undermine that objective. Secondly, as matter of interpretation of the language of schedule 4 itself, it is argued that the shift away from the language of the Land Registration Act 1925 means that an 'error in registration' can now be defined in terms that are perfectly independent of what the position might be in relation to unregistered land. Both arguments depend on the assumption that the 'principles of land registration', including the principle of the conclusiveness of the register, constitute a coherent and distinctive set of values on the basis of which questions as to the interpretation of the LRA 2002 can be resolved. The next section examines the validity of this assumption, so far as it relates to the principles often referred to as the 'principles of land registration', concludes that it is unworkable, and puts forward an alternative basis on which the shift in values represented by the LRA 2002 should be understood.

The 'principles of land registration'

The joint Report of the Law Commission and HM Land Registry which preceded the LRA 2002 states that the 'fundamental objective' of the Act is that:

> … the register should be a complete and accurate reflection of the state of the title of the land at any given time, so that it is possible to investigate title to land on line, with the absolute minimum of additional enquiries and inspections.[34]

[32] Ibid [43].
[33] *Ruoff and Roper* (n 29) [46.030].
[34] *Law Commission and HM Land Registry* (n 6) [1.5].

This statement expressly underpins many of the reforms implemented by the Act.[35] It can be seen as a variation on an ideal often referred to as 'the mirror principle', following Ruoff's account of the aims of a registration system: he explains that the register ought to be 'a mirror which reflects accurately and completely and beyond all argument the current facts that are material to a man's title'.[36] This metaphor of the mirror has been frequently drawn upon in the literature on the principles of land registration;[37] for example, the existence of overriding interests[38] has been explained as a 'crack in the mirror' necessitated by various policy considerations that prevent the mirror aspiration from being perfectly achieved.[39] While the Law Commission's formulation does not directly refer to the register as a 'mirror', the language of reflection can be seen as a submerged reference to the same metaphor.

However, as Professor Cooke has pointed out, if the register is a mirror, it is a peculiar one:

> The strange thing about this mirror is that it is an active one; what it reveals has been made true, at least to some extent, by the register itself.[40]

This follows from the dispositive effect of title registration, which has also been expressed to be a principle fundamental to the LRA 2002:

> It will be the fact of registration and registration alone that confers title. This is entirely in accordance with the fundamental principle of a conclusive register which underpins the Bill.[41]

Despite the claim that they are entirely in accordance with each other, these ideals appear to pull in opposite directions. This is because the objective of 'accuracy' makes sense only if there is an external reality which must be matched ('mirrored') by the register of title. If registration alone confers title, such an aspiration has no meaning as a standard by which success or failure can

[35] As evidenced by the frequency with which the Report refers back to this objective to explain specific policy choices: see *Law Commission and HM Land Registry* (n 6) [4.14], [7.43], [8.1], [8.58], and [9.29]. The Law Commission's recent work on easements, covenants and profits à prendre has also expressly drawn on this as a significant policy objective relevant to its proposals for reform of that area of law: see Law Commission, 'Easements, Covenants and Profits à Prendre' (Law Com Cp No 186) [2.16]–[2.17] for the general approach and [4.2], [4.8] and [8.12] for specific instances of reform proposals informed by this objective.

[36] T Ruoff, *An Englishman Looks at the Torrens System* (The Law Book Company of Australia, Sydney 1957) 8.

[37] See, for example, R Smith, *Property Law* (6th edn Longman, London 2008) 220 and M Dixon, *Modern Land Law* (5th edn Cavendish Publishing, London 2005) 33–34.

[38] This term is not used in the LRA 2002, but remains a useful shorthand term for unregistered rights that are binding on a registered proprietor of an estate in registered land (either after first registration or following a subsequent registered disposition): see the LRA 2002 sch 1 and 3.

[39] See D Hayton, *Registered Land* (Sweet & Maxwell, London 1981) 76.

[40] E Cooke, *The New Law of Land Registration* (Hart Publishing, Oxford 2003) 54.

[41] *Law Commission and HM Land Registry* (n 6) [1.8]. The LRA 2002 s 58 provides that 'if, on the entry of a person in the register as the proprietor of a legal estate, the legal estate would not otherwise be vested in him, it shall be deemed to be vested in him as a result of the registration.'

be measured: the register will always, by definition, be an accurate reflection of whatever has been registered. It is this tension which also underlies the problem of what Pamela O'Connor, following the language of the Scottish Law Commission, calls 'bijural ambiguity':

> Many title registration statutes are ambiguous because they attempt to incorporate two inconsistent propositions. The first is that only instruments which are valid under the ordinary rules are to be registered. The second is that registration confers title irrespective of the validity of the instruments.[42]

If this is right, it seems to follow that the principles of land registration – incorporating, as they do, two inconsistent propositions – are profoundly incoherent. However, these ideals are not in fact incoherent; rather, the problem with reconciling them arises because, understood as norms (ie reasons for action), they are directed to different subjects. The mirror principle is concerned with what the register ought to be. The principle of a conclusive register is concerned with how the register ought to be interpreted.

The distinction becomes clearer if title registration is compared to the alternative system of deeds registration. As Jean Howell points out, the distinction between a title register and a deeds register is the distinction between a record of facts – which the individual relying on the register must interpret to arrive at a legal conclusion – and a record of rights, which the individual relying on the register is entitled to accept as an authoritative interpretation of the legal consequences of the acts and transactions that have already taken place.[43] Registration under the LRA 2002 is both a fact that has legal consequences and an official interpretation of the legal meaning of other facts. The mirror principle is directed towards those officials whose role it is to interpret the acts and transactions of parties in order to arrive at a conclusion as to the rights that can then be registered. The ideal of a conclusive register is directed towards those officials (the courts) whose role it is to interpret the legal consequences of registration itself. The question of how these particular norms are to be related to each other, so as to provide an internally coherent model of 'land registration', can only be understood as part of an official task of balancing competing and desirable policy goals, such as static security and dynamic security.[44]

The problem with treating these policy goals as an account of the unique set of values which govern registered land is that they are, firstly, indeterminate (since they pull in opposite directions) and, secondly, not unique to registered land. As McFarlane points out, the clash between dynamic and static security – what he calls the 'basic tension' between the rights of an owner of property and those of a subsequent purchaser – is one which is fundamental to any system

[42] P O'Connor, 'Deferred and Immediate Indefeasibility: Bijural Ambiguity in Registered Land Title Systems' (2009) *Edin L Rev* 194, 197.

[43] See J Howell, 'Deeds Registration in England: A Complete Failure?' [1999] *CLJ* 366, 368–71.

[44] *O'Connor* (n 42) 221.

of property law.[45] While the LRA 2002 clearly creates a distinctively structured scheme within which these separate policy goals can be achieved by different officials, the bare fact that it aims to achieve both does not give any guidance on the proper interpretation of the Act in cases where achieving one would compromise the other.

One way of resolving this indeterminacy is turn our attention to the other possible subject of legal norms, ignored by the policy-oriented account of the legislation: the individual. Professor Penner has argued, following Raz, that the fundamental task of any legal system is to provide reasons for action to its subjects; given this, he argues that the best way to characterise a particular set of positive norms, within a given legal system, is by reference to the reasons for action that they provide to the individuals served by those norms.[46]

It is not necessary, for present purposes, to follow Penner in his view that an account of legal rules that focuses on the reasons for action that they give to the individual necessarily provides the best or most central account of the function of those rules.[47] Such conclusions depend on the purpose for which the given account of the law is being put forward. For example, if the aim is to evaluate possible avenues for legislative reform, an instrumental account of the different social and economic objectives served or capable of being served by the existing rules is likely to be valuable. However, when it comes to the judicial interpretation of the provisions of an existing statute, an account focused on the intended effect of the rules on the individual litigant before the court may be more appropriate.[48]

In order to arrive at such an account, this chapter draws on Professor Birks' taxonomy of private law, which classifies legal rules in terms of the rights and liabilities generated by various 'causative events'.[49] The question of whether causative event analysis of this type is the best approach to private law in general and property law in particular is highly controversial,[50] as are various elements of the map of the law suggested by Birks. This chapter assumes only that a classification by legal response to real-world events is a possible method of approaching a set of rules of law. It is also a useful approach in the present context because it focuses attention on the legal subjects to whose actions the law responds: as argued above, this enables an important gap in our current account of the land registration rules to be filled. Although it is not the only

[45] B McFarlane, *The Structure of Property Law* (Hart Publishing, Oxford 2008) 6.

[46] J Penner, *The Idea of Property in Law* (OUP, Oxford 1997) 7–13.

[47] Penner also suggests that reasons for action should be considered in terms of the interests of the individual that they ultimately serve. This chapter does not consider the reasons provided by the land registration rules in these terms, but only in the narrow sense of the sanctions or benefits they confer on individuals in response to various actions that they may take.

[48] See R Dworkin, *A Matter of Principle* (OUP, Oxford 1985) 375.

[49] P Birks, 'Definition and Division: A Meditation on Institutes 3.13' in P Birks (ed), *The Classification of Obligations* (Clarendon Press, Oxford 1997) 1.

[50] G Samuel, 'English Private Law: Old and New Thinking in The Taxonomy Debate' (2004) 24 *OJLS* 335; J Dietrich, 'What is "Lawyering"? The Challenge of Taxonomy' [2006] *CLJ* 549.

possible approach to classification of the legal material,[51] nor necessarily the most useful in every context, this chapter therefore adopts the basic assumption of the Birks taxonomy (ie that rights, both proprietary and personal, can be analysed as responses to events). The next section examines the land registration legislation from this perspective and locates the controversy about the scope of schedule 4 within this classification.

Rights in registered land as responses to events

The Birks taxonomy suggests that property rights are capable of arising in response to consent, wrongs, unjust enrichment and other events.[52] When and if property rights arise in response to wrongs or to unjust enrichment is controversial. There are also some cases where it is controversial whether 'intention' is the source of the particular right.[53] Since the controversial aspects of these cases are not peculiar to registered land, this chapter does not consider them. Instead, it focuses on certain specific events, the proprietary consequences of which are uncontroversial – the taking of possession[54] and express declarations of intent on the part of a current right-holder[55] – and on registration itself as an event generating rights and liabilities.

Express declarations of intention on the part of a right-holder

If A is the registered proprietor of a registered estate in land, he may wish to deal with that estate in various ways. He may want to give his title to an estate to B, sell it to C, or create a lesser interest (such a lease, an easement or a beneficial interest under a trust) in favour of D.[56] This section of the chapter examines the law's response to the two such expressions of an intention: gifts and sales of title to the whole estate.

[51] For an example of an alternative classification of (inter alia) the provisions of the LRA 2002, intended to answer a different question, see L Fox, O'Mahony and N Cobb, 'Taxonomies of Squatting: Unlawful Occupation in a New Legal Order' (2008) 71 *MLR* 878.

[52] P Birks, 'Equity in the Modern Law: An Exercise in Taxonomy' (1996) *UWALR* 1, 9.

[53] That is, where there are debates about the evidential basis of a court's decision as to intention (the 'common intention constructive trust' line of authority) and what the intention is that the right responds to (the 'presumed intention resulting trusts' line of authority).

[54] Which would fall within the 'other' category of the Birks taxonomy. See *Armory v Delamirie* (1772) 93 ER 664 (personal property) and *Asher v Whitlock* (1865) LR 1 QB 1 (unregistered land).

[55] Which would fall within the 'consent' category of the Birks taxonomy, since that category includes contracts, wills, conveyances and express declarations of trust.

[56] He will be entitled to make any of these dispositions if an equivalent disposition would be possible, in respect of the relevant estate, in unregistered land: see LRA 2002 s 23. The exception is a mortgage by demise or sub-demise which is no longer permissible with respect to registered land (LRA 2002 s 23(2)).

Gift

If A wishes to gratuitously transfer his title to B, he must express his intention to do so in the form of a deed. As in the case of unregistered land, if the purported transfer is made orally, or in some written form that does not qualify as a deed,[57] it will be void for the purposes of conveying the legal estate.[58] In the absence of consideration, the statement of intention will not create a contract either, even if it is in writing that satisfies the formality requirements for the creation of a contract for the disposition of an estate or interest in land.[59] As a result, in the absence of additional facts (such as those generating an estoppel), A's intention to benefit B will simply have no legal effect unless he expresses it in the prescribed form.

If A does express his intention to transfer his registered estate to B in the form of a deed, this will qualify as a purported 'transfer' of the registered estate within the meaning of the LRA 2002 section 27(2).[60] This means that it is a disposition which is required to be completed by registration for the purposes of the LRA 2002 section 27(1), and therefore will not operate at law until the relevant registration requirements are met.

Those requirements are set out in the LRA 2002 schedule 2; in the case of a transfer of the whole of the registered estate, they are simply that B must be entered on the register as the proprietor. In order to ensure that this happens, A and B must fill out a set of forms prescribed by the Land Registry[61] and B must make an application to the Land Registry to be entered as the proprietor. The making of the application generates a duty on the part of the applicant to inform the Registry about certain overriding interests which affect the estate, where he has actual knowledge of the existence of those interests.[62] If B makes the application in the proper form and discloses the all relevant information and there are no objections to the application from any quarter,[63] the registrar will enter him as the

[57] That is, if it does not comply with the requirements set out in the Law of Property (Miscellaneous Provisions) Act 1989 s 1.

[58] Law of Property Act 1925 s 52(1).

[59] Law of Property (Miscellaneous Provisions) Act 1989 s 2.

[60] In practice this distinction between deed and application to register arises only in a case where A does enter into a deed but fails to apply to register: where he does apply to register, the application will normally also be a deed (see n 61 below).

[61] LRR 2003 r 58; and see Land Registry, 'Form TR1: Transfer of whole of registered title(s)' (Land Registry, London 2009) <http://www1.landregistry.gov.uk/assets/library/documents/TR1.pdf> accessed 13 September 2010 and Land Registry, 'Form AP1: Application to change the register' (Land Registry, London 2009) <http://www1.landregistry.gov.uk/assets/library/documents/AP1.pdf> accessed 13 September 2010. In practice, there is unlikely to be a separation between the execution of the deed required by the Law of Property Act 1925 and the application to register: since Form TR1 requires the applicant to execute it as a deed, A's successful completion of his part of this form will be sufficient to satisfy the formality requirements of the Law of Property Act 1925.

[62] LRA 2002 s 71(b) and LRR 2002 r 57; see *Land Registry Form AP1* (n 61) panel 11, and Land Registry, 'Form DI: Disclosable overriding interests' (Land Registry, London 2009) <http://www1.landregistry.gov.uk/assets/library/documents/DI.pdf> accessed 13 September 2010.

[63] Under LRA 2002 s 73, anyone may object to an application to the registrar. LRR 2003 r 19 prescribes the form that such an objection must take.

registered proprietor of the estate. If there is an objection from a third party (say, if X asserts that A granted her an option to purchase the land and the purported transfer is in breach of her rights) and the registrar is not satisfied that the objection is groundless, it must be determined by agreement between the parties, by the withdrawal of the objection or decision by the adjudicator[64] in order for B's registration as proprietor to proceed. If there is no objection or if any objection is satisfactorily dealt with, B will be registered as proprietor of the estate.

This will result in the legal estate vesting in B[65] and B becoming entitled to exercise various powers in relation to that estate.[66] However, because B has not given valuable consideration, the LRA 2002 section 29 will not apply to the disposition in his favour. As a result, he will be bound by any estate or interest that was binding on A whether or not such interests appear on the register or have overriding status.[67]

Where B, for some reason, does not make the relevant application to Land Registry, the transfer will not operate at law. Since the purported transfer is in the form of a deed, it might be interpreted to be a binding covenant obliging A to complete the transfer to B by registration. However, since any such promise is gratuitous, it will not have automatic proprietary effect in equity under the rule in *Lysaght v Edwards*,[68] which applies only to agreements that are specifically enforceable. As a result, if A transfers the registered estate to a third party, B will not be entitled to require the third party to perform the agreement.[69]

On these facts, therefore, in terms of the legal outcome of compliance or non-compliance, the registration requirements have a very similar effect to that of the formality requirements that are also applicable to unregistered land.[70] It is worth noting that the outcome is similar in the case of chattels: in the absence of a contract, a deed, or delivery of possession, a gratuitous expression of an intention that legal title pass from A to B will not be effective in passing title to anything in English law.[71]

[64] For the role of the Adjudicator, see LRA 2002 ss 107–12.

[65] Assuming that the transfer is not flawed in any way, this result will follow from the combination of LRA 2002 s 23 (by which A has 'owner's powers' entitling him to make any disposition of the estate permitted by the general law, with the exception of a mortgage by demise or sub-demise) and s 27 (which provides that a conveyance will operate at law once the relevant registration requirements are met). If the transaction is flawed, s 58 will be engaged to produce the same result.

[66] LRA 2002 s 23.

[67] LRA 2002 s 28 provides that the priority of an interest affecting the registered estate will be unaffected by a disposition of that estate. If there are legal interests affecting A's estate, therefore, they will bind B under the rule that the first in time prevails. If there are equitable interests, they will bind B since they are first in time and he cannot have the benefit of the bona fide purchaser defence (being a volunteer).

[68] (1875–76) LR 2 Ch D 499 (Ch).

[69] Unless, as in *Mascall v Mascall* (1985) 50 P & CR 119 (CA), A has already done everything in his power to make the gift (ie filled in his part of the Land Registry forms etc). Where this is the situation, the rule in *Re Rose* [1952] Ch 499 (CA) will mean that A holds his registered estate on trust for B, who will therefore be able to bind A's successor in title if he is a donee or if B's interest is overriding (e.g. because he has been allowed into actual occupation).

[70] And, as noted above (n 61), in practice they tend to absorb those formality requirements.

[71] See *McFarlane* (n 45) 169–75.

There are, however, two important differences in the case of registered land. First, for A, expressing his intentions to the Land Registry is likely to involve a more onerous process than expressing his intentions to B in the form of a deed. Secondly, more broadly, the transaction is not purely private as between A and B; in order for it to have effect, any objections that a third party might have must be resolved either by negotiation, by adjudication or by satisfying the registrar that it is groundless. Thus, in the case of a gift, while the effects of a failure to comply with the registration requirements are not very different from the effects of a failure to comply with formality requirements found elsewhere in the law, the burden involved in complying is greater.

Sale

A's intention to transfer his registered estate to C in exchange for valuable consideration is subject to the same formality and registration requirements as a gratuitous transfer. However, there are significant differences in the consequences both of registration and of failure to register.

First, where there is a failure to register but an effective contract,[72] the contract will be personally enforceable as between A and C and may also have proprietary effects in equity.[73] That is, if A refuses to take the steps necessary to allow C to complete the transfer by registration, C may sue; and, if A transfers his estate to a third party who is a volunteer,[74] C will be entitled to sue the third party to achieve the same result.

Secondly, successful completion of registration will engage the LRA 2002 section 29(1). As a result, unlike B, C will not be subject to every interest in the land that bound A. Instead, she will be only be bound by 'protected' interests: that is, interests discoverable as notices on the register[75] and the interests listed in the LRA 2002 schedule 3. Of the interests listed in schedule 3, legal easements and profits created after 2003 will be binding on C if they have been exercised within the year prior to the disposition. If they have not been exercised within the past year, but she either knows about them or could have discovered them on a reasonably careful inspection of the land, she will be bound.[76] Similarly, she will not be bound by the interests of a person in actual occupation of the land if she made inquiries of that person and they failed to disclose the existence of their interest in circumstances where it would have been reasonable to expect them to do so. Further, even if she makes no such inquiries, she will not be bound if the actual occupation is not discoverable on a reasonably careful inspection of the land, unless she has actual knowledge of the interest held by the person in actual occupation.[77]

[72] That is, a contract that meets the formality requirements of the Law of Property (Miscellaneous Provisions) Act 1989 and is supported by valuable consideration.

[73] Under the rule in *Lysaght v Edwards* (1875–76) LR 2 Ch D 499 (Ch).

[74] That is, a third party who has no defence to C's claim under LRA 2002 s 29 or at common law.

[75] LRA 2002 s 29(1)(a)(i) and (iii).

[76] LRA 2002 sch 3 para 3.

[77] LRA 2002 sch 3 para 2.

A purchaser for valuable consideration therefore gains significant benefits by completing a disposition by registration, by inspecting the register of title and by engaging in a reasonably careful inspection of the land that is being purchased. It is the combination of these steps which enables her to escape the consequences of the nemo dat rule, which would otherwise mean that she is bound by pre-existing legal interests and by equitable interests of which she has notice. This outcome resembles the effect, in relation to equitable interests in other forms of property, of the defence of bona fide purchase of a legal interest for value and without notice.[78] It is different in that it applies to certain legal interests[79] and is considerably more sharply defined than that defence. However, this is a difference of scope rather than aim.[80] The purchaser is still rewarded for investigating the physical state of the land and its occupation, although the LRA 2002 gives her considerably more security if she does this than the old law did.

Possession

One of the fundamental differences between registered and unregistered land has been said to be the principle that, in registered land, 'registration and not possession is the basis of title'.[81] It is true that a registered proprietor need not rely on evidence of possession (either his own or that of his predecessor in title) in order to show that he has the best title available to registered land. The sweeping reforms of the law of adverse possession brought about by the LRA 2002[82] have also de-emphasised the importance of possession as the ultimate source of entitlement to land.

However, although reform has resulted in a considerable change in the policy of the law with respect to the consequences of long possession, there remains a great deal of continuity between the approach of the LRA 2002 and the rest of the law of property when it comes to the general significance of possession. This is demonstrated by the legal consequences of the physical possession of land, without more, and more significantly by the legal consequences of the physical possession of land when coupled with registration and in the absence of any other basis for entitlement.

[78] Apart from the various statutory and common law exceptions to the nemo dat principle that apply to the sale of goods: see A G Guest and others, *Benjamin's Sale of Goods* (7th edn Sweet & Maxwell, London 2009) ch 7.

[79] Albeit only to the very limited class of legal interests that are both capable of creation without registration (under the LRA 2002 s 27) and lacking in overriding status under sch 3. Certain implied and prescriptive easements are the most significant category of such interests.

[80] A point made by Lord Wilberforce in *Williams & Glyn's Bank v Boland* [1981] AC 487 (HL) 504: 'The purpose, in each system, is the same, namely, to safeguard the rights of persons in occupation, but the method used differs'.

[81] C Harpum, S Bridge and M Dixon, *Megarry and Wade, The Law of Real Property* (7th edn, Sweet & Maxwell, London 2008) [6-041].

[82] Summarised in *Law Commission and HM Land Registry* (n 6) Part 14.

The act of taking possession

It is true that the act of possession is no longer the root of title to registered land where 'title' is defined to mean evidence of the best title available.[83] However, it remains the case that possession generates a title to land, with or without registration, if title is understood in its broadest definition as referring to 'the conditions, within a particular property institution, which must be satisfied before a person can slot into the protection of its trespassory rules.'[84] Nothing in the LRA 2002 displaces the ordinary principle of relativity of title whereby a trespasser is entitled, by virtue of his possession, to the protection of the law against a third party who does not have a better right to possession. In fact, the LRA 2002 acknowledges the existence of this title since it provides that the effect of the registration of an adverse possessor as registered proprietor is to extinguish the title that he or she enjoyed at the time of application for registration.[85]

More broadly, although it radically shifts the balance of interests between a registered proprietor and an adverse possessor,[86] the LRA 2002 does not eliminate the concept that possession is, in principle, capable of generating a right to land that ought to be protected even against a party who originally had better title. The right of an adverse possessor to apply for registration as registered proprietor[87] and his entitlement to succeed if certain conditions are met[88] is, of course, a highly watered-down version of the right of an adverse possessor of unregistered land once all other titles have been extinguished by limitation. But it exists on a continuum with the rules that generate those more powerful rights and cannot be understood except in the context of a system in which possession generates rights.

Possession of a registered proprietor

As noted above, where registration (in the absence of any other ground of entitlement) is coupled with physical possession of the land, the LRA 2002 schedule 4 restricts the circumstances in which the register can be rectified in order to defeat the title of the registered proprietor. Rectification is possible only where the proprietor in possession consents; where he has, by his own fraud or lack of proper care, caused or substantially contributed to

[83] See B Rudden, 'The Terminology of Title' (1964) 80 *LQR* 63, 65 distinguishing the idea of title as 'a right to possession' from the idea of title as 'the best right to possession.'

[84] J Harris, *Property and Justice* (Oxford University Press, Oxford 1996) 39.

[85] LRA 2002 sch 6 para 9(1).

[86] Cf M Dixon, 'The Reform of Property Law and the Land Registration Act 2002: a Risk Assessment' [2003] *Conv* 136, 150, describing the 'emasculation of adverse possession in relation to registered land'.

[87] LRA 2002 sch 6 para 1.

[88] Either under LRA 2002 sch 6 para 5 or para 6.

the mistake that led to his registration in the absence of any other ground of entitlement; or where it would for any other reason be unjust to deny rectification.

The situation where the schedule is engaged arises where, for example, there has been a purported transfer to X from the previous registered proprietor, which has been accepted by the Land Registry as entitling her to be entered as registered proprietor, but that transfer has been forged by a third party. In these circumstances, the LRA 2002 section 58 will operate to vest the legal estate in X and section 23 will vest unlimited powers of disposition in respect of that estate in her, but it may be open to the former registered proprietor to apply for an alteration of the register for the purpose of correcting a mistake.

If X herself had forged the transfer, rectification would clearly be available, since she would have caused the mistake by her own fraud. In such a circumstance, the registrar is obliged to rectify the register unless there are exceptional circumstances which justify not rectifying it.[89] It is difficult to see what these would be in the case where X has committed fraud, although the existence of the registrar's power not to rectify is significant in terms of the discretion it allows the registrar (and/or a court reviewing his decision) to determine the legal consequences of a fraud or other error.

However, in the case where X is innocent – because the transfer to her was forged by a third party and the forgery would not have been discoverable by the exercise of proper care – the registrar's discretion is reduced. In the absence of X's consent, no rectification will be available unless the registrar determines that it would be unjust to do so; the default position is that rectification should be unavailable unless the case is deemed exceptional. The former registered proprietor may seek compensation for his loss under the indemnity provisions of the LRA 2002, unless the loss has been caused by his own fraud or lack of proper care, but he will not be able to recover the land itself.

Registration alone

This outcome is to be contrasted with the case where the same facts arise but X is not in possession. Here an alteration of the register will not count as a rectification. As a result, the registrar may decide to alter the register for the purpose of correcting the mistake that has led to X's registration as proprietor. He will not be obliged to do so. The registered proprietor who is not in possession, therefore, is at the mercy of the registrar's discretion in a way that the registered proprietor who is in possession is not.

[89] LRA 2002 sch 4 para 6(3).

Odogwu v Vastguide Ltd[90]

It is in the context of this scheme of rights and duties that the fact situation in cases such as *Odogwu*[91] must be analysed. In that case, Mr Odogwu had expressed no intention at all to grant Credit & Mercantile Ltd the charge over the property; the sole ground of their entitlement was registration. Vastguide Ltd, on the other hand, became registered proprietor on the basis of an expression of intention by Credit & Mercantile Ltd, combined with registration and with its own possession of the property. The argument that their registration was a mistake within the meaning of schedule 4 on these facts requires us to take the view that the Land Registry should not have registered Vastguide Ltd as proprietor of the house if it had been aware of the forgery which grounded Credit & Mercantile's title; that is, if the Land Registry had known of the forgery, they would not have treated Credit & Mercantile's statement of intention as a relevant source of rights in the property.

In my view, this approach to the facts of *Odogwu* is correct and the interpretation of the 'mistake' provision of the schedule put forward in Ruoff is misguided. As previously argued, the conclusiveness and the accuracy of the register are competing policy goals. Although the conclusiveness of the register is an important ideal, the underlying normative principle that it represents is protection of the reliance of a purchaser who has fulfilled the obligations imposed upon him by the registration rules. This reliance is protected even where the LRA 2002 schedule 4 is engaged and it is acknowledged that a 'mistake' has been made, due to the scope of the discretion exercisable by the court or the registrar when it comes to applying that schedule, as well the stronger protection that will be offered to a purchaser who is a registered proprietor in possession. If Vastguide Ltd had not been aware that it was relying on a forgery to acquire rights, rectification would not have been ordered against them. Further, if the courts took the view that they had no jurisdiction to rectify or alter the register in this situation, the underlying policy objective contained in the ideal of the accuracy of the register would not be protected: the failure to rectify or alter would mean that the register did not reflect the position as it would have been if all parties had fulfilled their duties to deal honestly with the Land Registry.

Conclusions

This analysis has aimed to demonstrate that the title registration rules cannot be fully understood except by reference to their interaction with the principles of English property law as a whole. Divergences arise on the basis that individuals are prima facie entitled to rely on the Land Registry's interpretation of the rights

[90] [2009] EWHC 3565 (Ch).
[91] Discussed above at the text to n 31.

to which they are entitled and the liabilities to which they are subject; as a result of this principle, considerable discretion is vested in various officials in order to ensure that reliance on the register does not lead to loss. However, this prima facie entitlement comes with a burden of assisting the Land Registry in arriving at accurate interpretations of the relevant rights and liabilities and the measure of accuracy, with rare exceptions, involves the application of principles that are similar or identical to those applicable to unregistered land. Questions such as the definition of a 'mistake' for the purposes of the LRA 2002 schedule 4 must be seen in the context of this fundamental continuity between the principles applicable to registered land and property principles generally.

14

Bijural Ambiguity and Values in Land Registration Systems

Matthew Harding and Robin Hickey*

Introduction

In her recent article in the *Edinburgh Law Review*, Pamela O'Connor explores some of the difficulties that courts across the Commonwealth have faced owing to the fact that land registration systems are typically what the Scottish Law Commission has described as 'bijural'.[1] Bijural systems, according to the Scottish Law Commission, are those in which rules of general law, whose function is to allocate property in land, operate alongside statutory rules that have the same function.[2] In her article, O'Connor notes that the difficulties for Commonwealth courts have arisen where a land registration statute within a bijural system does not make clear on its face the extent to which its statutory rules – especially those that provide that an act of registration confers a valid title on a disponee of an interest in registered land – replace the general law rules that operate in that system. Where a land registration statute is characterised by this sort of 'bijural ambiguity', O'Connor observes, 'sudden and abrupt rule change can occur, even against the weight of judicial authorities or long-standing consensus as to the meaning of the statutory provisions'.[3]

* University of Melbourne and Queen's University, Belfast. We are grateful to Ms Tanya Josev for excellent research assistance, and to the University of Melbourne for funding our research via an Early Career Research Grant awarded to Dr Harding and an International Visitors' Scheme Grant awarded to Dr Hickey. Thanks also to Professor Michael Bryan for his helpful comments on a draft.

[1] P O'Connor, 'Deferred and Immediate Indefeasibility: Bijural Ambiguity in Registered Land Title Systems' (2009) 13 *Edin L Rev* 194, 195, referring to Scottish Law Commission, 'Discussion Paper on Land Registration: Void and Voidable Titles' (Scots Law Com Dp No 125, 2004).

[2] *Scottish Law Commission* (n 1) [1.11] and [5.15]–[5.22]. See also E Cooke, 'Land Registration: void and voidable titles – a discussion of the Scottish Law Commission's paper' [2004] *Conv* 482, 487–88; P O'Connor, 'Registration of Invalid Dispositions: Who Gets the Property?' in E Cooke (ed), *Modern Studies in Property Law: Volume 3* (Hart Publishing, Oxford 2005) 45, 57.

[3] *O'Connor* (n 1) 221.

Bijural ambiguity occasions difficulties for courts chiefly in cases where two innocent parties dispute the allocation of property in registered land in light of the activities of a third party. The third party may have forged a disposition of a registered interest, or may have made a disposition of a registered interest to the detriment of the holder of an unregistered interest. O'Connor points out that disputes in cases of these types entail a competition between two imperatives: 'static security' and 'dynamic security'.[4] Giving effect to static security means resolving the dispute in favour of the holder of a registered or unregistered interest in the disputed land who stands to lose that interest owing to the activities of the third party; giving effect to dynamic security means resolving the dispute in favour of the disponee of a registered interest in the disputed land where the disposition in question has been caused by the activities of the third party. In her work, O'Connor reveals that, although land registration statutes across the Commonwealth have been designed to shift the focus of land law from static to dynamic security,[5] the persistence of bijural ambiguity in land registration systems has meant that courts have struggled to know exactly where the appropriate balance between the two imperatives is to be struck when determining disputes relating to the allocation of property in registered land.

Taking O'Connor's important work as our starting point, our aim in this chapter is to contribute to the literature on the question of how legislatures and courts do, and should, respond to the competing imperatives of static and dynamic security in bijural systems of land law. One way of making such a contribution might be to examine closely the provisions of various land registration statutes to ascertain the extent to which they generate bijural ambiguity as well as the extent to which they provide guidance to courts on how to deal with bijural ambiguity. That is not our approach in this chapter: we assume the bijural ambiguity of land registration systems, and accept that it generates indeterminacy in the interpretation of the provisions of land registration statutes. Rather than subjecting statutory provisions to close scrutiny, our chapter approaches the problem of bijural ambiguity from a philosophical perspective.

First, we argue that underlying the competition of static and dynamic security are several fundamental and incommensurable human values, so that the resolution of that competition in any given case may ultimately be a matter of political choice. Secondly, we propose that the bijural ambiguity of land registration systems has compelled courts to make these types of choices, and we explore some of the choices that courts have made, concentrating first on cases from the Torrens world entailing forged dispositions, and then on English cases relating to overriding interests in registered land. We conclude with four

[4] *O'Connor* (n 2) 47–48; P O'Connor, 'Registration of Title in England and Australia: A Theoretical and Comparative Analysis' in E Cooke (ed), *Modern Studies in Property Law: Volume 2* (Hart Publishing, Oxford 2003) 81, 85–86. O'Connor borrows the language of 'static security' and 'dynamic security' from R Demogue, 'Security' in F W Scott and J P Chamberlain (trs), A Fouillée and others (eds), *Modern French Legal Philosophy* (Boston Book Co, Boston 1916) ch XIII.

[5] *O'Connor* (n 1) 198.

tentative observations about the problem of bijural ambiguity, keeping our discussion of value considerations in view.

Values underlying static and dynamic security

One way of understanding the competition of static and dynamic security is to take into account considerations of human value that bear upon that competition.[6] It is likely that static and dynamic security are values in themselves: there would appear to be no reason to deny that the sense of comfort that a person derives from either type of security is an irreducible good, regardless of what consequences that sense of comfort might have. However, of more interest for present purposes is the range of values that underlie static and dynamic security; values that bear upon the justification of allocating property either to the claimant who invokes static security or to the claimant who invokes dynamic security. The relation between static and dynamic security and these underlying values is an instrumental one in the sense that static and dynamic security gain value because they enable the realisation of the values that underlie them.

One such value is personal identity, or, as it is sometimes referred to in the literature, personhood. The value of personal identity may assist in the justification of property to the extent that personhood is expressed in, and contingent upon, ongoing relations with things.[7] Some things – the best example is money, but the category includes all things that are held, in Bernard Rudden's language, as 'wealth'[8] – are unlikely to be bound up with personal identity in the way necessary for that value to have any justificatory force in an argument for property in the things in question. However, other things – a family home or business is an excellent example – are plausible candidates to feature in a personhood-based argument for property.[9] Personhood-based arguments are unlikely to supply a complete justification of property except in rare cases,[10] but personal identity may sometimes be a value underlying static and dynamic security in the land registration setting. For example, where the owner of a family home disputes the allocation of property in that home with a registered mortgagee whose mortgage has been

[6] G S Alexander and others, 'A Statement of Progressive Property' (2009) 94 *Cornell L Rev* 743.

[7] M J Radin, 'Property and Personhood' (1982) 34 *Stan L Rev* 957 reproduced in her *Reinterpreting Property* (University of Chicago Press, Chicago 1993) 35; M J Radin, 'Reconsidering Personhood' (1995) 74 *Or L Rev* 423; J W Harris, *Property and Justice* (Clarendon Press, Oxford 1996) 220–23; H Dagan, *Unjust Enrichment: A Study of Private Law and Public Values* (Cambridge University Press, Cambridge 1997) 40–49, 63–70.

[8] B Rudden, 'Things as Thing and Things as Wealth' (1994) 14 *OJLS* 81.

[9] On personal identity and the notion of home, see L Fox, *Conceptualising Home: Theories, Laws and Policies* (Hart Publishing, Oxford 2007) 167–73.

[10] *Harris* (n 7) 220–21; see also J Penner, *The Idea of Property in Law* (Clarendon Press, Oxford 1997) 126, 180–81, 205–6.

procured by third party forgery, it is arguable that the value of the personal identity of the home-owner underlies, and lends weight to, the imperative of static security in that case. By contrast, in such a case personhood does not underlie dynamic security, given that the mortgagee's interest is in the home as 'wealth'.

A second value underlying static and dynamic security is liberty. Indeed, in his work on security, René Demogue recognised this, stating that security was linked with the idea of 'absolute unlimited rights, with that sort of free zone, recognised by everybody, which is the basis of individualism'.[11] The value of liberty underlies static and dynamic security in two ways. First, as Demogue alluded to in the passage above, security with respect to her property enables a person to enjoy freedom from the intrusions of the world around her and especially from the interference of other persons.[12] A home, for example, represents for many a zone of privacy and retreat; a fact recognised by Article 8 of the European Convention on Human Rights: 'Everyone has the right to respect for his private and family life, his home and his correspondence.'[13] There is, then, a justificatory connection between negative liberty and property.[14] Secondly, a person whose property is secure may draw on the material benefits that that property provides in exercising her personal autonomy, formulating, executing and realising plans and goals, and exercising control over her affairs.[15] For example, a person may lend money on the security of a mortgage of land, and because she has the security of that mortgage, she may make plans with confidence that her wealth may be recovered by an action against the land if necessary. This is an example of property grounding the enjoyment of positive liberty.

Personal identity and liberty are individual values and, in a liberal community at least, their relevance to property and, in the setting of property law, to the competition of static and dynamic security is easy enough to appreciate. However, social values also bear upon that competition.[16] One such is utility. The history of utilitarian thinking reveals that the meaning of utility can be and has been contested. However, all utilitarian thinkers are in agreement on one point:

[11] *Demogue* (n 4) 419.

[12] J Waldron, *The Right to Private Property* (Clarendon Press, Oxford 1988) 295–96.

[13] Convention for the Protection of Human Rights and Fundamental Freedoms (European Convention on Human Rights, as amended) art 8. See also *Fox* (n 9) ch 10.

[14] On the distinction between negative and positive liberty, see I Berlin, 'Two Concepts of Liberty' in his *Four Essays on Liberty* (Oxford University Press, Oxford 1969) 118; C Taylor, 'What's Wrong with Negative Liberty' in his *Philosophy and the Human Sciences: Philosophical Papers 2* (Cambridge University Press, Cambridge 1985) 211.

[15] *Waldron* (n 12) 300–18; *Harris* (n 7), discussed in D D Lametti, 'The Morality of James Harris's Theory of Property' in T Endicott and others (eds), *Properties of Law: Essays in Honour of Jim Harris* (Oxford University Press, Oxford 2006) 138.

[16] For a theoretical account of why social values matter, see C Taylor, 'Atomism' in his *Philosophy and the Human Sciences: Philosophical Papers 2* (Cambridge University Press, Cambridge 1985) 187; C Taylor, 'Irreducibly Social Goods' in his *Philosophical Arguments* (Harvard University Press, Cambridge MA 1997) 127.

whatever utility is, and however it is to be measured, it is a value and it is to be maximised where possible. For present purposes, we are content to assume that utility means something like efficiency in the sense meant in classical 'law and economics' literature,[17] and to point to three demands that the value of utility, so understood, makes in the setting of the competition of static and dynamic security. First, all else being equal, utility demands that property be allocated to the claimant who values it most. Secondly, all else being equal, utility demands that a loss be allocated to the claimant who could most cheaply have invested resources to prevent the loss, because this will incentivise the claimant and others like the claimant to invest resources in the cheap prevention of future losses in similar cases. And finally, utility demands that property-allocating rules be clear and certain, so that resources may be organised productively with confidence that property in them is secure, and so that transactions can be carried out cheaply and quickly with confidence that they will be effective according to their terms.[18]

The values of personal identity, liberty and utility are just some of the values that underlie the competition of static and dynamic security in the setting of property law. We focus on them in this chapter not only because they are relevant to static and dynamic security, but also because they are fundamental, in the sense that they do not stand in an instrumental relation with deeper values. Being fundamental in this way, they are several, irreducible, and incommensurable.[19] To describe personal identity, liberty and utility as incommensurable is to point to the fact that 'reason has no judgment to make concerning their relative value.'[20] This is not to say that reason has no judgement to make concerning the value of each of personal identity, liberty and utility taken in isolation: indeed, in this chapter we deploy those three considerations on the strength of just such rational judgements as to their value. It is rather to say that, when personal identity, liberty and utility are considered alongside each other, there is no reason in addition to the reasons that support each in isolation that may be taken as a specific reason to prefer one over the others. Entailed in this is that there is no reason for ranking or ordering the three considerations once all the reasons supporting each of them are known with certainty. As Joseph Raz puts it, '"the correct way of balancing the competing values" does not exist.'[21]

The incommensurability of the values underlying the competition of static and dynamic security in the property law setting has two implications. First,

[17] See R A Posner, *Economic Analysis of Law* (7th edn Aspen Publishers, Austin 2007) 10–15.

[18] H Dagan, 'The Craft of Property' (2003) 91 CLR 1517, 1544–45, referring to M Mautner, '"The Eternal Triangles of the Law": Toward a Theory of Priorities in Conflicts Involving Remote Parties' (1991) 90 *Mich L Rev* 95.

[19] On value pluralism, see generally: *Berlin* (n 14) 170; C Taylor, 'The Diversity of Goods' in his *Philosophy and the Human Sciences: Philosophical Papers 2* (Cambridge University Press, Cambridge 1985) 230; H Dagan, 'The Limited Autonomy of Private Law' (2008) 56 *Am J Comp L* 809.

[20] J Raz, *The Morality of Freedom* (Clarendon Press, Oxford 1986) 324.

[21] J Raz, 'The Relevance of Coherence' (1992) 72 *BUL Rev* 273, 312.

any choice for one of those values over the others cannot, in the absence of other considerations, be rationally challenged. Secondly, with one exception, where one of those values underlies both the imperative of static security and the imperative of dynamic security in the setting of a particular dispute, no rational challenge can, in the absence of other considerations, be mounted to a choice either for static security or for dynamic security. The exception is the value of utility: although the value of utility is incommensurable with values like personal identity and liberty, it should – in theory at least – always be possible to measure one instance of utility against another, because the very concept of utility presupposes a determinate and universal method of calculation. However, once utility-utility conflicts are put to one side, it follows from the incommensurability of the values underlying the competition of static and dynamic security that any challenge to a choice for one of those values over the others, or for one instance of one of those values over another such instance, must be a political challenge, a bare assertion of preference. It follows that the choice itself must be a political choice.

Judicial choices among values in the land registration setting

In cases where two innocent parties dispute the allocation of property in registered land in light of the activities of a third party, the traditional response of Commonwealth courts has been to allocate property in accordance with what they have taken to be the meaning of specific provisions of land registration statutes. However, the bijural ambiguity of those statutes has meant that, while courts have typically presented their judgments in cases entailing disputes over registered land as detailed and technical analyses of statutory rules, they have been compelled to reach decisions about property-allocation in circumstances of considerable indeterminacy. This indeterminacy has led courts to allocate property in a variety of ways, in factually similar cases and even at different stages of appeal in the same case, notwithstanding a backdrop of similar, or even the very same, statutory provisions. In our view, it is arguable that this variety of responses to similar factual scenarios against an often similar legislative backdrop indicates the possibility that the decisions about property-allocation that courts have made when determining disputes over registered land are appropriately viewed as more-or-less conscious political choices among underlying incommensurable values. In this section of the chapter, we explore this idea with reference to two types of case: cases from the Torrens world entailing forged dispositions; and English cases about overriding interests in registered land.

Forged dispositions in the Torrens world

Traditional approaches

Traditionally, courts in the Torrens world have determined forged disposition cases by applying one of two approaches. The first approach was set out by the Privy Council in its 1891 decision in *Gibbs v Messer*,[22] a decision that was followed in New Zealand until the 1920s, in Australia until the 1960s, and that in Canada is followed even today. The second approach was also set out by the Privy Council, when it decided *Frazer v Walker* in 1967.[23] *Frazer v Walker* has proved popular in Australasia: the decision has been followed by Australian courts ever since it was handed down, and in New Zealand the rule that it stands for was applied even before it was handed down, and continues to be applied today.

In *Gibbs v Messer*, the Privy Council set out two rules relating to forged disposition cases. The first rule applies in a case where X takes a disposition from A, who appears to be a person identified by the register as in a position to make the disposition, and X then gets registered. In this kind of case, *Gibbs v Messer* stands for the proposition that if the instrument presented for registration turns out to be forged so that A is not in fact the person named in the register, X's title is invalid and must be removed from the register.[24] The second rule applies in a case where, by a forged instrument, a disposition with respect to A's interest in registered land is effected in favour of B, who gets registered and then makes a disposition in favour of X. In a case like this, the rule from *Gibbs v Messer* is that notwithstanding the forgery of A-B, the registration of B's interest generates a good root of title for X, X having taken a disposition from the person indicated by the register as in a position to effect the disposition. X's title is therefore valid and may be asserted against A, even once the effects of A-B are undone.[25] In Torrens parlance, this latter rule is known as the rule of 'deferred indefeasibility' of title.

In *Frazer v Walker*, the Privy Council confirmed that in a case of type A-B-X, in circumstances of forgery X's title is valid.[26] However, the Privy Council also held that in cases of type A-X, notwithstanding that a disposition has been forged, X's title is valid.[27] Indeed, the Privy Council expressed this rule with sufficient width that it applies in all A-X cases where A-X is void, even if not for forgery.[28] This rule from *Frazer v Walker* not only replaces the rule from

[22] *Gibbs v Messer* [1891] AC 248 (PC).
[23] *Frazer v Walker* [1967] 1 AC 569 (PC).
[24] *Gibbs* (n 22) 254–255, 257.
[25] Ibid.
[26] *Frazer* (n 23) 586.
[27] Ibid 584.
[28] See, eg, *Boyd v The Mayor of Wellington* [1924] NZLR 1174 (NZCA), a case that presaged *Frazer v Walker*.

Gibbs v Messer invalidating X's title in A-X cases entailing forged dispositions; it also makes otiose the rule of 'deferred indefeasibility' because it effectively transforms A-B-X cases into two cases of type A-X and renders the disposition in each of those two cases valid.[29] In Torrens parlance, it is known as the rule of 'immediate indefeasibility' of title.

Both *Gibbs v Messer* and *Frazer v Walker* rested on a close analysis of the provisions of the relevant Torrens statute: in the case of *Gibbs v Messer* this was the Transfer of Land Statute 1866 of the then colony of Victoria;[30] in *Frazer v Walker* it was the Land Transfer Act 1952 of New Zealand.[31] The applicable provisions of these two statutes were very similar.[32] That the Privy Council in *Frazer v Walker* chose a different rule to determine the A-X case than it had chosen in *Gibbs v Messer*, notwithstanding the similarity of the statutory provisions in both cases and the fact that they were carefully considered in each case, indicates that close scrutiny of the precise words of those statutory provisions is not likely to shed sufficient light on the two decisions. In our view, it is at least arguable that a more illuminating approach might be to try to understand the decisions with reference to the values underlying static and dynamic security.

In discerning what choice among underlying values *Gibbs v Messer* stands for, the first point to note is that *Gibbs v Messer* mediates between the competing imperatives of static and dynamic security in circumstances of forgery. In the A-X case, static security is preserved; in the A-B-X case, dynamic security is preserved. This via media is consistent with respect for the liberty of both disponors and disponees: disponors in the A-X case and disponees in the A-B-X case. Although the two rules from *Gibbs v Messer* are unable to preserve the liberty of both the disponor *and* the disponee in any given case, the fact that the first rule preserves disponor liberty and the rule of deferred indefeasibility preserves disponee liberty means that the two rules, when viewed as a package, may be reconciled with the liberty that underlies both static and dynamic security.

A second point that arises in light of the via media established in *Gibbs v Messer* is that the decision is indifferent to the value of personal identity. We have noted already that that value may underlie the claim to static security of a home-owner against a registered mortgagee in a forged disposition case. Whether or not *Gibbs v Messer* delivers static security to such a home-owner

[29] *Frazer* (n 23) 586.

[30] *Gibbs* (n 22). Although there is no reference to specific provisions of the Victorian statute in the ratio decidendi of *Gibbs v Messer*, in his judgment in the subsequent case of *Clements v Ellis* (1934) 51 CLR 217 (High Court of Australia) 238, Dixon J noted that he had read a 'shorthand report' of the argument in *Gibbs v Messer* and that the relevant provisions of the Victorian statute had been 'examined and discussed closely' by the Privy Council at that stage, Lord Watson's judgment on behalf of their Lordships serving as a 'brief, but exact' summary.

[31] *Frazer* (n 23) 579–83.

[32] Cf Transfer of Land Statute 1866 (29 Vic No 301) ss 49 and 138, and Land Transfer Act 1952 (NZ) ss 62 and 63.

depends on which of its two rules is applied to the case, and this of course depends on the form that the case happens to take. If the case is of type A-X, static security, and the value of personhood, is protected. But if the case is of type A-B-X, it is the dynamic security of the mortgagee that will be protected. With the value of personal identity in view, the two rules from *Gibbs v Messer* are thus arbitrary in their operation: from this it may be concluded that those rules are in all cases indifferent to personhood.

We argued above that the value of utility makes three demands in the setting of the competition of static and dynamic security.[33] *Gibbs v Messer* is not in alignment with the first of these: its two rules do not guarantee an allocation of property to the claimant who values it most, nor is that even a likely consequence of their application. However, it is arguable that *Gibbs v Messer* is sensitive to the second and third demands of utility. According to the second demand of utility, the cheapest preventer of a realised loss should bear it, so as to incentivise future efficient loss-prevention. In *Gibbs v Messer*, in discussing the rule that invalidates titles in A-X cases, the Privy Council stated that:

> … the duty of ascertaining the identity of … [A] with the person who stands on the register as proprietor, and of seeing that they get a genuine deed executed by … [A], rests with … [X]; and if … [X] accept[s] a forgery … [X] must bear the consequences.[34]

This strict duty, which is a concomitant of the rule applied in A-X cases to invalidate X's title in circumstances of forgery, functions as an incentive to parties in the position of X to take the steps necessary to ensure that the disposition is not forged,[35] and assumes that those parties are best-placed to take those steps. This indicates that the second demand of utility may underpin the imperative of static security that an application of the first rule from *Gibbs v Messer* gives effect to in A-X cases.

The third demand of utility in the setting of the competition of static and dynamic security is that the property rules that are applied in resolving that competition should be clear and certain, so as to ensure confidence in holdings and in transactions. In *Gibbs v Messer*, the Privy Council stated that, in its view, the object of the Victorian Transfer of Land Statute was 'to save persons dealing with registered proprietors from the trouble and expense of going behind the register, in order to investigate the history of their author's title, and to satisfy themselves of its validity.'[36] In other words, the Privy Council interpreted the statute so as to deliver certainty to a disponee in circumstances where, under the general law, that certainty was traditionally lacking, ie circumstances where

[33] Text to n 18.

[34] *Gibbs* (n 22) 258. See also *Katene Te Whakaruru v Public Trustee* (1893) 12 NZLR 651, 661.

[35] Being a strict duty, it is an especially powerful incentive. For a less powerful incentive, see the duty to take reasonable steps to ascertain the identity of a mortgagor that is imposed on mortgagees of registered land by: Real Property Act 1900 (NSW) s 56C (inserted by Real Property and Conveyancing Legislation Amendment Act 2009 (NSW) sch 1); Land Title Act 1994 (Qld) ss 11A, 11B, 187.

[36] *Gibbs* (n 22) 254.

a disponee had verified the identity of the disponor, but exhaustive title searches could not easily be performed. Clearly, then, the decision of the Privy Council in *Gibbs v Messer* was in at least one respect a response to the third demand of utility that we set out above.[37]

Turning to *Frazer v Walker*, it is clear that the rule of immediate indefeasibility endorsed in that case balances the values underlying static and dynamic security differently than the two rules from *Gibbs v Messer.* To begin with, because the rule prefers dynamic security over static security in all forged disposition cases rather than maintaining a via media between the two imperatives, it consistently preserves the liberty of the disponee at the expense of the liberty of the disponor. Moreover, it is strongly arguable that the rule of immediate indefeasibility is not indifferent to the value of personal identity. This is because in forged disposition cases of both type A-X and type A-B-X, where the dispute is between a home-owner and a registered mortgagee, the value of personal identity can only be in play in support of static security, given that a mortgagee always has an interest in land as 'wealth'. Because it validates a mortgagee's title in every case where a mortgage is the product of forgery – whether that case takes the form A-X or A-B-X – it is arguable that the rule of immediate indefeasibility is not indifferent regarding the value of personhood, and instead may discount that value.

In our view, the most significant difference between *Gibbs v Messer* and *Frazer v Walker*, having regard to underlying values, concerns the value of utility formalised in its three demands. Recall that the two rules from *Gibbs v Messer* do not guarantee an allocation of property to the person who values it most, and therefore they are insensitive to the first demand of utility. However, by imposing a strict duty on disponees to take the steps necessary to ensure that the disposition is not forged, the first rule from *Gibbs v Messer* incentivises efficient loss-prevention by compelling the cheapest preventer of a realised loss to bear it, assuming that the disponee is the cheapest loss-preventer: in this way it is sensitive to the second demand of utility. And *Gibbs v Messer* aims to deliver the certainty that utility demands in its third dimension, by assuring dynamic security to the disponee who has verified the identity of the disponor.

In a case where the value of personal identity underlies the imperative of static security, an argument might be made that the rule of immediate indefeasibility endorsed in *Frazer v Walker*, unlike the two rules from *Gibbs v Messer*, discounts the first demand of utility. This is because a person whose identity is bound up with their property in registered land is likely to value that property more than another person making a competing claim to property in the same land. Moreover, unlike the two rules from *Gibbs v Messer*, the rule of immediate indefeasibility may be insensitive to the second demand of utility. It is strongly arguable that the rule of immediate indefeasibility does not incentivise efficient loss-prevention, but rather allocates a loss to a disponor and, ultimately, to the public via the assurance fund in circumstances where neither the disponor nor

[37] Text to n 18.

the public (in the person of the Registrar) could have taken steps to prevent the loss from occurring, given the nature of forgery. There may be exceptional cases in which a disponor is the cheapest preventer of a realised loss, and indeed it is arguable that *Frazer v Walker* itself was such a case.[38] However, those cases are exceptional, especially in the setting of a dispute between a land owner and a mortgagee; in more typical cases the disponor is not aware, nor could she reasonably have been aware, of the circumstances of the forgery and consequently she cannot be regarded as the cheapest loss-preventer. Indeed, it might even be argued that the rule of immediate indefeasibility has incentivised practices, especially on the part of mortgagees, that make forgery, and the losses that flow from it, more likely.[39]

The chief concern underlying the rule of immediate indefeasibility is not the prevention of loss; it is maximising certainty as to the allocation of property in the event of forgery. This it achieves through delivering a valid title to the disponee in all cases, whether or not the disponee has verified the identity of the disponor. It would appear, then, that by choosing a rule of immediate indefeasibility in *Frazer v Walker*, the Privy Council placed great emphasis on the third demand of utility.

Recent developments

Recently, in the Canadian provinces of Ontario and British Columbia, Courts of Appeal have begun dealing with forged disposition cases in a new way, against a backdrop of bijural ambiguity. In Ontario, the relevant decision is *Lawrence v Wright*, decided in 2007;[40] in British Columbia it is *Gill v Bucholtz*, decided in 2009.[41]

Lawrence v Wright was an A-B-X case: by a forged instrument, registered land was transferred to a person using the alias 'Thomas Wright', and 'Wright' borrowed money from Maple Trust on security of a registered mortgage of that land. Belobaba J of the Ontario Superior Court of Justice set aside the transfer to 'Wright' for fraud but upheld Maple Trust's mortgage, on the basis of a rule of immediate indefeasibility that, for a short time, was part of the land law of Ontario.[42] In the Ontario Court of Appeal, the decision of Belobaba J was overturned. In her judgment for the Court, Gillese JA acknowledged that relevant provisions of Ontario's Land Titles Act 1990, sections 78(4) and 155, generated bijural ambiguity. On the one hand, Gillese JA thought that those provisions were capable of supporting the two rules from *Gibbs v Messer*.

[38] R Sackville, 'The Torrens System – Some Thoughts on Indefeasibility and Priorities' (1973) 47 *ALJ* 526, 531.

[39] See S Rodrick, 'Forgeries, False Attestations and Imposters: Torrens System Mortgages and the Fraud Exception to Indefeasibility' (2002) 7 *Deakin L Rev* 97.

[40] *Lawrence v Wright* (2007) 278 DLR (4th) 698 (Ont CA).

[41] *Gill v Bucholtz* (2009) 310 DLR (4th) 278 (BC CA).

[42] *Lawrence v Wright* 2006 CanLII 24129 (Ont SCJ).

On the other hand, she considered that the provisions supported another rule according to which, in an A-B-X case, X's title is invalid if A-B is forged and B is a party to the fraud, but may form a good root of title for Y in the event that X makes a disposition in Y's favour.[43] Pamela O'Connor, following Alan G Silverstein, has called this rule the rule of 'deferred indefeasibility plus'.[44] Significantly, in giving the reasons of the Court for adopting this rule of deferred indefeasibility plus, Gillese JA emphasised the 'policy reasons' that bore upon the case.[45] We return to this point below.

Like *Lawrence v Wright*, *Gill v Bucholtz* was an A-B-X case. An imposter pretending to be Gill transferred Gill's land by a forged transfer to a fellow fraudster, who then borrowed money on security of a registered mortgage over the land in favour of the Bucholtzs. In British Columbia, a rule of immediate indefeasibility protects the title of the disponee of an ownership interest in a forged disposition case, whether that case is of type A-X or A-B-X.[46] However, unlike in Australasian Torrens jurisdictions, British Columbia's Land Title Act 1996 does not extend the protection of this rule to the title of a mortgagee.[47] At trial, Barrow J of the Supreme Court of British Columbia interpreted the provisions of the Land Title Act relevant to a forged mortgage case, sections 25.1 and 26(1), as being consistent with the two rules from *Gibbs v Messer* and, on that basis, he applied the rule of deferred indefeasibility and upheld the Bucholtzs' mortgage as a result.[48]

The view taken by the British Columbia Court of Appeal of the meaning of sections 25.1 and 26(1) was quite different from that taken by Barrow J at trial, which indicates the presence of bijural ambiguity in those provisions of British Columbia's land registration statute. According to the approach taken by the Court of Appeal, in British Columbia, in either an A-X case or an A-B-X case, where X is a mortgagee X's title is invalid in circumstances of forgery. This is because, taken together, sections 25.1 and 26(1) of the Land Title Act preserve the general law rule of *nemo dat quod non habet* with respect to mortgages, 'even where the holder has relied on the register and dealt bona fide with a non-fictitious registered owner.'[49] Presumably, this rule extends not only further than the two rules from *Gibbs v Messer*, but also further than the rule of deferred

[43] *Lawrence* (n 40) [16]–[40].

[44] *O'Connor* (n 1) 209, citing AG Silverstein, 'Bill 152 – What Every Law Clerk (and Lawyer) Needs To Know' (17th Annual Conference of the Institute of Law Clerks of Ontario, 11 May 2007) <http://www.telus.assystrealestate.com/docs/en/ILCO_Bill152_paper_May2007.pdf> accessed 26 August 2010.

[45] *Lawrence* (n 40) [57]–[58].

[46] Land Title Act RSBC 1996 c 250 (as amended by Miscellaneous Statutes Amendment Act SBC 2005 c 35) s 23(2). See also *Heller v British Columbia (Registrar, Vancouver Land Registration District)* (1961) 26 DLR (2d) 154 (BC CA) 159–63.

[47] *Crédit Foncier Franco-Canadien v Bennett* (1963) 43 WWR 545 (BC CA); *Homewood Mortgage Investments Ltd v Lee* [2008] BCSC 512, BCWLD 6146.

[48] *Gill v Bucholtz* (2008) DLR (4th) 688 (BC SC). See also *Re Oehlerking Estate* [2008] BCSC 1648, [2009] BCWLD 1192 (BC SC).

[49] *Gill* (n 41) [26].

indefeasibility plus of *Lawrence v Wright*: in a case of type A-B-X, where A-B is void for forgery, and B-X takes the form of a mortgage, if X then transfers the mortgage to Y, even Y's registered title is invalid owing to the operation of the *nemo dat* rule. By contrast, in such circumstances Y's title as registered mortgagee would be protected by the application of the rule of deferred indefeasibility plus applied in *Lawrence v Wright*.

Lawrence v Wright and *Gill v Bucholtz* show that the law of Ontario and British Columbia now weighs more heavily than before in favour of static security. And indeed, subsequent developments have confirmed this. In *Lawrence v Wright*, Gillese JA appeared to take the view that X's title would be invalid in an A-B-X case only where X was party to the fraud,[50] but in the more recent decision of *Reviczky v Meleknia and HSBC Bank Canada*, the Ontario Superior Court of Justice declared a mortgage invalid in an A-B-X case in which both B and X were totally unaware of the fraud.[51] This decision is an even greater affirmation of the imperative of static security than *Lawrence v Wright* itself. Moreover, in October 2009 the Supreme Court of Canada refused leave to appeal from a case heard alongside *Gill v Bucholtz* in the British Columbia courts and decided on the same basis: *Re Oehlerking Estate*.[52] This was a strong signal that the ratio decidendi of *Gill v Bucholtz*, with its heavy emphasis on static security in forged mortgage cases, will be the law in British Columbia for the foreseeable future, in the absence of legislative intervention.

The response to forged disposition cases that has emerged recently in the law of Ontario and British Columbia balances the values of liberty, personal identity and utility differently than either the two rules from *Gibbs v Messer* or the rule of immediate indefeasibility from *Frazer v Walker*. To begin with, in Ontario and British Columbia, the liberty of disponors is preserved at the expense of the liberty of disponees, given that in all forged disposition cases (in Ontario regardless of the nature of the disposition and in British Columbia where the disponee is the holder of a registered mortgage) the imperative of static security will be given effect to.

Secondly, in cases where the dispute is between a home-owner and a mortgagee, it is arguable that in Ontario and British Columbia the value of personal identity has been apprehended via the courts making a distinction between an interest in registered land as 'thing' and an interest in the same land as 'wealth'. So much was acknowledged by Gillese JA in *Lawrence v Wright* in her discussion of the 'policy reasons' in favour of the rule of deferred indefeasibility plus that was endorsed in that case:

> Under the theory of immediate indefeasibility, the innocent homeowner has no defence to a mortgagee's action for possession. The homeowner is exposed to the loss

[50] *Lawrence* (n 40) [67]–[68].

[51] (2007) 287 DLR (4th) 193 (Ont SCJ).

[52] See *Re Oehlerking Estate* [2008] BCSC 1648, [2009] BCWLD 1192; *Re Oehlerking Estate* [2009] BCCA 138, [2009] BCWLD 2842, [2009] 7 WWR 468; *GET Acceptance Corporation v Land Title and Survey Authority of British Columbia* 2009 CanLII 57518 (SCC).

> of her home through eviction with the only available remedy being to make a claim for loss of value of the property from the [assurance] Fund. The idea that a person who buys a specific parcel of land with a specific house on it should be compensated in damages runs contrary to the notion that real property, in such circumstances, is not fungible. To see a lender compensated in damages does not offend that same notion.[53]

It must be noted that in Ontario the rule of deferred indefeasibility plus may, in exceptional cases, bring about a result inconsistent with the value of personhood: for example, think of an A-B-X case where X has taken a disposition of an ownership interest and has enjoyed possession of the land for some time before the forgery is discovered. However, given that the value of personhood typically underlies the imperative of static security, the rule of deferred indefeasibility plus is largely consistent with respect for that value.

As to the value of utility, *Lawrence v Wright* and *Gill v Bucholtz* appear to be sensitive to the first demand of utility – that property be allocated to the claimant who values it most – in their recognition that a mortgagee is likely to value registered land simply as fungible 'wealth', whereas a homeowner typically attributes value to land not only as 'wealth' but also because of the specific physical form that it takes. Moreover, with respect to the second and third demands of utility, the emerging treatment of forged disposition cases in Ontario and British Columbia is new and different. Recall that the concomitant of the first rule from *Gibbs v Messer* is that a disponee has a strict duty to ascertain the identity of the disponor: failure to discharge that duty means that the disponee's title is invalid. In Ontario, in an A-B-X case, that duty now extends beyond simply ascertaining the identity of B and demands that X ensure that even A-B is not forged. In British Columbia, if X is a mortgagee, this wider duty is imposed not only on X but also, if X transfers the mortgage to Y, on Y (and, potentially, further disponees who do not take an ownership interest). In both jurisdictions, then, great weight is now placed on the second demand of utility, the assumption being that X is the cheapest avoider of a realised loss in forged disposition cases both of type A-X and of type A-B-X, and even in circumstances where B is not a party to the forgery. In *Lawrence v Wright*, in her discussion of 'policy reasons', Gillese JA stated that:

> By interpreting the Act in accordance with the theory of deferred indefeasibility [plus], the law encourages lenders to be vigilant when making mortgages and places the burden of the fraud on the party that has the opportunity to avoid it, rather than the innocent homeowner who played no role in the perpetration of the fraud.[54]

In *Gill v Bucholtz*, Newbury JA indicated that the legislature had, in the design of the British Columbia's Land Title Act, chosen to allocate the losses occasioned by mortgage fraud to lenders rather than to homeowners;[55] one plausible

[53] *Lawrence* (n 40) [57].
[54] Ibid [58].
[55] *Gill* (n 41) [27].

interpretation of this choice is that it rested on the assumption that the second demand of utility would be best met thereby. Given the bijural ambiguity of the Land Title Act, we would suggest that the decision of the Court of Appeal in *Gill v Bucholtz* itself may be viewed as a choice that rested on that assumption and was, to that extent, responsive to the second demand of utility.

Any emphasis placed by the courts of Ontario and British Columbia on the second demand of utility in the setting of forged disposition cases has almost certainly been at the expense of the third demand of utility: the demand that property-allocating rules be clear and certain. The rule of immediate indefeasibility generates certainty that a disponee's title is valid in all forged disposition cases, and the rule of deferred indefeasibility generates such certainty in all A-B-X cases where X has verified the identity of B. By contrast, the rule of deferred indefeasibility plus and the *nemo dat* rule applied in Ontario and British Columbia respectively generate uncertainty even in A-B-X cases where X has verified the identity of B, because in such cases X's title is still invalid if A-B turns out to be forged. And in British Columbia, where X is a mortgagee and transfers that mortgage to Y, there will be similar uncertainty as to the validity of Y's title. Exactly how much uncertainty the rule of deferred indefeasibility plus and the *nemo dat* rule generate is a matter for debate.[56] But it can scarcely be denied that some additional uncertainty in A-B-X cases is the price paid, in Ontario and British Columbia, for the relatively high level of protection that those provinces now provide to static security and the values that underlie it.

Overriding interest cases in England and Wales

At this point we could turn our attention to English forgery cases to inquire whether differing value responses are evident there.[57] That course seems interesting,[58] but we avoid it here for the sake of expanding our analysis. For if it is arguable that in forgery cases generally the decision that a rule entails static or dynamic security has been achieved by courts making political choices amongst incommensurable values, it seems reasonable to suppose further that this practice has also occurred where different facts have reflected the same basic tension. A plausible example is provided by the interpretation of the provisions of successive English land registration statutes which have operated to resolve

[56] Compare B Ziff, 'Looking for Mr Wright: A Comment on *Lawrence v Wright*' (2007) 51 *RPR* (4th) 22, and B Bucknall, 'Real Estate Fraud and Systems of Title Registration: The Paradox of Certainty' (2008) 47 *CBLJ* 1.

[57] On English forgery cases generally see D Fox, 'Forgery and Alteration of the Register under the Land Registration Act 2002' in E Cooke (ed), *Modern Studies in Property Law: Volume 3* (Hart Publishing, Oxford 2005) 25.

[58] For example, the strong protection afforded in England and Wales to a registered proprietor in possession of land seems to suggest strong sensitivity to personhood, especially since this protection is routinely denied to mortgagees in possession: Land Registration Act 2002 ('LRA 2002') s 131, sch 4; E Cooke, *The New Law of Land Registration* (Hart Publishing, Oxford 2003) 130.

disputes between the disponee of a registered estate and the holder of an earlier unregistered interest in the land where the latter remains in actual occupation of the land at the date of the disposition. Under the terms of the Land Registration Act 2002, where such a disposition is made for valuable consideration and completed by registration, the unregistered interest might enjoy priority over the registered estate if it falls within a protected class of 'interests which override registered dispositions'.[59] So far as relates to our chosen example, this class includes unregistered interests of persons in actual occupation of land at the time of the disposition, save where inquiry was made of that person before the disposition and she failed to disclose the right when she could reasonably have been expected to do so.[60]

Williams & Glyn's Bank Ltd v Boland[61] is a seminal case on the interpretation of provisions relating to the overriding interests of persons in actual occupation.[62] In each of two consolidated appeals, a husband, who was sole registered proprietor of a family home, charged the home to secure business debts. The bank registered its charge, and upon default commenced possession proceedings which were resisted by the wife on the basis of a prior equitable interest consequent on her contribution to the purchase price of the home. Two arguments were at stake: first, that the interest of the wives, being necessarily an equitable interest under a trust for sale, was of a sort capable of taking effect as an overriding interest; and secondly, that in each case the wife was in 'actual occupation' of the land so as to protect her interest from the effects of subsequent registration in favour of the bank. Everything turned on the meanings attributed to 'interest' and 'actual occupation'. In attributing these meanings, the courts reached beyond the legislative provisions to the general law, and in so doing were subject to the same sort of bijural ambiguity that animates the forgery cases we have been considering.

At first instance in *Boland*, Templeman J found for the bank, placing a narrow construction on each of the key concepts.[63] Since an interest under a trust for sale was elsewhere in the Land Registration Act 1925 defined as a minor interest,[64] his Lordship made a categorical argument to hold that it could not also be considered an overriding interest.[65] And having decided that Mrs Boland could not possibly have held an overriding interest, he relied on unregistered title authorities to place a technical construction on 'actual occupation', holding that since Mrs Boland's occupation was 'wholly consistent' with the

[59] LRA 2002 s 29(2)(a)(ii), sch 3.

[60] LRA 2002 sch 3 para 2.

[61] [1981] AC 487 (HL).

[62] *Boland* was decided under the Land Registration Act 1925 ('LRA 1925'), but remains authoritative under the LRA 2002 insofar as it interprets 'actual occupation' and the 'interests' in land which might be protected by actual occupation: K J Gray and S F Gray, *Elements of Land Law* (5th edn OUP, Oxford 2008) [8.2.42].

[63] (1978) 36 P & CR 448 (Ch).

[64] LRA 1925 s 3(xv).

[65] (1978) 36 P & CR 448 (Ch) 453.

legal title offered to the bank,[66] she was not in actual occupation, and could not have protected any interest from the effects of the subsequent registration. The appellate courts drew much wider interpretations, on both counts. The mutual exclusivity of minor and overriding interests was rejected by construing the relevant statutory provisions from first principles: the important point was that only rights 'subsisting in reference' to the land could be overriding interests,[67] so the question whether the wives held overriding interests was to be answered by determining whether an equitable interest under a trust for sale could properly be considered as a right subsisting in registered land.[68] This question was answered affirmatively with argument on the intentions of cohabiting parties,[69] and by reference to the authorities.[70] Then 'actual occupation' was given its ordinary factual meaning.[71] What was required was physical presence on the land, which was clearly the case in respect of the wives in the instant appeals.[72] Indeed Lord Denning MR rejected any other conclusion as manifestly out of step with prevailing social realities.[73]

It seems arguable that these competing understandings of 'overriding interest' and 'actual occupation' reflect differing judicial perceptions of the values underlying the legislative provisions. Take first the intuitive suggestion that, insofar as it preserves static security in respect of family homes, the appellate judgments in *Boland* are sensitive to the value of personhood. Tellingly, in the bank's first instance victory, there was no mention of 'home' in the judgment. By contrast, the opening sentences of the Court of Appeal and House of Lords judgments make reference to the domestic situation of the defendants.[74] Moreover, throughout the judgments there are references which make clear that in each case the wife's interest in the premises was not primarily as 'wealth'. Rejecting the general argument that would render all interests under a trust for sale as interests only in the proceeds of sale, Lord Wilberforce thought that to describe in this way 'the interests of spouses in a house jointly bought to be lived in as a matrimonial home ... [was] just a little unreal'.[75] In the Court of Appeal, Lord Denning MR juxtaposed the wife's interest in the land as home

[66] Ibid 454, approving *Caunce v Caunce* [1969] 1 WLR 286 (Ch) 293.

[67] LRA 2002 speaks of interests 'relating to land': sch 3 para 2.

[68] [1979] Ch 312 (CA) 330, 336–37.

[69] Ibid 329.

[70] Most notably *Bull v Bull* [1955] 1 QB 234 (CA): see [1979] Ch 312 (CA) 330, 336, 341; [1981] AC 487 (HL) 507–8, 510–11. Also given were *Cook v Cook* [1962] P 235; *Cooper v Critchley* [1955] Ch 431 (CA); *Elias v Mitchell* [1972] Ch 652 (Ch); *Hodgson v Marks* [1971] Ch 892 (CA) and *Bridges v Mees* [1957] Ch 475 (Ch).

[71] [1979] Ch 312 (CA) 332; [1981] AC 487 (HL) 504–5, 510.

[72] [1979] Ch 312 (CA) 338, 342–43; [1981] AC 487 (HL) 505.

[73] [1979] Ch 312 (CA) 332.

[74] 'In these two cases a bank seeks to evict a man and his wife and family from their home. Can the bank do it?': ibid 326; '[T]hese appeals ... raise for decision the same question: whether a husband or wife ... who has a beneficial interest in the matrimonial home ... has an "overriding interest" binding on a mortgagee who claims possession of the matrimonial home': [1981] AC 487 (HL) 502.

[75] [1981] AC 487 (HL) 507.

to the bank's interest in its security by holding that the bank was 'not entitled to throw these families out into the street – simply to get the last penny of the husband's debt',[76] and spoke of the bank's social duty to 'recognise the integrity of the family home'.[77] That said, even in the face of clear opinion that the wives' interests could not fairly be represented in wealth terms, there is a sense in which we fail to give full account of those interests by saying that they are protected by a provision premised on the realisation of personhood. The wives had also contributed substantially to the purchase prices of the lands in question. Even if they were not *primarily* interested in the land as 'wealth', it would be going too far to suggest they had no interest in 'their investments' in a financial sense, and this much was recognised in the Court of Appeal.[78] Moreover, in the House of Lords, Lord Wilberforce was careful to generalise the point of law involved, arguing that the issue did not in any sense depend on the fact that the respondents were wives defending a home, and might equally well arise outside the matrimonial sphere.[79] So whilst it seems fair to argue that the judges in *Boland* were not indifferent to the value of personal identity, and that it figured in their construction of the relevant provisions, it might be too much to argue that this value was the major animator of those provisions.

It is perhaps more plausible to argue that the successive decisions in *Boland* laid competing emphases on utility demands and on the liberty of the parties. This is revealed mainly, though not exclusively, in different attitudes taken to the proposition that lenders should be bound to inquire whether there was someone additional to the borrower in actual occupation of land, and whether he or she claimed any beneficial interest in the land.[80] At first instance Templeman J referred to this position as 'impossible' and 'almost catastrophic'.[81] Even allowing for hyperbole, it seems clear that his intention was that banks should be free to make agreements on the strength of registered titles without inquiring behind the register. Insofar as this minimises constraints on would-be lenders, it preserves and increases their liberty in pursuing such transactions; and insofar as it expresses a preference for certainty, and particularly the certainty of dealing with the register, it is consonant with the third demand of utility.

By contrast, both appellate courts thought that the lender should have made inquiries in the instant case, and expressed the hope that lenders routinely

[76] [1979] Ch 312 (CA) 333.

[77] Ibid 332.

[78] Ibid 333.

[79] [1981] AC 487 (HL) 502; Law Commission, 'Property Law: The Implications of Williams and Glyn's Bank Ltd v Boland' (Law Com No 115, 1982) [7]. See M Conaglen, 'Mortgagee Powers Rhetoric' (2006) 69 *MLR* 583, arguing that, contrary to prevailing opinions, the decision in *Boland* was not primarily motivated by social justice concerns. Conaglen argues persuasively that it is much more accurately viewed as the product of 'a straightforward commonsense application of the statutory words contained in section 70(1)(g)' (599–600), to which we would add only that these interpretive applications reflect an appreciation of the values animating the legislation.

[80] (1978) 36 P & CR 448 (Ch) 454.

[81] Ibid.

would make such inquiries in the future.[82] The assumption underlying their reasoning holds it desirable that the existence of any overriding interest be firmly established by the disponee prior to the disposition, in order to avoid losses that might result from the persistence of unregistered interests. In the Court of Appeal, Lord Denning MR had framed the actions required of the bank in this sense as its 'duty',[83] but whether or not there is strictly an obligation to make inquiries prior to taking a registered disposition, the decision to preserve static security in a case where the bank does not make inquiries clearly provides a strong incentive to lenders to take such steps. This incentive recognises that the lender is in the best (and sometimes, the only) position to put in place measures directed at avoiding the loss, and in this sense it is responsive to the second demand of utility. It also reveals sympathy for the liberty of the unregistered interest holder. Where its inquiries reveal an actual occupant who claims to hold an adverse unregistered interest, ultimately a bank might require the occupant to join in the mortgage or waive her rights; or it might forgo the transaction altogether.[84] Each of these options impliedly stresses the autonomy of the unregistered interest holder in dealing with her property: she must consent (and must be given the opportunity to consent) to dealings with land in respect of which she has an interest before the dealing can fairly be conducted. In the event that her consent is not sought, the effect of the priority rule is to preserve static security, and in this sense her liberty is guaranteed.

For completeness we should note that the appellate decisions in *Boland* are sensitive to the liberty of the wives in a second, more general sense. The successive judgments take pains to identify the wives as property holders, arguing that shifts in social attitudes and practices late in the twentieth century had made it likely that both parties in a cohabiting relationship would contribute to the value of the home, and that on this basis both would expect to hold property rights in respect of it.[85] In both decisions we find arguments to suggest that, as a matter of principle, the property rights of the wives ought not to yield to the proprietary claim of another apart from where strictly necessary, and Lord Scarman recognised expressly that this bore on the courts' interpretative duty:

> ... it is our duty ... to give the [overriding interests] provision, if we properly can, a meaning which will work for, rather than against, rights conferred by Parliament, or recognised by judicial decision.[86]

So, we might say in sum that the appellate decisions are sensitive to the liberty of the wives and responsive to the second demand of utility. It is possible too

[82] [1981] AC 487 (HL) 508–9.
[83] [1979] Ch 312 (CA) 332.
[84] Ibid 339.
[85] In the House of Lords, Lord Wilberforce spoke of 'the diffusion of property and earning capacity': [1981] AC 487 (HL) 508. In the Court of Appeal, Ormrod LJ distinguished the facts of the present case from the deserted-wife's-equity cases by arguing that here the defendants relied 'upon their property rights as ordinary citizens': [1979] Ch 312 (CA) 333; and see 328.
[86] [1981] AC 487 (HL) 510.

that the decisions are concerned with (or at least, not absolutely neutral about) personhood, but equally it seems fair to say that liberty and utility were the major values animating consideration of the statutory rules.

Notice that insofar as this matrix of values provides an explanation of *Boland*, and a justification for the decision to preserve the property of the wives in that case, it also provides a lens through which to view and understand subsequent developments relating to overriding interests. Often *Boland* is heralded as a doctrinal high point, a judgment in the interests of social justice,[87] the effects of which have been substantially constrained by the restrictive practices and interpretations that have followed in its wake.[88] For example, later courts considered 'actual occupation' to bear a more restrictive meaning than the basic factual sense given in the various appellate judgments in *Boland*: it was not sufficient that the claimant be physically present on the land, the occupancy must also be apparent or 'patent'.[89] The effects of this development have been preserved in the Land Registration Act 2002, which denies overriding status to the interest of an actual occupant where the occupation 'would not have been obvious on a reasonably careful inspection of the land at the time of the disposition'.[90] Plainly this requirement of patency is directed to the possibility of making reasonable inquiries, and accordingly, although it is a departure from the interpretation of 'actual occupation' in *Boland*, it is no departure from judicial perception of the values underlying that interpretation. Utility demands that the disponee take steps to guard against losses, but this demand is only meaningful where the requisite steps are possible. In this sense the patency requirement is a rational extension of the political choice in *Boland*.

Four observations about bijural ambiguity and values

In the third section above, 'Judicial choice among values in the land registration setting', we presented the decisions of courts in cases entailing the competition of static and dynamic security in the land registration setting as political choices among underlying considerations of human value. To present those decisions as being about values is easier in some instances than in others: for example, in *Lawrence v Wright*, the court was explicit in having regard to value-based 'policy reasons' for its decision; whereas in *Frazer v Walker*, the analysis was technical and formal, with no reference to value considerations. Nonetheless, given that the cases we have discussed were decided against a backdrop of

[87] *Gray and Gray* (n 62) [8.2.101]–[8.2.103].

[88] Ibid [8.2.104]. See generally the description and references given by *Conaglen* (n 79) though there the propriety of this treatment of *Boland* is convincingly rejected.

[89] *Malory Enterprises Ltd v Cheshire Homes Ltd* [2002] Ch 216 (CA); *Abbey National v Cann* [1991] AC 56 (HL).

[90] LRA 2002 sch 3 para 2(c)(i); provided that the disponee does not have actual knowledge of the occupant's interest at the time of the disposition: LRA 2002 sch 3 para 2(c)(ii).

bijural ambiguity, we contend that some light may be cast upon all of them by thinking about them as choices among values. Moreover, since they have been 'core' or 'seminal' cases, the choices made in them are not a matter of marginal significance for land lawyers. Yet, apart from O'Connor's recent work on bijural ambiguity, the matters explored in this chapter have received little attention. In this final section, we make four observations, with the modest aim only of advancing the discussion on the problem of bijural ambiguity in light of underlying considerations of value.

First, in case 'political' is read pejoratively, we perceive no necessary problem in courts making the kinds of choices we have identified here. On the contrary, choosing among the values underlying the competition of static and dynamic security seems to us entirely an apt way for courts to respond to the indeterminacy generated by the bijural ambiguity of land registration systems. After all, if considerations of value bear upon that competition, and the relevant statutory provisions generate indeterminacy, why should courts refrain from resolving that indeterminacy by responding to the values in question? Courts often point to what they call 'public policy' considerations in resolving such indeterminacy, both in property law and in other areas of private law, and so far as these same devices are evident in the cases we have been discussing, they seem properly consistent with this practice.

Secondly, as we pointed out above,[91] because the values underlying static and dynamic security are largely incommensurable, it is not possible rationally to argue that any particular choice among them is wrong or invalid. The choice among values made in *Gibbs v Messer*, for example, is as valid as that made in *Gill v Bucholtz*: any preference for one of those choices over the other is just that, a preference. Given that choosing among underlying values is an apt way for courts to deal with the problem of indeterminacy that bijural ambiguity occasions, and given that no such choice may be impugned as wrong, it might be argued that courts ought to respond to bijural ambiguity by making choices among values openly and thoroughly, and not by disguising their choices as technical analyses of determinate rules. Such an argument might conclude, for example, that the decision of the Privy Council in *Frazer v Walker* ought to have been explicit about the value considerations surrounding the selection of a rule of immediate indefeasibility in that case.

Thirdly, there will sometimes be grounds for insisting that legislatures take steps to minimise the bijural ambiguity of land registration statutes, so that courts are not faced with the sort of indeterminacy that we have explored in this chapter. This will be so wherever there is a sense that the interpretive exercises of courts have resulted (or have the potential to result) in the 'sudden and abrupt rule change' that Pamela O'Connor has described in her work.[92] Such change is undesirable, as it cannot but lead to unpredictability in land law, and

[91] Text to n 19.

[92] *O'Connor* (n 1) 221.

unpredictability is to be minimised in any legal system where the requirements of the rule of law are taken seriously.

Where action is required to minimise bijural ambiguity, it seems to us, broadly, that there are at least two possible strategies. First, a legislature may itself deliberate upon and choose among relevant values and, in doing so, enact an unambiguous rule that courts may then apply in the resolution of the competition of static and dynamic security in individual cases. The strategy appears to have been adopted in Ontario, where the legislature intervened to put an end to upheavals in that province's land law, at around the time that the Ontario Court of Appeal decided *Lawrence v Wright*, by embracing bijuralism in its statute but eliminating bijural ambiguity in the specific provisions of that statute.[93] It is also arguable that in at least some Torrens jurisdictions, this first strategy has been deployed via the inclusion of comprehensive indemnity provisions in the land registration statute; the argument is that by including such provisions, the legislature has signalled its willingness to treat land as 'wealth', and has indicated that values like personhood and disponor liberty are not to be accorded great weight.[94] The first strategy entails the legislature making a one-off choice among underlying values that will then be applied by courts consistently across time to all cases of the same type.

A second strategy entails the legislature leaving courts to make choices among underlying values in the particular circumstances of individual disputes over the allocation of property in registered land, but doing so in a way that does not generate bijural ambiguity. This strategy has been adopted, with respect to forged disposition cases, by the legislature of Nova Scotia in the form of sections 34 and 35 of that province's Land Registration Act 2001. Those sections establish as a default the two rules from *Gibbs v Messer* in circumstances of forgery. However, they go on to empower a court to set aside the first rule from *Gibbs v Messer* in an appropriate A-X case having taken into account a range of considerations that requires deliberation on all of the values – personhood, liberty and utility – that we have discussed in this chapter.[95]

Fourthly and finally, in the event that a legislature does take steps to resolve bijural ambiguity, it seems important to observe that previous decisions of the judges offer a lens through which to consider legislative policy, and might provide grounds for critique. One of the chief lessons from our analysis of *Boland* is that interpretive and legislative developments since the House of Lords' decision in that case are in harmony with the perception of values indicated

[93] Land Titles Act RSO 1990 c L-5 (Ont) ss 78(4) and 155, as amended by the Ministry of Government Services Consumer Protection and Service Modernization Act SO 2006 c 34 (Ont).

[94] Further research is required to ascertain the true force of this argument. Even to the extent that the argument holds, however, the history of vacillation between different species of indefeasibility in the Torrens world indicates that any choice among underlying values reflected by indemnity provisions has not translated into unambiguous rules for courts to apply. On indemnity provisions generally, see S Cooper, 'The Versatility of State Indemnity Provisions' in M Dixon (ed), *Modern Studies in Property Law: Volume 5* (Hart Publishing, Oxford 2009) 35.

[95] Land Registration Act SNS 2001 c 6 (NS) ss 34 and 35.

by that decision. When this harmony is identified and expressed, it provides a justification of the policy of the Land Registration Act 2002, and ought to generate confidence in its provisions amongst the legal community. By the same token, if personhood had been understood to be the major value underlying *Boland* (as we might easily have assumed it to be), so the 2002 provisions might reasonably have been considered a departure from the political choice in *Boland*, and that might have justified some criticism of the new provisions. Either way, the point is that a perception of the values underlying decisions that resolve problems of bijural ambiguity creates a lens through which to understand and consider future resolutions of the same kind.

V

Theoretical Enquiries about Property

15

The *Numerus Clausus* Principle and Covenants Relating to Land

Ben McFarlane*

The Law Commission's continuing work on covenants relating to land makes clear that reform is in the air. Professor Cooke, the Law Commissioner responsible for the relevant project, has recently noted that 'there is a growing consensus that there is no reason in principle why positive obligations should not be proprietary, provided that certain concerns are taken seriously.'[1] The Law Commission's provisional proposal that this change should occur through the statutory recognition of a new form of legal interest in land[2] necessarily directs our attention to a fundamental principle of property law: the *numerus clausus* principle. This principle, long recognised as a core feature of civilian property law systems, has recently attracted a flurry of interest amongst scholars working in the United States.[3] Yet, at least since Rudden's seminal article of 1987,[4] the principle's application to English law has attracted surprisingly little attention. The purpose of this chapter is to put the principle at the heart of the debate about the reform of covenants relating to land. It is not suggested that the principle is to be used simply as a means to reject the widespread calls for reform. Rather, it will be argued that the nature

* Reader in Property Law, University of Oxford; Fellow and Tutor in Law, Trinity College, Oxford. I am grateful to Joshua Getzler for comments received on a draft of this chapter, for further comments received at the Modern Studies in Property Law Conference, and for the very helpful suggestions of an anonymous referee.

[1] E Cooke, 'To Restate or not to Restate: Old Wine, New Wineskins, Old Covenants, New Ideas' [2009] *Conv* 448, 460.

[2] See Law Commission, 'Easements, Covenants and Profits à Prendre' (Law Com Cp No 186, 2008) [8.42]–[8.49].

[3] For a useful summary of that literature, see N M Davidson, 'Standardization and Pluralism in Property Law' (2008) 61 *Vand L Rev* 1597. For European discussion, see B Akkermans, *The Principle of* Numerus Clausus *in European Property Law* (Intersentia, Belgium 2008).

[4] B Rudden, 'Economic Theory vs Property Law: The *Numerus Clausus* Problem' in J Eekelaar and J Bell (eds), *Oxford Essays in Jurisprudence* (3rd series, Clarendon Press, Oxford 1987).

and scope of any reform must pay careful attention to the nature and scope of the *numerus clausus* principle.

The chapter is organised into three parts. First, the definition of the *numerus clausus* principle is considered. The argument made here is that the principle can best be understood by focusing not on its functional effects, but rather on its conceptual underpinning. Second, the scope of the *numerus clausus* principle is examined by considering its varying application to two quite different forms of right: legal property rights on the one hand; and equitable property rights on the other. Third, the impact of the principle is considered: first, in relation to promises by an owner of land *not to* act in a particular way (negative covenants); second, in relation to promises by an owner of land *to* act in a particular way (positive covenants).

The *numerus clausus* principle

Definition

The *numerus clausus* principle is generally said to dictate that there is a fixed or closed list of property rights:[5] a right can be given proprietary status only if its content matches that of a right already admitted to the list. The principle can thus be seen to limit the power of A, a holder of property. A, whilst retaining his right to a thing, may reach an agreement with B that B is to have a particular right in relation to that thing. A and B may agree that B's right is to be enforceable not only against A, but also against third parties. If, however, the content of B's right does not match that of a right already included on the list of property rights, it will not have the effect desired by A and B.

The case of *Hill v Tupper*[6] provides an example of the principle's operation. A held an estate in the Basingstoke Canal. A made a contractual promise to B that he would have the exclusive right to put pleasure boats on the canal, and to hire out those boats. X, the landlord of an inn adjoining the canal, then also started to hire out pleasure boats on the canal. B claimed that X had thereby committed a wrong against B: X had 'wrongfully and unjustly disturbed … [B] in his possession, use and enjoyment' of the 'right and liberty' granted to B by A. The Exchequer Chamber rejected B's claim. It was held that, whilst the contract between A and B gave B a right against A, it gave B 'no right of action in his own name for any infringement of the supposed exclusive right'.[7] So, whilst X had interfered with A's right to exclusive possession of the canal, and had thus committed a wrong against A, X had committed no wrong against B.

[5] See eg W Swadling, 'Property' in Burrows (ed), *English Private Law* (2nd edn OUP, Oxford 2007) [4.09] and [4.129]. See too W Swadling, 'Opening the *Numerus Clausus*' (2000) 116 *LQR* 358.

[6] (1863) 2 H & C 122, 159 ER 51.

[7] Ibid 127.

It had been argued for B that: (i) if A had instead given B 'a right to cut turves, or to fish or to hunt [on A's land]' then any party interfering with such a right would have committed a wrong against B; and (ii) the right given to B by A was analogous to such a profit à prendre. Pollock CB's answer to that contention was curt:

> The answer is, the law will not allow it ...A new species of incorporeal hereditament cannot be created at the will and pleasure of the owner of property, but he must be content to accept the estate and the right to dispose of it subject to the law as settled by decisions or controlled by Act of Parliament.[8]

The *numerus clausus* principle may thus be seen to have two aspects. First, as we have seen, it operates as a limitation on A's power to create property rights. Second, it similarly limits the powers of a court: to adopt a term used by Merrill and Smith, it can operate as a form of 'judicial self-governance'.[9] This aspect of the rule can be clearly seen in English land law: whilst the Law of Property Act 1925 section 1 sets out a closed list of legal estates and interests in land, section 4(1) of the same Act, on a natural reading at least,[10] limits the list of permissible equitable interests in land to those existing before the coming into force of the Act. This second aspect of the rule's operation thus reduces, whilst not eliminating, an ambiguity in the description of the first aspect: when determining if the content of a right held by B 'matches' the content of an existing form of property right, a judge must look for, at least, a very close analogy to an admitted form of property right.[11]

Justification

In *Hill v Tupper*, the court made no explicit reference to the *numerus clausus* principle. Indeed, in common law jurisdictions at least, judges rarely, if ever, directly invoke the principle. Nonetheless, a tacit acceptance of the principle in common law decision-making has been demonstrated in academic surveys undertaken by, for example, Rudden (a general comparative study),[12] Edgeworth (focusing on Australia)[13] and Merrill and Smith (focusing on the United States).[14] The recognition of the principle by commentators, however, does not imply

[8] (1863) 2 H & C 122, 159 ER 51, 127–28.

[9] T W Merrill and H E Smith, 'Optimal Standardization in the Law of Property: The *Numerus Clausus* Principle' (2000–01) 110 *Yale LJ* 3, 9, 58–68.

[10] See A Briggs, 'Contractual Licences: A Reply' [1983] *Conv* 285, 290.

[11] This ambiguity in the operation of the principle is particularly clear when considering the content of easements: whilst the list of permissible easements has been said not to be closed, it cannot be considered to be wholly open.

[12] *Rudden* (n 4).

[13] B Edgeworth, 'The *Numerus Clausus* Principle in Contemporary Australian Property Law' (2006) 32 *Monash U L Rev* 387.

[14] *Merrill and Smith* (n 9).

its warm acceptance. Indeed, the very title of Rudden's article refers to 'The *Numerus Clausus* Problem': the absence of a straightforward justification for the principle and, in particular, the difficulty of reconciling it with an economic analysis of property law. Commentators, particularly in the United States, have attempted to rise to the challenge of providing an economic justification for the principle,[15] but doubts remain and have been powerfully expressed by, for example, Epstein.[16] In particular, the first aspect of the principle's operation has been contrasted with parties' freedom to contract: it runs contrary to the general assumption that market transactions are the best way to ensure resources are put to an efficient use, with price adjustments used to take account of the imposition of burdens on purchasers of property. One particularly acute question is whether the policy goals served by the principle, such as the need to limit information costs for third parties planning to acquire a right in relation to land, can now be adequately met by the simple device of a robust registration system that protects such a third party, if he pays for and registers his right, from a pre-existing but hidden property right.[17]

Further, the second aspect of the principle's operation may appear to depend not so much on judicial self-restraint as judicial abdication of a responsibility to consider seriously the claims for protection of parties, such as licensees of land, whose relationship to property does not fit within the existing categories of property right.[18] In this way, and simplifying greatly, the principle may be exposed to simultaneous attack both from those who wish current holders of property to have the greatest freedom to exploit their wealth as they wish, and also from those who wish to press the claims of more vulnerable parties who do not have the means to acquire a currently recognised form of property right.[19]

One approach to finding a justification for the principle, popular amongst economic theorists, is to look to the *effects* of the principle. For example, Hansmann and Kraakman begin their analysis of the principle by stating that:

> Property rights differ from contract rights in that a property right in an asset, unlike a contract right, can be enforced against subsequent transferees of other rights in the asset.[20]

[15] See eg *Merrill and Smith* (n 9); H Hansman and R Kraakman, 'Property, Contract, and Verification: The *Numerus Clausus* Problem and the Divisibility of Rights' (2002) 31 *J Legal Studies* S373; M Heller, 'The Tragedy of the Anticommons: Property in the Transition from Marx to Markets' (1998) 111 *Harvard L R* 621.

[16] See eg R Epstein, 'Notice and Freedom of Contract in the Law of Servitudes' (1981–2) 55 *S Cal L Rev* 1353; *Edgeworth* (n 13).

[17] This question is raised by Edgeworth (n 13).

[18] See eg K J Gray and S F Gray, 'The Rhetoric of Realty' in J Getzler (ed), *Rationalizing Property, Equity and Trusts: Essays in Honour of Edward Burn* (LexisNexis Butterworths, London 2003) 222; K J Gray and S F Gray, *Elements of Land Law* (4th edn OUP, Oxford 2005) [2.53]–[2.55].

[19] See eg C J Berger and J C Williams, *Property: Land Ownership and Use* (4th edn New York, 1997) 211.

[20] *Hansman and Kraakman* (n 15) S374.

On this view, the crucial effect of the principle is that it limits the burdens that may be imposed on a particular asset. It is important, however, to distinguish between two particular effects, each of which is commonly attributed to property rights. Penner, for example, has usefully contrasted 'trespassory' and 'successor' versions of rights *in rem*.[21] The question of 'successor' liability, of whether B's right could 'run with' a particular asset, is the one identified by Hansmann and Kraakman; however, that issue was not at stake in, for example, *Hill v Tupper*.[22] Rather, the issue was whether X, a party who had acquired no right from A, could be subject to a 'trespassory' liability for interfering with B's use of A's land. The role of the *numerus clausus* principle in limiting such tortious liability may be crucial to its justification.

Such a justification of the principle can be built not on its effects, but rather on its conceptual underpinning. A focus on this 'trespassory' liability suggests that the rationality of the *numerus clausus* principle may lie, at least in part, in the fact that it is an application of a wider and very simple principle: it is not generally the case that an agreement between A and B, or indeed any conduct of B alone, will impose a new duty or liability on X. There are of course exceptions to this general position: A's contractual duty to sing at B's theatre at particular times may deprive X, if he knows of the contract between A and B, of X's liberty to persuade A to sing at X's theatre at those times.[23] It is important to note, however, two crucial points about the manner in which A's contractual duty to B affects X. First, X's duty to B (a duty not to procure a breach by A of A's contract with B) is clearly different in content from A's duty to B (a duty to sing at B's theatre). It is not a duplication of A's duty, but is rather a negative, *ancillary* duty, imposed to protect the positive, primary duty owed by A to B.[24] Second, X's duty does not impose any strict liability on X: X is liable only if he procures conduct by A, believing that conduct of A to be a breach of A's contract with B.[25]

In contrast, if B acquires a property right, then X, along with the rest of the world, comes under the same prima facie duty to B; and X can be strictly liable for a breach of that duty. The acquisition of a property right thus provides the most striking exception to the general rule that an agreement between A and B, or indeed any conduct of B alone, cannot impose a new duty or liability on X. For example, the unilateral action of B in taking possession of a physical thing may impose a new duty on X, owed to B, not to interfere with that thing, whether or not X knows of B's action. In this case, in contrast to the contractual example, B's conduct imposes the same prima facie duty on the

[21] J Penner, 'Duty and Liability in Respect of Funds' in J Lowry and L Mistelis (eds), *Commercial Law: Perspectives and Practice* (LexisNexis Butterworths, London 2006).

[22] See the discussion above under 'The *Numerus Clausus* Principle'.

[23] See *Lumley v Gye* (1853) 2 El & Bl 216, 118 ER 1083.

[24] See further R Stevens, *Torts and Rights* (OUP, Oxford 2007) 281; B McFarlane, 'Equity, Obligations and Third Parties' (2008) *Sing J Legal Studies* 308.

[25] See eg *OBG Ltd v Allan* [2007] UKHL 21, [2008] 1 AC 1 [39] (Lord Hoffmann), discussing the decision in *British Industrial Plastics Ltd v Ferguson* [1940] 1 All ER 479 (HL).

rest of the world; and the duty is a strict one. The role of possession as the root of title is very widely accepted, but its effect in imposing a new, strict duty on X requires justification. It is important to emphasise that the primary effect of possession is to impose a prima facie duty of non-interference on the rest of the world: not to increase the legal powers of the possessor, but to limit the liberties of others. For example, even before taking possession of a physical thing, B has a liberty, as against anyone other than a party with a pre-existing right to the thing, to use that physical thing: so, in relation to a bike owned by A, each of B and X have, against the other, a liberty to ride, paint or even destroy the bike. B's taking of possession of the bike does not give him any further liberties against X, or indeed against anyone: it simply removes the pre-existing liberties of X, and others, as against B, to use the bike.[26]

B's taking of possession of a physical thing thus provides an exception to the general principle that B's unilateral action cannot impose a duty on X. It permits B to acquire a property right, consisting in the right to exclusive possession of the thing forever. The duration of B's right, continuing even if B loses possession of the thing, may have to be justified in terms of efficiency: as argued by, for example, Demsetz,[27] permitting B ongoing protection in relation to a resource may encourage B to make efficient use of that resource by internalising the long-term effects of its use. The taking of possession, of course, is not the only means by which B can acquire such a property right: A, a party who already has such a right, may transfer it to B. This provides a further exception to the general rule that A and B's conduct may not impose a new duty on X. The exception is, however, very limited in its effect on X: X's duty of non-interference with the physical thing simply shifts from A to B.[28]

In contrast, if A is permitted to retain his legal property right *and* to grant B such a right, this will have the effect, as Rudden has noted, of 'cloning claims'[29] and thus multiplying duties: in addition to his existing duty to A, X will come under a new duty to B.[30] The point is that X's pre-existing duty of non-interference is a duty owed to A: the acquisition of a further property right by B has a detrimental effect on X as it removes a liberty X previously held against B. The detriment to X in such cases is not merely theoretical. First, the power to enforce X's duty of non-interference is no longer in the sole control of A.[31] Second, the addition of

[26] See eg *Armory v Delamirie* (1722) 5 Stra 505, 93 ER 664; *Asher v Whitlock* (1865–66) LR 1 QB 1 (QB); *Costello v Chief Constable of Derbyshire* [2001] EWCA Civ 381, [2001] 1 WLR 1437.

[27] H Demsetz, 'Toward a Theory of Property Rights' (1967) 57 *Am Econ Rev* 347.

[28] This aspect of X's duty is captured by Penner's notion of a 'duty *in rem*': X's duty relates to a particular resource, and is not specific to the current holder of that resource: see J Penner, *The Idea of Property in Law* (OUP, Oxford 1997) 26–28.

[29] *Rudden* (n 4) 251–52.

[30] It should be noted that such a multiplication of duties will occur if B acquires actual possession of A's thing; but, in such a case, that multiplication depends on the fact of B's possession (and so can be justified on the basis discussed above) and not on A's exercise of a power to give B a right.

[31] This point was important in *Manchester Airport plc v Dutton* [2000] QB 133 (CA). It was clear that Mr Dutton owed a duty to A, the freehold owner of the land, not to remain on that land. It may, however, have been the case that A (the National Trust) would have been reluctant to bring

a duty to B exposes X, should he interfere with the thing, to a liability to pay damages as compensation for consequential loss suffered by B: such loss may go beyond any consequential loss suffered by A.[32] These concerns about the cloning of claims are clearly present in the reasoning of the court in *Hill v Tupper*, and also in the decision in *Stockport Waterworks Co v Potter*.[33] In that case, the majority explicitly refused to accept Bramwell B's argument that, given that X had in any case committed a wrong against A (a riparian owner) by polluting a river, X could not object to paying compensation to B, a non-riparian owner who had been granted rights by A and suffered loss as a result of the pollution.

The scope of the *numerus clausus* principle

Legal property rights

The analysis in the previous section suggests that Rudden was quite right to note that the *numerus clausus* principle conflicts with the starting point of economic analysis. Whereas such analysis demands specific reasons why A's power to create new property rights should be limited, the rationale of the *numerus clausus* instead requires compelling reasons to be found *before* A is given the power to add to the duties owed by X. As a starting point, it can be argued that, if B can acquire a particular right through his own, independent action (as by taking possession of a physical thing), then it should be possible for A to grant B such a right. The logic here is that a new duty can be imposed on X not simply because of A and B's intention to impose such a duty, but rather because the law has already acknowledged that, where B's right to use a thing has a particular content, the rest of the world is under a prima facie duty to B.

It is important to emphasise the limited consequences of the idea that A may have a power to grant B any property right that B could in any case acquire through his own, independent conduct. In relation to things other than land, the only right that can be independently acquired is itself a right to exclusive possession forever.[34] It seems, then, that when we move away from that core

proceedings to remove Mr Dutton and his fellow environmental protestors. The claimants, to whom A had given a licence to use the land, had no such hesitation in seeking to remove those protestors.

[32] This point was important in *Colour Quest Ltd v Total Downstream UK plc* [2010] EWCA Civ 180, [2010] 3 All ER 793 *sub nom Shell UK Ltd v Total UK Ltd* [2010] EWCA Civ 180, [2010] 3 All ER 793. It was clear that the defendants had a duty to compensate A, the freehold owner of the land, for any loss caused to A as a result of the defendants' interference with A's land. The question for the Court of Appeal was whether the defendants also owed a duty to B (a beneficiary of a trust of A's freehold) and so could be liable to pay for consequential loss suffered by B, and not by A.

[33] (1864) 3 H & C 300, 159 ER 545.

[34] For discussion of this point, see B McFarlane, *The Structure of Property Law* (Hart Publishing, Oxford 2008) 144–46. In relation to land, it seems that rules on prescription allow for the independent acquisition of an easement or profit à prendre; although the courts, of course, explain such rules as resting on a fictional grant by an owner of the servient land.

property right, it is difficult, if not impossible, to find a principled reason for the recognition of the right. Instead, the question becomes one of pure policy: is overall utility increased if the particular right claimed by B, such as a right of way over A's land, imposes a duty not only on A but also, prima facie, on the rest of the world? If so, A may then have the power to grant B such a property right; if not then, whatever the intentions of A and B, A's duty to B will not be shared by the rest of the world.

This brings us back to the two core aspects of the *numerus clausus* principle. First, A and B's intention that A's duty should also bind the rest of the world cannot, by itself, impose such a duty on third parties. As noted by Merrill and Smith,[35] A and B's creation of a duty prima facie binding the rest of the world creates externalities: not only is a previous liberty of X as against B removed, but information costs are increased for all other parties who may plan to act in regard to a particular thing and are therefore required to check if any party other than an owner has a property right in that thing. As Rose has put it, 'a property regime is "in rem", affecting not only the immediate owners but also the world around them – and the rest of the world may have something to say about [the] costs and benefits.'[36]

The second aspect of the *numerus clausus* principle concerns the powers not of the parties but of judges. It is unlikely that a particular court is best placed to perform the calculation as to whether the legal system is, overall, improved if a particular right is recognised as a property right. The question will, by definition, concern parties not before the court. Whilst a legislative recognition of a new form of property right can deal with those and other matters, judges are not as well placed to deal with this example of the 'problem of partial reform'.[37] This does not mean, however, that the *numerus clausus* principle should be used as an excuse for judges not properly to consider the claim that B's right should count as a property right. If a particular form of right, such as an easement, has been accepted as a property right, then it is appropriate for judges to reason analogically and to ask, for example, if an easement of parking is sufficiently analogous to existing forms of easements.[38] Indeed, Raz identifies such analogical thinking as a response to the very problem of partial reform.[39] Gray and Gray's concern that an unthinking application of the *numerus clausus* principle may lead to an abdication of judicial responsibility is, therefore, an important one. Equally urgent, however, is the need for the courts carefully to justify why, as an exception to the general rule, A's being under a duty to B leads to the rest of the world also being under a prima facie duty to B.

[35] *Merrill and Smith* (n 9).

[36] C Rose, 'Servitudes' (2009), Research Frontiers in Law and Economics, Arizona Legal Studies Discussion Paper No 09–13 <http://papers.ssrn.com/sol3/papers.cfm?abstract_id=137125158> accessed 29 September 2010.

[37] See J Raz, *The Authority of Law: Essays on Law and Morality* (OUP, Oxford 1979) 200.

[38] See eg *London & Blenheim Estates v Ladbroke Retail Parks* [1992] 1 WLR 1278 (Ch); *Moncrieff v Jamieson* [2007] 1 WLR 2620 (HL).

[39] Raz (n 37) 200.

Equitable property rights

The analysis above suggests a clear rationale for having a closed list of legal property rights. There may be a conceptual argument as to why the rest of the world should be under a prima facie duty to a possessor of a physical thing; but there is no such argument as to why A should have a power to grant to B any other form of property right. Rather, the question is whether the beneficial consequences of allowing A to have such a power outweigh the adverse consequences to X. In relation to equitable property rights, however, the picture appears to be rather different. It seems that B will acquire an equitable property right whenever A is under a duty to B, provided that duty relates to a specific, distinct claim-right or power held by A.[40] If A is under such a duty, the rest of the world comes under a prima facie liability to B: *if* X acquires A's right, or a right that depends on A's right then, *if* X acquires knowledge of A's prior duty whilst still holding that right or its product, X comes under a duty to B.[41]

On this view, developed in more detail elsewhere,[42] the concept of a duty-burdened right is central to both the definition and operation of equitable property rights. For example, if A declares a trust of a right, it is not the case that A separates out his pre-existing property right into a legal property right, now held by A as trustee, and an equitable property right, held by the beneficiary. After all, A can declare a trust of any form of right, even if it is a non-assignable personal right.[43] The Court of Appeal's analysis of the concept of an equitable lease in *Hammersmith & Fulham LBC v Alexander-David* is also of interest.[44] A, the local authority, had entered into a standard-form tenancy agreement with B, a minor. B argued that, as B could not hold a legal estate in the land, the purported grant operated as a declaration of trust and that, as a trustee, A was under particular duties to B. A argued that there was no room for a trust, as the occupation agreement instead operated as a grant of an equitable tenancy. That argument was rejected: Sullivan LJ, adopting a submission of counsel for the occupier, held that 'a landlord does not elect to grant an equitable tenancy; such a tenancy arises in certain specified circumstances, recognised by equity'.[45] This analysis is consistent with the view that, whilst a legal lease depends on a

[40] It seems that, if A's right is, in Hohfeld's terminology (see eg W N Hohfeld, *Fundamental Legal Conceptions as Applied in Judicial Reasoning* (Yale University Press, New Haven, 1946)), a liberty or immunity, then B cannot acquire an equitable property right in relation to A's right: see below, text at n 64.

[41] The limited nature of liability in knowing receipt (see eg *BCCI v Akindele* [2001] Ch 437 (CA)) demonstrates that X is not under a duty to B if X acquires knowledge of A's prior duty only after parting with the initial right or its product.

[42] See eg B McFarlane (n 34) 206–28, B McFarlane and R Stevens, 'The Nature of Equitable Property' (2010) 4 *Journal of Equity* 1.

[43] See eg *Don King v Warren* [2000] Ch 291 (CA); *Barbados Trust Company Ltd v Bank of Zambia* [2007] EWCA Civ 148, [2007] 2 All ER (Comm) 445 [43].

[44] [2009] EWCA Civ 259, [2010] 2 WLR 1126.

[45] Ibid [30].

grant by A (an actual or implied exercise of A's power to create a legal lease), an equitable lease instead arises where, due to A's conduct, A is under a duty to grant B a lease.

On this view, the *numerus clausus* principle does not, strictly speaking, apply to regulate the content of equitable property rights; there is no need for such a principle, as the content of such rights can be directly determined by applying a conceptual test. It is of course the case that the various forms of equitable property rights permitted by this principle can be grouped according to their content, and a list of such rights can thus be generated. No such list, however, can hide the diversity in the content of equitable property rights, particularly in those that may arise under a trust. In contrast to the position with legal property rights other than the right to exclusive possession forever, there is no need to undertake a consequentialist analysis of a claimed equitable property right in order to see if that right should be admitted to the list. Of course, this does not detract from the fact that, whenever B acquires an equitable property right as a result of A's conduct, an exception is made to the general principle that the conduct of A and B cannot, by itself, impose a new duty *or liability* on X. There is a higher level question as to whether the very existence of equitable property rights can be justified conceptually,[46] or whether it instead depends on the consequential advantages of recognising such rights.

The disadvantages caused to X by the recognition of the institution of equitable property rights must, of course, be compared to the advantages entailed by the existence of such rights. It is worth noting that the trust, in particular, is a form that has been greatly admired, not least by non-common law jurisdictions wishing to capture some of its benefits. The flexibility permitted by equitable property rights may be particularly appealing: as Worthington has noted, such rights allow for the distribution and fragmentation of the benefits of a particular right in ways that cannot be achieved by manipulation of the limited list of legal property rights.[47] In this way, equitable property rights can be used as a response to the closed list of legal property rights. For example, under the provisions of the Law of Property Act 1925, A has no power to divide his freehold into a succession of separate legal estates in land; but A can set up a trust under which the *benefit* of his freehold is so divided. This relegation of particular rights from legal property rights to equitable property rights would make no sense were it not for the different operation of each form of right. Whereas a legal property right may impose a strict prima facie duty on the rest of the world, this is not the case with equitable property rights. The existence of the latter form of right does impose a liability on X, but a duty on X arises only if X acquires a particular right and has or gains knowledge of A's initial duty to B.

[46] For consideration of this question, see eg L Smith, 'Philosophical Foundations of Proprietary Remedies' in R Chambers, C Mitchell and J Penner (eds), *Philosophical Foundations of the Law of Unjust Enrichment* (OUP, Oxford 2009).

[47] See S Worthington, *Equity* (2nd edn OUP, Oxford 2006) 73–77.

The impact of the *numerus clausus* principle

Restrictive covenants

Whilst it has been argued that the *numerus clausus* principle, strictly speaking, has no impact on the content of equitable property rights, the development of the restrictive covenant as a form of such right holds a number of useful lessons when considering the more general principle that, in turn, lies behind the *numerus clausus*. The first point is that the decision of the High Court of Chancery in *Tulk v Moxhay*[48] did not in itself establish the proprietary status of a restrictive covenant. As Lord Cottenham LC's judgment made clear:

> ... the question is, not whether the covenant runs with the land, but whether a party shall be permitted to use the land in a manner inconsistent with the contract entered into by his vendor, and with notice of which he purchased.[49]

B's protection in *Tulk v Moxhay* therefore seems to depend on a new right, arising as a result of X's conduct in purchasing A's land with notice of the agreement between A and B. This explains the fact that, in *Tulk*, as in cases immediately following it, little attention was paid to the precise content of the initial agreement: the focus was on the culpability of X's conduct, not on the nature of A's initial duty to B.[50] Restrictions on the content of B's right, in particular that it should impose only a negative duty on A, and that it should benefit some land of B, appeared later, when *Tulk* was re-analysed as a decision depending not on X's conduct, but instead on the creation, in the agreement between A and B, of a new form of equitable property right.

It is little surprise that such re-characterisation occurred. The essential point, which had already been made in *Keppell v Bailey*,[51] and was later emphasised by Diplock J in *Port Line Ltd v Ben Line Steamers Ltd*[52] and Browne-Wilkinson J in *Swiss Bank v Lloyds Bank*,[53] is that X's knowledge of a contract entered into by A and B, and imposing a duty on A in relation to a particular physical thing, cannot, by itself, impose the same duty on X if X later acquires a right in relation to that thing. The reasoning in *Tulk v Moxhay*, like the well known dictum of Knight Bruce LJ in *de Mattos v Gibson*,[54] can be seen as an intervention, on the ultimately unsuccessful side, in a debate as to whether a duty can be imposed on X simply as a result of X's acquisition of a right with knowledge of a previous contract relating to that right. As this debate concerns the circumstances in which B can acquire a new right against X as a result of X's conduct, it is not,

[48] (1848) 2 Ph 774, 41 ER 1143.
[49] Ibid 777–78.
[50] See eg *Catt v Tourle* (1868–69) LR 4 Ch App 654, and *Luker v Dennis* (1877) 7 Ch D 277 (Ch).
[51] (1834) 2 My & K 517, 39 ER 1042.
[52] [1958] 2 QB 146 (QB).
[53] [1979] Ch 548 (Ch).
[54] (1849) 4 De G & J 276, 45 ER 108.

strictly speaking, relevant to the *numerus clausus* principle. The resolution of the debate is, nonetheless, of great relevance to the general principle which lies behind the *numerus clausus*.

For example, it has been argued, not least by Epstein,[55] that a robust registration or notice system can perform the role traditionally allocated to the *numerus clausus* principle and thus permit A and B much greater, indeed nearly complete, freedom in creating new forms of property rights. There may be a sound economic rationale for such an approach, at least in the case of a potential successor in title planning to purchase a right from A, who can then discover B's right and make the necessary price adjustment. Yet, in cases where X acquires a right with knowledge of A and B's pre-existing contract, the courts have considered the very question of whether this knowledge suffices to impose a duty on X; and the conclusion has been that it does not.[56] It is therefore very difficult to say that, as a matter of principle, the *only* concern when considering the content of property rights is as to X's ability to discover such rights.

The second point about the development of restrictive covenants is that their re-analysis as equitable property rights is not free from difficulty. In a number of important ways, the content of restrictive covenants differs from that of other forms of equitable property right.[57] First, the restrictive covenant can exist only in relation to land. It could be said that, for example, an equitable lease or equitable easement shares that feature. In each of those cases, however, A, as a holder of an estate in land, has a power not available to an owner of property other than land: the power to create a lease or an easement. As A has that power, it is then possible for B to acquire an equitable property right if A comes under a duty to B to exercise that power in B's favour: in such a case, B has a right against A's power. The possibility of an equitable lease or equitable easement therefore flows from the fact that a holder of an estate in land can create legal property rights, such as a lease or easement, not recognised in relation to property other than land. The restrictive covenant differs as it is not contingent on any special power held only by those with property rights in land. Second, a restrictive covenant can be enforced only by a party who holds a right in land that benefits from the duty imposed by the covenant.[58] It could be said that an equitable easement shares this feature, but, in that case, the requirement flows from a condition imposed on the content of the legal property right. Third, uniquely

[55] *Epstein* (n 16). A more moderate form of that argument is made by Edgeworth (n 13).

[56] See eg *Port Line Ltd v Ben Line Steamers Ltd* [1958] 2 QB 146 (QB); *Swiss Bank v Lloyds Bank* [1979] Ch 548 (Ch).

[57] In this way, the analysis here supports Cooke's observation that the restrictive covenant is like the 'duck-billed platypus': see E Cooke 'The Consequences of Genetic Engineering' in ch 11 of this volume. Contrary to Cooke's suggestion, this is not due to the contractual origin of such rights; after all, many equitable property rights arise from agreements between A and B. Rather, it is the content of restrictive covenants, not the means by which such rights are acquired, which distinguishes them from other forms of equitable property right.

[58] See eg *London City Council v Allen* [1914] 3 KB 642 (CA).

amongst equitable property rights,[59] a restrictive covenant can impose a duty on X even if X acquires no right from A. In *Re Nisbet & Potts' Contract*,[60] the Court of Appeal held that X, a squatter later acquiring his own independent freehold in A's land, could be bound by a restrictive covenant made between A and B. This decision was criticised by Maitland[61] and, on a purely conceptual analysis of the nature of an equitable property right, it cannot be defended: as X did not acquire a right that depends on A's right, the fact that A's right was burdened by a duty to B can be of no consequence to X.[62] Cozens-Hardy LJ, however, gave a robust and consequentialist justification of the need to ensure that *all* successors of A, in possession as well as in title, are prima facie bound by a restrictive covenant:

> The value of estates in the neighbourhood of London and all large towns, and the amenity of those estates, depend almost entirely upon the continuance of the mutual restrictive covenants affecting the user and enjoyment of the land.[63]

Such a policy-based analysis is, in fact, the only way to justify the operation of the restrictive covenant, as it cannot be reconciled with the general *conceptual* test for an equitable property right. It seems to be the case that B cannot have a right against A's right if A's right is, rather than being a claim-right or a power, a liberty or an immunity.[64] For example, A, an owner of a book, has both a property right in the book and (inter alia) a liberty to read the book. It is of course possible for A to declare a trust of his ownership of the book. It is not, however, possible for A to declare a trust over only his liberty to read the book. If A were able to declare such a trust in favour of B, B could ensure that neither A, nor a third party acquiring ownership of the book from A, could read the book. This limit on the content of equitable property rights may be explained in one of two ways. It could be said that, conceptually, there is simply no means by which B's right can bind X, a party later acquiring ownership of the book from A. For, in such a case, X does not acquire a liberty to read the book as a result of that transfer: as against anyone other than A (or any other party with a pre-existing legal property right in the book), X already had such a liberty. As a result, the logic through which equitable property rights may bind a third party (ie that A was under a duty to B in relation to a certain right; and that

[59] Although note that the decision of the Court of Appeal in *Colour Quest Ltd v Total Downstream UK plc* [2010] EWCA Civ 180, [2010] 3 All ER 793 *sub nom Shell UK Ltd v Total UK Ltd* [2010] EWCA Civ 180, [2010] 3 All ER 793 suggests that a stranger may be under a duty to a beneficiary of a trust.

[60] [1906] 1 Ch 386 (CA).

[61] W Maitland, *Lectures on Equity* (1929) ch 12, 169–70.

[62] Of course, things would be different if B's right was also protected by ancillary duties owed to B by X as is the case, for example, when A is a trustee for B, and X comes under an ancillary duty not to dishonestly assist A in a breach of trust (see eg *Royal Brunei Airlines v Tan* [1995] 2 AC 378 (HL)): no such ancillary duty arose in *Re Nisbet & Potts' Contract* [1906] 1 Ch 386 (CA).

[63] *Re Nisbet & Potts' Contract* [1906] 1 Ch 386 (CA) 409.

[64] See B McFarlane and R Stevens, 'The Nature of Equitable Property' (2010) 4 *Journal of Equity* 1, 12 15.

the right has now passed to X) simply does not apply. From a consequentialist perspective, it could instead be said that the content of equitable property rights must be limited in order to avoid stultification of A's right: B therefore cannot have an equitable property right that amounts to no more than the ability to prevent A exercising a liberty. Indeed, the existence of such rights would raise an anticommons problem:[65] a situation in which parties without rights to use a particular resource are able to block its use by others. On this view, a particular conceptual limit on the content of equitable property rights may flow from a practical concern often said to lie behind the *numerus clausus* principle: the need to avoid stultification of resources.

The judicial recognition of the restrictive covenant, like that of any legal property right other than the right to exclusive possession forever, ultimately depends on a calculation that the benefits of allowing A and B to create such a right outweigh the disadvantages caused to third parties.[66] As to the benefits, the ability of A, a vendor selling part of his land, to enhance his retained land by keeping some control over the land sold off provides a short term means of freeing, rather than stultifying, the land market, and may have seemed particularly important at the time of the development of the restrictive covenant.[67] Further, the negative externalities imposed on future owners of the burdened land may perhaps be compensated by the positive externalities enjoyed by A's neighbours, who may also benefit from the restriction on the use of the burdened land. These effects, as in the case of easements, are linked to the fact that a party's enjoyment of his own land may, to some extent at least, involve some dependence on his neighbours.[68]

It is clear that, even if it can be justified through consequentialist reasoning, the restrictive covenant currently occupies a very awkward conceptual position amongst equitable property rights. As a result, the Law Commission's suggestion that restrictive covenants should be subsumed into legal property rights, whilst made for reasons unrelated to conceptual tidiness, has much to recommend it, provided that the extra costs imposed on A and B by the need to satisfy the heightened formality requirements (including the need for express identification of the benefited land) do not impede the practical usefulness of such rights.

[65] *Heller* (n 15).

[66] Indeed, in his analysis of the anticommons problem, *Heller* (n 15) 674–75, notes that an anticommons is not necessarily 'tragic', and refers to the example of a scheme of restrictive covenants in which each homeowner has a veto right to control the character of a neighbourhood, suggesting that, in such a case, the increase in property values may outweigh the negative externalities of the scheme.

[67] Without it, B may be reluctant to sell off parts of a large estate, for fear that his new neighbours might use their land in an undesirable way. The historical importance of this function of the restrictive covenant is considered by S Gardner, *An Introduction to Land Law* (2nd edn Hart Publishing, Oxford 2009) 181.

[68] This dependence is recognised, for example, by the Access to Neighbouring Land Act 1992, under which a court, if certain conditions are met, may make an 'access order' obliging A to allow B to enter A's land to carry out works 'reasonably necessary' for the preservation of 'all or part of B's land'.

If such a proposal were adopted, it will be useful to make clear, as it seems the Law Commission will do,[69] that the existing equitable rules under which a restrictive covenant can bind a third party are abolished; and also, lest the original doctrine of *Tulk v Moxhay* re-appear, that a third party's acquisition of a right in land with knowledge of a pre-existing agreement between A and B as to the use of that land should not, by itself, impose a duty on X.

Positive covenants

It was suggested above (under 'Restrictive Covenants') that the recognition of restrictive covenants as equitable property rights involves a distortion of the usual test for such rights and can only be justified on consequentialist grounds. The judicial admission of this new form of equitable property right, however, did not extend to positive covenants: such promises by A to perform a positive act were held binding on X only in the relatively brief period, following *Tulk v Moxhay*, in which enforcement was seen to depend on X's conduct, rather than on the nature of A and B's initial agreement.[70] This long-standing refusal to give proprietary effect to positive covenants was confirmed by the House of Lords in *Rhone v Stephens*.[71] Lord Templeman's reasoning in that case has been attacked as unconvincing.[72] Its essential point was that:

> Enforcement of a positive covenant lies in contract; a positive covenant compels an owner to exercise his rights. Enforcement of a negative covenant lies in property; a negative covenant deprives the owner of a right over property.[73]

This may seem to be a statement of a conclusion, rather than one of reasons for that conclusion. A link can be drawn, however, with Rudden's analysis of the different potential effects of a restrictive and a positive covenant.[74] A restrictive covenant clones, in B's favour, X's pre-existing duty to A. Before A and B's agreement, X has a duty to A not to make a particular use of the land. On acquiring A's right to the land, X's duty to A ceases and X would therefore expect to be free to use that land as he wishes. A and B's prior agreement, however, means that, before acquiring A's right to the land, X is also under a duty to B not to make a particular use of the land. A's transfer to X does not release X from that duty to B, and the advantages to X of that transfer are thus reduced: in this way, in Lord Templeman's words, '[r]estrictive covenants deprive an owner [X] of a right which he could otherwise exercise.'[75] In contrast, a positive covenant,

[69] See *Cooke* (n 1) fn 58.

[70] See eg *Morland v Cook* (1868) LR 6 Eq 252 (Ch); *Cooke v Chilcott* (1876) LR 3 Ch D 694 (Ch).

[71] [1994] 2 AC 310 (HL).

[72] See eg S Gardner, 'Two Maxims of Equity' [1995] *CLJ* 60; E Cooke, *Land Law* (OUP, Oxford, 2007) ch 8.

[73] [1994] 2 AC 310 (HL) 318.

[74] *Rudden* (n 4) 251–52.

[75] Above (n 73).

if allowed to bind X, does not simply multiply a duty which X already owed to A. If, by virtue of acquiring A's right to the land, X comes under a positive duty to B, X is bound by a wholly new duty, arising as a result of A's agreement with B. It is not simply the case that there has been a reduction in the advantages to X of the transfer of A's right; rather, that transfer imposes a distinct, separate disadvantage on X as, before the transfer, X had no duty, whether owed to A or anyone else, to (for example) repair a wall on A's land. This analysis may also explain the 'touch and concern' requirement, at least in its application to the land burdened by a restrictive covenant: a binding promise by A not to shop at Tesco, for example, would not give B a right capable of binding X, even if it incidentally benefited a business run from B's land. This is because X's liberty to shop at Tesco existed before, and is wholly independent of, his acquisition of a right from A. Further, the positive covenant is a particular concern given that, as Rudden noted: 'Duties-not are frequently imposed on us without our consent, as in the example just given [of A and B's entry into a restrictive covenant], or by the law of tort. Duties-to are not.'[76]

The basic principle underlying the *numerus clausus*, that a new duty or liability should not be imposed on X simply because of the conduct of others, is therefore of particular prominence when considering positive covenants. Certainly, Rudden is correct to note that the law of tort is sensitive to the distinction between negative and positive duties: Lord Hoffmann gives a persuasive explanation for this stance in *Stovin v Wise*.[77] It can be said that, as noted above, a positive covenant imposes a liability rather than a duty: *if* X acquires a particular right in land, he may then come under a duty to B. The decision in *Keppell v Bailey*[78] shows however that the mere fact of X's acquisition of a right in land with knowledge of a pre-existing positive covenant is not regarded as sufficient to impose a duty on X. Further, the notion that a particular positive duty is linked to the acquisition of a right in land may, as noted by Harris,[79] carry a whiff of feudalism and the 'domination-potential' such a system involves. In the United States, for example, concern has been expressed about the intrusive and controlling nature of covenants binding members of 'common interest communities'.[80] There is a particular risk that the link between holding a right in land and the imposition of a duty to act may undermine one or more of the key justifications for recognising property rights, such as the protection of X's autonomous choice,[81] privacy or independence. As noted by Rudden, this concern is most prominent where X's potential personal

[76] *Rudden* (n 4) 252. The criminal law, of course, makes the same distinction: see eg the discussion in *Airedale NHS Trust v Bland* [1993] AC 789 (HL).

[77] [1996] AC 923 (HL) 943–44.

[78] (1834) 2 My & K 517, 39 ER 1042, 535.

[79] J Harris, *Property and Justice* (OUP, Oxford 1996) 328.

[80] See eg *Rose* (n 36). Rose (n 36 fn 83), refers to Californian legislative intervention to protect the liberty of landowners, even in the face of a contrary term in a common interest community scheme, to keep a pet.

[81] See eg *Harris*, above (n 79) 172–73.

liability exceeds the value of the right he has acquired in the land and so puts X's other assets at risk.[82]

It would therefore be a mistake to see English law's current treatment of positive covenants as unprincipled. It can, of course, be pointed out that positive covenants can bind parties in privity of estate, but this exception is very hard to avoid once the lease itself is recognised a distinct form of assignable legal property right in land.[83] As impliedly noted by each of Rudden[84] and Lord Templeman,[85] if there is an anomaly, it is in the treatment of leasehold covenants. This does not, of course, prevent English law's stance from being criticised as inconvenient. Cooke gives a straightforward example:[86] B sells part of his land to A and A promises to maintain a boundary fence. The mere fact that A and B intended that A's successors in title should also be under a duty to maintain the fence does not mean that X, a later purchaser of A's land, will come under a duty to B to maintain the fence. There are, of course, a number of different devices that may be employed by A and B as responses to the refusal to recognise positive freehold covenants as property rights. Cooke has noted that these devices 'all work, to a greater or lesser extent'.[87] Nonetheless, it may be that the problems with these devices, and the inconvenience caused to A and B by employing them, can be used as part of a consequentalist argument that the benefits of allowing A and B, by entering into a positive covenant, to impose a liability on X, outweigh the disadvantages of giving A and B such a power.

This calculation must be the ultimate test of the Law Commission's suggestion that certain forms of positive covenant should count as legal property rights in land. The logic of the *numerus clausus* principle is that a convincing case must be made before A and B should be given such a power to impose a liability on X. The term liability is used because, unlike almost all other legal property rights, a positive covenant would not impose an immediate duty on the rest of the world; it would rather, like an equitable property right, impose a liability, whereas a duty would arise only on X's acquisition of a particular right in land. As a legal property right, a positive covenant would therefore be unusual; but not unprecedented: a rentcharge entered into before the Rentcharges Act 1977 is recognised by the Law of Property Act 1925 section 1(2)(b) as a legal interest in land and the duty to pay money imposed by such a right is not prima facie binding on the whole world, but only on successors to the party initially bound. The legislature would therefore be free to consider which particular successors would be prima facie bound by a positive covenant, and such decisions could be

[82] *Rudden* (n 4) 248.

[83] For example, it would be difficult to contemplate a situation in which the assignee of a tenant can claim to have acquired his lease free from the assignor's positive duty to pay rent.

[84] *Rudden* (n 4) 252.

[85] *Rhone v Stephens* [1994] 2 AC 310 (HL) 322.

[86] *Cooke* (n 1) 453 (the letters have been changed).

[87] Ibid 455. For an overview of the various devices, see Law Commission, 'Easements, Covenants and Profits à Prendre' (Law Com Cp No 186, 2008) [7.46]–[7.64].

informed by the economic concerns relevant to a consequentialist calculation. In this and other aspects of reform, the Law Commission can draw on the experience of other jurisdictions, such as Scotland,[88] the Republic of Ireland,[89] New Zealand[90] and Trinidad and Tobago.[91]

As is the case when considering if any particular right relating to land should count as a property right, the essentially consequentialist nature of the inquiry means that no knock-down argument can be made either for or against proprietary status. The principle identified here demands that a strong case must be made before a new type of proprietary right can be recognised, especially where A and B seek a power to impose a liability on X to perform a positive act. Two specific difficulties with legislative reform must also be factored into the analysis: first, the general difficulty of drafting appropriate legislation; second, the specific difficulty of reforming a rule that seems to stand in the way of A and B's intentions, and to which a number of exceptions already exist.

The first difficulty is compounded by the fact that, as noted by Rose[92] and also by Lord Brougham LC in *Keppell v Bailey*,[93] the content of a positive covenant is potentially unlimited. It is therefore essential that any legislation precisely defines those positive covenants that will be capable of counting as legal property rights. This task will be far from easy, given the need to come up with a specific statutory formula and the difficulty of anticipating the very varied duties, as 'infinite in variety as the imagination can make them'.[94] It is worth noting that the current US Restatement (Third) of Property: Servitudes, has taken the view that a positive covenant is valid if it is not 'illegal, unconstitutional, or against public policy'.[95] The requirement that a covenant must 'touch and concern' land has been dropped, and the person who challenges the covenant has the onus of showing that it is invalid. In addition, there is no need for the covenant to benefit any land of B: a covenant in gross is permitted, but B will need to show he has a 'legitimate interest' in seeking to enforce such a covenant.[96] The aim, in the words of Professor French, the Reporter responsible for the Restatement, is 'both to allow innovative uses of servitudes, and to encourage a judge who holds a servitude invalid to give a substantive rationale for the decision.'[97] It may be that such a light touch is permissible, and perhaps even preferable, in a Restatement, which is not a legislative instrument and instead aims to set out

[88] For discussion see the Scottish Law Commission, 'Report on Real Burdens' (Scot Law Com No 181, 2000).

[89] Land and Conveyancing Law Reform Act 2009 s 49(2).

[90] Property Law Act 2007 s 303.

[91] Land Law and Conveyancing Act 1981 s 118.

[92] *Rose* (n 36) 18.

[93] (1834) 2 My & K 517, 39 ER 1042, 535.

[94] See Lord Brougham in *Keppell v Bailey* (1834) 2 My & K 517, 39 ER 1042, 535.

[95] American Law Institute, *Restatement of the Law Third, Property (Servitudes)* (Philadelphia, PA 2000) s 3.1.

[96] Ibid s 8.1.

[97] S French, 'Highlights of the New Restatement (Third) of Property: Servitudes' (2000–2001) 35 *Real Prop Prob & Tr J* 225, 233.

a framework of principle that may apply across more than fifty jurisdictions. Nonetheless, the possibility of a consistent and transparent approach seems somewhat remote given the statement in section 3.1 of the Restatement that servitudes invalid on the grounds of public policy *include*, but are not limited to, a servitude that: (a) is arbitrary, spiteful or capricious; (b) unreasonably burdens a fundamental constitutional right; (c) imposes an unreasonable restraint on alienation; (d) imposes an unreasonable restraint on trade or competition; or (e) is unconscionable. A concern about any such ex post facto restraints on the content of covenants is that it is the party prima facie bound by the covenant who must take the initiative and risk the cost of arguing for the invalidity of the covenant, and must factor in the risk of failure when deciding whether to acquire a right in land. That same concern, of course, applies to the control mechanism, currently existing under the Law of Property Act 1925 section 84, under which a binding restrictive covenant may be discharged or modified. Indeed, whilst the suggestion would necessarily reduce the convenience of positive covenants to A and B, an alternative would be to acquire *prior* approval, by a tribunal if not necessarily a court, of the creation of a proprietary positive covenant. Whilst such an approach would be anathema to a critic like Epstein, it would represent a more limited departure from the general rule that an agreement between A and B cannot impose a liability or duty on X, and would allow the interests of potential third parties to be considered in advance and weighed alongside the need for the positive covenant. The proposal would, however, depend on a legislative formulation of the criteria to be applied by any such tribunal.[98] In suitable cases, it might even be possible for a 'buy out' clause to be inserted to allow any future party prima facie bound by the positive covenant to be released from the positive duty by a one-off payment to the holder(s) of the benefit of the covenant. One function of such a clause would be to prevent a positive covenant being used purely for 'ransom' value by its holder.

The second difficulty – affecting legislation that sets out to tackle a rule that seems to stand in the way of A and B's intentions, and to which a number of exceptions already exist – consists in a risk that reform, as well as bringing the difficulties of interpretation that any new Act entails, may introduce a mechanism that serves as an addition to, not a replacement for, the existing set of devices. For example, as noted by Stevens,[99] this difficulty arises in the context of reform to the privity rule in contract law. The problem may be due in part to the inherent conservatism of legal professionals, preferring tried and trusted methods to statutory innovations: this tendency seems to have limited the use of commonhold schemes, for example. The problem may be due to the particular

[98] I am grateful to an anonymous referee for drawing a parallel with the initial position under the Landlord and Tenant Act 1954 Pt II. Court approval was required to contract out of the security of tenure provisions. An important factor in the eventual abolition of the requirement was the failure to provide grounds on which such approval could be refused.

[99] R Stevens, 'The Contracts (Third Parties) Act 1999' (2004) 120 *LQR* 292.

advantages offered by the existing, if complicated, methods. For example, Cooke has noted that estate rentcharges, as permitted under the Rentcharges Act 1977 section 2(4), may continue to be available after any legislative reform of positive covenants:[100] an advantage of such rights, not shared by the proprietary positive covenant likely to be recommended by the Law Commission, is that the party holding the rentcharge need not hold any land benefiting from the performance of the positive obligation.

Conclusion

The *numerus clausus* principle has a number of important practical effects. For example, as noted by Merrill and Smith,[101] it can reduce information costs for third parties who wish to find out what burdens may affect them if they acquire a right in a physical thing. It is important, however, not to confuse an effect of a principle with its purpose. For it is clear that, as noted by Epstein[102] and Edgeworth,[103] the information-providing effect of the principle can instead be provided with robust registration and notice rules. It has been suggested here that the principle is in fact the product of a more general and simple idea: it is not generally the case that an agreement between A and B, or indeed any conduct of B alone, can impose a new duty or liability on X. Any exception to that principle, such as the power of A to create a legal or equitable property right, requires justification.

As noted above (under 'Positive covenants'), the idea on which the *numerus clausus* principle is based applies with particular force to the imposition of positive covenants. It may however be the case that, in carefully defined circumstances at least, the overall benefits of allowing such rights to count as legal property rights may outweigh the disadvantages to third parties. This view certainly seems to have been reached in some other jurisdictions. It may be that the best argument, which also has some effect in allowing the recognition of easements and restrictive covenants as rights capable of binding third parties, is based on the dependence which a party with a right in land necessarily has on the use made of neighbouring land. It is encouraging that the Law Commission aims to ensure that limits are placed on any new power of A and B to create proprietary positive covenants; as can be seen in its plan to reject the use of such covenants to enforce overage agreements,[104] allowing A and B a convenient means of reaching a desired result will not be the only goal of any reform. Nonetheless, the success of any such reform will depend on a careful assessment

[100] *Cooke* (n 1) fn 56.
[101] *Merrill and Smith* (n 9).
[102] *Epstein* (n 16).
[103] *Edgeworth* (n 13).
[104] *Cooke* (n 1) fn 33.

of the reasons for the stance currently taken by English law. In making the case for such reform, the Law Commission will have to show first that the benefits of any statutory reform outweigh the risks it entails, and second that there is a strong consequentialist justification for making a further exception to the general principle that an agreement of A and B should not, by itself, impose a duty or liability on X.

16

Conversion of Contractual Rights

Amy Goymour*

This chapter explores property law's outer edges from the perspective of the tort of conversion. As typically understood, conversion is the principal means whereby English law protects the ownership of chattels.[1] Recently, however, a minority in the House of Lords has suggested that conversion should be extended to protect intangible contractual rights. Acceptance of such an approach would see interferences with merely contractual rights remedied by a tort which has hitherto only remedied interferences with proprietary interests and could have radical implications for our understanding of the range of recognised proprietary interests. This chapter argues that such a development would be unprincipled and is unnecessary.

The current scope of conversion and the case for its extension

Conversion is a tort of strict liability which currently operates to protect legal possessory title to tangible goods against unauthorised interferences. As Lord Nicholls explained in *Kuwait Airways Corporation v Iraqi Airways Co*, conversion has three basic features:

> First, the defendant's conduct was inconsistent with the rights of the owner (or other person entitled to possession). Second, the conduct was deliberate, not accidental. Third, the conduct was so extensive an encroachment on the rights of the owner as to exclude him from use and possession of the goods.[2]

* I am enormously grateful to Stephen Watterson, Graham Virgo and two anonymous referees for their helpful comments; all errors are, of course, my own.

[1] *Kuwait Airways Corporation v Iraqi Airways Co (Nos 4 & 5)* [2002] AC 883 (HL) [77].

[2] Ibid [39].

A defendant who commits conversion must pay damages measured by reference to either the claimant's loss or the defendant's gain.[3] If the defendant retains the chattel, there is the further possibility that the court may order its 'delivery up' to the claimant instead. Thus described, conversion – even in relation to normal chattels – has an extensive reach. Being a tort of strict liability, it lies against someone who has innocently dealt with another's property. This can lead to harsh results. For example, someone who innocently buys a stolen watch as a present might be liable to its owner for the watch's full market value, even though the purchaser acted innocently and made no residual gain.[4]

In recent times, as increasing levels of wealth are held in *intangible* forms, such as bank accounts and shares,[5] the historic limitations on conversion's protective ambit have come under pressure. So far, however, the extent to which conversion has been adapted has been modest. Where intangible wealth is represented by a document, such as a cheque, conversion of the document now attracts damages beyond the negligible value of the piece of paper. The courts have developed a principle, known as the 'face value rule', whereby 'a document embodying or recording a debt or obligation should be treated as having the same value as the debt or obligation'.[6] So conversion of a cheque written for £1,000 will attract that sum in damages. By this means, conversion offers significant protection for intangible wealth. However, it is incomplete: because conversion assumes the existence of a document, the face value rule does not apply to contractual rights which have no documentary manifestation. These 'pure' rights are currently unprotected by the law of conversion; whether they should be is the focus of this chapter.

The case for extending the tort to pure contractual rights was made before the House of Lords in *OBG Ltd v Allan*.[7] The litigation concerned a pipe-laying company, OBG Ltd, in dire financial difficulties. Administrative receivers were appointed which rapidly sold off the company's chattels, and extracted prompt payment from OBG's debtors by agreeing settlements for significantly less than the full sums owed. It was subsequently discovered that the receivers' dealings with the company's assets were unlawful because their appointment was invalid.[8] OBG, by this time acting by a liquidator, therefore sued the receivers, inter alia, in conversion. The receivers, who had not known of the invalidity of their appointment at the time of their dealings, conceded that they were strictly liable for the market value of the company's chattels which they had sold. However, of greater value to OBG, accounting for about seventy percent of the company's assets, had been the contractual claims it held against its customers.

[3] Ibid [87].

[4] See S Milsom, *Historical Foundations of the Common Law* 2nd edn (Oxford, OUP, 1981) 378–79.

[5] See Office for National Statistics, *Social Trends No 38* (2008) 76; and L Rubin, 'Conversion of Choses in Action' (1941) 10 *Fordham L Rev* 415.

[6] See discussion in *OBG Ltd v Allan* [2005] EWCA Civ 106, [2005] QB 762 [76] and on appeal to the House of Lords: [2007] UKHL 21, [2008] 1 AC 1 [225]. See also *International Factors v Rodriguez* [1979] QB 351 (CA) 358.

[7] *OBG* [2007] UKHL 21, [2008] 1 AC 1.

[8] The charge, pursuant to which the appointment was made, did not exist.

OBG argued that conversion should apply to unlawful dealings with these pure contractual rights as much as to chattels, and that it made no sense on the facts for the tort to distinguish between the two forms of asset. The House of Lords was divided, but it rejected OBG's claim by a bare majority, deciding not to extend the tort of conversion judicially and to leave the option of reform instead to the Law Commission and Parliament.[9]

As this area is ripe for re-examination, the minority views of Lord Nicholls and Baroness Hale are significant. Baroness Hale relied on two arguments – a property argument and a comparative law argument.[10] First, she noted that conversion protects proprietary interests in goods. Observing that contractual rights display certain proprietary characteristics, such as the assignability of their benefit to third parties, she reasoned that they too should fall within the scope of conversion. With respect, this argument is unconvincing: it seems circular. Although contractual and proprietary rights do share certain characteristics, other important proprietary attributes are not exhibited by contractual rights – in particular, their enforceability against third parties. Contracts are generally not proprietary in this sense, and will only be generally enforceable against third parties if brought within conversion's protective ambit.[11] Baroness Hale's second argument was that English law might follow the lead of other legal systems, which have already extended conversion to protect intangible wealth.[12] Such comparative material is informative, but is not a compelling reason, without more, for reform.

Lord Nicholls offered a more substantive reason for extending the tort, termed here the 'analogy argument', that all forms of wealth – tangible and intangible, documented or undocumented – should be protected in a coherent fashion and that the law should avoid drawing bright lines between them.[13] Observing that conversion had already made the leap from tangibles to documentary intangibles via the face value rule, Lord Nicholls said that as a matter of substance the law already protects certain contractual rights. It would therefore lack 'rhyme and reason' not to extend the tort by analogy to pure contractual rights. At first sight, this argument is compelling. Indeed, on the facts of *OBG*, it might appear rational to treat the receivers' dealings with the chattels and the contracts in the same way. However, analogies are only as strong as their foundation. Lord Nicholls seemed to assume that the face value rule was a sure basis from which conversion could be extended to pure contractual rights; but on examination, this assumption looks doubtful.

[9] *OBG* (n 7) [94]–[107], [271] and [321]–[322].

[10] Ibid [308]–[318].

[11] For an alternative argument, see P Lee, 'Inducing Breach of Contract, Conversion and Contract as Property' [2009] *OJLS* 511.

[12] In particular, many American states protect intangible wealth by conversion. See, eg, *Thyroff v Nationwide Mutual Insurance Co* (2007) 832 NYS 2d 873 (electronic records); and *Kremen v Cohen* (2003) 337 F 3d 1024 (California) (domain name). See further L Hill, 'A New Found Haliday: The Conversion of Intangible Property' [1972] 511 *Utah L Rev* 511.

[13] *OBG* (n 7) [219]–[241].

The remainder of this chapter is divided into two main parts. The first part examines Lord Nicholls' assumption and advances an alternative view that the cases recognising conversion of documented contractual rights (the 'documents cases') themselves lack a coherent rationale. This finding casts significant doubt on his Lordship's analogy argument for the extension of the tort and, further, may indicate that conversion has already gone too far in protecting documentary rights. The second part searches for an alternative explanation for the documents cases, and suggests that they are susceptible to alternative analysis within the law of unjust enrichment. This is significant because unjust enrichment is well equipped for protecting wealth which is tied up in contractual rights generally, documentary or not. A desire not to discriminate between different forms of contractual rights was central to Lord Nicholls' analogy argument for extending conversion. That concern can arguably be met by relying on unjust enrichment, thereby obviating the need to extend conversion and potentially enabling conversion to revert to its original role of protecting possessory rights in ordinary chattels.

Conversion of documents

This part explores what it means to convert a document, and what lies behind the rule that damages are assessed at the document's face value. In one sense there is nothing remarkable about the law recognising conversion of documents because, as pieces of paper, documents are chattels. Any unauthorised dealing with another's cheque is thus an act of conversion.[14] And just as one might seek specific recovery of a unique vase by bringing a claim in conversion for delivery up, a conversion action might yield recovery of a misappropriated cheque.[15] However, in another sense, documents differ from ordinary chattels because their value lies not in their physical form, but in the intangible rights they represent, and it is these rights which are protected by the face value rule. If the rule has a rationale which is consistently applied in the cases, Lord Nicholls' argument for extending conversion to undocumented rights by analogy looks attractive. This section advances two possible theoretical models for the face value rule but finds that, when tested against the cases, both lack explanatory force. To keep within sensible limits, the analysis focuses on the cheque as a core example of a document to which the face value rule applies.[16]

[14] *Anonymous* (1698) 1 Salkeld 126, 91 ER 118.

[15] *Goggerley v Cuthbert* (1806) 2 Bos & P NR 170, 127 ER 589.

[16] For a discussion as to the range of documents to which the face value rule applies, see text to n 48 below.

Two possible explanatory models for the face value rule[17]

The embodied rights model

In *OBG*, Lord Nicholls suggested that conversion of a document was in reality conversion of a related underlying intangible right, and that the face value rule involves 'equating the value of a document ... with the value of the rights embodied or recorded in it'.[18] However, this immediately begs the question: exactly which of the claimant's underlying rights are supposedly converted where a cheque is interfered with? One theory – the 'embodied rights model' – treats conversion of a cheque as a direct interference with the rights 'embodied' in the document, ie the rights created by the document itself. For example, a cheque handed over for valuable consideration serves to create rights – 'embodied rights' – in favour of the payee and against the drawer.[19] A second, and broader, theory pretends that by interfering with a cheque, one interferes with *any* right belonging to the claimant, whether or not embodied in the document. For example, if the defendant steals the claimant's chequebook, he might be deemed to interfere with the contractual rights the claimant holds against his bank. Whilst the first theory seems plausible and is explored further here, this second theory must be dismissed at the outset. It provides a very loose explanation of the face value rule, which fails to articulate which of the claimant's rights are within the rule's ambit, and so hides as much as it reveals.

The consequential loss/gain model

The face value rule might be rationalised on an entirely different basis: the 'consequential loss/gain model'. According to this model, the document is treated as an ordinary chattel and damages are awarded by reference to the normal remedial measures applicable to conversion claims – ie as compensation for the consequential loss caused to the claimant, or as restitution of the defendant's gain. The face value rule might be a manifestation of these orthodox rules, with the document operating simply as a medium for causing loss or gain.

The implications of the models

If they were to fit the documents cases, either the embodied rights or the consequential loss/gain model might be a launch-pad for extending the tort of conversion. Adopting the embodied rights model, one might conclude that the courts' focus is *already* on the embodied intangible rights, and not just on the document itself. An extension of conversion beyond documentary contractual rights might

[17] See further S Douglas, 'Converting Contractual Rights' [2008] *LMCLQ* 129.
[18] *OBG* (n 7) [228].
[19] Bills of Exchange Act 1882 s 55.

then seem justifiable, as Lord Nicholls argued. Adopting the alternative consequential loss/gain model, one might argue for an extension of conversion by analogy to encompass non-documentary means of adversely affecting contractual rights, such as the unauthorised use of another's PIN number.

However, extending the tort by analogy, by reference to either of the two models, is only justified if the model can explain the documents cases. Yet, closer examination reveals that both models are wanting as explanations of the documents cases. To understand these deficiencies, it is necessary to explore the way in which the courts have applied the face value rule to cheques. The cases cluster around two core fact patterns – differing according to whether the claimant is the account holder and drawer of the cheque, or the payee.

Where claimant is account holder

Take first those cases where the claimant (A) holds an account on which a cheque is drawn, represented by Diagram 1:

If A wishes to make a cheque payment to B, he would normally draw a cheque on his account with the paying bank and issue it to B. B would then present the cheque to his collecting bank, which would provisionally credit his account and then collect the relevant sum from the paying bank. In turn, the paying bank would debit A's account, and the payment process would be complete.[20] If all goes to plan, the cheque payment cycle is a well-oiled machine. However, it runs into difficulties where the cheque is drawn or issued in an irregular fashion, for example owing to fraud or forgery. This is where the tort of conversion might come into play. In such circumstances, the law frequently assumes that A has retained a right to possess the cheque,[21] sufficient to give him standing to sue in conversion any party who deals with the cheque inconsistently with A's rights.

[20] See M Brindle and R Cox (eds), *Law of Bank Payments,* 3rd edn (London, Sweet and Maxwell, 2004) ch 7.

[21] Ibid 487–98. The cases are not consistent on this point and will be revisited in a future paper.

Application of the face value rule

Bringing a claim in conversion will be particularly advantageous to A if his bank has been able to debit his account despite the irregularity. This is often the case.[22] A cheque drawn by A operates as a mandate for the paying bank to pay out on the cheque and simultaneously debit A's account. Unfortunately for A, if the cheque has been drawn by an authorised signatory, it may be rare for an irregularity in its issue to invalidate the bank's mandate. Thus, the fact that a cheque was procured by B's fraud does not affect the bank's mandate. Neither is it invalidated if B, having been authorised to issue cheques on A's account, exceeds the bounds of his authority by writing a cheque in his own favour.[23] Similarly, A might write out a cheque but find that it has been stolen by B before A has issued it to B by delivery. Again, the paying bank is able to debit A's account.[24] In all these cases where an authorised signatory has written out the cheque, the document is valid despite the background irregularities.[25] As a result, A, having had his account debited, has a real financial incentive to bring a conversion claim.

In practice, the most likely target of A's conversion claim is the collecting bank whose liability is prima facie very extensive. By dealing with the cheque, albeit innocently, the bank exposes itself to liability assessed at the face value of the document.[26] However, this liability is greatly mitigated in practice by the Cheques Act 1957 section 4, which affords an immunity to the bank from any claim by the cheque's owner if it acted in good faith and without negligence.

The above has assumed that the irregularity in the issuing of the cheque had no impact on the paying bank's entitlement to debit A's account. However, certain irregularities are so extreme that they render the cheque void, and thereby negate the paying bank's entitlement to debit the customer's account. The key examples are forged cheques,[27] and cheques which are materially altered after being issued (for example, where the payee increases the amount payable from £3,000 to £30,000).[28] If the paying bank erroneously debits A's account in respect of a void cheque, A may seek an order from the court that his account

[22] *Brindle and Cox* (n 20) 576–610.

[23] *Lloyds Bank v The Chartered Bank of India, Australia and China* [1929] 1 KB 40 (CA); *Morison v London County & Westminster Bank* [1914] 3 KB 356 (CA). See also Bills of Exchange Act 1882 s 80 which further protects a paying bank against a potential liability to re-credit its customer's account where it acts in good faith and without negligence.

[24] Even though not issued, the document is still a 'cheque': *Dextra Bank and Trust Co Ltd v Bank of Jamaica* [2001] UKPC 50, [2002] 1 All ER (Comm) 193, 199; as such the paying bank is protected against its customer by the Bills of Exchange Act 1882 s 80, provided it acts in good faith and without negligence.

[25] But if the bank has notice of the irregularity or if the cheque has since been avoided, the bank is disabled from debiting A's account.

[26] *Underwood v Bank of Liverpool* [1924] 1 KB 775 (CA) 795.

[27] Bills of Exchange Act s 24. See, eg, *Tai Hing Cotton Mill Ltd v Liu Chong Hing Bank Ltd (No 2)* [1986] AC 519 (HL).

[28] Bills of Exchange Act 1882 s 61(1). See, eg, *Smith v Lloyds TSB* [2001] QB 541 (CA).

be re-credited. It follows that it is the paying bank, and not A, which normally loses out where payment is made on a void cheque.[29] If the paying bank wishes to recover the money it mistakenly paid on the void cheque, it might sue the recipient of the funds in unjust enrichment.[30] A, by contrast, has little incentive to bring a conversion action which, in any event, would yield no substantial recovery: the courts regard void documents as 'worthless piece[s] of paper' which do not attract face value damages.[31]

Evaluation of the face value rule

Unfortunately, neither the embodied rights model nor the consequential loss/gain model is a comfortable fit with the operation of the face value rule against the collecting bank in these cases.

Take first the embodied rights model, which assumes that conversion of a document equates to conversion of the rights it embodies. The model fails completely to explain A's conversion claim. When cheques are issued for valuable consideration, they generally create rights *in the payee* (B) to be paid by the drawer (A).[32] From A's perspective, the cheque embodies a *duty*, not a right; it is B who holds the rights which are embodied in the cheque, not A. Thus A's conversion claim cannot be for interference with any embodied rights. The only contractual rights which A holds are against his bank, as the bank's customer. Although A's rights against his bank might be *affected* by a misappropriation of a cheque drawn on his account, they cannot be understood as being *embodied* in that cheque form.

The consequential loss/gain model better explains the circumstances in which A has a claim for substantial damages. To recap, this model treats the cheque as an ordinary chattel – a piece of paper – and explains the face value rule on orthodox conversion principles, as either compensation for the claimant's loss or as restitution of the defendant's gain. As we saw above, where a cheque is wrongly drawn on A's account, the cheque is often valid despite the irregularity. Being valid, the cheque permits the paying bank to debit A's account and thereby to cause A loss. The collecting bank will have gained an equivalent sum. Hence, A's recovery of face value damages against the collecting bank could be equally characterised as compensation for A's loss or as restitution of the bank's gain. Some cases indeed suggest that the judges might be thinking in these terms. In *Morison v London County & Westminster Bank*,[33] for example, B had fraudulently drawn cheques on A's account by exceeding his authority as agent.

[29] However, exceptionally the customer's account might be debited if he breaches any contractual or common law obligations owed to the paying bank: *Greenwood v Martins Bank Ltd* [1933] AC 51 (HL); *London Joint Stock Bank Ltd v MacMillan* [1918] AC 777 (HL).

[30] *Barclays Bank Ltd v WJ Simms Son & Cooke (Southern) Ltd* [1980] QB 677 (Com Ct).

[31] *Smith* (n 28) 556.

[32] Bills of Exchange Act s 55.

[33] *Morison* (n 23).

Despite the agent's fraud, the cheques were valid; therefore, as they made their way around the payment cycle, A's account was lawfully debited by his bank, and the collecting bank received the relevant sum. The Court of Appeal found that A had a prima facie claim against the collecting bank for the face value of the cheques.[34] It was conceded that it was hard to rationalise this remedy, but Phillimore LJ nonetheless attempted to do so by suggesting that:

> … the cheques … are potential instruments whereby the sums may be drawn from [A's] bankers, and, if they get into any other hands than his, he [A] will be the loser to the extent of the sums which they represent [*ie a loss-based analysis of the remedy*]. It may be also that anyone who has obtained its value by presenting a cheque is estopped from asserting that it has only a nominal value [*ie a gains-based analysis*] (annotations added).[35]

Accordingly, the consequential loss/gain analysis might explain conversion claims in respect of cheques which are valid despite being irregularly drawn. However, the analysis can only partially explain the results in cases concerning void cheques. As we saw above, the courts refuse to apply the face value rule to forged or materially altered cheques because they are deemed to be worthless pieces of paper. As a result, the claimant is limited to the negligible value of the paper. The 'loss', but not the 'gain', aspect of the consequential loss/gain model offers a cogent explanation for this result. The facts of *Smith v Lloyds TSB* illustrate why.[36]

A had written out a cheque payable to the Inland Revenue. Before it was issued by delivery, the cheque was stolen by B, who fraudulently altered it into his own name, thereby voiding the cheque. The document subsequently made its way around the payment cycle: the collecting bank received the relevant sum from the paying bank, which then debited A's account. Upon discovering the fraud, A sued the collecting bank in conversion. The Court of Appeal refused to make a face value award because the cheque was void, but was careful to point out that A would not lose out, because it could demand that its account with the paying bank be re-credited. The result of the conversion claim makes sense if one focuses on the 'loss' aspect of the loss/gain analysis: A suffered no loss, because its account with the paying bank was not lawfully debited. However, if the loss/gain model is understood as giving the claimant in conversion a choice of remedy between compensation for his loss and restitution of the defendant's gain, the model cannot explain the result. Having suffered no loss, one might expect that the claimant could elect to recover the collecting bank's substantial gain; yet the Court of Appeal in *Smith* declined to apply the face value rule.

It would therefore appear that the courts are uncomfortable with awarding restitution on a strict liability basis where there is no corresponding loss to the

[34] However, on the facts the bank had a statutory defence: Bills of Exchange Act s 81, now Cheques Act 1957 s 4.

[35] *Morison* (n 23) 379.

[36] [2001] QB 541 (CA).

claimant. This means that, to fit the cases, the corresponding loss/gain model must be recast as a purely loss-based model. There is nothing intrinsically wrong with changing the model; however, by limiting recovery to the claimant's loss, it must be recognised that the damages available for conversion of documents become divorced from the orthodox conversion rule that damages are available on a loss *or* gain basis. As such, the model becomes less tidy as an explanation of the face value rule.

Even if recast as loss-based, the model might nonetheless break down in certain circumstances where the cheque is void. As explained above, the paying bank is not generally entitled to debit A's account if a cheque is void. However, if A has carelessly facilitated the forgery or alteration (for example, by leaving a copy of his signature next to a blank cheque) the paying bank might exceptionally be entitled, under the terms of the bank-customer agreement, to debit the account.[37] Clearly A would suffer loss; nevertheless, a conversion claim against the collecting bank would not appear to yield face value damages here because, being void, the cheque is deemed worthless. So even the loss-based model is at odds with the operation of the face value rule. Therefore, neither of the two models offers a full explanation of the rule in this context.

Where claimant is cheque payee

The second group of cases in which the face value rule is applied is more susceptible to rationalisation. Here, X lawfully issues a cheque payable to Y. Subsequently, Z acquires the cheque in irregular circumstances and presents it to his collecting bank. As before, that bank will collect the money from the paying bank which in turn will seek to debit X's account. Z might roguishly acquire the cheque in various ways. For example, Z might have stolen the cheque and forged an indorsement to himself,[38] or have purported to receive the cheque on Y's behalf but pay it into an account he has opened for his own benefit in a similar-sounding name.[39]

Diagram 2:

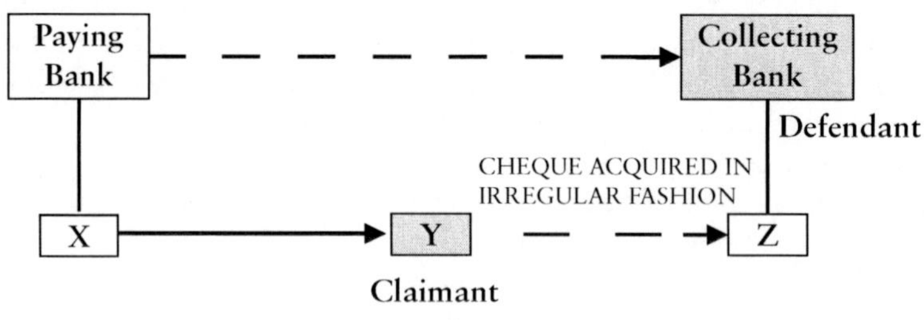

[37] See n 29 above.
[38] See, eg, *Linklaters v HSBC* [2003] EWHC 1113 (Comm), [2003] 2 Lloyd's Rep 545.
[39] See, eg, *Architects of Wine v Barclays Bank* [2007] EWCA Civ 239, [2007] 2 All ER (Comm) 285.

Application of the face value rule

In these cases, Y, as payee on the cheque, will normally have the best possessory title to the document and therefore title to sue in conversion. He may sue any party who deals with the cheque inconsistently with his rights. Once again, the most appealing defendant is the collecting bank, against which a claim for face value damages will normally lie.[40] But, as before, the claim will fail if the cheque is rendered void by Z's conduct (for then it is a worthless piece of paper) or if the collecting bank can invoke its immunity under the Cheques Act 1957 section 4.

Evaluation of conversion's face value rule

The embodied rights model goes a long way towards explaining the availability of the face value rule here. This is because when a cheque is issued for valuable consideration, it creates an obligation owed by X to Y which is embodied in the document.[41] By receiving payment on it, the collecting bank 'exhaust[s] the operation of the cheque'.[42] This makes it plausible to say that by converting the cheque the bank simultaneously converts Y's embodied rights.

Despite its immediate appeal, however, the embodied rights model has an important limitation. As the model assumes that by interfering with the document, one interferes with the embodied right, it only works if the cheque actually embodies a right held by the claimant. This is not always so. Most significantly, a cheque which is gifted – perhaps as a birthday present – rather than issued for valuable consideration, creates no embodied rights to payment against its drawer (here, X) or anyone else when it is handed over. A gifted cheque confers no right on the payee, but merely a power to be paid the relevant sum. There appear to be no authorities on conversion of gifted cheques, but the tenor of the cases suggests that the face value rule would apply.[43] If that is the case, the result cannot be explained by the embodied rights model.

The consequential loss/gain model offers a tidier fit. Take the loss measure first. Whether Y receives the cheque for consideration or as a gift, he loses something valuable (whether an embodied right or merely a power to acquire the stated sum) when the cheque is converted by the collecting bank, so a loss-based remedy would produce the desired result. In such cases the bank's gain

[40] *Arnold v The Cheque Bank* (1876) 1 CPD 57; *Underwood* (n 26); *Architects of Wine* (n 39).

[41] Bills of Exchange Act 1882 s 55.

[42] *Underwood* (n 26) 791.

[43] It would appear that in all of the documents cases where the claim is brought by the cheque payee, the claimant has in fact given valuable consideration for the cheque (see, eg, *Underwood* (n 26); *Gordon v London, City and Midland Bank* [1902] 1 KB 242 (CA); [1903] AC 240 (HL); and *Architects of Wine* (n 39). However, the giving of valuable consideration is not mentioned as a condition for the application of the face value rule; rather it would appear that it is the *validity* of the cheque which is important.

will normally mirror the claimant's loss, so a gain-based remedy would produce the same outcome.

Pulling together the observations so far, it would appear that the embodied rights model is weak: it can only explain claims brought by a cheque payee (Y), and only where he has given valuable consideration. The consequential loss/gain model better fits the documents cases, but it is not all-encompassing. The courts appear to apply the face value rule only where the claimant has suffered loss, and not where the defendant has gained but the claimant has not suffered loss. To fit the cases, the consequential loss/gain model must therefore be recast as a loss-based model. Yet, there is a further significant decision which not even this amended model can cope with: *International Factors v Rodrigez.*[44]

Diagram 3: International Factors v Rodriguez

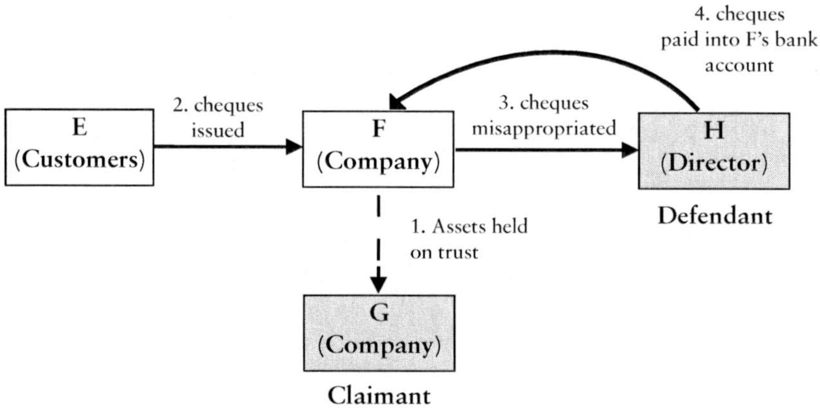

F company assigned all its book debts to G company. The parties agreed that any property sent to F would thereafter be held on trust for G and immediately handed over. Customers of F (E) still owed money, and so sent cheques to F in order to settle their debts. In breach of the assignment agreement, F's wayward director, H, misappropriated the cheques and paid them into F's bank account. G sought to recover the relevant sums. By this stage F was in liquidation and not worth suing, so G instead brought a claim in conversion against H. The Court of Appeal found H liable for the face value of the cheques.[45]

The result cannot today be explained by the embodied rights model because, in a subsequent decision, the Court of Appeal has made it clear that conversion protects legal and not equitable interests.[46] In *Rodriguez,* the claimant G had

[44] *International Factors v Rodriguez* [1979] QB 351 (CA).

[45] Note that the Court of Appeal found that the assignment gave G a possessory right in the cheques, sufficient to bring a claim in conversion.

[46] *MCC Proceeds Inc v Lehman Bros International (Europe)* [1998] 4 All ER 675 (CA). Note that *Colour Quest Ltd v Total Downstream UK plc* [2010] EWCA Civ 180, [2010] 3 All ER 793 *sub nom*

no entitlement at law to the rights embodied in the cheques: those rights still belonged legally to F, which held them on trust for G.

The consequential loss/gain model also fails to explain *Rodriguez*, for there was neither loss to the claimant G nor gain to the defendant H: H had not personally gained, having paid the money into F company's bank account rather than his own; and the Court of Appeal expressly found that the claimant assignee G had suffered no loss. The customers (E) had tendered the cheques in payment of their debts to the original creditor, F. However, following the assignment, E should have paid G instead and, by paying the wrong party, E failed to discharge their debts, which remained owing to the claimant G. Counsel for the defendant expressly argued that damages should be limited to the claimant's actual loss. This was dismissed by the Court of Appeal, which decided that the fact the claimant had suffered no loss was 'no ground upon which the defendant [could] escape from paying damages in full'.[47]

Whilst it remains good law, *Rodriguez* is a final nail in the coffin for both explanatory models. The courts seem to assume that the face value rule is self-justifying, and therefore apply it in a blanket fashion without questioning its underlying principles. This is problematic, for a rule which has no obvious rationale risks producing unsatisfactory results. Indeed, *Rodriguez* might be a case in point: it is not obvious that a party which has received no gain should be strictly liable to a party which has suffered no loss.

Further, without a discernable rationale, it is difficult to predict the limits of the face value rule and, in particular, to which types of documents it might apply. To date, it has been applied not only to cheques but also to bankers' drafts,[48] warrants issued by the government in relation to farming subsidies,[49] share certificates[50] and post office orders.[51] These documents are generally dispositive: they serve to create rights. However, there are suggestions in *OBG* that the rule may extend to 'any document which is specially prepared in the ordinary course of business as evidence of a debt or obligation'.[52] If so, the rule has the potential to be very wide-ranging by extending, for example, to 'IOU' notes or invoices. It is unlikely that the conversion of either of these documents, which are evidentiary but not dispositive, will impact substantially on the owner's contractual rights; and a common sense approach might dictate that substantial damages should not be available. But it is quite possible that, without the guidance of an underlying principle, the face value rule would apply here too.

Shell UK Ltd v Total UK Ltd [2010] EWCA Civ 180, [2010] 3 All ER 793, which accepted that the tort of negligence might protect equitable as well as legal owners, might have future implications for the tort of conversion.

[47] *Rodriguez* (n 44) 359. See also 354 and 358–59.

[48] See, eg, *Lipkin Gorman v Karpnale Ltd* [1991] 2 AC 548 (HL).

[49] *Marquess of Bute v Barclays Bank* [1955] 1 QB 202 (QB).

[50] *Malkins Nominees v Societé Financière Mirelis* [2004] EWHC 2631 (Ch).

[51] *The Fine Art Society v The Union Bank of London* (1886) 17 QBD 705 (CA).

[52] *OBG* (n 7) [226], endorsing A Dugdale and M Jones (eds), *Clerk & Lindsell on Torts* 19th edn (London, Sweet and Maxwell, 2006) [17–35]. See also *OBG* (n 7) [310] and [321].

Implications for the possible extension of conversion

These findings have serious consequences for Lord Nicholls' argument that conversion should extend to undocumented rights by analogy with the documents cases. Problems arise from three different perspectives.

First, from a theoretical angle, because it is hard to find a coherent justification for the award of substantial damages in the documents cases, any further extension of the tort by analogy would be like building a house on sand – as Lord Hoffmann recognised in *OBG*. He said that the current documents cases are 'an insecure base on which to erect a comprehensive system of strict liability for interference with choses in action'.[53]

Secondly, it is clear that once the need for a chattel (here, a document) is removed, neither of the theoretical models for the face value rule provide a precise or coherent practical test for how conversion might work in relation to contractual rights.[54] English law has carefully worked out over the centuries what it means to convert possessory rights to tangible goods. However, that body of law cannot simply be lifted and applied to cases concerning intangible rights where there is no physical document. The current need for a document imposes a well-defined practical limit on the sorts of conduct that constitutes conversion. If we remove the need for a document, it is difficult to ascertain the bounds of the tort under either theoretical model. The embodied rights model concerns conversion of contractual rights via a document. Without the document, the model would seem to render actionable in conversion *any* interference with another's contractual rights. An extended version of the consequential loss model would look similar: that model is all about the misuse of a document which causes loss. If the tort of conversion were extended by removing the requirement of a document, arguably any act which adversely affects a contractual right would be actionable.[55] Under both models, it is unclear what in practice would constitute a sufficient interference.[56]

One particular question that would have to be answered is whether, to convert contractual rights, the defendant must interfere with the rights as a matter of law, or merely as a matter of fact. The facts of *OBG* itself illustrate that distinction. It will be remembered that invalidly appointed receivers settled debts owed to the claimant company for less than their full value. The invalidity

[53] *OBG* (n 7) [106].

[54] Some American states have tried to overcome this problem by extending conversion only to those undocumented rights which are typically 'merged in a documented': see *Kremen v Cohen* (2003) 337 F 3d 1024.

[55] Eg unauthorised use of the claimant's PIN might cause his account to be debited: where the customer has been negligent in revealing his PIN number to someone else, the bank might be entitled to debit the customer's account.

[56] There are also practical issues when it comes to remedies. The remedy of delivery up, for example, is sometimes available for conversion of a document. It is unclear whether that remedy could translate to pure contractual rights.

in the receivers' appointment had an important effect: they were not lawfully empowered to settle OBG's contracts. OBG's legal rights against its debtors were therefore not legally affected by the settlement arrived at by their receivers. However, in practical terms, OBG had been severely disadvantaged: it would not have been viable, in a business sense, to have pursued its customers for the payment of debts which had purportedly been settled.[57] Significantly, the House of Lords seemed to assume, without discussion, that conversion, if extended to intangible rights, would lie on these facts. If so, conversion starts looking like a tort with few defined limits – it would in effect impose strict liability for any factual interference with a contractual right.

Thirdly, these practical problems in turn raise serious policy concerns. When the requirement of a document is removed, the floodgates open, and conversion starts looking like strict liability for causing pure economic loss. When we look across to negligence and the economic torts, we see that tort law generally restricts liability for pure economic loss and confines recovery to carefully defined circumstances.[58] There is a real concern that the law of conversion, if extended, would swallow up these other torts together with their subtle ways of protecting contractual economic interests.

These three concerns mean that we must resist the temptation to extend conversion to pure contractual rights by analogy with the documents cases, however enticing that development might have seemed on the facts of *OBG*. Yet, it cannot be denied that Lord Nicholls' premise for the analogy argument – that the law should give equivalent protection to documentary and pure contractual rights – is logically appealing. An extension of conversion is not the right way to meet that concern; a more attractive solution might be to withdraw conversion's protection from contractual rights (even documentary ones) altogether. For this to be possible, we would have to find an alternative explanation for the documents cases. The next section explores whether the documents cases are susceptible to alternative analysis within the economic torts and unjust enrichment and suggests that the latter offers a rational explanation for the documents cases and, further, might be an appropriate vehicle for protecting pure contractual rights as well.

Alternative analyses of the documents cases

Economic torts

The economic torts frequently protect contractual interests, and so are an obvious starting-point in our search for an alternative analysis of the cases

[57] *OBG* (n 7) [92].
[58] See *Clerk and Lindsell* (n 52) [8–83] to [8–110] and ch 28.

where documented rights are converted. Unfortunately, however, the economic torts do not do the work required. Just two of the economic torts are considered here, the others being too far removed from the context.

Inducing breach of contract

The House of Lords in *OBG* defined the tort of inducing breach of contract as a form of assistance liability, parasitic upon someone else's breach of contract.[59] To be liable, the defendant must assist another's breach of contract, intending this result or knowing that it will arise, and the claimant must suffer actual rather than nominal damage. So defined, this tort cannot provide an alternative explanation for the documents cases. The major obstacle is the difficulty of finding a primary breach of contract which the defendant is alleged to have induced.

Take first those documents cases, depicted by Diagram 1 above, where the claimant (A) holds the account on which the relevant cheque was irregularly drawn.[60] As discussed earlier, if the cheque is valid despite the irregularity, A can generally recover face value damages from the collecting bank. A's only contractual rights are those against his paying bank, so if the inducement tort is to apply, those rights must be breached. Normally, there is no breach: the paying bank is entitled to debit A's account because, the cheque being valid, the bank acts within its customer's mandate.[61] So this type of documents case does not lend itself to analysis within the tort of inducing breach of contract.

A different analysis is required for those documents claims brought by the payee of the cheque, as depicted by Diagram 2 above.[62] Here, the claimant cheque payee (Y) might hold two types of contractual right against the drawer of the cheque (X). First, before the cheque was issued, X might have owed an obligation, for example to pay for goods sold, in discharge of which he offered the cheque. The terms of the underlying contract will determine whether this obligation subsists or is discharged when the cheque is offered. Secondly, as discussed above, the cheque itself creates embodied contractual rights. The tort of inducing breach of contract can only explain the defendant collecting bank's liability if the bank causes X to breach either of the two possible contractual duties he owes to Y. However, this does not happen in the typical case where a cheque is converted. Consider *Architects of Wine v Barclays Bank*, which involves facts typical of these cases. There, Y's cheque was fraudulently taken by a fraudster, Z, and paid into Z's account with the defendant collecting bank, which had been set up in a name similar to Y's. The bank was liable for the

[59] *OBG* (n 7) [39]–[44]. See further H Carty, *An Analysis of the Economic Torts* (Oxford, OUP, 2001) 55.

[60] See diagram accompanying n 20 above.

[61] If the bank had unlawfully debited the customer's account, the customer would require the bank to re-credit the account. It is arguable that the bank has acted in breach of contract. However, it is factually unlikely for the defendant collecting bank to have intended to induce the breach.

[62] See diagram near to n 39 above.

cheque's face value. On these facts, whilst it might be said that Y had *lost* its embodied rights against X, it could not be said that X had *breached* either of its contractual duties. It follows that the collecting bank could not have committed the tort of inducing breach of contract, as strictly defined in *OBG*.

Furthermore, even if we could find a breach of contract in the documents cases, the inducement tort is narrowly focused on defendants who intend to induce a breach. A collecting bank rarely intends or knows about the relevant breach. One case perhaps stands alone as satisfying the requirement – *International Factors v Rodriguez*[63] – but there the defendant was an individual and not a bank. The defendant director intentionally caused the company he worked for to breach the terms of its assignment to the claimant. However, even here a claim on the inducement tort would have failed because, as discussed above, the claimant had suffered no loss.

Causing loss by unlawful means

The tort of causing loss by unlawful means fares no better in explaining the documents cases. According to the House of Lords in *OBG*, this economic tort finds liability where there is: '(a) a wrongful interference with the actions of a third party in which the claimant has an economic interest and (b) an intention thereby to cause loss to the claimant'.[64]

Their Lordships made it clear that an interference is only 'wrongful' if it is independently actionable by the third party. However, in the documents cases, the defendant collecting bank commits no wrong other than conversion. That being so, the unlawful means tort cannot be used to explain the documents cases as an alternative to, and independently of, the tort of conversion.

Unjust enrichment

Whilst the economic torts cannot help explain the documents cases, it is contended here that the law of unjust enrichment can. Lord Hoffmann discussed this possibility in obiter dicta in *OBG* but suggested that unjust enrichment, at least in its formulation as an action for money had and received, could not stretch to these sorts of cases.[65] It is argued here that we need not be as pessimistic as Lord Hoffmann and that, according to modern analysis, unjust enrichment is a good fit with the documents cases.[66]

[63] *Rodriguez* (n 44).

[64] *OBG* (n 7) [47].

[65] Ibid [103]–[105]. It should be noted that on the facts of *OBG* itself, an unjust enrichment claim would not have been available, and therefore the point was not raised by counsel: the defendant receivers were not themselves 'enriched' by the settlement of OBG's contracts; it was the contractual debtors who had benefited from the receivers' actions.

[66] See F Harper, F James and O Gray, *The Law of Torts* 3rd edn (New York, Aspen Publishers, 1996) ch 2.13.

To bring an unjust enrichment claim, the claimant must prove that the defendant is enriched; that the enrichment was at his (the claimant's) expense; and that the enrichment was unjust.[67] Liability is strict, but subject to defences, most significantly change of position. A successful unjust enrichment claim results in the defendant owing a personal restitutionary liability to the claimant. On examination, the ingredients of an unjust enrichment claim map neatly onto the common factual configurations of the documents cases.

Enrichment

The first condition, that the defendant be enriched, is satisfied in the documents cases by the defendant collecting bank receiving money on the cheque. It might appear that the collecting bank merely acts as agent for its fraudulent customer in receiving the funds on the cheque, thereby enriching its customer rather than itself. However, the law of unjust enrichment gives the claimant a choice: he can either sue the collecting bank's customer, as the principal,[68] or he can sue the agent collecting bank by treating it as a beneficial recipient of the funds, which it owes to its customer.[69]

At the claimant's expense

The second condition requires the defendant's enrichment to have come from the claimant. This condition is wrought with controversies. For example, it is unclear whether the claimant must have suffered a loss which corresponds to the defendant's gain.[70] Also disputed is whether the defendant's enrichment must come *directly* from the claimant; or whether it is sufficient for the defendant's enrichment to be causally, albeit indirectly, at the claimant's expense.[71] Notwithstanding these controversies, in the documents cases it is possible to analyse the defendant's enrichment as being at the claimant's expense.

Take first those cases, depicted by Diagram 1 above, where the claimant is the account holder (A).[72] In such cases, Lord Hoffmann in obiter dicta (and without the benefit of argument on the point) seemed to doubt that the recipient of the money is enriched at A's expense.[73] His Lordship gave two examples to illustrate

[67] *Banque Financière de la Cité v Parc (Battersea) Ltd* [1999] AC 221 (HL) 227.

[68] *Coulthurst v Sweet* (1866) LR 1 CP 649.

[69] *Kleinwort Sons and Co v Dunlop Rubber Co* (1907) 97 LT 263 (HL). See M Bryan, 'Recovering Misdirected Money from Banks: Ministerial Receipt at Law and in Equity' in F Rose (ed), *Restitution and Banking Law* (Oxford, Mansfield Press, 1998).

[70] Compare the competing views in M McInnes, 'Interceptive Subtraction, Unjust Enrichment and Wrongs – A Reply to Professor Birks?' [2003] *CLJ* 697; and G Virgo, *The Principles of the Law of Restitution* 2nd edn (Oxford, OUP, 2006) 112–15.

[71] See, eg, A Burrows, *The Law of Restitution* 2nd edn (Oxford, OUP, 2002) 31–42; *Virgo* (n 70) 105–12.

[72] See diagram accompanying n 20 above.

[73] *OBG* (n 7) [103]–[104].

his point. First, he discussed what might happen where a paying bank pays a defendant some money which its customer, A, had deposited, erroneously believing the customer to have instructed it to do so.[74] His Lordship said that here the defendant's enrichment would not be at A's expense. This conclusion seems correct because, by acting without A's authority, the bank is disabled from debiting A's account. Therefore, if anyone is to bring an unjust enrichment claim here, it should be the paying bank.

Lord Hoffmann's second example implied that the same reasoning would negate an unjust enrichment analysis for cases involving cheques. He used the *Morison* case as an illustration.[75] It will be remembered that A gave B authority to draw cheques on A's account. B exceeded that authority by drawing cheques in his own favour which he paid into the defendant collecting bank. The defendant bank was prima facie liable for the cheque's face value. With respect, Lord Hoffmann's suggestion that A cannot bring an unjust enrichment claim here is doubtful. This is because in *Morison*, in contrast to his first example, the paying bank could lawfully debit A's bank account, so any gain received by the collecting bank should be understood as being at claimant A's expense.[76] This is so notwithstanding that it was A's bank, rather than A, which actually made the transfer. Two different explanations lead to this conclusion. First, by making a lawful payment from a customer's account, a paying bank acts as the customer's agent. Hence, the enrichment can be treated as directly conferred by the customer (A), thereby rendering him the proper party to sue in unjust enrichment.[77] A second explanation relies on the theory of 'interceptive subtraction'.[78] Where an enrichment destined for one party (here A) ends up in the hands of another (here the collecting bank), the latter is, for the purposes of a claim in unjust enrichment, enriched at *A*'s expense, even thought the payment is actually made by the paying bank. Significantly, the availability of an unjust enrichment claim here is entirely consistent with the case law. For example, in *Niru Battery Manufacturing Co v Milestone Trading Ltd (No.2)*, Moore-Bick J gave this very scenario as an example of such liability.[79] Perhaps more remarkably, *Morison* itself contemplates the availability of an unjust enrichment claim.[80] It is unclear why Lord Hoffmann seemed to think that unjust enrichment was unavailable as

[74] See, eg, *Rogers v Kelly* (1809) 2 Camp 123.

[75] *Morison* (n 23).

[76] See text to n 33 above.

[77] See C Mitchell, 'Banks, Agency, and Unjust Enrichment' in J Lowry and L Mistelis (eds), *Commercial Law: Perspectives and Practice* (London, Butterworths, 2006); D Fox, *Property Rights in Money* (Oxford, OUP, 2008) 176; L Smith 'Tracing and Electronic Funds Transfers' in F Rose (ed), *Restitution and Banking Law* (n 69). Cf *Hollicourt v Bank of Ireland* [2001] Ch 555 (CA).

[78] See P Birks, *Unjust Enrichment* 2nd edn (Oxford, OUP, 2005) 75–78.

[79] [2003] EWHC 1032 (Comm), [2003] 2 All ER [14].

[80] Both conversion and unjust enrichment were pleaded. Although the decision, that the collecting bank was prima facie liable, was ultimately based on conversion, the Court of Appeal suggested that the same result would have pertained on an unjust enrichment analysis. Cf *Ogden v Benas* (1873–74) LR 9 CP 513.

an explanation for the *Morison* case. Perhaps his Lordship meant that in 1914, when *Morison* was decided, unjust enrichment was immature as a subject and that it was conceived as having limited capacity to deal with cases such as these. Today there seems to be no reason why unjust enrichment would not work.

Before leaving the 'at the expense of' enquiry, it is worth considering what might happen where cheques drawn on A's account are void for forgery or material alteration. Such cheques do not attract face value damages when A sues in conversion.[81] An unjust enrichment analysis leads to the same outcome. The paying bank cannot generally debit the customer's account for such cheques. Hence any money received by the collecting bank is at the paying bank's, and not the customer's, expense.[82] And any unjust enrichment claim against the recipient of the funds should be brought by the bank, and not by its customer.[83]

In the other category of documents cases, depicted by Diagram 2 above,[84] we see the cheque payee (Y) bringing the conversion claim against the collecting bank, which collects payment under the cheque and in so doing exhausts the cheque. Here, an enrichment which was destined for Y, as payee of the cheque, has been intercepted; and a theory of interceptive subtraction might be employed to explain why the collecting bank's enrichment is at Y's expense.[85]

The enrichment is unjust

For the enrichment to be unjust, English law requires the claimant to prove the presence of an unjust factor.[86] If the claimant participated in the conferral of the enrichment, he might call on the unjust factors of duress, undue influence or mistake to demonstrate that his intention was vitiated by the circumstances. In many cheques cases, however, the claimant has no involvement in the events at all. Where this is the case, finding an unjust factor is trickier: the courts have so far failed to articulate the ground of restitution in these cases. A case in point is *Lipkin Gorman v Karpnale*,[87] where claimant solicitors were deprived of assets without their knowledge by a fraudulent employee who ultimately paid them

[81] See text to n 31 above.

[82] *Rogers* (n 74).

[83] By exception, *Agip (Africa) Ltd v Jackson* [1991] Ch 547 (CA) allowed the claimant, whose Tunisian bank had wrongly paid out money on his account, to sue the recipient of the funds directly: the claimant had tried to sue its bank in the Tunisian courts, and failed; the Court of Appeal said that 'for practical purposes' it made sense to treat the bank as having paid away the claimant's money under a lawful mandate. Cf *Burrows* (n 71) 32.

[84] See diagram near to n 39 above.

[85] See text to n 78 above. The technical analysis will differ according to whether Y had initially received the cheque as a gift or for valuable consideration. If the former, Y will lose the *power* to receive the relevant payment (see text to n 43 above); if the latter, Y will in addition lose his *embodied rights* to receive the payment (see text to n 19 above). In both cases, the collecting bank's enrichment can be understood as being at Y's expense.

[86] *Deutsche Morgan Grenfell Group Plc v Inland Revenue Commissioners* [2006] UKHL 49, [2007] 1 AC 558 [21].

[87] [1991] 2 AC 548 (HL).

to a gambling club. The House of Lords recognised that the solicitors had a claim in unjust enrichment against the club but omitted to articulate the unjust factor. Nonetheless, because the claim succeeded, an unjust factor was present, and that unjust factor, however we articulate it, should ground recovery in the documents cases.

Much academic ink has been spilt over how best to formulate the unjust factor in *Lipkin Gorman*. Burrows has suggested that 'ignorance' explains the case because the solicitors were unaware of the misappropriation.[88] More recent work has suggested that the unjust factor should specifically acknowledge that the enrichment occurred in circumstances which were *unauthorised* by the claimant: Edelman and Degeling have recommended that 'unauthorised disposal of another's assets' fits the bill.[89] In the same vein, Chambers and Penner have argued that the unjust factor should be 'lack of authority'.[90] The latter two options seem preferable for they best depict what is happening in the documents cases where the claimant was unaware of the interference with his cheque. Either could be adopted as an appropriate label for the unjust factor.

Conclusions on possible application of unjust enrichment

So it appears that generally the documents cases might be re-analysed within the law of unjust enrichment, which offers a more principled explanation than conversion's face value rule. This insight has some important consequences when related back to Lord Nicholls' concerns in *OBG*. In essence, his Lordship was concerned to ensure that undocumented rights were protected by the law as well as documented rights currently are; his solution was to expand conversion to achieve that objective. However, that objective is arguably already met by unjust enrichment, which protects documentary and pure contractual rights alike. This might relieve the pressure for conversion to expand. Moreover, to meet Lord Nicholls' legitimate concern not to draw bright lines between the protection of documented and undocumented wealth, perhaps we should do the reverse of what he suggests: rather than extending conversion to all contractual rights, it should protect none, not even documentary rights. The tort would then be confined to ordinary chattels, such as bicycles and artwork,[91] and unjust enrichment would do the work of protecting intangible wealth; documentary or not.

Of course, this suggestion can only be sensibly proposed if contractual rights – and documentary ones in particular – would in practice be adequately

[88] *Burrows* (n 71) ch 4.

[89] S Degeling and J Edelman, 'What is an Unjust Factor?' in S Degeling and J Edelman (eds), *Unjust Enrichment in Commercial Law* (Sydney, Thomson Reuters, 2008).

[90] R Chambers and J Penner, 'Ignorance' in S Degeling and J Edelman (ed), *Unjust Enrichment in Commercial Law* (Sydney, Thomson Reuters, 2008). See further Mitchell (n 77) 114–15.

[91] The possible redundancy of conversion in relation to documentary intangibles inevitably raises the question of whether the tort performs a useful role even in relation to ordinary chattels. That question must be visited another day.

protected by unjust enrichment. The next section argues that, in the most part, they would.

Does unjust enrichment give sufficient protection to documentary contractual rights?

To evaluate the capacity of unjust enrichment to protect documentary rights, it is instructive to assess whether analysing the documents cases in this way would produce different results. Six differences can be identified. In some situations, unjust enrichment provides a greater level of protection than conversion; in other situations it is the other way around. In those cases which unjust enrichment cannot reach, it is necessary to evaluate whether conversion is performing a useful function, and therefore whether it should retain a residual role.

First, the *Rodriguez* case applied conversion's face value rule even though there was neither loss to the claimant nor gain to the defendant. Analysed as unjust enrichment, the claim would inevitably fail: the defendant had not gained. It is questionable whether the law should render someone liable in tort where they have caused neither loss nor gain. This is especially so where the defendant is an innocent convertor. The rigid application of the face value rule in *Rodriguez* seems to go too far in imposing liability. Unjust enrichment would appear better-equipped to produce a fair result.

Secondly, substantially different results might arise where the claimant's loss exceeds the defendant's gain. Analysed as unjust enrichment, the claim would be capped at the defendant's gain. However, it is likely that the face value rule for conversion would allow recovery for the document's face value even if the defendant does not gain by that sum.[92] Where the recipient acts innocently, thinking he is entitled to payment under the cheque, arguably unjust enrichment produces the fairer result: why should someone who deals with a cheque without fault be liable to pay back more than he received?[93] This looks like strict liability for causing pure economic loss, which is objectionable on policy grounds for reasons discussed above.[94] It would seem that here again unjust enrichment offers a more nuanced and sensitive approach to liability. The situation might, however, be different if the defendant acts with fault or intention. There, a loss-based measure of damages seems much less objectionable. Indeed, negligence and the economic torts allow recovery for pure economic loss where the defendant acts with a degree of fault. So if we abolish conversion's face value rule, it might nonetheless be appropriate to retain some kind of fault-based tort which protects against loss caused to contractual rights.

[92] This possibility seems to have been countenanced in *Alsager v Close* (1842) 10 M & W 576, 584 and 604.

[93] Of course, this criticism could also be levelled at conversion of chattels. But the point is particularly pertinent in relation to cheques, where the loss looks to be purely economic.

[94] Text to n 58 above.

Thirdly, unjust enrichment sometimes imposes liability where conversion would not. For example, the claimant might negligently leave a chequebook in a public area, together with a copy of his signature. An opportunist might draw up a cheque in his favour by forging the claimant's signature, and then present it at a defendant collecting bank. The claimant's account might be debited[95] and the defendant collecting bank will receive the payment. An unjust enrichment claim would be available; but a claim in conversion would not yield substantial damages because the cheque, being void, is a worthless piece of paper.[96] It would seem entirely appropriate to allow recovery here, subject to appropriate defences. And once again, unjust enrichment provides an appropriate solution. Nothing would be lost by abolishing the face value rule.

Fourthly, a claimant who loses his document might desire its return, rather than a damages award. Conversion can facilitate this, in the form of the discretionary delivery up remedy,[97] but unjust enrichment cannot. Here, unusually, it is conversion which produces the desired outcome. Take, for example, a claimant who has bought a National Lottery ticket and has selected the winning numbers. The lottery rules state that claiming a prize is conditional on producing the winning ticket. Imagine that the defendant takes the claimant's winning ticket. If he cashes it in, both conversion and unjust enrichment would render the defendant liable. However, the defendant might simply withhold the ticket without cashing it in. Here, the claimant will want the ticket back. Conversion can readily secure that result. Unjust enrichment might achieve it but only indirectly: the claimant could argue that the defendant is unjustly enriched to the extent of the potential prize money payable on the ticket.[98] Without cashing in the ticket, the defendant would be unlikely to have the resources to satisfy that claim, and might be indirectly forced to surrender the ticket. To this particular problem, conversion, with its remedy of delivery up, offers a better practical solution than unjust enrichment. Even against an innocent recipient, it is appropriate that a claimant can recover his property. Therefore, even if we abolish conversion's face value rule, it might be appropriate to retain the delivery up remedy for documents.

Fifthly, the bases of the claims in conversion and unjust enrichment are different. For conversion, the claimant must prove a right to possession; for unjust enrichment, the claimant needs to prove an operative unjust factor, but does not need to prove that he still has a title.[99] The rules on transfer of title and the unjust factors are different. It is generally easier to establish an unjust factor than it is

[95] See n 29 and text to n 37 above.

[96] *Smith* (n 28).

[97] *Goggerley v Cuthbert* (1806) 2 Bos & PNR 170, 127 ER 589.

[98] Relying on *McDonald v Coys of Kensington* [2004] EWCA Civ 47, [2004] 1 WLR 2775.

[99] Indeed, it has been argued that the claimant's retention of title precludes an unjust enrichment claim: W Swadling, 'A Claim in Restitution' [1996] *LMCLQ* 63. However, this view seems misconceived: R Stevens 'Three Enrichment Issues' in A Burrows and Lord Rodger (eds), *Mapping the Law* (Oxford, OUP, 2006) 62–64.

to demonstrate that the claimant retains a possessory title against the defendant. The case of *Midland Bank v Brown Shipley* illustrates the difference.[100] The claimant banks had been fraudulently induced by a fraudster to issue bankers' drafts in favour of the defendant bank. The defendant bank collected the sums on the drafts, and paid them out to the fraudsters. On discovering the fraud, the claimants sued the defendant bank in conversion. The claim failed on the basis that the claimants had not laboured under a sufficiently fundamental mistake to prevent title to the drafts from passing to the defendants. Nonetheless, Waller J opined in obiter dicta that the claimant might have had a prima facie claim in unjust enrichment,[101] as the drafts had been handed over pursuant to a mistake of fact. A lesser form of mistake sufficed for the unjust enrichment claim than was required for the title-based conversion claim.

Thus, unjust enrichment sometimes emerges as a broader cause of action than conversion. It might be argued that it imposes liability too widely. However, that risk is averted by the readily available defence of change of position. It is suggested here that unjust enrichment—with its unjust factors—is better equipped at dealing with the documents cases than conversion and that conversion's requirement that the claimant has a possessory title seems to be too narrow. Evidence for this is found in some conversion cases, where the courts, desiring the claimant to succeed, have artificially constructed a possessory right in his favour. For example, in *Midland Bank v Reckitt*[102] the claimant's solicitor acted outside his authority by issuing cheques on the claimant's account to himself. A successful conversion claim was brought against the solicitor's collecting bank. Unfortunately, Lord Atkin's explanation for the claimant's possessory right in the cheque is somewhat unconvincing. He said that the claimant would have sufficient possession if one could say that, had the claimant gone into the bank when the solicitor was signing the cheque, he could have demanded the cheque back immediately.[103] This test is unpersuasive: whilst it is true that the claimant had a possessory right against the *solicitor*, he arguably did not against the *defendant bank* at the point in time when the bank was alleged to have converted the cheque by dealing with it, because it is conceivable that the solicitor had apparent authority to transfer title to the cheque. Lord Atkin's test perhaps reveals that it might be appropriate to abandon questions of possessory title to pieces of paper in these cases: a more open inquiry into whether the defendant has been unjustly enriched at the claimant's expense might be preferable.

Finally, the two types of claim attract markedly different defences. It is generally easier to defend a claim framed as unjust enrichment than conversion. A conversion claim normally succeeds in the documents cases unless the

[100] *Midland Bank v Brown Shipley* [1991] 2 All ER 690 (Com Ct). See also *Perpetual Trustees Australia Ltd v Heperu* [2009] NSWCA 84.

[101] *Midland Bank* (n 100) 585. The unjust enrichment claim would nonetheless have failed owing to the defendant's change of position.

[102] *Midland Bank v Reckitt* [1933] AC 1 (HL).

[103] Ibid 14.

defendant has the protection of the Cheques Act 1957. The most important provision for these purposes is section 4 which, it will be remembered, protects a bank which collects money on a cheque in good faith and without negligence. Defendants which are not banks do not enjoy this protection. Contrast that with the unjust enrichment claim, which is defeated by a number of defences, most significantly change of position,[104] which is available when a recipient has changed its position in good faith as a result of the enrichment.[105] Currently this defence is unavailable against a conversion claim.[106] Further, the section 4 defence applies to claims brought in unjust enrichment as it does to conversion. The differing availability of the defences has a significant impact on the likely success of the two types of claim. To see why, it is instructive to consider separately claims brought against collecting banks and claims against other recipients.

We should consider first the collecting bank's position. It is protected from liability in conversion by section 4. This defence is both narrower and broader than change of position. On the one hand, the change of position defence is narrower because it requires the defendant to have actually changed its position. This can be contrasted with the section 4 defence which protects the collecting bank even if it retains the money received and has not otherwise prejudicially altered its position. On the other hand, the section 4 defence is narrower because it is defeated by the bank's negligence, whereas change of position and the agent's defence are not.[107] These differences mean that if the documents cases are recast as unjust enrichment liability then, if it has paid the money away, the bank could get away with negligence, whereas it could not if the claim was in conversion. That might not be desirable: arguably, the policy behind section 4 is that banks only deserve protection from liability (of whatever sort) where they act without negligence. This problem, however, need not inhibit an unjust enrichment analysis of the documents cases. If we want to uphold the policy concerns of section 4, we could adjust the operation of the change of position defence where banks are concerned such that they are disqualified from its operation if negligent.

We should then consider those claims which arise outside the banking context. Here, where the claim is framed as conversion, the defendant has no defence if he has changed his position, however innocent he might have been. If the claim is framed as unjust enrichment, he does. Therefore a re-conceptualisation of

[104] Also relevant is the defence of 'payment over by an agent' which arises, in the agency context, on similar grounds to change of position: E Bant, *The Change of Position Defence* (Hart Publishing, Oxford 2009) ch 3.

[105] *Lipkin Gorman* (n 48).

[106] *Test Claimants in the FII Group Litigation v HM Revenue and Customs* [2008] EWHC 2893 (Ch), not discussed on appeal: [2010] EWCA Civ 103 (noted A Goymour and G Virgo [2010] *CLJ* 232).

[107] See eg *Linklaters v HSBC* [2003] EWHC 1113 (Comm), [2003] 2 Lloyd's Rep 545 where the defendant bank had been negligent so could not rely on s 4 but arguably it had changed its position in good faith.

the cheques cases as unjust enrichment might produce substantially different outcomes. Take, for example, a scenario where twin sisters, Emily and Elizabeth Smith, live in the same house. A birthday cheque for £100 is sent to Emily, payable to 'E Smith'. Elizabeth mistakenly thinks the cheque is hers, pays it into her bank account, and subsequently spends the gifted sum on a luxury spa day. Emily later realises the £100 was intended for her and brings a claim against her sister for that sum. Analysed as conversion, Elizabeth is liable to Emily for the cheque's face value.[108] Despite her innocence, Elizabeth cannot rely on the change of position defence. However, that defence would work if Emily's claim is analysed as unjust enrichment. Again, it seems to be unjust enrichment which produces the more desirable outcome here, for it softens the blow for those who innocently receive the amount intended to be paid to another by means of a cheque.

We might conclude that if conversion ceased to be applicable, documentary rights would be adequately protected by the law of unjust enrichment except in two situations, where there is arguably a residual role for conversion. First, conversion's remedy of delivery up may be useful in allowing a document to be recovered in specie. It should be possible to retain this feature of conversion in relation to documents whilst at the same withdrawing the availability of substantial damages. Secondly, unjust enrichment does not provide for recovery where the claimant's loss exceeds the defendant's gain. It was suggested above that it would be appropriate to impose liability here, but not on a strict liability basis. To be consistent with other torts which remedy pure economic loss, to recover here arguably the claimant should have to prove that the defendant has acted with fault, set at an appropriate level. Perhaps the time has come to recognise a new tort to deal with such cases. Although this proposed fault-based liability might be understood as a modified form of conversion, it would be better to recognise that, having a fault requirement, it is intrinsically different to conversion, and therefore should form a new species of economic tort. The shape of the new tort would have to be carefully worked out, so that it fits alongside, without eclipsing, the current economic torts. Space precludes a detailed study of its possible formulation here, but in broad terms it would seek to impose liability for intentionally causing loss to another's contractual rights.

Conclusions

The aim of this chapter was to evaluate whether Lord Nicholls was right in *OBG* that the tort of conversion ought to be extended to pure contractual rights, by analogy with the protection it confers on documentary rights. At one level, his Lordship's argument is compelling: it is desirable that all contractual

[108] See text to n 43 above.

rights (documentary and pure) attract similar legal protection. However, the analysis in this chapter of the documents cases, and of other bases of private law liability, suggests that it is neither necessary nor desirable for conversion to be the vehicle for providing this protection. It would, instead, be better for the law to develop along the following, very different, lines.

First, the analogy argument should be rejected as a reason for extending conversion to pure contractual rights. As the current application of conversion to documentary rights cannot be rationalised by a consistent theory; it would be theoretically unjustifiable and practically unworkable to build on a body of law which cannot be fully understood and explained.

Secondly, because there is merit in giving equivalent protection to documentary and pure contractual rights alike, it is argued that conversion should protect neither, and that the face value rule should be abolished. In short, the tort should be contracted, rather than expanded, in order to meet Lord Nicholls' broad policy concerns.

Thirdly, the gap created by the abolition of the face value rule can be filled, in the most part, by the law of unjust enrichment, which offers a more principled basis for recovery and, in addition, is able to protect documentary and pure contractual rights on equivalent terms. For those cases where unjust enrichment cannot reach and where it would be desirable to impose liability, it is suggested that a new fault-based tort be developed.

Returning full circle to where this chapter began – to the facts in *OBG* – it can be seen that these proposals produce a desirable result, for the innocent receivers would not be liable for settling the claimant's contractual rights.[109] Only if they had acted with fault might there be a case for imposing liability for causing economic loss to contractual rights, via a new fault-based tort.

The upshot of these proposals is that the tort of conversion is confined to its natural territory of protecting possessory interests in ordinary chattels, which is where its life began. Although society is undoubtedly holding more and more wealth in intangible forms, conversion is not the appropriate tool for coping with that change. A further desirable outcome of these proposals is that in pulling the tort back from protecting contractual rights, there is no need to confront the dilemma of whether, if it were to protect these rights, conversion would be elevating contractual interests into a new category of proprietary right.

[109] See Lord Hoffmann's argument to this effect in *OBG* (n 7) [107].

17

Intellectual Property and the Concept of Dematerialised Property

Andreas Rahmatian*

Introduction

Property theorists, when discussing the legal side of property, generally seem in tacit agreement that there is a unitary law of property whereby land, personal property and intellectual property are instances of general principles on which the whole law of property rests.[1] In the area of doctrinal law this does not quite seem to be the case in practice, at least in England and Wales,[2] where land, personal property (generally rather neglected in scholarship)[3] and intellectual property are studied in different academic subjects separated from one another, which makes combining and overarching scholarship more difficult. Nevertheless, in the view of the author the unitary approach is correct, but property theorists tend to stop short of putting their professed methodology into practice, either by referring to intellectual property as part of property but then excluding it largely from further discussion,[4] by not going into detail as

* Mag iur et phil, Dr iur (Vienna), LLM (London), Solicitor (England & Wales). Senior Lecturer in Law, University of Glasgow.

[1] J W Harris, *Property and Justice* (OUP, Oxford 1996) 3–4, 6; it also appears from J E Penner, *The Idea of Property in Law* (OUP, Oxford 1997) 68–74, J Waldron, *The Right to Private Property* (Clarendon Press, Oxford 1988) 33, S E Munzer, *A Theory of Property* (CUP, Cambridge 1990) 16.

[2] In Scotland the tendency to a unitary law of property seems to prevail, as a result of the Roman law tradition in this jurisdiction, see K G C Reid, *The Law of Property in Scotland* (Butterworths, Edinburgh 1996) [1], but there are also reservations to one of its roots, the Roman property law schema of things (*res*), as was expounded by Gaius, Inst 2, 12–14, see G L Gretton, 'Ownership and its Objects' (2007) 71 *Rabels Zeitschrift für ausländisches und internationales Privatrecht* 805, 826, 831.

[3] S Worthington, *Personal Property Law: Text, Cases and Materials* (Hart Publishing, Oxford 2000) v (preface): 'Personal Property Law Is One of the Most Neglected and Least Understood Aspects of English Law.' Similarly, A Pretto-Sakmann, *Boundaries of Personal Property* (Hart Publishing, Oxford 2005) 15–17.

[4] See *Waldron* (n 1) 33 and 35, with a notable absence of intellectual property in the summary at 59. There is also little discussion in A M Honoré, 'Ownership' in A G Guest (ed), *Oxford Essays*

to the specific characteristics that intellectual property as incorporeal property inevitably entails,[5] or by maintaining that intellectual property is an akin, but still rather different, species when compared with tangible property.[6] More recently, it has even been claimed that intellectual property is not property at all because intellectual property rights do not confer rights against tangible things – objects that can be physically located.[7]

This chapter seeks to apply property principles, as developed in legal theories on property, to intellectual property and in this way tries to redress the balance in academic discourse somewhat: intellectual property is property, with all the advantages and dangers which originate from that quality. It is arguably even accurate to say that the legal concept of property rights in general is more easily understood when looking at intellectual property rights first, although that is obviously exactly reversing the historical development of property law. First, the notion of property in contemporary property law with an emphasis on the concept of dematerialised property will be discussed: on the basis of a more modern relational property concept (traces of this idea can already be found in the eighteenth century), one can define property rights as rights against persons (that is, the world at large) in relation to things. A property right (*ius in rem*, real right) is an abstract legal concept which relates to an object. The object is itself an abstract legal conceptualisation, but may have a corresponding tangible item in the material world. These principles will be applied to intellectual property, more specifically, to copyright, patents and trade marks. The idea that intellectual property rights are property rights may appear straightforward, but is in fact controversial, as already indicated. A general discussion of the viewpoints of some of the critics[8] will be followed by arguments against their concerns. It needs to be noted that the following discussion refers to property *in law* only,[9] that is, the idea of property in legal systems; it does not seek a philosophical justification of intellectual property rights as being property rights, and it does not discuss the manifestly relevant political, social and economic concerns which invariably come to the fore when practical aspects of the nature of intellectual property rights as 'property' are

in Jurisprudence (1st series, OUP, Oxford 1961) 129, 131; similarly so in *Gretton* (n 2) 846–47. The brief discussion in *Harris* (n 1) 42–47 is among the longest one can find with property theorists.

[5] See *Munzer* (n 1) 16, 33 and 303 for only passing reference of copyright, patents and trade marks. Gray's 'excludability' criterion (see K J Gray, 'Property in Thin Air' (1991) 50 *CLJ* 268) is not too appropriate for intellectual property either.

[6] *Penner* (n 1) 119–20.

[7] B McFarlane, *The Structure of Property Law* (Hart Publishing, Oxford 2008) 132, 134–35.

[8] There is also criticism against the proprietary nature of especially copyright from intellectual property specialists, see P Drahos, *A Philosophy of Intellectual Property* (Ashgate Publishing, Aldershot 1996) 200, 213, 223; R Deazley, *Rethinking Copyright. History, Theory, Language* (Edward Elgar, Cheltenham 2006) 143, 162, but mainly on the basis of legal policy and the legal history of copyright, rather than property theory. Therefore their views are disregarded in the present context.

[9] The same approach is taken in *Penner* (n 1) 2.

looked at. This scholarly reduction is inevitable to keep the subject within manageable proportions.

Property and property rights in general: the legal concept of dematerialised property

The meaning of the term 'property' and the idea of relational property

It is common knowledge that the ambiguous term 'property' has at least three different meanings in law:[10] (1) the sum of the assets, or the 'wherewithal'[11] of a person;[12] (2) the right in relation to an object or 'thing' (*res*) which is enforceable *erga omnes* and is usually named *ius in rem* (right in a thing), real right or proprietary right; (3) the object or 'thing' which that real right refers to.[13] Even from this short description one notices that real rights are ultimately always rights against, or more broadly, legal relations between, persons. Thus property rights are rights against persons (in a sociological context: *over* persons)[14] in relation to things. Property lawyers, particularly in the Anglo-Saxon world, seem to take pride in the destruction of the layperson's idea that property rights are just rights of persons to things,[15] and point out that these are in fact complex relations conferring rights against everyone except the holder of the property right. However, that very familiar discussion can be passed over in the present context. The relational concept of property rights can be traced back to thinkers of the eighteenth century,[16] such as Kames,[17] and, very clearly, Kant.[18]

[10] One of the earliest clear accounts on this point can be found with the Scottish jurist, judge and philosopher Lord Kames (1696–1782). See Lord Kames, *Historical Law-Tracts* (2nd edn printed for A Kincaid, 1761) (facsimile reprint, Edition Legal Classics Library 1988) 88 and note. See also A Rahmatian, 'The Property Theory of Lord Kames (Henry Home)' (2006) 2 *Int JLC* 180.

[11] *Penner* (n 1) 129.

[12] 'Assets' or '*patrimonium*' or 'wherewithal' is the sum total of assets minus the liabilities allocated by law to a person in the form of tangible and intangible (including purely intangible) objects (rights and obligations), which constitutes the person's estate and which can typically be expressed in a monetary value, for example in the case of succession or insolvency.

[13] 'Property' is occasionally also used in a fourth meaning: it can denote ownership, thus a particular type of property right (see eg Sale of Goods Act 1979 s 61, and M Bridge, *Personal Property Law* (3rd edn OUP, Oxford 2002) 30, 81. This imprecise and confusing use of the term 'property' should be avoided.

[14] Compare M Cohen, 'Property and Sovereignty' (1927–28) 13 *Cornell LQ* 12, 14.

[15] For an overview of that discussion, see eg *Gretton* (n 2) 829–30. See also *Waldron* (n 1) 27.

[16] If not earlier, eg potentially in Stair: J D Stair, *Institutions of the Law of Scotland*, D Walker (ed) (University Presses of Edinburgh and Glasgow, Edinburgh 1981) I, 1, 22. The concept must have been tacitly accepted in some unfocused way by the eighteenth century and was clearly not invented by the leading US academic and property law expert Joseph W Singer, as some academic texts nevertheless seem to suggest.

But a relational concept of property (rights) does not mean that real rights can be explained away as merely particular manifestations of personal rights, as Hohfeld attempted.[19] In his view a right *in rem* is split into a multitude of identical individual rights *in personam* held by the right holder against everyone else who has a corresponding duty to respect this real right. The artificiality of this concept with regard to a property right becomes particularly apparent in the case of a property transfer: when an object of property is transferred from one person to another, according to Hohfeld, everyone else exchanges one duty against the transferor A for another against the transferee B:[20] is that a parallel transfer of identical rights from A against everyone in the world and simultaneously a parallel transfer of correlative duties in respect of A to B with the whole world of duty-holders? One can see that this idea is highly theoretical and not suitable for the analysis of property rights: the more appropriate view is that a transfer leads to a change of the rights and duties of A and B only.[21] Hohfeld's theory has been criticised aptly[22] and will not be pursued further in the following. Property rights are, like personal rights, ultimately rights against persons, but, unlike personal rights, rights against *all* persons except the right-holder.

Property rights and objects of property rights as legal concepts

The first meaning of 'property' as 'assets' is not particularly problematic in this context, but the second and third definitions of property and the relationship between them are of central importance. First, it is necessary to ascertain what the object (*res*) of the real right is. Any definition in this regard will inevitably involve a *petitio principii*, because it becomes apparent that the 'object' or '*res*' is a conceptual creation of the law, in that the real rights which are attached to the object and supposedly protect it, actually create the object for the purpose of the law. Thus the object can notionally not be separated from the real right in it. This needs to be explained, perhaps more easily with the example of tangible property, although the principle applies to any type of property.

[17] Eg *Kames* (n 10) 82 (property is a purely mental conception and to be distinguished from – factual and physical – possession), also in Lord Kames (Henry Home), *Elucidations respecting the Common and Statute Law of Scotland* (Printed for William Creech, Edinburgh 1777) (facsimile reprint, Routledge/Thoemmes Press 1993) 228, art 33. Kames's *Elucidations* referred to here have to be read in connection with Kames's *Elements of Criticism* (a rather unexpected reference in a legal context) from which Kames's relational concept of property becomes more apparent. See also *Rahmatian* (n 10) 181.

[18] I Kant, *Die Metaphysik der Sitten* (*Metaphysics of Morals*) W Weischedel (ed) (Werkausgabe Band VIII) (Frankfurt am Main, Suhrkamp Taschenbuch Verlag, 1977) *Rechtslehre* § 11 371–72.

[19] W N Hohfeld, *Fundamental Legal Conceptions* (Yale University Press, New Haven 1966) 72–73.

[20] *Penner* (n 1) 23.

[21] *Penner* (n 1) 23, followed by *Rahmatian* (n 10) 180.

[22] *Harris* (n 1) 122–24; *Penner* (n 1) 23–24; R B Grantham and C E F Rickett, 'Property Rights as a Legally Significant Event' (2003) 62 *CLJ* 728.

The Real Right

If we look at a plot of land, or a car, they do not change their physical appearance when they are owned by someone (theoretically) for the first time, or when ownership[23] changes, for example as a result of a sale and subsequent transfer of proprietary entitlements in them. The land or the car as (someone's) 'property' are the object of a legal conception,[24] and from a normative position one would have to say that it is the abstract legal conception 'real right' which enables the law to identify and recognise material objects of the physical world, to incorporate them into its normative system by categorising them as a 'things' (*res*), and subsequently to allocate them to persons as 'owners'. Roman law-based legal systems reduce conceptually the physical world into abstract and conceptual 'persons' and 'things' (and actions as relations between persons and persons to things),[25] but also English law effectively adheres to the same pattern without being expressly indebted to the Romanist systematisation.[26] It follows from this conception that real rights in an object of the material world do not physically exist; what exists in the real world is a certain social behaviour of human beings in relation to other humans and with regard to a certain material object, which manifests the right in the object claimed. It is the social behaviour of human beings in relation to one another; their performance, enforced (instigated) by the law (and its sanctions in case of non-compliance) which makes the normative idea of a real right a reality, and thus translates the normative 'ought' into a material 'is'.[27] Thus a transfer of ownership in a car is actually a change of behaviour of the persons involved: the transferee asserts his entitlement by certain visual acts (driving away and leaving the car in his garage etc), and all others respect his entitlement (including now the transferor). This shows that real rights are really behavioural relations between persons ordered by the law. The abstract and normative right of 'ownership' (in an untechnical sense), an 'ought', is converted into the 'is' of the material world especially by the human conduct of 'possession'. Thus if I claim that it is 'my' land, I show

[23] Or what is un-technically called 'ownership' in English law; see *Bridge* (n 13) 28, with regard to land; J W Harris, 'Ownership of Land in English Law' in N MacCormick and P Birks (eds), *The Legal Mind. Essays for Tony Honoré* (Oxford, Clarendon Press, 1986) 148.

[24] Compare *Kames* (n 17) (*Elucidations*) 228, art 33.

[25] B Nicholas, *An Introduction to Roman Law* (Clarendon Press, Oxford 1975) 34, 60, on Gaius's system of *personae-res-actiones* (Gaius Inst I, 8); for a comparative study in relation to modern jurisdictions, see eg *Gretton* (n 2) 804, 807. Gaius's schema is used in a quite exemplary way in the Austrian ABGB (*Allgemeines Bürgerliches Gesetzbuch*, General Civil Code), see §§ 14, 285, 291, 859.

[26] F H Lawson and B Rudden, *The Law of Property* (3rd edn OUP, Oxford 2002) 5, 19–20; N E Simmonds, 'Reason, History and Privilege: Blackstone's Debt to Natural Law' (1988) 105 *Zeitschrift der Savigny-Stiftung für Rechtsgeschichte* (Germanistische Abteilung) 206, on the influence of the Roman law on Blackstone. See also *Gretton* (n 2) 831.

[27] The logical obstacle of deducing conclusions from an 'ought' to an 'is' is a problem beyond the scope of this chapter. See D Hume, *A Treatise of Human Nature*, reprinted in L A Selby-Bigge (ed) (Clarendon Press, Oxford 1960) book 3, 1, 1, at 469.

my entitlement through acts of possession, such as planting apple trees and harvesting them; if it is 'my' chair, I show my entitlement through possession by literally sitting on it, for example. It is trite to say that the social behaviour in the material world can be deceptive, not only because a right may be claimed wrongly or pretended, but also because the visible and overt acts of behaviour are not necessarily clear informers of the actual underlying legal relation. There is only a finite number of simple human behaviours available which are able to signify a real right, and such behaviours are often too crude to denote precisely the fine distinctions of (proprietary and non-proprietary) entitlements the law recognises: having possession of a chair may mean that I own it,[28] or that I am merely a bailee,[29] or that I am only a licensee of a conference organiser who owns the chair and permits me to sit on it for the time of the conference.[30] In many cases the simple human conduct needs to be supplemented by other forms of conduct (registration and other formalities, which perform a 'channelling function')[31] to create a social reality that denotes the legal relations. These matters need not be discussed further.

Real rights are behavioural patterns in relation to objects, or put differently, relations between persons with respect to things as the law imagines and organises them. It is these behavioural patterns which incorporate these objects into the law as objects of 'property'. The substance of such real rights is often referred to as a 'bundle of rights',[32] a concept that is not without its difficulties,[33] but one could rephrase the bundle of rights concept in the following, arguably unproblematic, way: the substance of a real right can be split in a Spinozist manner into a number of attributes that turn the real right into concrete individualised real rights. The attributes are aspects of the whole that is the substance of the real right, they are not actually independent 'sticks' bundled together. The concrete real rights are determined and delineated as to their existence/extent and content by an *external* and an *internal* aspect which can be regarded as coinciding sides of the same coin.

The *internal* side of real rights is expressed in the content of the real right, and that content is created by the powers that the real right confers and the duties it entails. These powers and duties that form the content

[28] Compare *Bridge* (n 13) 29.

[29] Compare *Bridge* (n 13) 33, 35.

[30] In this case the human conduct denotes either a personal right (contract) or a bare licence, thus not a possessory or proprietary right at all, see eg K J Gray and S F Gray, *Elements of Land Law* (5th edn OUP, Oxford 2009) 1288–90.

[31] That is, the formalities offer 'channels for the legally effective expression of intention'. See L Fuller, 'Consideration and Form' (1941) 41 *Colum L Rev* 801, discussing the 'channelling function' (with reference to R von Ihering) as providing a simple external test so that certain human acts are easily diagnosed as being legally recognised and enforceable.

[32] Eg *Gray* (n 5) 252; *Munzer* (n 1) 16, 23.

[33] See J E Penner, 'The "Bundle of Rights" Picture of Property' (1996) 43 *UCLA L Rev* 739–40, 796, asserting that the 'bundle of rights' concept suggests wrongly that property is a bundle of lesser units, a structural composite, and a matter of degree, what it is not.

of the real right depend on:[34] (a) the type of the real right (eg ownership, restricted real right: mortgage, easement); (b) the object of the real right or *res*, particularly whether it is intangible or tangible, and in the latter case, the physical characteristics of the *res* (thus the real right in relation to a plot of land confers the power to grow potatoes, for instance, while a copyright does not); (c) restrictions by private law which are often the result of the location or physical characteristics of the object of property (right of way as of necessity of a land-locked plot of land,[35] rules regarding the use of the common parts in a block of flats);[36] (d) public law restrictions (eg planning laws). As to (a), the basic and most far-reaching type of real right is ownership.[37] The powers/duties of ownership can be listed as what Honoré calls 'the standard incidents of ownership'.[38] They include the right to possess, the right to use and to alienate,[39] the right to manage and to obtain an income, the right to the capital, the liability to execution for debt and others.[40] These incidents depend on the type of *res*; thus, for example, ownership in relation to a copyright can obviously not involve possession.[41]

The *external* side of real rights materialises in the right to exclude everybody except the right holder from the object of the real right:[42] the real right 'binds the world', is enforceable against everyone in accordance with the type of the real right in question (thus the mortgagee's rights are more limited than the owner's rights). As a consequence, a corresponding duty against the right holder arises in the (presumptive) intruder to respect the real right and, through that, the object of the real right.[43] This also shows that property rights are eventually legal relations between persons. The realisation of the property right is effectively the legal relationship which comes into existence between the holder of the real right, having especially the right to exclude, and the third party, having the

[34] *Rahmatian* (n 10) 187.

[35] In English land law, see eg *Clark v Cogge* (1606) Croke Jac 170; 79 ER 149 (KB). See *Gray and Gray* (n 30) 649 for further references.

[36] Restrictive and positive covenants in relation to leasehold property under English law; law of the tenement in Scots law: Tenements (Scotland) Act 2004.

[37] The definitions of ownership are similar in civilian and in common law systems and are effectively bland statements emphasising the widest possible power that a real right can confer: ownership is at the same time the most powerful proprietary right and a residual category which can only be defined in relation to lesser rights (see eg the relevant sections in modern civil codes in the Roman law tradition: § 903 German BGB (*Bürgerliches Gesetzbuch*, Civil Code), § 354 Austrian ABGB (General Civil Code), art 544 French Code Civil, art 641 Swiss ZGB (*Zivilgesetzbuch*, Civil Code). From a common law viewpoint, one may say with *Honoré* (n 4) 108, that ownership is the greatest possible interest in a thing which a mature legal system recognises.

[38] *Honoré* (n 4) 112.

[39] Not everyone sees the right of alienation as an instance of ownership, for example *Penner* (n 33) 760.

[40] *Honoré* (n 4) 113–24.

[41] See Paulus D 41,2,3 pr: '*Possideri autem possunt, quae sunt corporalia*' (One can only possess corporeal things). Compare also *Penner* (n 33) 756.

[42] See *Rahmatian* (n 10) 182–83.

[43] On the close connection between real right and object of the real right or *res*, see immediately further below: 'The property object (*Res*)'.

corresponding duty to respect the right as the individual potential encroacher. Thus there is no continually existing abstract Hohfeldian correlative duty to the claim-right, but the duty only arises in a concrete form when the third party is in an actual position to encroach on the individual real right: these duties are expressed especially in the rules of trespass and conversion for land and chattels, and in the infringement provisions for intellectual property rights.[44]

The Property Object (*Res*)

If property objects are only the creation of the real rights attached to them, what is now the concrete meaning of 'thing' or '*res*'? The real right may be reified by the physical thing, eg the chair, but this is only a convenient 'social crutch' for the actors in the physical world and not conceptually necessary for the law. In law a chair is only one realisation of the abstract and normative legal concept of 'thing' or 'chattel'. The law typifies the individual object as a 'thing', and this typification of the thing is the method by which the law recognises an object of the material world as technically a 'thing' or 'property' for the purpose of the law: in this way the law is able to incorporate the material phenomenon of an object into its normative world. Thus it is conceptually insignificant whether the object of the real right is an object in the physical world or an object as conceptualised by the law's categories. This is the idea of dematerialised property. An apple does not exist in the normative world of the law by virtue of its mere existence in the material world. For the purpose of the law, the apple 'exists' only because property rights are attached to it, triggering the behaviour of one person exercising power over the thing in question ('owner') and all others respecting such exercise of power by way of non-interference (a right binding the world, *erga omnes*). Only if and when property rights are attached to the apple does it become typified as 'property' or 'a thing/*res*' and the law is capable of perceiving it and incorporating it into the abstract-normative system of 'persons' and 'things', that is, relations between persons (*ius in personam*) and between persons in relation to things (*ius in rem*). The fact that the *res* can be represented by something incorporeal, such as in case of intellectual property rights, is conceptually irrelevant.

Therefore, if there are no property rights, not even potentially, in the *res*, there is no *res* in property law. This view presupposes that real rights are legal creations only; they have no 'natural' existence beyond the law and are subject to constant legal change as to their existence, extent and duration.[45]

[44] The similarity of trespass and infringement rules has been expressed eg recently in the musical copyright case *Fisher v Brooker* [2009] UKHL 41, [2009] 1 WLR 1764 [17]: 'Where there is trespass… to land or goods, or a comparable invasion of intangible property rights, the court's natural response is to grant injunctive relief …'. Compare also Copyright, Designs and Patents Act 1988 s 96 (2).

[45] Thus, a limited duration of rights, such as with intellectual property, does not deprive such rights of their proprietary quality.

Property rights are conventional, not natural, rights:[46] they are invented, not reflected by the law. The real rights are the conceptual means that create the normative notion of 'property' (meaning a property-object or *res*). This sounds bizarre, because the law would be unreasonable and probably unworkable if it were not responsive to social realities and did not recognise physical objects as 'property' in law. However, this principle applies not only in a positive way in relation to objects in which there is an existing real right, but even in a negative way in relation to objects where there is no such real right. Things in the real world which in law cannot be owned by anyone come into existence in the normative world by way of a negative definition: real rights could, but specifically *should not*, attach to certain objects (for religious, moral or practical reasons, '*res extra patrimonium*').[47] In such a situation the law chooses to mirror certain existing moral norms, without, however, deriving from such moral norms. The denial of real rights (to a person or a person in law) in relation to a certain physical object (sacred object etc) presupposes the normative concept of real rights in order to negate real rights subsequently in relation to the specific object. This argument becomes less bizarre if the object of the real right is not a (corporeal) thing in the material world but an object only as conceptualised by the law's categories, for there is nothing material which is directly[48] reified by the legal notion of 'object' (*res*), and in such a case it becomes even more apparent that it is the enforceable real right which effectively creates the notional object by defining and protecting it. Thus, strictly speaking from a conceptual point of view, one can indeed use the terms 'property right' and 'property' interchangeably, whereby the latter stresses more the aspect of reification through a (tangible) object while the former refers to a (formalised) behavioural pattern. Objects that depend for their existence on legal concepts are often reified by formalities to enable human actors to recognise and operate on them. Where debts or other interests are involved, normative formalities effectuate the reification: debts can be reified in the formalised paper of a negotiable instrument to ensure practically unassailable transfer;[49] subsisting equitable interests can only be transferred in writing.[50] In case of intellectual property, registration

[46] *Hume* (n 27) book 3, part 2, 491; J Bentham, 'Principles of the Civil Code' in R Hildreth (tr), *The Theory of Legislation* (7th edn Kegan Paul, London 1891) 111–13. The position stated here deliberately stands against any natural law conception of property rights, as can be found especially with classical theorists, such as Grotius, Locke or Kames. Blackstone is ambiguous, but seems to have regarded property as an artifice, W Blackstone, *Commentaries on the Laws of England. Book The Second. Of the Rights of Things* (A Strahan, London 1800) Comm II, 1, at 2: 'there is no foundation in nature or in natural law, why a set of words upon parchment should convey the dominion of land'.

[47] For Roman law, see M Kaser, *Das Römische Privatrecht I. Das altrömische, das vorklassische und das klassische Recht* (2nd edn C H Beck, München 1971) 377.

[48] On the reification process in case of intellectual property rights, see below under 'Intellectual property rights as dematerialised property'.

[49] Bill of Exchange Act 1882 s 29.

[50] Law of Property Act 1925 s 53(1)(c).

may effectuate its reification where the intellectual property right is subject to registration requirements (patents, registered trade marks, registered designs). Copyright arises without any formality,[51] so a formality rule bringing about reification would be in relation to assignment.[52] Generally, intellectual property assignments (not only of copyright) have to comply with the requisite statutory formalities to be valid.[53]

If an object in question is a material thing, it is defined by its physical characteristics ('properties'), and the real rights in it are conceptual; but if the object is a legal concept, the law also has to provide further conceptual defining points which enable the recognition of that concept (for example, in case of an express private trust: certainty of intention, certainty of subject-matter, certainty of objects).[54] These further legal conceptual criteria for the determination of the actual (notional) object of the real right cannot be severed from the real rights themselves in it. For the law, however, every *res* is a notion, whether it is referring to – and thus being directly reified by – a certain individual material item or whether the *res* is a legal notion itself. This conceptualisation of dematerialised property may sound modern, but already at an early stage in history the feudal system of land-holding necessitated the notion of abstract dematerialised property and property rights: feudal English land law contained the notion of 'tenure', which led to the idea of the 'estate' in the land in more modern times.[55] Thus, even with regard to tangible property the law has been able to interpose an abstract construct between the right-holder and the object which emphasises the general rule that 'property' is not the physical thing but a bundle of different rights in the thing which form its abstract legal representation:[56] one owns an estate in the land, since the land itself is (notionally) owned by the Crown through a mediated, indirect, relationship.[57] Under the concept of dematerialised property, the *res* can (and often will) be reified by a tangible object, but the *res* itself is the creation of the

[51] And must do so; see Berne Convention for the Protection of Literary and Artistic Works (Berne Convention) (as revised) (Paris Text 1971) art 5(2).

[52] The fixation requirement in copyright can also fulfil a reifying role. It is debateable whether fixation is really a formality (it is not considered as such by the Berne Convention art 2(2)), and even if so, then it does not apply consistently: one should bear in mind that fixation is not required for broadcasts (Copyright, Designs and Patents Act s 6) and does not normally apply in author's rights systems.

[53] Assignments must be in writing, signed by the assignor, eg copyright, Copyright, Designs and Patents Act 1988 s 90(3); trade marks, Trade Marks Act 1994 s 24(3); patents, Patents Act 1977 s 30(6). There are also formality rules regarding the charging, assignment by way of security, and mortgaging of intellectual property.

[54] *Knight v Knight* (1840) 3 Beav 148 (Ch), 173; 49 ER 58, 69.

[55] C Harpum, S Bridge and M Dixon, *Megarry and Wade, The Law of Real Property* (7th edn Sweet & Maxwell, London 2008) 22–23, 35, 38; *Gray and Gray* (n 30) 57.

[56] Honoré says that according to one school of thought, 'we ought always to speak of owning rights over material objects, never of owning the objects themselves', which seems to express a similar idea. See *Honoré* (n 4) 131.

[57] *Gray and Gray* (n 30) 57. This also excludes actual private ownership of land in English land law in the form of *dominium*; see also *Harris* (n 23) 148.

law as much as the real rights attached to it. The physical thing may represent, but does not constitute, the *res* in law. In many cases, the physical thing, if there is one, does *not* even *directly* represent the *res*, but acts merely as an *indirect* reifier. The most obvious example is intellectual property, or: the intellectual property *right*.

Intellectual property rights as dematerialised property

Whilst tangible things have a real and continued existence in the material world independent of the abstract legal conception surrounding and relating to them, intellectual property is purely an abstract creation of the law with no material existence at all and entirely the product of the legal conception which brings it about. The intellectual property-object has no direct reification in the physical world,[58] and the law cannot build upon facts or realities, such as the size or extent of the material thing, the ability to hand it over to another person for the purpose of delivery etc; and the law cannot attach legal consequences that take account of the physical characteristics of the thing (registration for transfer of a plot of land, delivery of a chattel to create a pledge, or retention of possession of a chattel to exercise a lien,[59] limitation of the extent of a right against trespass by the borders of the land etc). It is up to the law to delineate the extent and the properties of its abstract creation, and that inevitably melts together with the second legal conception; the rights in the intellectual property object, the *iura in rem*. That shows particularly well that the rights *in rem* effectively create the *res* as a legal concept for the incorporation of a thing (whether material or conceptual) into the normative framework of the law. A copyright or patent 'exists' *exclusively normatively*, through the rights in it: if the rights in the intellectual property were subtracted, there would nothing be left, especially not a physical thing in the material world to which these subtracted rights would otherwise relate. The object of an intellectual property right is exclusively defined normatively. The idea of the abstract normative *res* can be shown particularly well with regard to the statutory intellectual property rights, of which the most important ones (copyright, patents, registered trade marks) will be considered first, with emphasis on copyright, because this is the conceptually most complicated intellectual property right. Statutory intellectual property rights are property rights by virtue of legislation,[60] and in England

[58] Thus a written text is only an *indirect* reification of the copyright-property in it (and the copyright is detached from this particular specimen of the text); the physical page is *direct* reifier of the personal property right in it.

[59] *Bridge* (n 13) 170, 175.

[60] Copyright, Designs and Patents Act 1988 s 1 (copyright), s 213 (unregistered designs); Trade Marks Act 1994 s 2 (trade marks); Patents Act 1977 s 30(1) (patents); Registered Designs Act 1949 ss 1(2) and 2 (registered designs).

and Wales they are normally also defined as *choses in action*.[61] For present purposes, it is irrelevant in which way the property right, sometimes referred to as a (legal) monopoly right,[62] comes into existence, whether by grant following a successful application (patents, registered trade marks, registered designs), or automatically (copyright, unregistered designs). Only the existence of the right is relevant, so that it can be enjoyed and is protected against infringement. Statutory provisions also define patent and trade mark *applications* as property.[63]

The matter is less straightforward in relation to common law rights in the context of intellectual property (passing-off, protection of confidential information), and the problem is potentially also a challenge to the generally agreed idea of a *numerus clausus* of property rights.

Copyright: the copyright-right and the copyright-*res*

Copyright can be a *res* or object of property rights in law, and as the law stands at present, it expressly is.[64] The copyright-*res* is an abstract legal concept itself and a fine example of dematerialised property. A copyright is protected and thereby created by the real rights of copyright with no direct material refier which could represent it, unlike a car or land. The material object 'book' is the direct reifier of the personal/moveable property right[65] in it, but only an indirect reifier of the copyright in it. The existence, extent and the limits of the copyright-property are determined by the law only.[66] The criteria for the creation of copyright-property under UK copyright law are the well-known protection criteria: broadly, a creation is protected by copyright if it constitutes an original work that is recorded

[61] Intellectual property rights are normally regarded as *choses in action* (in England and Wales; in Scotland they would be incorporeal moveable property. See Patents Act 1977 s 31; Copyright, Designs and Patents Act 1988 ss 90 and 222; Trade Marks Act 1994 s 22). Patents are apparently not *choses in action*, see Patents Act 1977 s 30(1). Cornish questions why patents should be different: W R Cornish and D Llewelyn, *Intellectual Property: Patents, Copyright, Trade Marks and Allied Rights* (6th edn Sweet & Maxwell, London 2007) 279, footnote 55. See further the discussion in A Firth and J Fitzgerald, 'Equitable Assignments in Relation to Intellectual property' (1999) 2 *IPQ* 231. In the present context of the concept of dematerialised property, the matter is of limited importance.

[62] Intellectual property rights are not monopolies in an economist's sense, see eg E W Kitch, 'Property Rights in Inventions, Writings, and Marks' (1990) 13 *Harv J L & Pub Pol'y* 122, although they may be instrumental in bringing about economic monopolies.

[63] Patents Act 1977 s 30(1); Trade Marks Act 1994 s 27.

[64] Copyright, Designs and Patents Act 1988 s 1.

[65] The term 'personal property' is the term in English law for what is called moveable property in Scots law and Roman law-based private law systems on the European continent. Technically, 'personal property' and 'moveable property' are not identical terms, see *Bridge* (n 13) 3–8, 10. However, in the present context the overlap of their meanings is so broad that these terms can be used interchangeably.

[66] For example, a text in a book is normatively defined and categorised as (an original) 'literary work'. Were that not the case, the text would not 'exist' for the purpose of copyright law. How artificial such normative definitions sometimes are can be shown by the fact that computer programmes are 'literary works' in the eyes of copyright law (Copyright, Designs and Patents Act 1988 s 3(1)(b)).

in some permanent form.[67] A 'work' is a creation (in a broad sense) of the human mind which falls into one or more of the eight categories the law provides;[68] 'original'[69] means not deriving (substantially) from a pre-existing work, but being the product of one's own (limited) skill, labour, effort, financial expenditure etc;[70] 'recorded' refers to the requirement of a physical existence of the work through which it is expressed (fixation).[71] Once these criteria are fulfilled, the copyright-property comes into existence, or 'copyright arises', but it only arises by virtue of the real rights attached to it, specified as 'acts restricted to the copyright owner' in the Copyright, Designs and Patents Act 1988, sections 16-27. These provisions delineate the extent and the properties of the abstract creation 'copyright', so the real rights or *iura in rem* inevitably melt together with the *res* or copyright itself. Thus the terms 'intellectual property' and 'intellectual property right' can be used interchangeably even more justifiably than in case of tangible property.

In intellectual property, the external or exclusionary aspect of the real rights dominates. It is obvious that a purely notional realm defines itself and its area of protection in exclusionary terms, thus negatively or in a tortious way: the realm of protection emerges as soon as all possible trespassory acts are subtracted.[72] The rules which define such acts as trespassory together put up the notional fence and exclude everybody except the right holder from the realm of protection. In copyright these tortious or trespassory acts include copying of the work, issuing copies of the work to the public, performance of the work.[73] When someone other than the right holder copies without authorisation, he steps over the notional fence of the copyright in question. The notional fence is thus formed by the sum of all trespassory acts and delineates the extent of the realm of the copyright-*res*. If there is no notional fence or remaining area, the copyright-*res* does not exist or no longer exists (in law), as is with works that have passed into the public domain. One

[67] Compare A Rahmatian, 'Copyright and Commodification' (2005) 27 *EIPR* 372. This short formula obviously has to be seen as a short-hand expression. Not all works require originality in the copyright sense (entrepreneurial works) and broadcasts need not be recorded for protection: see L Bently and B Sherman, *Intellectual Property Law* (3rd edn OUP, Oxford 2009) 92.

[68] Literary, dramatic, musical, artistic works (Copyright, Designs and Patents Act 1988 ss 1, 3–4); sound recordings (s 5A), films (s 5B), broadcasts (s 6), published editions (typographical works) (s 8).

[69] In case of the entrepreneurial works (Copyright, Designs and Patents Act 1988 ss 5–8), the requirement is 'not being copied' (Copyright, Designs and Patents Act 1988 ss 5A(2), 5B(4), 6(6), 8(2)), rather than originality. For a discussion of differences as a result of this lower threshold, see *Bently and Sherman* (n 67) 111.

[70] Copyright, Designs and Patents Act 1988 s1(1)(a); *University of London Press v University Tutorial Press* [1916] 2 Ch 601 (Ch); *Ladbroke (Football) Ltd v William Hill (Football) Ltd* [1964] 1 WLR 273 (HL) 277.

[71] Copyright, Designs and Patents Act 1988 s 3(2).

[72] For instance, as regards land, looking into someone's garden from the street without a licence does not trigger a trespassory action, while entering the land does: a copyright equivalent would be – reading a book without permission: no trespassory action, photocopying: trespassory action (infringement).

[73] See Copyright, Designs and Patents Act 1988 s 16 and following sections.

can see the purely normative definition of the *res* in law:[74] the poem out of copyright is very much extant in the real world, but a *nullum* in copyright law,[75] except for the fact that it has an impact on future works that seek protection: where a work derives (substantially)[76] from a pre-existing work in the public domain, its copyright-originality[77] is denied and no copyright protection is available.[78] But there is no infringement of the pre-existing work because the pre-existing *res* has become a *nullum* in law: there are no rights in it or trespassory acts left which would delineate a remainder, the notional realm of protection.

The concept of copyright protection is similar to the protection of tangible property, especially in relation to the right of ownership under English law, being a tortious protection or *negative* protection of ownership. Intellectual property infringement provisions are tortious, especially trespassory,[79] in nature, and they share this feature with the protection of ownership rights in real[80] and personal[81] property in English law; thus intellectual property protection is in this respect conceptually consistent. In civil law countries, where the concept of ownership (protection) is the *positive* Roman law concept of protection,[82] property is principally safeguarded through the real (not personal) action for recovery of property or *rei vindicatio* in respect of tangible property.[83] This is a central element of ownership and the most important ownership right.[84] But intellectual property as purely intangible property cannot be possessed and delivered physically in civil law countries either, nor can a dispossession take place which a court action would need to seek to reverse, so there is only the option of a tortious remedy. Remedies in civil law countries against intellectual property infringement would also be regarded as tortious in nature if the

[74] See above under 'Property and property rights in general: the legal concept of dematerialised property'.

[75] One could say that the poem is an (i) original (ii) literary work that is (iii) fixed and (iv) outside the granted term of protection, and while (i)–(iii) form the *res* as its constituents, (iv) reduces the *res* to a *nullum* as is characteristic of property rights that are limited in time.

[76] This is a normative term; as is well-known, derivative works can be regarded as original and may obtain copyright protection, see *Bently and Sherman* (n 67) 98.

[77] *University of London Press v University Tutorial Press* [1916] 2 Ch 601 (Ch) 608.

[78] Compare A Rahmatian, 'Music and Creativity as Perceived by Copyright Law' (2005) 3 *IPQ* 292.

[79] *Harris* (n 1) 45.

[80] *Harris* (n 23) 144–45.

[81] R Goode, *Commercial Law* (3rd edn Penguin Books, London 2004) 31–33; *Bridge* (n 13) 47.

[82] Based on the idea of the *dominium* where the real right of ownership emanates centrally from this idea. Ownership is not just defined as the outcome of the (non)availability of trespassory actions, see (with regard to property in general) *Rahmatian* (n 10) 182–83.

[83] Owing to the fact that there cannot be a dispossession or a *rei vidicatio* with regard to the incorporeal copyright, Lord Kames mistakenly held in the Scottish case *Hinton v Donaldson* (27 July 1773) that copyright cannot be a property right, see, with references, *Rahmatian* (n 10) 200.

[84] For this reason, in some legal systems the right containing the real action cannot be assigned separately from the transfer of ownership in the thing to which the real action relates (eg Austria), or the assignment of the real action can be a method of transfer of ownership (eg Germany, if a third party possesses the thing in question at the time of the transfer, German BGB (German Civil Code) § 931).

categories of English law were used.[85] Courts in civil law countries recognise the need for strong and specific infringement provisions (eg rules regarding injunctions and damages) for intellectual property rights because their incorporeal nature makes it very difficult to protect them otherwise.[86]

The fact that, with intellectual property rights, the external or exclusionary aspect of the real right dominates should not lead to a neglect of the internal aspect of the real right. Intellectual property rights are not just 'negative rights', that is, rights to prevent others from doing certain things.[87] In the case of copyright (and mutatis mutandis with all intellectual property rights), the positive, internal aspect of the real right is the right to use, especially in the form of the right to assign or license.[88]

Patents

Many relevant points have already been discussed above in the context of copyright. A main difference to copyright is that patents require a successful application to come into existence. The content of this application (once it is granted as a patent), is essential in the determination of the content and extent of the property right, that is, the dematerialised property 'patent' in question. Patents are monopolies in inventions that are new and involve an inventive step.[89] The extent and content of the monopoly sought/granted is delineated and demarcated by two components in the 'specification' of the patent application:[90] (a) the 'description' which describes and thereby fully discloses the invention in such a way that a person skilled in the art is enabled to work the invention;[91] (b) the 'claims' in which the applicant for the patent seeks protection for the elements of his invention which are new and involve an inventive step when compared with the prior art. The claims set out the scope for legal protection conferred by the patent, whereby the description

[85] See eg with regard to copyright, Germany: UrhG 1965 (*Urheberrechtsgesetz 1965*, Author's Rights Act 1965), § 97 and following sections, France: CPI 1992 (*Code de la propriété intellectuelle 1992*, Intellectual Property Code 1992) art L 331 and following articles. See also A Rahmatian, 'Contracts Infringing Intellectual Property Rights' (2003) 4 *IPQ* 427.

[86] For example, the Austrian Supreme Court (OGH) with regard to copyright (author's right) and its liquidated damages provision for infringements in § 87(3) UrhG 1936 (*Urheberrechtsgesetz 1936*, Austrian Author's Rights Act 1936), OGH 1998/05/26, SZ 71/92 (available on the Austrian Federal Chancellery website, Legal Information System, RIS: http://www.ris.bka.gv.at/Judikatur/), but the principle applies to all intellectual property rights.

[87] That is however the view in *Cornish and Llewelyn* (n 61) 6 and 501.

[88] For a discussion of these rights in several copyright systems within the EU, see A Rahmatian, 'Dealing with Rights in Copyright-protected Works: Assignments and Licences' in E Derclaye (ed), *Research Handbook on the Future of EU Copyright* (Edward Elgar, Cheltenham 2009) 286.

[89] Patents Act 1977 ss 1(1), 2 and 3.

[90] Compare *Bently and Sherman* (n 67) 360.

[91] *Biogen v Medeva* [1997] RPC 1 (HL) 47.

must support the claims.[92] The claims delineate and define the invention and set out the notional territory for which the owner (patentee) will be able to claim protection against infringement. Or, put differently from a property theorist's angle: the claims create, by way of language (supplemented by technical drawings), the extent and content of the purely intangible property right and object, or the *res* in question, that is, the *patent* in relation to a particular invention. In law the patent-*res* is denoted by the claims, not by, for instance, a physical machine which exemplifies the patented invention. Hence, judges, when looking at the ambit of the claims in a patent infringement action, determine their scope by interpreting the claims and the description as a whole;[93] thus they look at the text, supported by the technical drawings,[94] not at a machine or other material object.[95] Also for this reason, both statute and case law stress that claims have to define the matter for which the applicant seeks protection and must be clear and concise.[96] It is the words in the claims which create the *res*, not the properties of a physical object. The infringing activities against which the scope of protection is compared, are set out in section 60 of the Patents Act 1977.

Thus a patent specification or the claims are not the direct reification of the property 'patent', nor is it a machine or a part of it which incorporates the patent. However, the claims in particular are the essential representation of the content and extent of the patent rights. It is the text (description and claims), if sanctioned by a successful application, which creates the patent (property) right and symbolises it, not a prototype machine which may exist in the physical world. In this respect, the patent documentation shares certain similarities with the debts embodied in a bill of exchange and the rights flowing from the formalities of this embodiment.[97] It is often quite difficult indeed, if not impossible, to identify an exact corresponding object in the material world which acts as a reifier of the imaginary normative concept of the property-object in intellectual property law.

[92] Patents Act 1977 s 14(5)(c).

[93] Patents Act 1977 s 125, citing art 69 of the protocol to the Convention on the Grant of European Patents (European Patent Convention).

[94] The text ultimately tends to prevail in case of possible conflicting interpretations, see *Van der Lely NV v Bamfords Ltd* [1963] RPC 61 (HL).

[95] The comparison as to whether a defendant's activities constituted an infringement of a patent has to be made between the claims in the patent (not the devices/products made by the claimant-patentee) and the device made and sold by the defendant, *Buchanan v Alba Diagnostics Ltd* [2001] RPC 43 (Inner House) [58]–[60], affirmed by *Buchanan v Alba Diagnostics Ltd* [2004] UKHL 5, 2004 SC (HL) 9 (this point was not before the House of Lords).

[96] Patents Act 1977 s 14(5)(a) and (b). *Kirin-Amgen v Hoechst Marion Roussel* [2005] RPC 9 (HL), especially [125]–[126]. What is relevant is that the skilled person must regard the claims as clear: *Bayer CropScience/Safeners*, T1020/98 [2003] OJ EPO 533, 542–43 (European Patent Office, Technical Board of Appeal).

[97] Compare Bills of Exchange Act 1882 s 3(1) and (2).

Registered Trade Marks

Registered trade marks tend to be a less complex example of dematerialised property. However, although it is in the nature of trade marks that they are supposed to denote something (especially the origin and quality of a product/service),[98] it is not necessarily clear which *res* or property (right) they actually denote. Nowadays, trade marks, the actual signs, are generally regarded as property in their own right,[99] which is reflected especially well in their dilution protection.[100] The property 'registered trade mark' is relatively easily created by way of an application for registration, whereby the sign for which protection is sought must not fall within one of the absolute grounds for refusal of registration (the sign is inherently flawed, eg not capable of graphic representation or not capable of distinguishing),[101] or one of the relative grounds for refusal of registration (broadly, the sign is per se unobjectionable, but it conflicts with an earlier already registered trade mark by being identical or confusingly similar).[102] The ambit of the property right is set out in the infringement provisions[103] which largely reflect the relative grounds for refusal of registration. The question as to whether use of a sign is identical/similar and therefore potentially infringing is ascertained in the light of the appearance (in a wide sense)[104] of the signs/trade marks at issue. The property right extends to, say, a particular drawing of a fox terrier looking into a gramophone horn (for example the famous trade mark 'HMV – His Master's Voice').

But this is not the real or intended ambit of the trade mark property right (the picture or painting as such would usually attract copyright protection in any case). Trade mark protection originates from the protection against passing-off which protects the proprietary interest of the business goodwill,[105] so that initially the sign itself did not obtain property protection.[106] This idea of the sign connected with the goodwill is also a reason for the fact that until recently

[98] See *Cornish and Llewelyn* (n 61) 620, for an overview of the functions of trade marks.

[99] Trade Marks Act 1994 s 22; *Bently and Sherman* (n 67) 959–60.

[100] Eg for the US: R N Klieger, 'Trade Mark Dilution: The Whittling Away of the Rational Basis for Trade Mark Protection' (1996–1997) 58 *U Pitt L Rev* 789, 792, 794, 831, 839.

[101] Trade Marks Act 1994 s 3.

[102] Trade Marks Act 1994 s 5.

[103] Trade Marks Act 1994 ss 9 and 10.

[104] 'Appearance' has to be understood in the sense of any type of perception in the material world, because sound marks can now also be registered, see *Shield Mark BV v Kist (t/a Memex)* [2004] RPC 315 (ECJ); their graphic representation is, for example, through notation of the music.

[105] Compare *Reckitt and Colman Products v Borden Inc* [1990] 1 WLR 491 (HL) 511: 'The fact that the proprietary right which is protected by the action [of passing-off] is in the goodwill rather than in the get-up distinguishes the protection afforded by the common law to a trader from that afforded by statute to the registered holder of a trade mark who enjoys a permanent monopoly therein.' Thus with a registered trade mark, the property right is (also) in the registered sign itself, while in the case of passing-off, the business goodwill only, not the get-up of a product, is the intellectual property.

[106] For example in the United States, see: S J Liddy, 'The Problem of State Trade Mark Registrations' (1949) 39 *Trade Mark Reporter* 667, 669, and L H Johnston, 'Drifting Toward Trade Marks Rights in Gross' (1995) 85 *Trade Mark Reporter* 19, 21–22.

many European countries prohibited the transfer of the trade mark without the transfer of the business in connection.[107] The actual nature and extent of business goodwill is difficult to ascertain, but it can roughly be described as the 'benefit and advantage of the good name, reputation, and connection of a business'.[108] Thus the trade mark depicts the property right 'business goodwill' first and foremost, and rather at a less central level, the *res* 'sign' which it represents. The object of trade mark protection, the *res*, is fundamentally the goodwill, typically of a business, and that is symbolised, but hardly specifically reified, by a 'sign capable of being represented graphically'.[109] The sign, still most typically consisting of words and images or a combination of these, *denotes* the concept of 'goodwill', but it is not itself the goodwill, the principal object of the proprietary trade mark right.[110] A trade mark is a simple and quick way to visualise the notional *res* 'goodwill' symbolically in the material world, a short-hand signifier, but not a material object of the goodwill. Parallels with a promissory note, a banknote or a bill of exchange arise. The law recognises, however, that the trade mark has a separate existence beside its purpose as a signifier for goodwill: this is shown by the statutory definition of a trade mark as property in its own right,[111] and by the fact that the sign itself may be subject to copyright protection. Thus the trade mark is indirect reifier for the business goodwill through its origin, quality and communication functions, and direct reifier for itself as a graphic representation. Unlike a painting (in this regard from the viewpoint of copyright), the *res* 'sign' is socially imbued with a particular purpose, that of denoting a certain goodwill, a purpose an ordinary picture or painting (or word) would not have. This again shows that property rights can only be social relations which create, and determine the content and meaning of, 'things' and rights in them *erga omnes*. It is inessential for the concept 'property' as such whether such 'things/*res*' have a corporeal counterpart in the material world and the way in which that corporeal object is understood.

Common law rights with regard to intellectual property: the *numerus clausus* problem

Statutory intellectual property rights are property rights because the law – in the UK at least – defines them as such (in the case of copyright, patents, trade marks

[107] This is now permitted; see Community Trade Mark Regulation art 17(1), UK: Trade Marks Act 1994 s 24(1). However, see eg the rebuttable presumption in Germany: Markengesetz 1994 § 27(2).

[108] For the UK this well-known definition can be found in *IRC v Muller & Co's Margarine* [1901] AC 217 (HL) 224. See also *Bently and Sherman* (n 67) 729.

[109] This is the statutory definition of the registered trade mark, Trade Marks Act 1994 s 1.

[110] The trade mark as the signifier of goodwill is the typical case. But a trade mark may be perceived by the parties of a certain bargain as denoting something else: this is the case if the trade mark is assigned without the goodwill of a business or, to some extent at least, if the assignment is partial (Trade Marks Act 1994 s 24(1) and (2)).

[111] Trade Marks Act 1994 s 2.

and designs)[112] or assigns certain powers to these rights which are functionally powers of property, as discussed,[113] and thereby renders the rights permanent, enforceable against everyone and alienable.

What makes a right a property right is difficult to define. Civil law countries are in a better position in this regard, because codified systems provide an exhaustive list or a *numerus clausus* as to what constitutes a property right (ownership, mortgages, easements and the like).[114] The common law systems effectively operate such a *numerus clausus* in all but name;[115] for example, whether in English law an activity in question qualifies as an easement, and is thus the exercise of a property right, is determined by the *Re Ellenborough Park* test.[116] The courts effectively shape the *numerus clausus* when deciding whether an event or activity is property.[117] The common law generally uses rules of thumb: characteristic of a property right is that it is identifiable, has a certain permanence, is enforceable against everyone or 'binds the world' and is (typically) alienable.[118] The latter criterion is not necessarily free from circularity. Rights have been identified as property rights, because they are alienable, but it is in fact their proprietary quality that makes them alienable.[119]

As with traditional property, the *numerus clausus* of intellectual property rights can only be a snapshot of a given jurisdiction at a given point in time. It is by no means immutable but subject to historical development, especially judicial interpretation. The way in which some judgments have dealt with certain phenomena indicates that the courts are prepared to treat them effectively as property,[120] for example, information,[121] or confidential information in breach

[112] Copyright, Designs and Patents Act 1988 s 1 (copyright), s 213 (unregistered designs); Trade Marks Act 1994 s 2 (trade marks); Patents Act 1977 s 30(1) (patents); Registered Designs Act 1949 ss 1(2) and 2 (registered designs).

[113] See above under 'Intellectual Property as Dematerialised Property'.

[114] B Rudden, 'Economic Theory vs Property Law: The *Numerus Clausus* Problem' in J Eekelaar and J Bell (eds), *Oxford Essays in Jurisprudence* (3rd series, Clarendon Press, Oxford 1987) 243. For Germany, H Prütting, *Sachenrecht* (33rd edn C H Beck, München 2008) 8; V Jänich, *Geistiges Eigentum: eine Komplementärerscheinung zum Sacheigentum?* (Jus privatum… vol 66, Mohr Siebeck,Tübingen 2002) 234. Especially the area of security rights shows that the statutory list of property rights in the German BGB (Civil Code) is in reality not exhaustive.

[115] *Rudden* (n 114) 244, with references to English case law.

[116] Providing that the following are requirements for a valid easement: (1) Dominant and servient tenements, (2) the easement must accommodate the dominant tenement, (3) the owners of the dominant and servient tenements must be different persons, (4) the right must be capable of forming the subject-matter of a grant. See *Re Ellenborough Park* [1956] Ch 131 (CA) 140. See also *Gray and Gray* (n 30) 601–2.

[117] Eg no property or quasi-property in a spectacle: *Victoria Park Racing and Recreation Grounds v Taylor* (1937) 58 CLR 479 (High Court of Australia) 496.

[118] *National Provincial Bank v Ainsworth* [1965] AC 1175 (HL) 1247–48.

[119] *Gray* (n 5) 293.

[120] See example by Lord Devlin with regard to copyright in *Ladbroke (Football) Ltd v William Hill (Football) Ltd* [1964] 1 WLR 273 (HL) 291: a shop window arrangement of wine bottles (no copyright), making a list (potentially copyright).

[121] Eg in the US case *International News Service v Associated Press* (1918) 248 US 251 (US SC) 236.

of confidence actions.[122] Where the subject-matter of a passing-off action is an unregistered trade mark or goodwill of any other kind, the proprietary nature of a given 'goodwill' is conceptually beyond doubt.[123] Such interpretations open up the closed list of intellectual property rights by treating certain claims functionally as proprietary rights without necessarily calling them such. The law chooses whether a phenomenon is property or not, and therefore an intellectual property right can be extended or restricted in its scope at any time. There is no qualitative difference in principle either whether an intellectual property right is a common law right[124] or a statutory right (registered trade marks, patents, designs, copyright), these are merely different means of legal form. Intellectual property rights bring to light that the idea of the *numerus clausus* of property rights can only be a guiding yardstick, not a strict rule.

The critics: intellectual property is not property or 'lesser' property

The fact that intellectual property rights have no tangible existence or no direct tangible reifier has led some property theorists to believe that intellectual property rights are not property rights at all or are property rights of a lesser nature. McFarlane generally believes that property rights can only relate to physical objects, which by definition excludes intellectual property from being property.[125] As to copyright he says:

> … strictly speaking, [the copyright owner] … does not have a right against a *thing*. His copyright does not relate to any physical object that can be located; instead it relates to a form of expression. So I can have Ownership of *a copy of this book* (a specific thing); but … even though I wrote it, I cannot have Ownership of *the book* (the form in which I have expressed a set of ideas).[126]

The rejection of the concept of dematerialised property, together with the problem of reification of different real rights in relation to a tangible object may provoke such misconceptions. The physical book itself is the material reifier of someone's personal/moveable property right (a real right) to the *res*, here exemplified by the book. Besides, the book, as any other copy of the book, a

[122] *Mustad v Allcock* [1963] 3 All ER 416 (HL); *Lac Minerals v International Corona Resources* (1989) 61 DLR (4th) 14 (Supreme Court of Canada). Both cases may be of limited importance only as precedents, see *Cornish and Llewelyn* (n 61) 342–43.

[123] See eg *Reckitt and Colman Products v Borden Inc* [1990] 1 WLR 491 (HL) 511; *Bently and Sherman* (n 67) 729 and 743.

[124] For example, the common law copyright which existed in the US at state law level, to the extent which it has not been pre-empted by Copyright Act 1976 s 301. Thus common law copyright is very limited in the US (ie works not fixed in tangible medium of expression).

[125] *McFarlane* (n 7) 132.

[126] *McFarlane* (n 7) 134.

photocopy, or a copy of the text on the internet, also acts as an indirect reifier[127] of someone's (usually someone else's) copyright-property right in relation to the 'literary work'[128] which the text of the book constitutes. The term 'literary work' is normative-constitutive: this is the way in which the law normatively turns any text, being my poem, someone else's poem, a novel, a newspaper article, a table or compilation, a computer program and other works which would not normally be regarded as works of literature, into a *res*, provided they are also 'original' (in the meaning of copyright) and recorded. Copyright law typifies all these possible written expressions of the human mind as abstract objects of property by categorising them as 'literary works'[129] and turning them into objects of a property right. This enables the law to recognise the varieties of human expression within its system of conceptual 'persons' and 'things'.[130] In McFarlane's example it is in fact irrelevant whether the copyright owner has a right against a physical object. His example remains incorrect if the outmoded requirement of corporality for a property right were maintained, for in case of a painting, for example, the relevant copyright very much 'relates to a physical object that can be located',[131] more than in the case of a literary work as it appears in/through a book. But that is not a relevant factor anyway; what matters is that the object 'painting' and the object 'copyright-artistic work' are two different things (*res*) in law, one a chattel (canvas) and the other one the artistic expression it displays, whereby the chattel as direct reifier of the notional personal (moveable) property right also acts as an indirect reifier of the notional copyright: in this way the chattel represents, but does not constitute, the copyright in the painting.[132]

Harris and Penner have a less extreme approach. Harris says that property rules allocate rights to scarce resources,[133] whereby intellectual property rights create an artificial scarcity, because 'ideas' (in an untechnical sense), once they are in the public domain through publication or otherwise, cease to be scarce. Intellectual property creates an artificial scarcity by developing trespassory rules which protect the author from unauthorised use of his ideas comprised within his work and in this way grant the author an ownership interest in them.[134]

In fact, intellectual property rights do not create more of an artificial scarcity than rights to tangible property. Copyright, for example, is not interested in the

[127] Compare *Harris* (n 1) 45.

[128] Copyright, Designs and Patents Act 1988 s 3.

[129] And the law normatively sets out the extent and limits of this category in its definition in Copyright, Designs and Patents Act s 3(1).

[130] *Rahmatian* (n 78) 282.

[131] *McFarlane* (n 7) 134.

[132] The chattel does not 'constitute' the personal property-*res* either, but represents it as its *direct* reifier. Since the law constructs property relations entirely normatively, every physical object can only *represent* property rights in the property object (or the *res* in law) and the property-object itself, but it cannot *be* property.

[133] *Harris* (n 1) 12 and 24.

[134] *Harris* (n 1) 43.

raw material of the 'idea', but what has specifically been done with it (a certain novel, piece of music, sculpture etc); it is not relevant what *could* have been done with it by others, but what *has* actually individually been done.[135] That realisation is scarce, if not unique, and not artificially so: not the law makes the expression scarce, the expression is scarce by itself and the law attaches property rights to it because of this scarcity. However, the distinction between artificial scarcity (intellectual property) and natural scarcity (tangible property) is unconvincing in any case, since one could argue that material resources may also be made scarce because of the property rights attached to them, typically in connection with the economic powers of markets.

Penner describes intellectual property rights as rights to monopolies, and since these rights clearly correlate to duties *in rem*, he concedes that they have the features of a property right.[136] But then he proceeds to say that 'patents are not property rights in ideas, nor copyrights property rights in expressions'[137] and claims at one point that the idea 'that intellectual property constitutes property in ideas (patents) or expressions (copyright)' is an 'idiotic fiction'.[138] This indicates a conceptual confusion about intellectual property. It is true, copyright does not protect ideas, nor does patent law, and there is little point using the elusive term 'idea' to refer to an invention which is new and involves an inventive step.[139] But, against Penner's proposition,[140] copyright *does* protect the specific expression of the idea used (though not the idea as such):[141] the way in which a plot of a story (idea) was individually used and worded to form a novel, the way in which a harmonic progression was applied in a specific melody line, and so on. Copyright does not prevent the enjoyment of the result of the application of an 'idea' (reading a book, looking at a painting); it prevents the actual re-use of that very application of the 'idea' in substantially the same way.[142] That 'application of an idea' is the 'expression', being the conceptual property object (*res*) and the exclusive right, enforceable against everyone, over that object. This type of protection is a proprietarian one through 'trespassory rules', to use Harris's term.[143] The situation in patent law is similar: discoveries, scientific theories or mathematical methods are excluded from patentability,[144] while their technical

[135] Harris's argument in this respect misses the point; see *Harris* (n 1) 43.

[136] *Penner* (n 1) 109 and 119.

[137] *Penner* (n 1) 119.

[138] *Penner* (n 1) 118.

[139] Compare Patents Act 1977 s 1.

[140] Whether Penner uses the term 'expression' in the specific technical meaning of copyright law, is, however, unclear.

[141] Compare US Copyright Act 1976 § 102(b); TRIPS Agreement art 9(2). The UK has no express statutory rule in this regard.

[142] This is a general outline of the principles for the purpose of a discussion of the object of property within property theory. It should not suggest that especially issues of non-literal copying in copyright are easy to resolve. On that see eg *Cornish and Llewelyn* (n 61) 457.

[143] *Harris* (n 1) 45.

[144] Patents Act 1977 s 1(2)(a).

application or an invention directed to the technical effect of such discoveries etc is not.[145]

Conclusion

A property right (*ius in rem*, real right) is an abstract legal concept which relates to an object, referred to as 'thing' or '*res*', or imprecisely, but commonly, 'property'. This object of property is a product of legal categorisation; it may be represented by a physical thing or it can be an abstract legal creation itself, as is the case with an intellectual property right. In any event, for the law the 'property-object' (whether tangible, intangible or purely intangible) is the product of a legal conceptualisation. The law (private law) creates any *res* or thing, whether corporeal or not, through the legal concept of real rights. That enables legal recognition of the *res* in question. The material object (if there is one) only becomes a *res* in law if real rights are attached to it. Therefore, real rights and *res* are both 'property', and particularly with (purely intangible) intellectual property, property rights and property objects merge into one. The abstract conceptual *res* typically has a reifier to make it recognisable in the material world and for the purpose of social interactions. This reifier can be a corporeal object, in which case it is a direct reifier (a table being a direct reifier and incident of a *res*, chattel), but, for example in case of copyright, a chattel may act not only as *direct* reifier of the notional personal (moveable) property right (eg a canvas of a painting, the score of a symphony, the paper of a manuscript), but also as an *indirect* reifier of the notional copyright (artistic work, musical work, literary work). The chattel in question represents directly the personal/moveable property (but does not *constitute* it, because the *res* remains a legal concept), and, in addition, the chattel represents indirectly the copyright in the work which is expressed and recorded in the chattel in question (a painting, sculpture etc). Critics have questioned or denied entirely the proprietary nature of intellectual property rights, generally as a result of either a misconception as to the actual scope of protection of these rights, or because they have not taken the abstract conceptual nature of the idea of property to its logical conclusion. Their views are quite in contrast with every day legal reality, not only with regard to intellectual property rights, but also in relation to debts, company shares and the like.

[145] *Aerotel v Telco Holdings* [2007] EWCA Civ 1371, [2007] 1 All ER 225; *Chiron Corp v Organon Teknika Ltd (No 3)* [1994] FSR 202 (Ch Patents) 239.

Index